Walt Disney's

Donald Duck

by Carl Barks

Publisher and Executive Editor: GARY GROTH
Senior Editor: J. MICHAEL CATRON
Color Editor: JASON T. MILES
Colorist: RICH TOMMASO
Series Design: JACOB COVEY
Volume Design: KEELI McCARTHY
Production: PAUL BARESH
Editorial Consultant: DAVID GERSTEIN
Associate Publisher: ERIC REYNOLDS

– – – – – – – – – – – – – – – – – – –

Walt Disney's Donald Duck: "The Ghost Sheriff of Last Gasp" is copyright © 2016 Disney Enterprises, Inc.
All contents copyright © 2016 Disney Enterprises, Inc. unless otherwise noted. All rights reserved.
This is Volume 15 of *The Complete Carl Barks Disney Library*. Permission to quote or reproduce material
for reviews must be obtained from the publisher.

Fantagraphics Books, Inc.
7563 Lake City Way NE
Seattle WA 98115

Visit us at fantagraphics.com or (800) 657-1100. Follow us on Twitter at @fantagraphics
and on Facebook at facebook.com/fantagraphics.

Special thanks to Thomas Jensen and Kim Weston.

First printing, November 2016
ISBN 978-1-60699-953-0

Printed in Malaysia
Library of Congress Control Number: 2016941731

Now available in this series:
Walt Disney's Donald Duck: "Christmas on Bear Mountain" (Vol. 5)
Walt Disney's Donald Duck: "The Old Castle's Secret" (Vol. 6)
Walt Disney's Donald Duck: "Lost in the Andes" (Vol. 7)
Walt Disney's Donald Duck: "Trail of the Unicorn" (Vol. 8)
Walt Disney's Donald Duck: "The Pixilated Parrot" (Vol. 9)
Walt Disney's Donald Duck: "Terror of the Beagle Boys" (Vol. 10)
Walt Disney's Donald Duck: "A Christmas for Shacktown" (Vol. 11)
Walt Disney's Uncle Scrooge: "Only a Poor Old Man" (Vol. 12)
Walt Disney's Donald Duck: "Trick or Treat" (Vol. 13)
Walt Disney's Uncle Scrooge: "The Seven Cities of Gold" (Vol. 14)
Walt Disney's Donald Duck: "The Ghost Sheriff of Last Gasp" (Vol. 15)

– – – – – – – – – – – – – – – – – – –

Boxed sets of some titles are available at select locations.

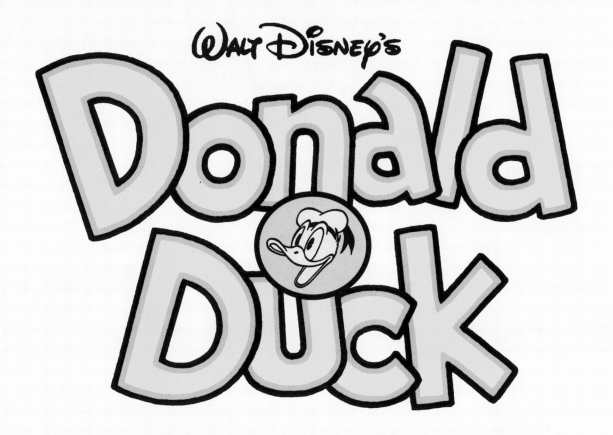

WALT DISNEY's

Donald Duck

"The Ghost Sheriff of Last Gasp"

by Carl Barks

FANTAGRAPHICS BOOKS
SEATTLE

Contents

*All comics stories written and drawn by Carl Barks, except as noted.
All comics stories colored by Rich Tommaso.*

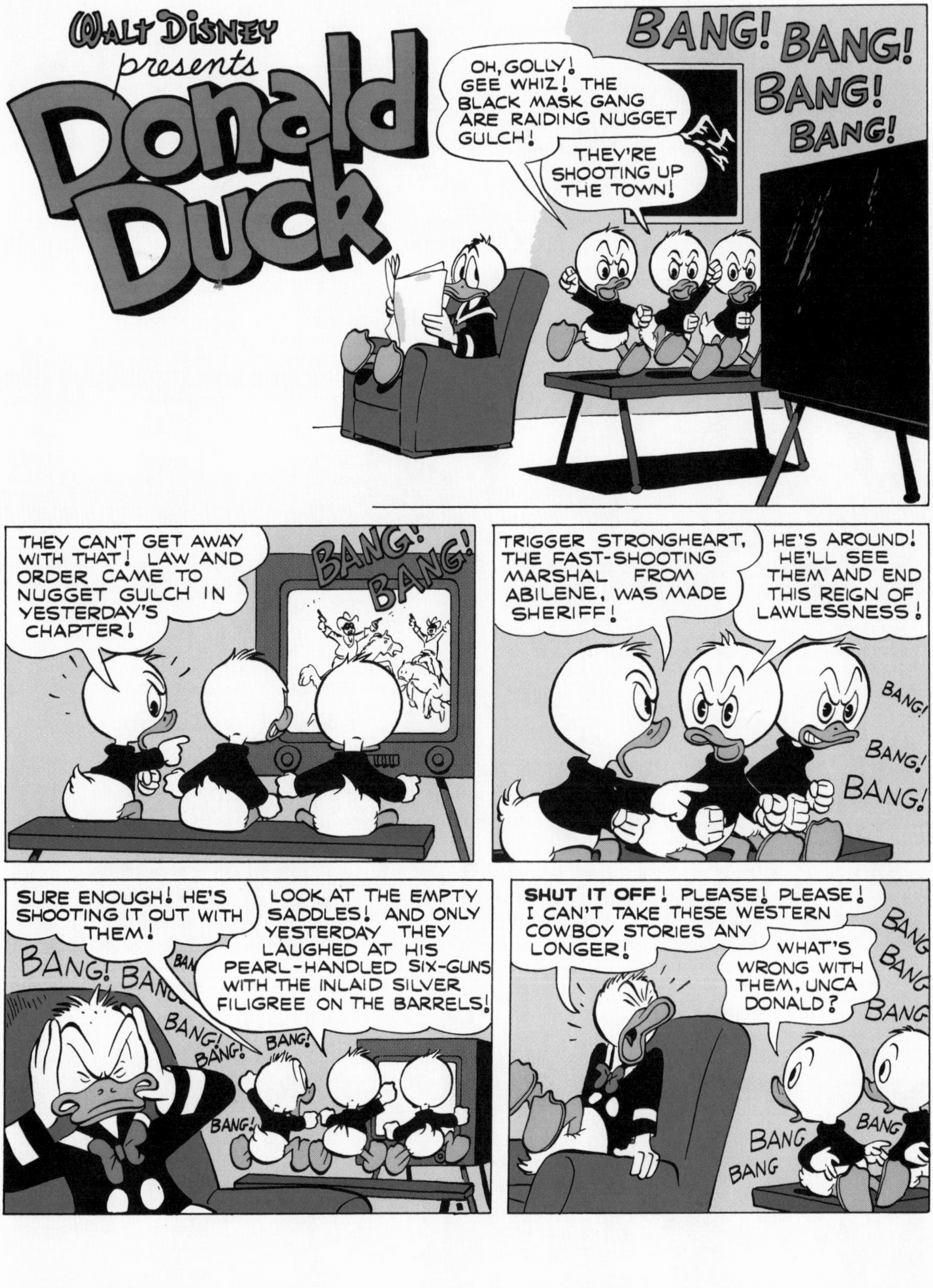
WALT DISNEY presents
Donald Duck
BANG! BANG! BANG! BANG!
OH, GOLLY! GEE WHIZ! THE BLACK MASK GANG ARE RAIDING NUGGET GULCH!
THEY'RE SHOOTING UP THE TOWN!
THEY CAN'T GET AWAY WITH THAT! LAW AND ORDER CAME TO NUGGET GULCH IN YESTERDAY'S CHAPTER!
BANG! BANG!
TRIGGER STRONGHEART, THE FAST-SHOOTING MARSHAL FROM ABILENE, WAS MADE SHERIFF!
HE'S AROUND! HE'LL SEE THEM AND END THIS REIGN OF LAWLESSNESS!
BANG! BANG! BANG!
SURE ENOUGH! HE'S SHOOTING IT OUT WITH THEM!
LOOK AT THE EMPTY SADDLES! AND ONLY YESTERDAY THEY LAUGHED AT HIS PEARL-HANDLED SIX-GUNS WITH THE INLAID SILVER FILIGREE ON THE BARRELS!
BANG! BANG! BANG! BANG! BANG! BANG!
SHUT IT OFF! PLEASE! PLEASE! I CAN'T TAKE THESE WESTERN COWBOY STORIES ANY LONGER!
WHAT'S WRONG WITH THEM, UNCA DONALD?
BANG BANG BANG BANG BANG BANG

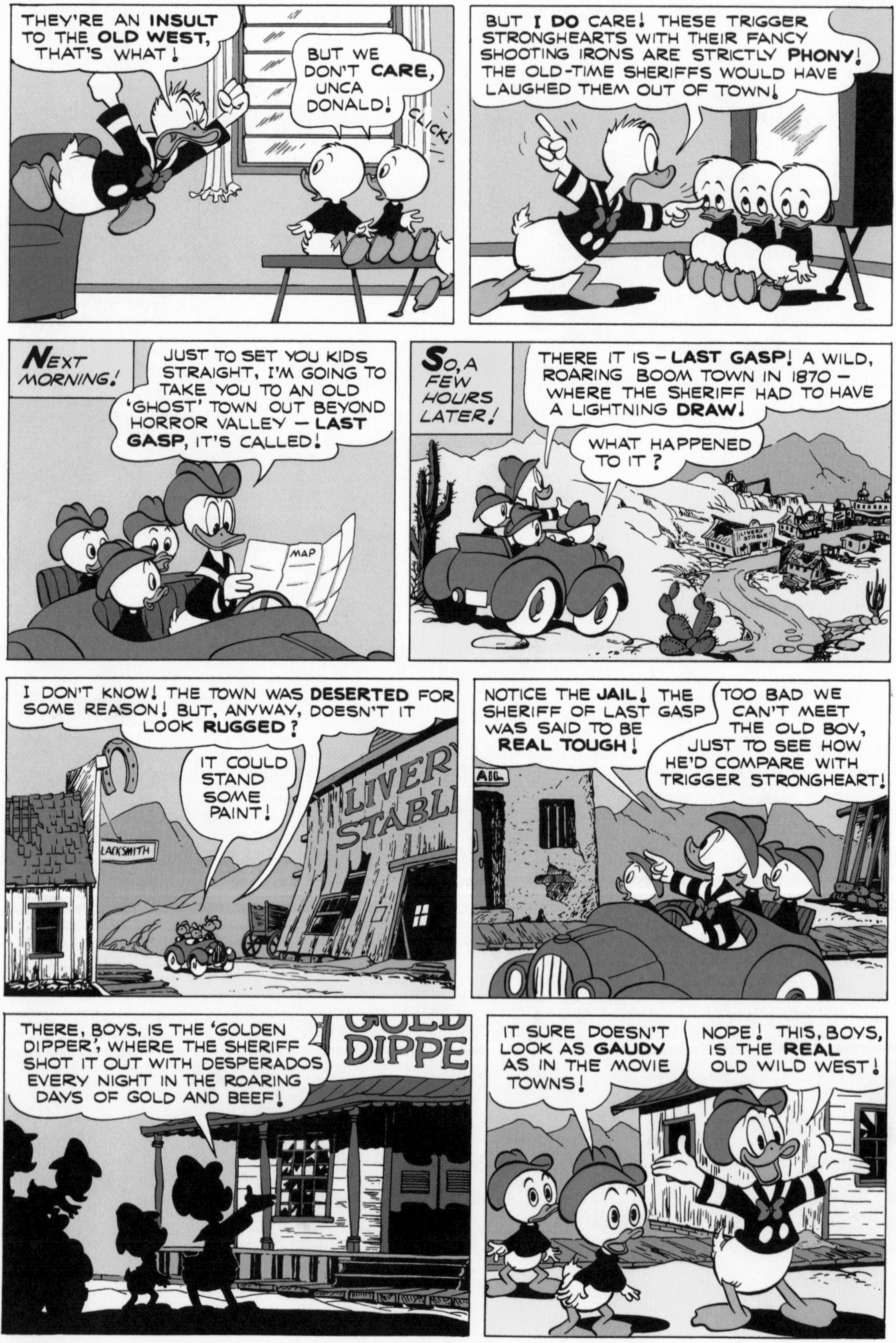
THEY'RE AN INSULT TO THE OLD WEST, THAT'S WHAT!
BUT WE DON'T CARE, UNCA DONALD!
CLICK!
BUT I DO CARE! THESE TRIGGER STRONGHEARTS WITH THEIR FANCY SHOOTING IRONS ARE STRICTLY PHONY! THE OLD-TIME SHERIFFS WOULD HAVE LAUGHED THEM OUT OF TOWN!
NEXT MORNING!
JUST TO SET YOU KIDS STRAIGHT, I'M GOING TO TAKE YOU TO AN OLD 'GHOST' TOWN OUT BEYOND HORROR VALLEY — LAST GASP, IT'S CALLED!
MAP
SO, A FEW HOURS LATER!
THERE IT IS — LAST GASP! A WILD, ROARING BOOM TOWN IN 1870 — WHERE THE SHERIFF HAD TO HAVE A LIGHTNING DRAW!
WHAT HAPPENED TO IT?
I DON'T KNOW! THE TOWN WAS DESERTED FOR SOME REASON! BUT, ANYWAY, DOESN'T IT LOOK RUGGED?
IT COULD STAND SOME PAINT!
LACKSMITH
LIVERY STABL
NOTICE THE JAIL! THE SHERIFF OF LAST GASP WAS SAID TO BE REAL TOUGH!
TOO BAD WE CAN'T MEET THE OLD BOY, JUST TO SEE HOW HE'D COMPARE WITH TRIGGER STRONGHEART!
AIL
THERE, BOYS, IS THE 'GOLDEN DIPPER', WHERE THE SHERIFF SHOT IT OUT WITH DESPERADOS EVERY NIGHT IN THE ROARING DAYS OF GOLD AND BEEF!
DIPPE
IT SURE DOESN'T LOOK AS GAUDY AS IN THE MOVIE TOWNS!
NOPE! THIS, BOYS, IS THE REAL OLD WILD WEST!

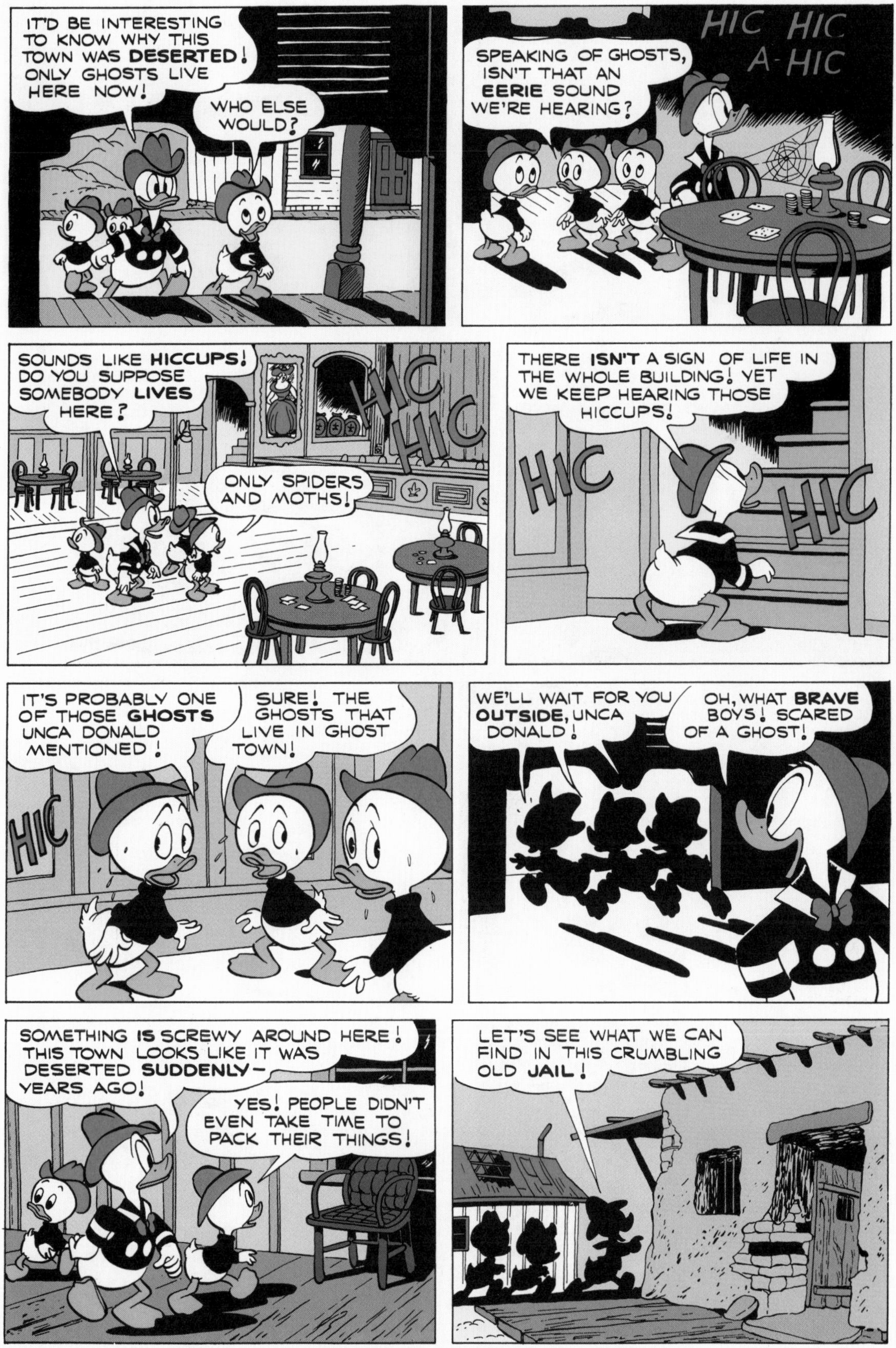

IT'D BE INTERESTING TO KNOW WHY THIS TOWN WAS **DESERTED**! ONLY GHOSTS LIVE HERE NOW!
WHO ELSE WOULD?
HIC HIC A-HIC
SPEAKING OF GHOSTS, ISN'T THAT AN **EERIE** SOUND WE'RE HEARING?
SOUNDS LIKE **HICCUPS**! DO YOU SUPPOSE SOMEBODY **LIVES** HERE?
HIC HIC
ONLY SPIDERS AND MOTHS!
THERE **ISN'T** A SIGN OF LIFE IN THE WHOLE BUILDING! YET WE KEEP HEARING THOSE HICCUPS!
HIC
HIC
IT'S PROBABLY ONE OF THOSE **GHOSTS** UNCA DONALD MENTIONED!
SURE! THE GHOSTS THAT LIVE IN GHOST TOWN!
HIC
WE'LL WAIT FOR YOU **OUTSIDE**, UNCA DONALD!
OH, WHAT **BRAVE** BOYS! SCARED OF A GHOST!
SOMETHING **IS** SCREWY AROUND HERE! THIS TOWN LOOKS LIKE IT WAS DESERTED **SUDDENLY**—YEARS AGO!
YES! PEOPLE DIDN'T EVEN TAKE TIME TO PACK THEIR THINGS!
LET'S SEE WHAT WE CAN FIND IN THIS CRUMBLING OLD **JAIL**!

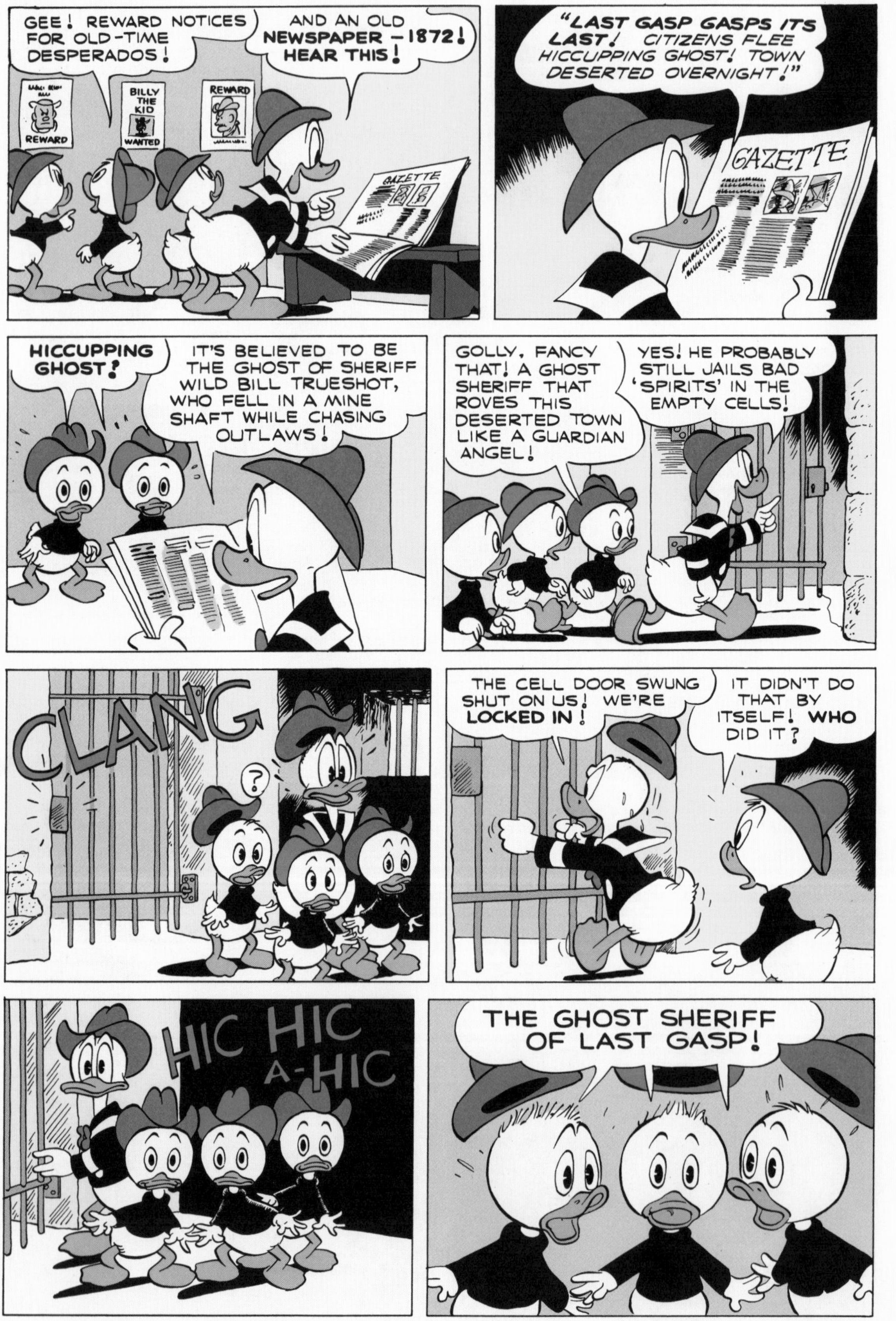
GEE! REWARD NOTICES FOR OLD-TIME DESPERADOS!
AND AN OLD NEWSPAPER —1872! HEAR THIS!
REWARD
BILLY THE KID WANTED
REWARD
GAZETTE
"LAST GASP GASPS ITS LAST! CITIZENS FLEE HICCUPPING GHOST! TOWN DESERTED OVERNIGHT!"
GAZETTE
HICCUPPING GHOST?
IT'S BELIEVED TO BE THE GHOST OF SHERIFF WILD BILL TRUESHOT, WHO FELL IN A MINE SHAFT WHILE CHASING OUTLAWS!
GOLLY, FANCY THAT! A GHOST SHERIFF THAT ROVES THIS DESERTED TOWN LIKE A GUARDIAN ANGEL!
YES! HE PROBABLY STILL JAILS BAD 'SPIRITS' IN THE EMPTY CELLS!
CLANG
?
THE CELL DOOR SWUNG SHUT ON US! WE'RE LOCKED IN!
IT DIDN'T DO THAT BY ITSELF! WHO DID IT?
HIC HIC A-HIC
THE GHOST SHERIFF OF LAST GASP!

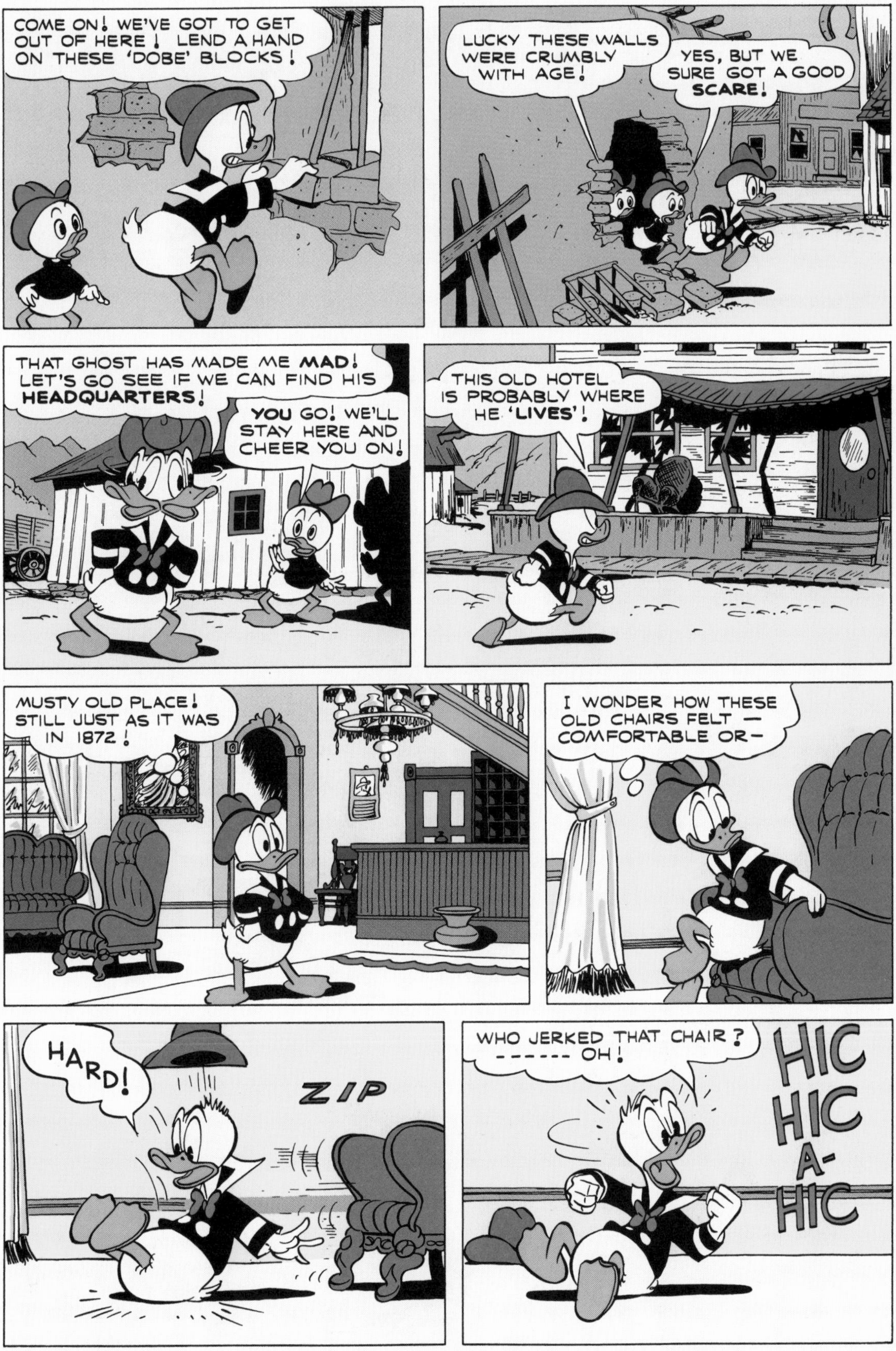
COME ON! WE'VE GOT TO GET OUT OF HERE! LEND A HAND ON THESE 'DOBE' BLOCKS!
LUCKY THESE WALLS WERE CRUMBLY WITH AGE!
YES, BUT WE SURE GOT A GOOD SCARE!
THAT GHOST HAS MADE ME MAD! LET'S GO SEE IF WE CAN FIND HIS HEADQUARTERS!
YOU GO! WE'LL STAY HERE AND CHEER YOU ON!
THIS OLD HOTEL IS PROBABLY WHERE HE 'LIVES'!
MUSTY OLD PLACE! STILL JUST AS IT WAS IN 1872!
I WONDER HOW THESE OLD CHAIRS FELT — COMFORTABLE OR—
HARD!
ZIP
WHO JERKED THAT CHAIR? ------ OH!
HIC
HIC
HIC
A-
HIC

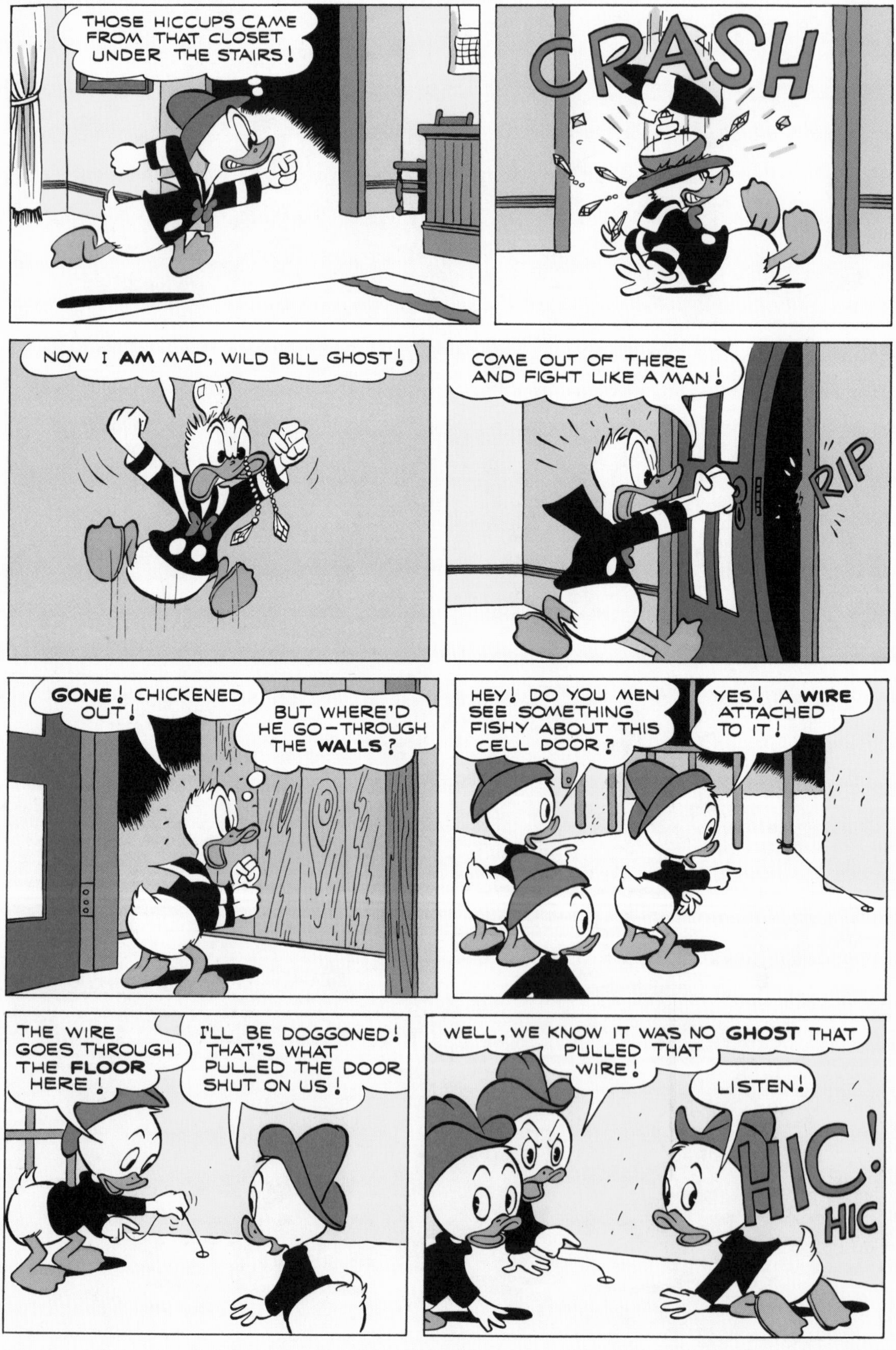
THOSE HICCUPS CAME FROM THAT CLOSET UNDER THE STAIRS!
CRASH
NOW I AM MAD, WILD BILL GHOST!
COME OUT OF THERE AND FIGHT LIKE A MAN!
RIP
GONE! CHICKENED OUT!
BUT WHERE'D HE GO—THROUGH THE WALLS?
HEY! DO YOU MEN SEE SOMETHING FISHY ABOUT THIS CELL DOOR?
YES! A WIRE ATTACHED TO IT!
THE WIRE GOES THROUGH THE FLOOR HERE!
I'LL BE DOGGONED! THAT'S WHAT PULLED THE DOOR SHUT ON US!
WELL, WE KNOW IT WAS NO GHOST THAT PULLED THAT WIRE!
LISTEN!
HIC!
HIC

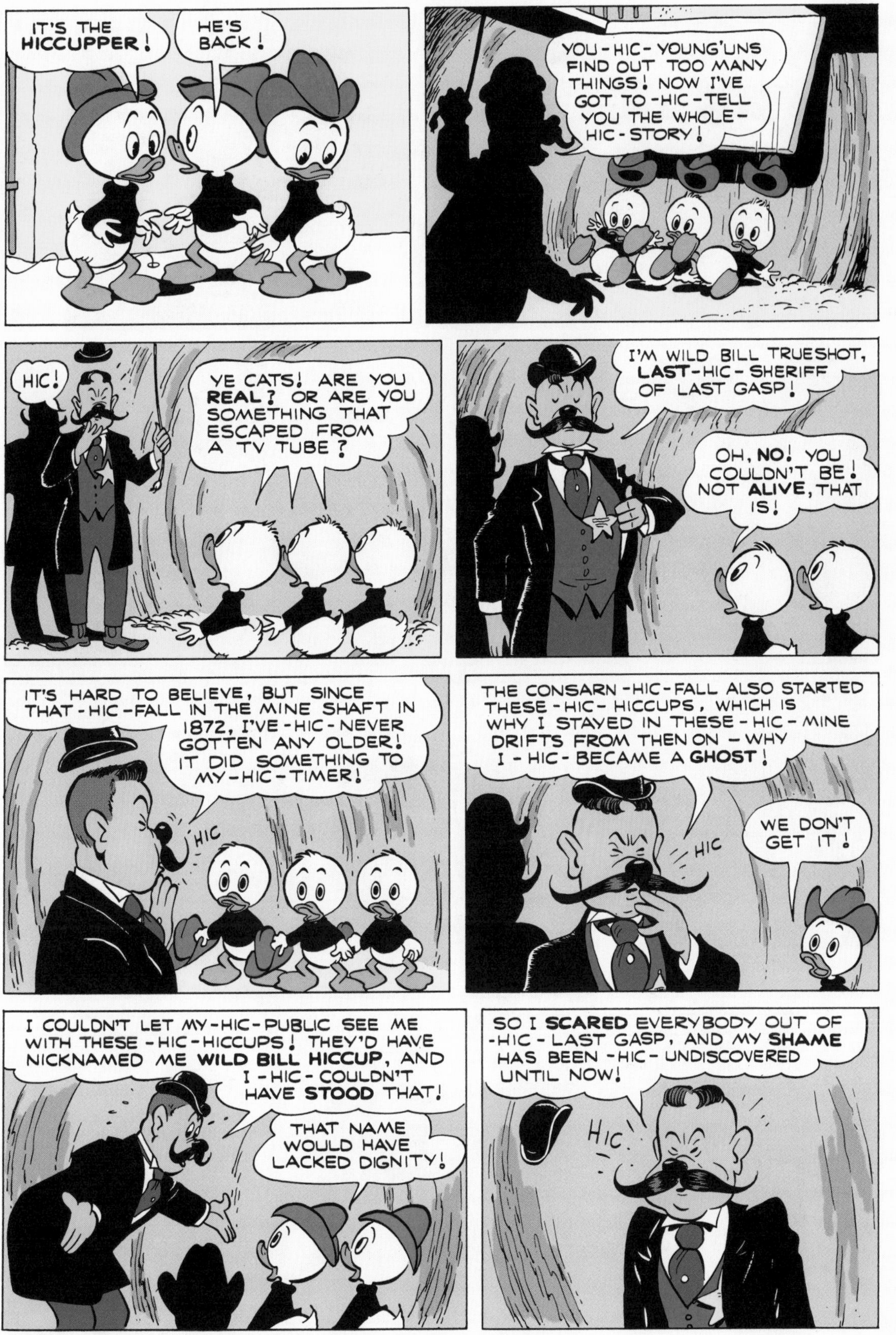
IT'S THE HICCUPPER!
HE'S BACK!
YOU-HIC-YOUNG'UNS FIND OUT TOO MANY THINGS! NOW I'VE GOT TO-HIC-TELL YOU THE WHOLE-HIC-STORY!
HIC!
YE CATS! ARE YOU REAL? OR ARE YOU SOMETHING THAT ESCAPED FROM A TV TUBE?
I'M WILD BILL TRUESHOT, LAST-HIC-SHERIFF OF LAST GASP!
OH, NO! YOU COULDN'T BE! NOT ALIVE, THAT IS!
IT'S HARD TO BELIEVE, BUT SINCE THAT-HIC-FALL IN THE MINE SHAFT IN 1872, I'VE-HIC-NEVER GOTTEN ANY OLDER! IT DID SOMETHING TO MY-HIC-TIMER!
HIC
THE CONSARN-HIC-FALL ALSO STARTED THESE-HIC-HICCUPS, WHICH IS WHY I STAYED IN THESE-HIC-MINE DRIFTS FROM THEN ON - WHY I-HIC-BECAME A GHOST!
HIC
WE DON'T GET IT!
I COULDN'T LET MY-HIC-PUBLIC SEE ME WITH THESE-HIC-HICCUPS! THEY'D HAVE NICKNAMED ME WILD BILL HICCUP, AND I-HIC-COULDN'T HAVE STOOD THAT!
THAT NAME WOULD HAVE LACKED DIGNITY!
SO I SCARED EVERYBODY OUT OF -HIC-LAST GASP, AND MY SHAME HAS BEEN -HIC- UNDISCOVERED UNTIL NOW!
HIC

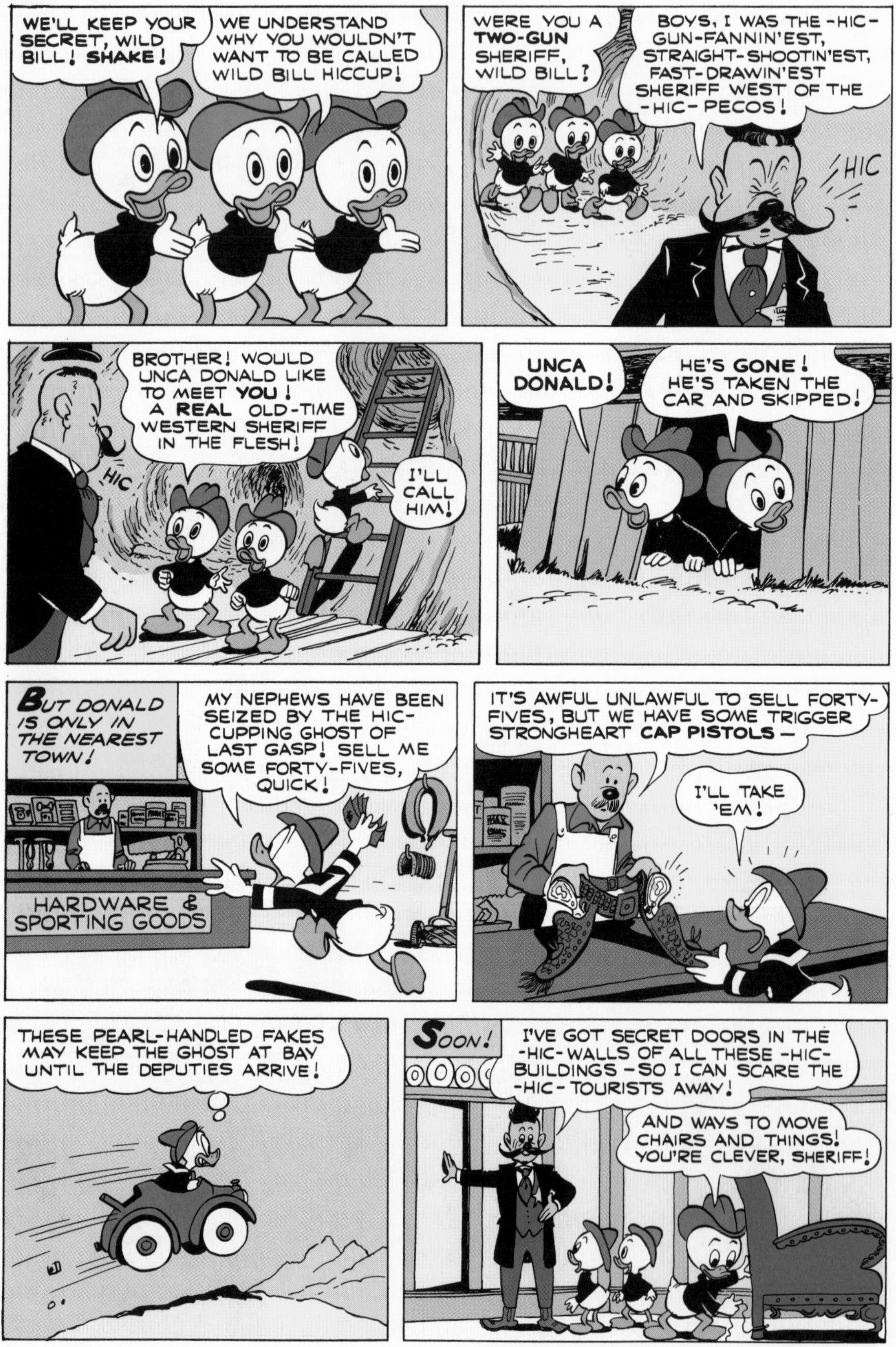
WE'LL KEEP YOUR SECRET, WILD BILL! SHAKE!
WE UNDERSTAND WHY YOU WOULDN'T WANT TO BE CALLED WILD BILL HICCUP!
WERE YOU A TWO-GUN SHERIFF, WILD BILL?
BOYS, I WAS THE -HIC- GUN-FANNIN'EST, STRAIGHT-SHOOTIN'EST, FAST-DRAWIN'EST SHERIFF WEST OF THE -HIC- PECOS!
HIC
BROTHER! WOULD UNCA DONALD LIKE TO MEET YOU! A REAL OLD-TIME WESTERN SHERIFF IN THE FLESH!
HIC
I'LL CALL HIM!
UNCA DONALD!
HE'S GONE! HE'S TAKEN THE CAR AND SKIPPED!
BUT DONALD IS ONLY IN THE NEAREST TOWN!
MY NEPHEWS HAVE BEEN SEIZED BY THE HIC-CUPPING GHOST OF LAST GASP! SELL ME SOME FORTY-FIVES, QUICK!
HARDWARE & SPORTING GOODS
IT'S AWFUL UNLAWFUL TO SELL FORTY-FIVES, BUT WE HAVE SOME TRIGGER STRONGHEART CAP PISTOLS—
I'LL TAKE 'EM!
THESE PEARL-HANDLED FAKES MAY KEEP THE GHOST AT BAY UNTIL THE DEPUTIES ARRIVE!
SOON!
I'VE GOT SECRET DOORS IN THE -HIC- WALLS OF ALL THESE -HIC- BUILDINGS—SO I CAN SCARE THE -HIC- TOURISTS AWAY!
AND WAYS TO MOVE CHAIRS AND THINGS! YOU'RE CLEVER, SHERIFF!

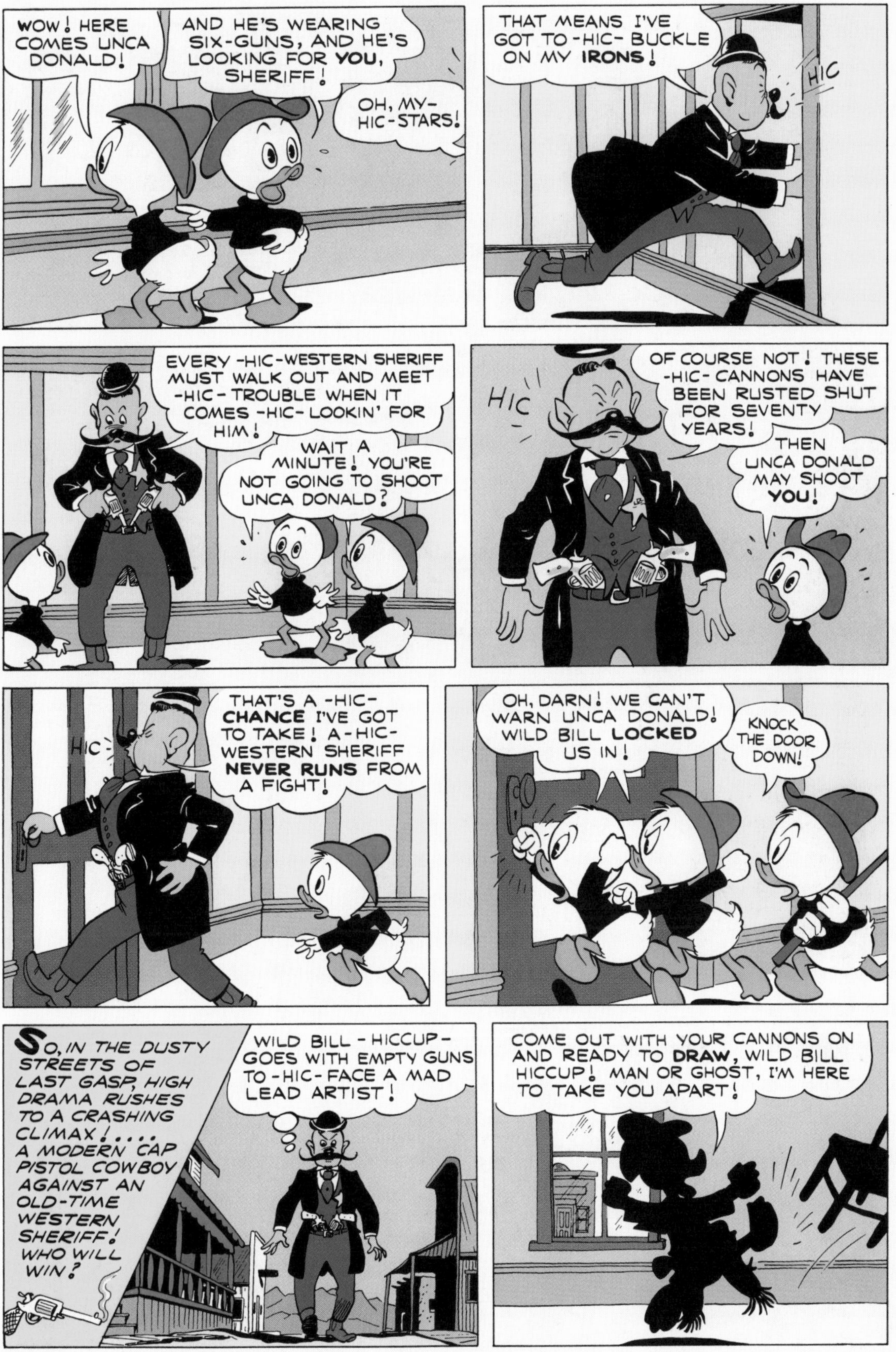
WOW! HERE COMES UNCA DONALD!
AND HE'S WEARING SIX-GUNS, AND HE'S LOOKING FOR YOU, SHERIFF!
OH, MY- HIC-STARS!
THAT MEANS I'VE GOT TO -HIC- BUCKLE ON MY IRONS!
HIC
EVERY -HIC-WESTERN SHERIFF MUST WALK OUT AND MEET -HIC- TROUBLE WHEN IT COMES -HIC- LOOKIN' FOR HIM!
WAIT A MINUTE! YOU'RE NOT GOING TO SHOOT UNCA DONALD?
HIC
OF COURSE NOT! THESE -HIC- CANNONS HAVE BEEN RUSTED SHUT FOR SEVENTY YEARS!
THEN UNCA DONALD MAY SHOOT YOU!
HIC
THAT'S A -HIC- CHANCE I'VE GOT TO TAKE! A-HIC- WESTERN SHERIFF NEVER RUNS FROM A FIGHT!
OH, DARN! WE CAN'T WARN UNCA DONALD! WILD BILL LOCKED US IN!
KNOCK THE DOOR DOWN!
SO, IN THE DUSTY STREETS OF LAST GASP, HIGH DRAMA RUSHES TO A CRASHING CLIMAX!.... A MODERN CAP PISTOL COWBOY AGAINST AN OLD-TIME WESTERN SHERIFF! WHO WILL WIN?
WILD BILL -HICCUP- GOES WITH EMPTY GUNS TO -HIC- FACE A MAD LEAD ARTIST!
COME OUT WITH YOUR CANNONS ON AND READY TO DRAW, WILD BILL HICCUP! MAN OR GHOST, I'M HERE TO TAKE YOU APART!

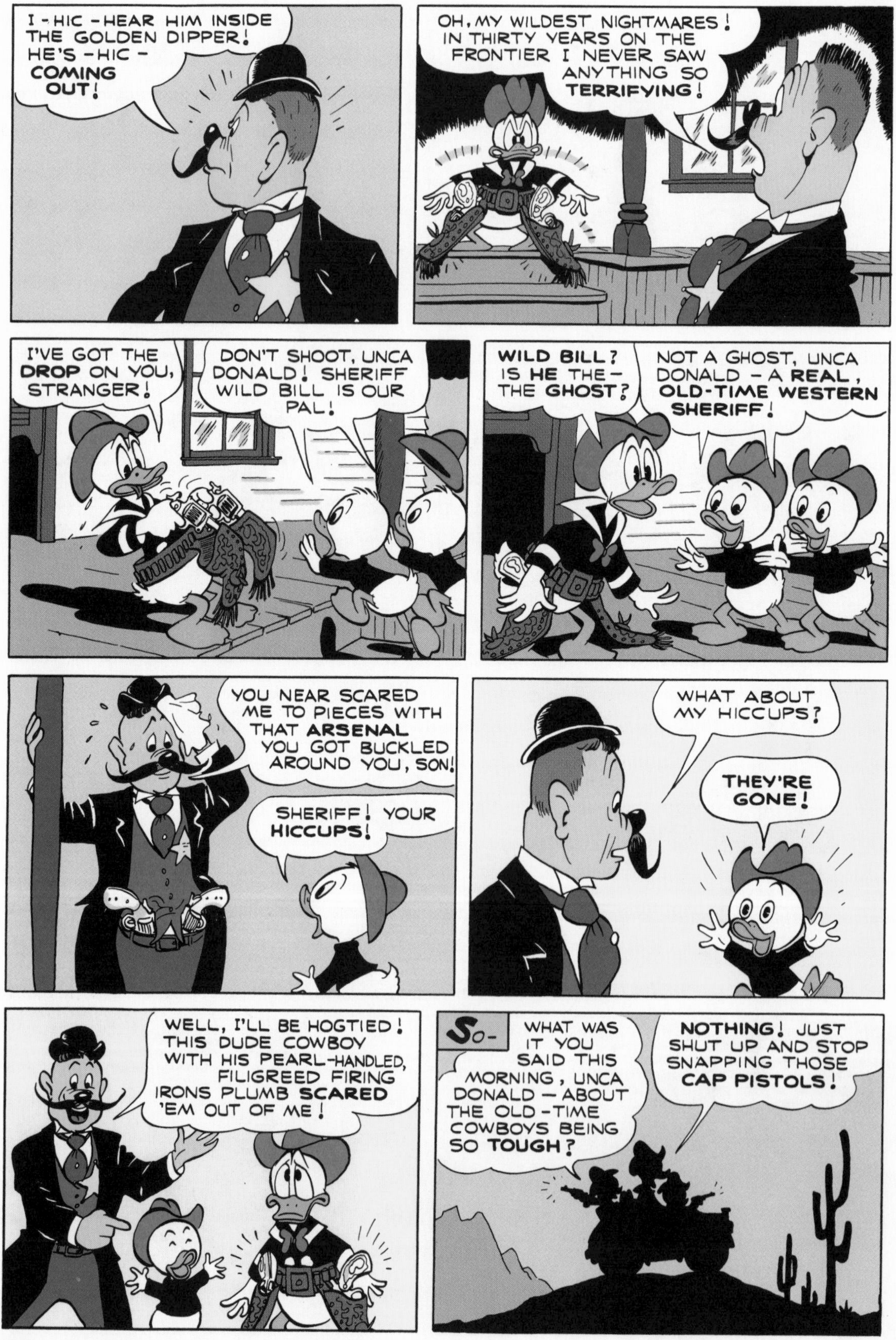
I-HIC-HEAR HIM INSIDE THE GOLDEN DIPPER! HE'S-HIC- **COMING OUT!**
OH, MY WILDEST NIGHTMARES! IN THIRTY YEARS ON THE FRONTIER I NEVER SAW ANYTHING SO **TERRIFYING!**
I'VE GOT THE **DROP** ON YOU, STRANGER!
DON'T SHOOT, UNCA DONALD! SHERIFF WILD BILL IS OUR PAL!
WILD BILL? IS **HE** THE-THE **GHOST?**
NOT A GHOST, UNCA DONALD - A **REAL, OLD-TIME WESTERN SHERIFF!**
YOU NEAR SCARED ME TO PIECES WITH THAT **ARSENAL** YOU GOT BUCKLED AROUND YOU, SON!
SHERIFF! YOUR **HICCUPS!**
WHAT ABOUT MY HICCUPS?
THEY'RE GONE!
WELL, I'LL BE HOGTIED! THIS DUDE COWBOY WITH HIS PEARL-HANDLED, FILIGREED FIRING IRONS PLUMB **SCARED** 'EM OUT OF ME!
SO-
WHAT WAS IT YOU SAID THIS MORNING, UNCA DONALD - ABOUT THE OLD-TIME COWBOYS BEING SO **TOUGH?**
NOTHING! JUST SHUT UP AND STOP SNAPPING THOSE **CAP PISTOLS!**

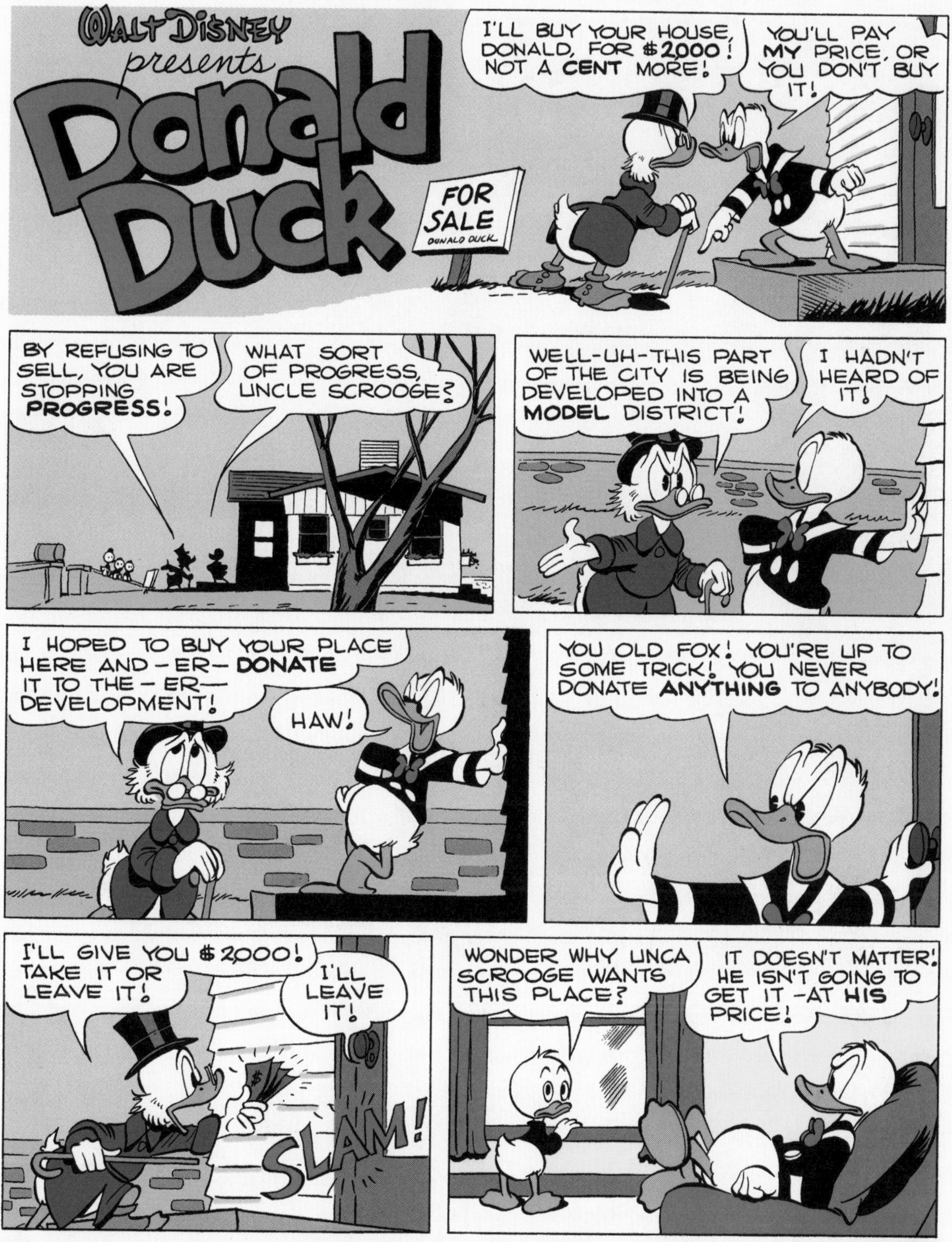
WALT DISNEY
presents
Donald Duck
FOR SALE
DONALD DUCK
I'LL BUY YOUR HOUSE, DONALD, FOR $2000! NOT A CENT MORE!
YOU'LL PAY MY PRICE, OR YOU DON'T BUY IT!
BY REFUSING TO SELL, YOU ARE STOPPING PROGRESS!
WHAT SORT OF PROGRESS, UNCLE SCROOGE?
WELL-UH-THIS PART OF THE CITY IS BEING DEVELOPED INTO A MODEL DISTRICT!
I HADN'T HEARD OF IT!
I HOPED TO BUY YOUR PLACE HERE AND-ER-DONATE IT TO THE-ER-DEVELOPMENT!
HAW!
YOU OLD FOX! YOU'RE UP TO SOME TRICK! YOU NEVER DONATE ANYTHING TO ANYBODY!
I'LL GIVE YOU $2000! TAKE IT OR LEAVE IT!
I'LL LEAVE IT!
SLAM!
WONDER WHY UNCA SCROOGE WANTS THIS PLACE?
IT DOESN'T MATTER! HE ISN'T GOING TO GET IT-AT HIS PRICE!

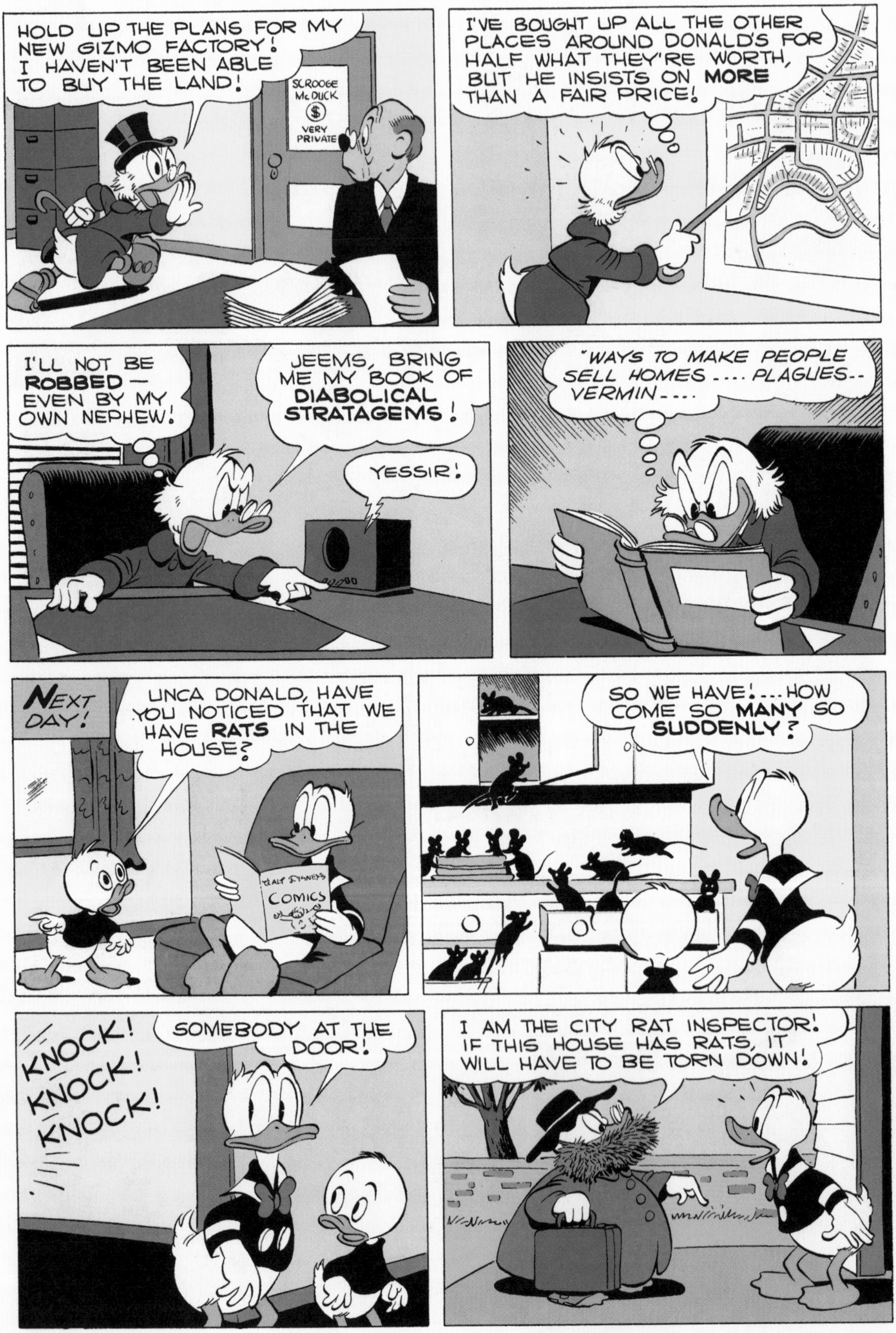
HOLD UP THE PLANS FOR MY NEW GIZMO FACTORY! I HAVEN'T BEEN ABLE TO BUY THE LAND!
SCROOGE McDUCK $ VERY PRIVATE
I'VE BOUGHT UP ALL THE OTHER PLACES AROUND DONALD'S FOR HALF WHAT THEY'RE WORTH, BUT HE INSISTS ON **MORE** THAN A FAIR PRICE!
I'LL NOT BE **ROBBED** — EVEN BY MY OWN NEPHEW!
JEEMS, BRING ME MY BOOK OF **DIABOLICAL STRATAGEMS**!
YESSIR!
"WAYS TO MAKE PEOPLE SELL HOMES .... PLAGUES-- VERMIN....
NEXT DAY!
UNCA DONALD, HAVE YOU NOTICED THAT WE HAVE **RATS** IN THE HOUSE?
WALT DISNEY'S COMICS
SO WE HAVE!...HOW COME SO **MANY** SO **SUDDENLY**?
KNOCK! KNOCK! KNOCK!
SOMEBODY AT THE DOOR!
I AM THE CITY RAT INSPECTOR! IF THIS HOUSE HAS RATS, IT WILL HAVE TO BE TORN DOWN!

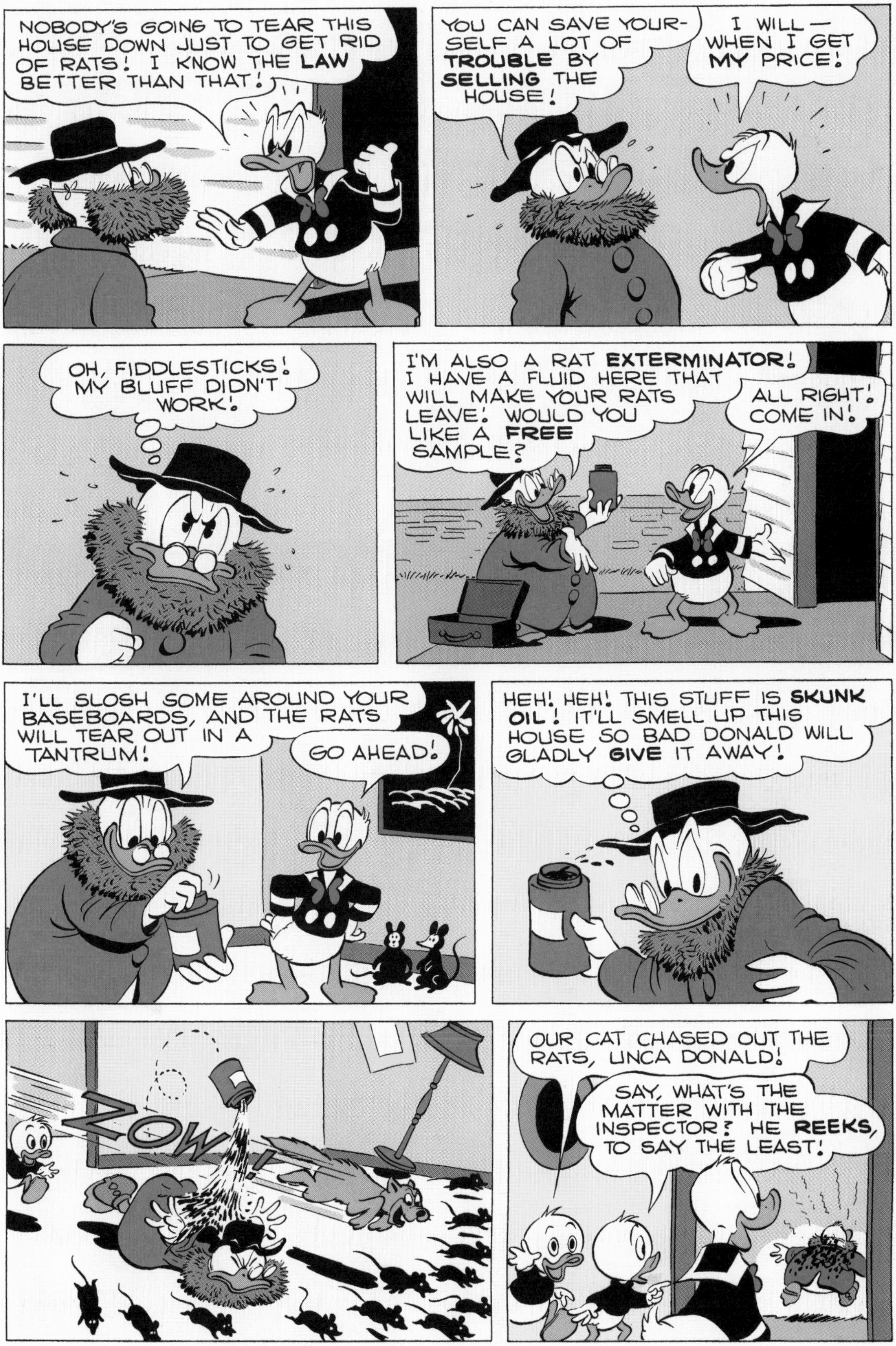
NOBODY'S GOING TO TEAR THIS HOUSE DOWN JUST TO GET RID OF RATS! I KNOW THE **LAW** BETTER THAN THAT!
YOU CAN SAVE YOURSELF A LOT OF **TROUBLE** BY **SELLING** THE HOUSE!
I WILL — WHEN I GET **MY** PRICE!
OH, FIDDLESTICKS! MY BLUFF DIDN'T WORK!
I'M ALSO A RAT **EXTERMINATOR**! I HAVE A FLUID HERE THAT WILL MAKE YOUR RATS LEAVE! WOULD YOU LIKE A **FREE** SAMPLE?
ALL RIGHT! COME IN!
I'LL SLOSH SOME AROUND YOUR BASEBOARDS, AND THE RATS WILL TEAR OUT IN A TANTRUM!
GO AHEAD!
HEH! HEH! THIS STUFF IS **SKUNK OIL**! IT'LL SMELL UP THIS HOUSE SO BAD DONALD WILL GLADLY **GIVE** IT AWAY!
ZOWIE!
OUR CAT CHASED OUT THE RATS, UNCA DONALD!
SAY, WHAT'S THE MATTER WITH THE INSPECTOR? HE **REEKS**, TO SAY THE LEAST!

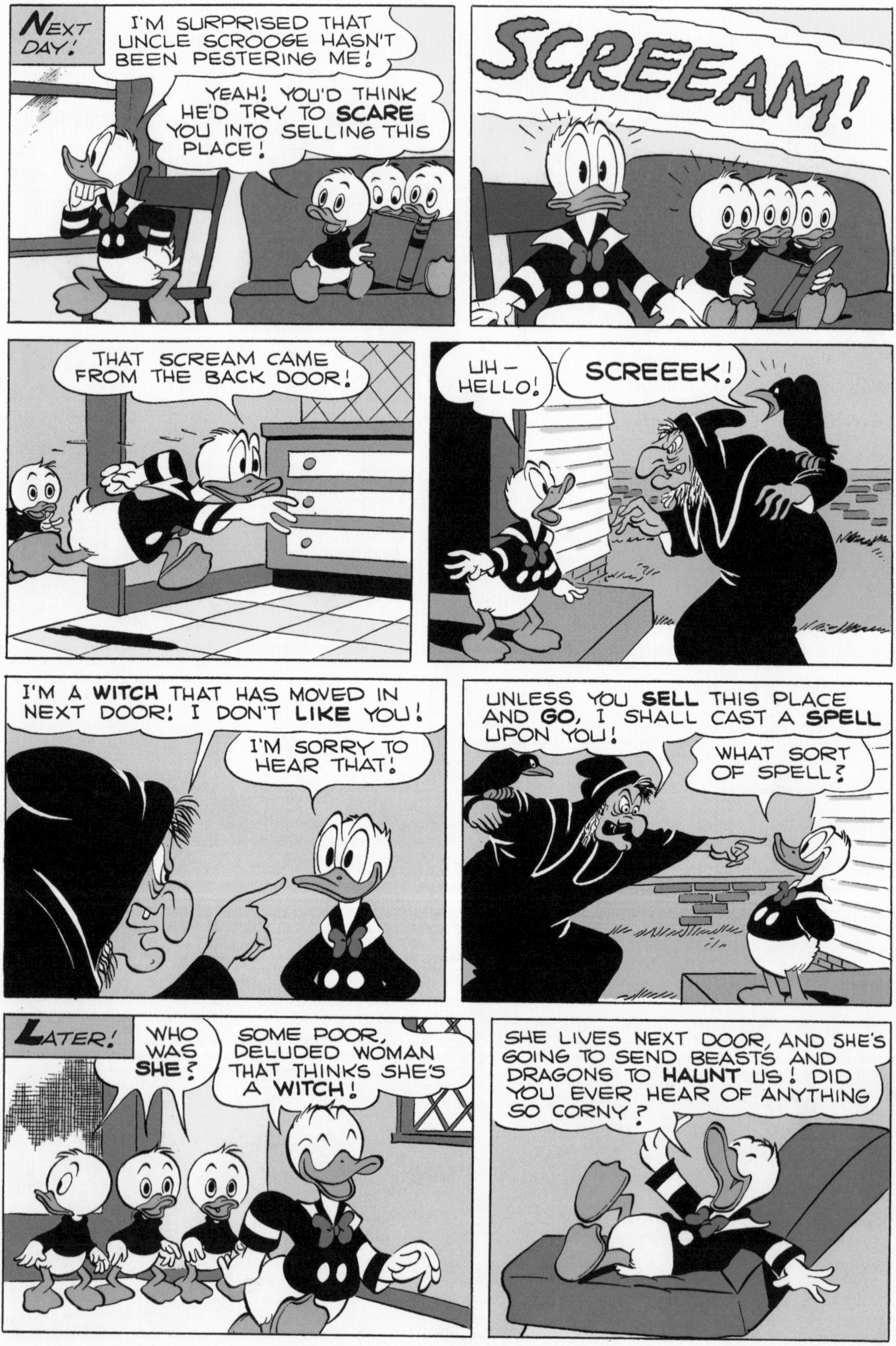
NEXT DAY!
I'M SURPRISED THAT UNCLE SCROOGE HASN'T BEEN PESTERING ME!
YEAH! YOU'D THINK HE'D TRY TO SCARE YOU INTO SELLING THIS PLACE!
SCREEAM!
THAT SCREAM CAME FROM THE BACK DOOR!
UH — HELLO!
SCREEEK!
I'M A WITCH THAT HAS MOVED IN NEXT DOOR! I DON'T LIKE YOU!
I'M SORRY TO HEAR THAT!
UNLESS YOU SELL THIS PLACE AND GO, I SHALL CAST A SPELL UPON YOU!
WHAT SORT OF SPELL?
LATER!
WHO WAS SHE?
SOME POOR, DELUDED WOMAN THAT THINKS SHE'S A WITCH!
SHE LIVES NEXT DOOR, AND SHE'S GOING TO SEND BEASTS AND DRAGONS TO HAUNT US! DID YOU EVER HEAR OF ANYTHING SO CORNY?

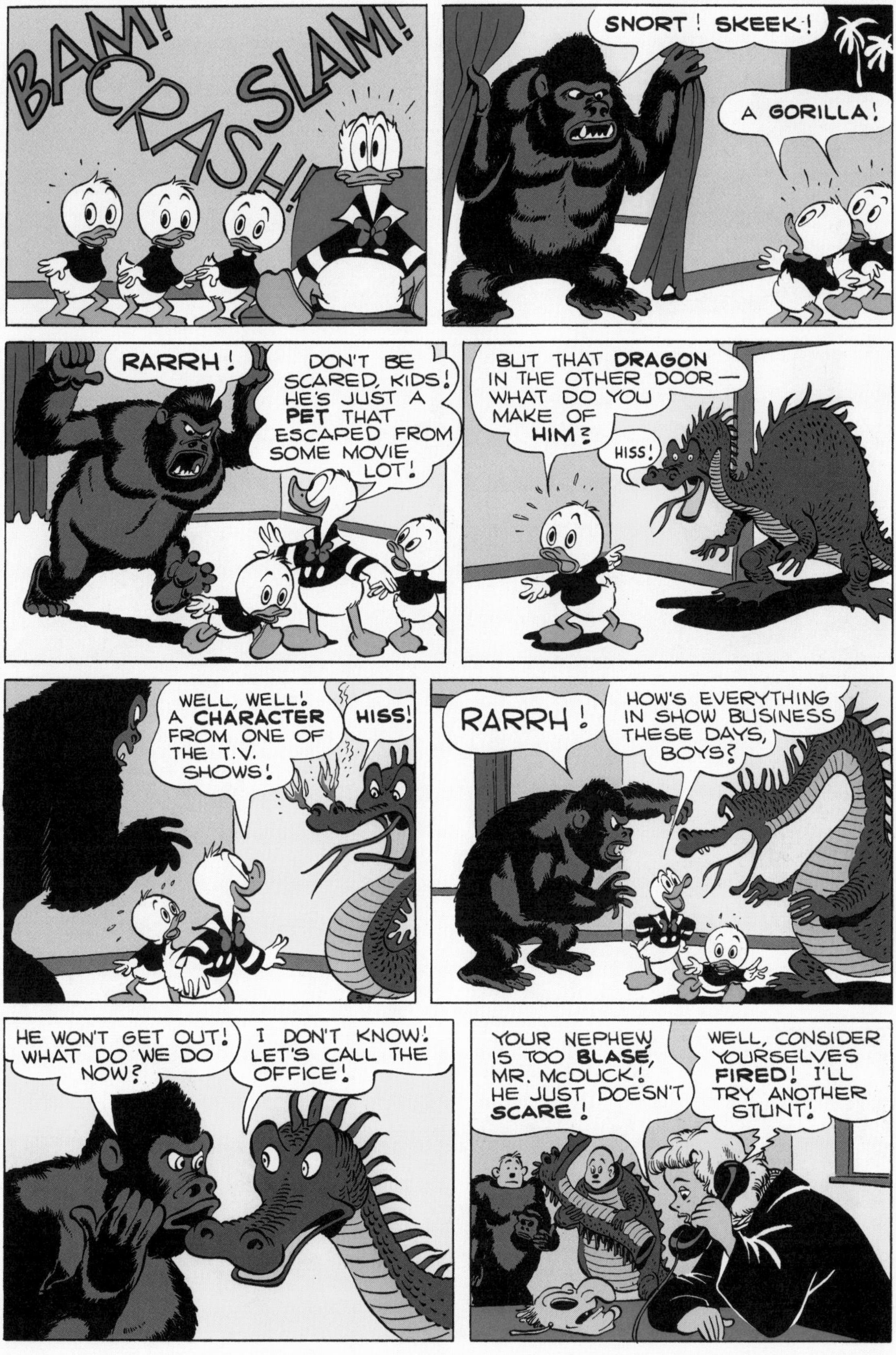
BAM! CRASH! SLAM!
SNORT! SKEEK!
A GORILLA!
RARRH!
DON'T BE SCARED, KIDS! HE'S JUST A PET THAT ESCAPED FROM SOME MOVIE LOT!
BUT THAT DRAGON IN THE OTHER DOOR — WHAT DO YOU MAKE OF HIM?
HISS!
WELL, WELL! A CHARACTER FROM ONE OF THE T.V. SHOWS!
HISS!
RARRH!
HOW'S EVERYTHING IN SHOW BUSINESS THESE DAYS, BOYS?
HE WON'T GET OUT! WHAT DO WE DO NOW?
I DON'T KNOW! LET'S CALL THE OFFICE!
YOUR NEPHEW IS TOO BLASÉ, MR. McDUCK! HE JUST DOESN'T SCARE!
WELL, CONSIDER YOURSELVES FIRED! I'LL TRY ANOTHER STUNT!

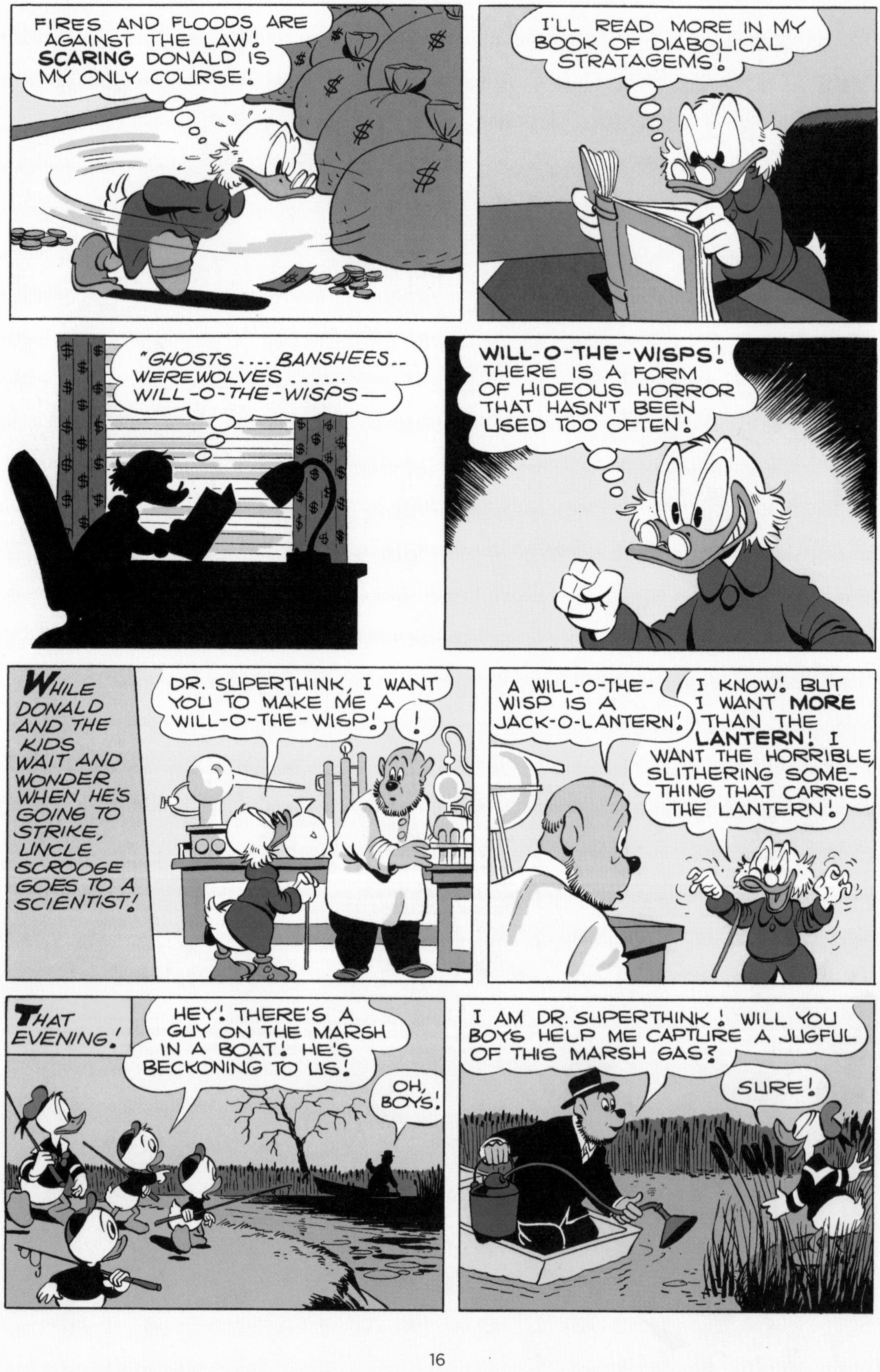
FIRES AND FLOODS ARE AGAINST THE LAW! SCARING DONALD IS MY ONLY COURSE!
I'LL READ MORE IN MY BOOK OF DIABOLICAL STRATAGEMS!
"GHOSTS .... BANSHEES.. WEREWOLVES ...... WILL-O-THE-WISPS—
WILL-O-THE-WISPS! THERE IS A FORM OF HIDEOUS HORROR THAT HASN'T BEEN USED TOO OFTEN!
WHILE DONALD AND THE KIDS WAIT AND WONDER WHEN HE'S GOING TO STRIKE, UNCLE SCROOGE GOES TO A SCIENTIST!
DR. SUPERTHINK, I WANT YOU TO MAKE ME A WILL-O-THE-WISP!
!
A WILL-O-THE-WISP IS A JACK-O-LANTERN!
I KNOW! BUT I WANT MORE THAN THE LANTERN! I WANT THE HORRIBLE, SLITHERING SOMETHING THAT CARRIES THE LANTERN!
THAT EVENING!
HEY! THERE'S A GUY ON THE MARSH IN A BOAT! HE'S BECKONING TO US!
OH, BOYS!
I AM DR. SUPERTHINK! WILL YOU BOYS HELP ME CAPTURE A JUGFUL OF THIS MARSH GAS?
SURE!

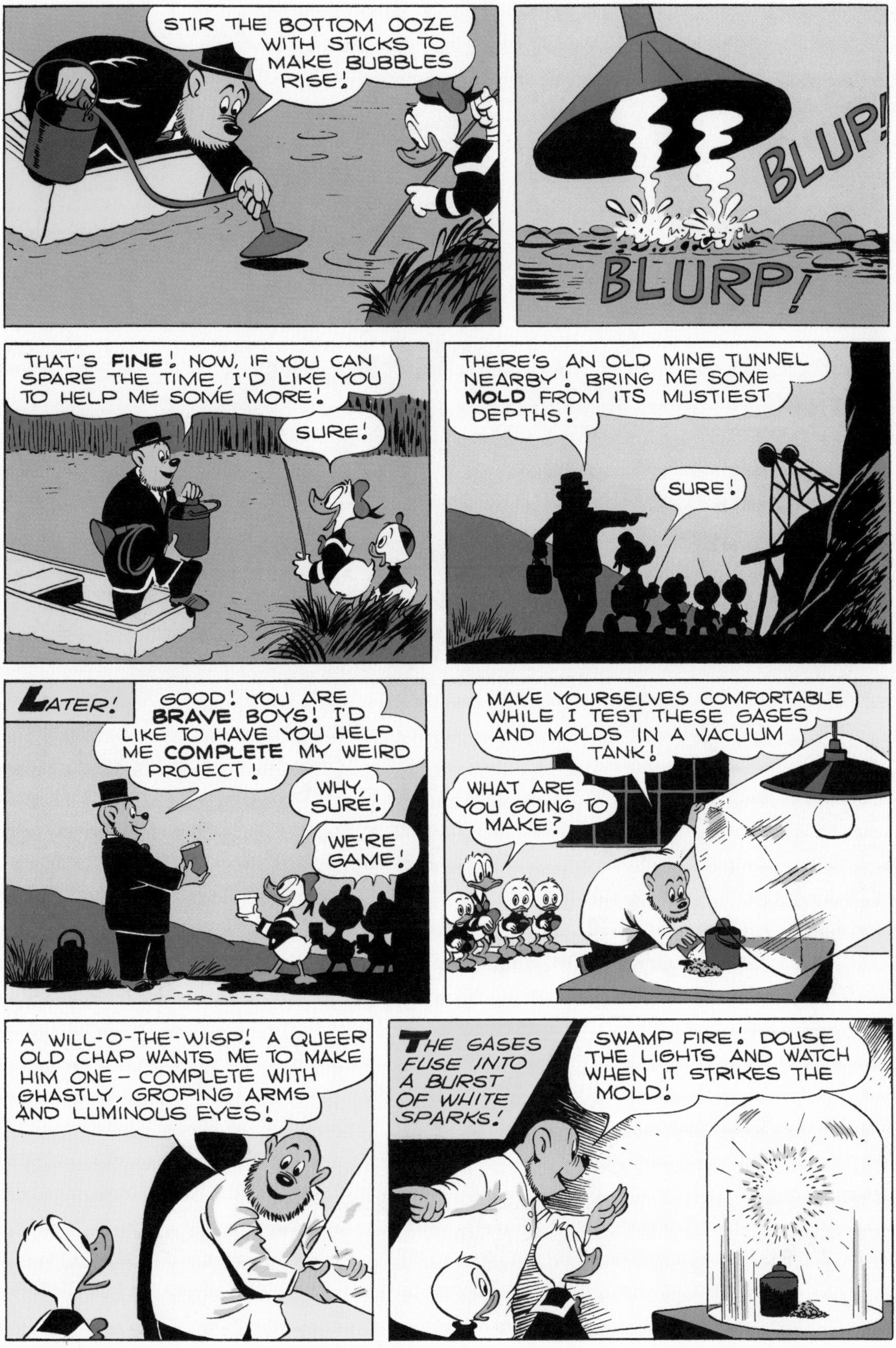
STIR THE BOTTOM OOZE WITH STICKS TO MAKE BUBBLES RISE!
BLUP!
BLURP!
THAT'S FINE! NOW, IF YOU CAN SPARE THE TIME, I'D LIKE YOU TO HELP ME SOME MORE!
SURE!
THERE'S AN OLD MINE TUNNEL NEARBY! BRING ME SOME MOLD FROM ITS MUSTIEST DEPTHS!
SURE!
LATER!
GOOD! YOU ARE BRAVE BOYS! I'D LIKE TO HAVE YOU HELP ME COMPLETE MY WEIRD PROJECT!
WHY, SURE!
WE'RE GAME!
MAKE YOURSELVES COMFORTABLE WHILE I TEST THESE GASES AND MOLDS IN A VACUUM TANK!
WHAT ARE YOU GOING TO MAKE?
A WILL-O-THE-WISP! A QUEER OLD CHAP WANTS ME TO MAKE HIM ONE – COMPLETE WITH GHASTLY, GROPING ARMS AND LUMINOUS EYES!
THE GASES FUSE INTO A BURST OF WHITE SPARKS!
SWAMP FIRE! DOUSE THE LIGHTS AND WATCH WHEN IT STRIKES THE MOLD!

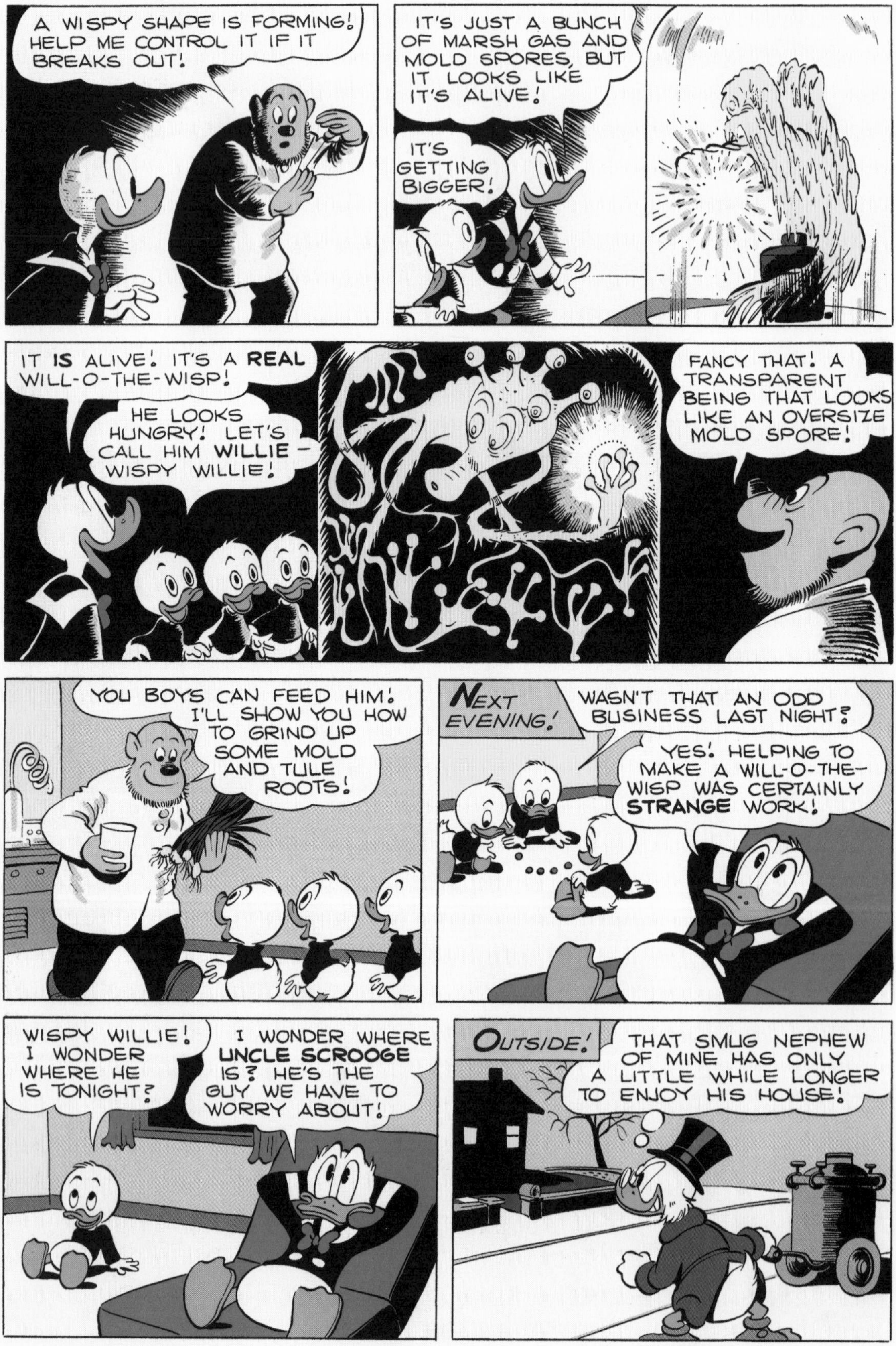
A WISPY SHAPE IS FORMING! HELP ME CONTROL IT IF IT BREAKS OUT!
IT'S JUST A BUNCH OF MARSH GAS AND MOLD SPORES, BUT IT LOOKS LIKE IT'S ALIVE!
IT'S GETTING BIGGER!
IT IS ALIVE! IT'S A REAL WILL-O-THE-WISP!
HE LOOKS HUNGRY! LET'S CALL HIM WILLIE — WISPY WILLIE!
FANCY THAT! A TRANSPARENT BEING THAT LOOKS LIKE AN OVERSIZE MOLD SPORE!
YOU BOYS CAN FEED HIM! I'LL SHOW YOU HOW TO GRIND UP SOME MOLD AND TULE ROOTS!
NEXT EVENING!
WASN'T THAT AN ODD BUSINESS LAST NIGHT?
YES! HELPING TO MAKE A WILL-O-THE-WISP WAS CERTAINLY STRANGE WORK!
WISPY WILLIE! I WONDER WHERE HE IS TONIGHT?
I WONDER WHERE UNCLE SCROOGE IS? HE'S THE GUY WE HAVE TO WORRY ABOUT!
OUTSIDE!
THAT SMUG NEPHEW OF MINE HAS ONLY A LITTLE WHILE LONGER TO ENJOY HIS HOUSE!

THIS HORRIBLE WILL-O-THE-WISP THAT I HAD MADE UP WILL SCARE DONALD CLEAR OUT OF THE COUNTY!

GET GOING, YOU SHIVERY SPECTACLE! GO UP THERE AND GLOWER THROUGH THE WINDOW!

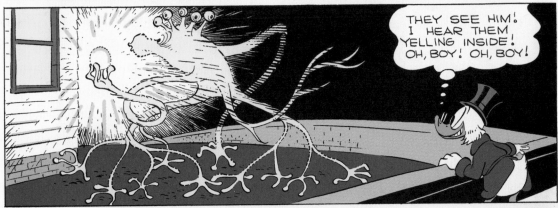

THEY SEE HIM! I HEAR THEM YELLING INSIDE! OH, BOY! OH, BOY!

NO LIVING THING CAN STAND THE HORROR OF SUCH A SIGHT! MY NEPHEWS WILL NEVER STOP RUNNING!

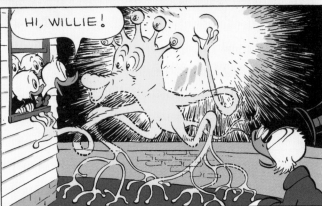

HI, WILLIE!

WHAT'S THE MATTER, OLD FELLA? HUNGRY? WE'LL GET YOU SOME TULE ROOTS!

THE ONLY EXPLANATION IS THAT I WAS BORN A HUNDRED YEARS TOO LATE!

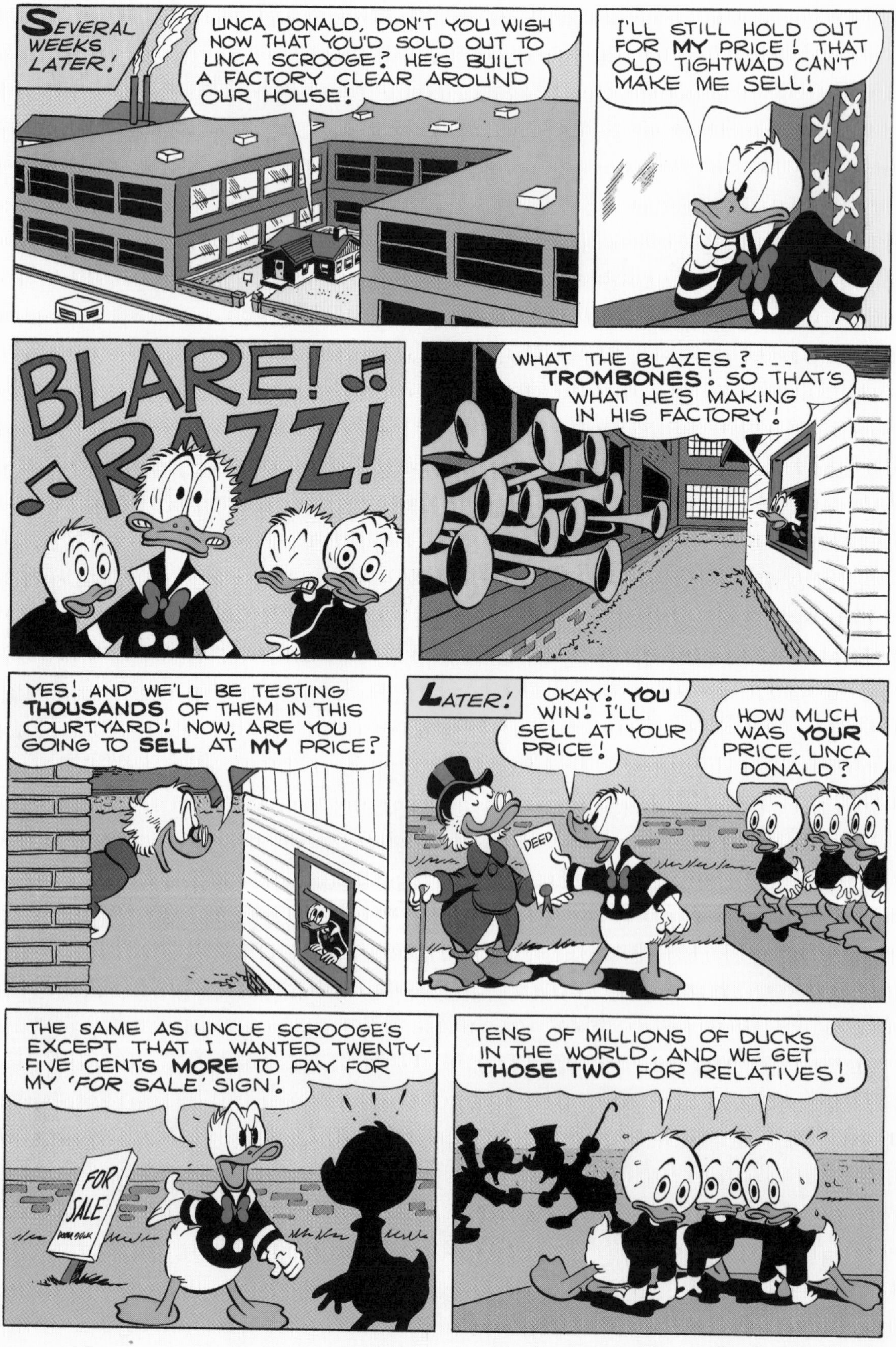
SEVERAL WEEKS LATER!
UNCA DONALD, DON'T YOU WISH NOW THAT YOU'D SOLD OUT TO UNCA SCROOGE? HE'S BUILT A FACTORY CLEAR AROUND OUR HOUSE!
I'LL STILL HOLD OUT FOR **MY** PRICE! THAT OLD TIGHTWAD CAN'T MAKE ME SELL!
BLARE! RAZZ!
WHAT THE BLAZES?--- **TROMBONES**! SO THAT'S WHAT HE'S MAKING IN HIS FACTORY!
YES! AND WE'LL BE TESTING **THOUSANDS** OF THEM IN THIS COURTYARD! NOW, ARE YOU GOING TO **SELL** AT **MY** PRICE?
LATER!
OKAY! **YOU** WIN! I'LL SELL AT YOUR PRICE!
HOW MUCH WAS **YOUR** PRICE, UNCA DONALD?
DEED
THE SAME AS UNCLE SCROOGE'S EXCEPT THAT I WANTED TWENTY-FIVE CENTS **MORE** TO PAY FOR MY '*FOR SALE*' SIGN!
FOR SALE
TENS OF MILLIONS OF DUCKS IN THE WORLD, AND WE GET **THOSE TWO** FOR RELATIVES!

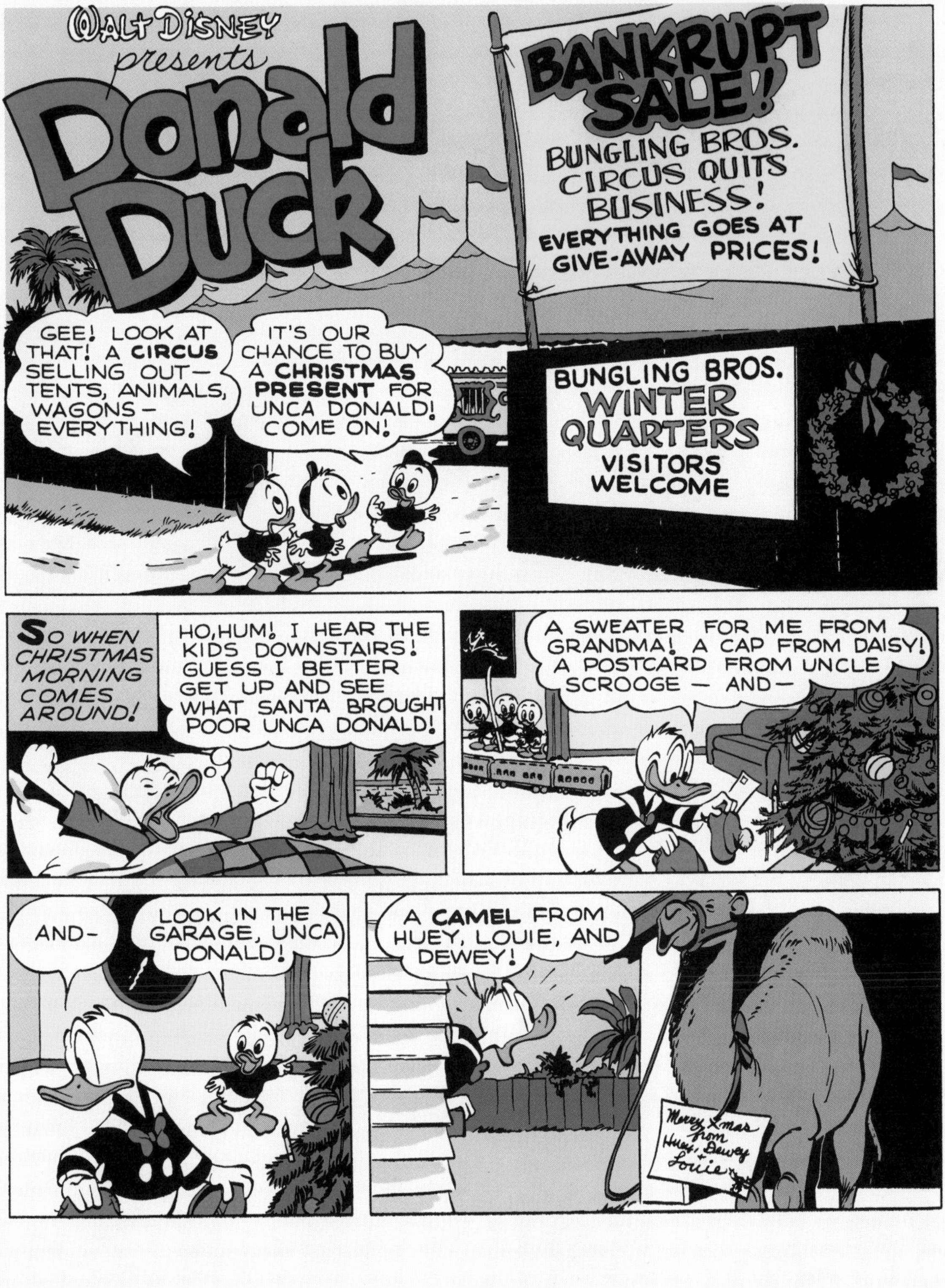
WALT DISNEY presents
Donald Duck
BANKRUPT SALE!
BUNGLING BROS. CIRCUS QUITS BUSINESS!
EVERYTHING GOES AT GIVE-AWAY PRICES!
GEE! LOOK AT THAT! A CIRCUS SELLING OUT— TENTS, ANIMALS, WAGONS— EVERYTHING!
IT'S OUR CHANCE TO BUY A CHRISTMAS PRESENT FOR UNCA DONALD! COME ON!
BUNGLING BROS. WINTER QUARTERS VISITORS WELCOME
SO WHEN CHRISTMAS MORNING COMES AROUND!
HO,HUM! I HEAR THE KIDS DOWNSTAIRS! GUESS I BETTER GET UP AND SEE WHAT SANTA BROUGHT POOR UNCA DONALD!
A SWEATER FOR ME FROM GRANDMA! A CAP FROM DAISY! A POSTCARD FROM UNCLE SCROOGE — AND—
AND—
LOOK IN THE GARAGE, UNCA DONALD!
A CAMEL FROM HUEY, LOUIE, AND DEWEY!
Merry Xmas from Huey, Dewey + Louie

A **CAMEL**! **WHY** A CAMEL?

WE THOUGHT IT'D MAKE YOU A **USEFUL** PET, UNCA DONALD!

OH!

DON'T YOU LIKE YOUR PRESENT, UNCA DONALD?

UH — UM — YES! BUT DIDN'T HE COST A **LOT** OF MONEY?

ONLY **FIFTY CENTS**! IF WE'D HAD TWO DOLLARS, WE COULD HAVE BOUGHT AN **ELEPHANT**!

WHAT DID I EVER DO TO DESERVE SUCH A **GRAND** GIFT? I'LL HAVE TO BE CAREFUL AFTER THIS!

HE CAN PULL THE LAWNMOWER AND TAKE YOU FOR RIDES IN THE PARK!

AND HE CAN **EAT** A TON OF HAY EVERY WEEK!

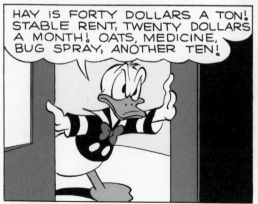

HAY IS FORTY DOLLARS A TON! STABLE RENT, TWENTY DOLLARS A MONTH! OATS, MEDICINE, BUG SPRAY, ANOTHER TEN!

YOU BETTER THINK OF SOMETHING **BIG** HE CAN DO, OR I'LL SELL HIM FOR **CAMELBURGERS**!

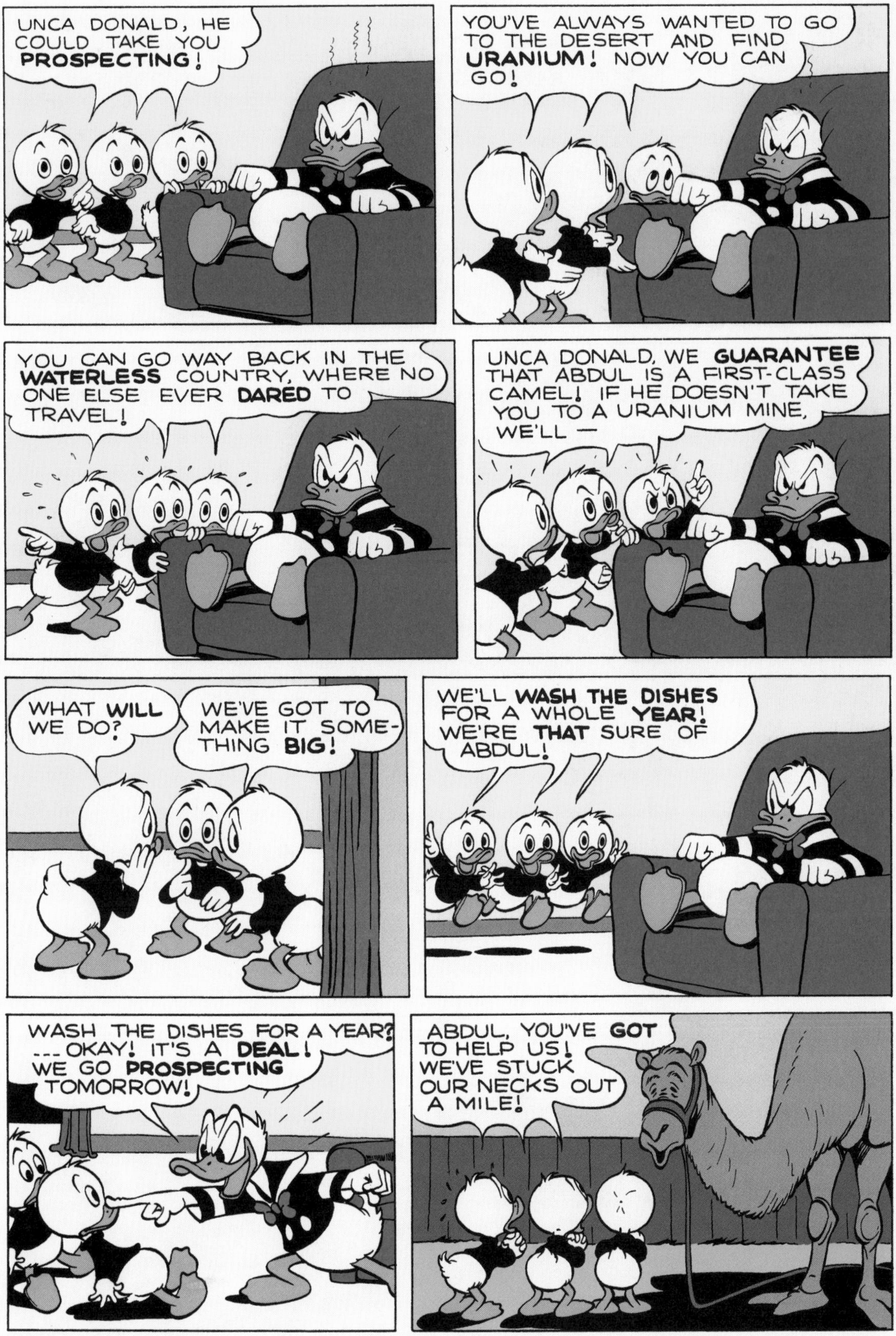
UNCA DONALD, HE COULD TAKE YOU PROSPECTING!
YOU'VE ALWAYS WANTED TO GO TO THE DESERT AND FIND URANIUM! NOW YOU CAN GO!
YOU CAN GO WAY BACK IN THE WATERLESS COUNTRY, WHERE NO ONE ELSE EVER DARED TO TRAVEL!
UNCA DONALD, WE GUARANTEE THAT ABDUL IS A FIRST-CLASS CAMEL! IF HE DOESN'T TAKE YOU TO A URANIUM MINE, WE'LL —
WHAT WILL WE DO?
WE'VE GOT TO MAKE IT SOMETHING BIG!
WE'LL WASH THE DISHES FOR A WHOLE YEAR! WE'RE THAT SURE OF ABDUL!
WASH THE DISHES FOR A YEAR? ...OKAY! IT'S A DEAL! WE GO PROSPECTING TOMORROW!
ABDUL, YOU'VE GOT TO HELP US! WE'VE STUCK OUR NECKS OUT A MILE!

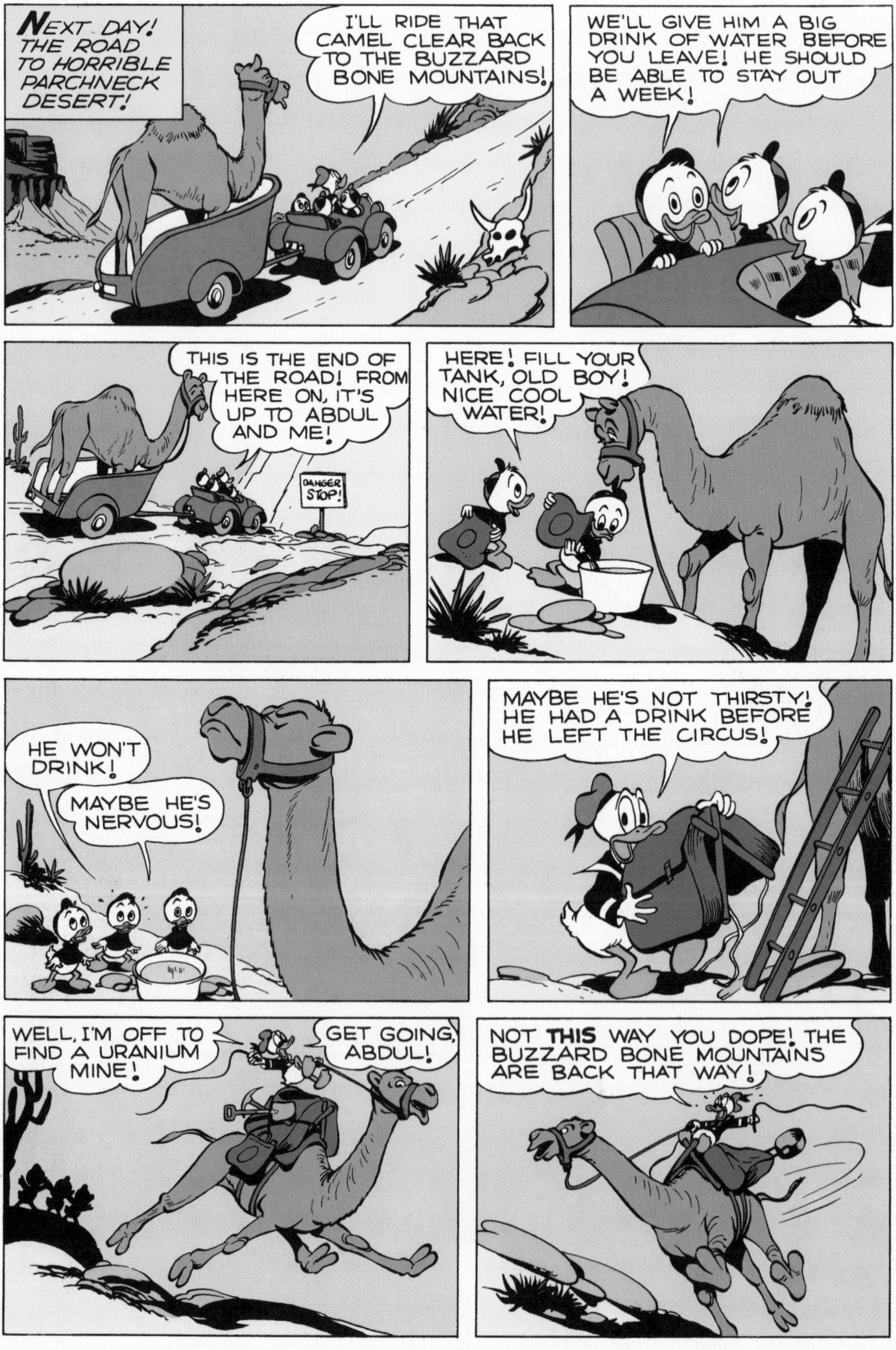
NEXT DAY! THE ROAD TO HORRIBLE PARCHNECK DESERT!
I'LL RIDE THAT CAMEL CLEAR BACK TO THE BUZZARD BONE MOUNTAINS!
WE'LL GIVE HIM A BIG DRINK OF WATER BEFORE YOU LEAVE! HE SHOULD BE ABLE TO STAY OUT A WEEK!
THIS IS THE END OF THE ROAD! FROM HERE ON, IT'S UP TO ABDUL AND ME!
DANGER STOP!
HERE! FILL YOUR TANK, OLD BOY! NICE COOL WATER!
HE WON'T DRINK!
MAYBE HE'S NERVOUS!
MAYBE HE'S NOT THIRSTY! HE HAD A DRINK BEFORE HE LEFT THE CIRCUS!
WELL, I'M OFF TO FIND A URANIUM MINE!
GET GOING, ABDUL!
NOT **THIS** WAY YOU DOPE! THE BUZZARD BONE MOUNTAINS ARE BACK THAT WAY!

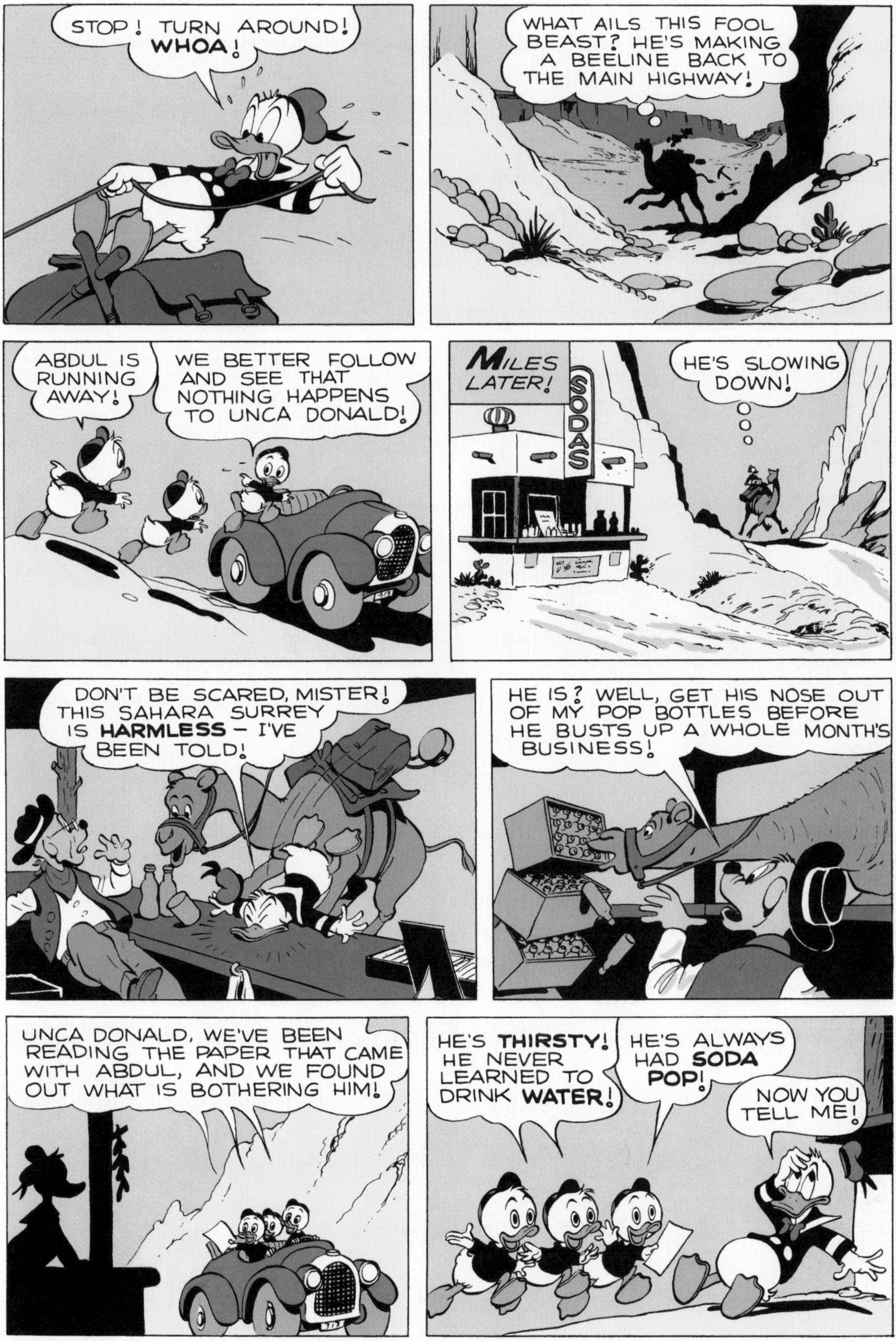
STOP! TURN AROUND! WHOA!
WHAT AILS THIS FOOL BEAST? HE'S MAKING A BEELINE BACK TO THE MAIN HIGHWAY!
ABDUL IS RUNNING AWAY!
WE BETTER FOLLOW AND SEE THAT NOTHING HAPPENS TO UNCA DONALD!
MILES LATER!
SODAS
HE'S SLOWING DOWN!
DON'T BE SCARED, MISTER! THIS SAHARA SURREY IS HARMLESS – I'VE BEEN TOLD!
HE IS? WELL, GET HIS NOSE OUT OF MY POP BOTTLES BEFORE HE BUSTS UP A WHOLE MONTH'S BUSINESS!
UNCA DONALD, WE'VE BEEN READING THE PAPER THAT CAME WITH ABDUL, AND WE FOUND OUT WHAT IS BOTHERING HIM!
HE'S THIRSTY! HE NEVER LEARNED TO DRINK WATER!
HE'S ALWAYS HAD SODA POP!
NOW YOU TELL ME!

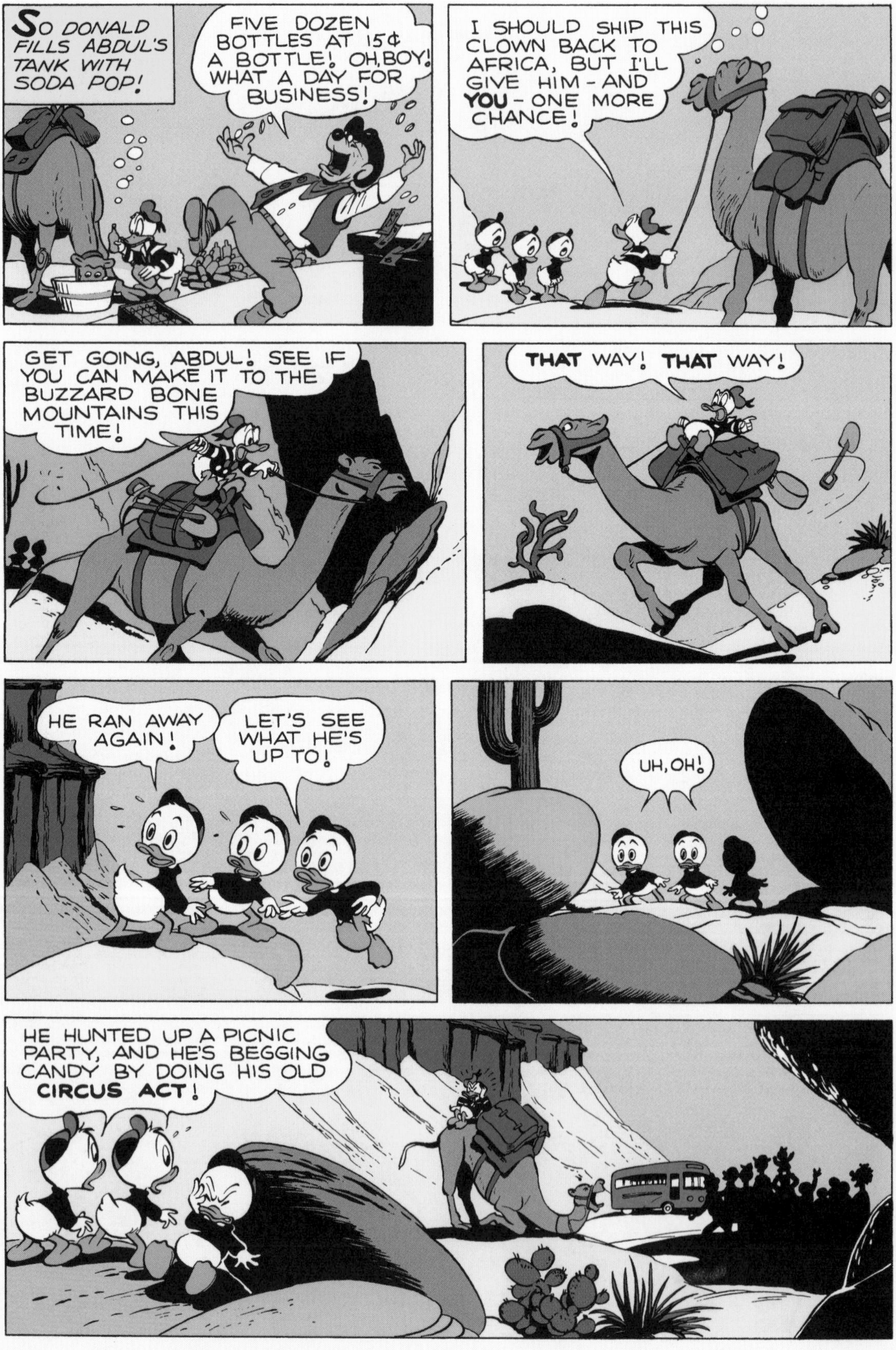
SO DONALD FILLS ABDUL'S TANK WITH SODA POP!
FIVE DOZEN BOTTLES AT 15¢ A BOTTLE! OH, BOY! WHAT A DAY FOR BUSINESS!
I SHOULD SHIP THIS CLOWN BACK TO AFRICA, BUT I'LL GIVE HIM - AND **YOU** - ONE MORE CHANCE!
GET GOING, ABDUL! SEE IF YOU CAN MAKE IT TO THE BUZZARD BONE MOUNTAINS THIS TIME!
THAT WAY! **THAT** WAY!
HE RAN AWAY AGAIN!
LET'S SEE WHAT HE'S UP TO!
UH, OH!
HE HUNTED UP A PICNIC PARTY, AND HE'S BEGGING CANDY BY DOING HIS OLD **CIRCUS ACT**!

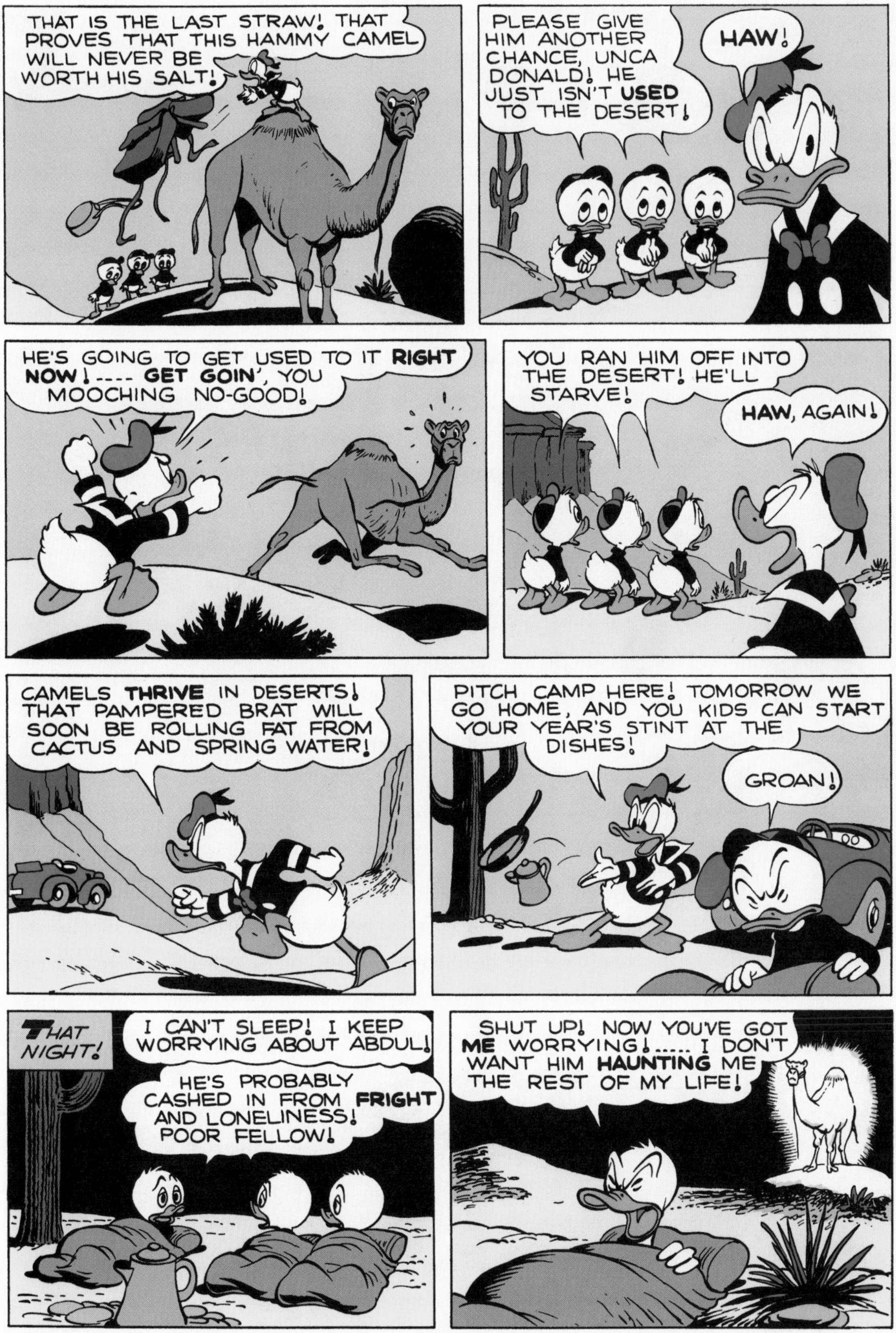
THAT IS THE LAST STRAW! THAT PROVES THAT THIS HAMMY CAMEL WILL NEVER BE WORTH HIS SALT!
PLEASE GIVE HIM ANOTHER CHANCE, UNCA DONALD! HE JUST ISN'T USED TO THE DESERT!
HAW!
HE'S GOING TO GET USED TO IT RIGHT NOW!---- GET GOIN', YOU MOOCHING NO-GOOD!
YOU RAN HIM OFF INTO THE DESERT! HE'LL STARVE!
HAW, AGAIN!
CAMELS THRIVE IN DESERTS! THAT PAMPERED BRAT WILL SOON BE ROLLING FAT FROM CACTUS AND SPRING WATER!
PITCH CAMP HERE! TOMORROW WE GO HOME, AND YOU KIDS CAN START YOUR YEAR'S STINT AT THE DISHES!
GROAN!
THAT NIGHT!
I CAN'T SLEEP! I KEEP WORRYING ABOUT ABDUL!
HE'S PROBABLY CASHED IN FROM FRIGHT AND LONELINESS! POOR FELLOW!
SHUT UP! NOW YOU'VE GOT ME WORRYING!..... I DON'T WANT HIM HAUNTING ME THE REST OF MY LIFE!

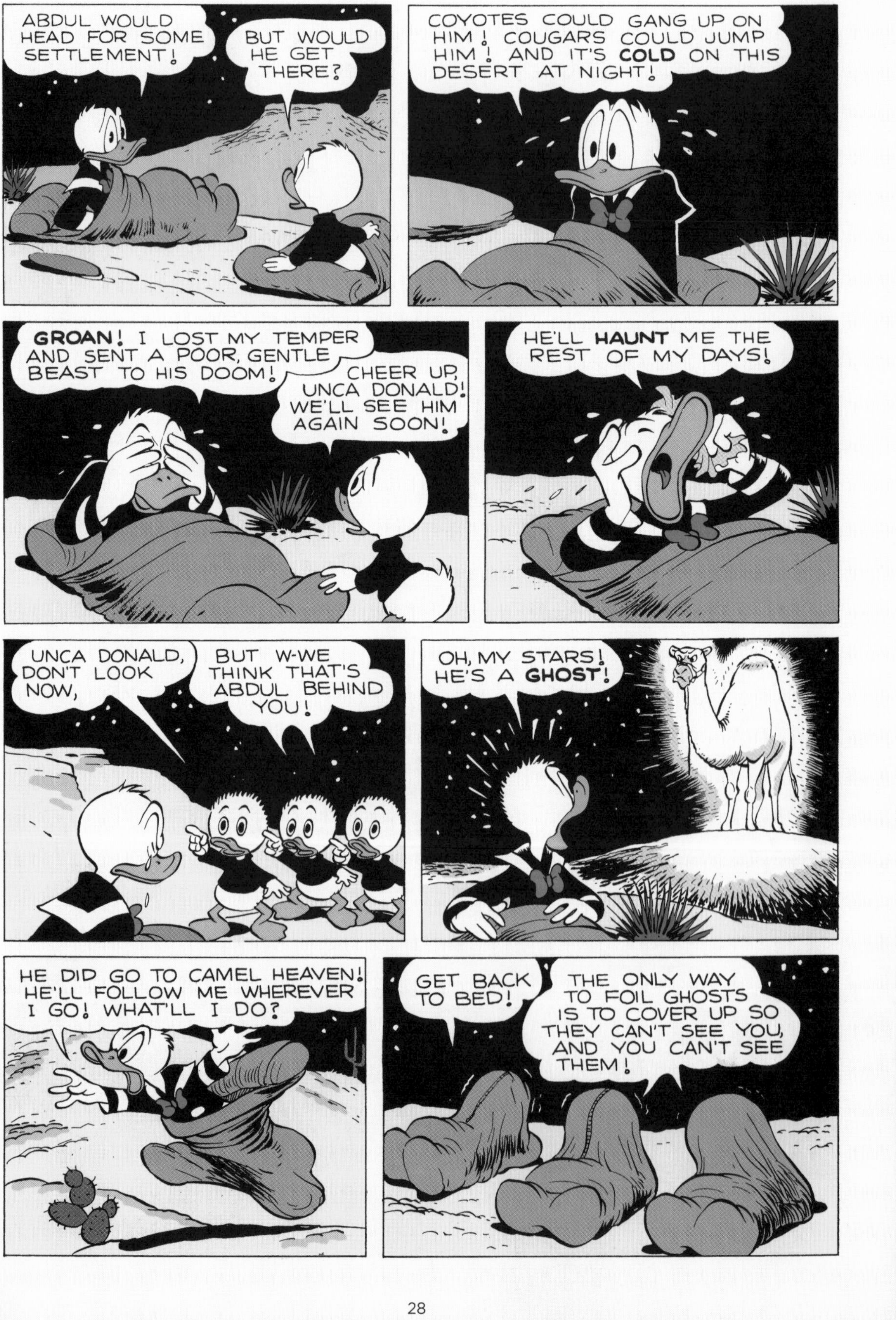
ABDUL WOULD HEAD FOR SOME SETTLEMENT!
BUT WOULD HE GET THERE?
COYOTES COULD GANG UP ON HIM! COUGARS COULD JUMP HIM! AND IT'S COLD ON THIS DESERT AT NIGHT!
GROAN! I LOST MY TEMPER AND SENT A POOR, GENTLE BEAST TO HIS DOOM!
CHEER UP, UNCA DONALD! WE'LL SEE HIM AGAIN SOON!
HE'LL HAUNT ME THE REST OF MY DAYS!
UNCA DONALD, DON'T LOOK NOW,
BUT W-WE THINK THAT'S ABDUL BEHIND YOU!
OH, MY STARS! HE'S A GHOST!
HE DID GO TO CAMEL HEAVEN! HE'LL FOLLOW ME WHEREVER I GO! WHAT'LL I DO?
GET BACK TO BED!
THE ONLY WAY TO FOIL GHOSTS IS TO COVER UP SO THEY CAN'T SEE YOU, AND YOU CAN'T SEE THEM!

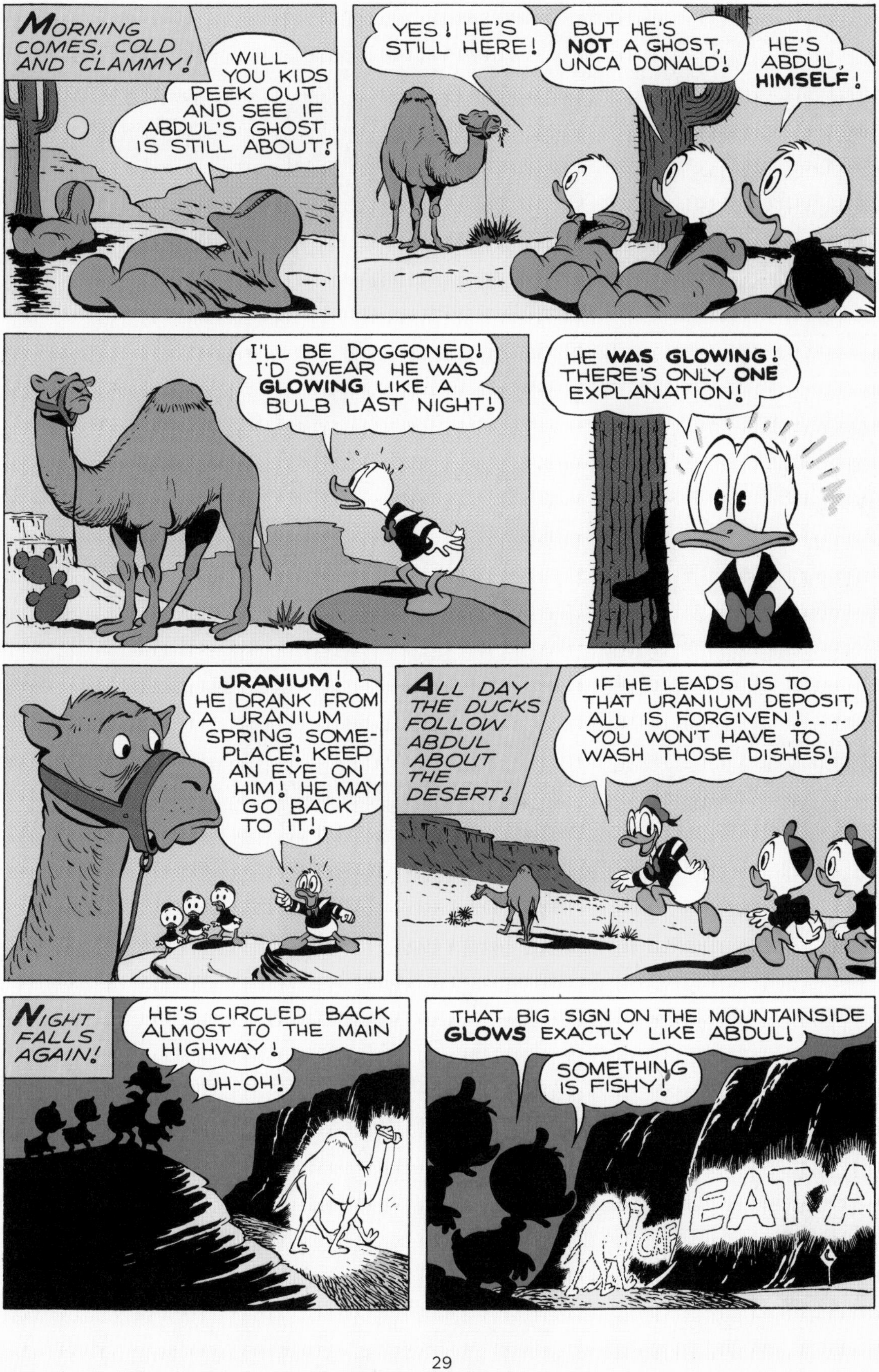
MORNING COMES, COLD AND CLAMMY!
WILL YOU KIDS PEEK OUT AND SEE IF ABDUL'S GHOST IS STILL ABOUT?
YES! HE'S STILL HERE!
BUT HE'S NOT A GHOST, UNCA DONALD!
HE'S ABDUL, HIMSELF!
I'LL BE DOGGONED! I'D SWEAR HE WAS GLOWING LIKE A BULB LAST NIGHT!
HE WAS GLOWING! THERE'S ONLY ONE EXPLANATION!
URANIUM! HE DRANK FROM A URANIUM SPRING SOME-PLACE! KEEP AN EYE ON HIM! HE MAY GO BACK TO IT!
ALL DAY THE DUCKS FOLLOW ABDUL ABOUT THE DESERT!
IF HE LEADS US TO THAT URANIUM DEPOSIT, ALL IS FORGIVEN!.... YOU WON'T HAVE TO WASH THOSE DISHES!
NIGHT FALLS AGAIN!
HE'S CIRCLED BACK ALMOST TO THE MAIN HIGHWAY!
UH-OH!
THAT BIG SIGN ON THE MOUNTAINSIDE GLOWS EXACTLY LIKE ABDUL!
SOMETHING IS FISHY!
CAFE
EAT A

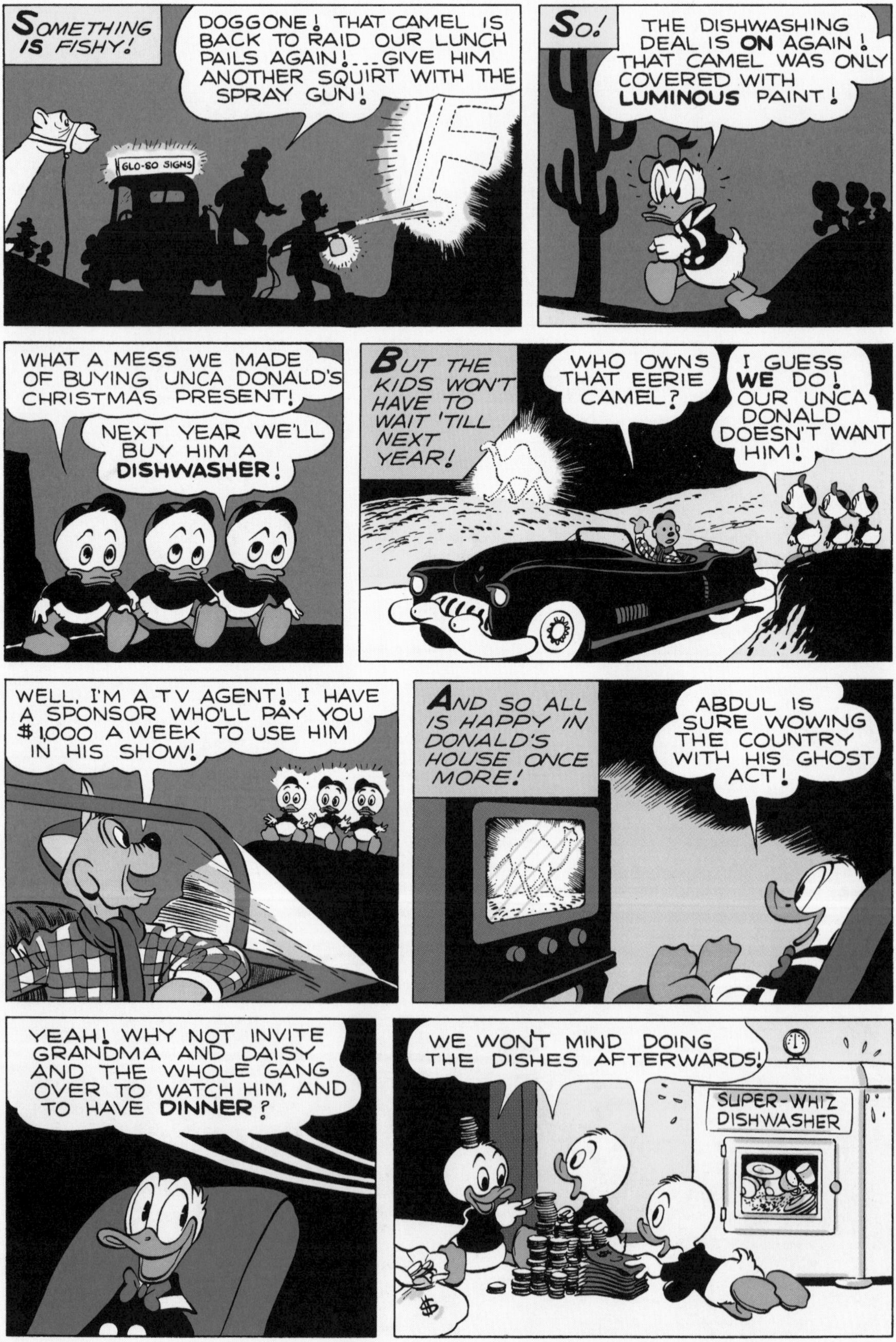
SOMETHING IS FISHY!
DOGGONE! THAT CAMEL IS BACK TO RAID OUR LUNCH PAILS AGAIN!...GIVE HIM ANOTHER SQUIRT WITH THE SPRAY GUN!
GLO-SO SIGNS
SO!
THE DISHWASHING DEAL IS ON AGAIN! THAT CAMEL WAS ONLY COVERED WITH LUMINOUS PAINT!
WHAT A MESS WE MADE OF BUYING UNCA DONALD'S CHRISTMAS PRESENT!
NEXT YEAR WE'LL BUY HIM A DISHWASHER!
BUT THE KIDS WON'T HAVE TO WAIT 'TILL NEXT YEAR!
WHO OWNS THAT EERIE CAMEL?
I GUESS WE DO! OUR UNCA DONALD DOESN'T WANT HIM!
WELL, I'M A TV AGENT! I HAVE A SPONSOR WHO'LL PAY YOU $1,000 A WEEK TO USE HIM IN HIS SHOW!
AND SO ALL IS HAPPY IN DONALD'S HOUSE ONCE MORE!
ABDUL IS SURE WOWING THE COUNTRY WITH HIS GHOST ACT!
YEAH! WHY NOT INVITE GRANDMA AND DAISY AND THE WHOLE GANG OVER TO WATCH HIM, AND TO HAVE DINNER?
WE WON'T MIND DOING THE DISHES AFTERWARDS!
SUPER-WHIZ DISHWASHER

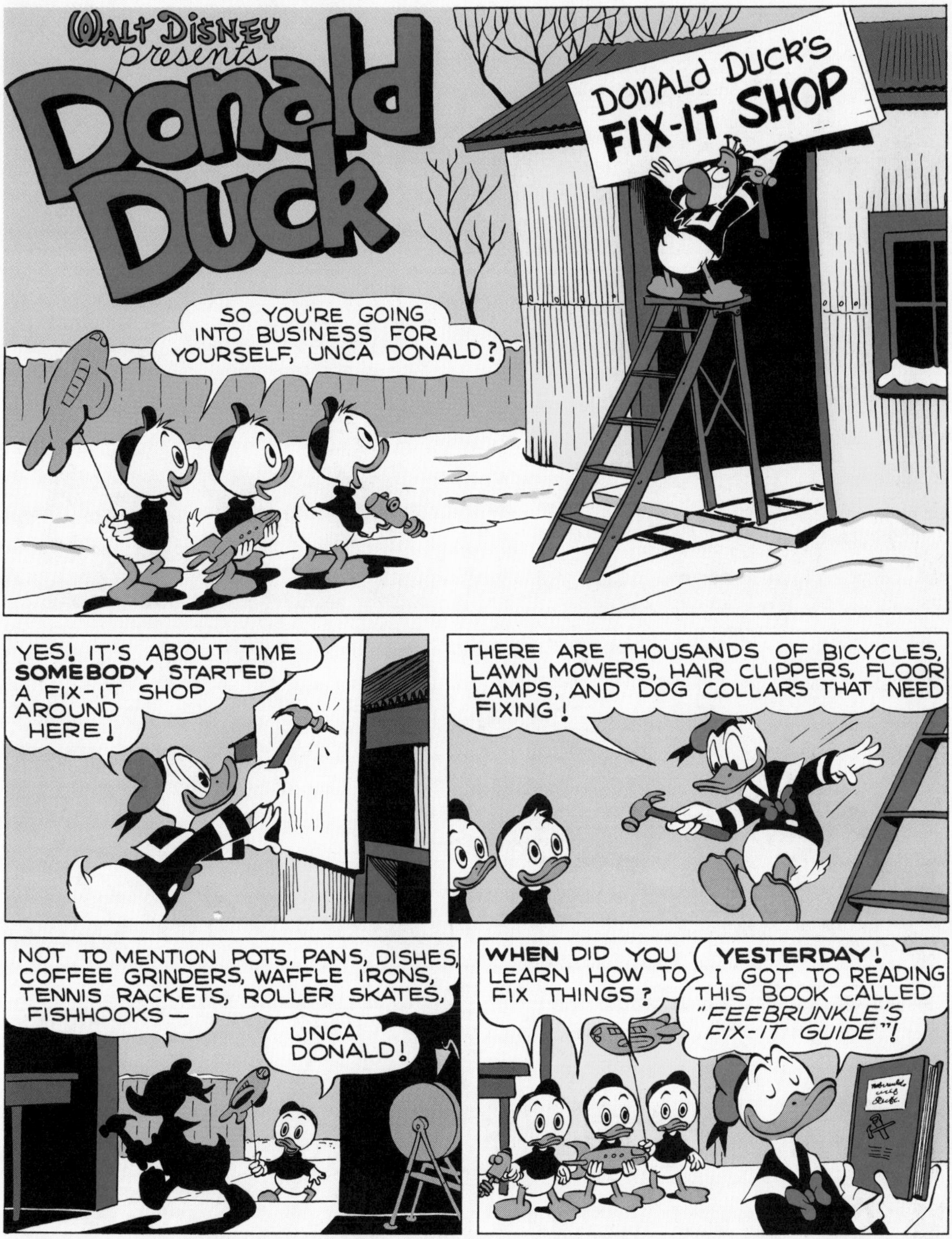
WALT DISNEY
presents
Donald Duck
DONALD DUCK'S FIX-IT SHOP
SO YOU'RE GOING INTO BUSINESS FOR YOURSELF, UNCA DONALD?
YES! IT'S ABOUT TIME SOMEBODY STARTED A FIX-IT SHOP AROUND HERE!
THERE ARE THOUSANDS OF BICYCLES, LAWN MOWERS, HAIR CLIPPERS, FLOOR LAMPS, AND DOG COLLARS THAT NEED FIXING!
NOT TO MENTION POTS, PANS, DISHES, COFFEE GRINDERS, WAFFLE IRONS, TENNIS RACKETS, ROLLER SKATES, FISHHOOKS—
UNCA DONALD!
WHEN DID YOU LEARN HOW TO FIX THINGS?
YESTERDAY! I GOT TO READING THIS BOOK CALLED "FEEBRUNKLE'S FIX-IT GUIDE"!

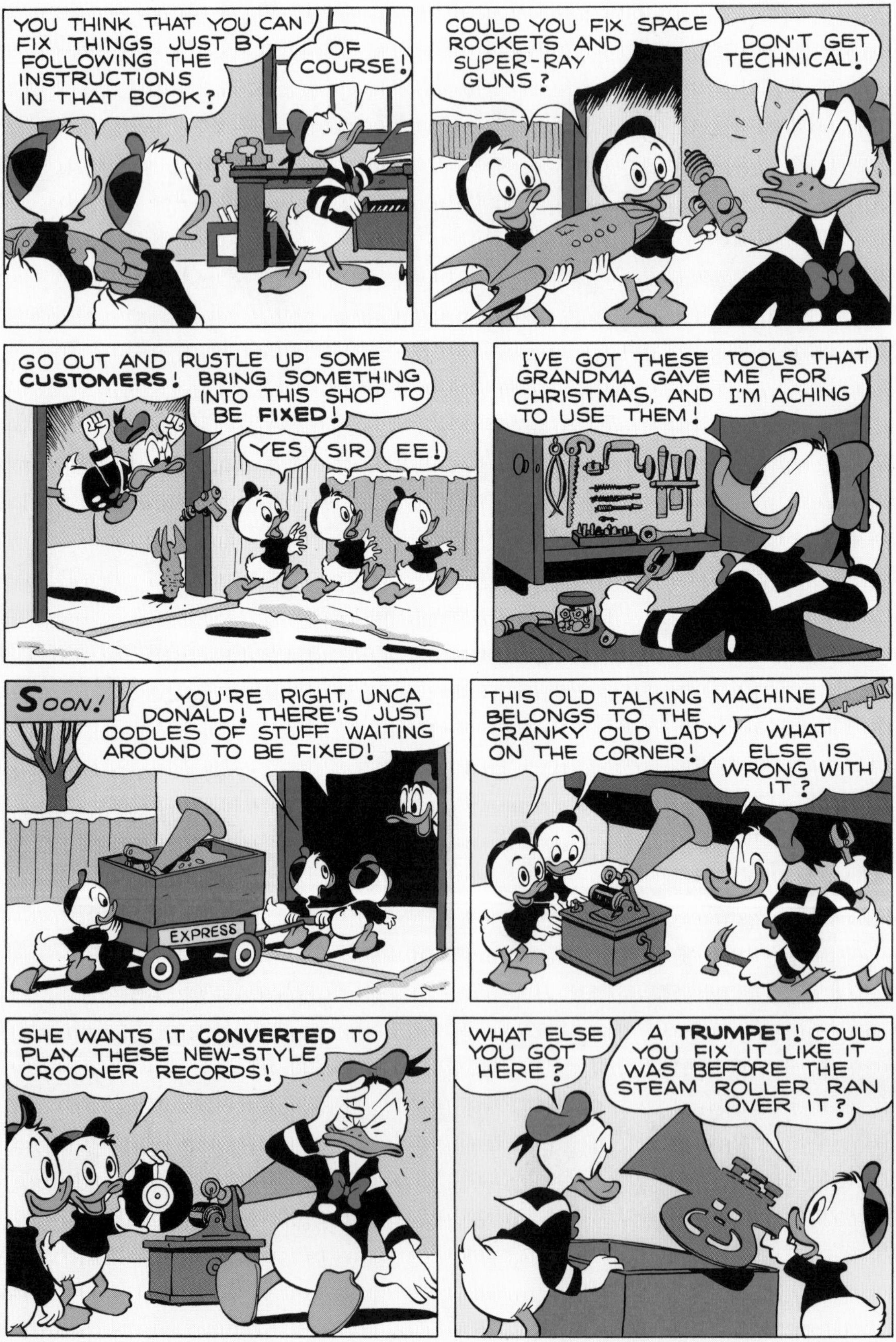
YOU THINK THAT YOU CAN FIX THINGS JUST BY FOLLOWING THE INSTRUCTIONS IN THAT BOOK?
OF COURSE!
COULD YOU FIX SPACE ROCKETS AND SUPER-RAY GUNS?
DON'T GET TECHNICAL!
GO OUT AND RUSTLE UP SOME **CUSTOMERS**! BRING SOMETHING INTO THIS SHOP TO BE **FIXED**!
YES
SIR
EE!
I'VE GOT THESE TOOLS THAT GRANDMA GAVE ME FOR CHRISTMAS, AND I'M ACHING TO USE THEM!
SOON!
YOU'RE RIGHT, UNCA DONALD! THERE'S JUST OODLES OF STUFF WAITING AROUND TO BE FIXED!
EXPRESS
THIS OLD TALKING MACHINE BELONGS TO THE CRANKY OLD LADY ON THE CORNER!
WHAT ELSE IS WRONG WITH IT?
SHE WANTS IT **CONVERTED** TO PLAY THESE NEW-STYLE CROONER RECORDS!
WHAT ELSE YOU GOT HERE?
A **TRUMPET**! COULD YOU FIX IT LIKE IT WAS BEFORE THE STEAM ROLLER RAN OVER IT?

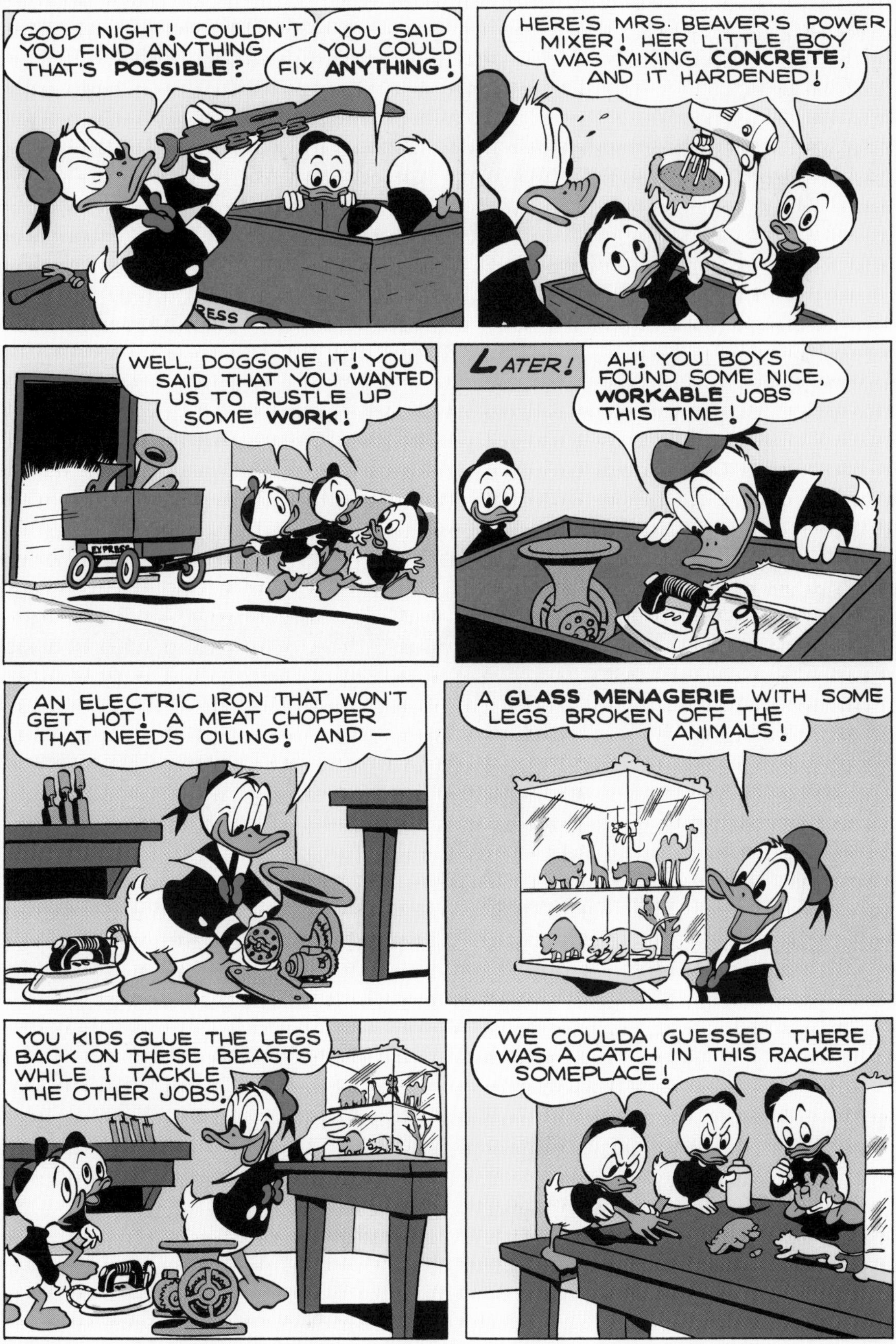
GOOD NIGHT! COULDN'T YOU FIND ANYTHING THAT'S POSSIBLE?
YOU SAID YOU COULD FIX ANYTHING!
HERE'S MRS. BEAVER'S POWER MIXER! HER LITTLE BOY WAS MIXING CONCRETE, AND IT HARDENED!
WELL, DOGGONE IT! YOU SAID THAT YOU WANTED US TO RUSTLE UP SOME WORK!
EXPRESS
LATER!
AH! YOU BOYS FOUND SOME NICE, WORKABLE JOBS THIS TIME!
AN ELECTRIC IRON THAT WON'T GET HOT! A MEAT CHOPPER THAT NEEDS OILING! AND—
A GLASS MENAGERIE WITH SOME LEGS BROKEN OFF THE ANIMALS!
YOU KIDS GLUE THE LEGS BACK ON THESE BEASTS WHILE I TACKLE THE OTHER JOBS!
WE COULDA GUESSED THERE WAS A CATCH IN THIS RACKET SOMEPLACE!

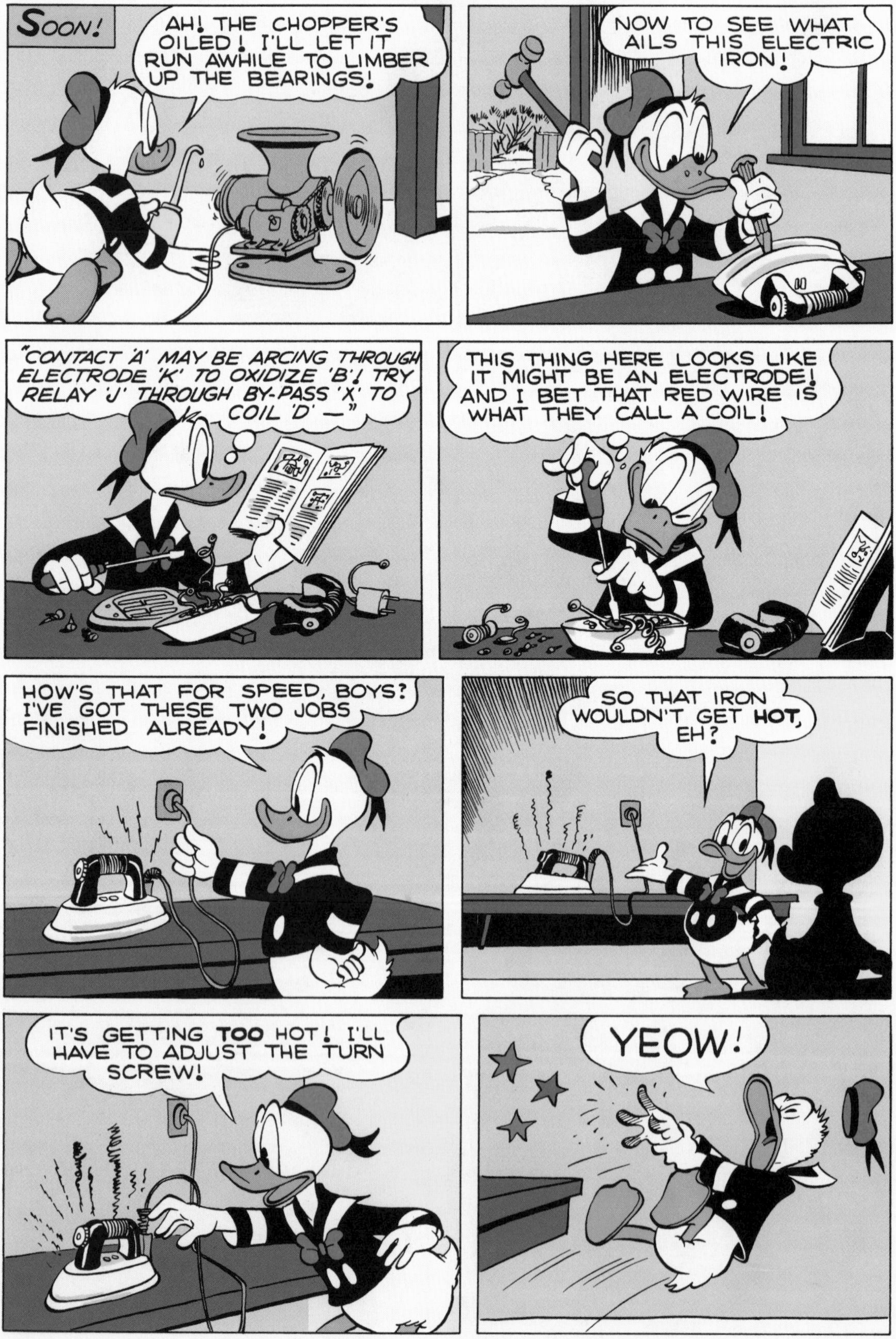
SOON!
AH! THE CHOPPER'S OILED! I'LL LET IT RUN AWHILE TO LIMBER UP THE BEARINGS!
NOW TO SEE WHAT AILS THIS ELECTRIC IRON!
"CONTACT 'A' MAY BE ARCING THROUGH ELECTRODE 'K' TO OXIDIZE 'B'! TRY RELAY 'J' THROUGH BY-PASS 'X' TO COIL 'D' —"
THIS THING HERE LOOKS LIKE IT MIGHT BE AN ELECTRODE! AND I BET THAT RED WIRE IS WHAT THEY CALL A COIL!
HOW'S THAT FOR SPEED, BOYS? I'VE GOT THESE TWO JOBS FINISHED ALREADY!
SO THAT IRON WOULDN'T GET **HOT**, EH?
IT'S GETTING **TOO** HOT! I'LL HAVE TO ADJUST THE TURN SCREW!
YEOW!

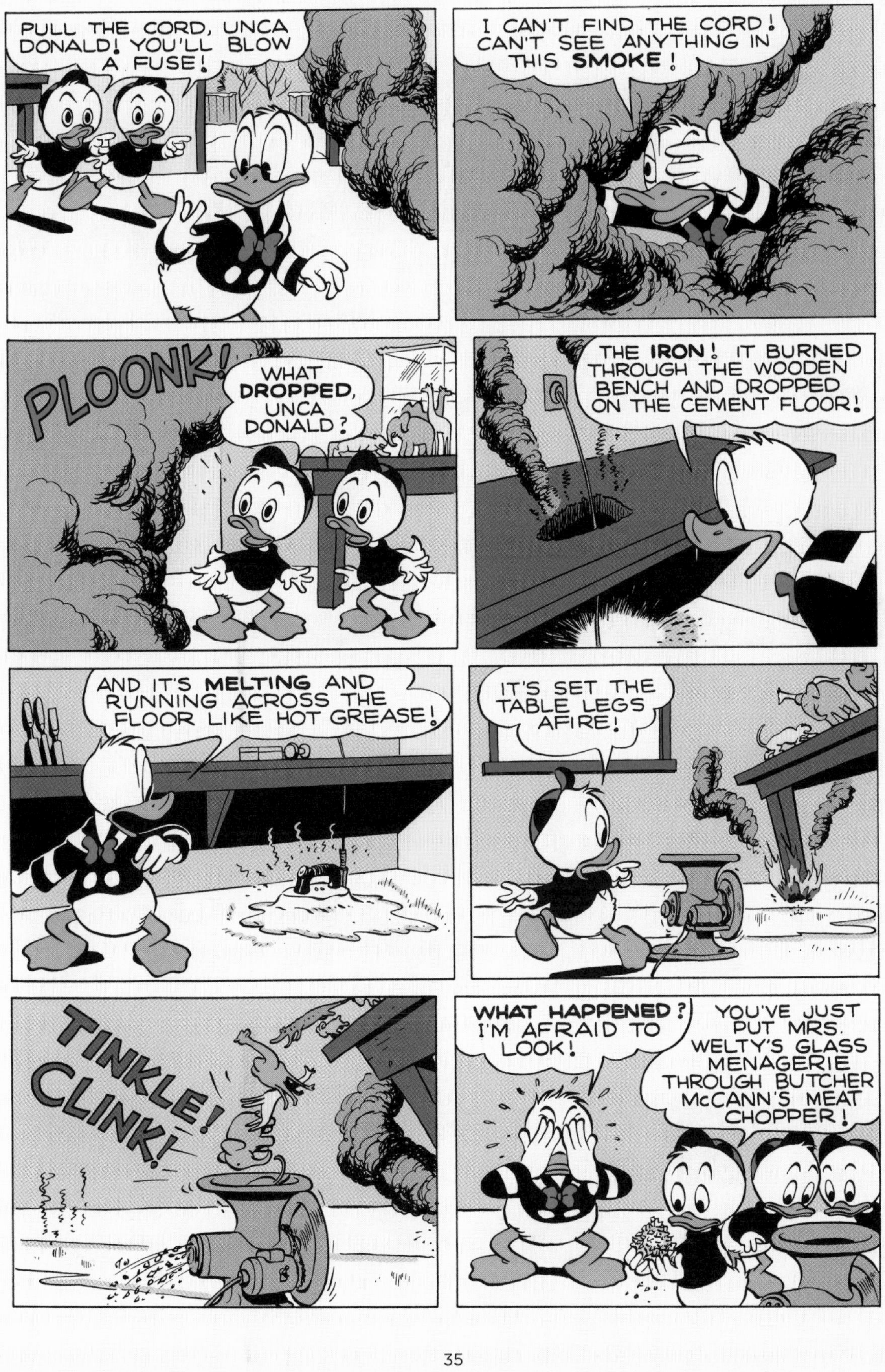
PULL THE CORD, UNCA DONALD! YOU'LL BLOW A FUSE!
I CAN'T FIND THE CORD! CAN'T SEE ANYTHING IN THIS SMOKE!
PLOONK!
WHAT DROPPED, UNCA DONALD?
THE IRON! IT BURNED THROUGH THE WOODEN BENCH AND DROPPED ON THE CEMENT FLOOR!
AND IT'S MELTING AND RUNNING ACROSS THE FLOOR LIKE HOT GREASE!
IT'S SET THE TABLE LEGS AFIRE!
TINKLE! CLINK!
WHAT HAPPENED? I'M AFRAID TO LOOK!
YOU'VE JUST PUT MRS. WELTY'S GLASS MENAGERIE THROUGH BUTCHER McCANN'S MEAT CHOPPER!

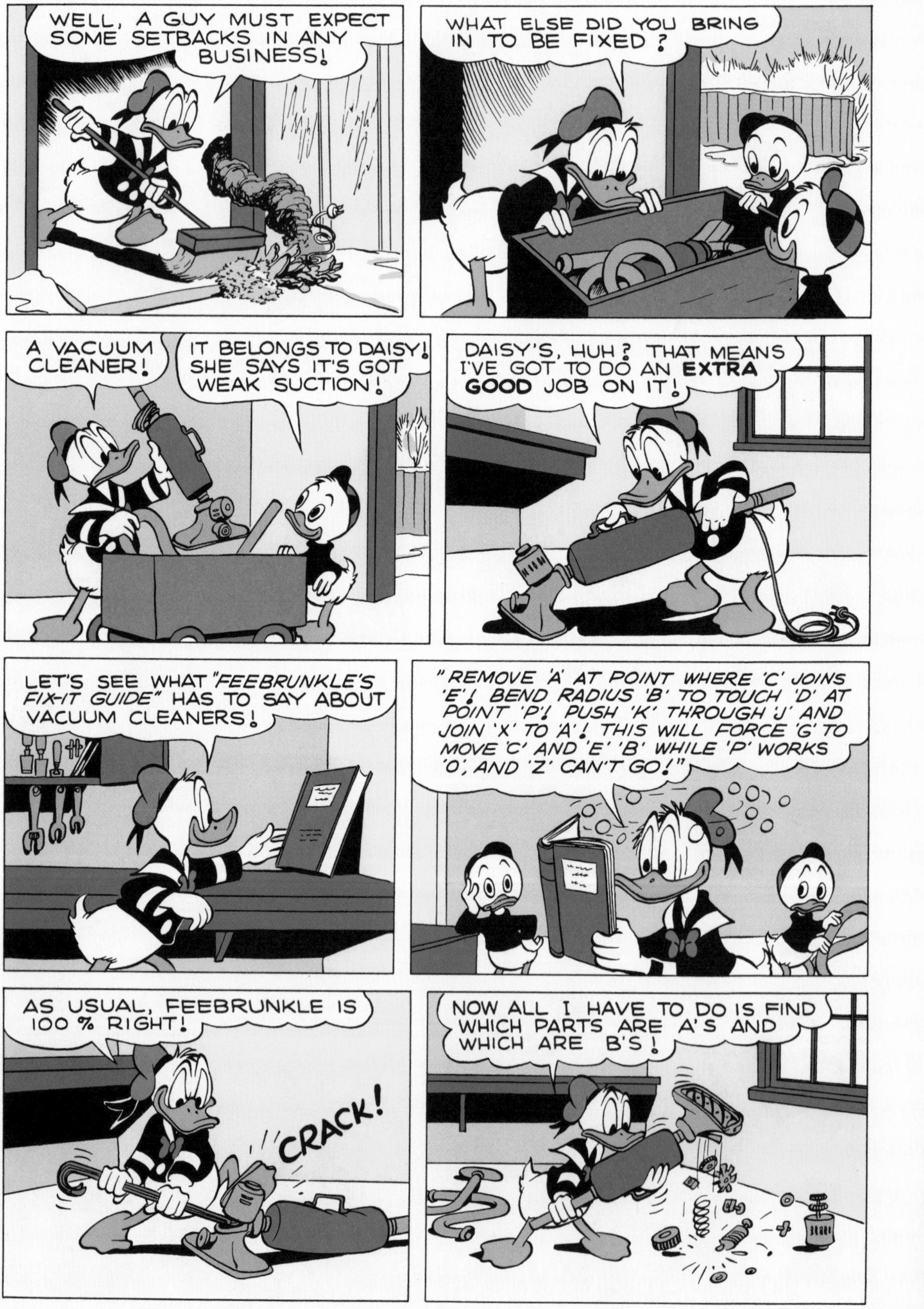
WELL, A GUY MUST EXPECT SOME SETBACKS IN ANY BUSINESS!
WHAT ELSE DID YOU BRING IN TO BE FIXED?
A VACUUM CLEANER!
IT BELONGS TO DAISY! SHE SAYS IT'S GOT WEAK SUCTION!
DAISY'S, HUH? THAT MEANS I'VE GOT TO DO AN EXTRA GOOD JOB ON IT!
LET'S SEE WHAT "FEEBRUNKLE'S FIX-IT GUIDE" HAS TO SAY ABOUT VACUUM CLEANERS!
"REMOVE 'A' AT POINT WHERE 'C' JOINS 'E'! BEND RADIUS 'B' TO TOUCH 'D' AT POINT 'P'! PUSH 'K' THROUGH 'J' AND JOIN 'X' TO 'A'! THIS WILL FORCE 'G' TO MOVE 'C' AND 'E' 'B' WHILE 'P' WORKS 'O', AND 'Z' CAN'T GO!"
AS USUAL, FEEBRUNKLE IS 100 % RIGHT!
CRACK!
NOW ALL I HAVE TO DO IS FIND WHICH PARTS ARE A'S AND WHICH ARE B'S!

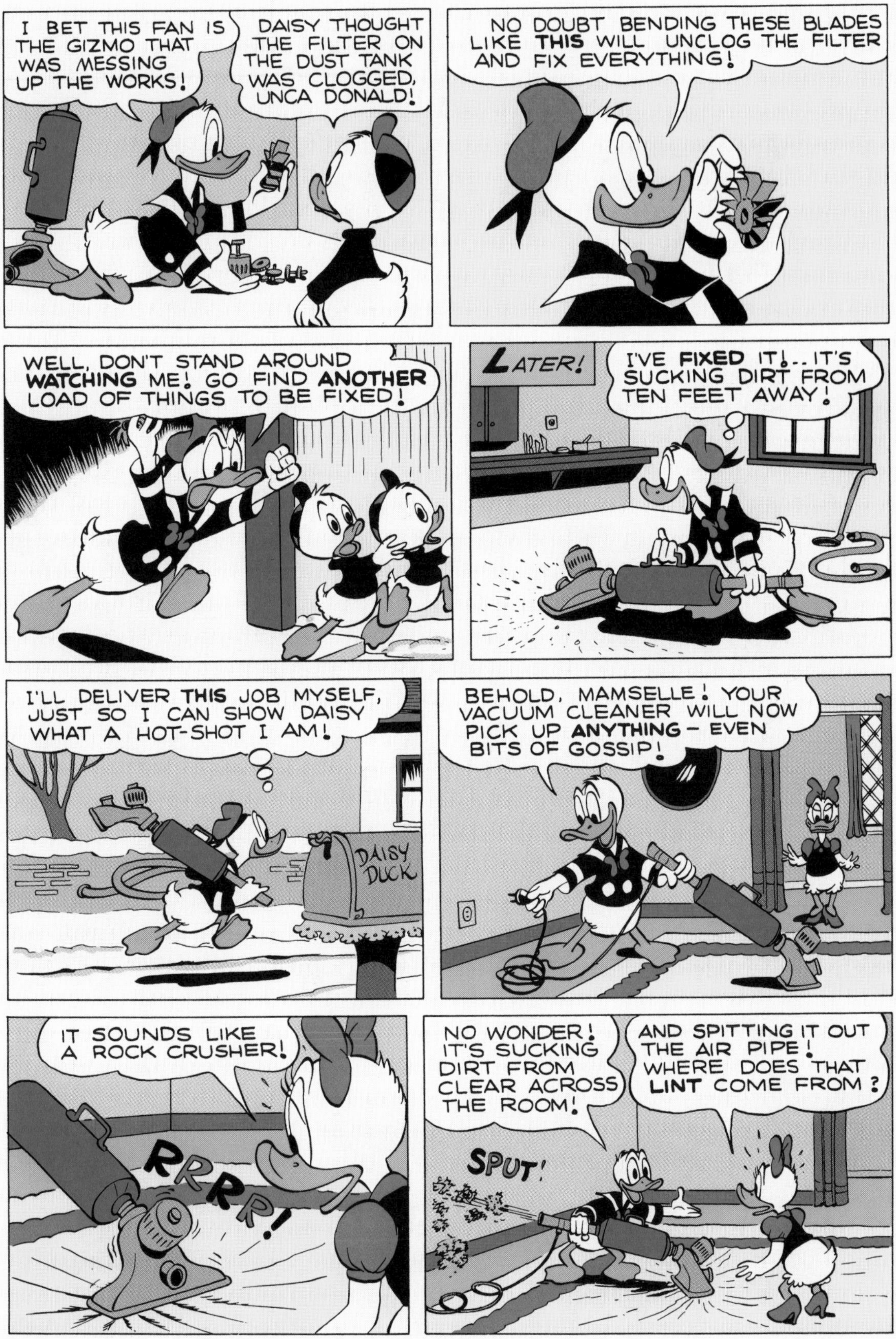
I BET THIS FAN IS THE GIZMO THAT WAS MESSING UP THE WORKS!
DAISY THOUGHT THE FILTER ON THE DUST TANK WAS CLOGGED, UNCA DONALD!
NO DOUBT BENDING THESE BLADES LIKE **THIS** WILL UNCLOG THE FILTER AND FIX EVERYTHING!
WELL, DON'T STAND AROUND **WATCHING** ME! GO FIND **ANOTHER** LOAD OF THINGS TO BE FIXED!
LATER!
I'VE **FIXED** IT!.. IT'S SUCKING DIRT FROM TEN FEET AWAY!
I'LL DELIVER **THIS** JOB MYSELF, JUST SO I CAN SHOW DAISY WHAT A HOT-SHOT I AM!
DAISY DUCK
BEHOLD, MAMSELLE! YOUR VACUUM CLEANER WILL NOW PICK UP **ANYTHING** – EVEN BITS OF GOSSIP!
IT SOUNDS LIKE A ROCK CRUSHER!
RRRR!
NO WONDER! IT'S SUCKING DIRT FROM CLEAR ACROSS THE ROOM!
AND SPITTING IT OUT THE AIR PIPE! WHERE DOES THAT **LINT** COME FROM?
SPUT!

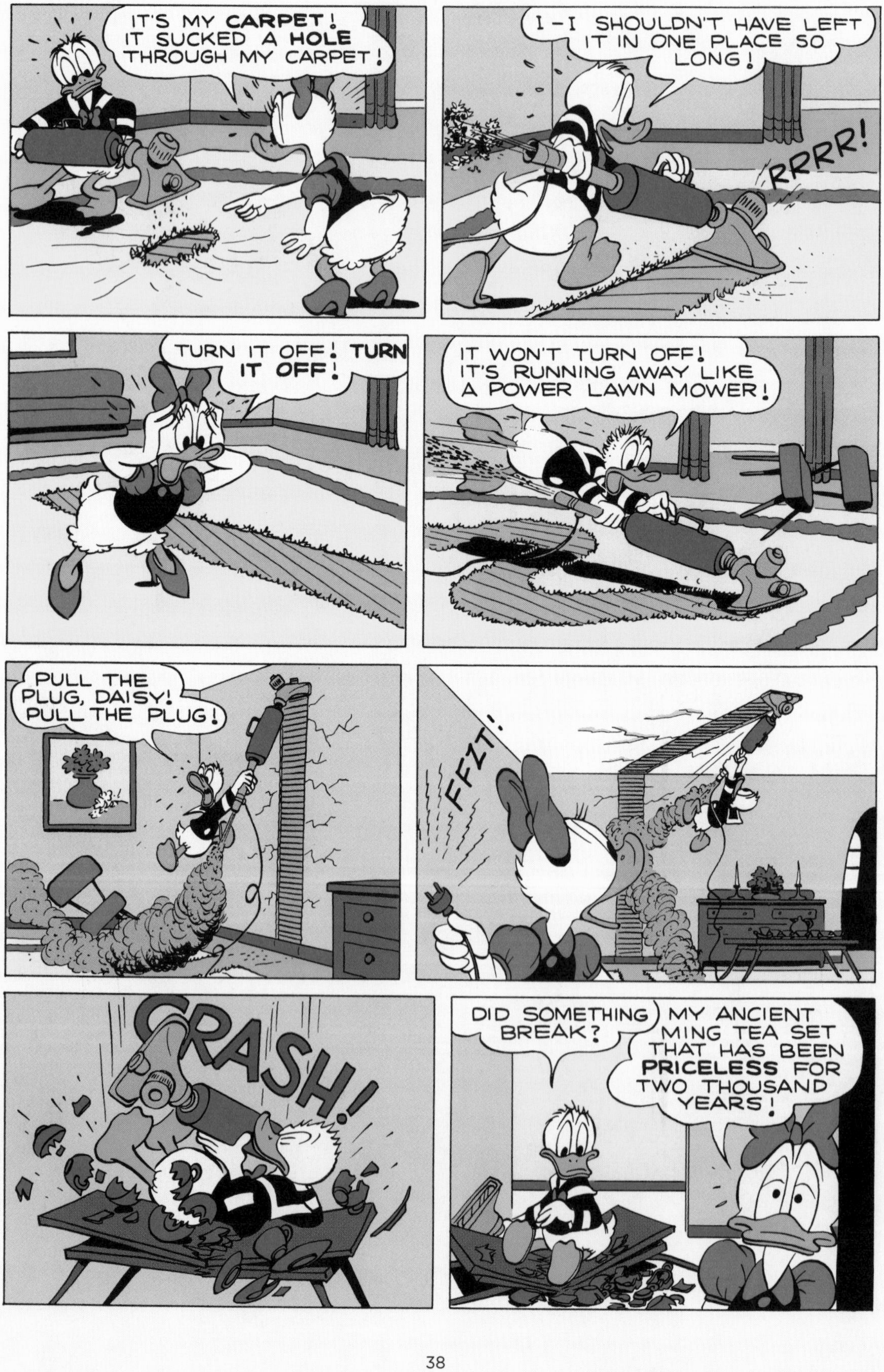
IT'S MY CARPET! IT SUCKED A HOLE THROUGH MY CARPET!
I-I SHOULDN'T HAVE LEFT IT IN ONE PLACE SO LONG!
RRRR!
TURN IT OFF! TURN IT OFF!
IT WON'T TURN OFF! IT'S RUNNING AWAY LIKE A POWER LAWN MOWER!
PULL THE PLUG, DAISY! PULL THE PLUG!
FFZT!
CRASH!
DID SOMETHING BREAK?
MY ANCIENT MING TEA SET THAT HAS BEEN PRICELESS FOR TWO THOUSAND YEARS!

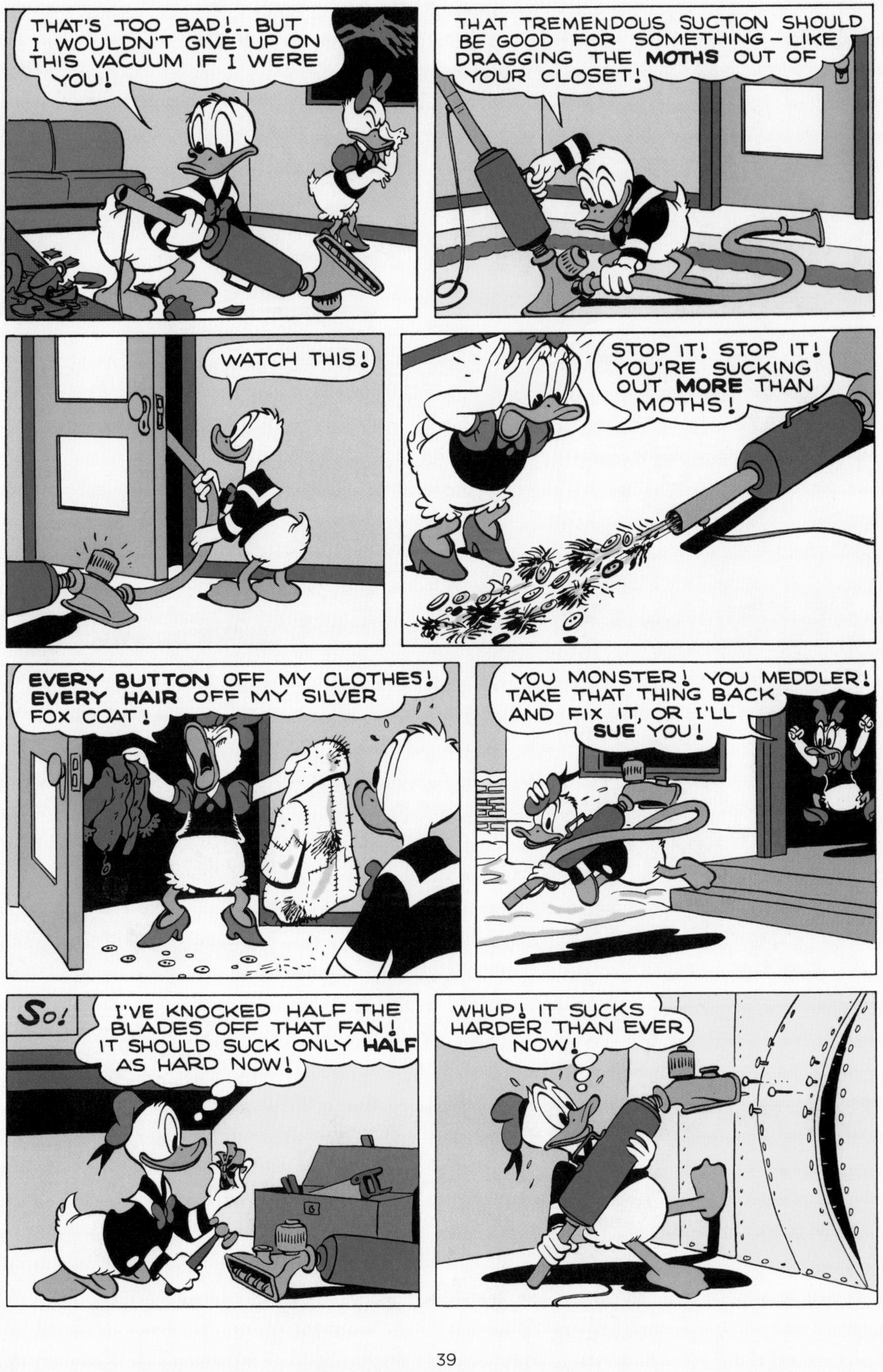
THAT'S TOO BAD!.. BUT I WOULDN'T GIVE UP ON THIS VACUUM IF I WERE YOU!
THAT TREMENDOUS SUCTION SHOULD BE GOOD FOR SOMETHING – LIKE DRAGGING THE **MOTHS** OUT OF YOUR CLOSET!
WATCH THIS!
STOP IT! STOP IT! YOU'RE SUCKING OUT **MORE** THAN MOTHS!
EVERY BUTTON OFF MY CLOTHES! **EVERY HAIR** OFF MY SILVER FOX COAT!
YOU MONSTER! YOU MEDDLER! TAKE THAT THING BACK AND FIX IT, OR I'LL **SUE** YOU!
So!
I'VE KNOCKED HALF THE BLADES OFF THAT FAN! IT SHOULD SUCK ONLY **HALF** AS HARD NOW!
WHUP! IT SUCKS HARDER THAN EVER NOW!

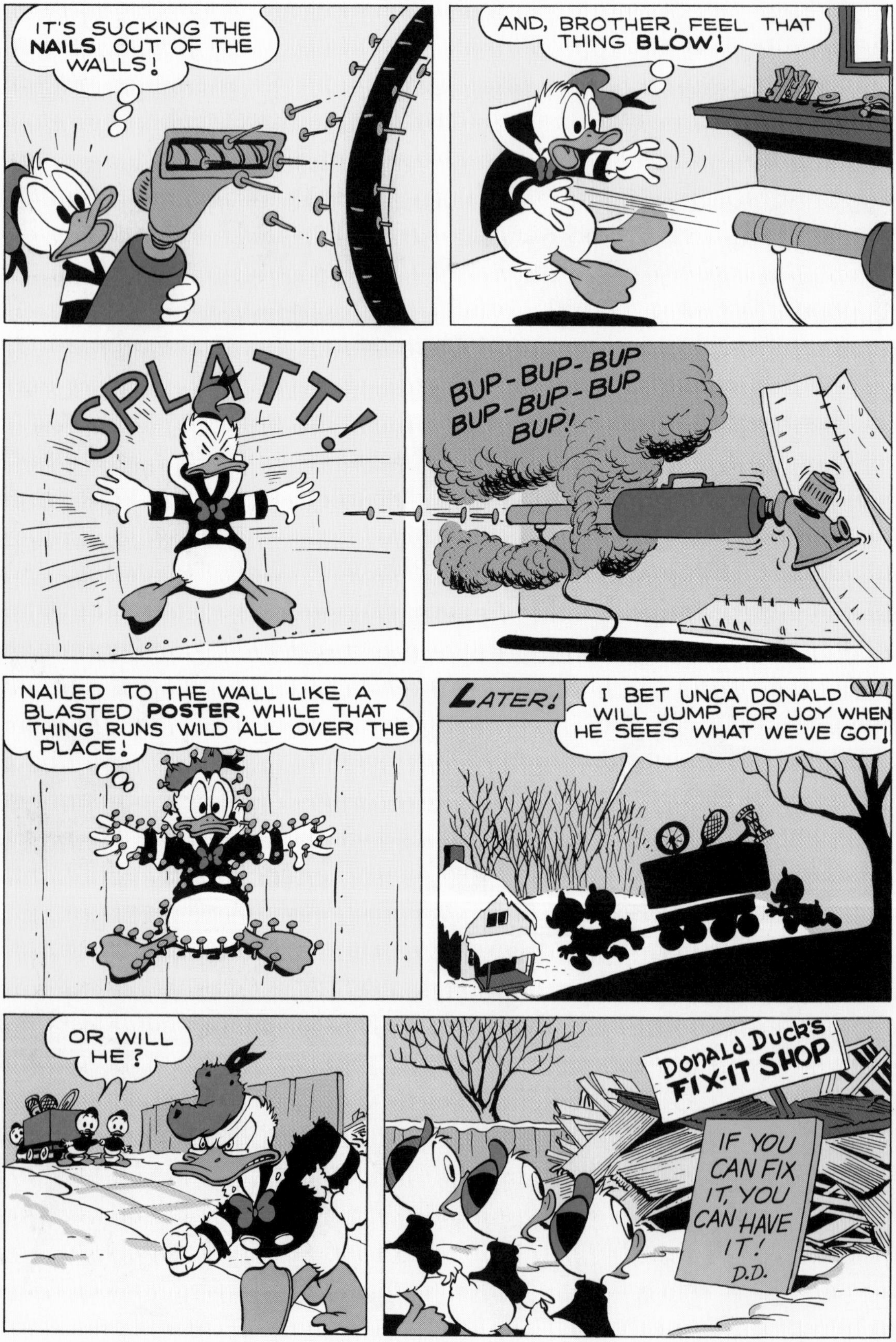
IT'S SUCKING THE NAILS OUT OF THE WALLS!
AND, BROTHER, FEEL THAT THING BLOW!
SPLATT!
BUP-BUP-BUP BUP-BUP-BUP BUP!
NAILED TO THE WALL LIKE A BLASTED POSTER, WHILE THAT THING RUNS WILD ALL OVER THE PLACE!
LATER!
I BET UNCA DONALD WILL JUMP FOR JOY WHEN HE SEES WHAT WE'VE GOT!
OR WILL HE?
Donald Duck's FIX-IT SHOP
IF YOU CAN FIX IT, YOU CAN HAVE IT! D.D.

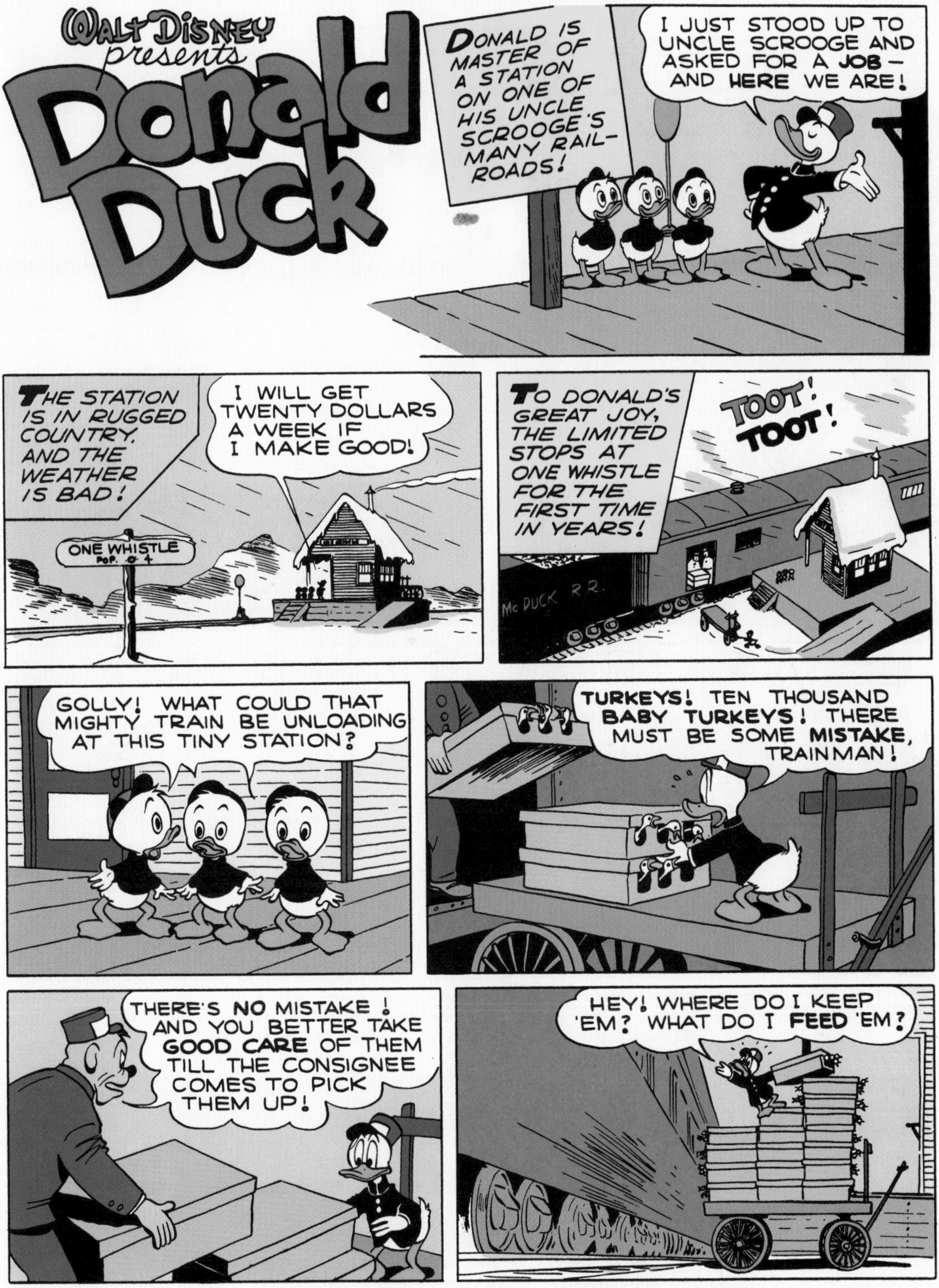
WALT DISNEY presents
Donald Duck
DONALD IS MASTER OF A STATION ON ONE OF HIS UNCLE SCROOGE'S MANY RAIL-ROADS!
I JUST STOOD UP TO UNCLE SCROOGE AND ASKED FOR A JOB — AND HERE WE ARE!
THE STATION IS IN RUGGED COUNTRY, AND THE WEATHER IS BAD!
I WILL GET TWENTY DOLLARS A WEEK IF I MAKE GOOD!
ONE WHISTLE POP. 4
TO DONALD'S GREAT JOY, THE LIMITED STOPS AT ONE WHISTLE FOR THE FIRST TIME IN YEARS!
TOOT! TOOT!
McDUCK R.R.
GOLLY! WHAT COULD THAT MIGHTY TRAIN BE UNLOADING AT THIS TINY STATION?
TURKEYS! TEN THOUSAND BABY TURKEYS! THERE MUST BE SOME MISTAKE, TRAINMAN!
THERE'S NO MISTAKE! AND YOU BETTER TAKE GOOD CARE OF THEM TILL THE CONSIGNEE COMES TO PICK THEM UP!
HEY! WHERE DO I KEEP 'EM? WHAT DO I FEED 'EM?

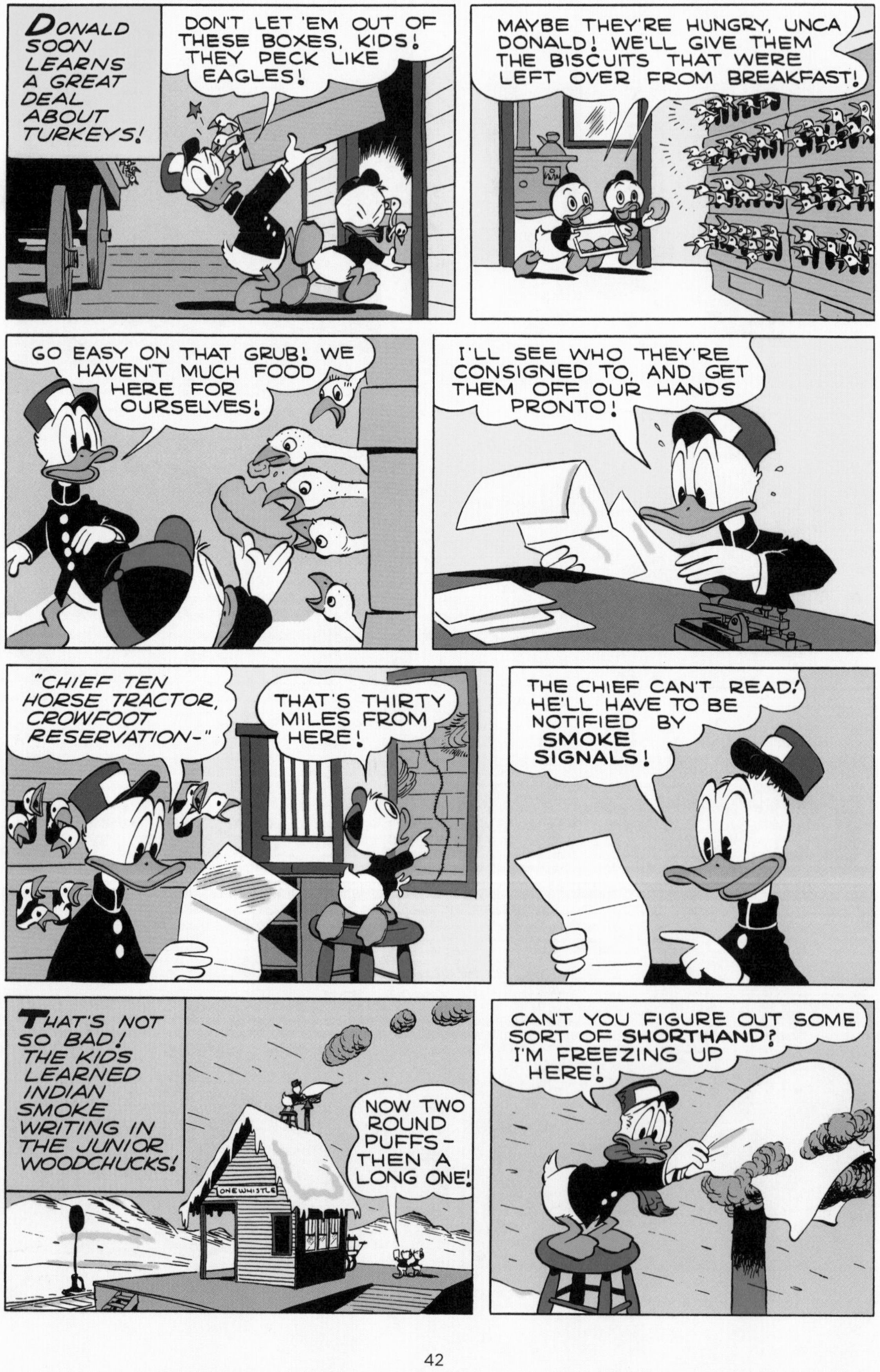
DONALD SOON LEARNS A GREAT DEAL ABOUT TURKEYS!
DON'T LET 'EM OUT OF THESE BOXES, KIDS! THEY PECK LIKE EAGLES!
MAYBE THEY'RE HUNGRY, UNCA DONALD! WE'LL GIVE THEM THE BISCUITS THAT WERE LEFT OVER FROM BREAKFAST!
GO EASY ON THAT GRUB! WE HAVEN'T MUCH FOOD HERE FOR OURSELVES!
I'LL SEE WHO THEY'RE CONSIGNED TO, AND GET THEM OFF OUR HANDS PRONTO!
"CHIEF TEN HORSE TRACTOR, CROWFOOT RESERVATION-"
THAT'S THIRTY MILES FROM HERE!
THE CHIEF CAN'T READ! HE'LL HAVE TO BE NOTIFIED BY SMOKE SIGNALS!
THAT'S NOT SO BAD! THE KIDS LEARNED INDIAN SMOKE WRITING IN THE JUNIOR WOODCHUCKS!
ONEWHISTLE
NOW TWO ROUND PUFFS - THEN A LONG ONE!
CAN'T YOU FIGURE OUT SOME SORT OF SHORTHAND? I'M FREEZING UP HERE!

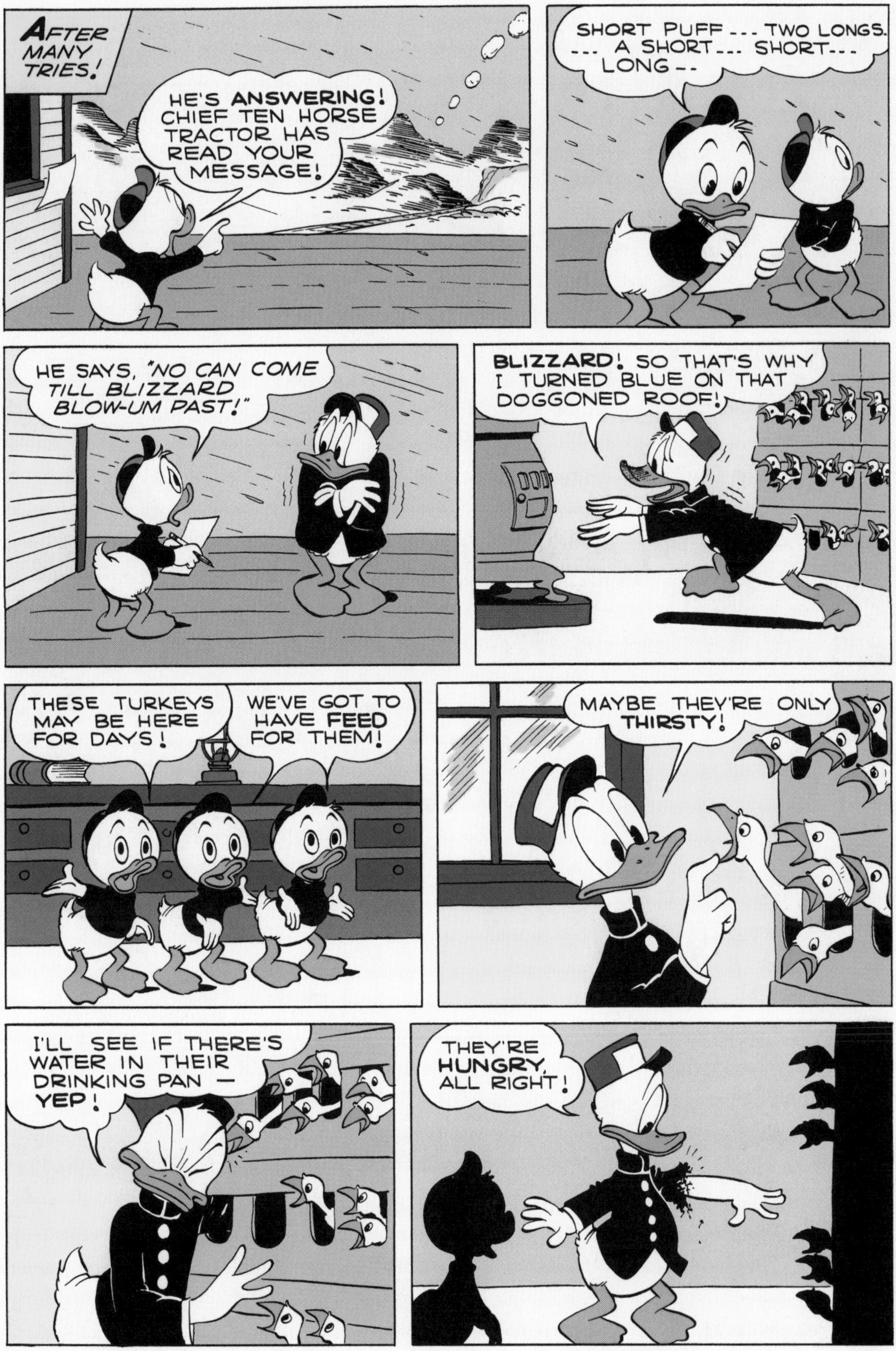
AFTER MANY TRIES!
HE'S ANSWERING! CHIEF TEN HORSE TRACTOR HAS READ YOUR MESSAGE!
SHORT PUFF --- TWO LONGS. --- A SHORT --- SHORT --- LONG --
HE SAYS, "NO CAN COME TILL BLIZZARD BLOW-UM PAST!"
BLIZZARD! SO THAT'S WHY I TURNED BLUE ON THAT DOGGONED ROOF!
THESE TURKEYS MAY BE HERE FOR DAYS!
WE'VE GOT TO HAVE FEED FOR THEM!
MAYBE THEY'RE ONLY THIRSTY!
I'LL SEE IF THERE'S WATER IN THEIR DRINKING PAN — YEP!
THEY'RE HUNGRY, ALL RIGHT!

HERE'S ALL THE FOOD WE HAVE IN THE KITCHEN!

GIVE IT TO THEM **RAW!** DARNED IF I'LL BAKE 'EM ANY CAKES AN' PIES!

SEND ME TEN SACKS OF TURKEY FEED ON THE NEXT TRAIN—

CLICK! CLICK!

CLICK! CLICK! CLICK! CLACK! CLACK! CLICK!

THEY SAY THE STORES ARE CLOSED FOR THE WEEK END! BEST THEY CAN DO IS TO SEND US TEN DOZEN **COCONUTS** TOMORROW!

TEN THOUSAND TURKEYS PECKING COCONUTS!.... LET'S NOT **THINK** OF IT TILL WE HAVE TO FACE IT!

EVENING!

PEEP KEOWK PEEP PEEP KEOWK KEOW KEBEEPK PEEP KEOWK

THE TURKEYS ARE **SHIVERING!** THERE ISN'T ENOUGH **HEAT** IN HERE TO KEEP THEM WARM!

PEEP! KEOWK! PEEP!

THEN, WE'VE GOT TO COVER THEM WITH **BLANKETS — OUR BLANKETS!** COME ON! GET THE COVERS OFF YOUR BED!

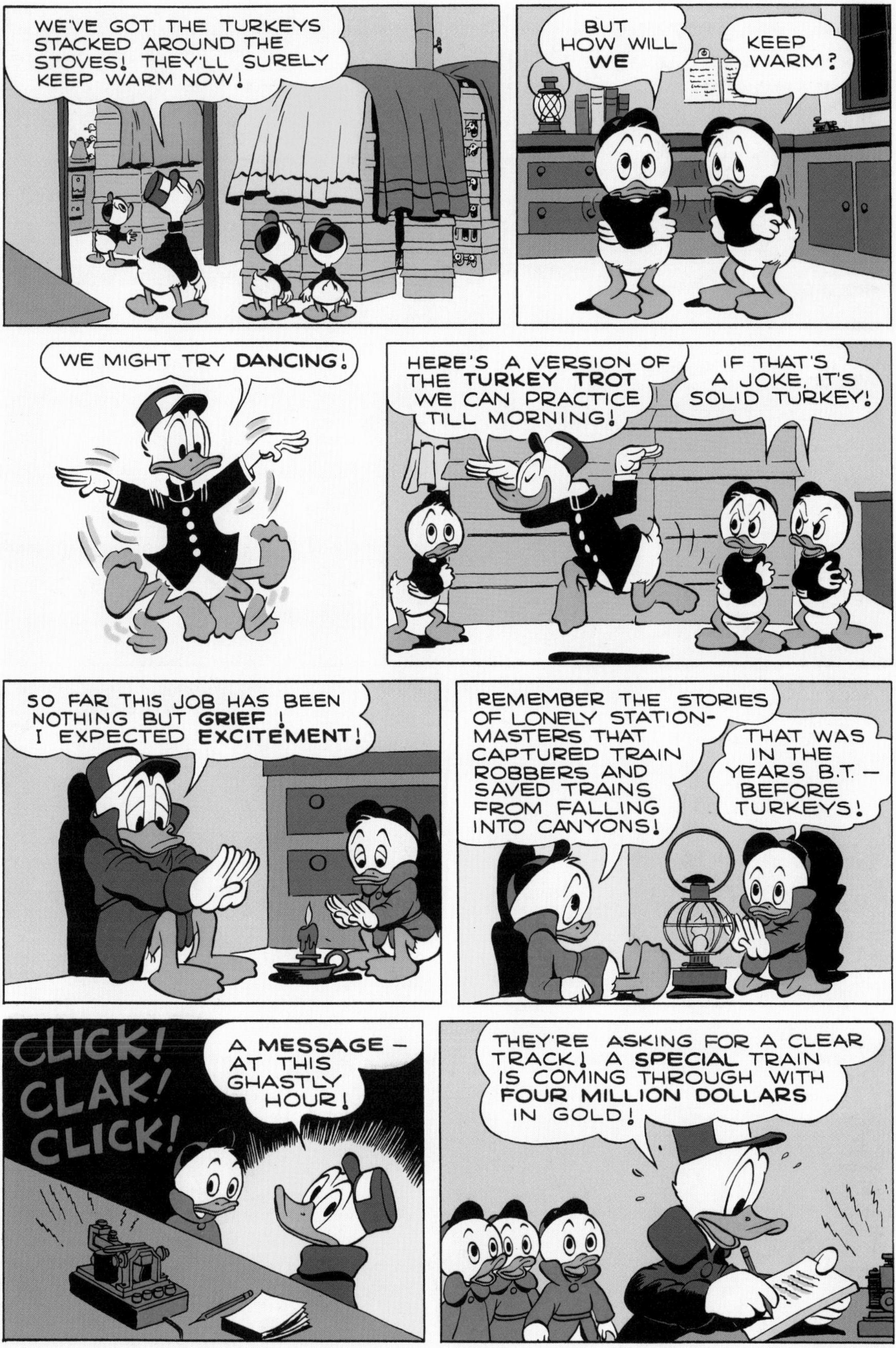
WE'VE GOT THE TURKEYS STACKED AROUND THE STOVES! THEY'LL SURELY KEEP WARM NOW!
BUT HOW WILL WE
KEEP WARM?
WE MIGHT TRY DANCING!
HERE'S A VERSION OF THE TURKEY TROT WE CAN PRACTICE TILL MORNING!
IF THAT'S A JOKE, IT'S SOLID TURKEY!
SO FAR THIS JOB HAS BEEN NOTHING BUT GRIEF! I EXPECTED EXCITEMENT!
REMEMBER THE STORIES OF LONELY STATION-MASTERS THAT CAPTURED TRAIN ROBBERS AND SAVED TRAINS FROM FALLING INTO CANYONS!
THAT WAS IN THE YEARS B.T. — BEFORE TURKEYS!
CLICK! CLAK! CLICK!
A MESSAGE — AT THIS GHASTLY HOUR!
THEY'RE ASKING FOR A CLEAR TRACK! A SPECIAL TRAIN IS COMING THROUGH WITH FOUR MILLION DOLLARS IN GOLD!

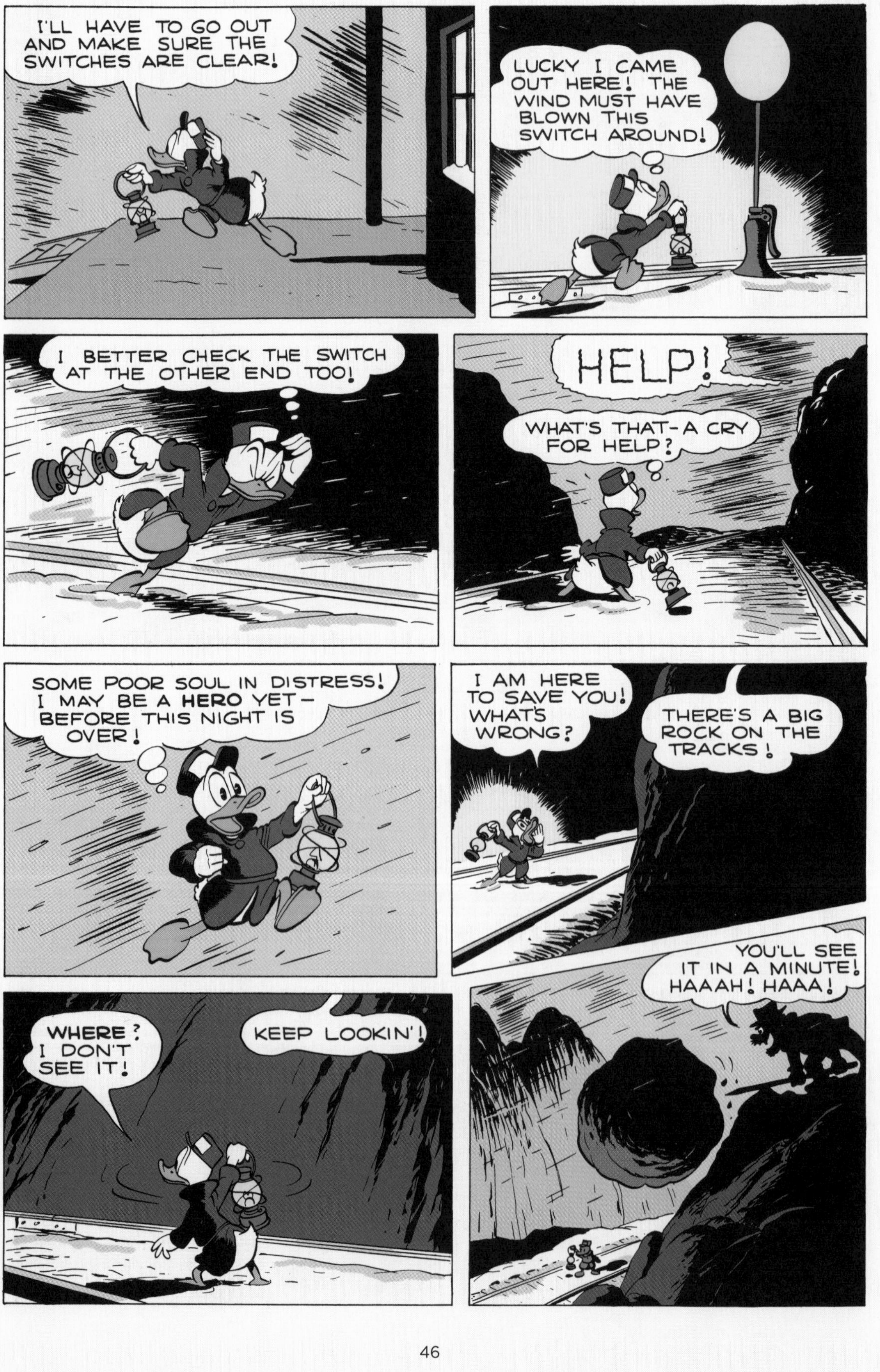
I'LL HAVE TO GO OUT AND MAKE SURE THE SWITCHES ARE CLEAR!
LUCKY I CAME OUT HERE! THE WIND MUST HAVE BLOWN THIS SWITCH AROUND!
I BETTER CHECK THE SWITCH AT THE OTHER END TOO!
HELP!
WHAT'S THAT—A CRY FOR HELP?
SOME POOR SOUL IN DISTRESS! I MAY BE A **HERO** YET— BEFORE THIS NIGHT IS OVER!
I AM HERE TO SAVE YOU! WHAT'S WRONG?
THERE'S A BIG ROCK ON THE TRACKS!
WHERE? I DON'T SEE IT!
KEEP LOOKIN'!
YOU'LL SEE IT IN A MINUTE! HAAAH! HAAA!

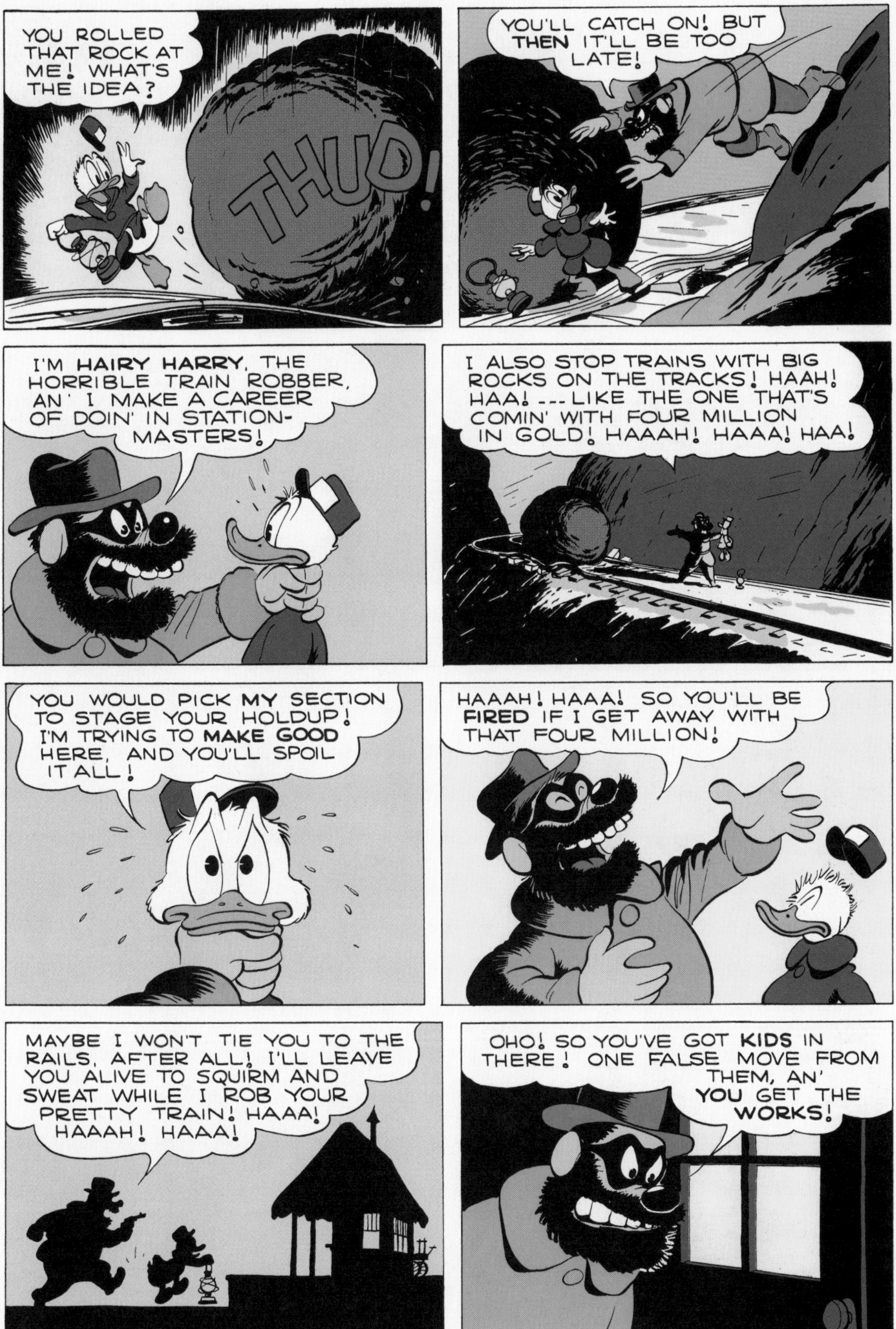
YOU ROLLED THAT ROCK AT ME! WHAT'S THE IDEA?
THUD!
YOU'LL CATCH ON! BUT THEN IT'LL BE TOO LATE!
I'M HAIRY HARRY, THE HORRIBLE TRAIN ROBBER, AN' I MAKE A CAREER OF DOIN' IN STATION-MASTERS!
I ALSO STOP TRAINS WITH BIG ROCKS ON THE TRACKS! HAAH! HAA! --- LIKE THE ONE THAT'S COMIN' WITH FOUR MILLION IN GOLD! HAAAH! HAAA! HAA!
YOU WOULD PICK MY SECTION TO STAGE YOUR HOLDUP! I'M TRYING TO MAKE GOOD HERE, AND YOU'LL SPOIL IT ALL!
HAAAH! HAAA! SO YOU'LL BE FIRED IF I GET AWAY WITH THAT FOUR MILLION!
MAYBE I WON'T TIE YOU TO THE RAILS, AFTER ALL! I'LL LEAVE YOU ALIVE TO SQUIRM AND SWEAT WHILE I ROB YOUR PRETTY TRAIN! HAAA! HAAAH! HAAA!
OHO! SO YOU'VE GOT KIDS IN THERE! ONE FALSE MOVE FROM THEM, AN' YOU GET THE WORKS!

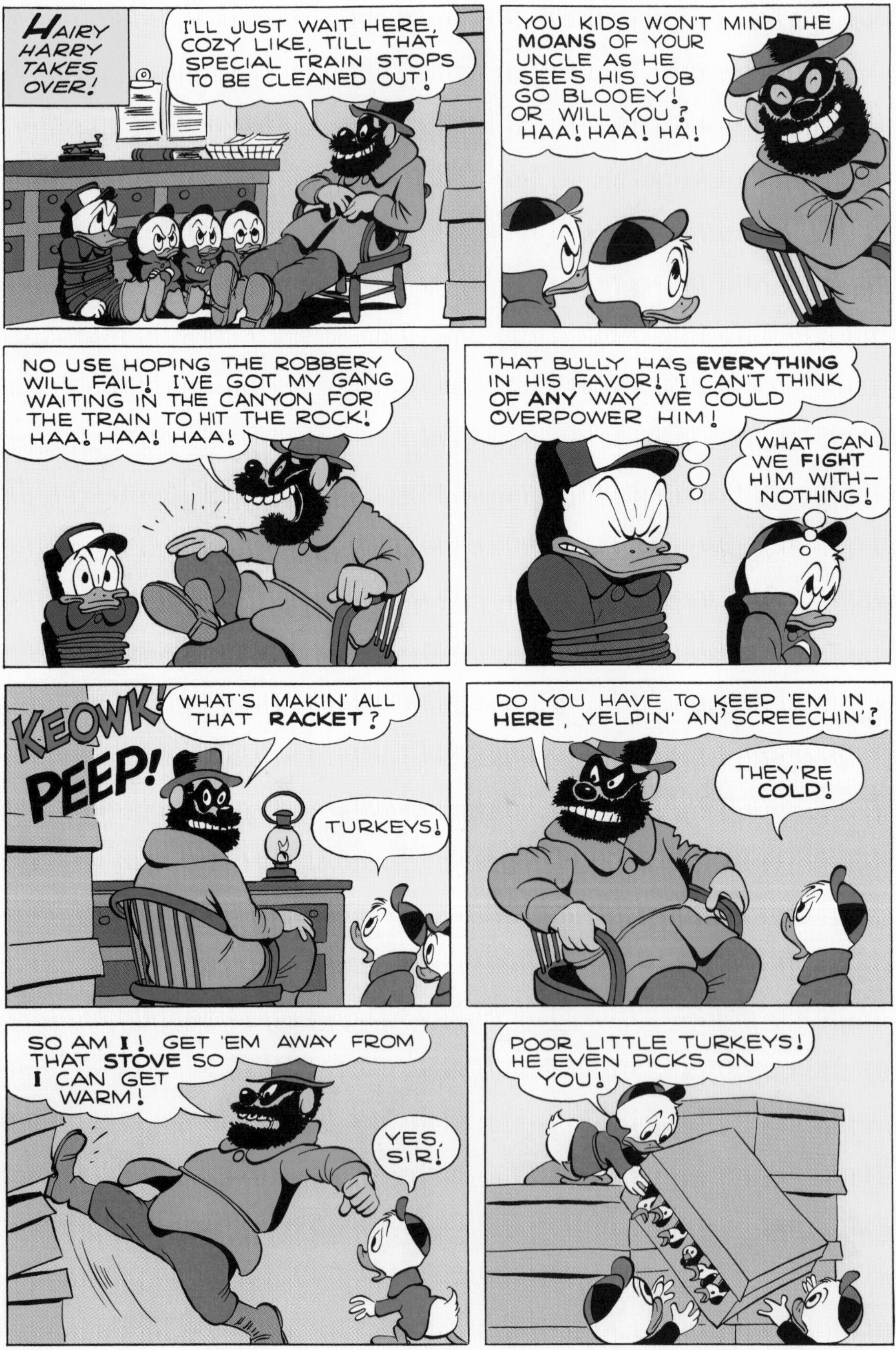
HAIRY HARRY TAKES OVER!
I'LL JUST WAIT HERE, COZY LIKE, TILL THAT SPECIAL TRAIN STOPS TO BE CLEANED OUT!
YOU KIDS WON'T MIND THE MOANS OF YOUR UNCLE AS HE SEES HIS JOB GO BLOOEY! OR WILL YOU? HAA! HAA! HA!
NO USE HOPING THE ROBBERY WILL FAIL! I'VE GOT MY GANG WAITING IN THE CANYON FOR THE TRAIN TO HIT THE ROCK! HAA! HAA! HAA!
THAT BULLY HAS EVERYTHING IN HIS FAVOR! I CAN'T THINK OF ANY WAY WE COULD OVERPOWER HIM!
WHAT CAN WE FIGHT HIM WITH— NOTHING!
KEOWK!
PEEP!
WHAT'S MAKIN' ALL THAT RACKET?
TURKEYS!
DO YOU HAVE TO KEEP 'EM IN HERE, YELPIN' AN' SCREECHIN'?
THEY'RE COLD!
SO AM I! GET 'EM AWAY FROM THAT STOVE SO I CAN GET WARM!
YES, SIR!
POOR LITTLE TURKEYS! HE EVEN PICKS ON YOU!

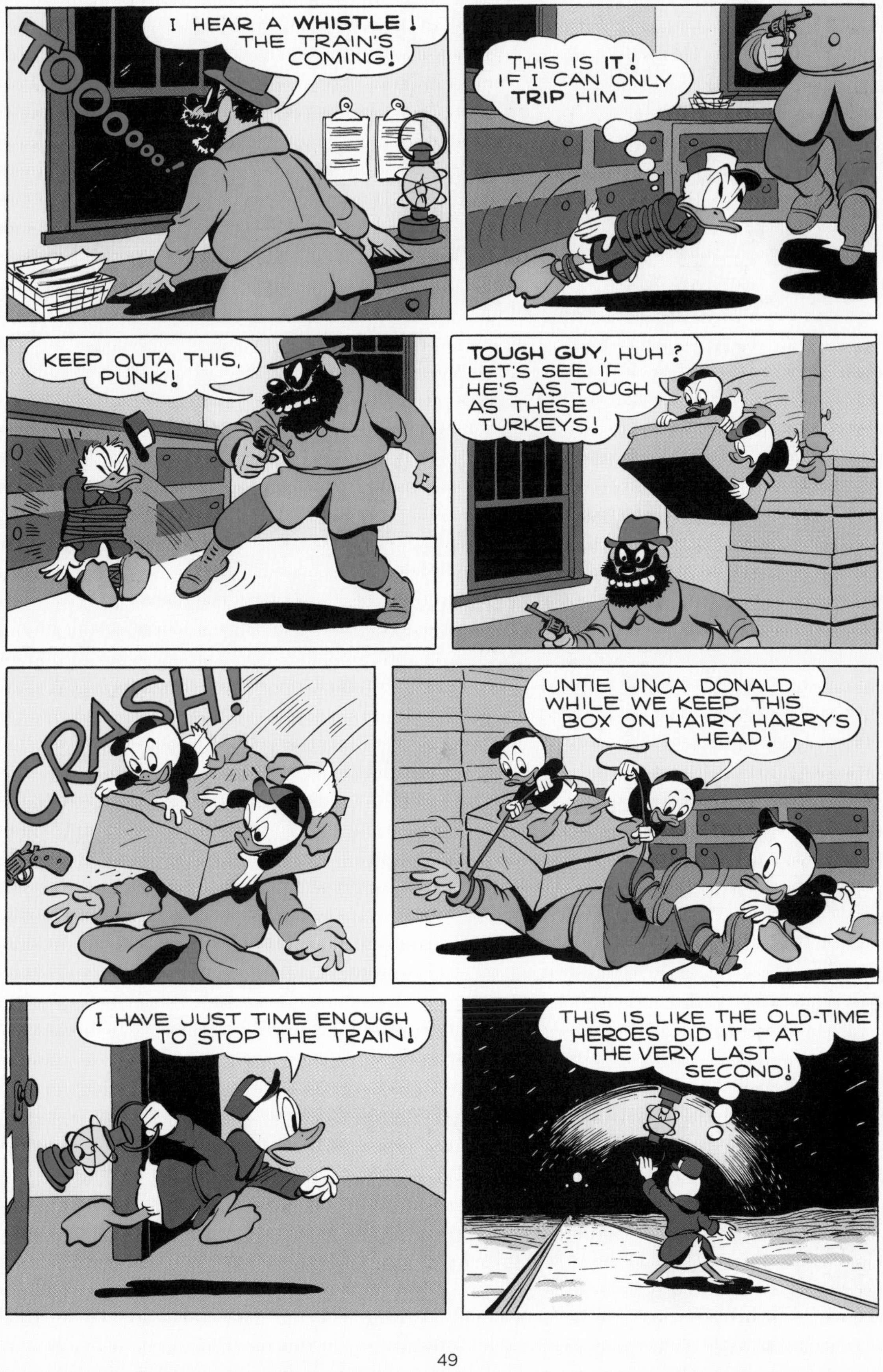
TOOOooo!
I HEAR A WHISTLE! THE TRAIN'S COMING!
THIS IS IT! IF I CAN ONLY TRIP HIM—
KEEP OUTA THIS, PUNK!
TOUGH GUY, HUH? LET'S SEE IF HE'S AS TOUGH AS THESE TURKEYS!
CRASH!
UNTIE UNCA DONALD WHILE WE KEEP THIS BOX ON HAIRY HARRY'S HEAD!
I HAVE JUST TIME ENOUGH TO STOP THE TRAIN!
THIS IS LIKE THE OLD-TIME HEROES DID IT—AT THE VERY LAST SECOND!

WELL! UNCLE SCROOGE HIMSELF!

WHAT'S THE IDEA, STOPPING THE **SPECIAL** AT THIS PEANUT STATION?

BECAUSE THERE'S A BIG ROCK ON THE TRACK AND **HAIRY HARRY'S** GANG ARE WAITING IN THE CANYON TO ROB YOU!

YOU WOULDN'T BE MAKING ALL THIS UP, WOULD YOU — TRYING TO LOOK GOOD ON YOUR NEW JOB?

HAIRY HARRY, HIMSELF, IS INSIDE! COME AND ASK HIM!

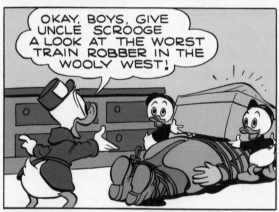

OKAY, BOYS, GIVE UNCLE SCROOGE A LOOK AT THE WORST TRAIN ROBBER IN THE WOOLY WEST!

THAT **SLICK-FACED** OAF IS **HAIRY HARRY** ???

HE'S **CHANGED!** HIS **BEARD** IS GONE!

AFTER ALL, UNCA DONALD! THOSE TURKEYS WOULD EAT **ANYTHING!**

So DONALD GETS ON THE PAY ROLL STEADY! THE STORM BLOWS AWAY, AND CHIEF TEN HORSE TRACTOR COMES AFTER HIS TURKEYS! IT IS GOOD TO BE ALIVE!

AND AFTER ONLY SIXTY YEARS OF THIS, UNCLE SCROOGE WILL LET ME RETIRE ON A PENSION OF $20 A MONTH!

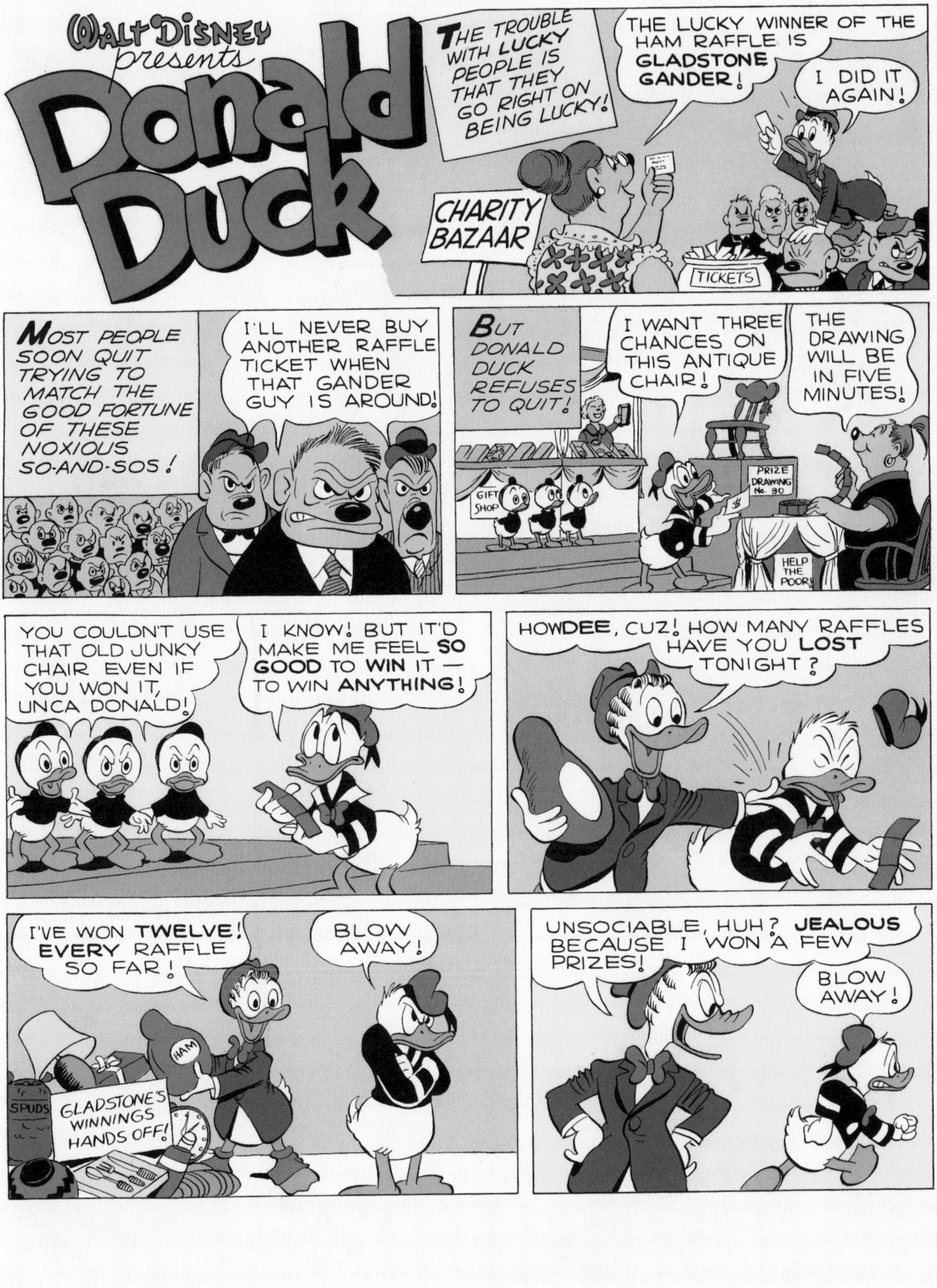
WALT DISNEY presents
Donald Duck
THE TROUBLE WITH LUCKY PEOPLE IS THAT THEY GO RIGHT ON BEING LUCKY!
THE LUCKY WINNER OF THE HAM RAFFLE IS GLADSTONE GANDER!
I DID IT AGAIN!
CHARITY BAZAAR
TICKETS
MOST PEOPLE SOON QUIT TRYING TO MATCH THE GOOD FORTUNE OF THESE NOXIOUS SO-AND-SOS!
I'LL NEVER BUY ANOTHER RAFFLE TICKET WHEN THAT GANDER GUY IS AROUND!
BUT DONALD DUCK REFUSES TO QUIT!
I WANT THREE CHANCES ON THIS ANTIQUE CHAIR!
THE DRAWING WILL BE IN FIVE MINUTES!
GIFT SHOP
PRIZE DRAWING No. 30
HELP THE POOR!
YOU COULDN'T USE THAT OLD JUNKY CHAIR EVEN IF YOU WON IT, UNCA DONALD!
I KNOW! BUT IT'D MAKE ME FEEL SO GOOD TO WIN IT — TO WIN ANYTHING!
HOWDEE, CUZ! HOW MANY RAFFLES HAVE YOU LOST TONIGHT?
I'VE WON TWELVE! EVERY RAFFLE SO FAR!
BLOW AWAY!
HAM
SPUDS
GLADSTONE'S WINNINGS HANDS OFF!
UNSOCIABLE, HUH? JEALOUS BECAUSE I WON A FEW PRIZES!
BLOW AWAY!

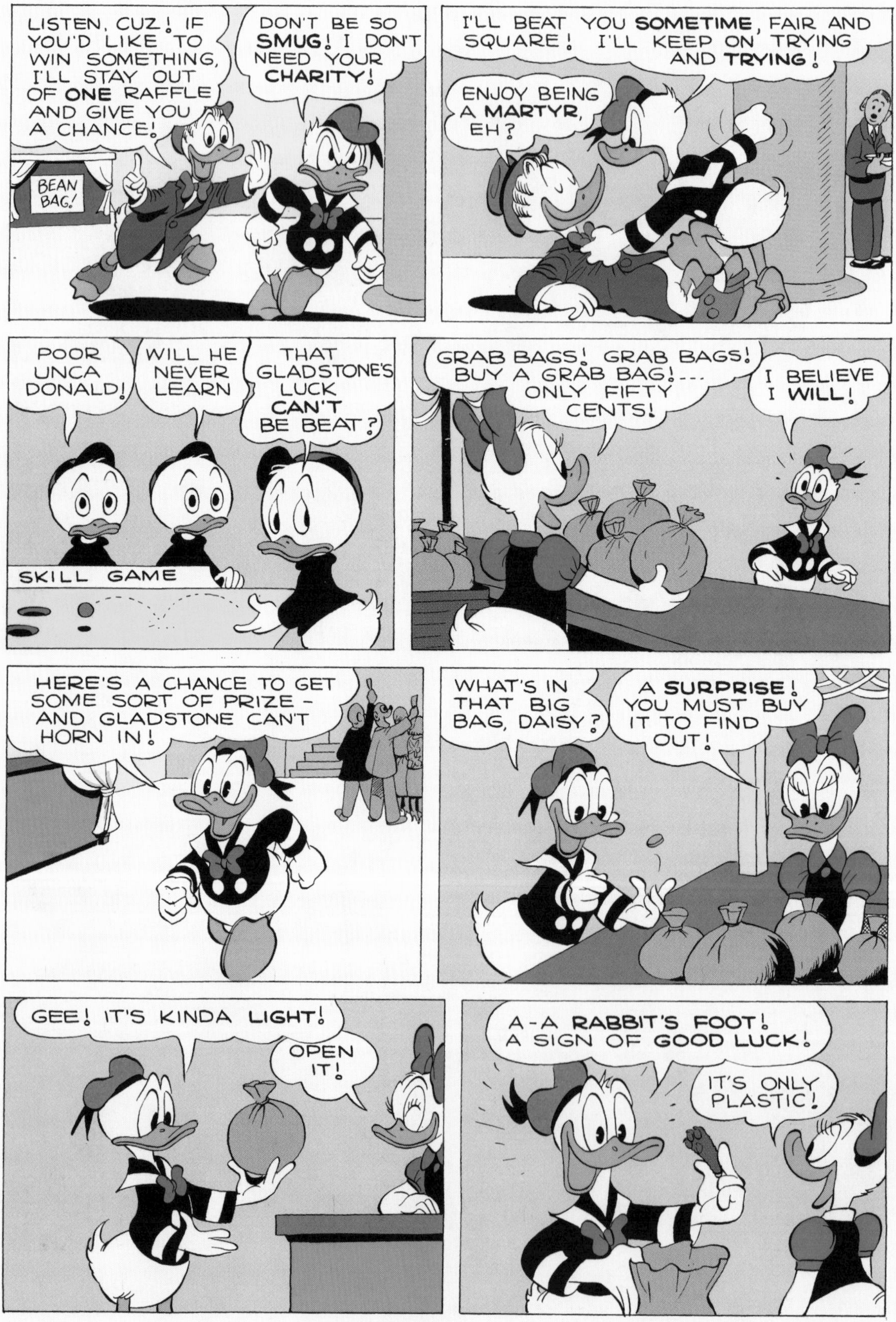

LISTEN, CUZ! IF YOU'D LIKE TO WIN SOMETHING, I'LL STAY OUT OF **ONE** RAFFLE AND GIVE YOU A CHANCE!
BEAN BAG!
DON'T BE SO **SMUG**! I DON'T NEED YOUR **CHARITY**!
I'LL BEAT YOU **SOMETIME**, FAIR AND SQUARE! I'LL KEEP ON TRYING AND **TRYING**!
ENJOY BEING A **MARTYR**, EH?
POOR UNCA DONALD!
WILL HE NEVER LEARN
THAT GLADSTONE'S LUCK **CAN'T** BE BEAT?
SKILL GAME
GRAB BAGS! GRAB BAGS! BUY A GRAB BAG!--- ONLY FIFTY CENTS!
I BELIEVE I **WILL**!
HERE'S A CHANCE TO GET SOME SORT OF PRIZE – AND GLADSTONE CAN'T HORN IN!
WHAT'S IN THAT BIG BAG, DAISY?
A **SURPRISE**! YOU MUST BUY IT TO FIND OUT!
GEE! IT'S KINDA **LIGHT**!
OPEN IT!
A-A **RABBIT'S FOOT**! A SIGN OF **GOOD LUCK**!
IT'S ONLY PLASTIC!

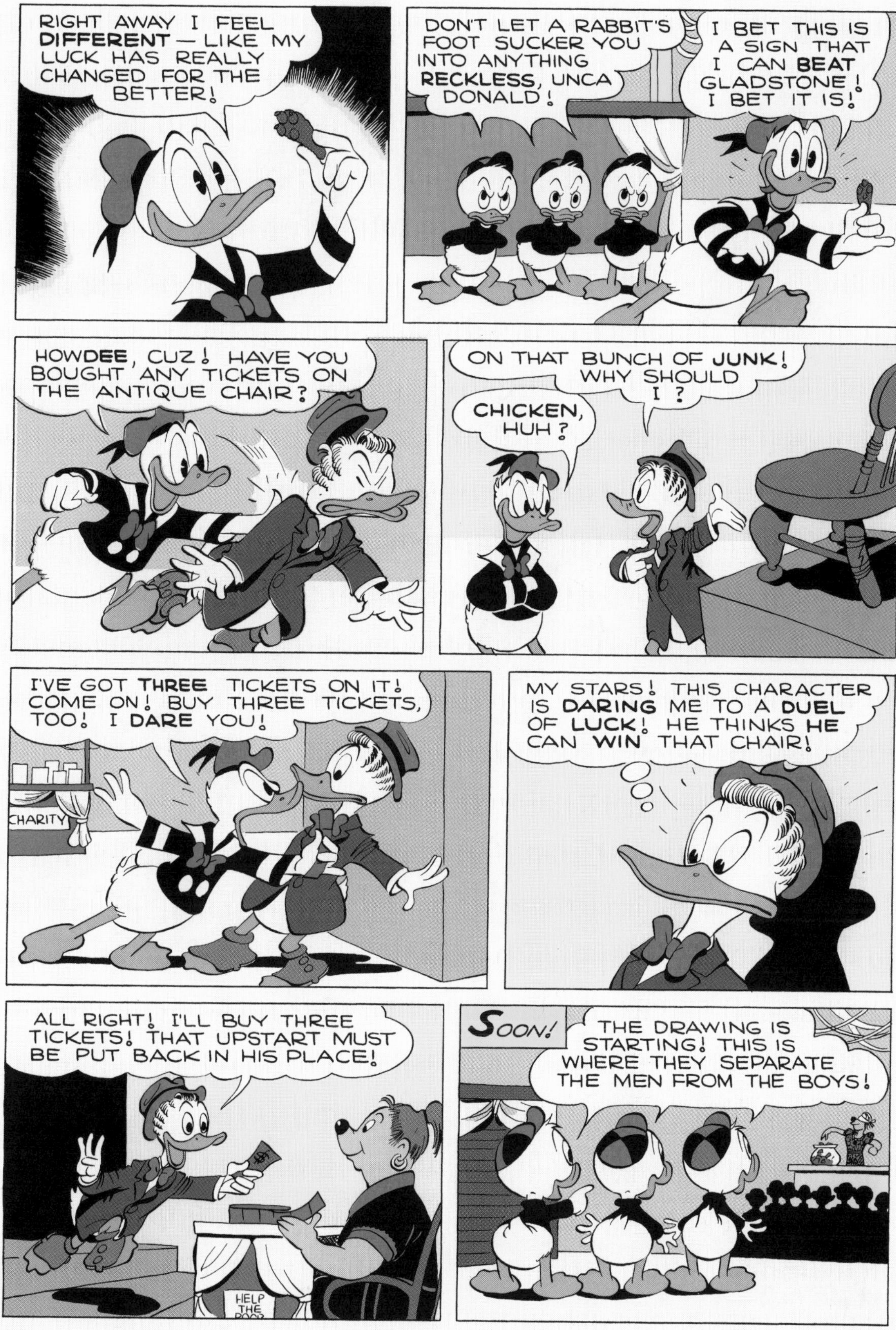
RIGHT AWAY I FEEL DIFFERENT — LIKE MY LUCK HAS REALLY CHANGED FOR THE BETTER!
DON'T LET A RABBIT'S FOOT SUCKER YOU INTO ANYTHING RECKLESS, UNCA DONALD!
I BET THIS IS A SIGN THAT I CAN BEAT GLADSTONE! I BET IT IS!
HOWDEE, CUZ! HAVE YOU BOUGHT ANY TICKETS ON THE ANTIQUE CHAIR?
ON THAT BUNCH OF JUNK! WHY SHOULD I?
CHICKEN, HUH?
I'VE GOT THREE TICKETS ON IT! COME ON! BUY THREE TICKETS, TOO! I DARE YOU!
CHARITY
MY STARS! THIS CHARACTER IS DARING ME TO A DUEL OF LUCK! HE THINKS HE CAN WIN THAT CHAIR!
ALL RIGHT! I'LL BUY THREE TICKETS! THAT UPSTART MUST BE PUT BACK IN HIS PLACE!
HELP THE
SOON!
THE DRAWING IS STARTING! THIS IS WHERE THEY SEPARATE THE MEN FROM THE BOYS!

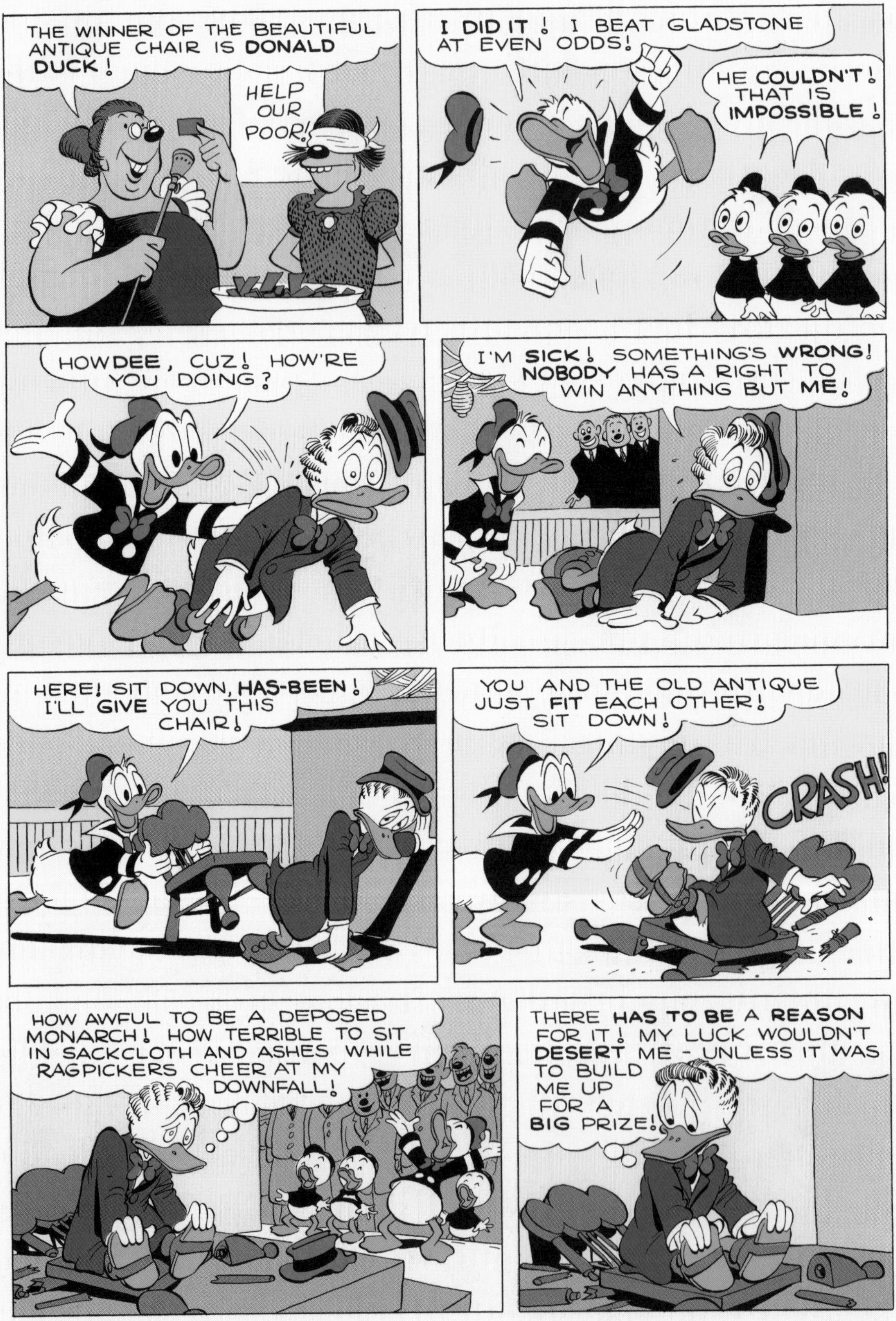
THE WINNER OF THE BEAUTIFUL ANTIQUE CHAIR IS DONALD DUCK!
HELP OUR POOR!
I DID IT! I BEAT GLADSTONE AT EVEN ODDS!
HE COULDN'T! THAT IS IMPOSSIBLE!
HOWDEE, CUZ! HOW'RE YOU DOING?
I'M SICK! SOMETHING'S WRONG! NOBODY HAS A RIGHT TO WIN ANYTHING BUT ME!
HERE! SIT DOWN, HAS-BEEN! I'LL GIVE YOU THIS CHAIR!
YOU AND THE OLD ANTIQUE JUST FIT EACH OTHER! SIT DOWN!
CRASH!
HOW AWFUL TO BE A DEPOSED MONARCH! HOW TERRIBLE TO SIT IN SACKCLOTH AND ASHES WHILE RAGPICKERS CHEER AT MY DOWNFALL!
THERE HAS TO BE A REASON FOR IT! MY LUCK WOULDN'T DESERT ME - UNLESS IT WAS TO BUILD ME UP FOR A BIG PRIZE!

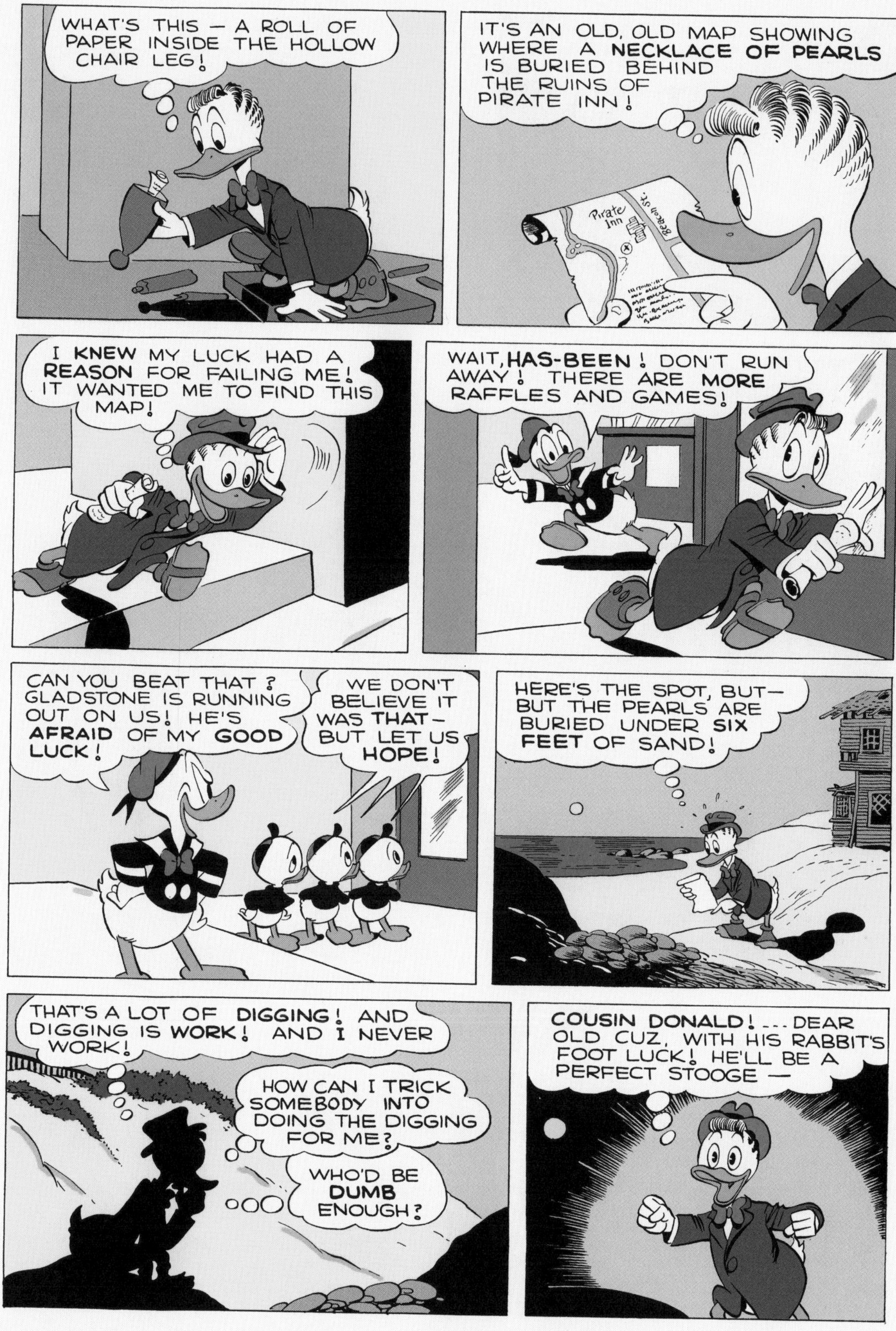
WHAT'S THIS — A ROLL OF PAPER INSIDE THE HOLLOW CHAIR LEG!
IT'S AN OLD, OLD MAP SHOWING WHERE A **NECKLACE OF PEARLS** IS BURIED BEHIND THE RUINS OF PIRATE INN!
Pirate Inn
Beacon St.
I **KNEW** MY LUCK HAD A **REASON** FOR FAILING ME! IT WANTED ME TO FIND THIS MAP!
WAIT, **HAS-BEEN**! DON'T RUN AWAY! THERE ARE **MORE** RAFFLES AND GAMES!
CAN YOU BEAT THAT? GLADSTONE IS RUNNING OUT ON US! HE'S **AFRAID** OF MY **GOOD LUCK**!
WE DON'T BELIEVE IT WAS **THAT**— BUT LET US **HOPE**!
HERE'S THE SPOT, BUT— BUT THE PEARLS ARE BURIED UNDER **SIX FEET** OF SAND!
THAT'S A LOT OF **DIGGING**! AND DIGGING IS **WORK**! AND **I** NEVER WORK!
HOW CAN I TRICK SOMEBODY **INTO** DOING THE DIGGING FOR ME?
WHO'D BE **DUMB** ENOUGH?
COUSIN DONALD! ... DEAR OLD CUZ, WITH HIS RABBIT'S FOOT LUCK! HE'LL BE A PERFECT STOOGE —

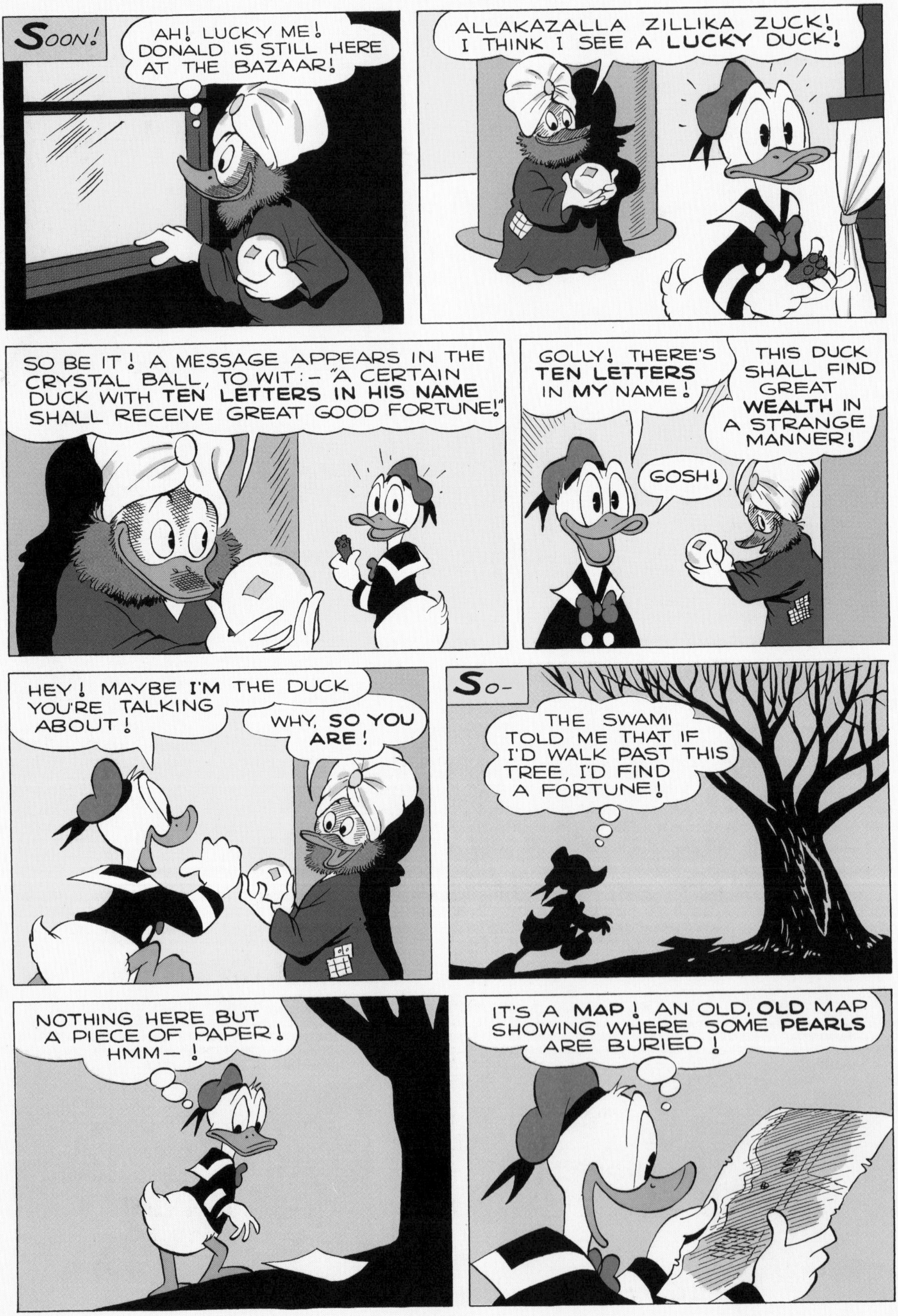
SOON!
AH! LUCKY ME! DONALD IS STILL HERE AT THE BAZAAR!
ALLAKAZALLA ZILLIKA ZUCK! I THINK I SEE A LUCKY DUCK!
SO BE IT! A MESSAGE APPEARS IN THE CRYSTAL BALL, TO WIT:– "A CERTAIN DUCK WITH TEN LETTERS IN HIS NAME SHALL RECEIVE GREAT GOOD FORTUNE!"
GOLLY! THERE'S TEN LETTERS IN MY NAME!
THIS DUCK SHALL FIND GREAT WEALTH IN A STRANGE MANNER!
GOSH!
HEY! MAYBE I'M THE DUCK YOU'RE TALKING ABOUT!
WHY, SO YOU ARE!
SO–
THE SWAMI TOLD ME THAT IF I'D WALK PAST THIS TREE, I'D FIND A FORTUNE!
NOTHING HERE BUT A PIECE OF PAPER! HMM–!
IT'S A MAP! AN OLD, OLD MAP SHOWING WHERE SOME PEARLS ARE BURIED!

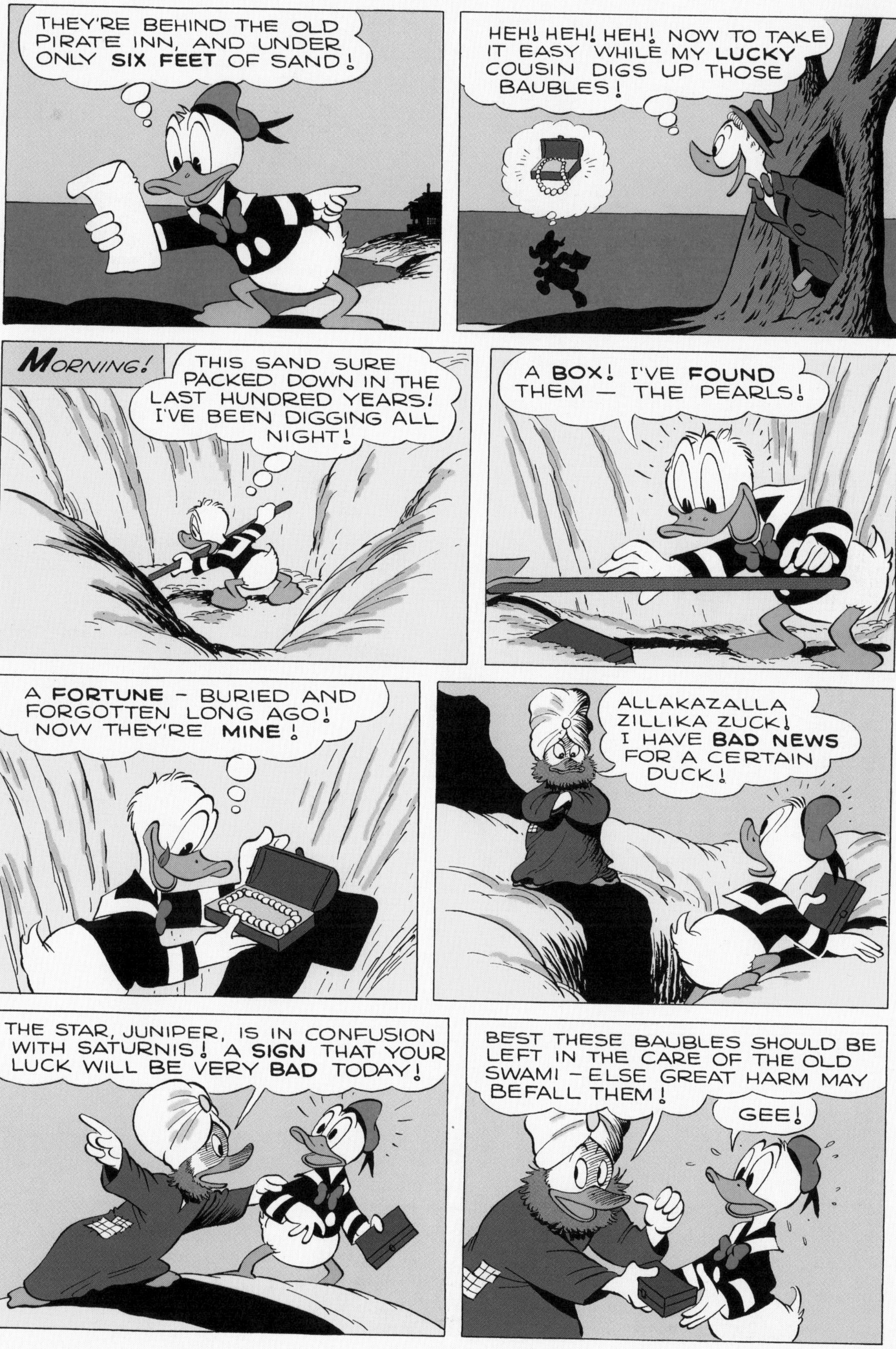
THEY'RE BEHIND THE OLD PIRATE INN, AND UNDER ONLY **SIX FEET** OF SAND!
HEH! HEH! HEH! NOW TO TAKE IT EASY WHILE MY **LUCKY** COUSIN DIGS UP THOSE BAUBLES!
MORNING!
THIS SAND SURE PACKED DOWN IN THE LAST HUNDRED YEARS! I'VE BEEN DIGGING ALL NIGHT!
A **BOX**! I'VE **FOUND** THEM — THE PEARLS!
A **FORTUNE** - BURIED AND FORGOTTEN LONG AGO! NOW THEY'RE **MINE**!
ALLAKAZALLA ZILLIKA ZUCK! I HAVE **BAD NEWS** FOR A CERTAIN DUCK!
THE STAR, JUNIPER, IS IN CONFUSION WITH SATURNIS! A **SIGN** THAT YOUR LUCK WILL BE VERY **BAD** TODAY!
BEST THESE BAUBLES SHOULD BE LEFT IN THE CARE OF THE OLD SWAMI - ELSE GREAT HARM MAY BEFALL THEM!
GEE!

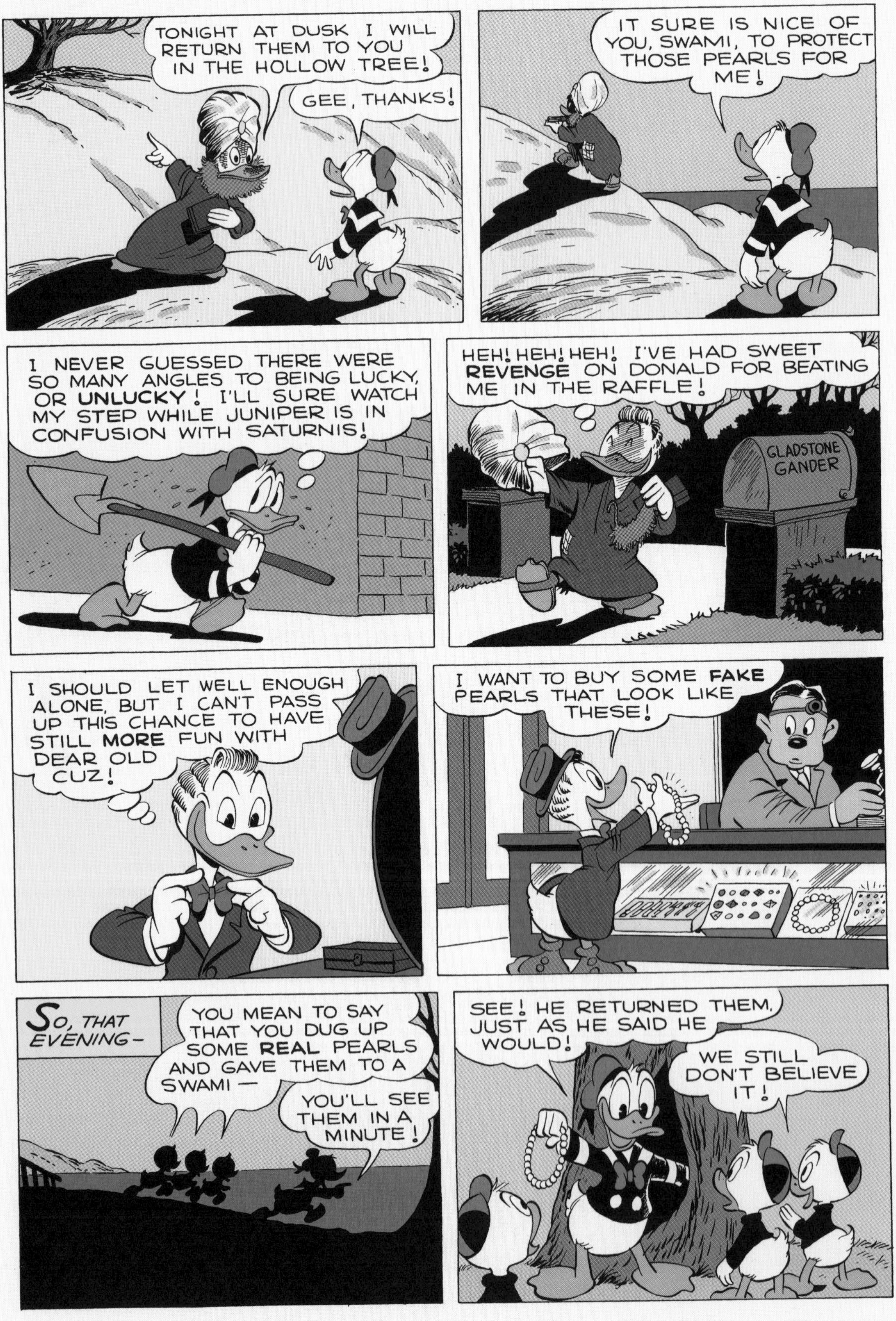
TONIGHT AT DUSK I WILL RETURN THEM TO YOU IN THE HOLLOW TREE!
GEE, THANKS!
IT SURE IS NICE OF YOU, SWAMI, TO PROTECT THOSE PEARLS FOR ME!
I NEVER GUESSED THERE WERE SO MANY ANGLES TO BEING LUCKY, OR UNLUCKY! I'LL SURE WATCH MY STEP WHILE JUNIPER IS IN CONFUSION WITH SATURNIS!
HEH! HEH! HEH! I'VE HAD SWEET REVENGE ON DONALD FOR BEATING ME IN THE RAFFLE!
GLADSTONE GANDER
I SHOULD LET WELL ENOUGH ALONE, BUT I CAN'T PASS UP THIS CHANCE TO HAVE STILL MORE FUN WITH DEAR OLD CUZ!
I WANT TO BUY SOME FAKE PEARLS THAT LOOK LIKE THESE!
SO, THAT EVENING—
YOU MEAN TO SAY THAT YOU DUG UP SOME REAL PEARLS AND GAVE THEM TO A SWAMI—
YOU'LL SEE THEM IN A MINUTE!
SEE! HE RETURNED THEM, JUST AS HE SAID HE WOULD!
WE STILL DON'T BELIEVE IT!

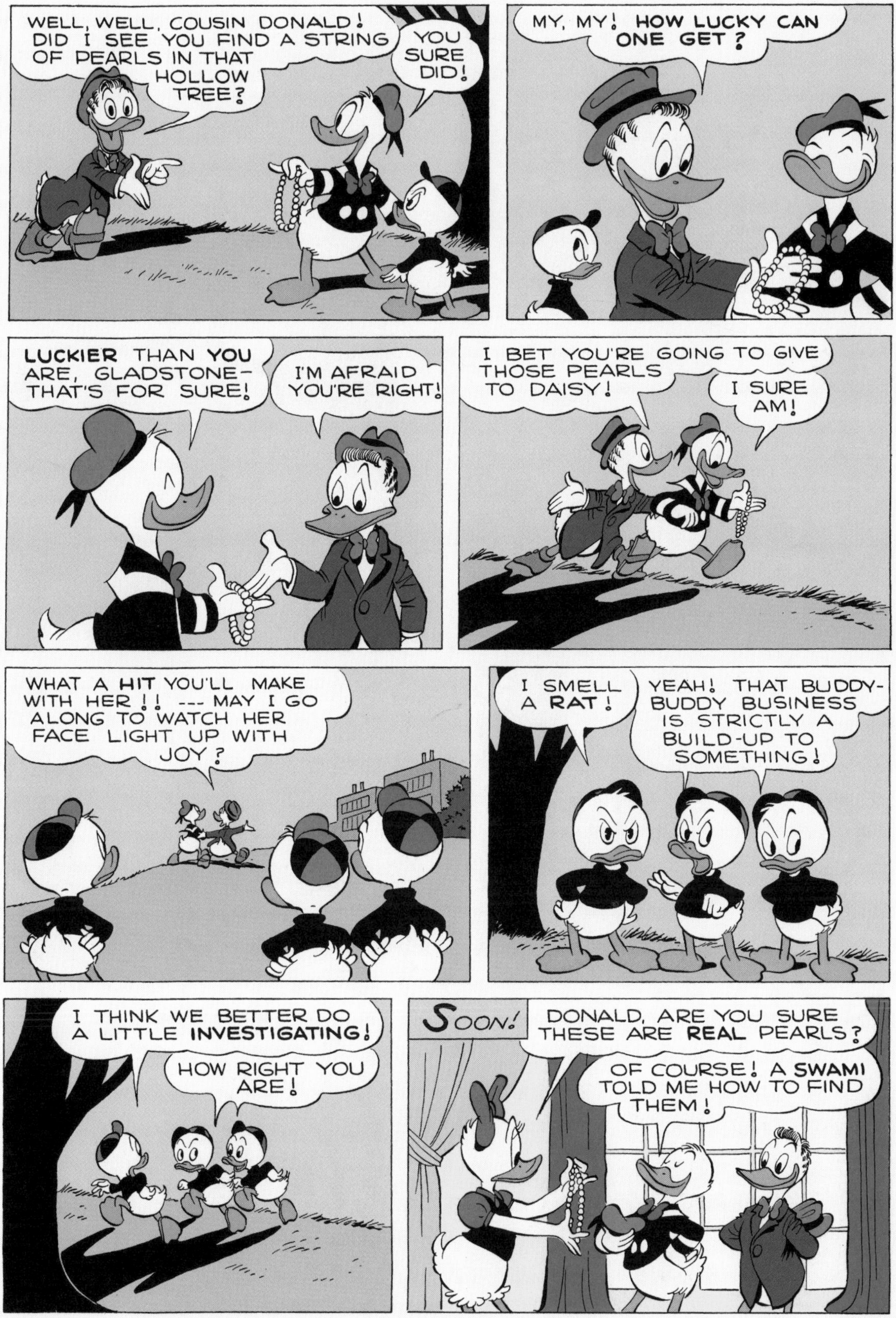
WELL, WELL, COUSIN DONALD! DID I SEE YOU FIND A STRING OF PEARLS IN THAT HOLLOW TREE?
YOU SURE DID!
MY, MY! HOW LUCKY CAN ONE GET?
LUCKIER THAN YOU ARE, GLADSTONE— THAT'S FOR SURE!
I'M AFRAID YOU'RE RIGHT!
I BET YOU'RE GOING TO GIVE THOSE PEARLS TO DAISY!
I SURE AM!
WHAT A HIT YOU'LL MAKE WITH HER!! --- MAY I GO ALONG TO WATCH HER FACE LIGHT UP WITH JOY?
I SMELL A RAT!
YEAH! THAT BUDDY-BUDDY BUSINESS IS STRICTLY A BUILD-UP TO SOMETHING!
I THINK WE BETTER DO A LITTLE INVESTIGATING!
HOW RIGHT YOU ARE!
SOON!
DONALD, ARE YOU SURE THESE ARE REAL PEARLS?
OF COURSE! A SWAMI TOLD ME HOW TO FIND THEM!

WHY WOULD A SWAMI TELL YOU HOW TO FIND PEARLS?

WHY- UH- BECAUSE I'VE SUDDENLY BECOME LUCKY- I GUESS!

HA! YOU'RE LUCKY YOU DIDN'T PUT THEM IN YOUR MOUTH! THEY'RE NOTHING BUT FLOUR AND GLUE!

THEY'RE DISSOLVING!

HAW! HAW! HAW! MY LUCKY COUSIN! HE DUG SAND ALL NIGHT TO FIND SOME FAKE PEARLS! HAW! HAW! HAW!

I DID FIND REAL PEARLS! THAT SWAMI SWINDLED ME OUT OF THE REAL ONES!

PSST! UNCA DONALD! COME HERE!

DID YOU EVER SEE THIS COSTUME BEFORE? WE FOUND IT AT GLADSTONE'S PLACE!

THE SWAMI'S CLOTHES AND THE PEARLS!

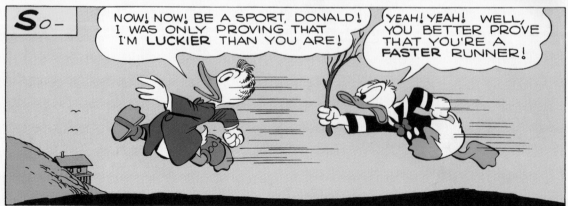

SO-

NOW! NOW! BE A SPORT, DONALD! I WAS ONLY PROVING THAT I'M LUCKIER THAN YOU ARE!

YEAH! YEAH! WELL, YOU BETTER PROVE THAT YOU'RE A FASTER RUNNER!

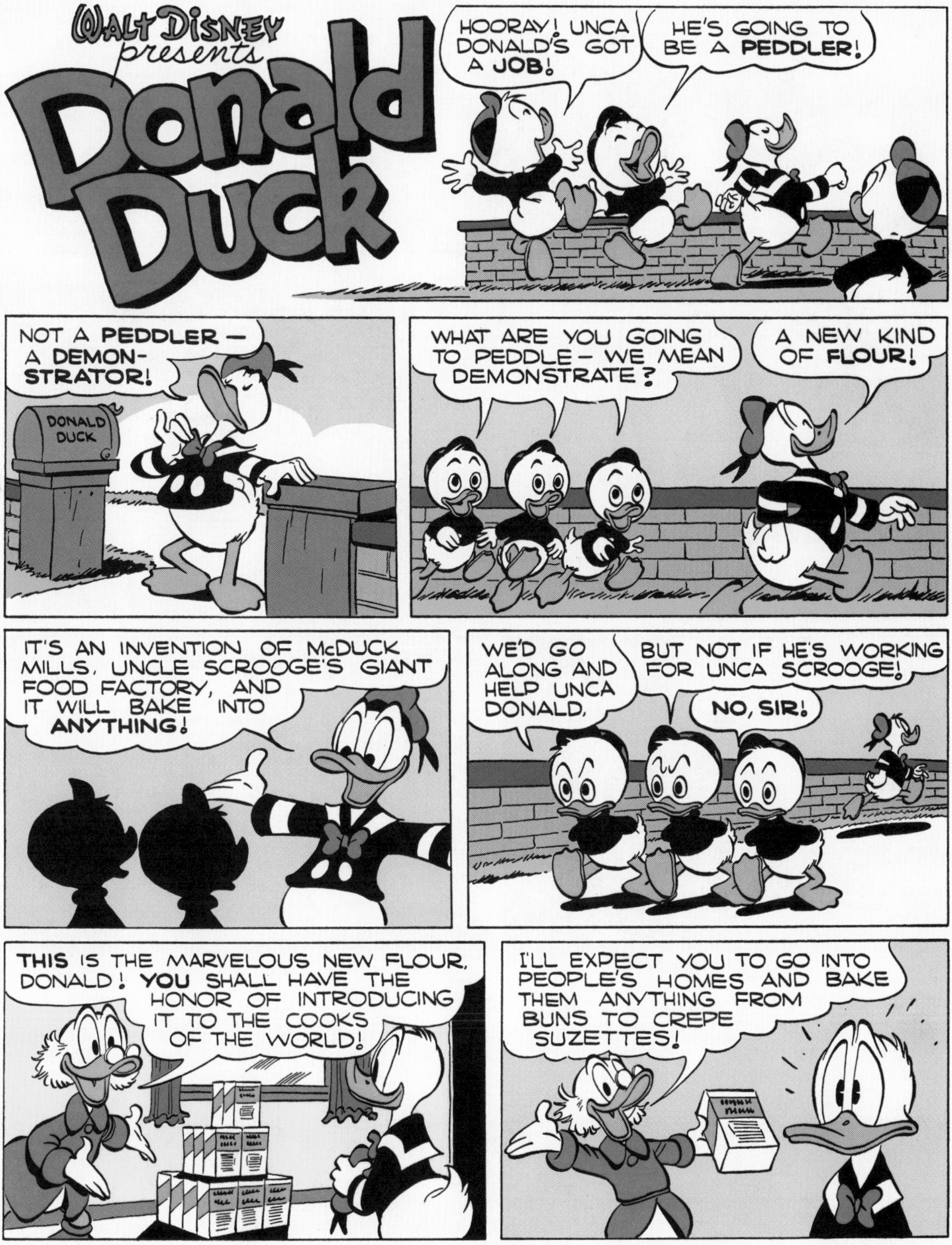
WALT DISNEY presents
Donald Duck
HOORAY! UNCA DONALD'S GOT A JOB!
HE'S GOING TO BE A PEDDLER!
NOT A PEDDLER — A DEMON-STRATOR!
DONALD DUCK
WHAT ARE YOU GOING TO PEDDLE — WE MEAN DEMONSTRATE?
A NEW KIND OF FLOUR!
IT'S AN INVENTION OF McDUCK MILLS, UNCLE SCROOGE'S GIANT FOOD FACTORY, AND IT WILL BAKE INTO ANYTHING!
WE'D GO ALONG AND HELP UNCA DONALD,
BUT NOT IF HE'S WORKING FOR UNCA SCROOGE!
NO, SIR!
THIS IS THE MARVELOUS NEW FLOUR, DONALD! YOU SHALL HAVE THE HONOR OF INTRODUCING IT TO THE COOKS OF THE WORLD!
I'LL EXPECT YOU TO GO INTO PEOPLE'S HOMES AND BAKE THEM ANYTHING FROM BUNS TO CREPE SUZETTES!

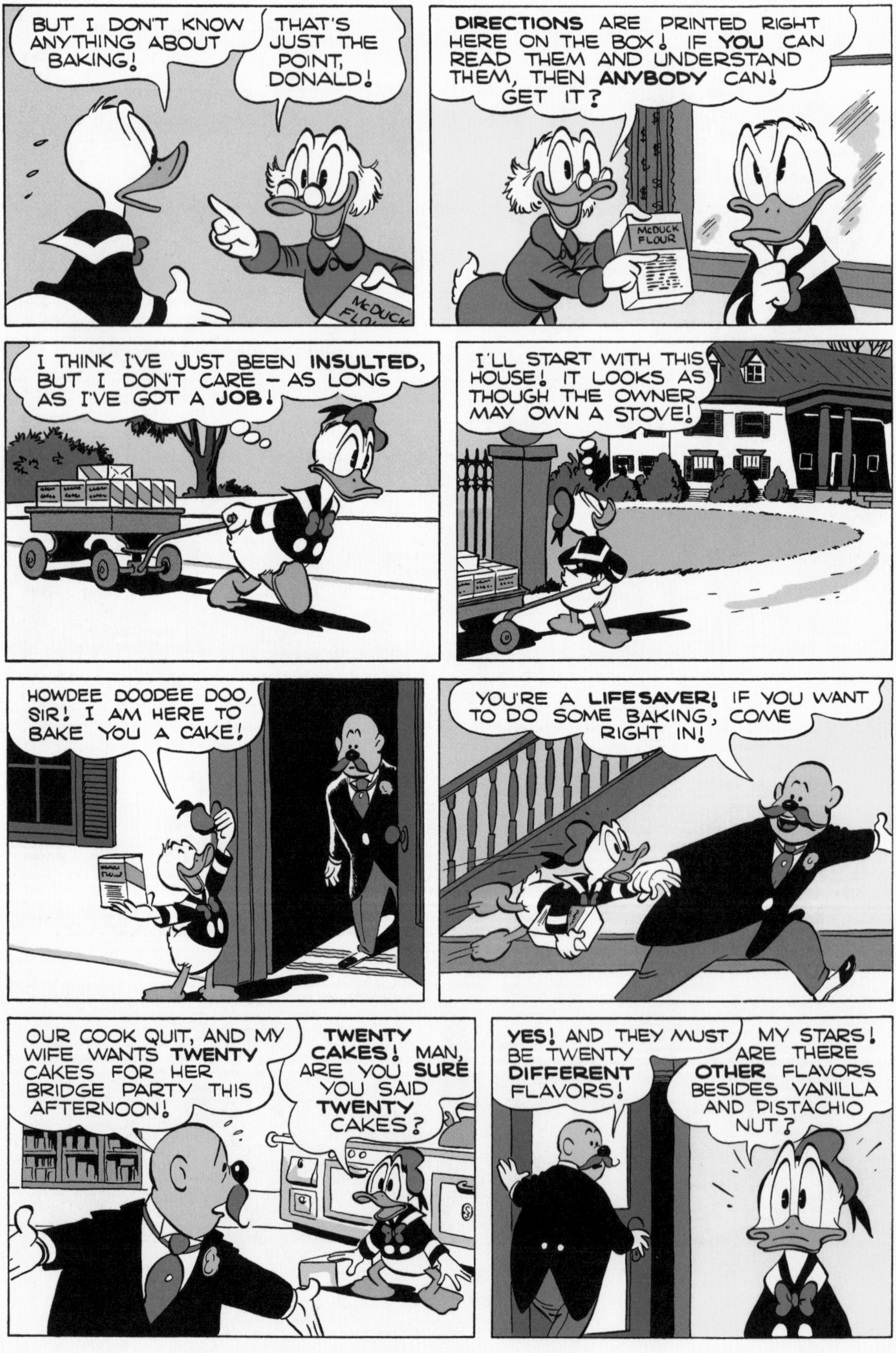
BUT I DON'T KNOW ANYTHING ABOUT BAKING!
THAT'S JUST THE POINT, DONALD!
McDUCK FLOUR
DIRECTIONS ARE PRINTED RIGHT HERE ON THE BOX! IF YOU CAN READ THEM AND UNDERSTAND THEM, THEN ANYBODY CAN! GET IT?
McDUCK FLOUR
I THINK I'VE JUST BEEN INSULTED, BUT I DON'T CARE — AS LONG AS I'VE GOT A JOB!
I'LL START WITH THIS HOUSE! IT LOOKS AS THOUGH THE OWNER MAY OWN A STOVE!
HOWDEE DOODEE DOO, SIR! I AM HERE TO BAKE YOU A CAKE!
YOU'RE A LIFESAVER! IF YOU WANT TO DO SOME BAKING, COME RIGHT IN!
OUR COOK QUIT, AND MY WIFE WANTS TWENTY CAKES FOR HER BRIDGE PARTY THIS AFTERNOON!
TWENTY CAKES! MAN, ARE YOU SURE YOU SAID TWENTY CAKES?
YES! AND THEY MUST BE TWENTY DIFFERENT FLAVORS!
MY STARS! ARE THERE OTHER FLAVORS BESIDES VANILLA AND PISTACHIO NUT?

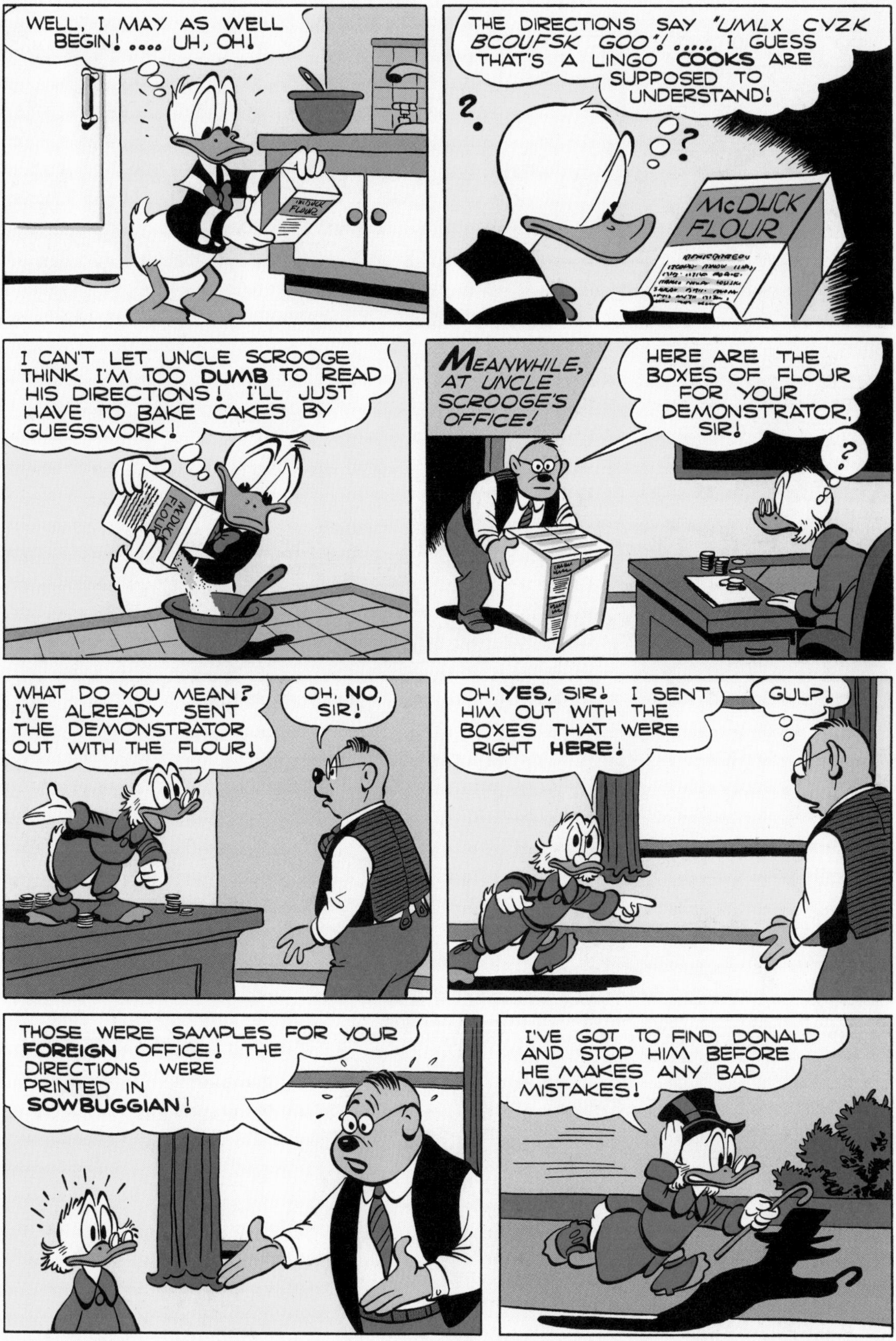
WELL, I MAY AS WELL BEGIN! ..... UH, OH!
McDUCK FLOUR
THE DIRECTIONS SAY "UMLX CYZK BCOUFSK GOO"! ..... I GUESS THAT'S A LINGO COOKS ARE SUPPOSED TO UNDERSTAND!
McDUCK FLOUR
I CAN'T LET UNCLE SCROOGE THINK I'M TOO DUMB TO READ HIS DIRECTIONS! I'LL JUST HAVE TO BAKE CAKES BY GUESSWORK!
McDUCK FLOUR
MEANWHILE, AT UNCLE SCROOGE'S OFFICE!
HERE ARE THE BOXES OF FLOUR FOR YOUR DEMONSTRATOR, SIR!
WHAT DO YOU MEAN? I'VE ALREADY SENT THE DEMONSTRATOR OUT WITH THE FLOUR!
OH, NO, SIR!
OH, YES, SIR! I SENT HIM OUT WITH THE BOXES THAT WERE RIGHT HERE!
GULP!
THOSE WERE SAMPLES FOR YOUR FOREIGN OFFICE! THE DIRECTIONS WERE PRINTED IN SOWBUGGIAN!
I'VE GOT TO FIND DONALD AND STOP HIM BEFORE HE MAKES ANY BAD MISTAKES!

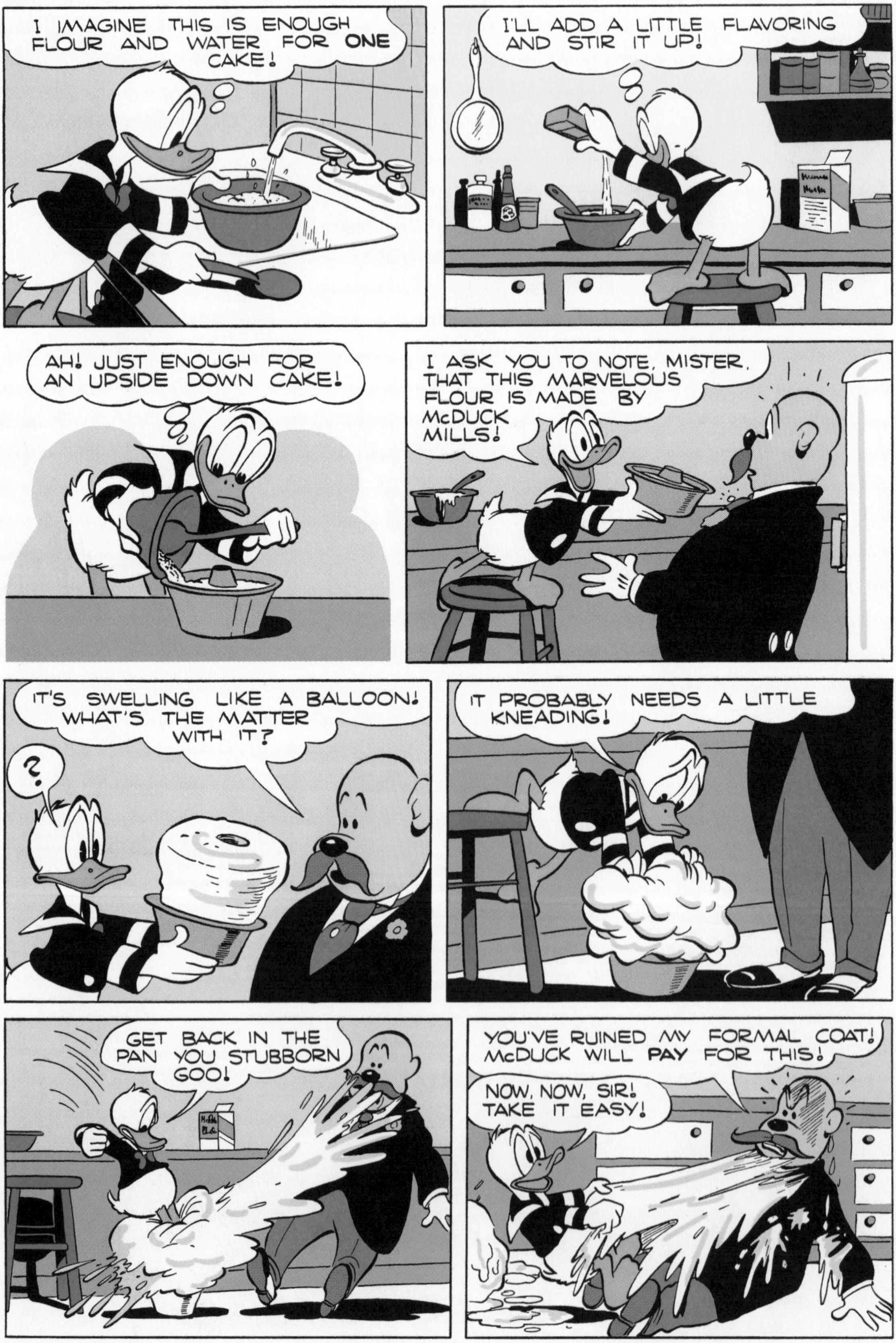
I IMAGINE THIS IS ENOUGH FLOUR AND WATER FOR **ONE** CAKE!
I'LL ADD A LITTLE FLAVORING AND STIR IT UP!
AH! JUST ENOUGH FOR AN UPSIDE DOWN CAKE!
I ASK YOU TO NOTE, MISTER, THAT THIS MARVELOUS FLOUR IS MADE BY McDUCK MILLS!
IT'S SWELLING LIKE A BALLOON! WHAT'S THE MATTER WITH IT?
?
IT PROBABLY NEEDS A LITTLE KNEADING!
GET BACK IN THE PAN YOU STUBBORN GOO!
YOU'VE RUINED MY FORMAL COAT! McDUCK WILL **PAY** FOR THIS!
NOW, NOW, SIR! TAKE IT EASY!

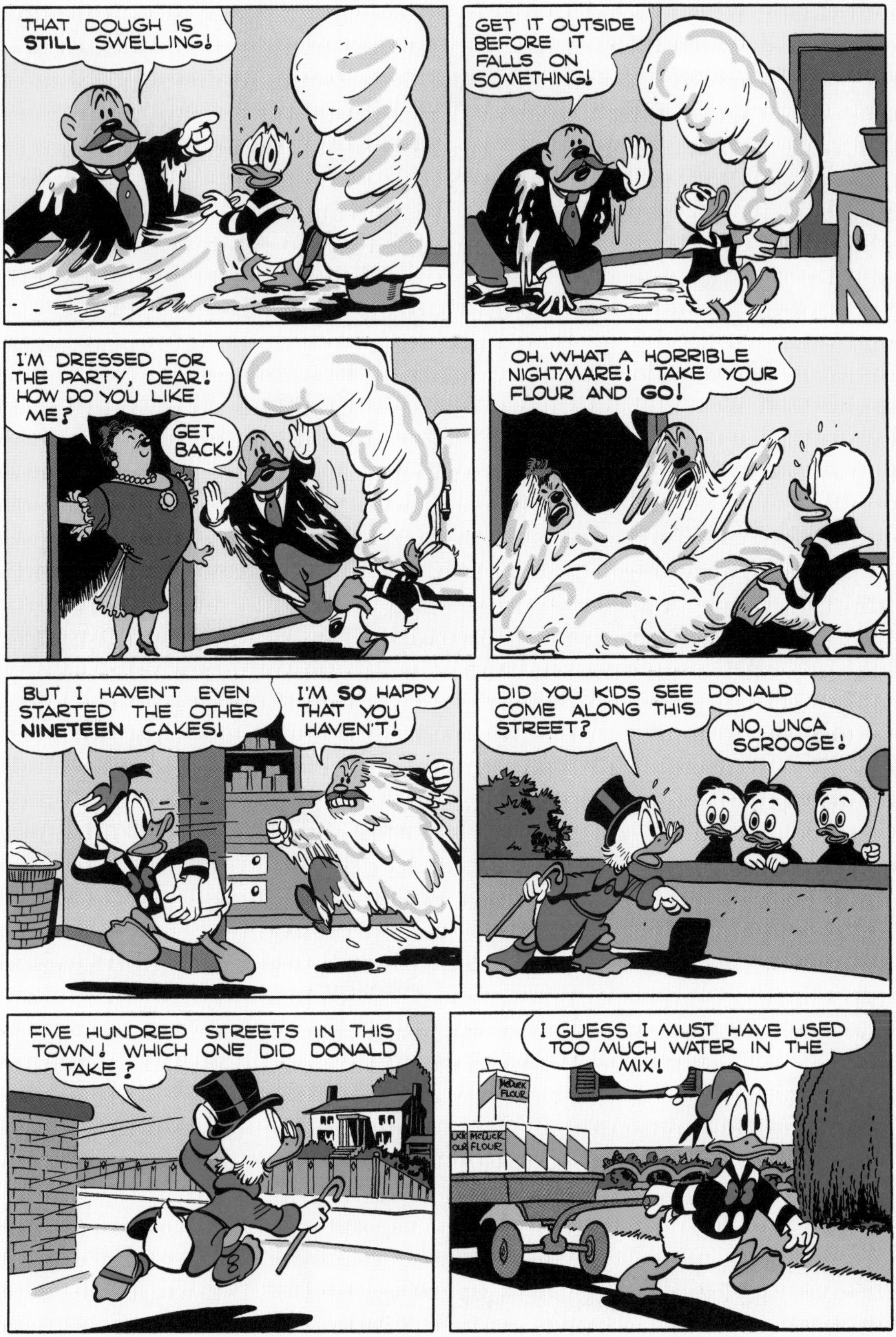

THAT DOUGH IS STILL SWELLING!
GET IT OUTSIDE BEFORE IT FALLS ON SOMETHING!
I'M DRESSED FOR THE PARTY, DEAR! HOW DO YOU LIKE ME?
GET BACK!
OH. WHAT A HORRIBLE NIGHTMARE! TAKE YOUR FLOUR AND GO!
BUT I HAVEN'T EVEN STARTED THE OTHER NINETEEN CAKES!
I'M SO HAPPY THAT YOU HAVEN'T!
DID YOU KIDS SEE DONALD COME ALONG THIS STREET?
NO, UNCA SCROOGE!
FIVE HUNDRED STREETS IN THIS TOWN! WHICH ONE DID DONALD TAKE?
I GUESS I MUST HAVE USED TOO MUCH WATER IN THE MIX!
McDUCK FLOUR
McDUCK FLOUR

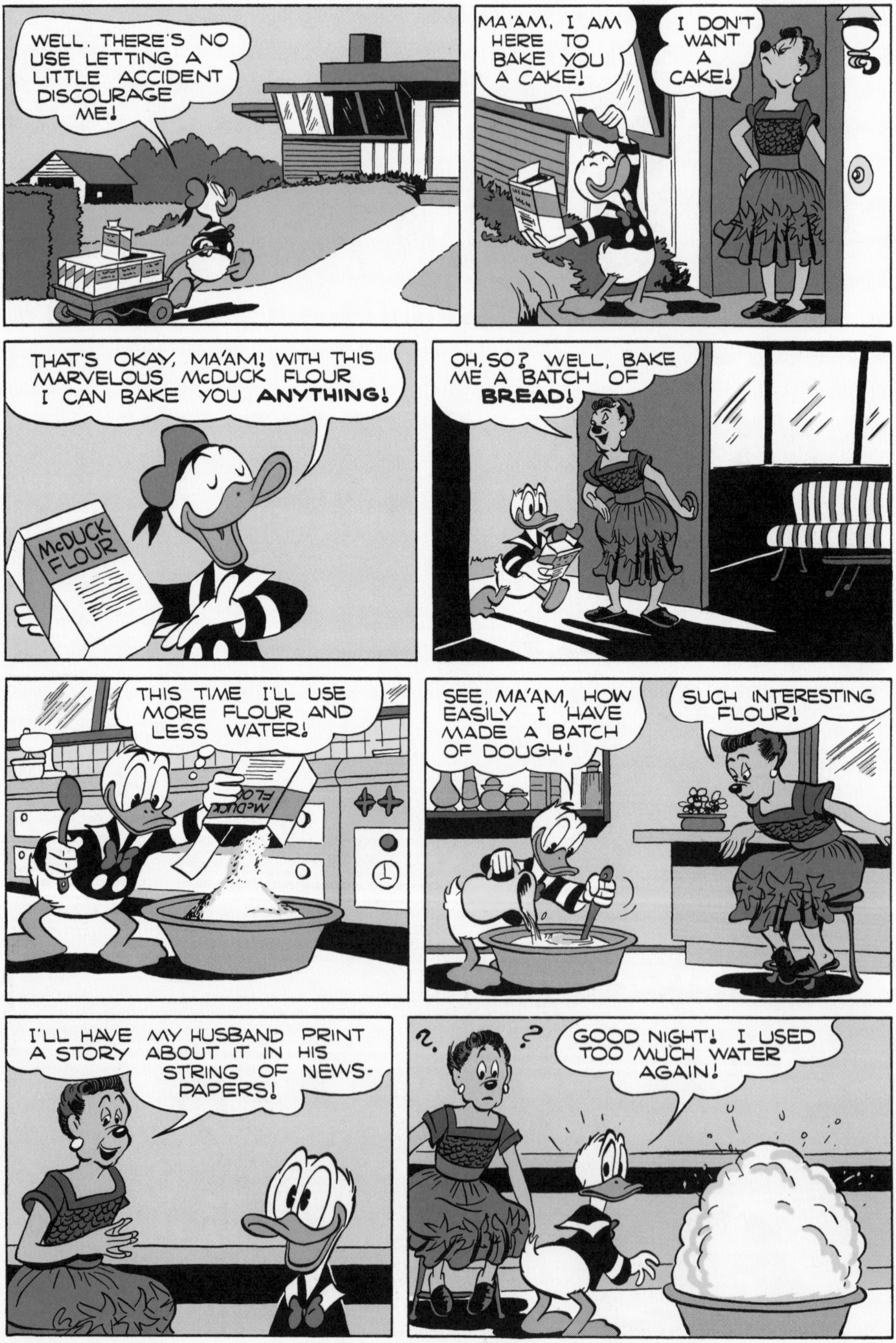
WELL, THERE'S NO USE LETTING A LITTLE ACCIDENT DISCOURAGE ME!
MA'AM, I AM HERE TO BAKE YOU A CAKE!
I DON'T WANT A CAKE!
McDUCK FLOUR
THAT'S OKAY, MA'AM! WITH THIS MARVELOUS McDUCK FLOUR I CAN BAKE YOU **ANYTHING!**
OH, SO? WELL, BAKE ME A BATCH OF **BREAD!**
THIS TIME I'LL USE MORE FLOUR AND LESS WATER!
SEE, MA'AM, HOW EASILY I HAVE MADE A BATCH OF DOUGH!
SUCH INTERESTING FLOUR!
I'LL HAVE MY HUSBAND PRINT A STORY ABOUT IT IN HIS STRING OF NEWS-PAPERS!
?
?
GOOD NIGHT! I USED TOO MUCH WATER AGAIN!

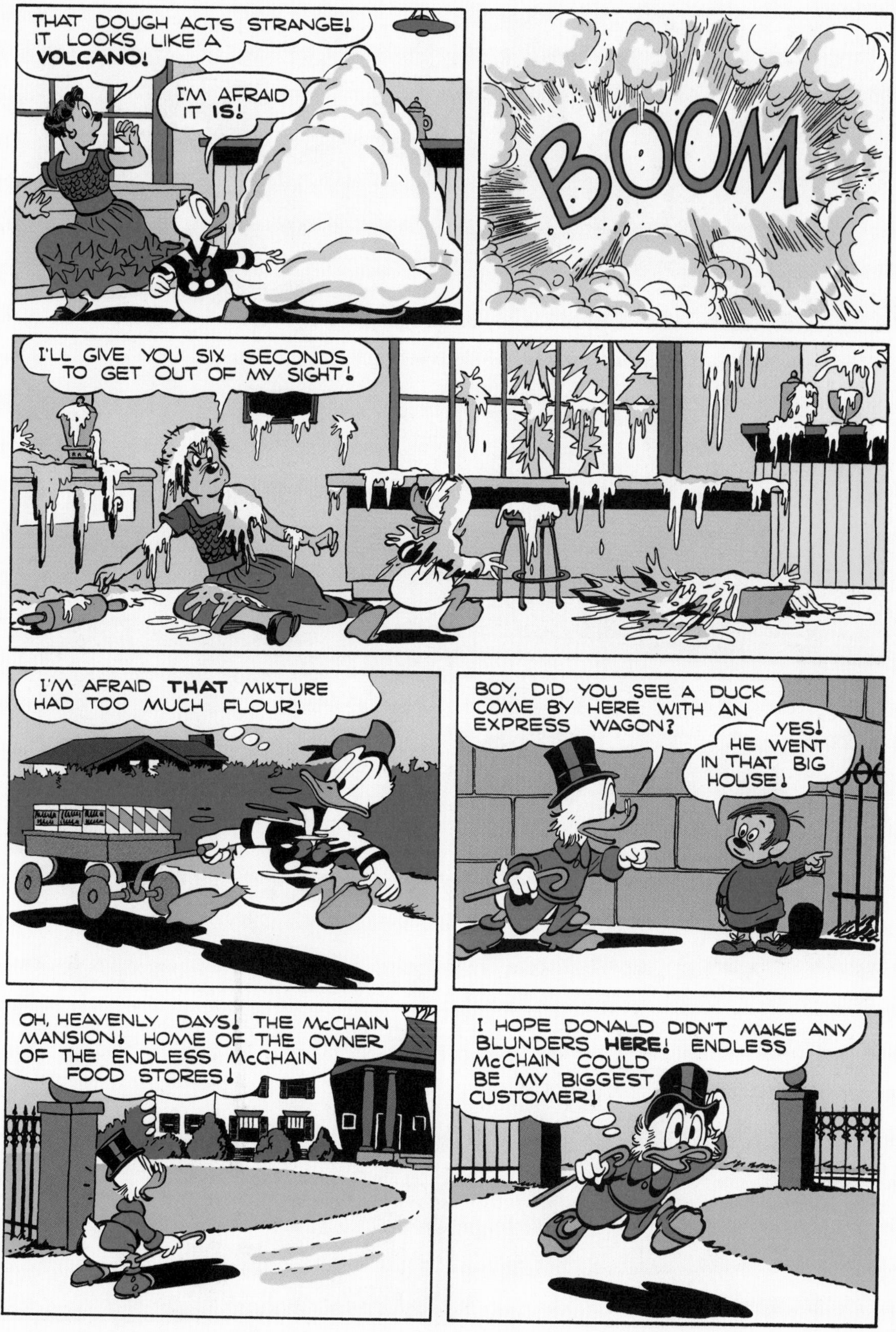
THAT DOUGH ACTS STRANGE! IT LOOKS LIKE A **VOLCANO!**
I'M AFRAID IT **IS!**
BOOM
I'LL GIVE YOU SIX SECONDS TO GET OUT OF MY SIGHT!
I'M AFRAID **THAT** MIXTURE HAD TOO MUCH FLOUR!
BOY, DID YOU SEE A DUCK COME BY HERE WITH AN EXPRESS WAGON?
YES! HE WENT IN THAT BIG HOUSE!
OH, HEAVENLY DAYS! THE McCHAIN MANSION! HOME OF THE OWNER OF THE ENDLESS McCHAIN FOOD STORES!
I HOPE DONALD DIDN'T MAKE ANY BLUNDERS **HERE!** ENDLESS McCHAIN COULD BE MY BIGGEST CUSTOMER!

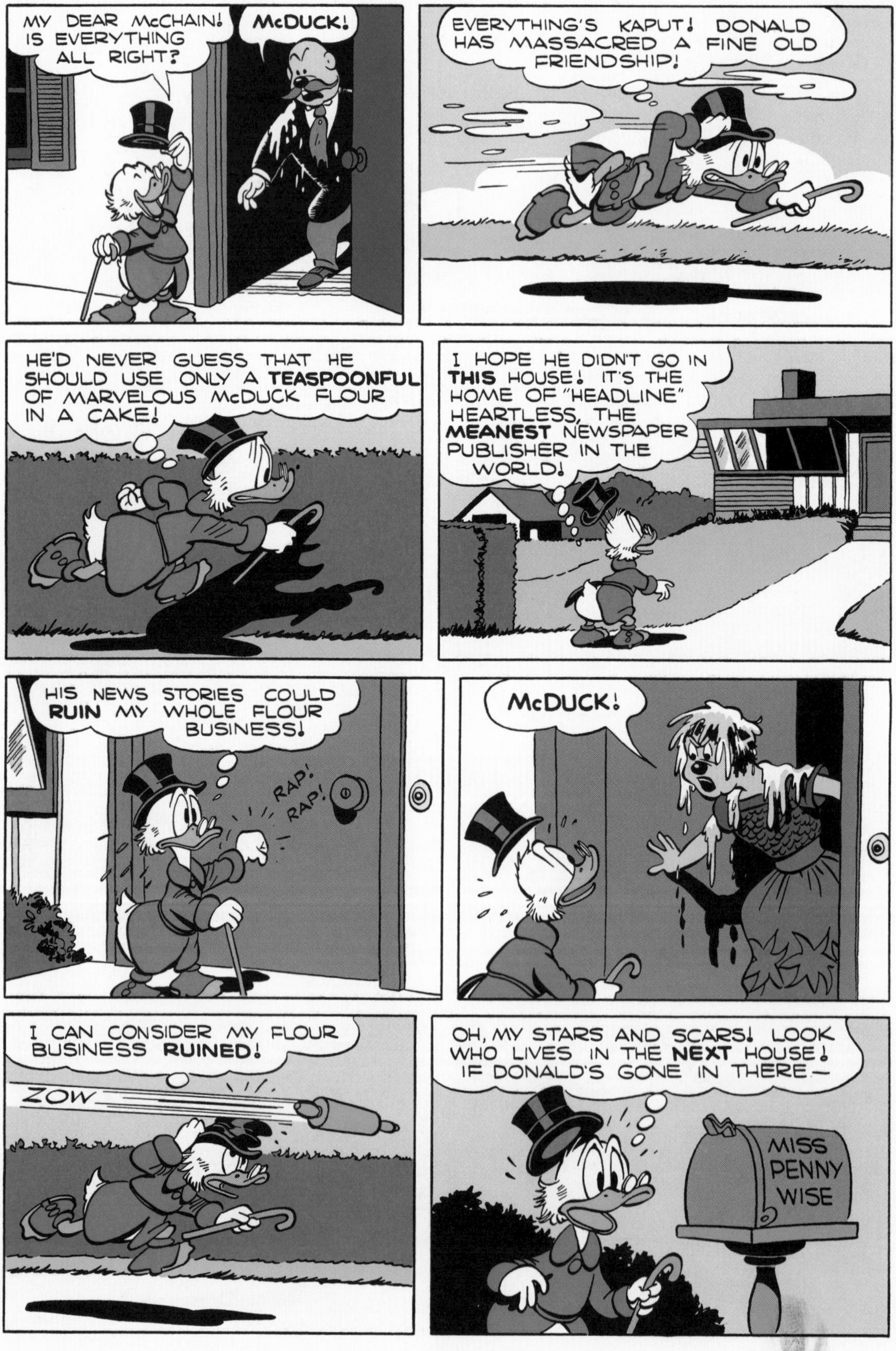

MY DEAR McCHAIN! IS EVERYTHING ALL RIGHT?
McDUCK!
EVERYTHING'S KAPUT! DONALD HAS MASSACRED A FINE OLD FRIENDSHIP!
HE'D NEVER GUESS THAT HE SHOULD USE ONLY A TEASPOONFUL OF MARVELOUS McDUCK FLOUR IN A CAKE!
I HOPE HE DIDN'T GO IN THIS HOUSE! IT'S THE HOME OF "HEADLINE" HEARTLESS, THE MEANEST NEWSPAPER PUBLISHER IN THE WORLD!
HIS NEWS STORIES COULD RUIN MY WHOLE FLOUR BUSINESS!
RAP! RAP!
McDUCK!
I CAN CONSIDER MY FLOUR BUSINESS RUINED!
ZOW
OH, MY STARS AND SCARS! LOOK WHO LIVES IN THE NEXT HOUSE! IF DONALD'S GONE IN THERE—
MISS PENNY WISE

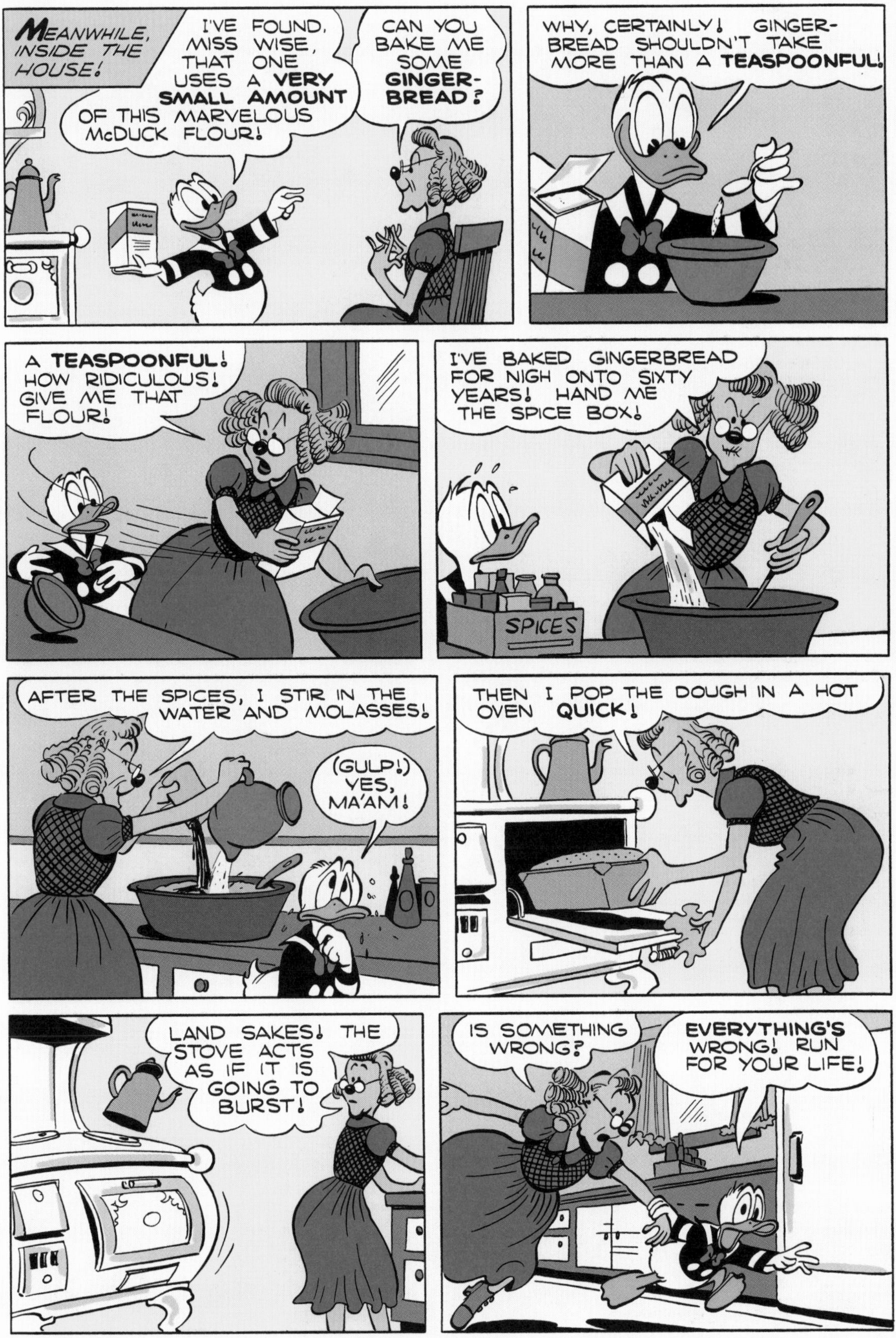
MEANWHILE, INSIDE THE HOUSE!
I'VE FOUND, MISS WISE, THAT ONE USES A VERY SMALL AMOUNT OF THIS MARVELOUS McDUCK FLOUR!
CAN YOU BAKE ME SOME GINGER-BREAD?
WHY, CERTAINLY! GINGER-BREAD SHOULDN'T TAKE MORE THAN A TEASPOONFUL!
A TEASPOONFUL! HOW RIDICULOUS! GIVE ME THAT FLOUR!
I'VE BAKED GINGERBREAD FOR NIGH ONTO SIXTY YEARS! HAND ME THE SPICE BOX!
SPICES
AFTER THE SPICES, I STIR IN THE WATER AND MOLASSES!
(GULP!) YES, MA'AM!
THEN I POP THE DOUGH IN A HOT OVEN QUICK!
LAND SAKES! THE STOVE ACTS AS IF IT IS GOING TO BURST!
IS SOMETHING WRONG?
EVERYTHING'S WRONG! RUN FOR YOUR LIFE!

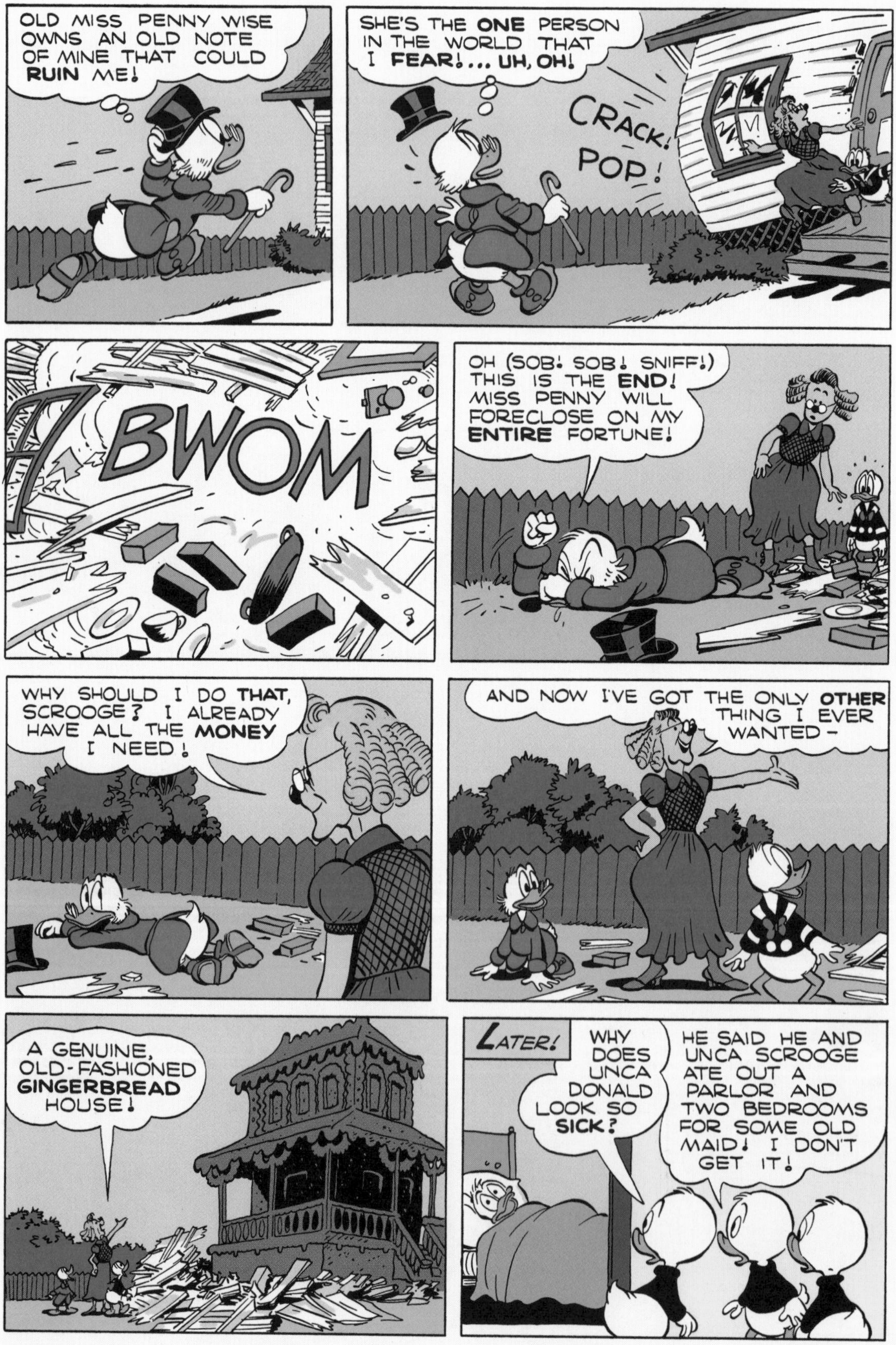
OLD MISS PENNY WISE OWNS AN OLD NOTE OF MINE THAT COULD **RUIN** ME!
SHE'S THE **ONE** PERSON IN THE WORLD THAT I **FEAR!... UH, OH!**
CRACK!
POP!
BWOM
OH (SOB! SOB! SNIFF!) THIS IS THE **END!** MISS PENNY WILL FORECLOSE ON MY **ENTIRE** FORTUNE!
WHY SHOULD I DO **THAT,** SCROOGE? I ALREADY HAVE ALL THE **MONEY** I NEED!
AND NOW I'VE GOT THE ONLY **OTHER** THING I EVER WANTED –
A GENUINE, OLD-FASHIONED **GINGERBREAD** HOUSE!
LATER!
WHY DOES UNCA DONALD LOOK SO **SICK?**
HE SAID HE AND UNCA SCROOGE ATE OUT A PARLOR AND TWO BEDROOMS FOR SOME OLD MAID! I DON'T GET IT!

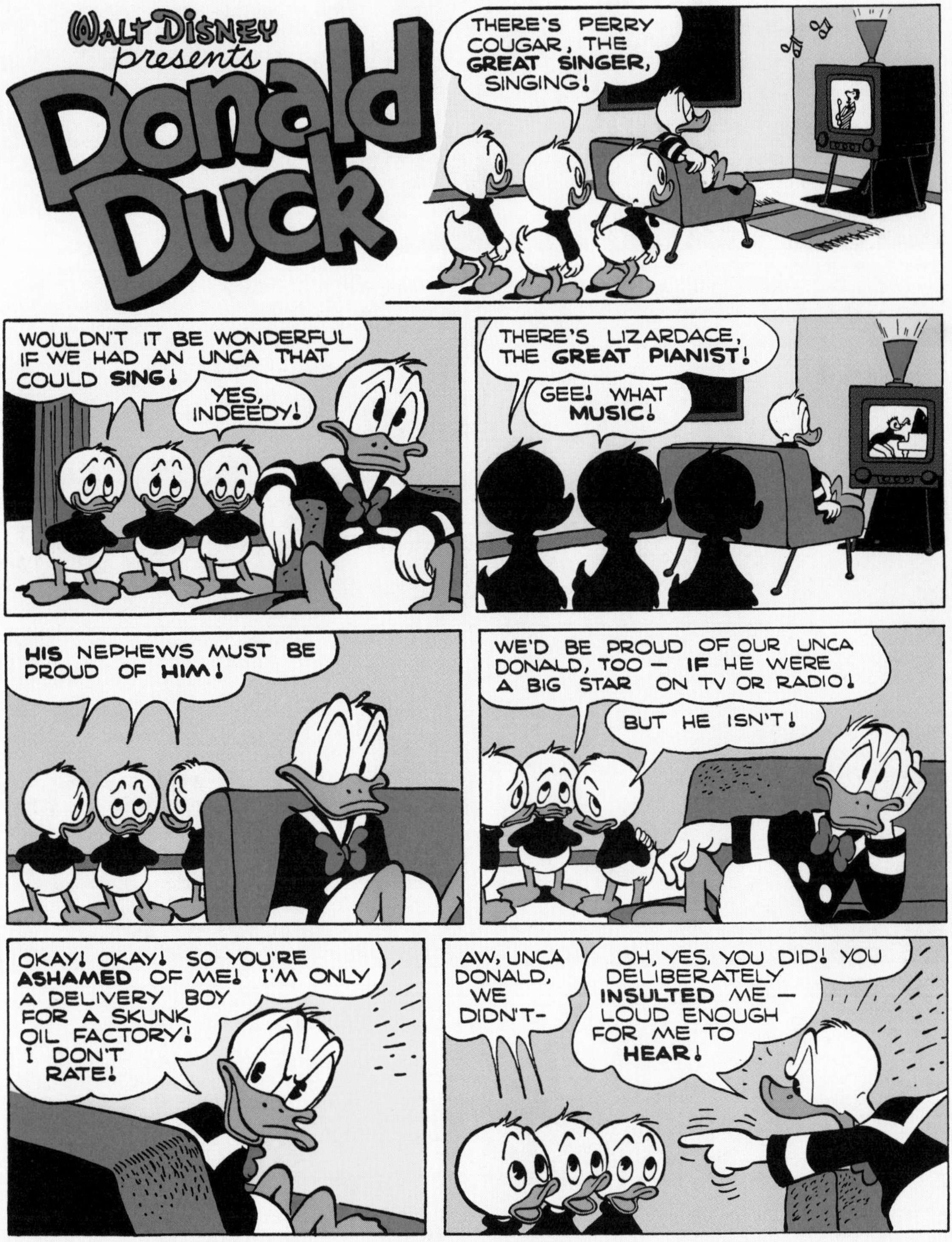
WALT DISNEY presents
Donald Duck
THERE'S PERRY COUGAR, THE GREAT SINGER, SINGING!
WOULDN'T IT BE WONDERFUL IF WE HAD AN UNCA THAT COULD SING!
YES, INDEEDY!
THERE'S LIZARDACE, THE GREAT PIANIST!
GEE! WHAT MUSIC!
HIS NEPHEWS MUST BE PROUD OF HIM!
WE'D BE PROUD OF OUR UNCA DONALD, TOO — IF HE WERE A BIG STAR ON TV OR RADIO!
BUT HE ISN'T!
OKAY! OKAY! SO YOU'RE ASHAMED OF ME! I'M ONLY A DELIVERY BOY FOR A SKUNK OIL FACTORY! I DON'T RATE!
AW, UNCA DONALD, WE DIDN'T-
OH, YES, YOU DID! YOU DELIBERATELY INSULTED ME — LOUD ENOUGH FOR ME TO HEAR!

WHAT A FINE WAY TO TREAT YOUR HARD-WORKING UNCLE! IF YOU HAD ANY **SHAME**, YOU'D HIDE YOUR FACES IN IT!

NOW, GO OUT AND PLAY! I WANT TO **SLEEP** THROUGH THIS MUSICAL SHOW SO I'LL BE AWAKE FOR THE WRESTLING LATER!

UNCA DONALD WILL NEVER AMOUNT TO MUCH!

HE'LL ALWAYS BE A DELIVERY BOY FOR THE SKUNK OIL FACTORY!

WE HAVEN'T BEEN ABLE TO INSULT HIM INTO IMPROVING HIS WAY OF LIFE!

HE HAS NO **PRIDE**!

WAIT! DON'T BURY OUR HOPES **YET**! THERE'S **ONE** WAY WE HAVEN'T TRIED!

LET'S SEE IF WE CAN FIRE HIS AMBITION BY **FLATTERY**!

SAY! THAT'S THE KIND OF COACHING **NOBODY** CAN RESIST!

NEXT MORNING!

OH, THE VILLAIN ONWARD STOLE ... ♫ WHILE A WICKED SMILE HE SMOLE! ♫

WAS THAT **YOU** SINGING, UNCA DONALD?

WE THOUGHT IT WAS PERRY COUGAR!

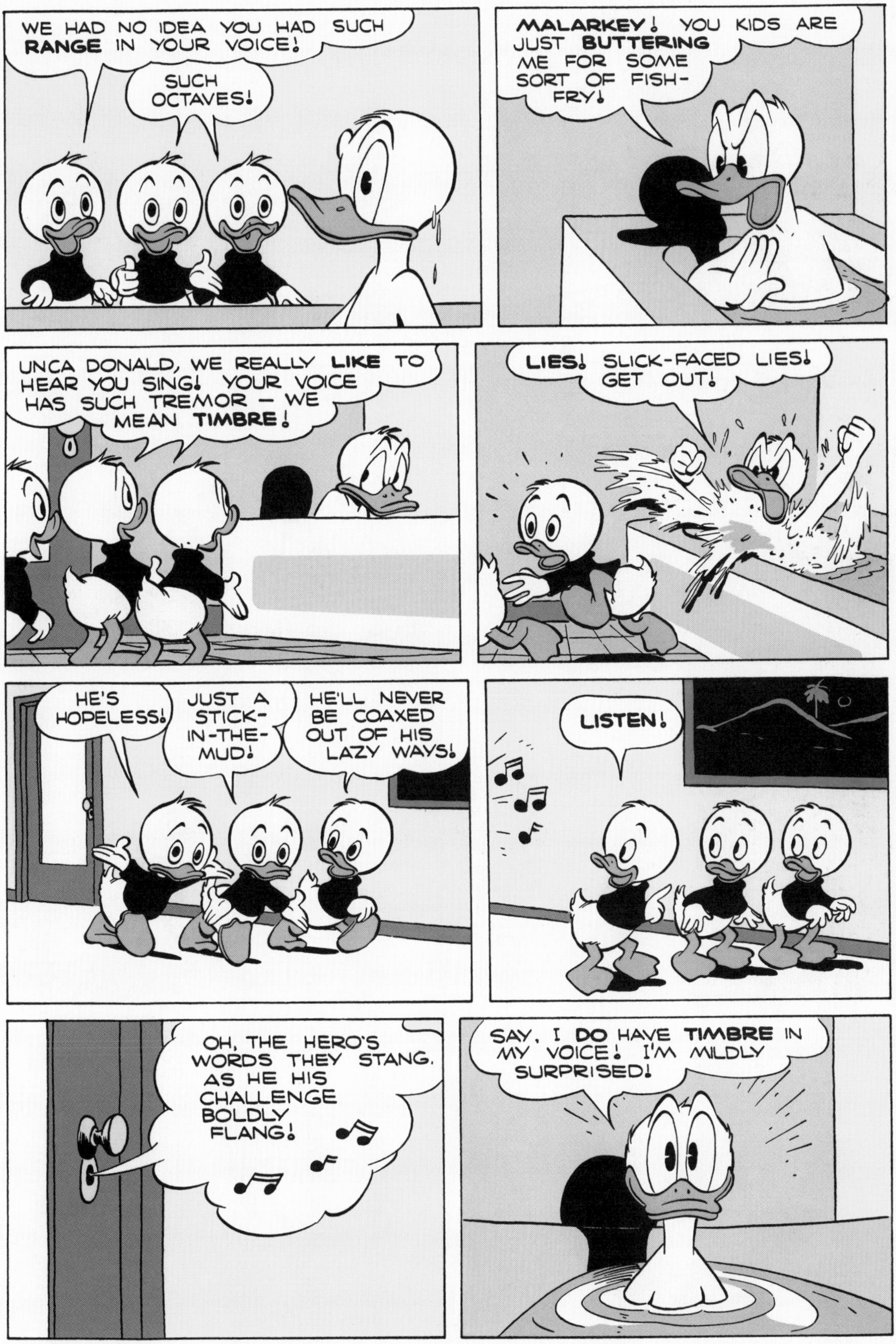
WE HAD NO IDEA YOU HAD SUCH RANGE IN YOUR VOICE!
SUCH OCTAVES!
MALARKEY! YOU KIDS ARE JUST BUTTERING ME FOR SOME SORT OF FISH-FRY!
UNCA DONALD, WE REALLY LIKE TO HEAR YOU SING! YOUR VOICE HAS SUCH TREMOR — WE MEAN TIMBRE!
LIES! SLICK-FACED LIES! GET OUT!
HE'S HOPELESS!
JUST A STICK-IN-THE-MUD!
HE'LL NEVER BE COAXED OUT OF HIS LAZY WAYS!
LISTEN!
OH, THE HERO'S WORDS THEY STANG, AS HE HIS CHALLENGE BOLDLY FLANG!
SAY, I DO HAVE TIMBRE IN MY VOICE! I'M MILDLY SURPRISED!

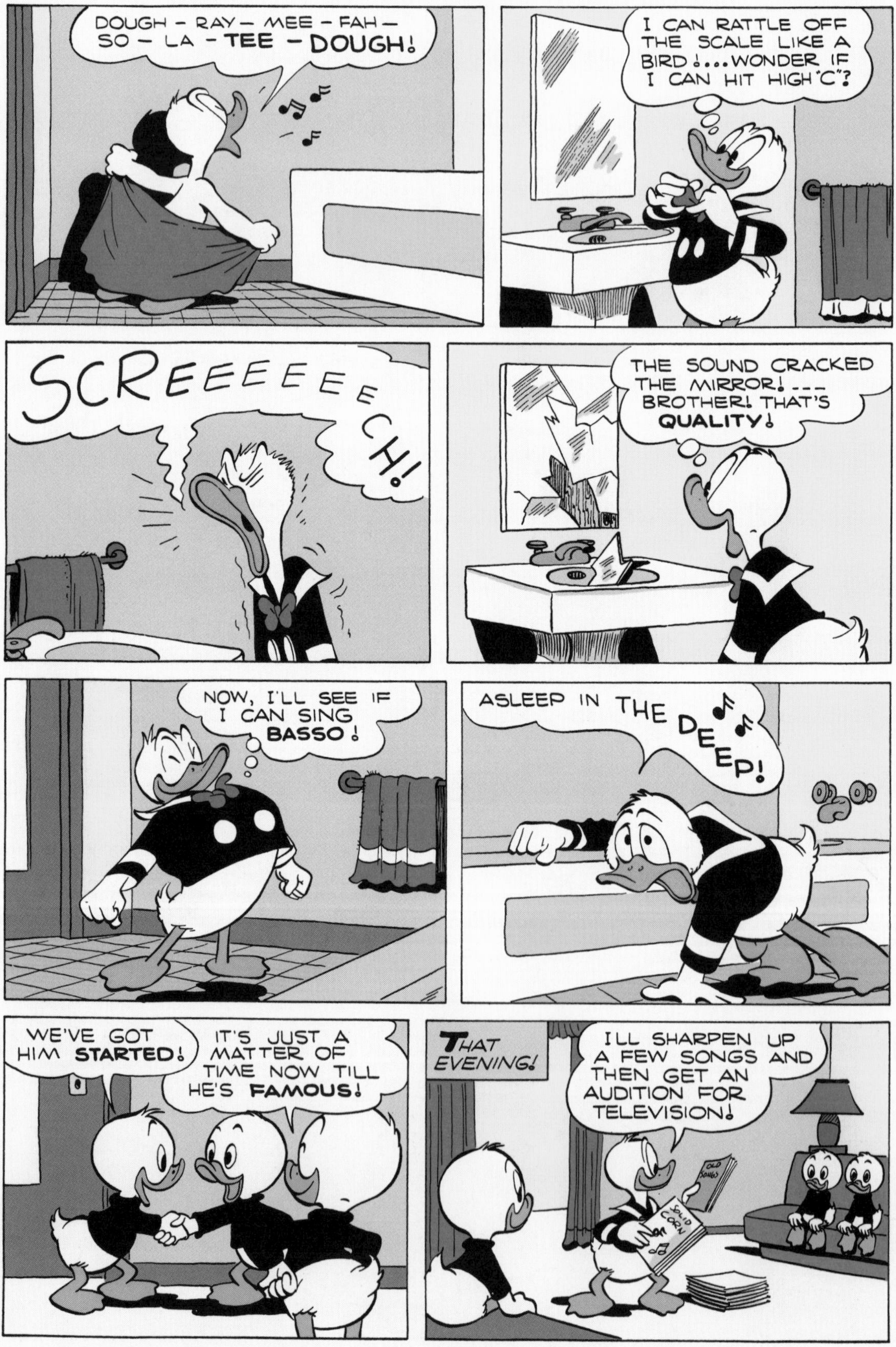
DOUGH - RAY - MEE - FAH - SO - LA - TEE - DOUGH!
I CAN RATTLE OFF THE SCALE LIKE A BIRD!... WONDER IF I CAN HIT HIGH "C"?
SCREEEEEEECH!
THE SOUND CRACKED THE MIRROR! --- BROTHER! THAT'S QUALITY!
NOW, I'LL SEE IF I CAN SING BASSO!
ASLEEP IN THE DEEP!
WE'VE GOT HIM STARTED!
IT'S JUST A MATTER OF TIME NOW TILL HE'S FAMOUS!
THAT EVENING!
I'LL SHARPEN UP A FEW SONGS AND THEN GET AN AUDITION FOR TELEVISION!
OLD SONGS
SOLID CORN

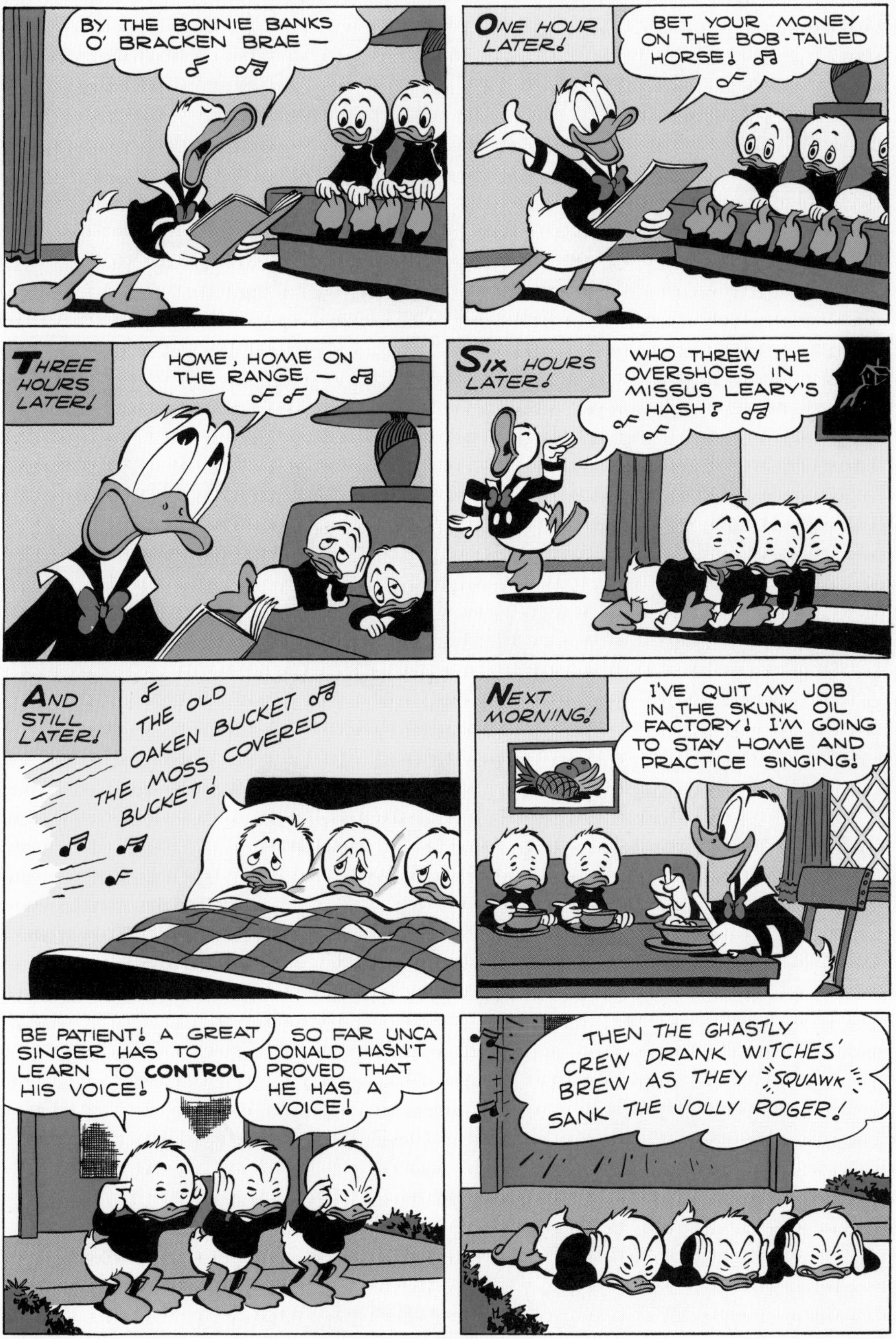
BY THE BONNIE BANKS O' BRACKEN BRAE —
ONE HOUR LATER!
BET YOUR MONEY ON THE BOB-TAILED HORSE!
THREE HOURS LATER!
HOME, HOME ON THE RANGE —
SIX HOURS LATER!
WHO THREW THE OVERSHOES IN MISSUS LEARY'S HASH?
AND STILL LATER!
THE OLD OAKEN BUCKET THE MOSS COVERED BUCKET!
NEXT MORNING!
I'VE QUIT MY JOB IN THE SKUNK OIL FACTORY! I'M GOING TO STAY HOME AND PRACTICE SINGING!
BE PATIENT! A GREAT SINGER HAS TO LEARN TO CONTROL HIS VOICE!
SO FAR UNCA DONALD HASN'T PROVED THAT HE HAS A VOICE!
THEN THE GHASTLY CREW DRANK WITCHES' BREW AS THEY SQUAWK SANK THE JOLLY ROGER!

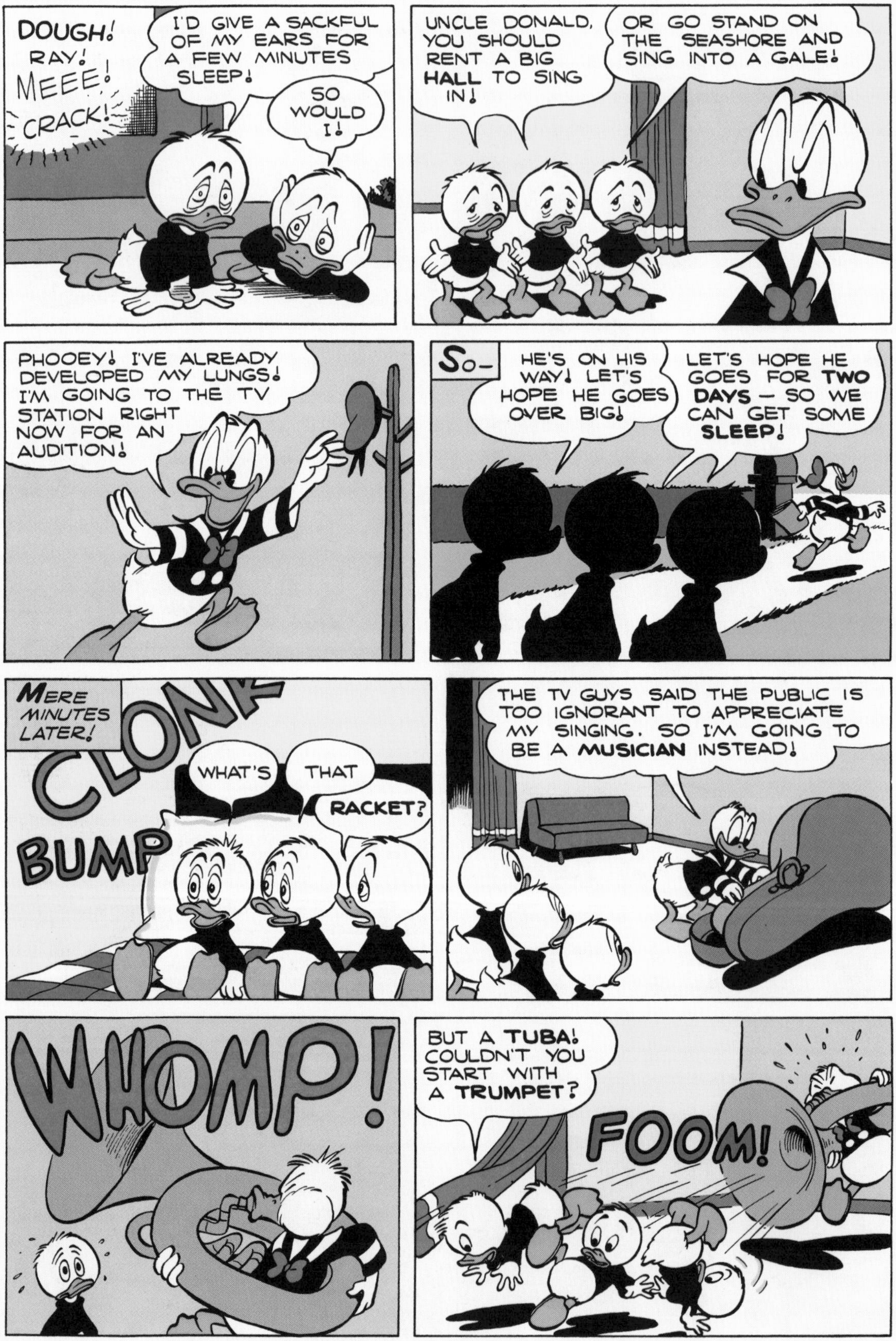
DOUGH! RAY! MEEE! CRACK!
I'D GIVE A SACKFUL OF MY EARS FOR A FEW MINUTES SLEEP!
SO WOULD I!
UNCLE DONALD, YOU SHOULD RENT A BIG HALL TO SING IN!
OR GO STAND ON THE SEASHORE AND SING INTO A GALE!
PHOOEY! I'VE ALREADY DEVELOPED MY LUNGS! I'M GOING TO THE TV STATION RIGHT NOW FOR AN AUDITION!
SO–
HE'S ON HIS WAY! LET'S HOPE HE GOES OVER BIG!
LET'S HOPE HE GOES FOR TWO DAYS – SO WE CAN GET SOME SLEEP!
MERE MINUTES LATER!
CLONK
BUMP
WHAT'S
THAT
RACKET?
THE TV GUYS SAID THE PUBLIC IS TOO IGNORANT TO APPRECIATE MY SINGING. SO I'M GOING TO BE A MUSICIAN INSTEAD!
WHOMP!
BUT A TUBA! COULDN'T YOU START WITH A TRUMPET?
FOOM!

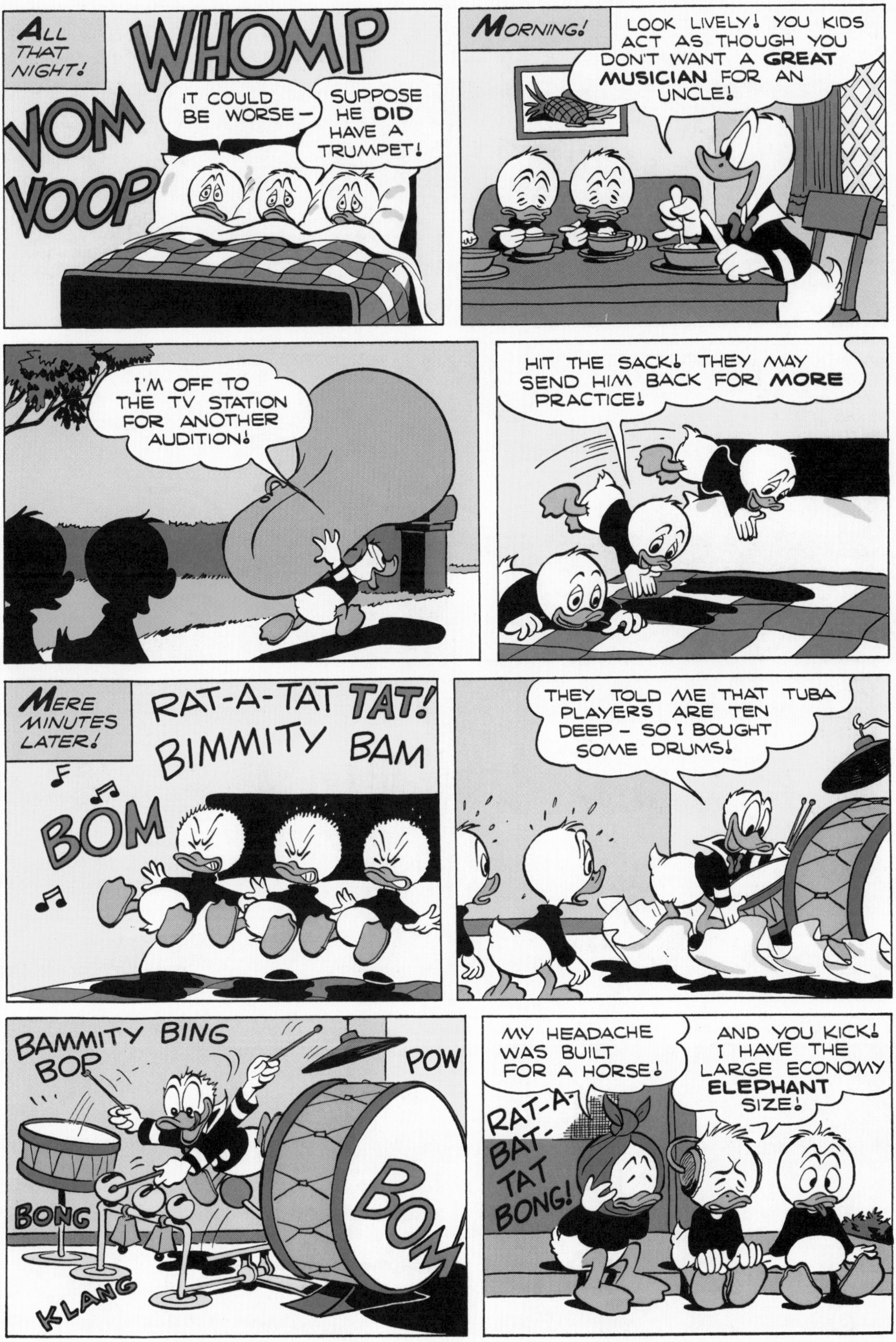

ALL THAT NIGHT!
WHOMP
VOM
VOOP
IT COULD BE WORSE—
SUPPOSE HE DID HAVE A TRUMPET!
MORNING!
LOOK LIVELY! YOU KIDS ACT AS THOUGH YOU DON'T WANT A GREAT MUSICIAN FOR AN UNCLE!
I'M OFF TO THE TV STATION FOR ANOTHER AUDITION!
HIT THE SACK! THEY MAY SEND HIM BACK FOR MORE PRACTICE!
MERE MINUTES LATER!
RAT-A-TAT TAT!
BIMMITY BAM
BOM
THEY TOLD ME THAT TUBA PLAYERS ARE TEN DEEP – SO I BOUGHT SOME DRUMS!
BAMMITY BING BOP
POW
BONG
BOM
KLANG
MY HEADACHE WAS BUILT FOR A HORSE!
AND YOU KICK! I HAVE THE LARGE ECONOMY ELEPHANT SIZE!
RAT-A-BAT-TAT BONG!

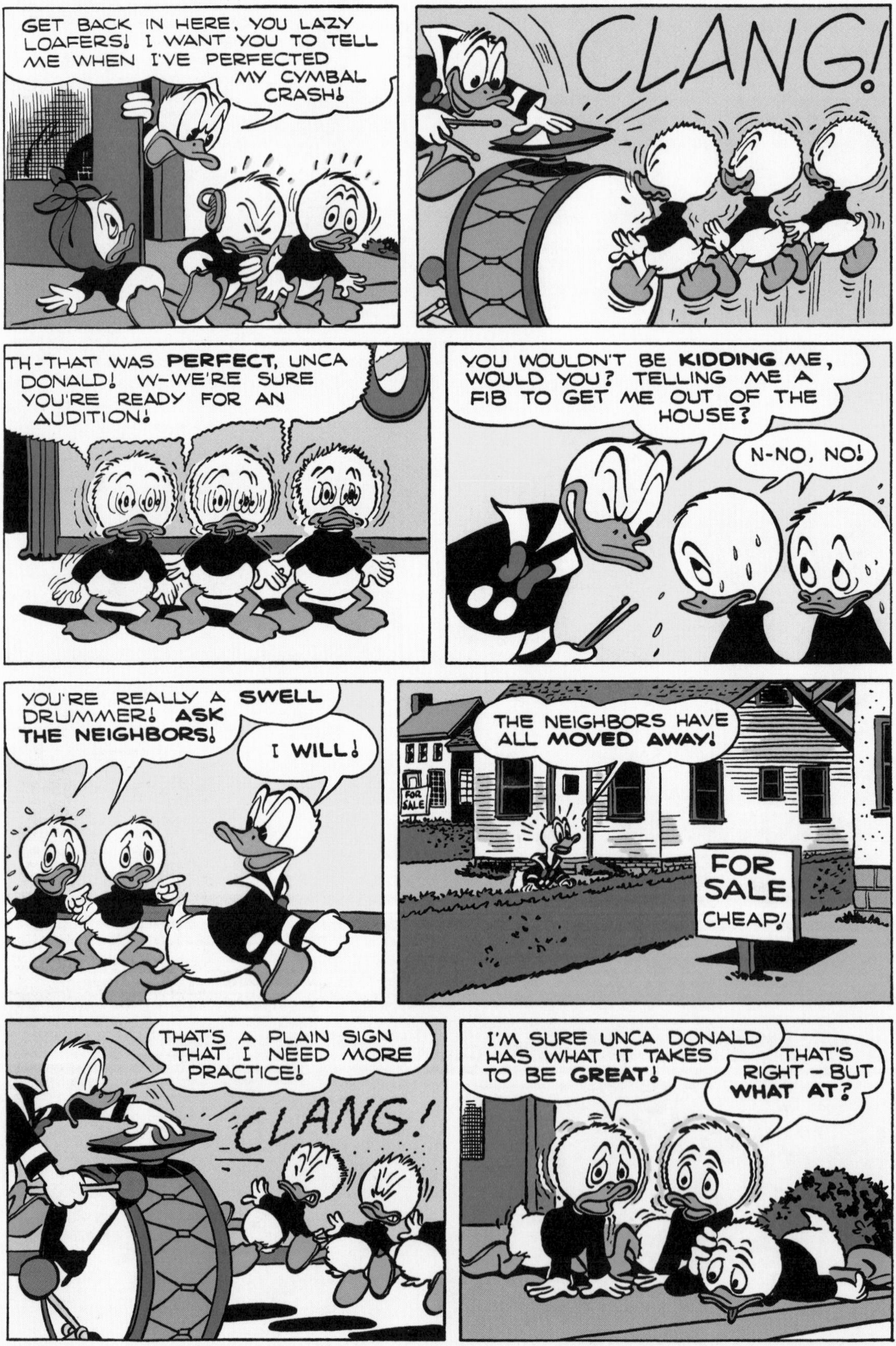
GET BACK IN HERE, YOU LAZY LOAFERS! I WANT YOU TO TELL ME WHEN I'VE PERFECTED MY CYMBAL CRASH!
CLANG!
TH-THAT WAS PERFECT, UNCA DONALD! W-WE'RE SURE YOU'RE READY FOR AN AUDITION!
YOU WOULDN'T BE KIDDING ME, WOULD YOU? TELLING ME A FIB TO GET ME OUT OF THE HOUSE?
N-NO, NO!
YOU'RE REALLY A SWELL DRUMMER! ASK THE NEIGHBORS!
I WILL!
THE NEIGHBORS HAVE ALL MOVED AWAY!
FOR SALE
FOR SALE CHEAP!
THAT'S A PLAIN SIGN THAT I NEED MORE PRACTICE!
CLANG!
I'M SURE UNCA DONALD HAS WHAT IT TAKES TO BE GREAT!
THAT'S RIGHT — BUT WHAT AT?

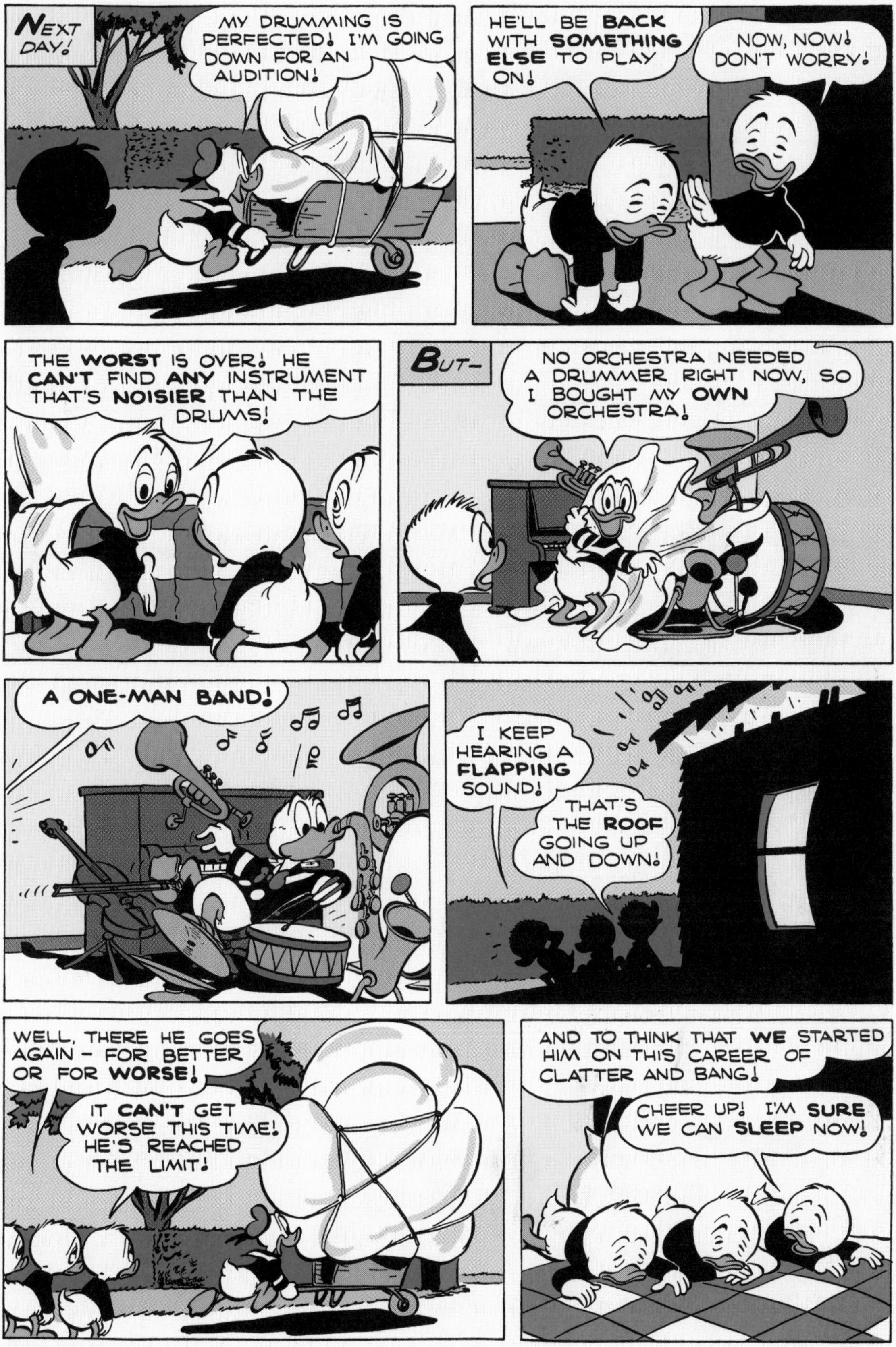
NEXT DAY!
MY DRUMMING IS PERFECTED! I'M GOING DOWN FOR AN AUDITION!
HE'LL BE BACK WITH SOMETHING ELSE TO PLAY ON!
NOW, NOW! DON'T WORRY!
THE WORST IS OVER! HE CAN'T FIND ANY INSTRUMENT THAT'S NOISIER THAN THE DRUMS!
BUT–
NO ORCHESTRA NEEDED A DRUMMER RIGHT NOW, SO I BOUGHT MY OWN ORCHESTRA!
A ONE-MAN BAND!
I KEEP HEARING A FLAPPING SOUND!
THAT'S THE ROOF GOING UP AND DOWN!
WELL, THERE HE GOES AGAIN – FOR BETTER OR FOR WORSE!
IT CAN'T GET WORSE THIS TIME! HE'S REACHED THE LIMIT!
AND TO THINK THAT WE STARTED HIM ON THIS CAREER OF CLATTER AND BANG!
CHEER UP! I'M SURE WE CAN SLEEP NOW!

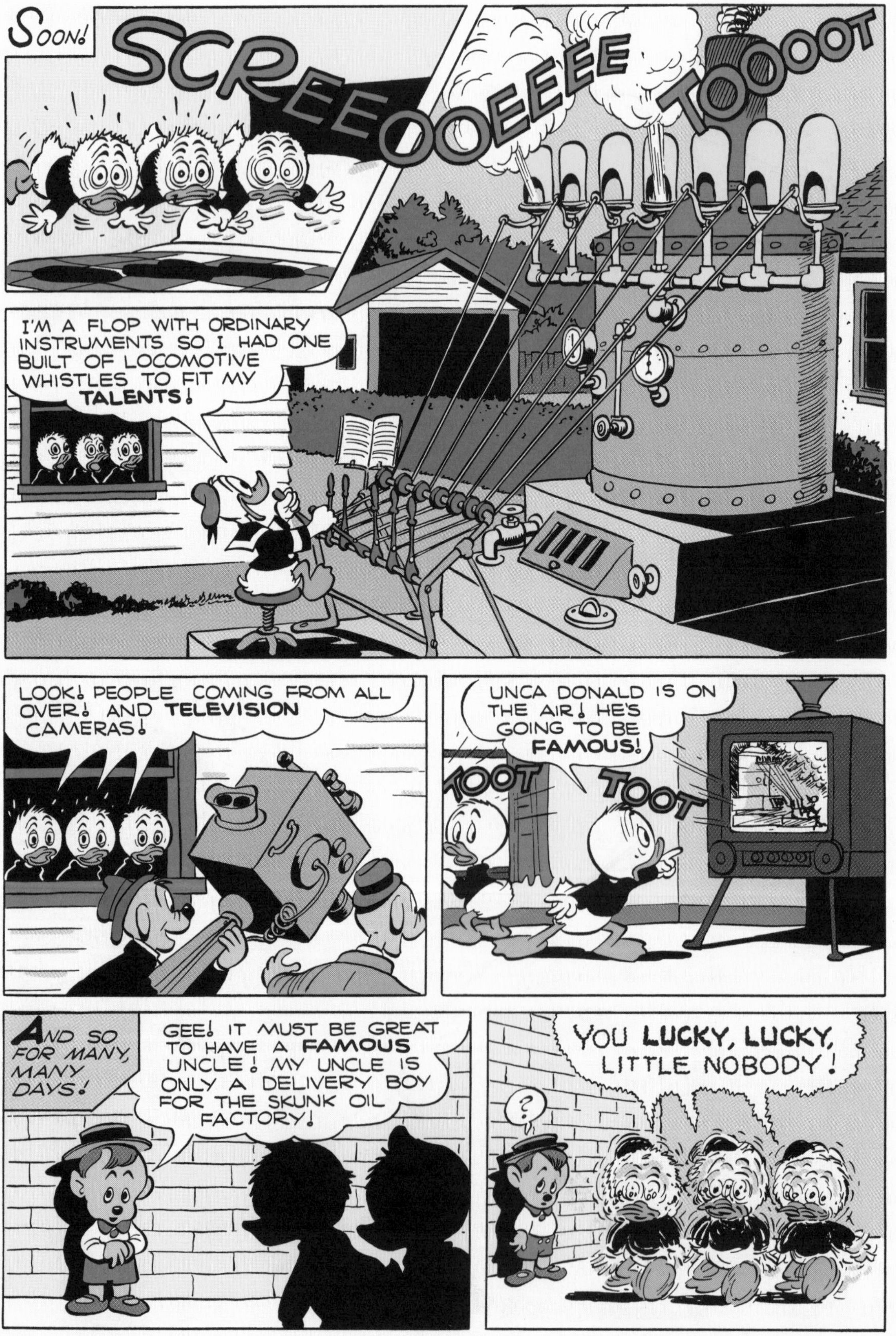
SOON!
SCREEOOEEEEE TOOOOT
I'M A FLOP WITH ORDINARY INSTRUMENTS SO I HAD ONE BUILT OF LOCOMOTIVE WHISTLES TO FIT MY **TALENTS**!
LOOK! PEOPLE COMING FROM ALL OVER! AND **TELEVISION** CAMERAS!
UNCA DONALD IS ON THE AIR! HE'S GOING TO BE **FAMOUS**!
TOOT
TOOT
AND SO FOR MANY, MANY DAYS!
GEE! IT MUST BE GREAT TO HAVE A **FAMOUS** UNCLE! MY UNCLE IS ONLY A DELIVERY BOY FOR THE SKUNK OIL FACTORY!
?
YOU **LUCKY, LUCKY,** LITTLE NOBODY!

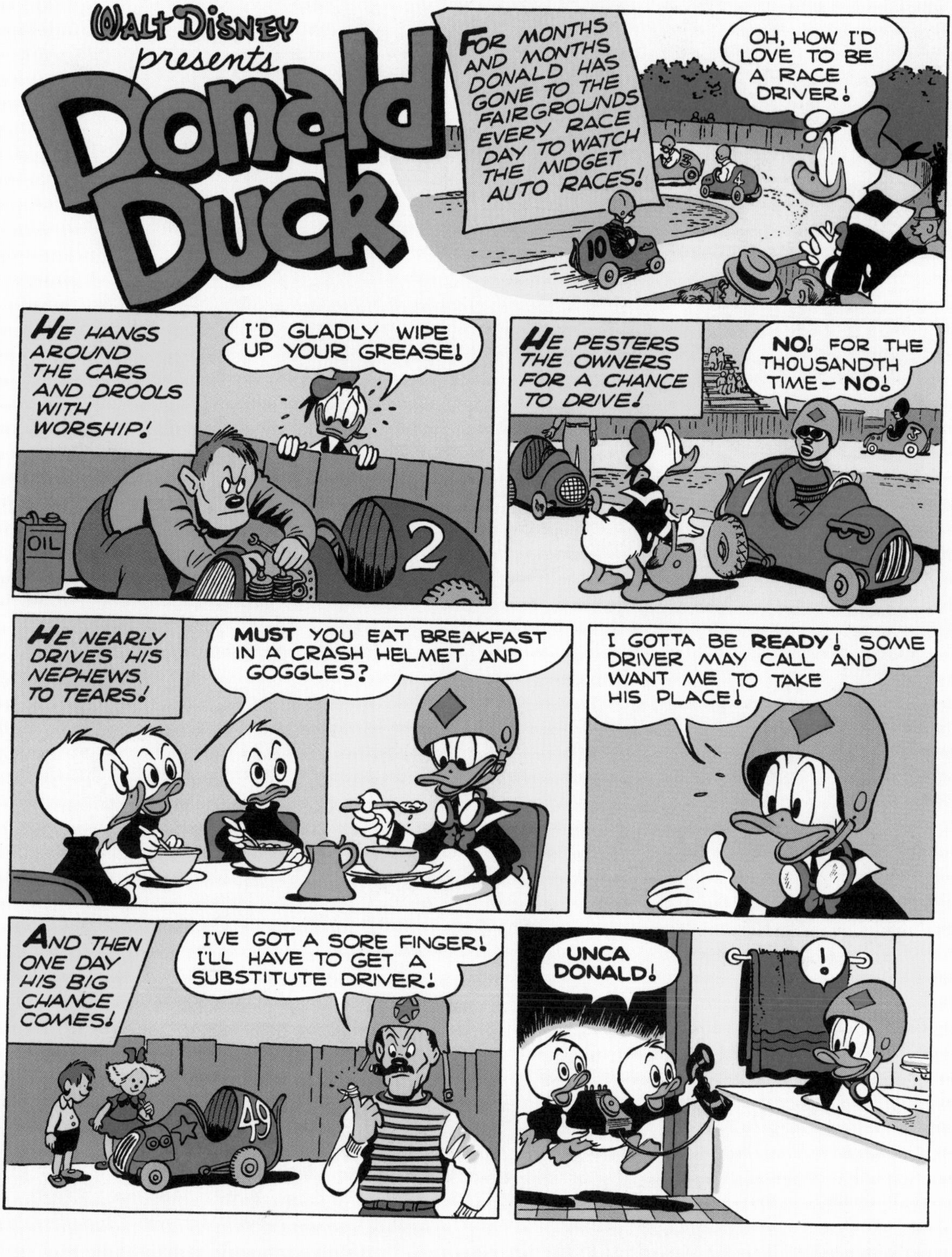
WALT DISNEY
presents
Donald Duck
FOR MONTHS AND MONTHS DONALD HAS GONE TO THE FAIRGROUNDS EVERY RACE DAY TO WATCH THE MIDGET AUTO RACES!
OH, HOW I'D LOVE TO BE A RACE DRIVER!
HE HANGS AROUND THE CARS AND DROOLS WITH WORSHIP!
I'D GLADLY WIPE UP YOUR GREASE!
OIL
HE PESTERS THE OWNERS FOR A CHANCE TO DRIVE!
NO! FOR THE THOUSANDTH TIME—NO!
HE NEARLY DRIVES HIS NEPHEWS TO TEARS!
MUST YOU EAT BREAKFAST IN A CRASH HELMET AND GOGGLES?
I GOTTA BE READY! SOME DRIVER MAY CALL AND WANT ME TO TAKE HIS PLACE!
AND THEN ONE DAY HIS BIG CHANCE COMES!
I'VE GOT A SORE FINGER! I'LL HAVE TO GET A SUBSTITUTE DRIVER!
UNCA DONALD!
!

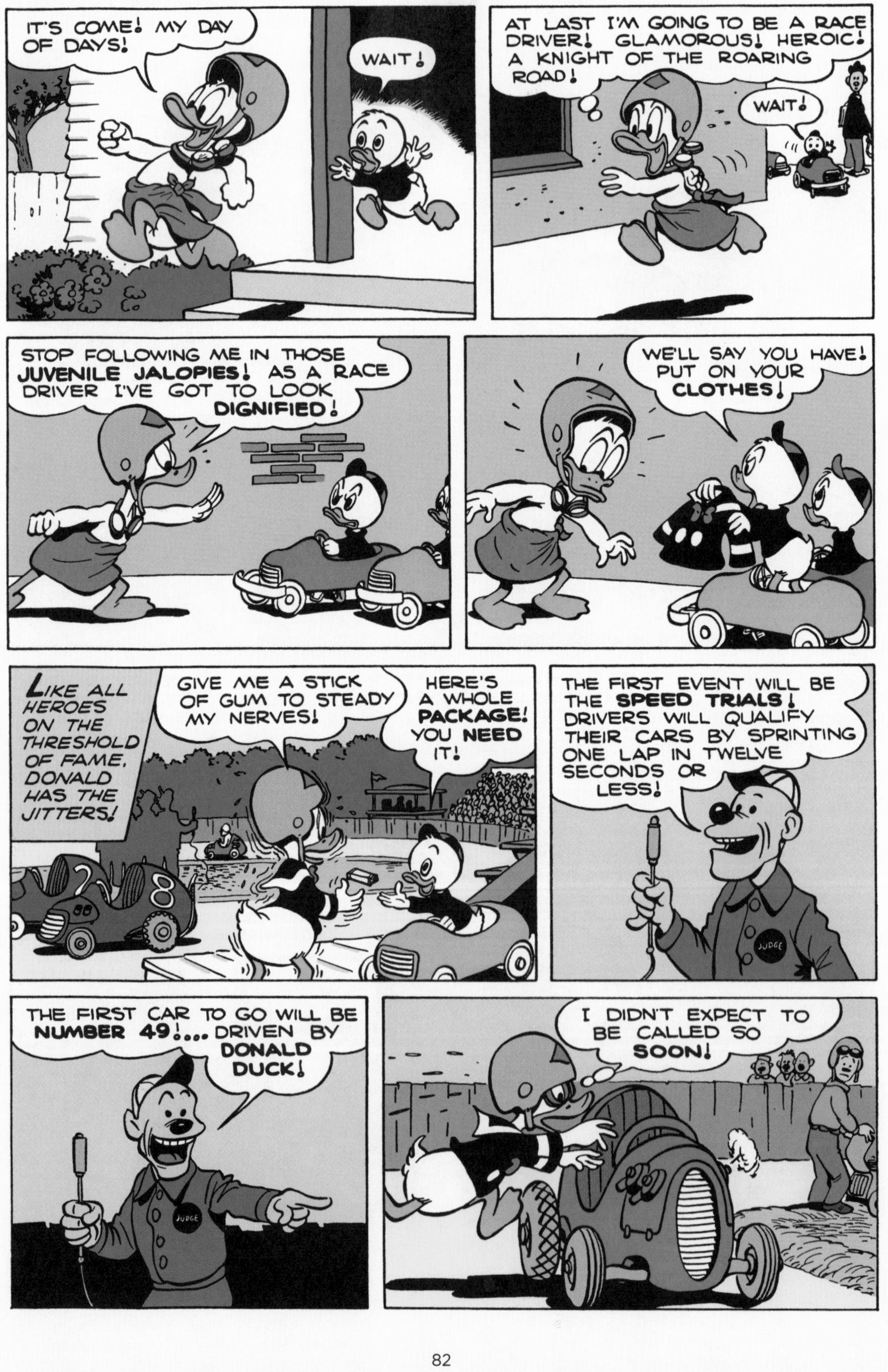
IT'S COME! MY DAY OF DAYS!
WAIT!
AT LAST I'M GOING TO BE A RACE DRIVER! GLAMOROUS! HEROIC! A KNIGHT OF THE ROARING ROAD!
WAIT!
STOP FOLLOWING ME IN THOSE **JUVENILE JALOPIES!** AS A RACE DRIVER I'VE GOT TO LOOK **DIGNIFIED!**
WE'LL SAY YOU HAVE! PUT ON YOUR **CLOTHES!**
LIKE ALL HEROES ON THE THRESHOLD OF FAME, DONALD HAS THE JITTERS!
GIVE ME A STICK OF GUM TO STEADY MY NERVES!
HERE'S A WHOLE **PACKAGE!** YOU **NEED** IT!
THE FIRST EVENT WILL BE THE **SPEED TRIALS!** DRIVERS WILL QUALIFY THEIR CARS BY SPRINTING ONE LAP IN TWELVE SECONDS OR LESS!
JUDGE
THE FIRST CAR TO GO WILL BE **NUMBER 49!...** DRIVEN BY **DONALD DUCK!**
JUDGE
I DIDN'T EXPECT TO BE CALLED SO **SOON!**

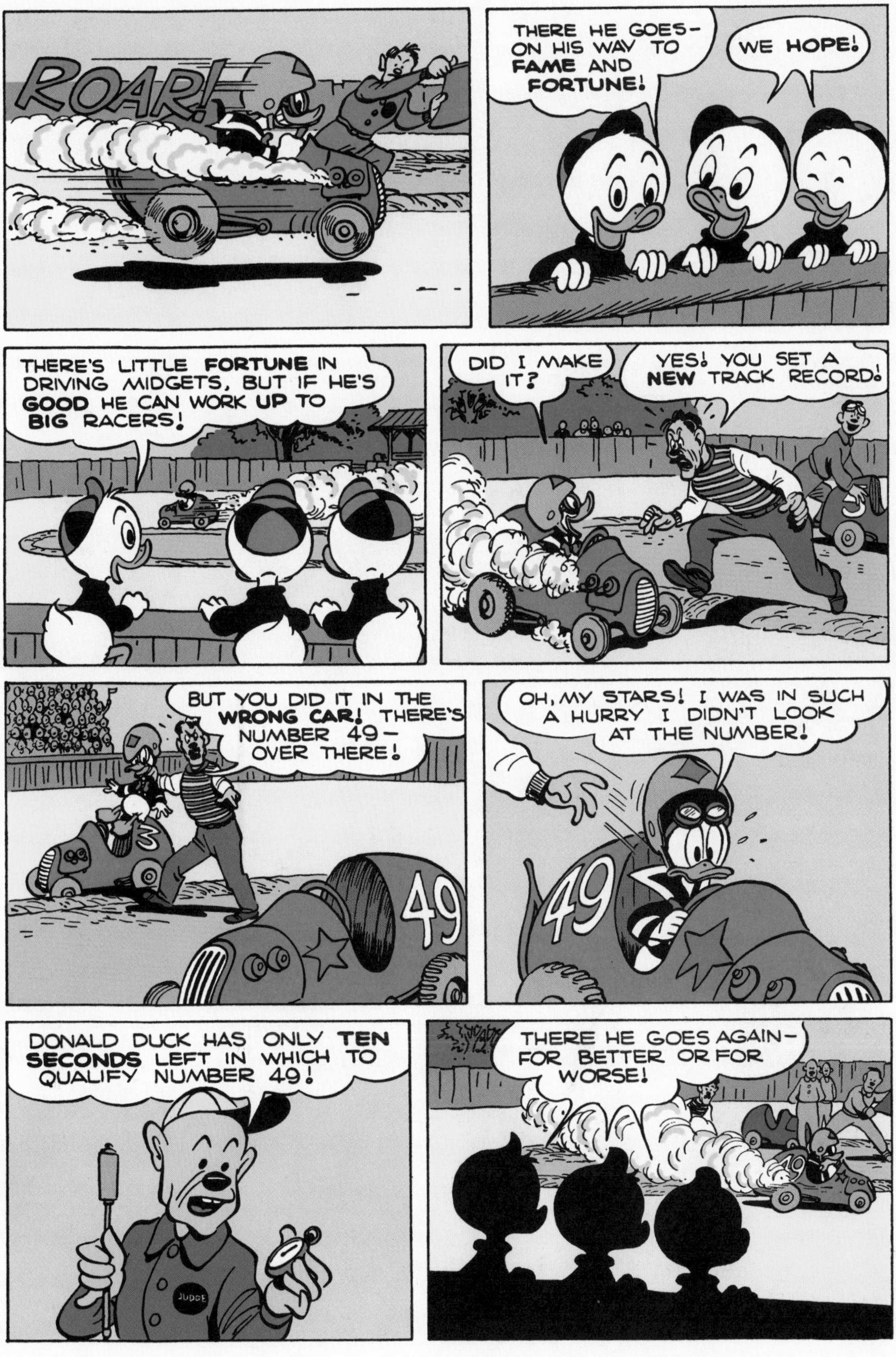
ROAR!
THERE HE GOES- ON HIS WAY TO FAME AND FORTUNE!
WE HOPE!
THERE'S LITTLE FORTUNE IN DRIVING MIDGETS, BUT IF HE'S GOOD HE CAN WORK UP TO BIG RACERS!
DID I MAKE IT?
YES! YOU SET A NEW TRACK RECORD!
BUT YOU DID IT IN THE WRONG CAR! THERE'S NUMBER 49- OVER THERE!
OH, MY STARS! I WAS IN SUCH A HURRY I DIDN'T LOOK AT THE NUMBER!
DONALD DUCK HAS ONLY TEN SECONDS LEFT IN WHICH TO QUALIFY NUMBER 49!
JUDGE
THERE HE GOES AGAIN- FOR BETTER OR FOR WORSE!

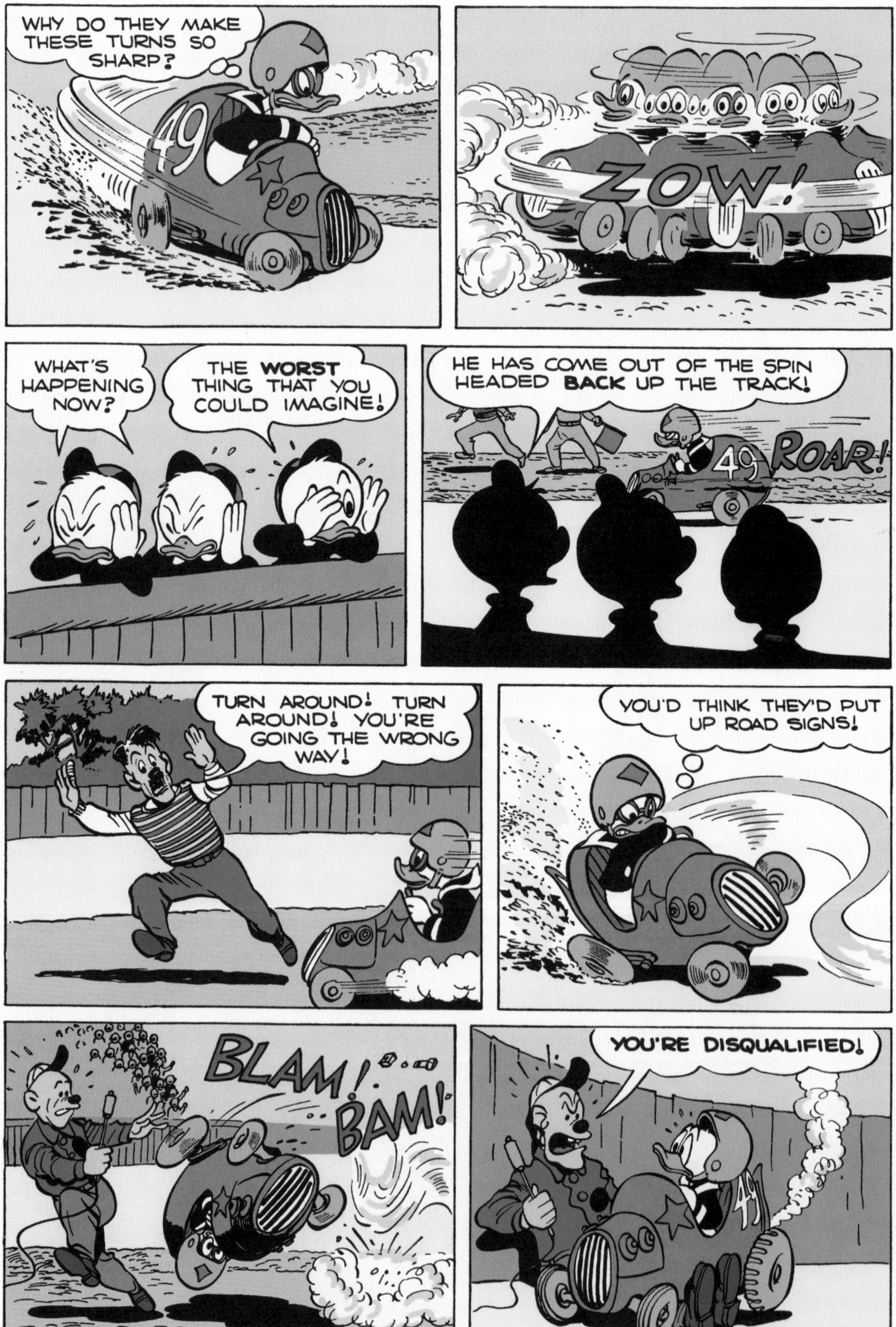
WHY DO THEY MAKE THESE TURNS SO SHARP?
49
ZOW!
WHAT'S HAPPENING NOW?
THE WORST THING THAT YOU COULD IMAGINE!
HE HAS COME OUT OF THE SPIN HEADED BACK UP THE TRACK!
49
ROAR!
TURN AROUND! TURN AROUND! YOU'RE GOING THE WRONG WAY!
YOU'D THINK THEY'D PUT UP ROAD SIGNS!
BLAM!
BAM!
YOU'RE DISQUALIFIED!
49

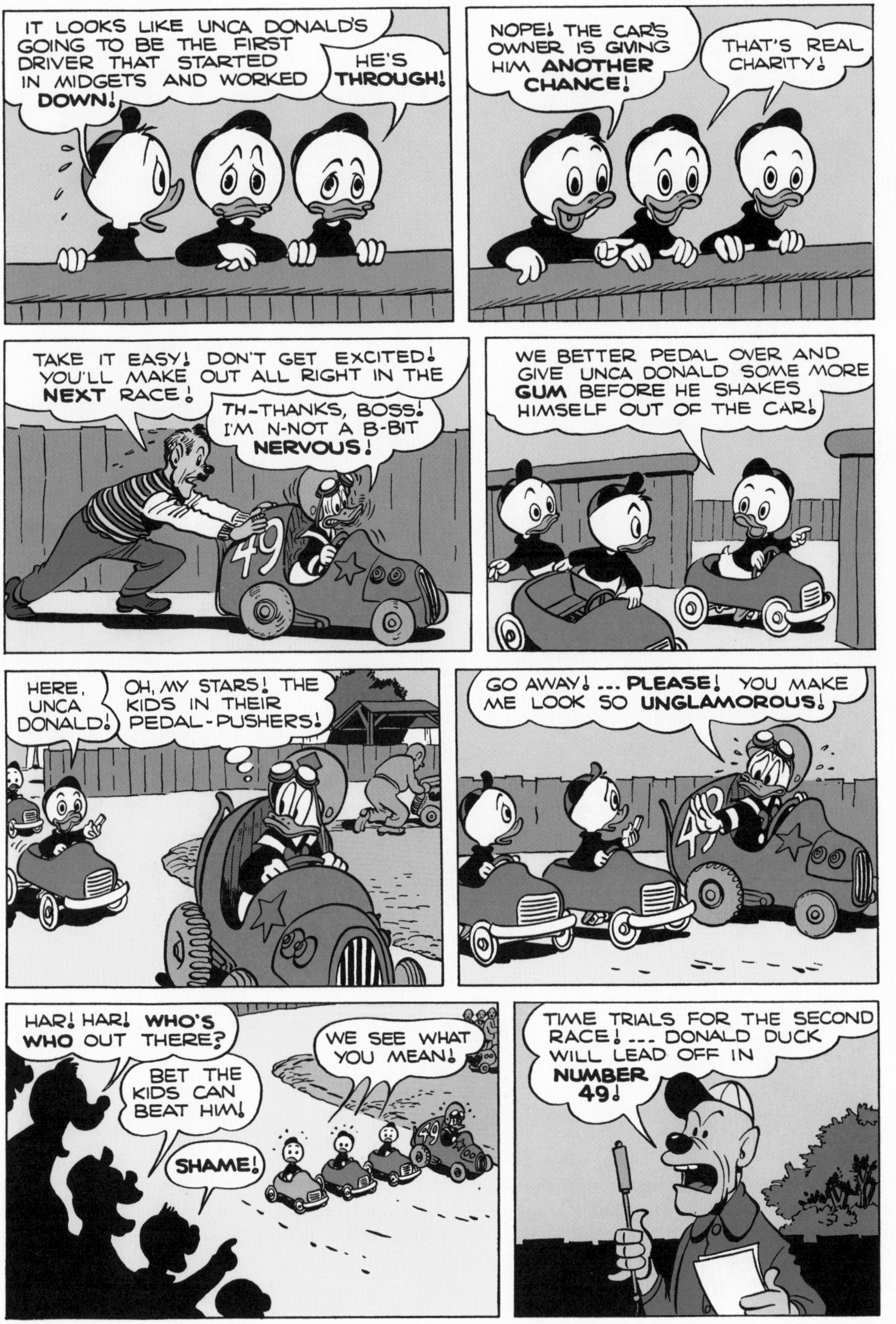

IT LOOKS LIKE UNCA DONALD'S GOING TO BE THE FIRST DRIVER THAT STARTED IN MIDGETS AND WORKED **DOWN**!
HE'S **THROUGH**!
NOPE! THE CAR'S OWNER IS GIVING HIM **ANOTHER CHANCE**!
THAT'S REAL CHARITY!
TAKE IT EASY! DON'T GET EXCITED! YOU'LL MAKE OUT ALL RIGHT IN THE **NEXT** RACE!
TH-THANKS, BOSS! I'M N-NOT A B-BIT **NERVOUS**!
WE BETTER PEDAL OVER AND GIVE UNCA DONALD SOME MORE **GUM** BEFORE HE SHAKES HIMSELF OUT OF THE CAR!
HERE, UNCA DONALD!
OH, MY STARS! THE KIDS IN THEIR PEDAL-PUSHERS!
GO AWAY! ... **PLEASE**! YOU MAKE ME LOOK SO **UNGLAMOROUS**!
HAR! HAR! **WHO'S WHO** OUT THERE?
BET THE KIDS CAN BEAT HIM!
WE SEE WHAT YOU MEAN!
SHAME!
TIME TRIALS FOR THE SECOND RACE! ... DONALD DUCK WILL LEAD OFF IN **NUMBER 49**!

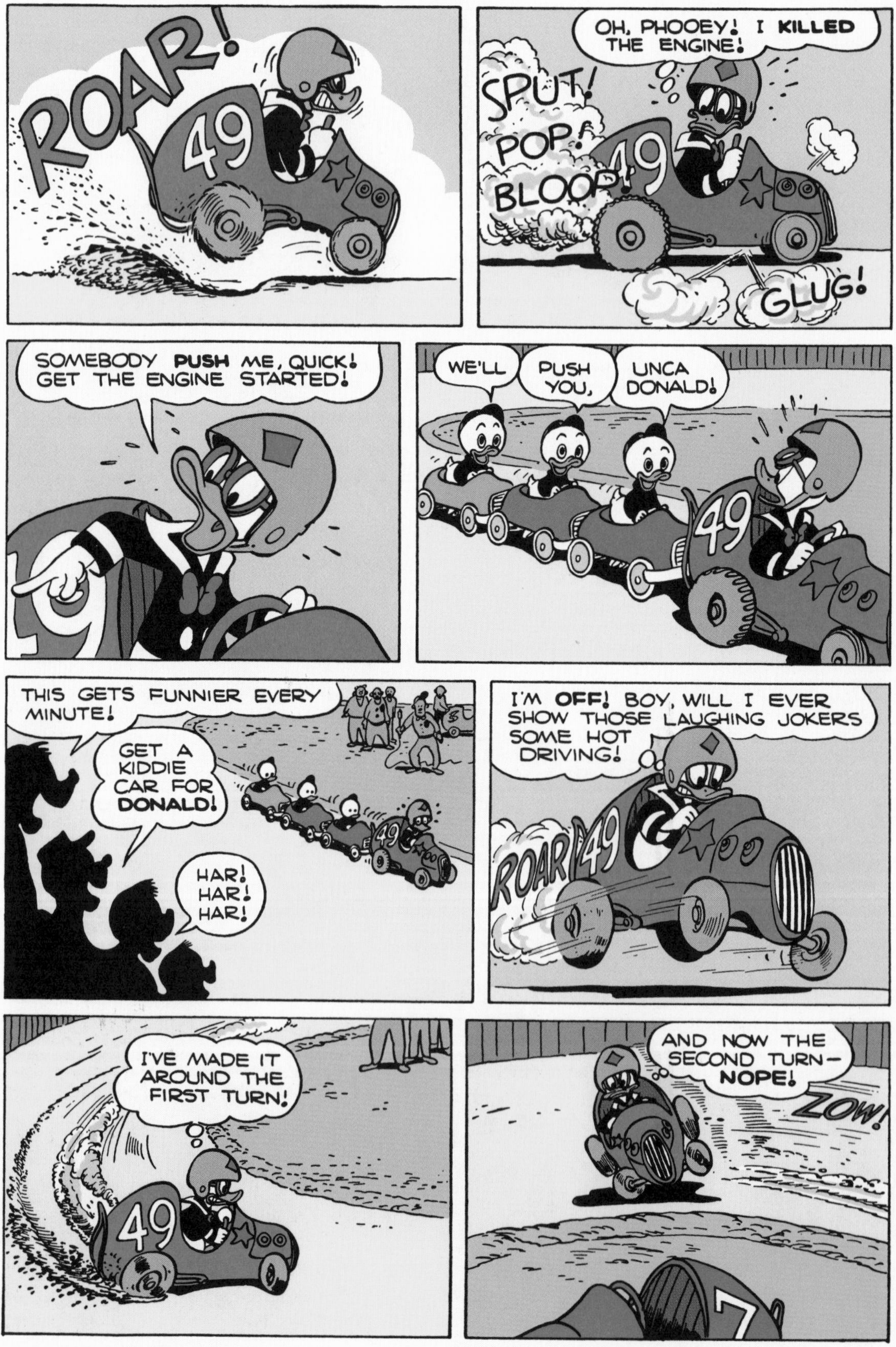
ROAR!
OH, PHOOEY! I KILLED THE ENGINE!
SPUT!
POP!
BLOOP!
GLUG!
SOMEBODY PUSH ME, QUICK! GET THE ENGINE STARTED!
WE'LL
PUSH YOU,
UNCA DONALD!
THIS GETS FUNNIER EVERY MINUTE!
GET A KIDDIE CAR FOR DONALD!
HAR! HAR! HAR!
I'M OFF! BOY, WILL I EVER SHOW THOSE LAUGHING JOKERS SOME HOT DRIVING!
ROAR
I'VE MADE IT AROUND THE FIRST TURN!
AND NOW THE SECOND TURN— NOPE!
ZOW!

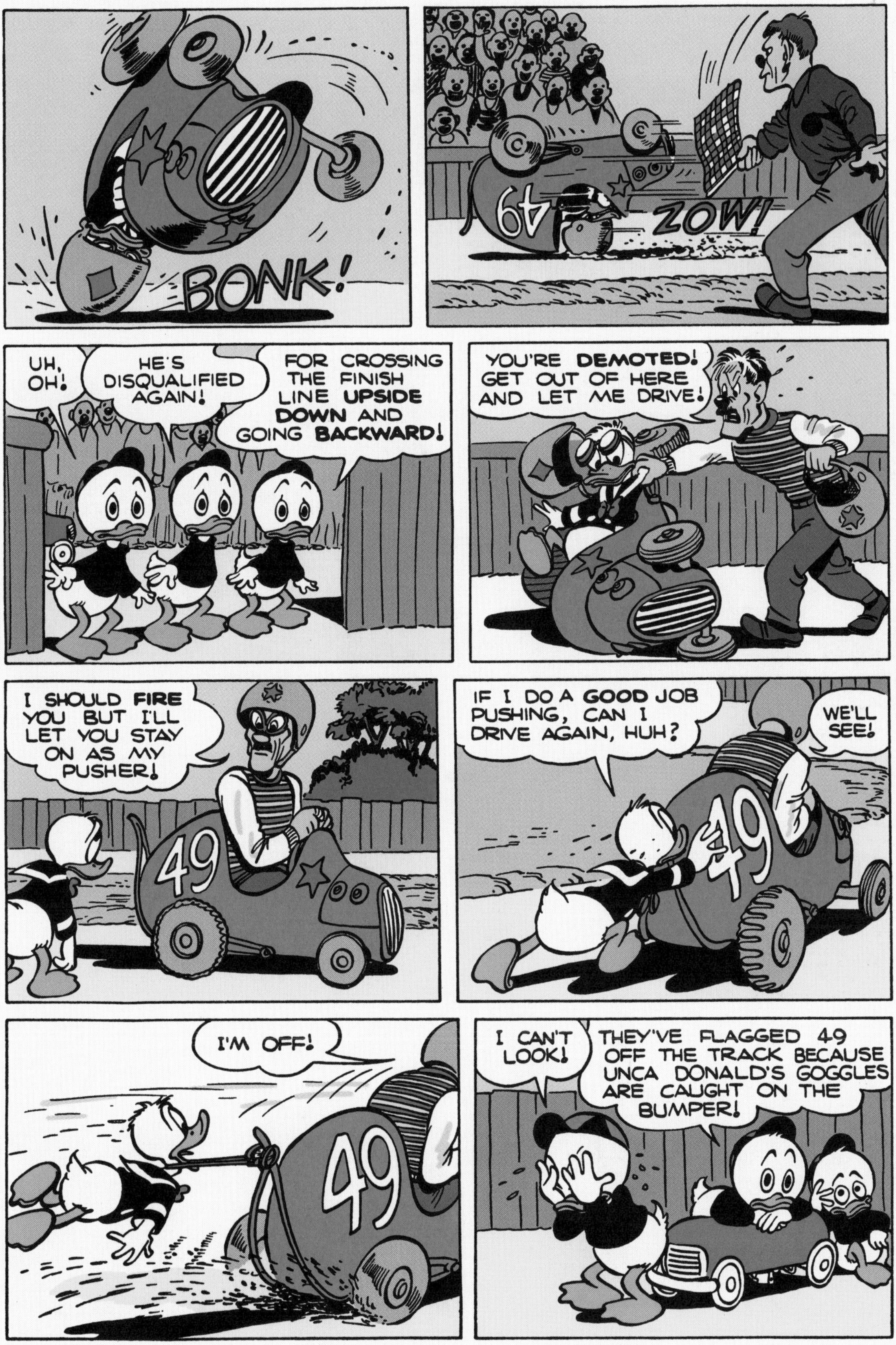
BONK!
ZOW!
49
UH, OH!
HE'S DISQUALIFIED AGAIN!
FOR CROSSING THE FINISH LINE UPSIDE DOWN AND GOING BACKWARD!
YOU'RE DEMOTED! GET OUT OF HERE AND LET ME DRIVE!
I SHOULD FIRE YOU BUT I'LL LET YOU STAY ON AS MY PUSHER!
49
IF I DO A GOOD JOB PUSHING, CAN I DRIVE AGAIN, HUH?
WE'LL SEE!
49
I'M OFF!
49
I CAN'T LOOK!
THEY'VE FLAGGED 49 OFF THE TRACK BECAUSE UNCA DONALD'S GOGGLES ARE CAUGHT ON THE BUMPER!

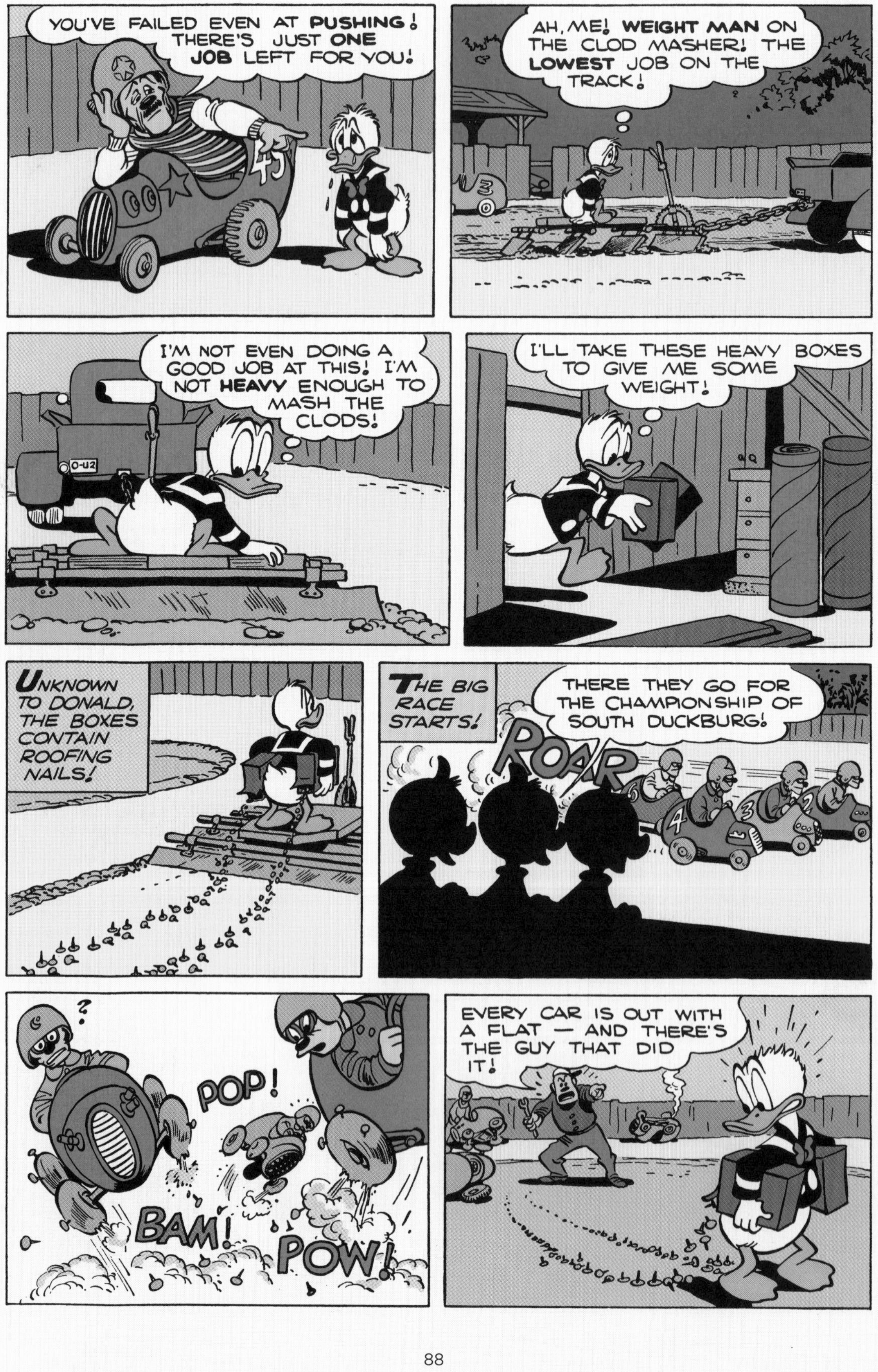
YOU'VE FAILED EVEN AT PUSHING! THERE'S JUST ONE JOB LEFT FOR YOU!
AH, ME! WEIGHT MAN ON THE CLOD MASHER! THE LOWEST JOB ON THE TRACK!
I'M NOT EVEN DOING A GOOD JOB AT THIS! I'M NOT HEAVY ENOUGH TO MASH THE CLODS!
I'LL TAKE THESE HEAVY BOXES TO GIVE ME SOME WEIGHT!
UNKNOWN TO DONALD, THE BOXES CONTAIN ROOFING NAILS!
THE BIG RACE STARTS!
THERE THEY GO FOR THE CHAMPIONSHIP OF SOUTH DUCKBURG!
ROAR
POP!
BAM!
POW!
EVERY CAR IS OUT WITH A FLAT — AND THERE'S THE GUY THAT DID IT!

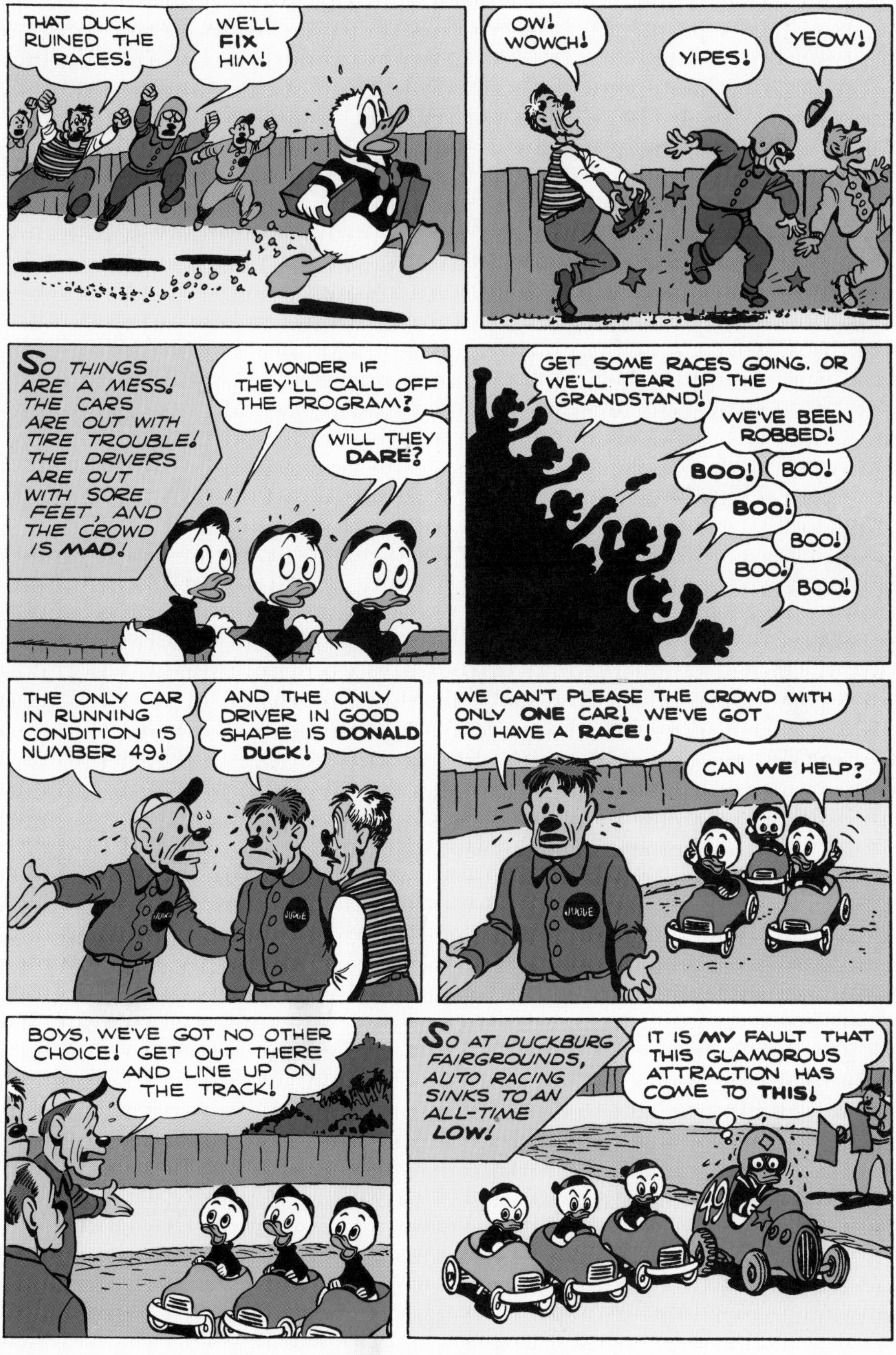
THAT DUCK RUINED THE RACES!
WE'LL FIX HIM!
OW! WOWCH!
YIPES!
YEOW!
SO THINGS ARE A MESS! THE CARS ARE OUT WITH TIRE TROUBLE! THE DRIVERS ARE OUT WITH SORE FEET, AND THE CROWD IS MAD!
I WONDER IF THEY'LL CALL OFF THE PROGRAM?
WILL THEY DARE?
GET SOME RACES GOING, OR WE'LL TEAR UP THE GRANDSTAND!
WE'VE BEEN ROBBED!
BOO!
BOO!
BOO!
BOO!
BOO!
BOO!
THE ONLY CAR IN RUNNING CONDITION IS NUMBER 49!
AND THE ONLY DRIVER IN GOOD SHAPE IS DONALD DUCK!
WE CAN'T PLEASE THE CROWD WITH ONLY ONE CAR! WE'VE GOT TO HAVE A RACE!
CAN WE HELP?
BOYS, WE'VE GOT NO OTHER CHOICE! GET OUT THERE AND LINE UP ON THE TRACK!
SO AT DUCKBURG FAIRGROUNDS, AUTO RACING SINKS TO AN ALL-TIME LOW!
IT IS MY FAULT THAT THIS GLAMOROUS ATTRACTION HAS COME TO THIS!
49

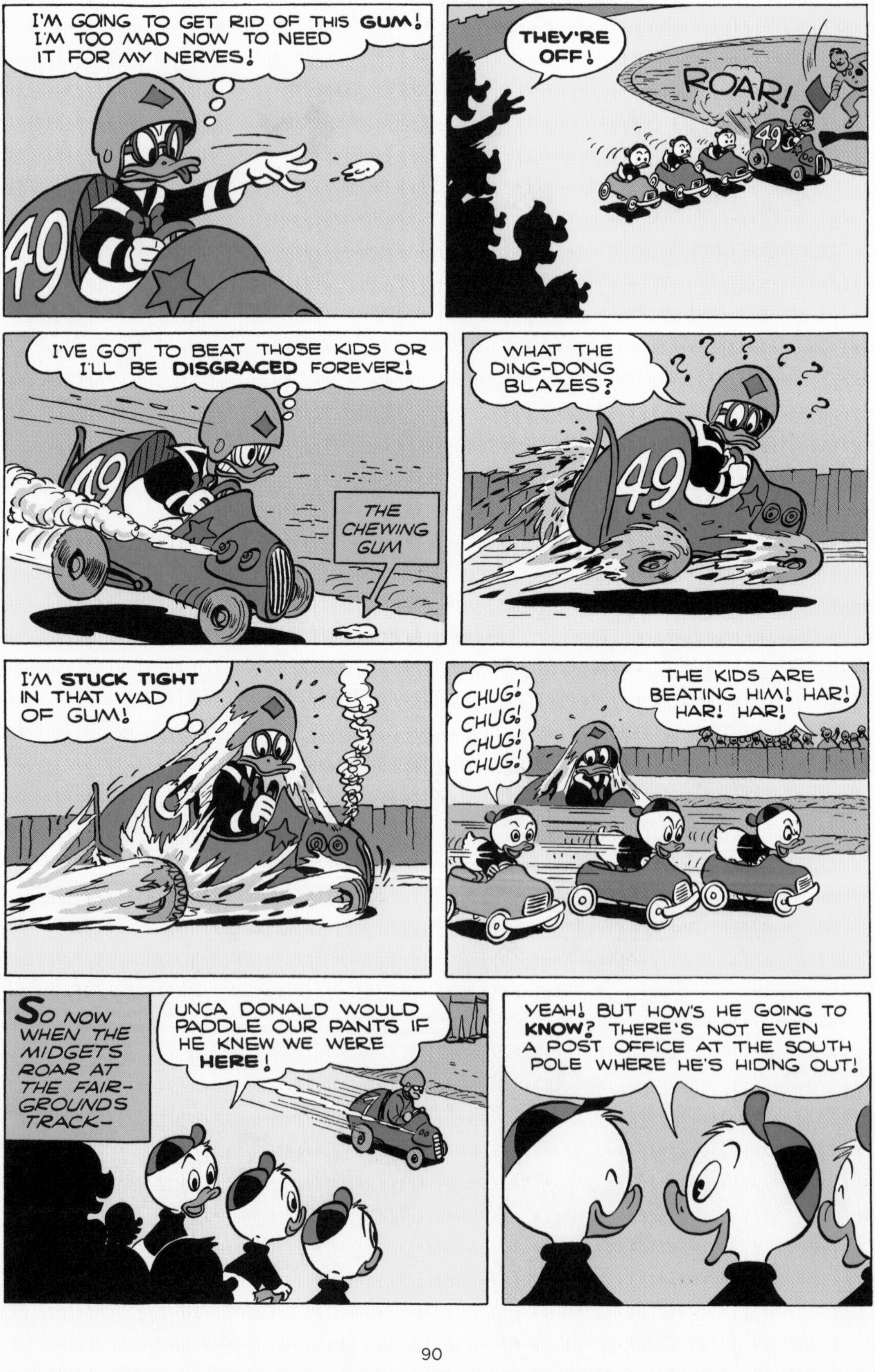
I'M GOING TO GET RID OF THIS **GUM**! I'M TOO MAD NOW TO NEED IT FOR MY NERVES!
THEY'RE OFF!
ROAR!
49
I'VE GOT TO BEAT THOSE KIDS OR I'LL BE **DISGRACED** FOREVER!
THE CHEWING GUM
WHAT THE DING-DONG BLAZES?
I'M **STUCK TIGHT** IN THAT WAD OF GUM!
CHUG! CHUG! CHUG! CHUG!
THE KIDS ARE BEATING HIM! HAR! HAR! HAR!
SO NOW WHEN THE MIDGETS ROAR AT THE FAIR-GROUNDS TRACK—
UNCA DONALD WOULD PADDLE OUR PANTS IF HE KNEW WE WERE **HERE**!
YEAH! BUT HOW'S HE GOING TO **KNOW**? THERE'S NOT EVEN A POST OFFICE AT THE SOUTH POLE WHERE HE'S HIDING OUT!

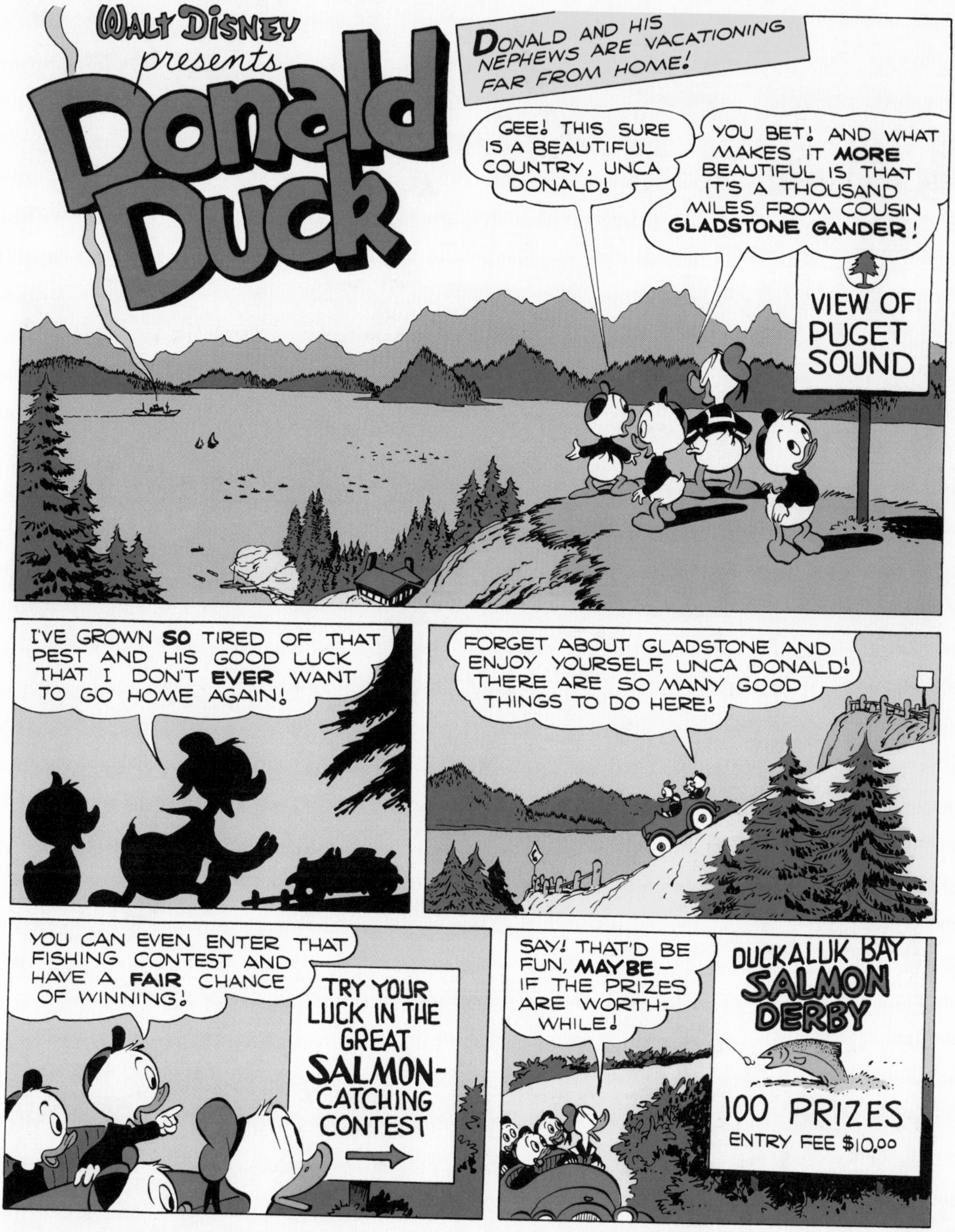
WALT DISNEY
presents
Donald Duck
DONALD AND HIS NEPHEWS ARE VACATIONING FAR FROM HOME!
GEE! THIS SURE IS A BEAUTIFUL COUNTRY, UNCA DONALD!
YOU BET! AND WHAT MAKES IT **MORE** BEAUTIFUL IS THAT IT'S A THOUSAND MILES FROM COUSIN **GLADSTONE GANDER**!
VIEW OF PUGET SOUND
I'VE GROWN **SO** TIRED OF THAT PEST AND HIS GOOD LUCK THAT I DON'T **EVER** WANT TO GO HOME AGAIN!
FORGET ABOUT GLADSTONE AND ENJOY YOURSELF, UNCA DONALD! THERE ARE SO MANY GOOD THINGS TO DO HERE!
YOU CAN EVEN ENTER THAT FISHING CONTEST AND HAVE A **FAIR** CHANCE OF WINNING!
TRY YOUR LUCK IN THE GREAT SALMON-CATCHING CONTEST
SAY! THAT'D BE FUN, **MAYBE**— IF THE PRIZES ARE WORTH-WHILE!
DUCKALUK BAY SALMON DERBY
100 PRIZES
ENTRY FEE $10.00

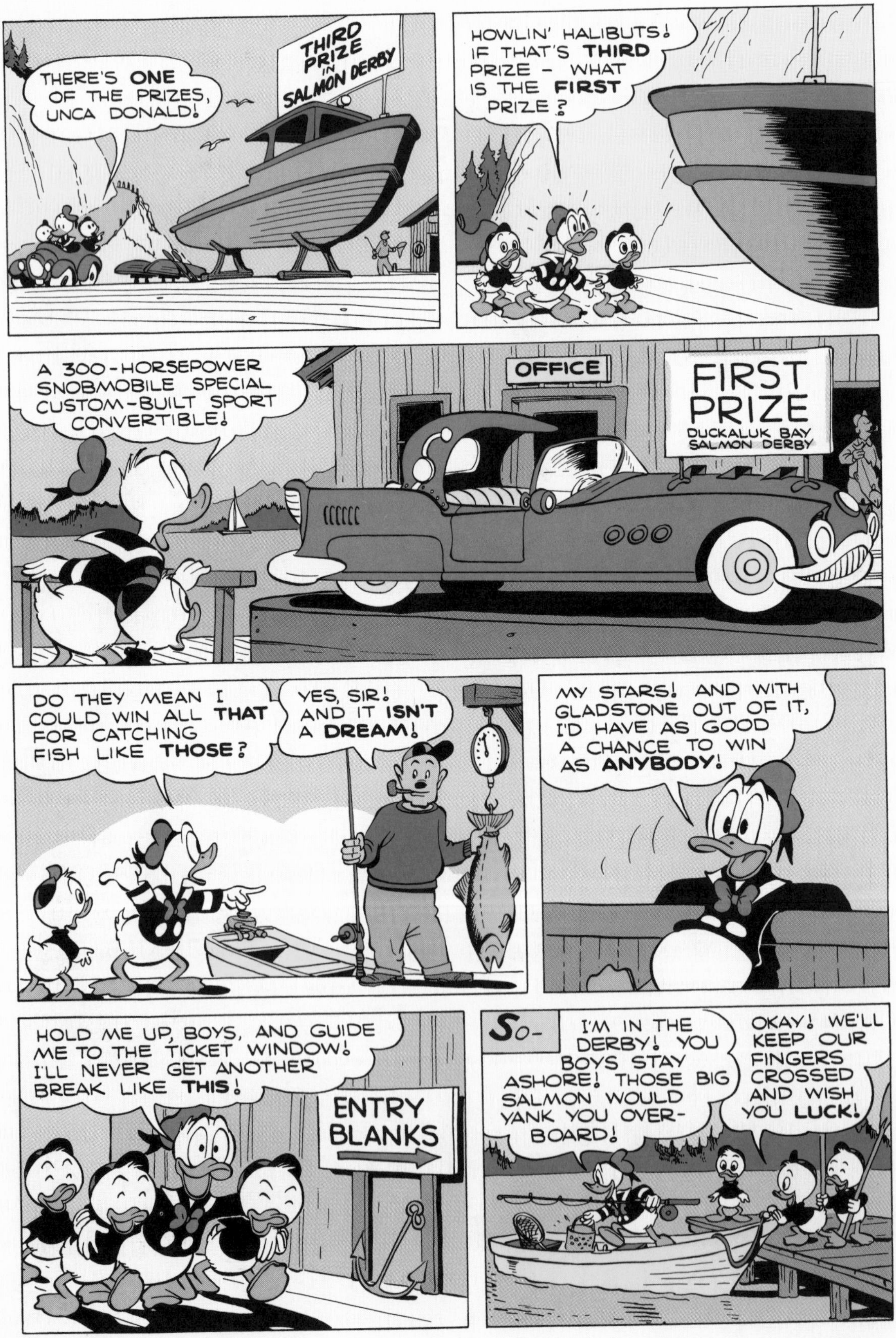
THIRD PRIZE IN SALMON DERBY
THERE'S ONE OF THE PRIZES, UNCA DONALD!
HOWLIN' HALIBUTS! IF THAT'S THIRD PRIZE - WHAT IS THE FIRST PRIZE?
A 300-HORSEPOWER SNOBMOBILE SPECIAL CUSTOM-BUILT SPORT CONVERTIBLE!
OFFICE
FIRST PRIZE DUCKALUK BAY SALMON DERBY
DO THEY MEAN I COULD WIN ALL THAT FOR CATCHING FISH LIKE THOSE?
YES, SIR! AND IT ISN'T A DREAM!
MY STARS! AND WITH GLADSTONE OUT OF IT, I'D HAVE AS GOOD A CHANCE TO WIN AS ANYBODY!
HOLD ME UP, BOYS, AND GUIDE ME TO THE TICKET WINDOW! I'LL NEVER GET ANOTHER BREAK LIKE THIS!
ENTRY BLANKS
SO-
I'M IN THE DERBY! YOU BOYS STAY ASHORE! THOSE BIG SALMON WOULD YANK YOU OVER-BOARD!
OKAY! WE'LL KEEP OUR FINGERS CROSSED AND WISH YOU LUCK!

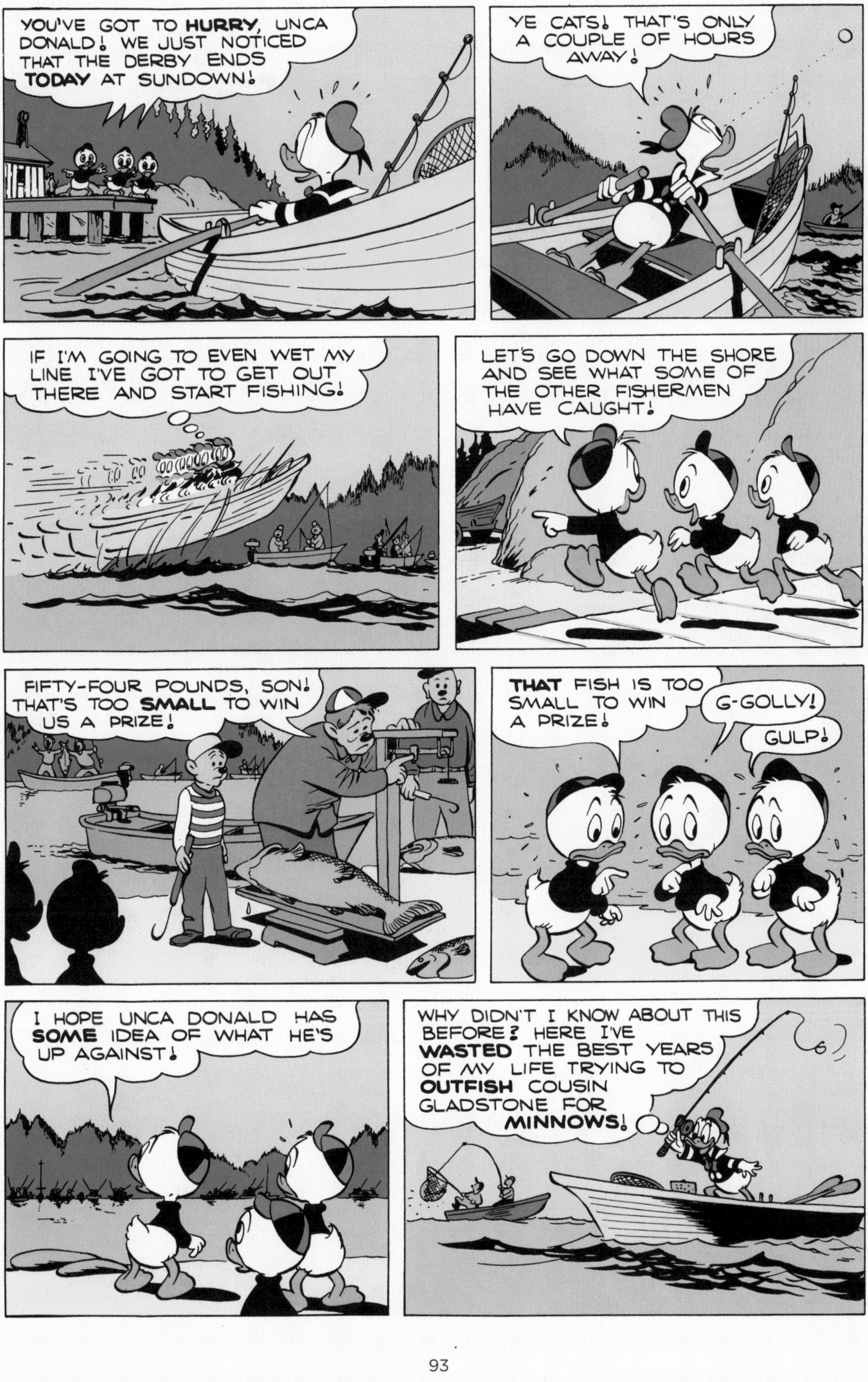
YOU'VE GOT TO **HURRY**, UNCA DONALD! WE JUST NOTICED THAT THE DERBY ENDS **TODAY** AT SUNDOWN!
YE CATS! THAT'S ONLY A COUPLE OF HOURS AWAY!
IF I'M GOING TO EVEN WET MY LINE I'VE GOT TO GET OUT THERE AND START FISHING!
LET'S GO DOWN THE SHORE AND SEE WHAT SOME OF THE OTHER FISHERMEN HAVE CAUGHT!
FIFTY-FOUR POUNDS, SON! THAT'S TOO **SMALL** TO WIN US A PRIZE!
THAT FISH IS TOO SMALL TO WIN A PRIZE!
G-GOLLY!
GULP!
I HOPE UNCA DONALD HAS **SOME** IDEA OF WHAT HE'S UP AGAINST!
WHY DIDN'T I KNOW ABOUT THIS BEFORE? HERE I'VE **WASTED** THE BEST YEARS OF MY LIFE TRYING TO **OUTFISH** COUSIN GLADSTONE FOR **MINNOWS**!

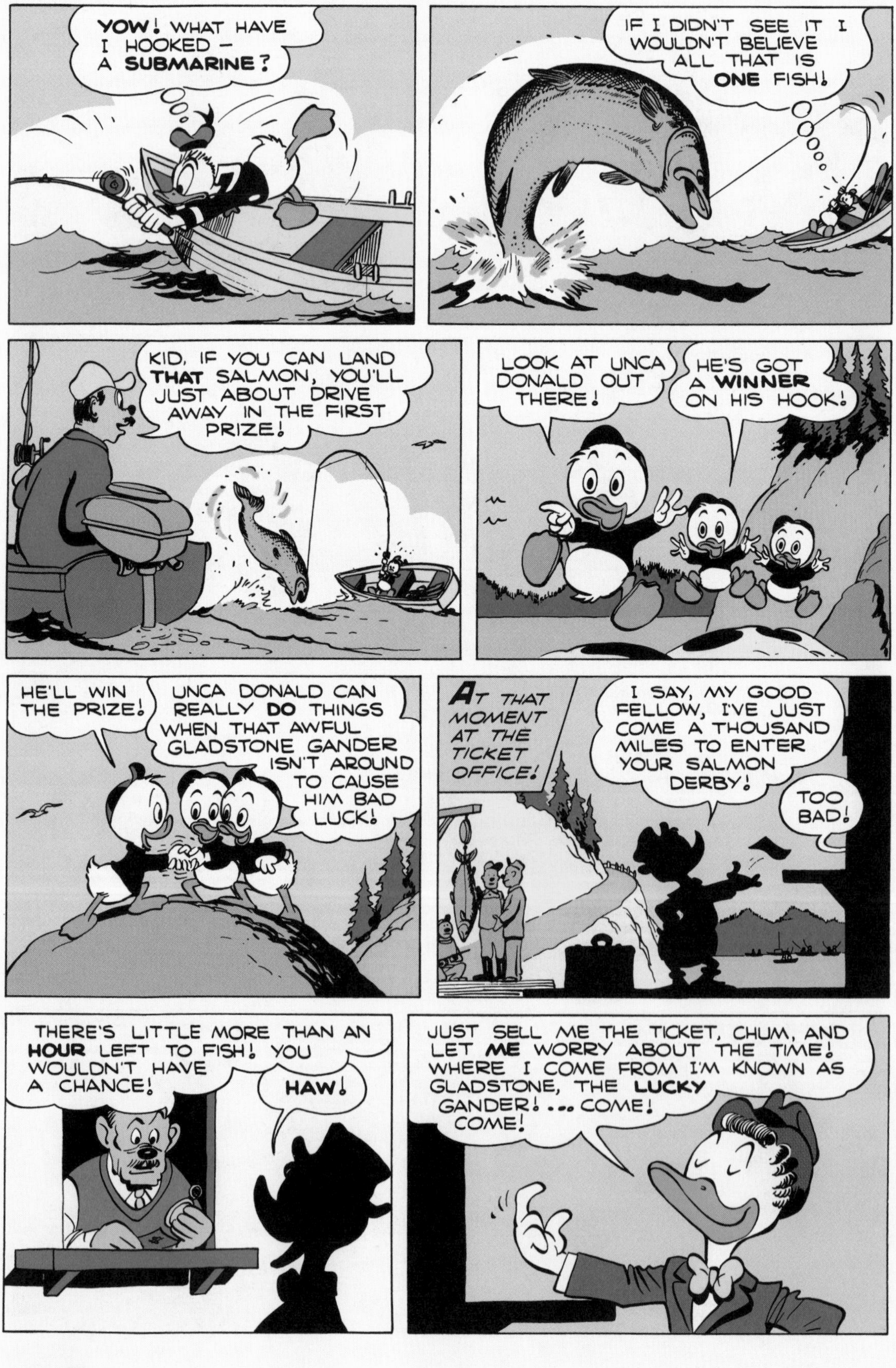
YOW! WHAT HAVE I HOOKED – A SUBMARINE?
IF I DIDN'T SEE IT I WOULDN'T BELIEVE ALL THAT IS ONE FISH!
KID, IF YOU CAN LAND THAT SALMON, YOU'LL JUST ABOUT DRIVE AWAY IN THE FIRST PRIZE!
LOOK AT UNCA DONALD OUT THERE!
HE'S GOT A WINNER ON HIS HOOK!
HE'LL WIN THE PRIZE!
UNCA DONALD CAN REALLY DO THINGS WHEN THAT AWFUL GLADSTONE GANDER ISN'T AROUND TO CAUSE HIM BAD LUCK!
AT THAT MOMENT AT THE TICKET OFFICE!
I SAY, MY GOOD FELLOW, I'VE JUST COME A THOUSAND MILES TO ENTER YOUR SALMON DERBY!
TOO BAD!
THERE'S LITTLE MORE THAN AN HOUR LEFT TO FISH! YOU WOULDN'T HAVE A CHANCE!
HAW!
JUST SELL ME THE TICKET, CHUM, AND LET ME WORRY ABOUT THE TIME! WHERE I COME FROM I'M KNOWN AS GLADSTONE, THE LUCKY GANDER! ... COME! COME!

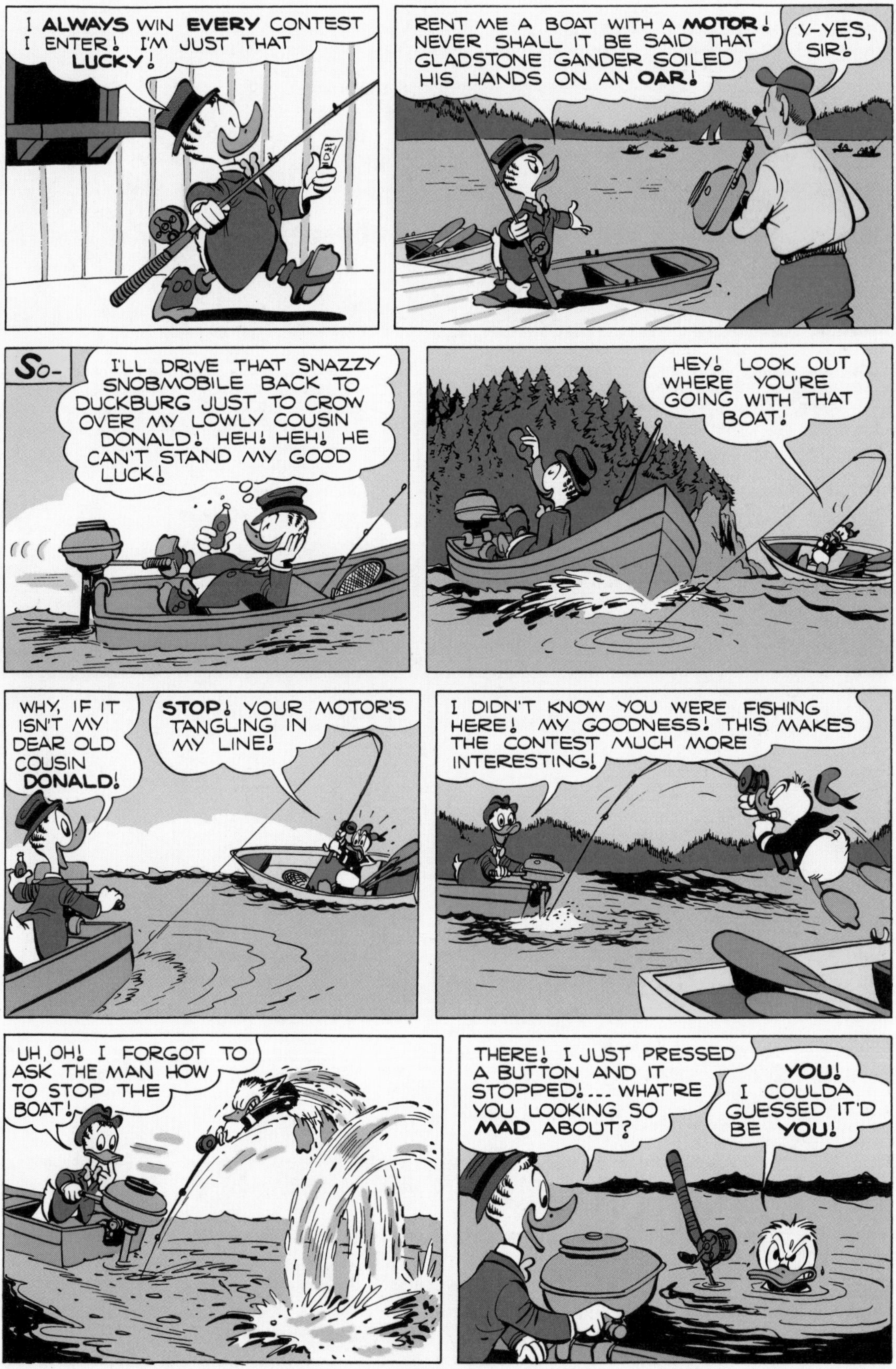
I ALWAYS WIN EVERY CONTEST I ENTER! I'M JUST THAT LUCKY!
RENT ME A BOAT WITH A MOTOR! NEVER SHALL IT BE SAID THAT GLADSTONE GANDER SOILED HIS HANDS ON AN OAR!
Y-YES, SIR!
SO-
I'LL DRIVE THAT SNAZZY SNOBMOBILE BACK TO DUCKBURG JUST TO CROW OVER MY LOWLY COUSIN DONALD! HEH! HEH! HE CAN'T STAND MY GOOD LUCK!
HEY! LOOK OUT WHERE YOU'RE GOING WITH THAT BOAT!
WHY, IF IT ISN'T MY DEAR OLD COUSIN DONALD!
STOP! YOUR MOTOR'S TANGLING IN MY LINE!
I DIDN'T KNOW YOU WERE FISHING HERE! MY GOODNESS! THIS MAKES THE CONTEST MUCH MORE INTERESTING!
UH, OH! I FORGOT TO ASK THE MAN HOW TO STOP THE BOAT!
THERE! I JUST PRESSED A BUTTON AND IT STOPPED!... WHAT'RE YOU LOOKING SO MAD ABOUT?
YOU! I COULDA GUESSED IT'D BE YOU!

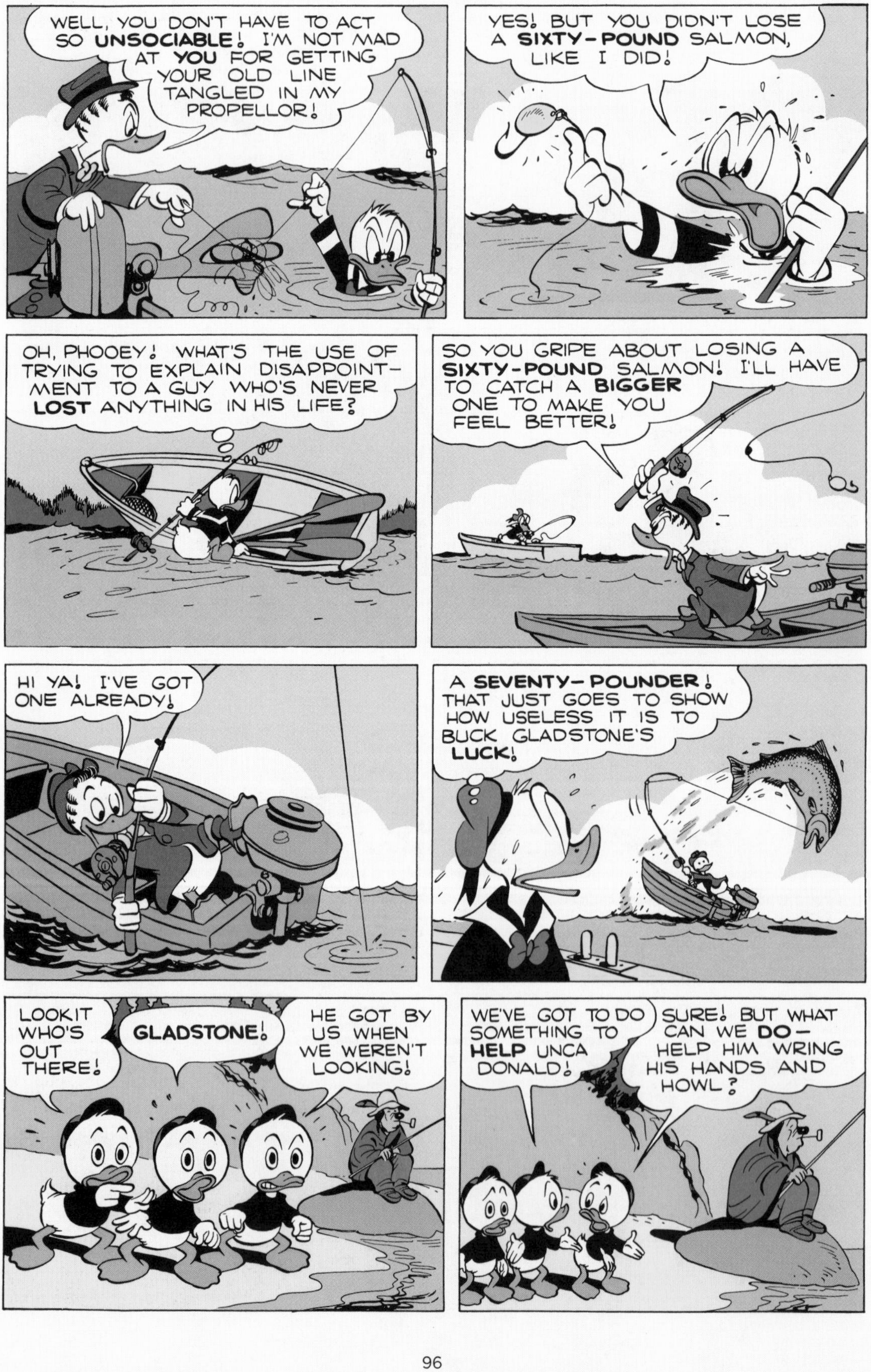
WELL, YOU DON'T HAVE TO ACT SO **UNSOCIABLE**! I'M NOT MAD AT **YOU** FOR GETTING YOUR OLD LINE TANGLED IN MY PROPELLOR!
YES! BUT YOU DIDN'T LOSE A **SIXTY-POUND** SALMON, LIKE I DID!
OH, PHOOEY! WHAT'S THE USE OF TRYING TO EXPLAIN DISAPPOINT-MENT TO A GUY WHO'S NEVER **LOST** ANYTHING IN HIS LIFE?
SO YOU GRIPE ABOUT LOSING A **SIXTY-POUND** SALMON! I'LL HAVE TO CATCH A **BIGGER** ONE TO MAKE YOU FEEL BETTER!
HI YA! I'VE GOT ONE ALREADY!
A **SEVENTY-POUNDER**! THAT JUST GOES TO SHOW HOW USELESS IT IS TO BUCK GLADSTONE'S **LUCK**!
LOOKIT WHO'S OUT THERE!
GLADSTONE!
HE GOT BY US WHEN WE WEREN'T LOOKING!
WE'VE GOT TO DO SOMETHING TO **HELP** UNCA DONALD!
SURE! BUT WHAT CAN WE **DO**— HELP HIM WRING HIS HANDS AND HOWL?

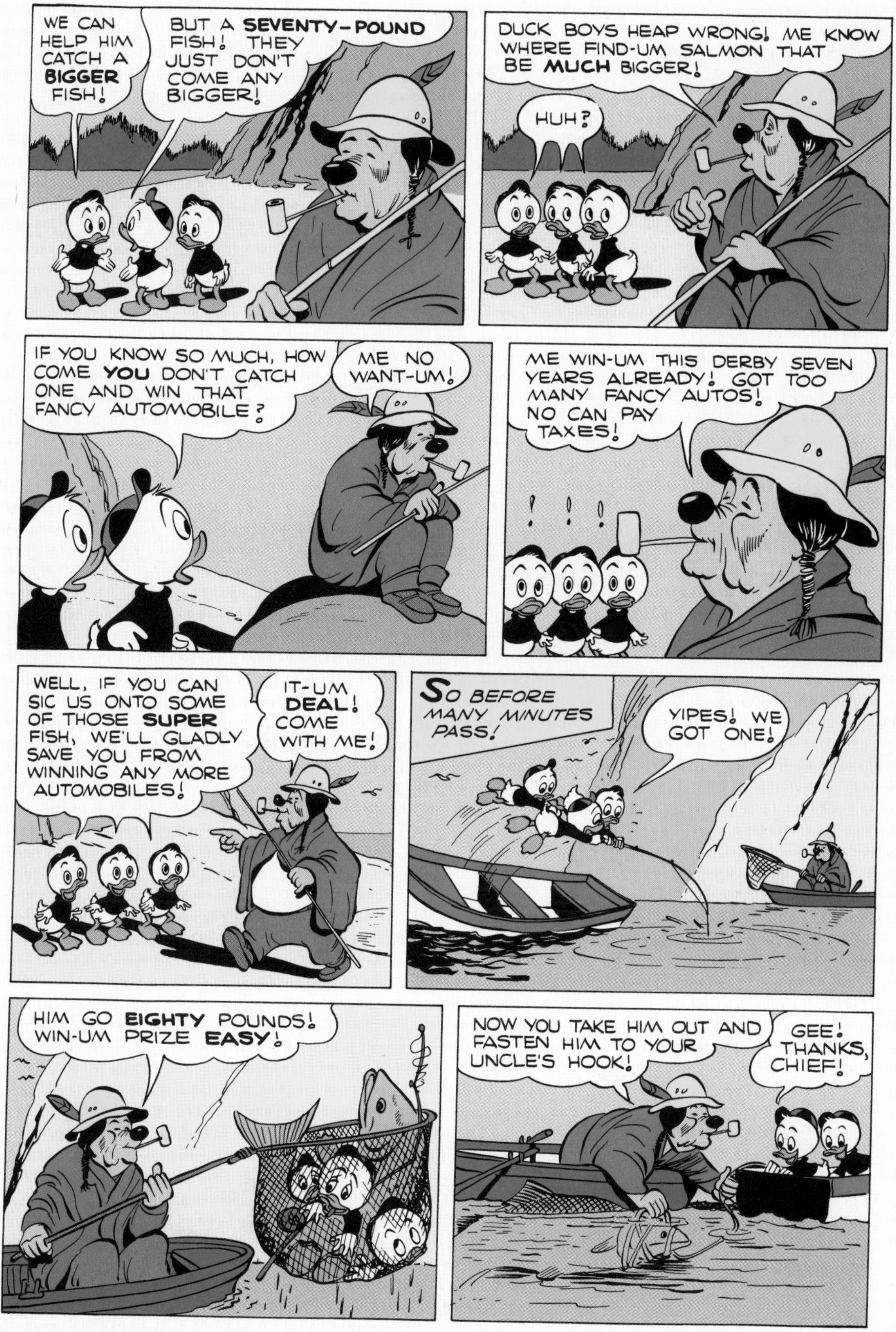
WE CAN HELP HIM CATCH A BIGGER FISH!
BUT A SEVENTY-POUND FISH! THEY JUST DON'T COME ANY BIGGER!
DUCK BOYS HEAP WRONG! ME KNOW WHERE FIND-UM SALMON THAT BE MUCH BIGGER!
HUH?
IF YOU KNOW SO MUCH, HOW COME YOU DON'T CATCH ONE AND WIN THAT FANCY AUTOMOBILE?
ME NO WANT-UM!
ME WIN-UM THIS DERBY SEVEN YEARS ALREADY! GOT TOO MANY FANCY AUTOS! NO CAN PAY TAXES!
! ! !
WELL, IF YOU CAN SIC US ONTO SOME OF THOSE SUPER FISH, WE'LL GLADLY SAVE YOU FROM WINNING ANY MORE AUTOMOBILES!
IT-UM DEAL! COME WITH ME!
SO BEFORE MANY MINUTES PASS!
YIPES! WE GOT ONE!
HIM GO EIGHTY POUNDS! WIN-UM PRIZE EASY!
NOW YOU TAKE HIM OUT AND FASTEN HIM TO YOUR UNCLE'S HOOK!
GEE! THANKS, CHIEF!

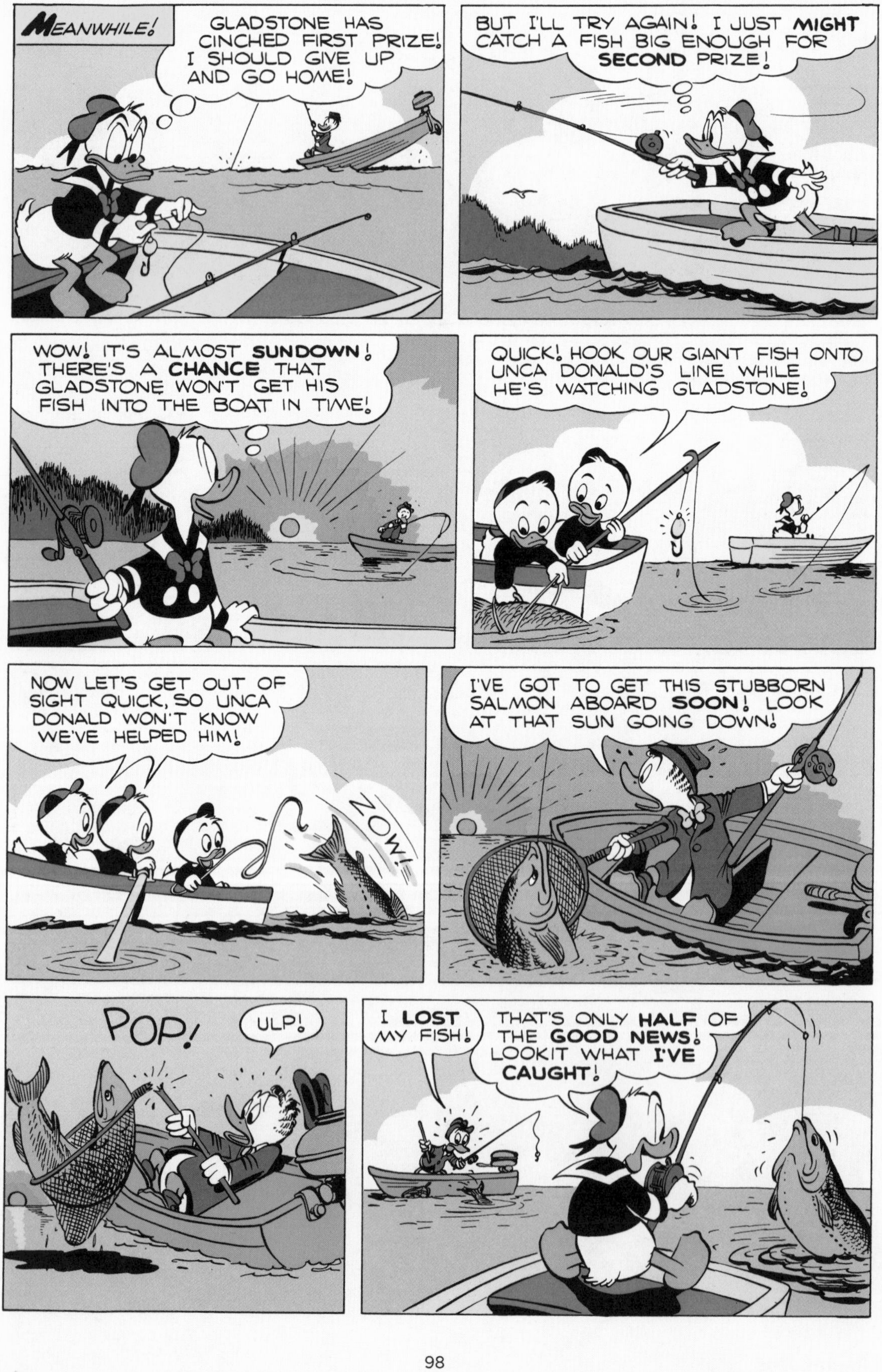
MEANWHILE!
GLADSTONE HAS CINCHED FIRST PRIZE! I SHOULD GIVE UP AND GO HOME!
BUT I'LL TRY AGAIN! I JUST **MIGHT** CATCH A FISH BIG ENOUGH FOR **SECOND** PRIZE!
WOW! IT'S ALMOST **SUNDOWN**! THERE'S A **CHANCE** THAT GLADSTONE WON'T GET HIS FISH INTO THE BOAT IN TIME!
QUICK! HOOK OUR GIANT FISH ONTO UNCA DONALD'S LINE WHILE HE'S WATCHING GLADSTONE!
NOW LET'S GET OUT OF SIGHT QUICK, SO UNCA DONALD WON'T KNOW WE'VE HELPED HIM!
ZOW!
I'VE GOT TO GET THIS STUBBORN SALMON ABOARD **SOON**! LOOK AT THAT SUN GOING DOWN!
POP!
ULP!
I **LOST** MY FISH!
THAT'S ONLY **HALF** OF THE **GOOD NEWS**! LOOKIT WHAT **I'VE CAUGHT**!

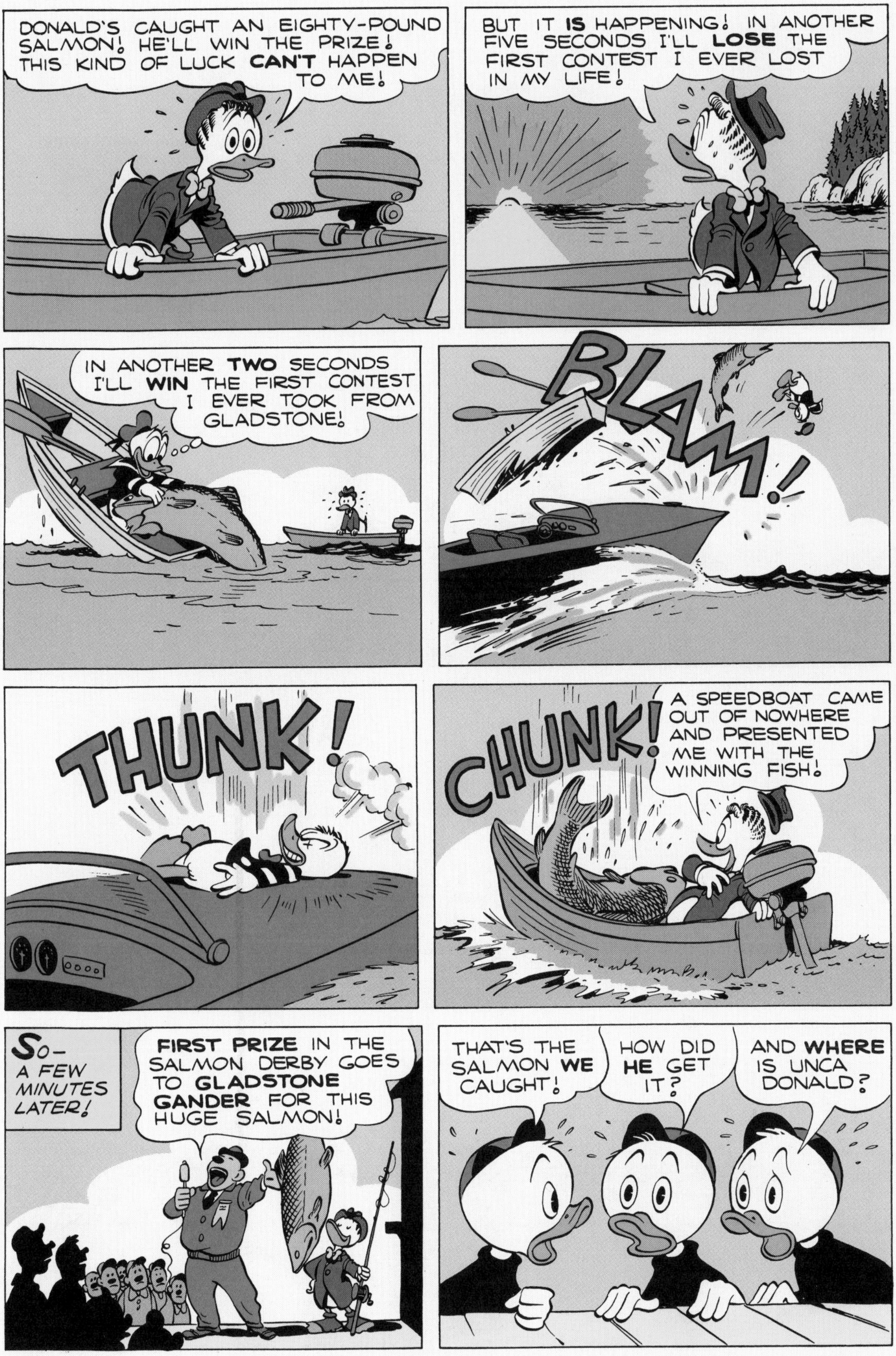
DONALD'S CAUGHT AN EIGHTY-POUND SALMON! HE'LL WIN THE PRIZE! THIS KIND OF LUCK **CAN'T** HAPPEN TO ME!
BUT IT **IS** HAPPENING! IN ANOTHER FIVE SECONDS I'LL **LOSE** THE FIRST CONTEST I EVER LOST IN MY LIFE!
IN ANOTHER **TWO** SECONDS I'LL **WIN** THE FIRST CONTEST I EVER TOOK FROM GLADSTONE!
BLAM!
THUNK!
CHUNK!
A SPEEDBOAT CAME OUT OF NOWHERE AND PRESENTED ME WITH THE WINNING FISH!
SO— A FEW MINUTES LATER!
FIRST PRIZE IN THE SALMON DERBY GOES TO **GLADSTONE GANDER** FOR THIS HUGE SALMON!
THAT'S THE SALMON **WE** CAUGHT!
HOW DID **HE** GET IT?
AND **WHERE** IS UNCA DONALD?

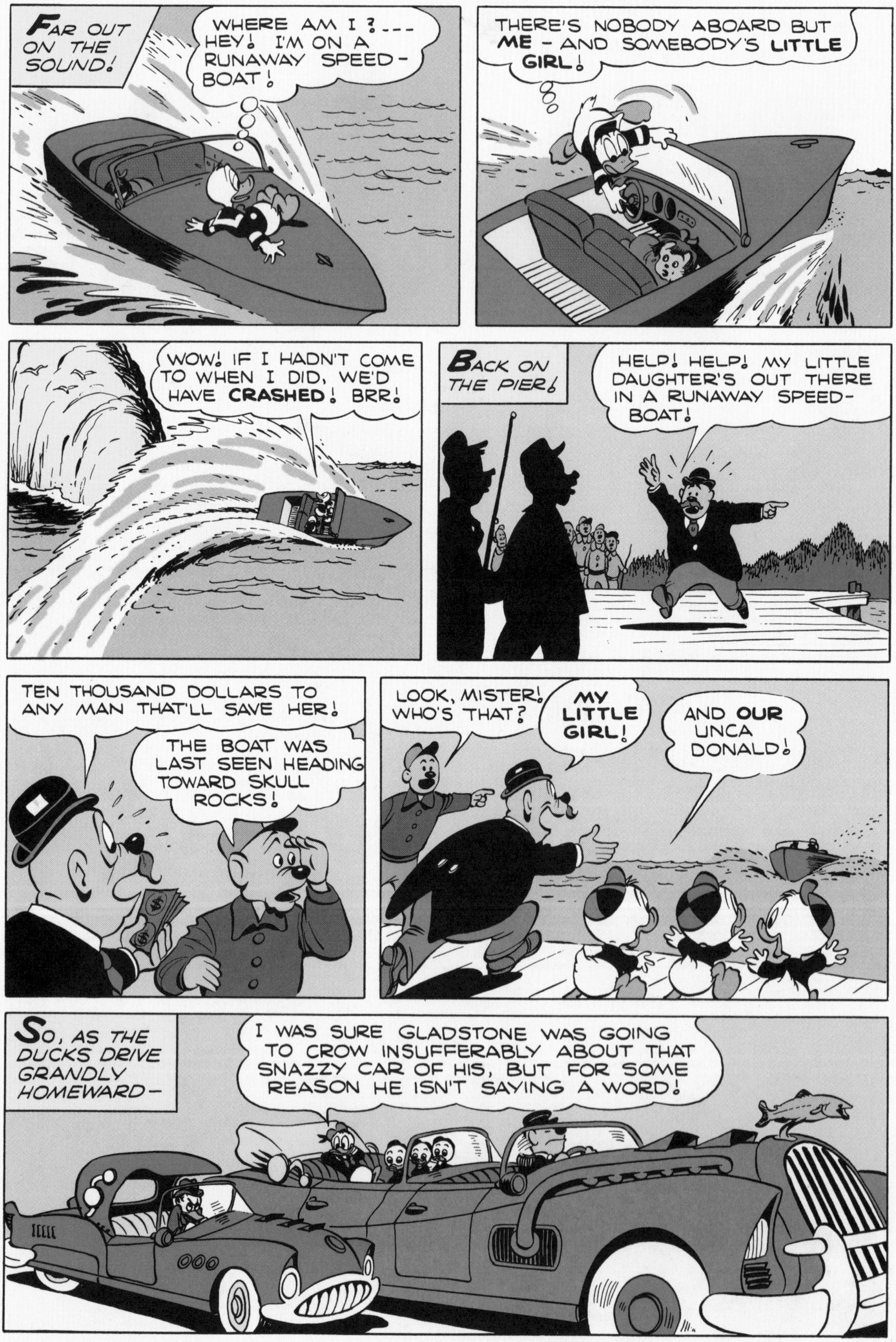
FAR OUT ON THE SOUND!
WHERE AM I ? - - - HEY! I'M ON A RUNAWAY SPEED-BOAT!
THERE'S NOBODY ABOARD BUT ME - AND SOMEBODY'S LITTLE GIRL!
WOW! IF I HADN'T COME TO WHEN I DID, WE'D HAVE CRASHED! BRR!
BACK ON THE PIER!
HELP! HELP! MY LITTLE DAUGHTER'S OUT THERE IN A RUNAWAY SPEED-BOAT!
TEN THOUSAND DOLLARS TO ANY MAN THAT'LL SAVE HER!
THE BOAT WAS LAST SEEN HEADING TOWARD SKULL ROCKS!
LOOK, MISTER! WHO'S THAT?
MY LITTLE GIRL!
AND OUR UNCA DONALD!
SO, AS THE DUCKS DRIVE GRANDLY HOMEWARD—
I WAS SURE GLADSTONE WAS GOING TO CROW INSUFFERABLY ABOUT THAT SNAZZY CAR OF HIS, BUT FOR SOME REASON HE ISN'T SAYING A WORD!

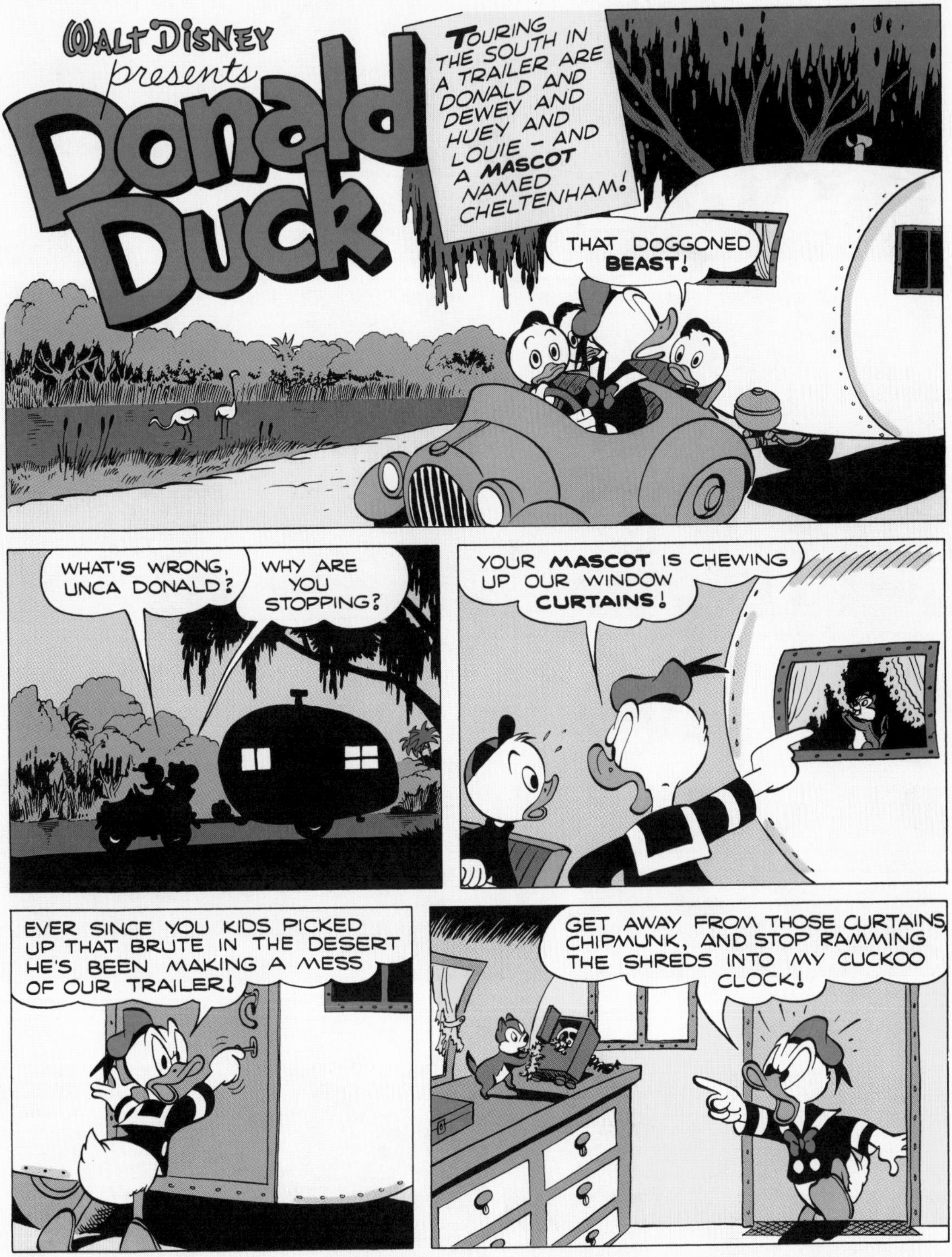
WALT DISNEY
presents
Donald Duck
TOURING THE SOUTH IN A TRAILER ARE DONALD AND DEWEY AND HUEY AND LOUIE – AND A MASCOT NAMED CHELTENHAM!
THAT DOGGONED BEAST!
WHAT'S WRONG, UNCA DONALD?
WHY ARE YOU STOPPING?
YOUR MASCOT IS CHEWING UP OUR WINDOW CURTAINS!
EVER SINCE YOU KIDS PICKED UP THAT BRUTE IN THE DESERT HE'S BEEN MAKING A MESS OF OUR TRAILER!
GET AWAY FROM THOSE CURTAINS, CHIPMUNK, AND STOP RAMMING THE SHREDS INTO MY CUCKOO CLOCK!

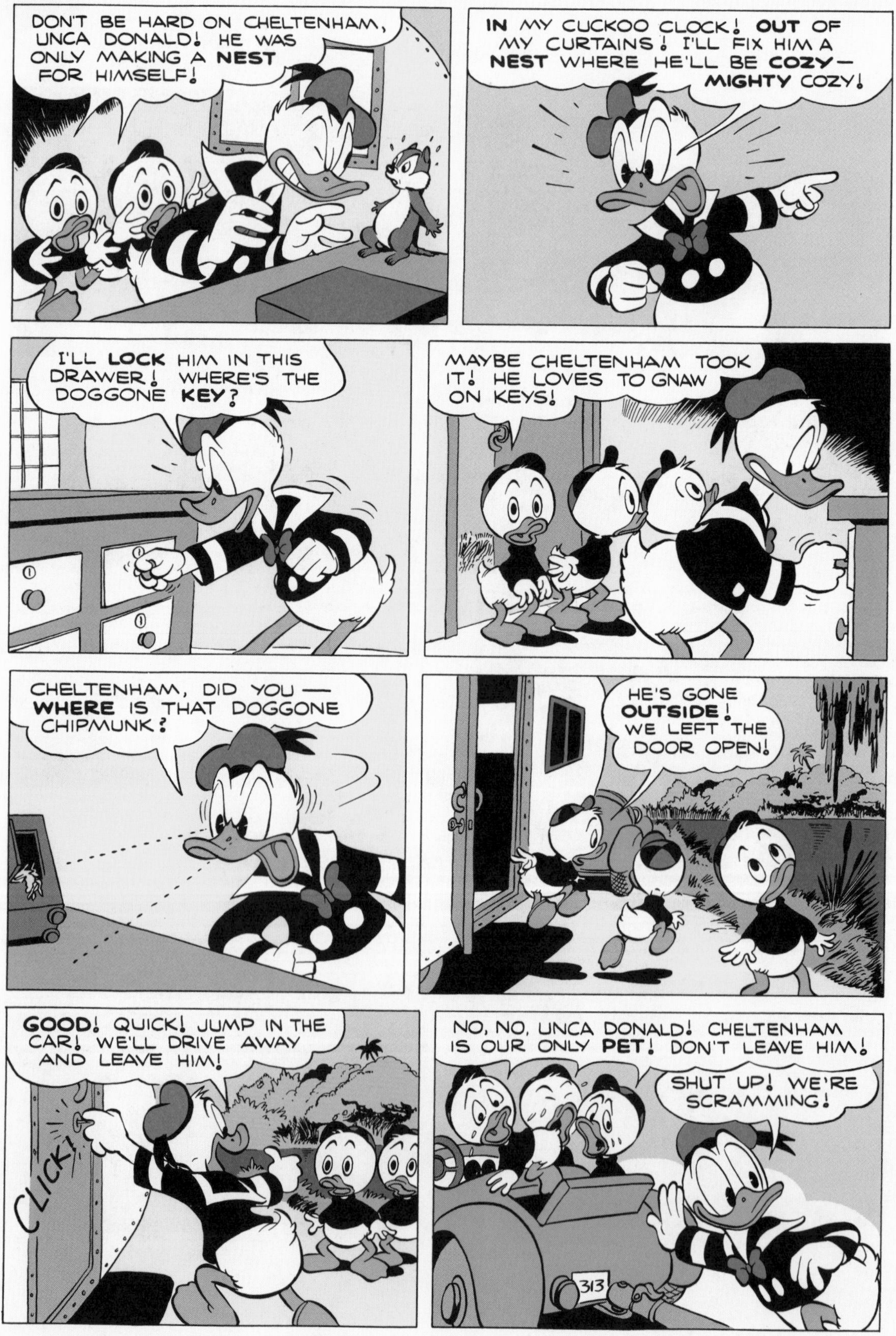
DON'T BE HARD ON CHELTENHAM, UNCA DONALD! HE WAS ONLY MAKING A NEST FOR HIMSELF!
IN MY CUCKOO CLOCK! OUT OF MY CURTAINS! I'LL FIX HIM A NEST WHERE HE'LL BE COZY— MIGHTY COZY!
I'LL LOCK HIM IN THIS DRAWER! WHERE'S THE DOGGONE KEY?
MAYBE CHELTENHAM TOOK IT! HE LOVES TO GNAW ON KEYS!
CHELTENHAM, DID YOU— WHERE IS THAT DOGGONE CHIPMUNK?
HE'S GONE OUTSIDE! WE LEFT THE DOOR OPEN!
GOOD! QUICK! JUMP IN THE CAR! WE'LL DRIVE AWAY AND LEAVE HIM!
CLICK!
NO, NO, UNCA DONALD! CHELTENHAM IS OUR ONLY PET! DON'T LEAVE HIM!
SHUT UP! WE'RE SCRAMMING!
313

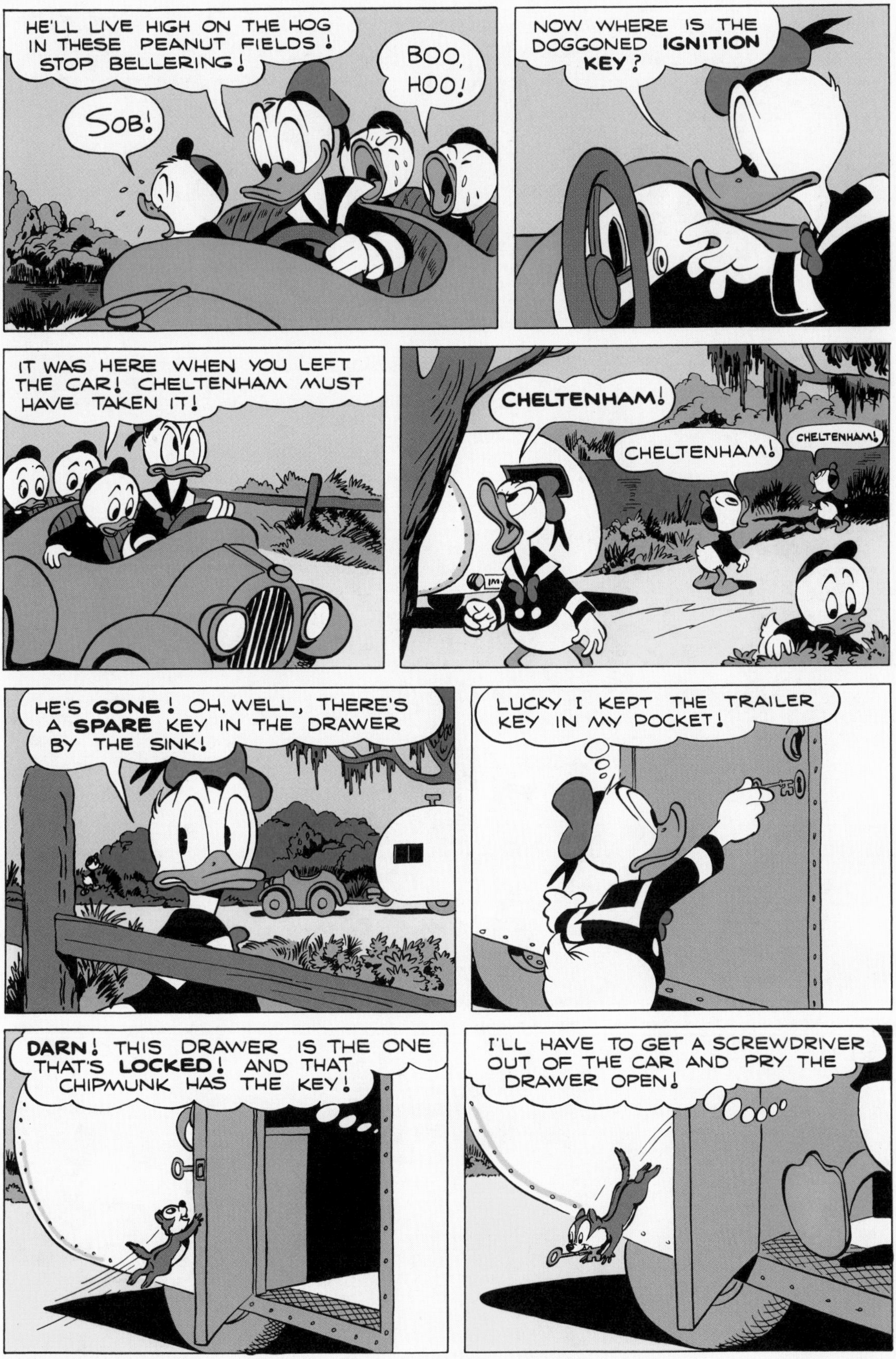
HE'LL LIVE HIGH ON THE HOG IN THESE PEANUT FIELDS! STOP BELLERING!
BOO, HOO!
SOB!
NOW WHERE IS THE DOGGONED IGNITION KEY?
IT WAS HERE WHEN YOU LEFT THE CAR! CHELTENHAM MUST HAVE TAKEN IT!
CHELTENHAM!
CHELTENHAM!
CHELTENHAM!
HE'S GONE! OH, WELL, THERE'S A SPARE KEY IN THE DRAWER BY THE SINK!
LUCKY I KEPT THE TRAILER KEY IN MY POCKET!
DARN! THIS DRAWER IS THE ONE THAT'S LOCKED! AND THAT CHIPMUNK HAS THE KEY!
I'LL HAVE TO GET A SCREWDRIVER OUT OF THE CAR AND PRY THE DRAWER OPEN!

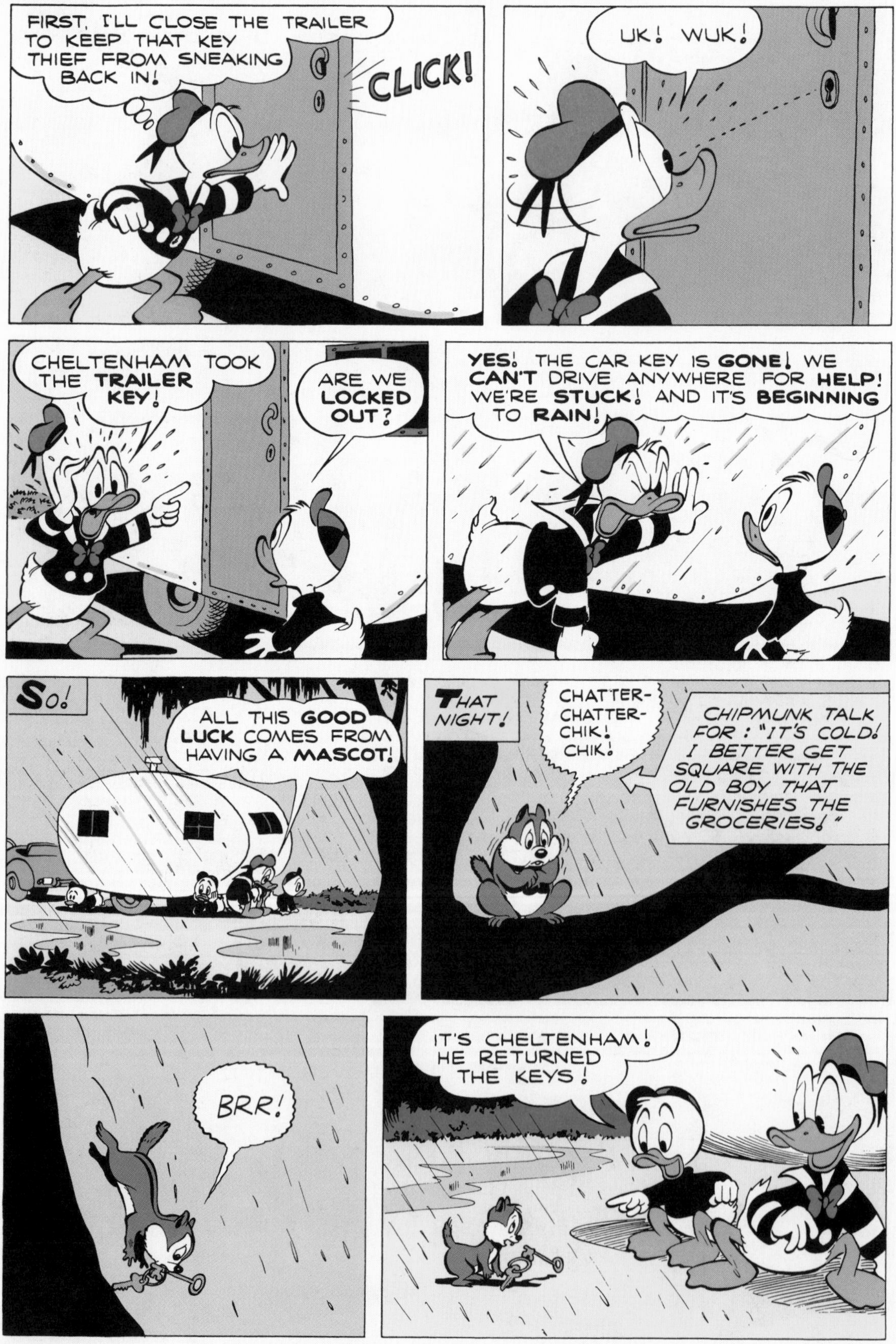
FIRST, I'LL CLOSE THE TRAILER TO KEEP THAT KEY THIEF FROM SNEAKING BACK IN!
CLICK!
UK! WUK!
CHELTENHAM TOOK THE TRAILER KEY!
ARE WE LOCKED OUT?
YES! THE CAR KEY IS GONE! WE CAN'T DRIVE ANYWHERE FOR HELP! WE'RE STUCK! AND IT'S BEGINNING TO RAIN!
SO!
ALL THIS GOOD LUCK COMES FROM HAVING A MASCOT!
THAT NIGHT!
CHATTER-CHATTER-CHIK! CHIK!
CHIPMUNK TALK FOR: "IT'S COLD! I BETTER GET SQUARE WITH THE OLD BOY THAT FURNISHES THE GROCERIES!"
BRR!
IT'S CHELTENHAM! HE RETURNED THE KEYS!

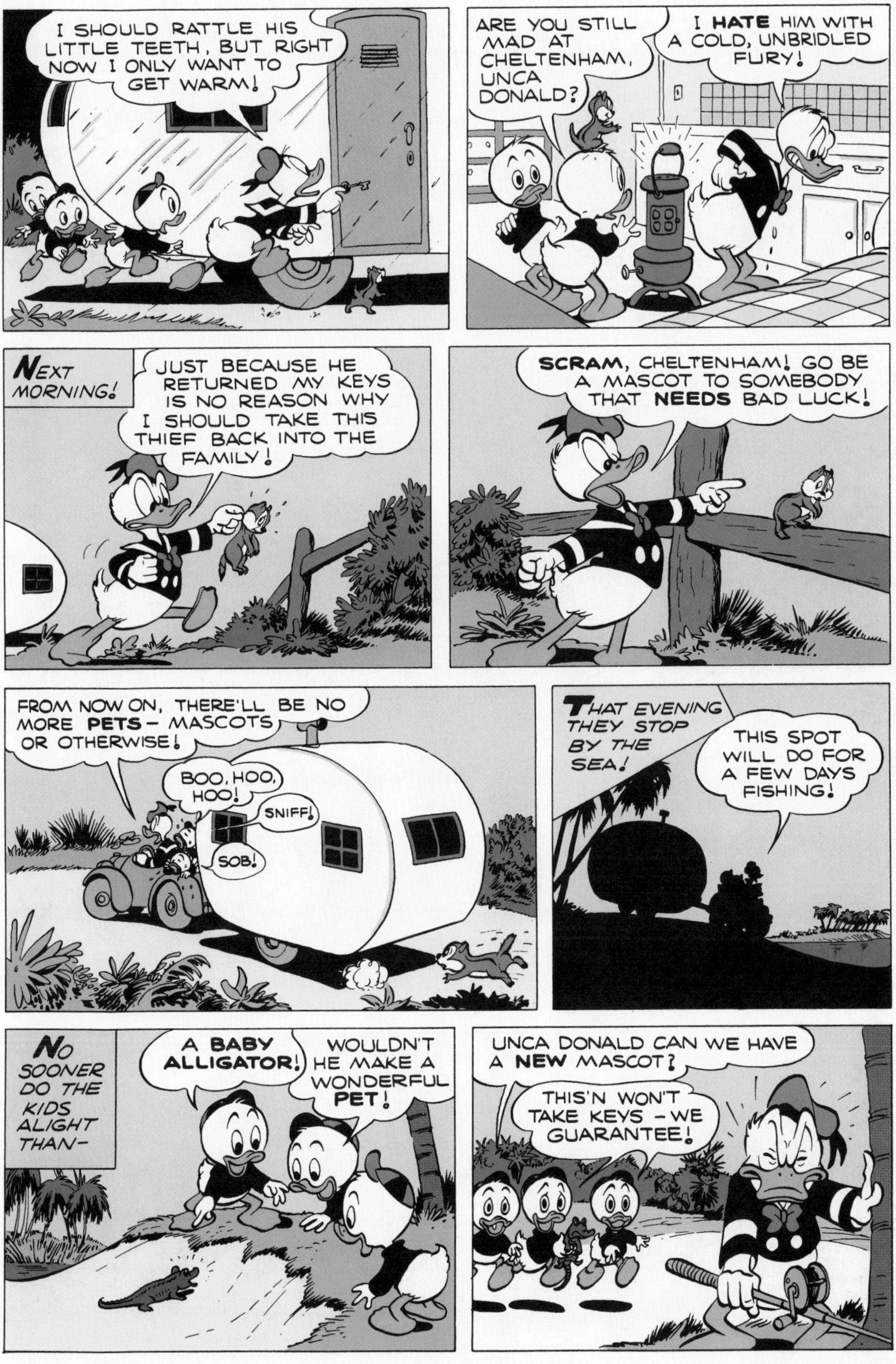

I SHOULD RATTLE HIS LITTLE TEETH, BUT RIGHT NOW I ONLY WANT TO GET WARM!
ARE YOU STILL MAD AT CHELTENHAM, UNCA DONALD?
I HATE HIM WITH A COLD, UNBRIDLED FURY!
NEXT MORNING!
JUST BECAUSE HE RETURNED MY KEYS IS NO REASON WHY I SHOULD TAKE THIS THIEF BACK INTO THE FAMILY!
SCRAM, CHELTENHAM! GO BE A MASCOT TO SOMEBODY THAT NEEDS BAD LUCK!
FROM NOW ON, THERE'LL BE NO MORE PETS— MASCOTS OR OTHERWISE!
BOO, HOO, HOO!
SNIFF!
SOB!
THAT EVENING THEY STOP BY THE SEA!
THIS SPOT WILL DO FOR A FEW DAYS FISHING!
NO SOONER DO THE KIDS ALIGHT THAN—
A BABY ALLIGATOR!
WOULDN'T HE MAKE A WONDERFUL PET!
UNCA DONALD CAN WE HAVE A NEW MASCOT?
THIS'N WON'T TAKE KEYS —WE GUARANTEE!

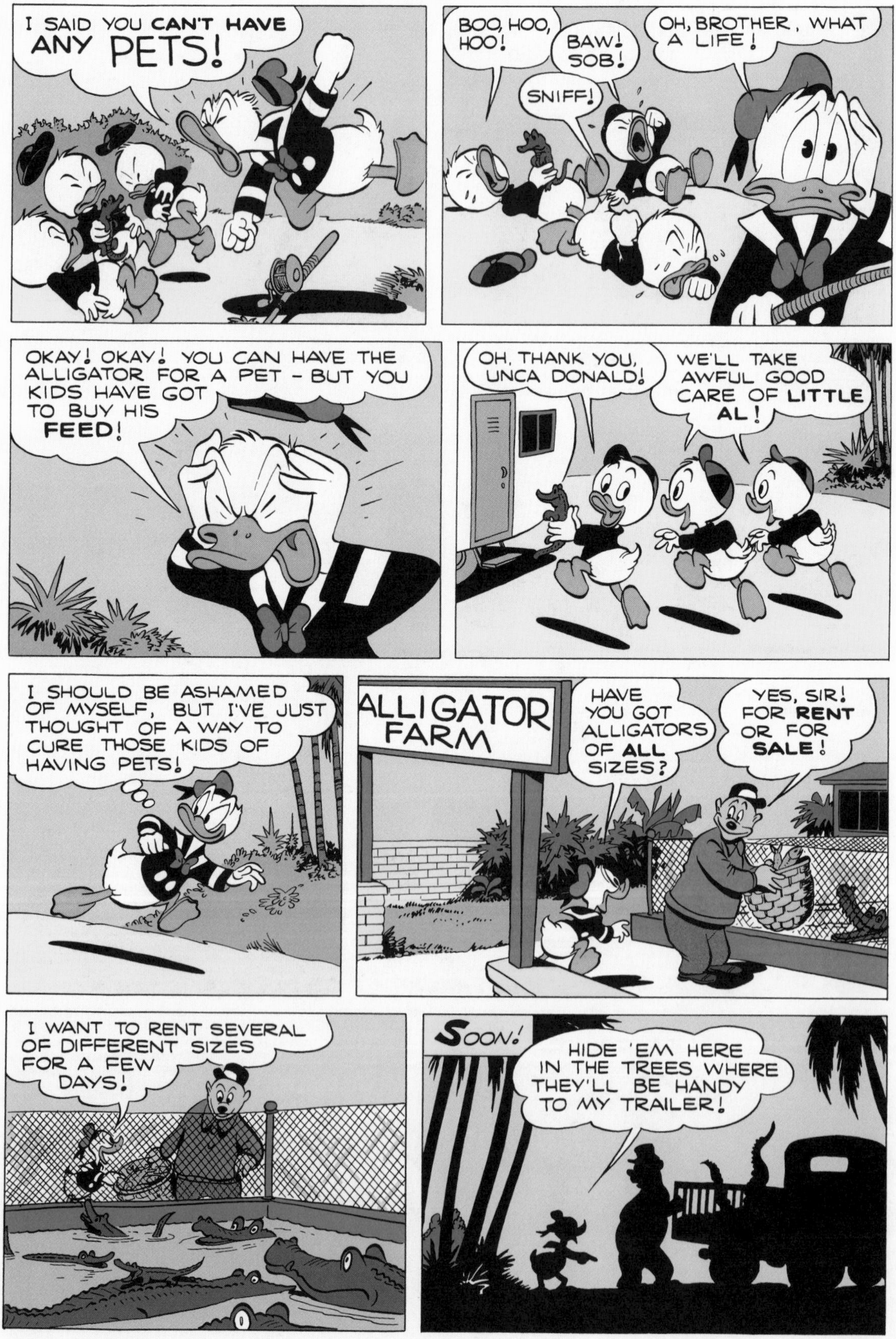
I SAID YOU CAN'T HAVE ANY PETS!
BOO, HOO, HOO!
BAW! SOB!
SNIFF!
OH, BROTHER, WHAT A LIFE!
OKAY! OKAY! YOU CAN HAVE THE ALLIGATOR FOR A PET – BUT YOU KIDS HAVE GOT TO BUY HIS FEED!
OH, THANK YOU, UNCA DONALD!
WE'LL TAKE AWFUL GOOD CARE OF LITTLE AL!
I SHOULD BE ASHAMED OF MYSELF, BUT I'VE JUST THOUGHT OF A WAY TO CURE THOSE KIDS OF HAVING PETS!
ALLIGATOR FARM
HAVE YOU GOT ALLIGATORS OF ALL SIZES?
YES, SIR! FOR RENT OR FOR SALE!
I WANT TO RENT SEVERAL OF DIFFERENT SIZES FOR A FEW DAYS!
SOON!
HIDE 'EM HERE IN THE TREES WHERE THEY'LL BE HANDY TO MY TRAILER!

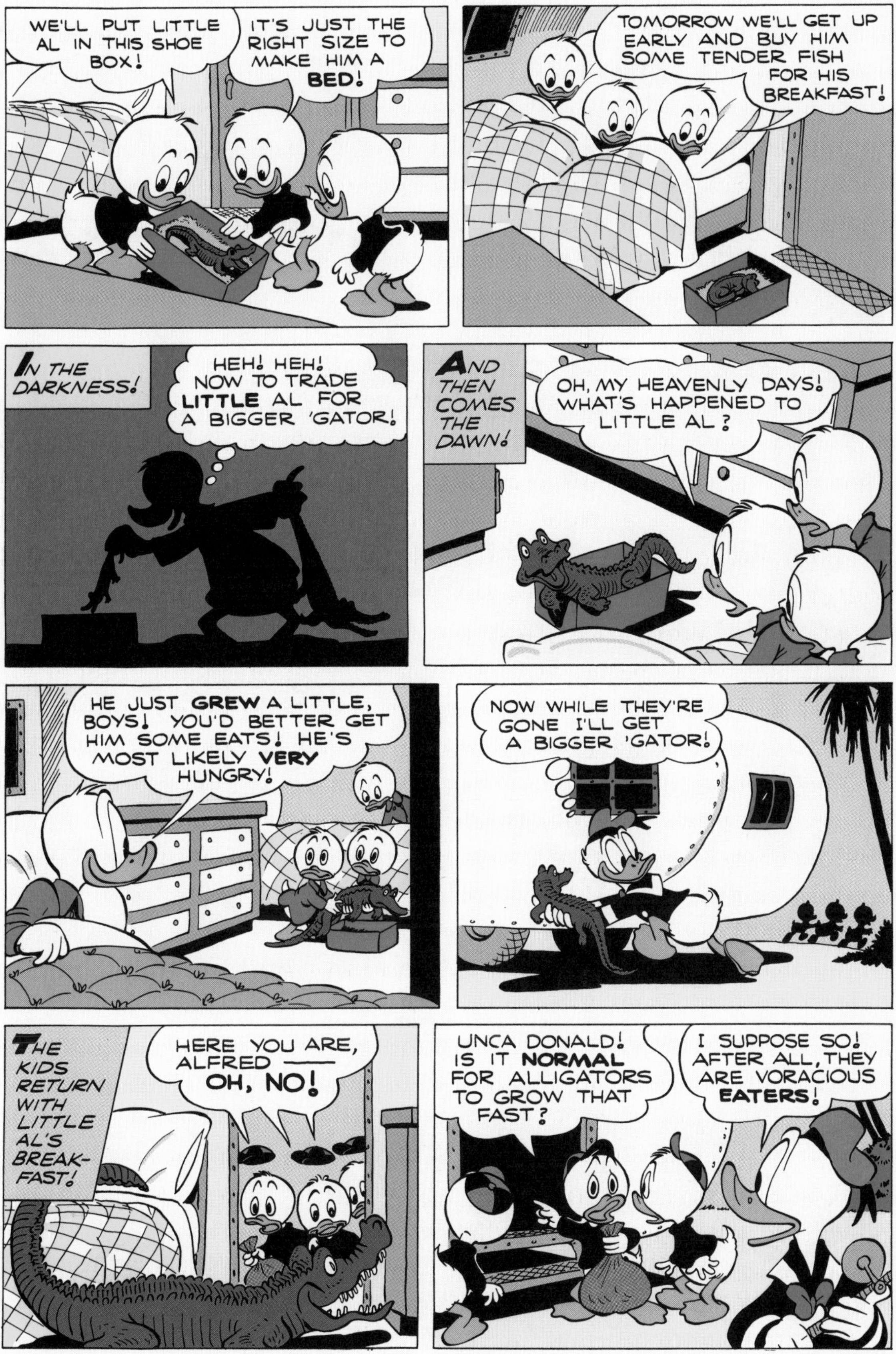
WE'LL PUT LITTLE AL IN THIS SHOE BOX!
IT'S JUST THE RIGHT SIZE TO MAKE HIM A BED!
TOMORROW WE'LL GET UP EARLY AND BUY HIM SOME TENDER FISH FOR HIS BREAKFAST!
IN THE DARKNESS!
HEH! HEH! NOW TO TRADE LITTLE AL FOR A BIGGER 'GATOR!
AND THEN COMES THE DAWN!
OH, MY HEAVENLY DAYS! WHAT'S HAPPENED TO LITTLE AL?
HE JUST GREW A LITTLE, BOYS! YOU'D BETTER GET HIM SOME EATS! HE'S MOST LIKELY VERY HUNGRY!
NOW WHILE THEY'RE GONE I'LL GET A BIGGER 'GATOR!
THE KIDS RETURN WITH LITTLE AL'S BREAK-FAST!
HERE YOU ARE, ALFRED — OH, NO!
UNCA DONALD! IS IT NORMAL FOR ALLIGATORS TO GROW THAT FAST?
I SUPPOSE SO! AFTER ALL, THEY ARE VORACIOUS EATERS!

THAT **PET** LOOKS **STARVED!** I'M SURE YOU DIDN'T BRING HIM ENOUGH FISH!

OH, GOLLY! GOLLY! THIS COULD BECOME **EXPENSIVE!**

WE'VE BOUGHT A **DOLLAR'S** WORTH OF FISH ALREADY!

HEH! HEH! HEH! LIFE'S BITTER LESSONS! TSK! TSK!

*A*GAIN THE KIDS RETURN!

THIS LOAD OF FISH SHOULD FILL ALFRED!

IT'LL **HAVE TO** — OR WE'LL GO **BROKE!**

SAY NO MORE! WE'RE **BANKRUPT!**

UNCA DONALD, CAN WE GIVE ALFRED TO SOME **MILLIONAIRE?** WE'VE DECIDED WE — THAT IS — WE —

DON'T WANT ANY MORE **PETS,** HUH?

THAT'S RIGHT, UNCA DONALD! **NO MORE PETS!**

VERY WELL! THAT'S A **RULE** IN THIS FAMILY FROM NOW ON!

*A*ND SO IT IS UNTIL THAT AFTERNOON!

HELLO, YOU LITTLE SAWED-OFF MESS OF SHARK BAIT!

ISN'T THAT **CUTE!**

JIM'S PET SHOP

TALKING MYNAH BIRD $5.00

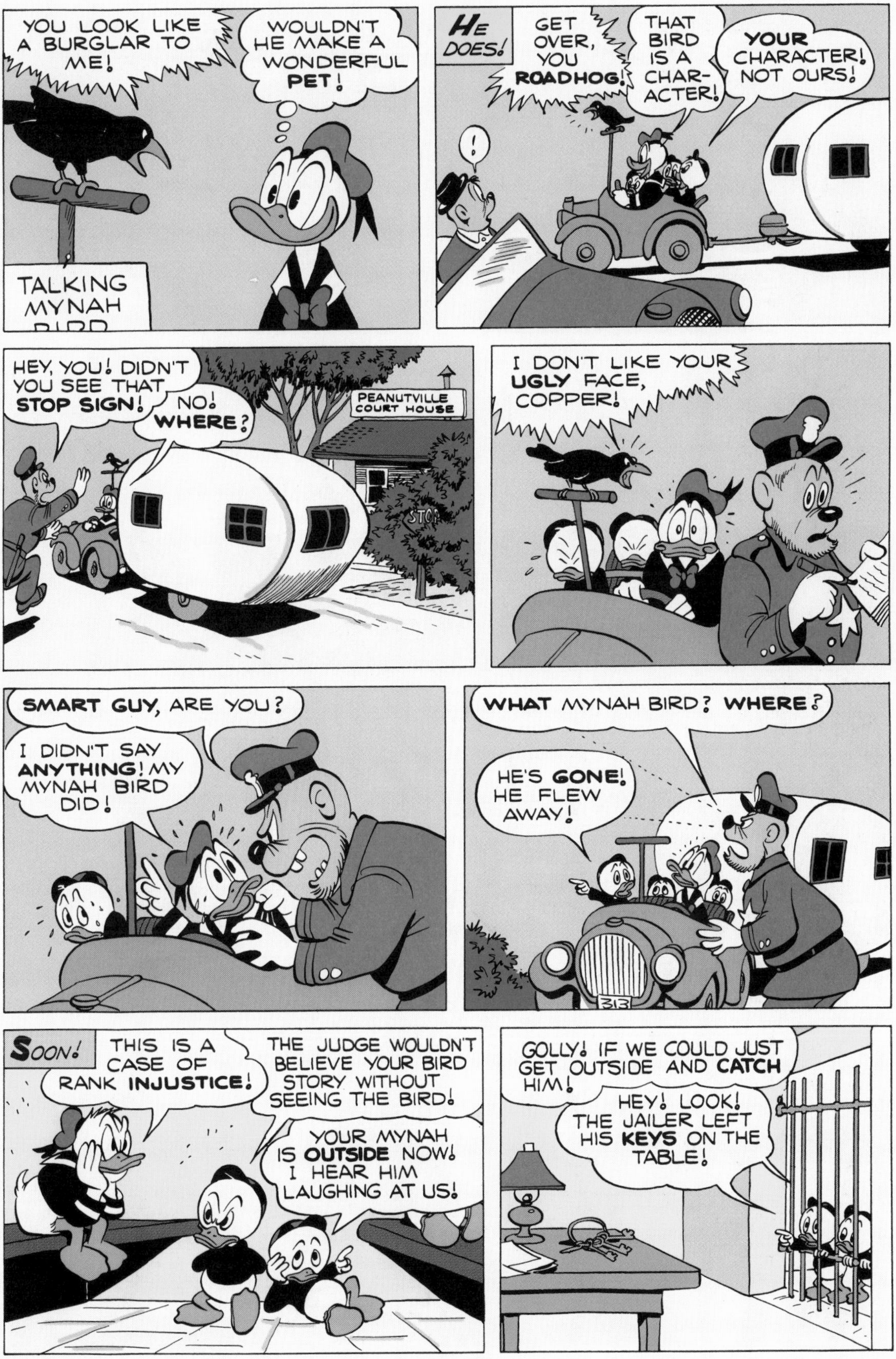
YOU LOOK LIKE A BURGLAR TO ME!
WOULDN'T HE MAKE A WONDERFUL **PET**!
TALKING MYNAH
HE DOES!
GET OVER, YOU **ROADHOG**!
THAT BIRD IS A CHARACTER!
YOUR CHARACTER! NOT OURS!
!
HEY, YOU! DIDN'T YOU SEE THAT **STOP SIGN**!
NO! **WHERE**?
PEANUTVILLE COURT HOUSE
STOP
I DON'T LIKE YOUR **UGLY** FACE, COPPER!
SMART GUY, ARE YOU?
I DIDN'T SAY **ANYTHING**! MY MYNAH BIRD DID!
WHAT MYNAH BIRD? **WHERE**?
HE'S **GONE**! HE FLEW AWAY!
313
SOON!
THIS IS A CASE OF RANK **INJUSTICE**!
THE JUDGE WOULDN'T BELIEVE YOUR BIRD STORY WITHOUT SEEING THE BIRD!
YOUR MYNAH IS **OUTSIDE** NOW! I HEAR HIM LAUGHING AT US!
GOLLY! IF WE COULD JUST GET OUTSIDE AND **CATCH** HIM!
HEY! LOOK! THE JAILER LEFT HIS **KEYS** ON THE TABLE!

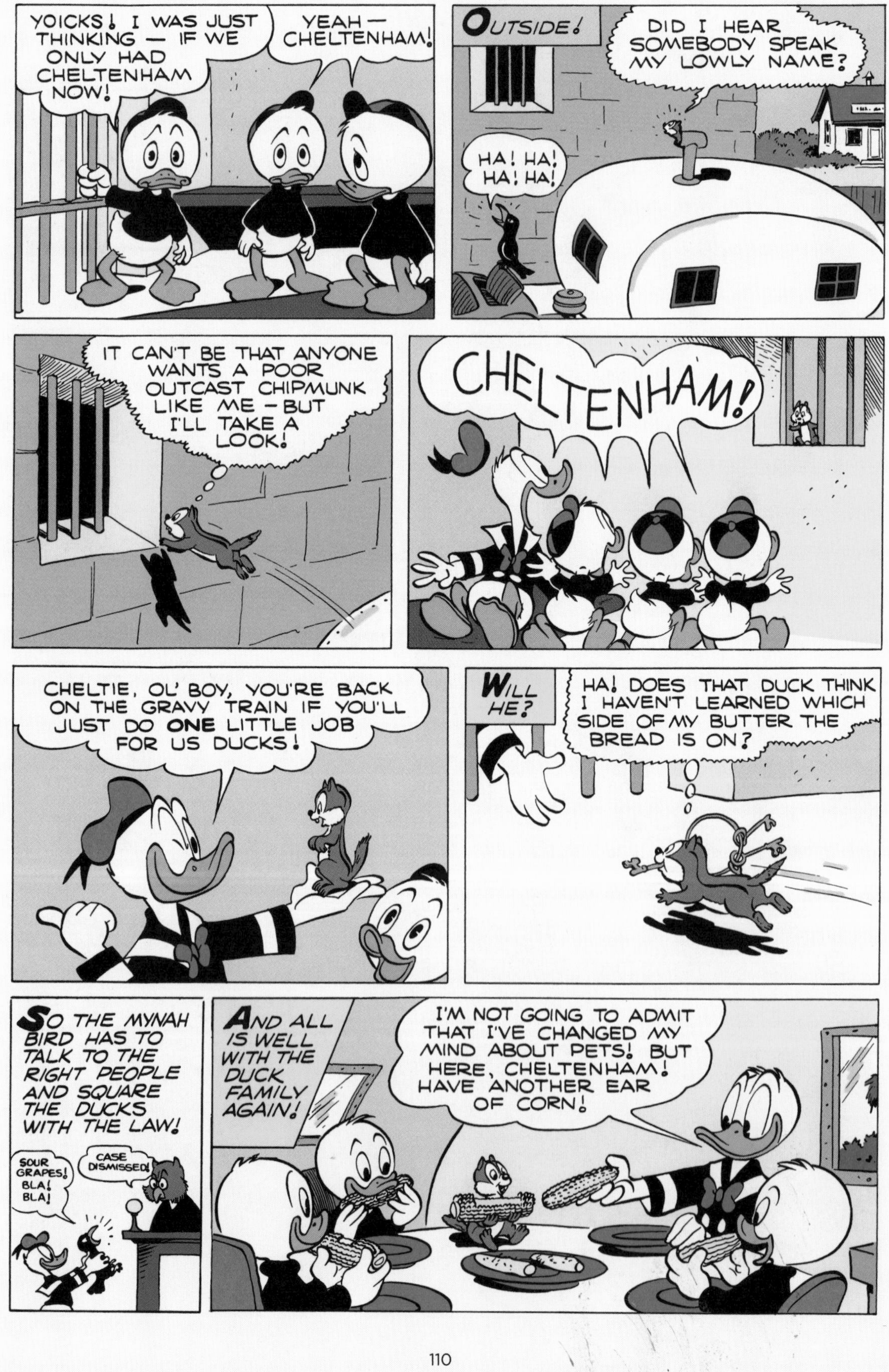
YOICKS! I WAS JUST THINKING — IF WE ONLY HAD CHELTENHAM NOW!
YEAH — CHELTENHAM!
OUTSIDE!
DID I HEAR SOMEBODY SPEAK MY LOWLY NAME?
HA! HA! HA! HA!
IT CAN'T BE THAT ANYONE WANTS A POOR OUTCAST CHIPMUNK LIKE ME — BUT I'LL TAKE A LOOK!
CHELTENHAM!
CHELTIE, OL' BOY, YOU'RE BACK ON THE GRAVY TRAIN IF YOU'LL JUST DO ONE LITTLE JOB FOR US DUCKS!
WILL HE?
HA! DOES THAT DUCK THINK I HAVEN'T LEARNED WHICH SIDE OF MY BUTTER THE BREAD IS ON?
SO THE MYNAH BIRD HAS TO TALK TO THE RIGHT PEOPLE AND SQUARE THE DUCKS WITH THE LAW!
SOUR GRAPES! BLA! BLA!
CASE DISMISSED!
AND ALL IS WELL WITH THE DUCK FAMILY AGAIN!
I'M NOT GOING TO ADMIT THAT I'VE CHANGED MY MIND ABOUT PETS! BUT HERE, CHELTENHAM! HAVE ANOTHER EAR OF CORN!

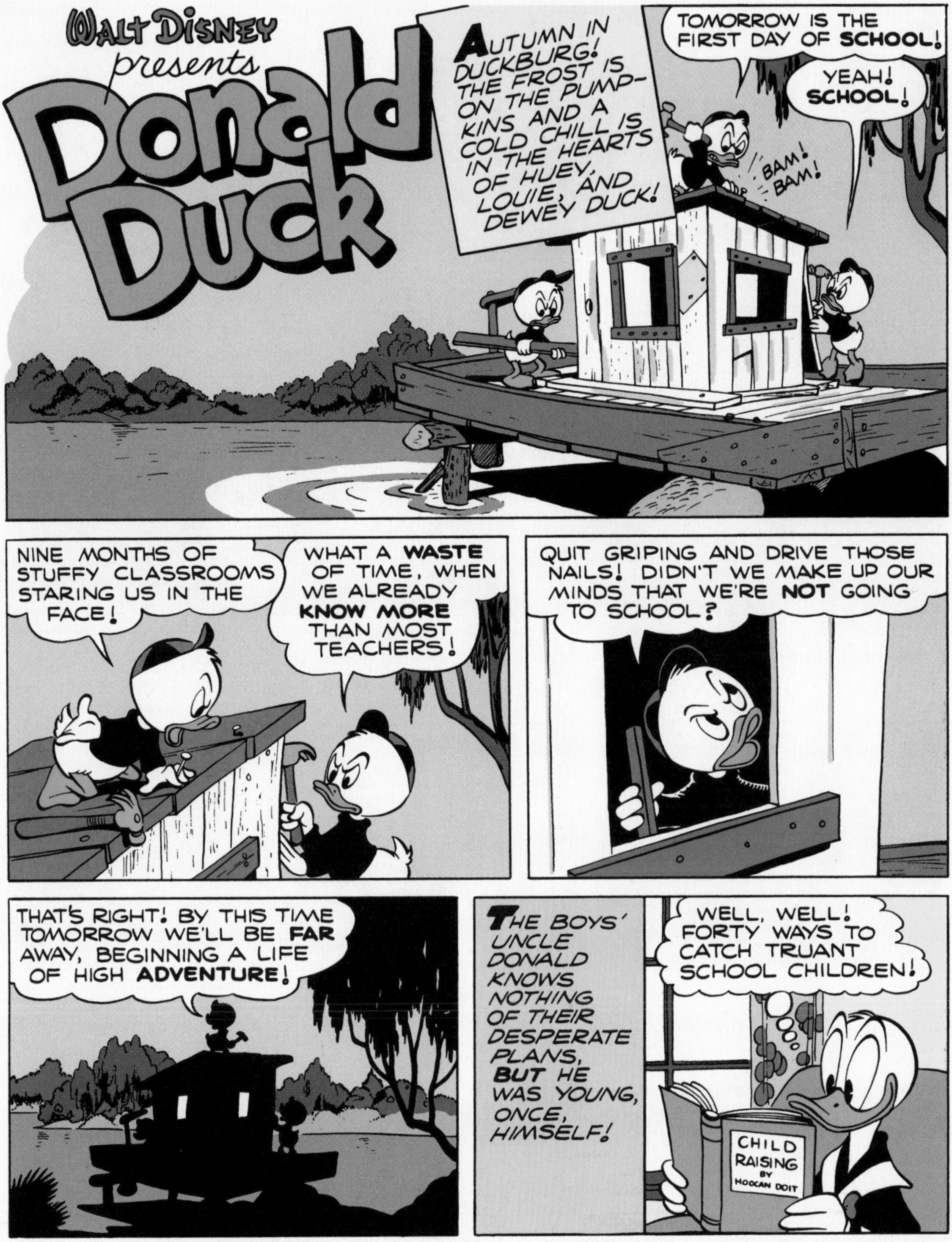
WALT DISNEY
presents
Donald Duck
AUTUMN IN DUCKBURG! THE FROST IS ON THE PUMPKINS AND A COLD CHILL IS IN THE HEARTS OF HUEY, LOUIE, AND DEWEY DUCK!
TOMORROW IS THE FIRST DAY OF SCHOOL!
YEAH! SCHOOL!
BAM! BAM!
NINE MONTHS OF STUFFY CLASSROOMS STARING US IN THE FACE!
WHAT A WASTE OF TIME, WHEN WE ALREADY KNOW MORE THAN MOST TEACHERS!
QUIT GRIPING AND DRIVE THOSE NAILS! DIDN'T WE MAKE UP OUR MINDS THAT WE'RE NOT GOING TO SCHOOL?
THAT'S RIGHT! BY THIS TIME TOMORROW WE'LL BE FAR AWAY, BEGINNING A LIFE OF HIGH ADVENTURE!
THE BOYS' UNCLE DONALD KNOWS NOTHING OF THEIR DESPERATE PLANS, BUT HE WAS YOUNG, ONCE, HIMSELF!
WELL, WELL! FORTY WAYS TO CATCH TRUANT SCHOOL CHILDREN!
CHILD RAISING BY HOOCAN DOIT

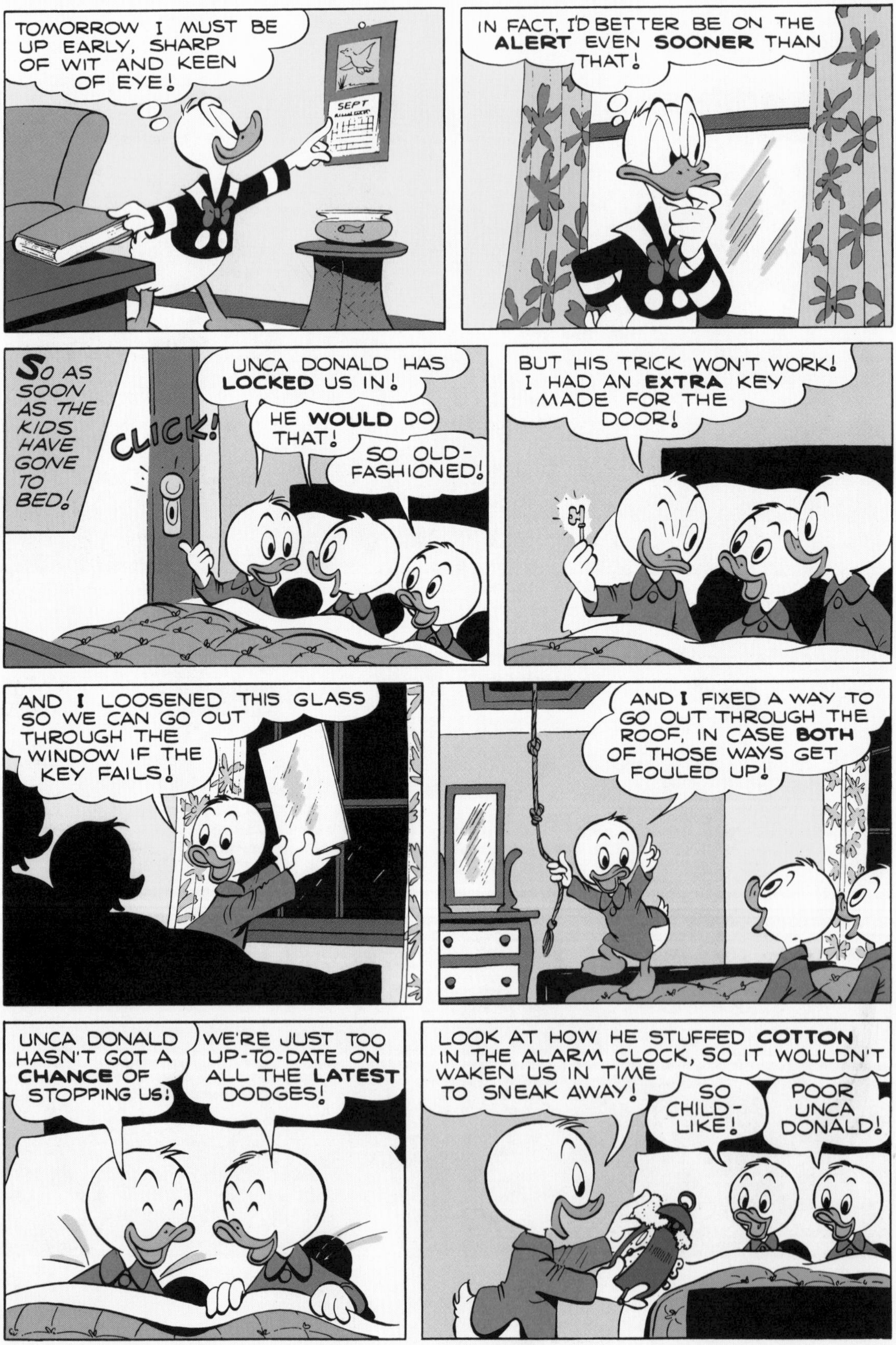
TOMORROW I MUST BE UP EARLY, SHARP OF WIT AND KEEN OF EYE!
SEPT
IN FACT, I'D BETTER BE ON THE ALERT EVEN SOONER THAN THAT!
SO AS SOON AS THE KIDS HAVE GONE TO BED!
CLICK!
UNCA DONALD HAS LOCKED US IN!
HE WOULD DO THAT!
SO OLD-FASHIONED!
BUT HIS TRICK WON'T WORK! I HAD AN EXTRA KEY MADE FOR THE DOOR!
AND I LOOSENED THIS GLASS SO WE CAN GO OUT THROUGH THE WINDOW IF THE KEY FAILS!
AND I FIXED A WAY TO GO OUT THROUGH THE ROOF, IN CASE BOTH OF THOSE WAYS GET FOULED UP!
UNCA DONALD HASN'T GOT A CHANCE OF STOPPING US!
WE'RE JUST TOO UP-TO-DATE ON ALL THE LATEST DODGES!
LOOK AT HOW HE STUFFED COTTON IN THE ALARM CLOCK, SO IT WOULDN'T WAKEN US IN TIME TO SNEAK AWAY!
SO CHILD-LIKE!
POOR UNCA DONALD!

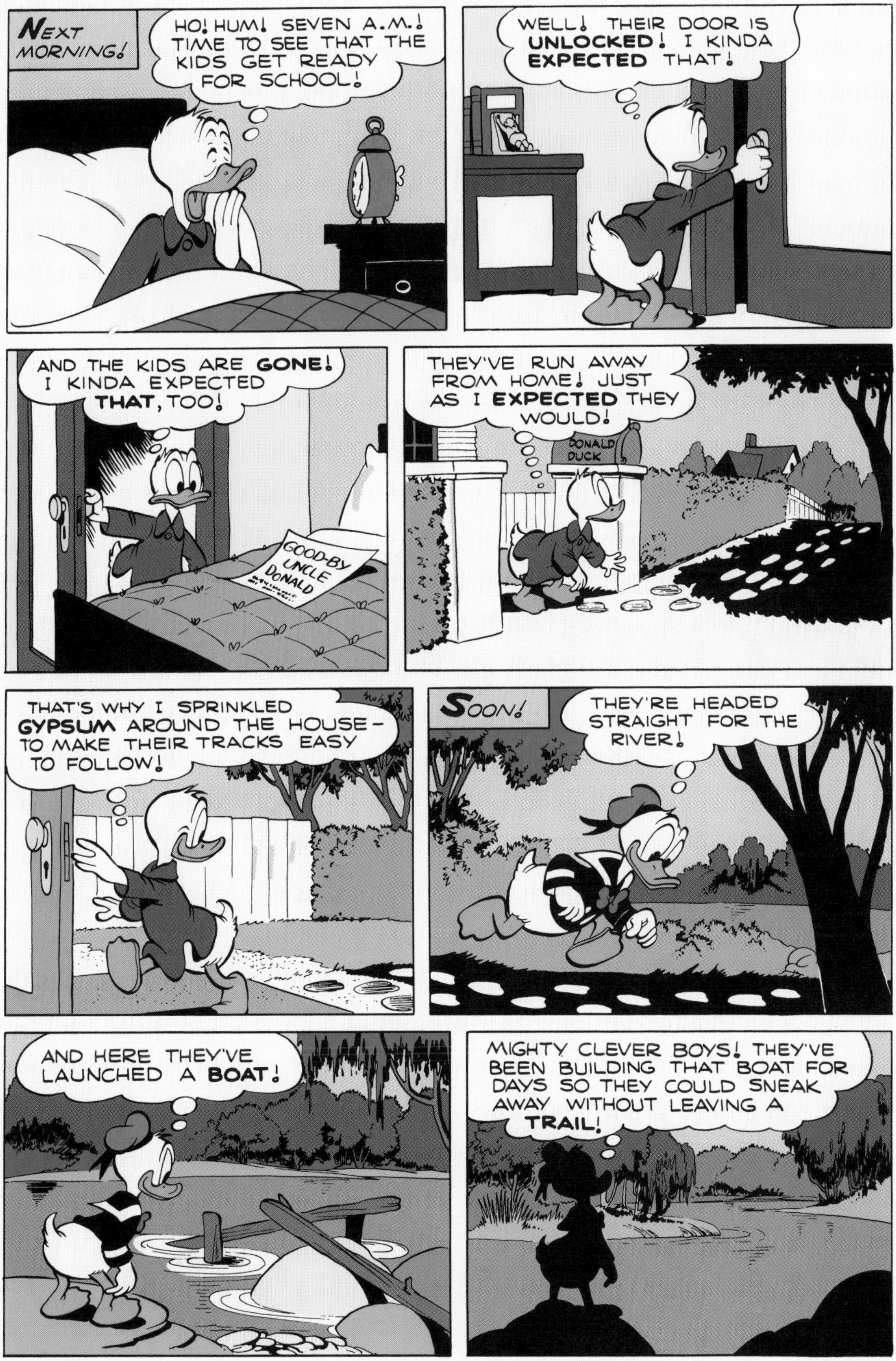
NEXT MORNING!
HO! HUM! SEVEN A.M.! TIME TO SEE THAT THE KIDS GET READY FOR SCHOOL!
WELL! THEIR DOOR IS UNLOCKED! I KINDA EXPECTED THAT!
AND THE KIDS ARE GONE! I KINDA EXPECTED THAT, TOO!
GOOD-BY UNCLE DONALD
THEY'VE RUN AWAY FROM HOME! JUST AS I EXPECTED THEY WOULD!
DONALD DUCK
THAT'S WHY I SPRINKLED GYPSUM AROUND THE HOUSE— TO MAKE THEIR TRACKS EASY TO FOLLOW!
SOON!
THEY'RE HEADED STRAIGHT FOR THE RIVER!
AND HERE THEY'VE LAUNCHED A BOAT!
MIGHTY CLEVER BOYS! THEY'VE BEEN BUILDING THAT BOAT FOR DAYS SO THEY COULD SNEAK AWAY WITHOUT LEAVING A TRAIL!

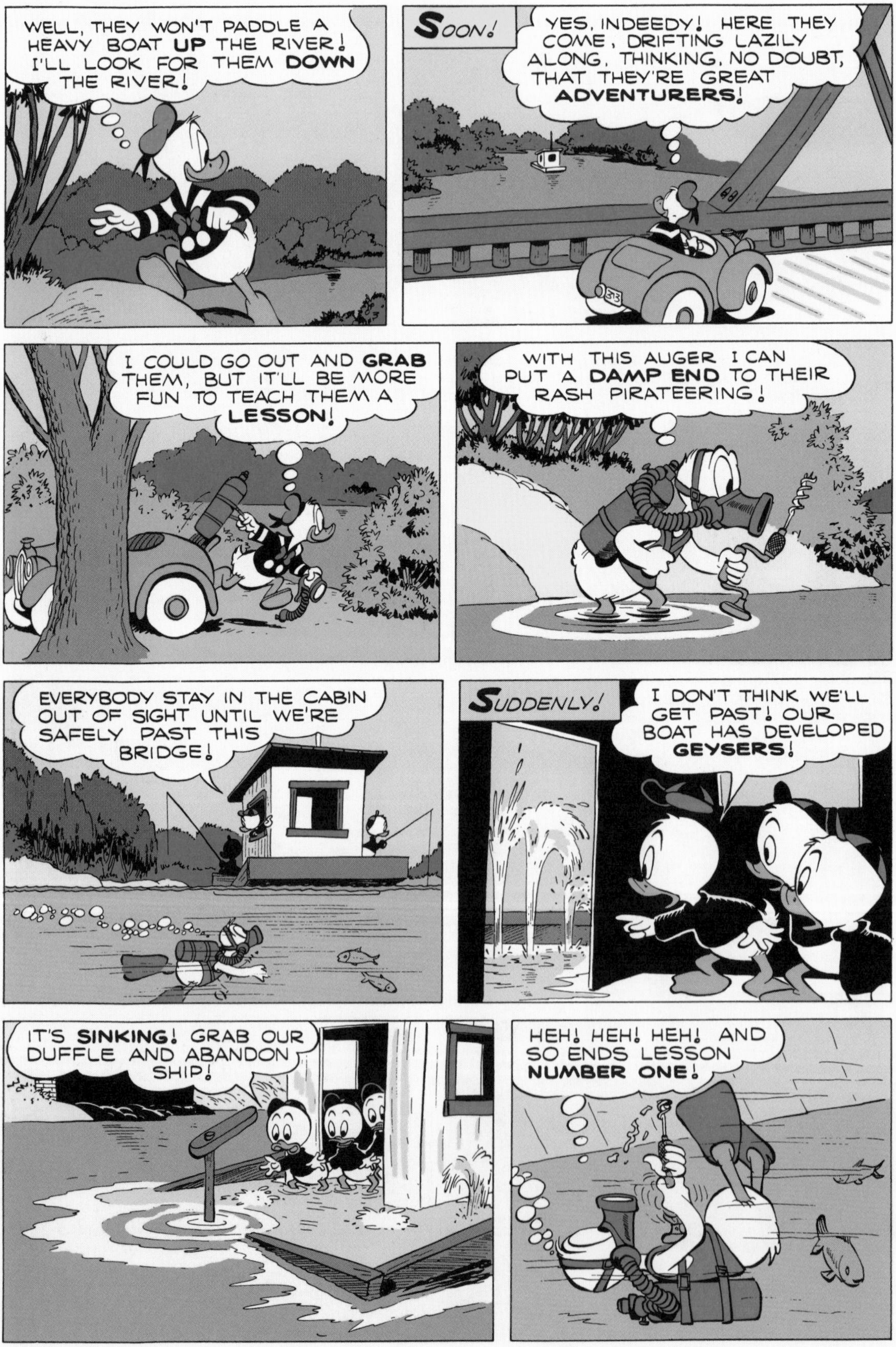
WELL, THEY WON'T PADDLE A HEAVY BOAT **UP** THE RIVER! I'LL LOOK FOR THEM **DOWN** THE RIVER!
SOON!
YES, INDEEDY! HERE THEY COME, DRIFTING LAZILY ALONG, THINKING, NO DOUBT, THAT THEY'RE GREAT **ADVENTURERS**!
I COULD GO OUT AND **GRAB** THEM, BUT IT'LL BE MORE FUN TO TEACH THEM A **LESSON**!
WITH THIS AUGER I CAN PUT A **DAMP END** TO THEIR RASH PIRATEERING!
EVERYBODY STAY IN THE CABIN OUT OF SIGHT UNTIL WE'RE SAFELY PAST THIS BRIDGE!
SUDDENLY!
I DON'T THINK WE'LL GET PAST! OUR BOAT HAS DEVELOPED **GEYSERS**!
IT'S **SINKING**! GRAB OUR DUFFLE AND ABANDON SHIP!
HEH! HEH! HEH! AND SO ENDS LESSON **NUMBER ONE**!

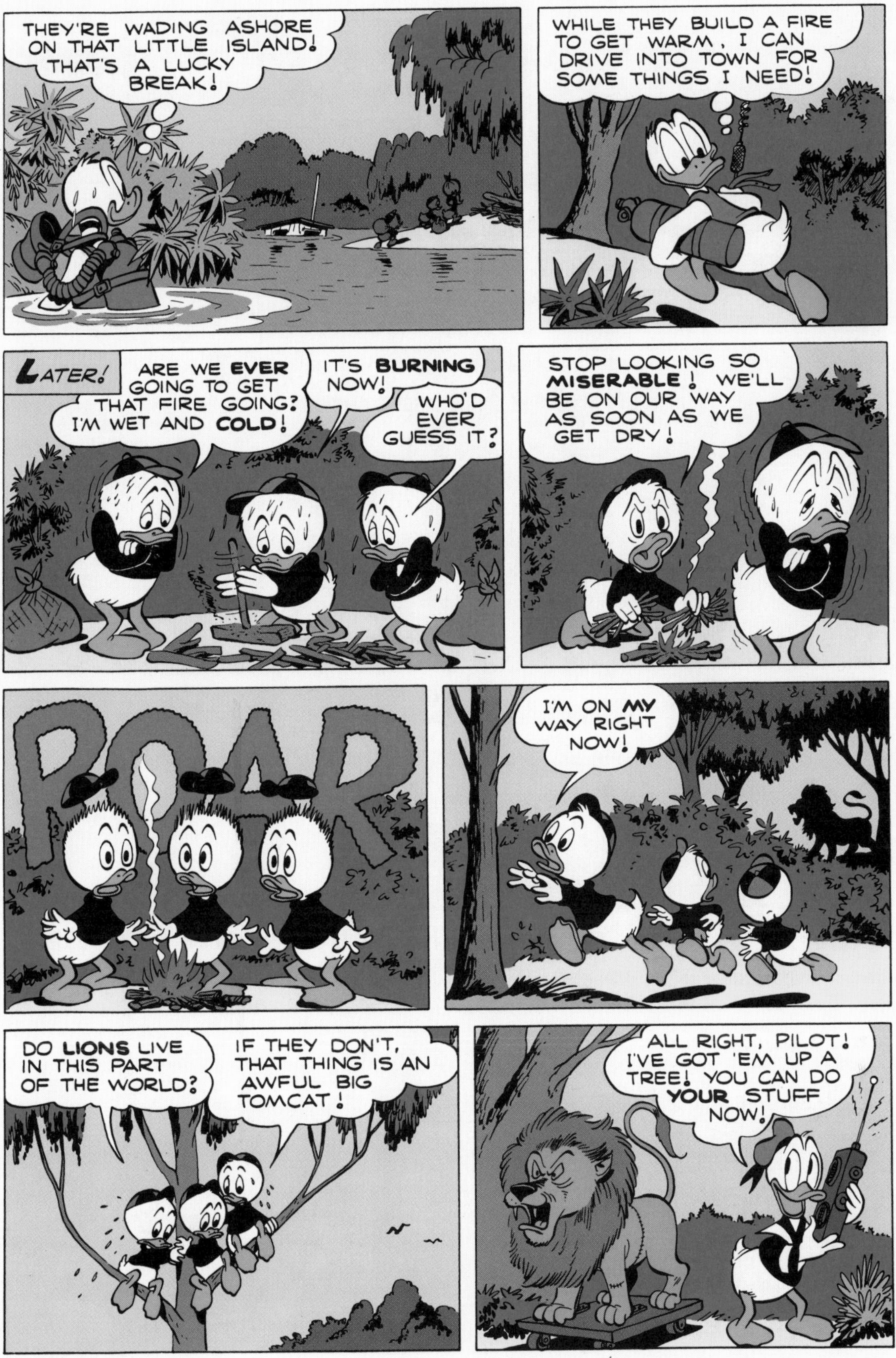
THEY'RE WADING ASHORE ON THAT LITTLE ISLAND! THAT'S A LUCKY BREAK!
WHILE THEY BUILD A FIRE TO GET WARM, I CAN DRIVE INTO TOWN FOR SOME THINGS I NEED!
LATER!
ARE WE EVER GOING TO GET THAT FIRE GOING? I'M WET AND COLD!
IT'S BURNING NOW!
WHO'D EVER GUESS IT?
STOP LOOKING SO MISERABLE! WE'LL BE ON OUR WAY AS SOON AS WE GET DRY!
ROAR
I'M ON MY WAY RIGHT NOW!
DO LIONS LIVE IN THIS PART OF THE WORLD?
IF THEY DON'T, THAT THING IS AN AWFUL BIG TOMCAT!
ALL RIGHT, PILOT! I'VE GOT 'EM UP A TREE! YOU CAN DO YOUR STUFF NOW!

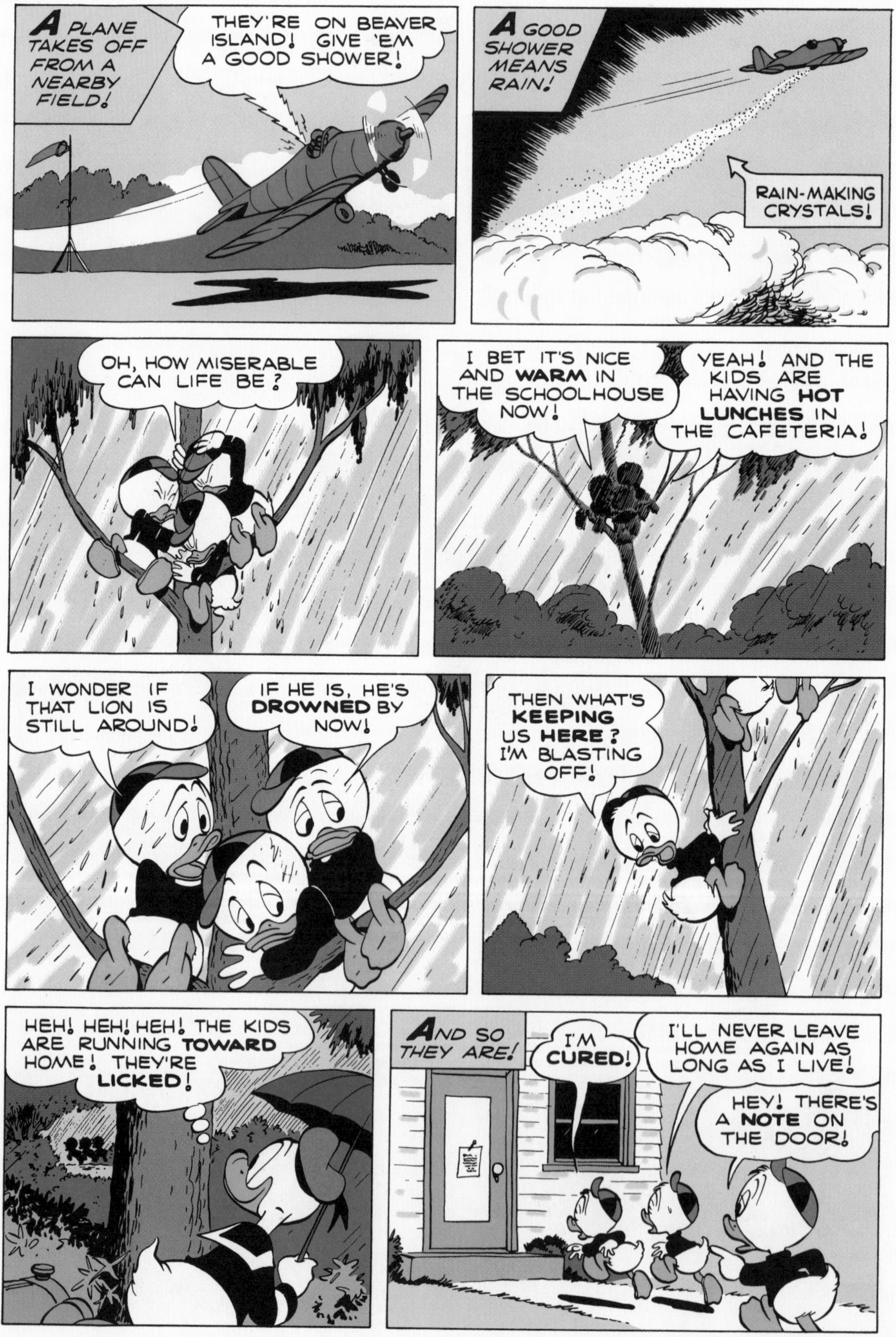
A PLANE TAKES OFF FROM A NEARBY FIELD!
THEY'RE ON BEAVER ISLAND! GIVE 'EM A GOOD SHOWER!
A GOOD SHOWER MEANS RAIN!
RAIN-MAKING CRYSTALS!
OH, HOW MISERABLE CAN LIFE BE?
I BET IT'S NICE AND WARM IN THE SCHOOLHOUSE NOW!
YEAH! AND THE KIDS ARE HAVING HOT LUNCHES IN THE CAFETERIA!
I WONDER IF THAT LION IS STILL AROUND!
IF HE IS, HE'S DROWNED BY NOW!
THEN WHAT'S KEEPING US HERE? I'M BLASTING OFF!
HEH! HEH! HEH! THE KIDS ARE RUNNING TOWARD HOME! THEY'RE LICKED!
AND SO THEY ARE!
I'M CURED!
I'LL NEVER LEAVE HOME AGAIN AS LONG AS I LIVE!
HEY! THERE'S A NOTE ON THE DOOR!

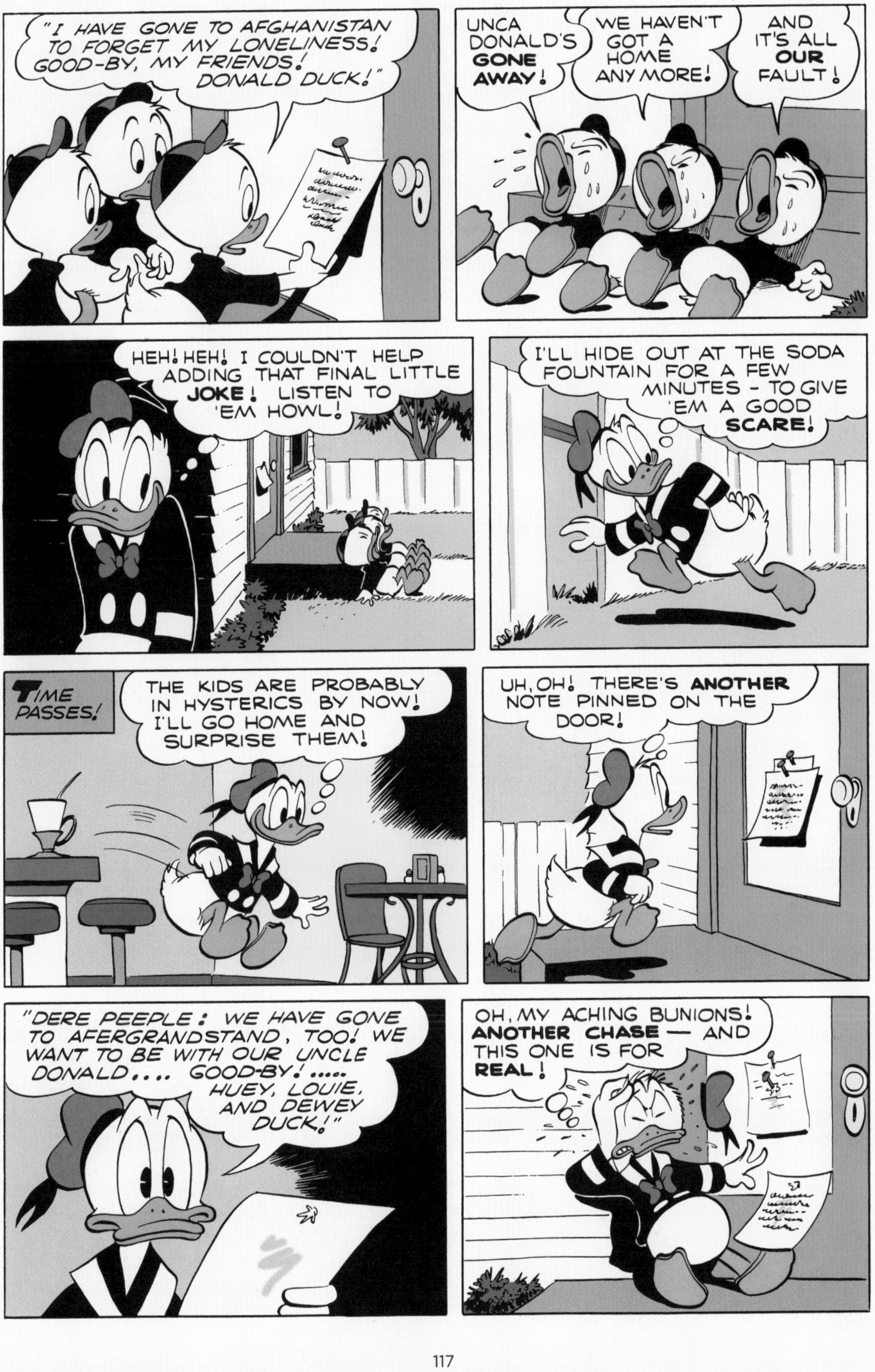
"I HAVE GONE TO AFGHANISTAN TO FORGET MY LONELINESS! GOOD-BY, MY FRIENDS! DONALD DUCK!"
UNCA DONALD'S GONE AWAY!
WE HAVEN'T GOT A HOME ANY MORE!
AND IT'S ALL OUR FAULT!
HEH! HEH! I COULDN'T HELP ADDING THAT FINAL LITTLE JOKE! LISTEN TO 'EM HOWL!
I'LL HIDE OUT AT THE SODA FOUNTAIN FOR A FEW MINUTES - TO GIVE 'EM A GOOD SCARE!
TIME PASSES!
THE KIDS ARE PROBABLY IN HYSTERICS BY NOW! I'LL GO HOME AND SURPRISE THEM!
UH, OH! THERE'S ANOTHER NOTE PINNED ON THE DOOR!
"DERE PEEPLE: WE HAVE GONE TO AFERGRANDSTAND, TOO! WE WANT TO BE WITH OUR UNCLE DONALD.... GOOD-BY!..... HUEY, LOUIE, AND DEWEY DUCK!"
OH, MY ACHING BUNIONS! ANOTHER CHASE — AND THIS ONE IS FOR REAL!

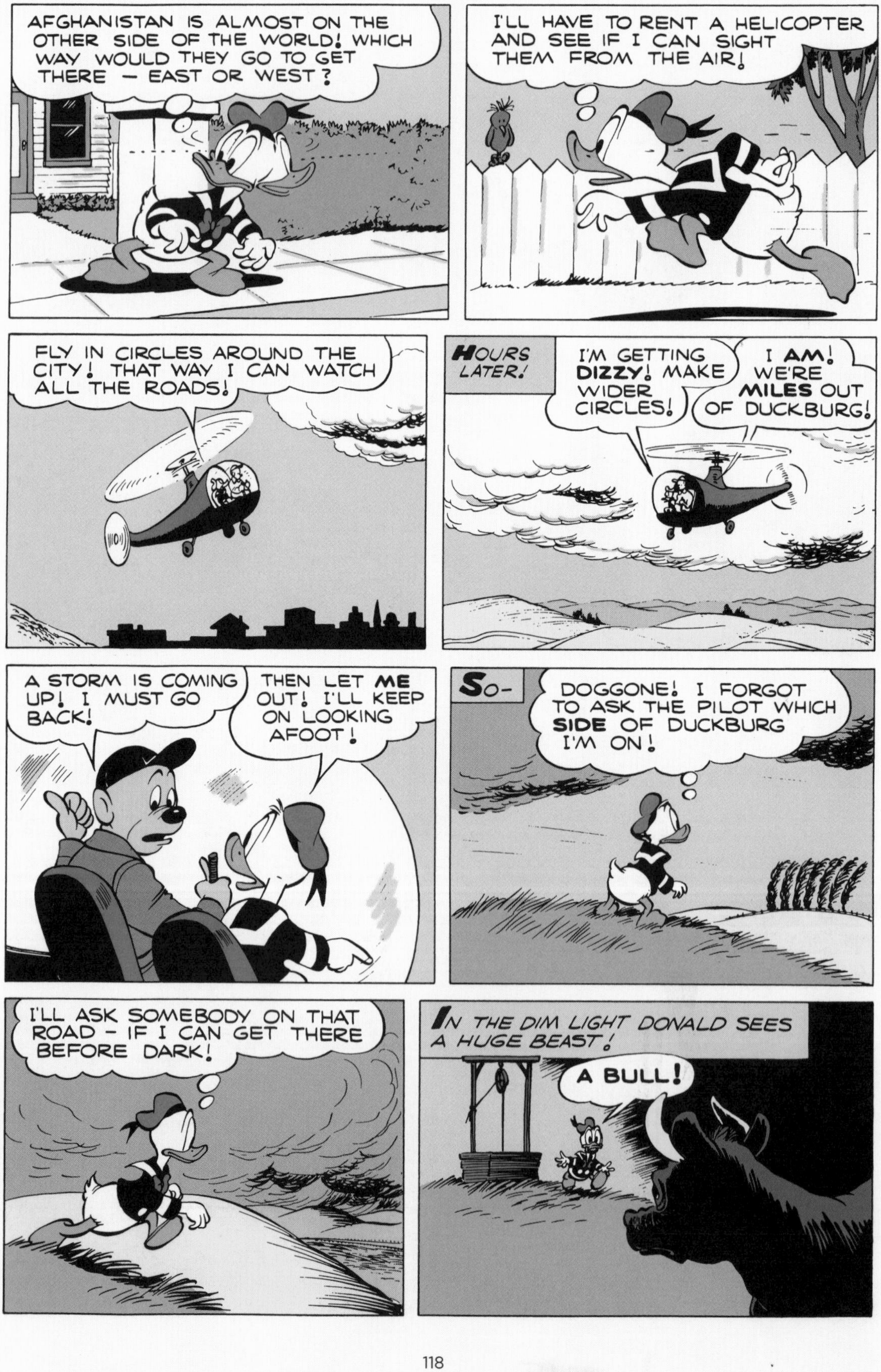
AFGHANISTAN IS ALMOST ON THE OTHER SIDE OF THE WORLD! WHICH WAY WOULD THEY GO TO GET THERE – EAST OR WEST?
I'LL HAVE TO RENT A HELICOPTER AND SEE IF I CAN SIGHT THEM FROM THE AIR!
FLY IN CIRCLES AROUND THE CITY! THAT WAY I CAN WATCH ALL THE ROADS!
HOURS LATER!
I'M GETTING DIZZY! MAKE WIDER CIRCLES!
I AM! WE'RE MILES OUT OF DUCKBURG!
A STORM IS COMING UP! I MUST GO BACK!
THEN LET ME OUT! I'LL KEEP ON LOOKING AFOOT!
SO-
DOGGONE! I FORGOT TO ASK THE PILOT WHICH SIDE OF DUCKBURG I'M ON!
I'LL ASK SOMEBODY ON THAT ROAD – IF I CAN GET THERE BEFORE DARK!
IN THE DIM LIGHT DONALD SEES A HUGE BEAST!
A BULL!

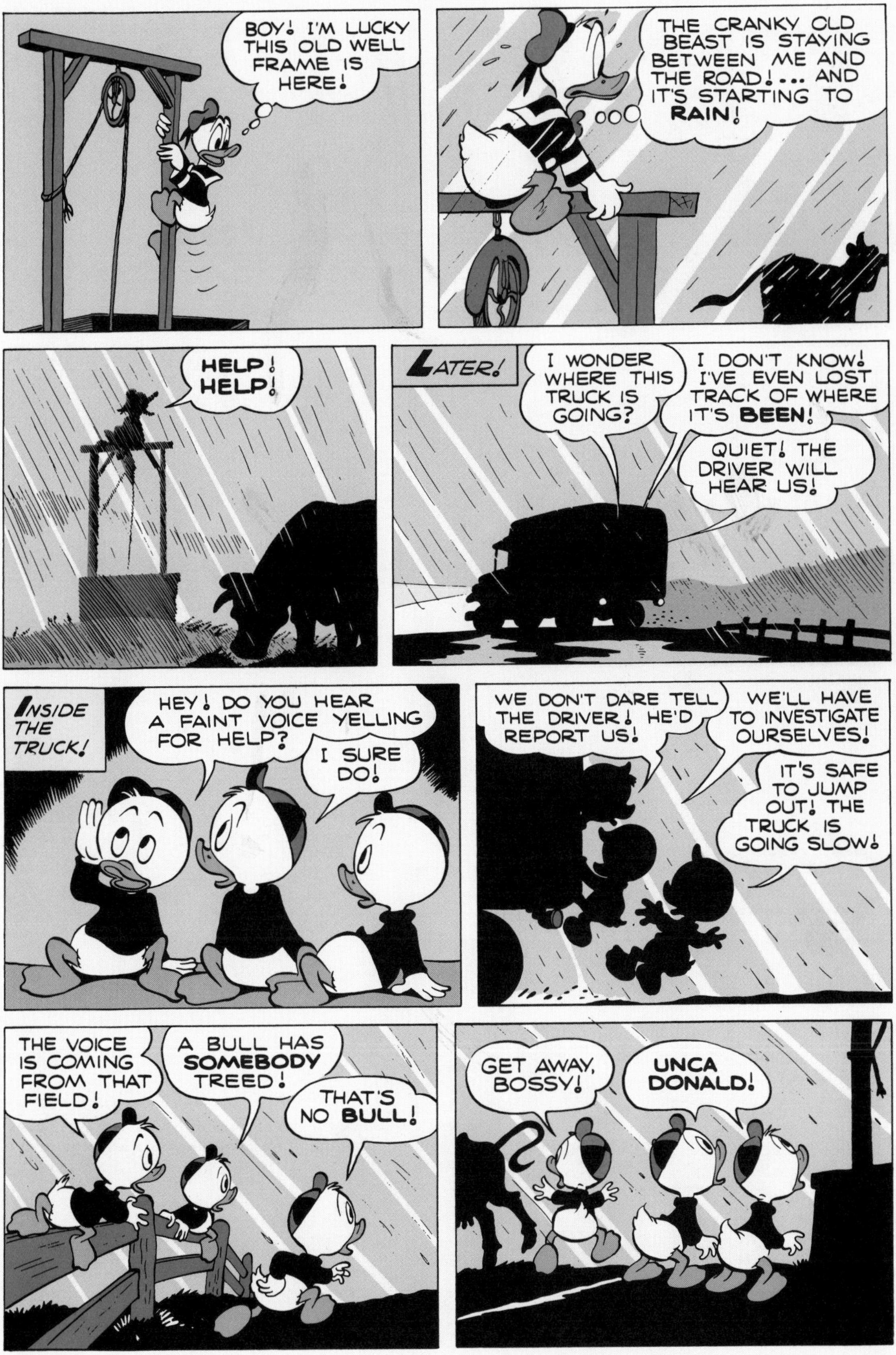
BOY! I'M LUCKY THIS OLD WELL FRAME IS HERE!
THE CRANKY OLD BEAST IS STAYING BETWEEN ME AND THE ROAD! ... AND IT'S STARTING TO RAIN!
HELP! HELP!
LATER!
I WONDER WHERE THIS TRUCK IS GOING?
I DON'T KNOW! I'VE EVEN LOST TRACK OF WHERE IT'S BEEN!
QUIET! THE DRIVER WILL HEAR US!
INSIDE THE TRUCK!
HEY! DO YOU HEAR A FAINT VOICE YELLING FOR HELP?
I SURE DO!
WE DON'T DARE TELL THE DRIVER! HE'D REPORT US!
WE'LL HAVE TO INVESTIGATE OURSELVES!
IT'S SAFE TO JUMP OUT! THE TRUCK IS GOING SLOW!
THE VOICE IS COMING FROM THAT FIELD!
A BULL HAS SOMEBODY TREED!
THAT'S NO BULL!
GET AWAY, BOSSY!
UNCA DONALD!

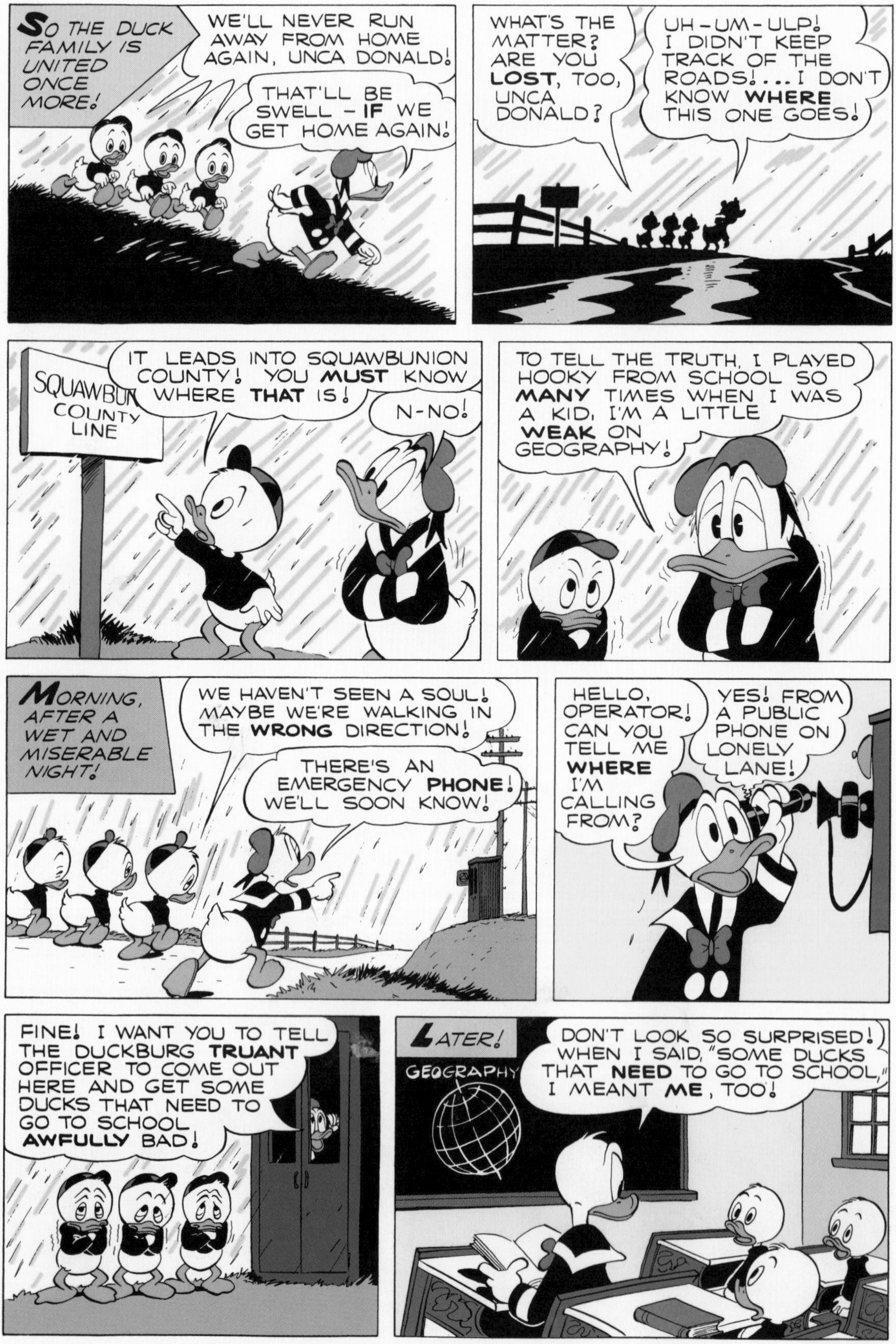
SO THE DUCK FAMILY IS UNITED ONCE MORE!
WE'LL NEVER RUN AWAY FROM HOME AGAIN, UNCA DONALD!
THAT'LL BE SWELL – IF WE GET HOME AGAIN!
WHAT'S THE MATTER? ARE YOU LOST, TOO, UNCA DONALD?
UH – UM – ULP! I DIDN'T KEEP TRACK OF THE ROADS! ... I DON'T KNOW WHERE THIS ONE GOES!
SQUAWBUN COUNTY LINE
IT LEADS INTO SQUAWBUNION COUNTY! YOU MUST KNOW WHERE THAT IS!
N-NO!
TO TELL THE TRUTH, I PLAYED HOOKY FROM SCHOOL SO MANY TIMES WHEN I WAS A KID, I'M A LITTLE WEAK ON GEOGRAPHY!
MORNING, AFTER A WET AND MISERABLE NIGHT!
WE HAVEN'T SEEN A SOUL! MAYBE WE'RE WALKING IN THE WRONG DIRECTION!
THERE'S AN EMERGENCY PHONE! WE'LL SOON KNOW!
HELLO, OPERATOR! CAN YOU TELL ME WHERE I'M CALLING FROM?
YES! FROM A PUBLIC PHONE ON LONELY LANE!
FINE! I WANT YOU TO TELL THE DUCKBURG TRUANT OFFICER TO COME OUT HERE AND GET SOME DUCKS THAT NEED TO GO TO SCHOOL AWFULLY BAD!
LATER!
GEOGRAPHY
DON'T LOOK SO SURPRISED! WHEN I SAID, "SOME DUCKS THAT NEED TO GO TO SCHOOL," I MEANT ME, TOO!

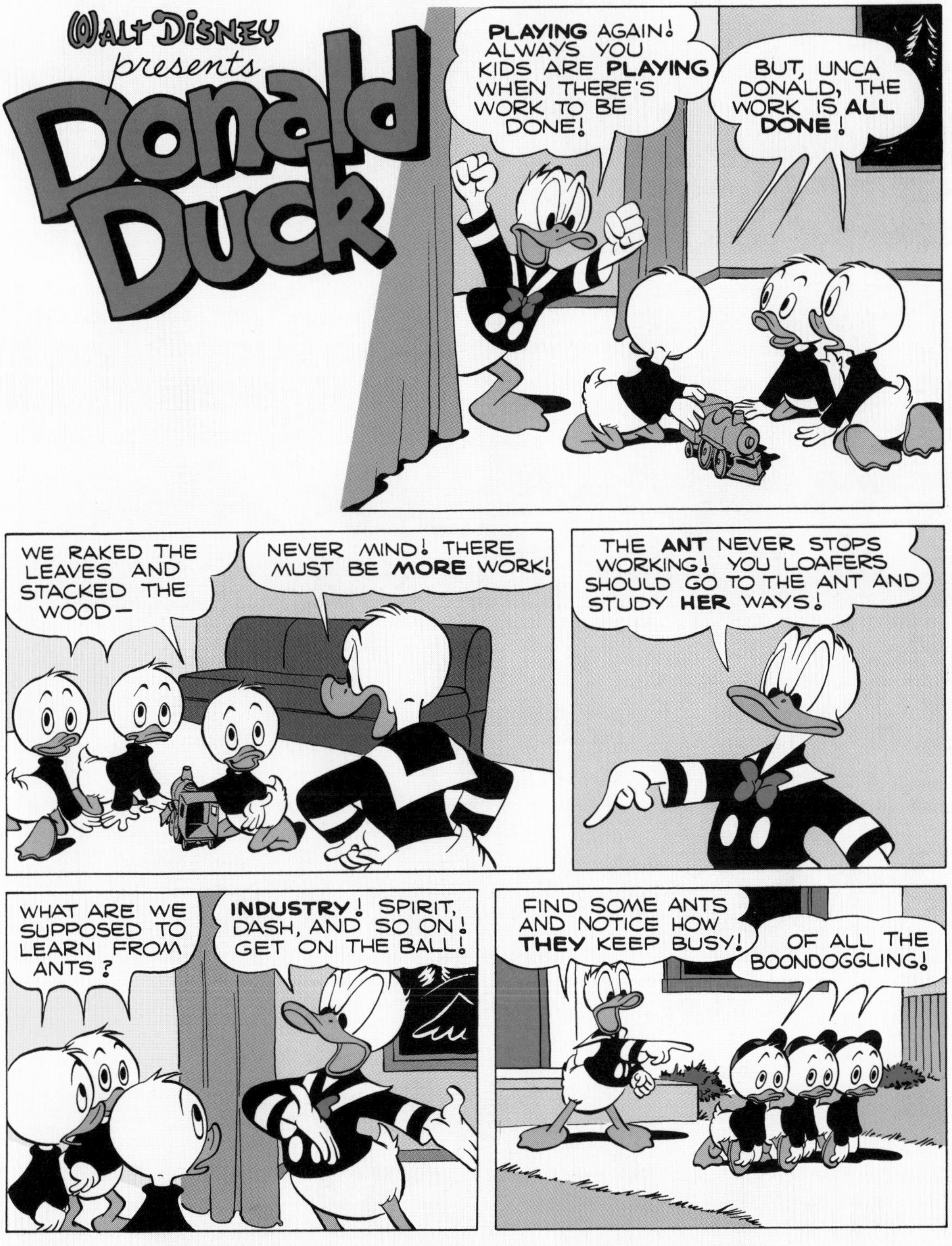
WALT DISNEY presents
Donald Duck
PLAYING AGAIN! ALWAYS YOU KIDS ARE PLAYING WHEN THERE'S WORK TO BE DONE!
BUT, UNCA DONALD, THE WORK IS ALL DONE!
WE RAKED THE LEAVES AND STACKED THE WOOD—
NEVER MIND! THERE MUST BE MORE WORK!
THE ANT NEVER STOPS WORKING! YOU LOAFERS SHOULD GO TO THE ANT AND STUDY HER WAYS!
WHAT ARE WE SUPPOSED TO LEARN FROM ANTS?
INDUSTRY! SPIRIT, DASH, AND SO ON! GET ON THE BALL!
FIND SOME ANTS AND NOTICE HOW THEY KEEP BUSY!
OF ALL THE BOONDOGGLING!

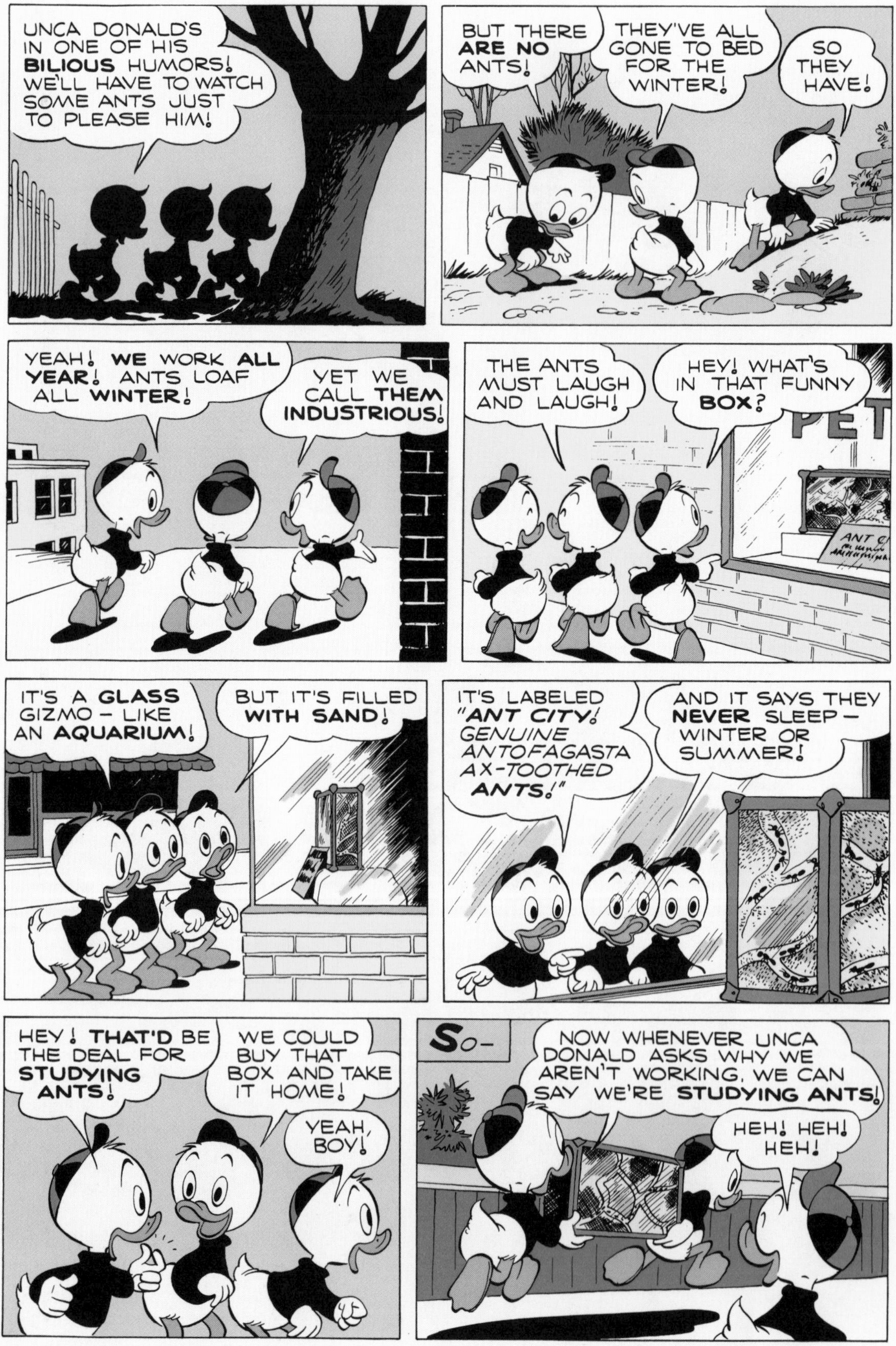
UNCA DONALD'S IN ONE OF HIS BILIOUS HUMORS! WE'LL HAVE TO WATCH SOME ANTS JUST TO PLEASE HIM!
BUT THERE ARE NO ANTS!
THEY'VE ALL GONE TO BED FOR THE WINTER!
SO THEY HAVE!
YEAH! WE WORK ALL YEAR! ANTS LOAF ALL WINTER!
YET WE CALL THEM INDUSTRIOUS!
THE ANTS MUST LAUGH AND LAUGH!
HEY! WHAT'S IN THAT FUNNY BOX?
PET
IT'S A GLASS GIZMO – LIKE AN AQUARIUM!
BUT IT'S FILLED WITH SAND!
IT'S LABELED "ANT CITY! GENUINE ANTOFAGASTA AX-TOOTHED ANTS!"
AND IT SAYS THEY NEVER SLEEP – WINTER OR SUMMER!
HEY! THAT'D BE THE DEAL FOR STUDYING ANTS!
WE COULD BUY THAT BOX AND TAKE IT HOME!
YEAH, BOY!
SO–
NOW WHENEVER UNCA DONALD ASKS WHY WE AREN'T WORKING, WE CAN SAY WE'RE STUDYING ANTS!
HEH! HEH! HEH!

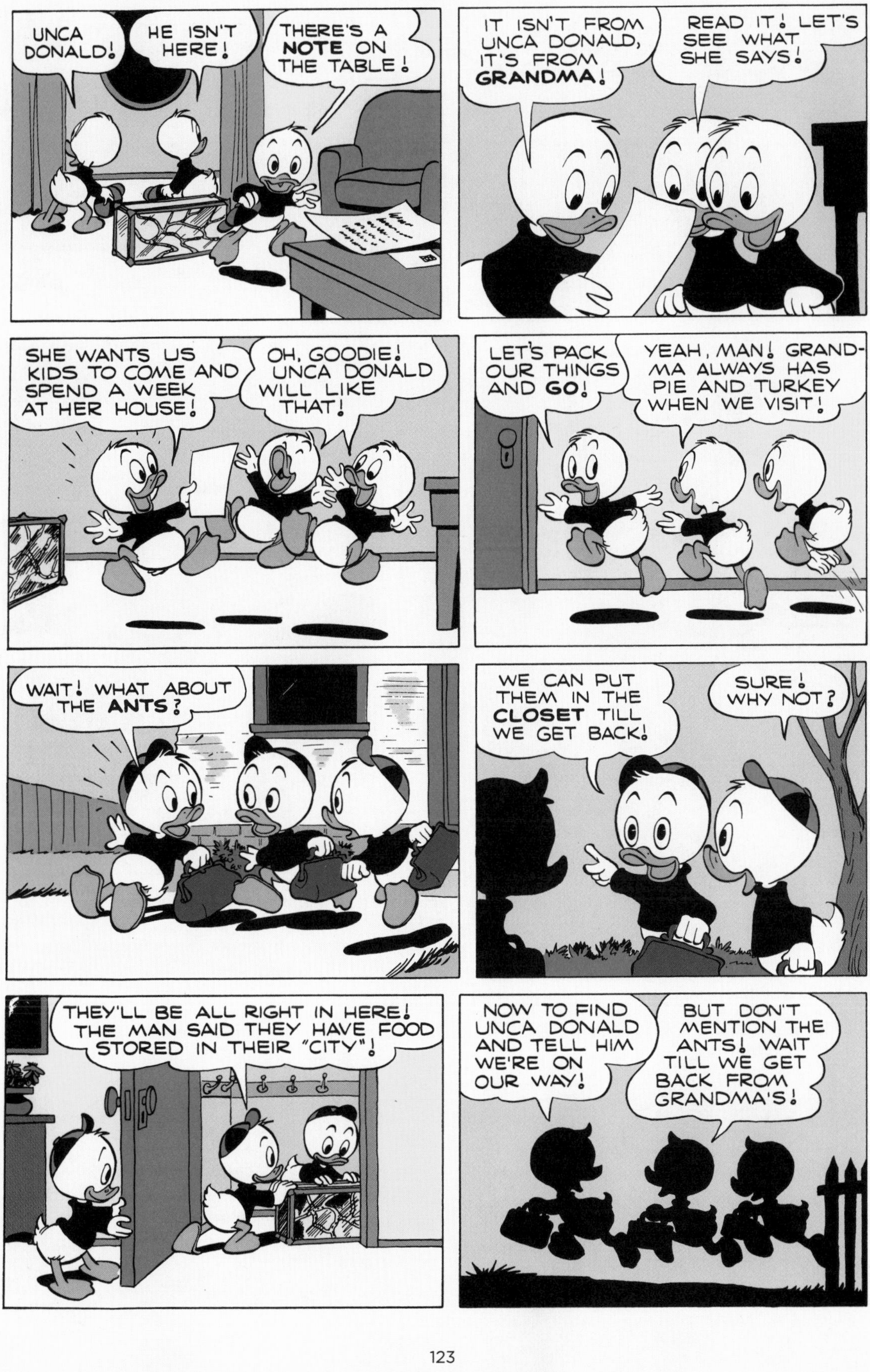
UNCA DONALD!
HE ISN'T HERE!
THERE'S A **NOTE** ON THE TABLE!
IT ISN'T FROM UNCA DONALD, IT'S FROM **GRANDMA**!
READ IT! LET'S SEE WHAT SHE SAYS!
SHE WANTS US KIDS TO COME AND SPEND A WEEK AT HER HOUSE!
OH, GOODIE! UNCA DONALD WILL LIKE THAT!
LET'S PACK OUR THINGS AND **GO**!
YEAH, MAN! GRANDMA ALWAYS HAS PIE AND TURKEY WHEN WE VISIT!
WAIT! WHAT ABOUT THE **ANTS**?
WE CAN PUT THEM IN THE **CLOSET** TILL WE GET BACK!
SURE! WHY NOT?
THEY'LL BE ALL RIGHT IN HERE! THE MAN SAID THEY HAVE FOOD STORED IN THEIR "CITY"!
NOW TO FIND UNCA DONALD AND TELL HIM WE'RE ON OUR WAY!
BUT DON'T MENTION THE ANTS! WAIT TILL WE GET BACK FROM GRANDMA'S!

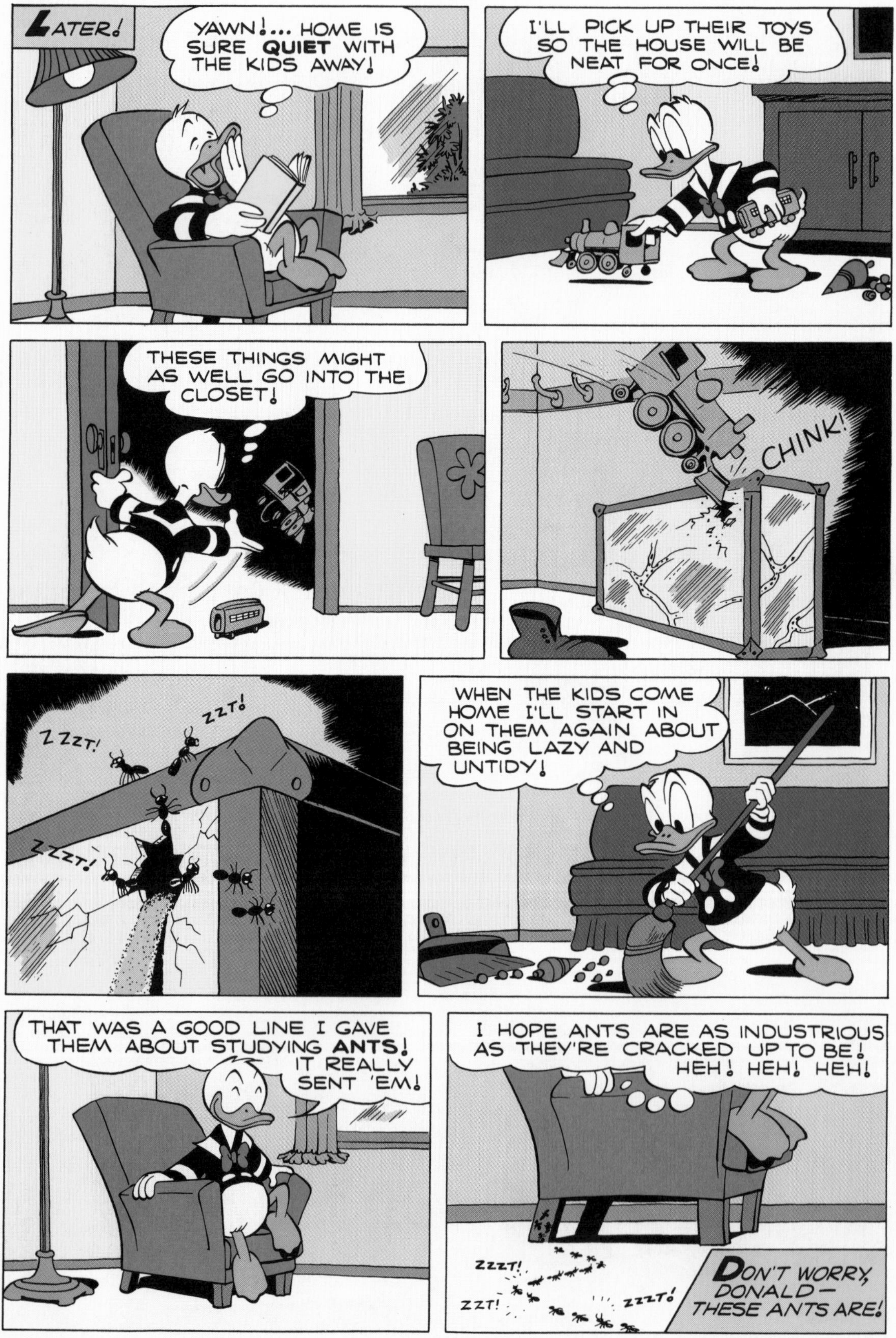
LATER!
YAWN!... HOME IS SURE **QUIET** WITH THE KIDS AWAY!
I'LL PICK UP THEIR TOYS SO THE HOUSE WILL BE NEAT FOR ONCE!
THESE THINGS MIGHT AS WELL GO INTO THE CLOSET!
CHINK!
ZZZT!
ZZT!
ZZZT!
WHEN THE KIDS COME HOME I'LL START IN ON THEM AGAIN ABOUT BEING LAZY AND UNTIDY!
THAT WAS A GOOD LINE I GAVE THEM ABOUT STUDYING **ANTS**! IT REALLY SENT 'EM!
I HOPE ANTS ARE AS INDUSTRIOUS AS THEY'RE CRACKED UP TO BE! HEH! HEH! HEH!
ZZZT!
ZZT!
ZZZT!
DON'T WORRY, DONALD— THESE ANTS ARE!

THE FAVORITE DIET OF THE ANTOFAGASTA AX-TOOTHED ANT IS **WOOD**!

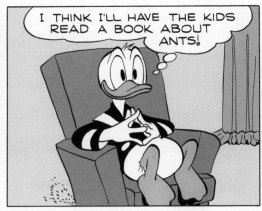

I THINK I'LL HAVE THE KIDS READ A BOOK ABOUT ANTS!

CRASH!

WHAT THE DINGDONG DOOZLEFEATHERS?

OHO! **ANTS**!.....BIG BROAD-CHESTED FELLOWS, TOO!

JUST THE KIND I CAN **SWAT** WITHOUT FEELING THAT I'M A BIG BULLY!

SLAM! BIFF! BAM!

CLONK!

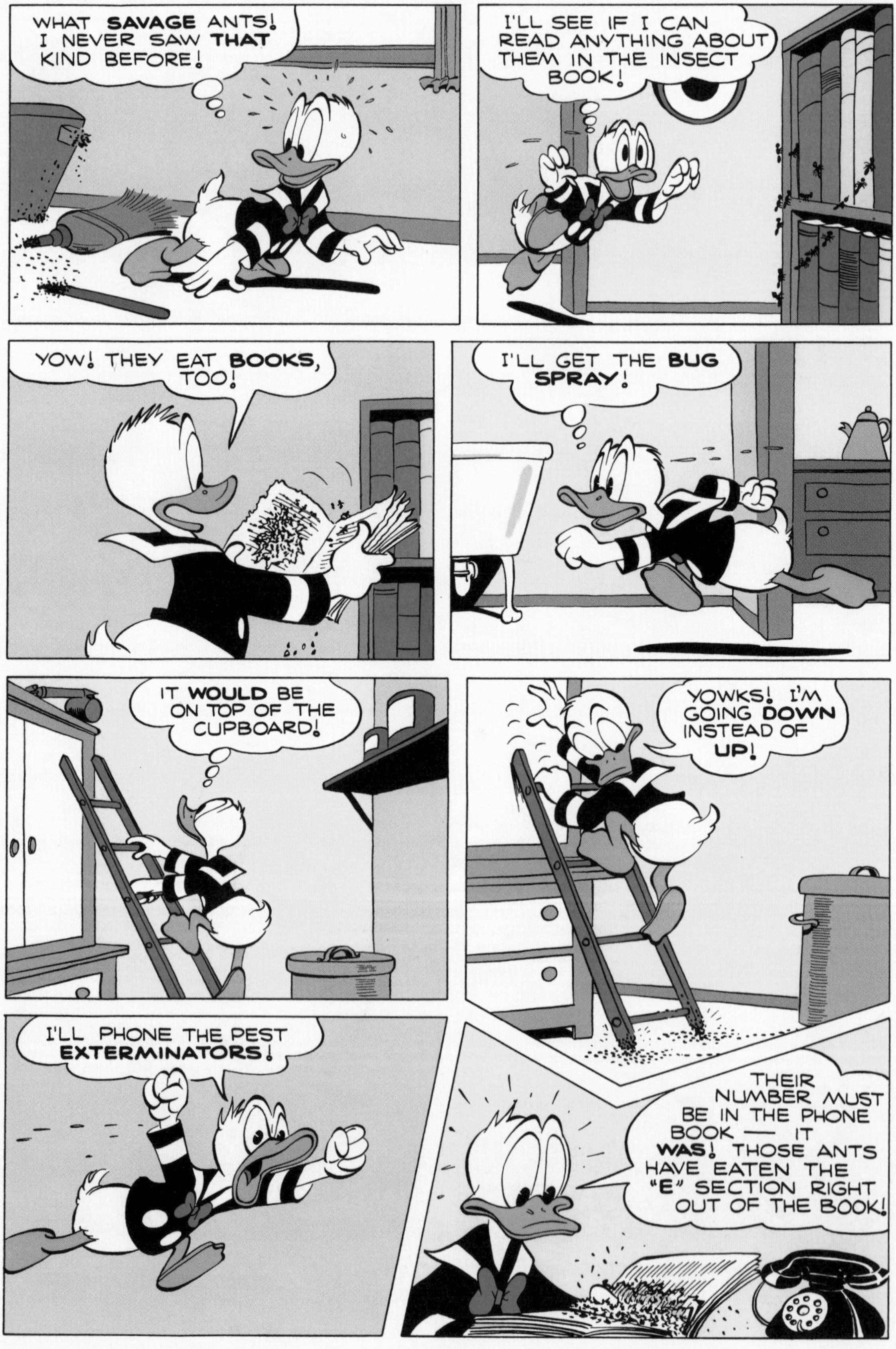

WHAT SAVAGE ANTS! I NEVER SAW THAT KIND BEFORE!
I'LL SEE IF I CAN READ ANYTHING ABOUT THEM IN THE INSECT BOOK!
YOW! THEY EAT BOOKS, TOO!
I'LL GET THE BUG SPRAY!
IT WOULD BE ON TOP OF THE CUPBOARD!
YOWKS! I'M GOING DOWN INSTEAD OF UP!
I'LL PHONE THE PEST EXTERMINATORS!
THEIR NUMBER MUST BE IN THE PHONE BOOK — IT WAS! THOSE ANTS HAVE EATEN THE "E" SECTION RIGHT OUT OF THE BOOK!

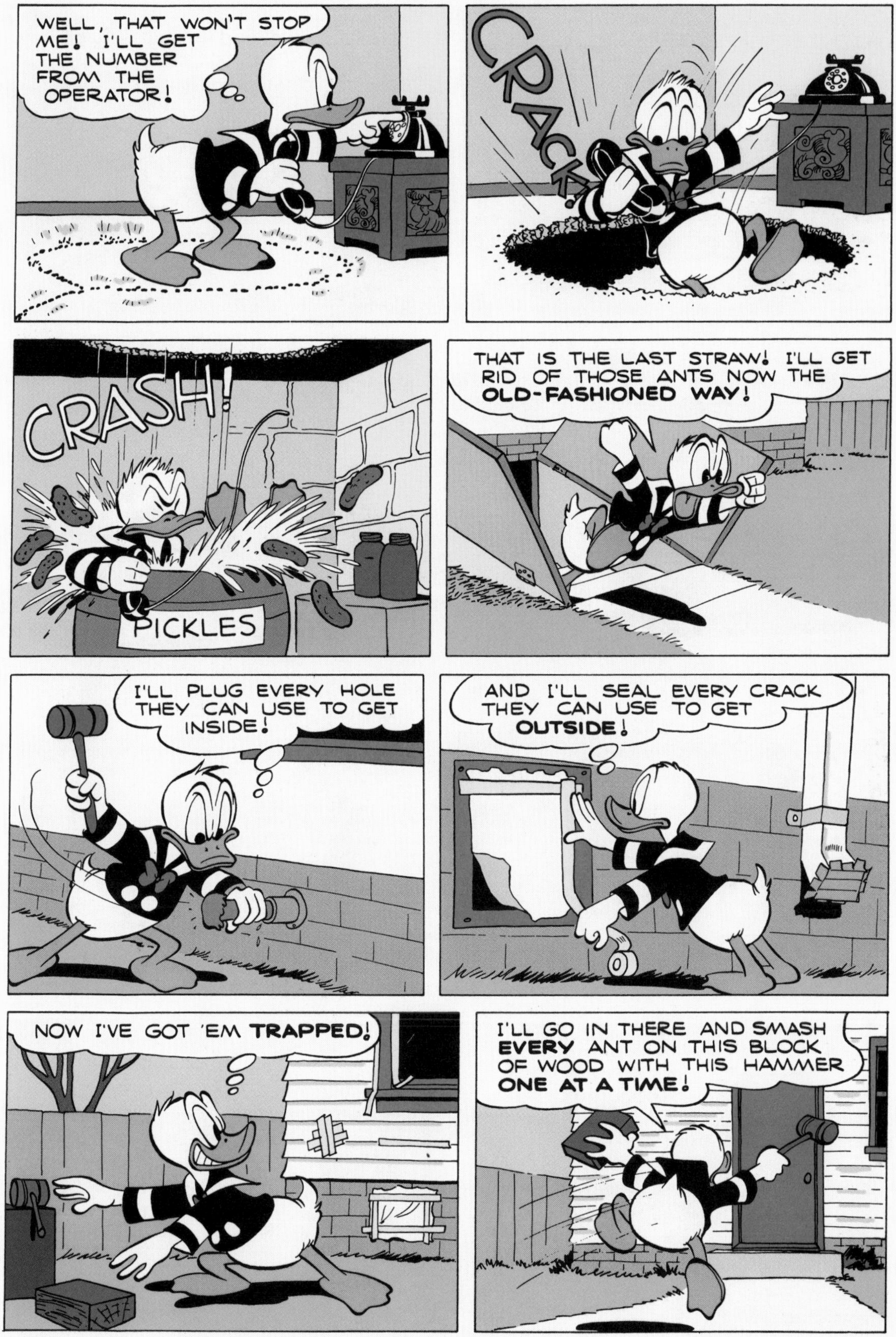
WELL, THAT WON'T STOP ME! I'LL GET THE NUMBER FROM THE OPERATOR!
CRACK
CRASH!
PICKLES
THAT IS THE LAST STRAW! I'LL GET RID OF THOSE ANTS NOW THE **OLD-FASHIONED WAY!**
I'LL PLUG EVERY HOLE THEY CAN USE TO GET INSIDE!
AND I'LL SEAL EVERY CRACK THEY CAN USE TO GET **OUTSIDE!**
NOW I'VE GOT 'EM **TRAPPED!**
I'LL GO IN THERE AND SMASH **EVERY** ANT ON THIS BLOCK OF WOOD WITH THIS HAMMER **ONE AT A TIME!**

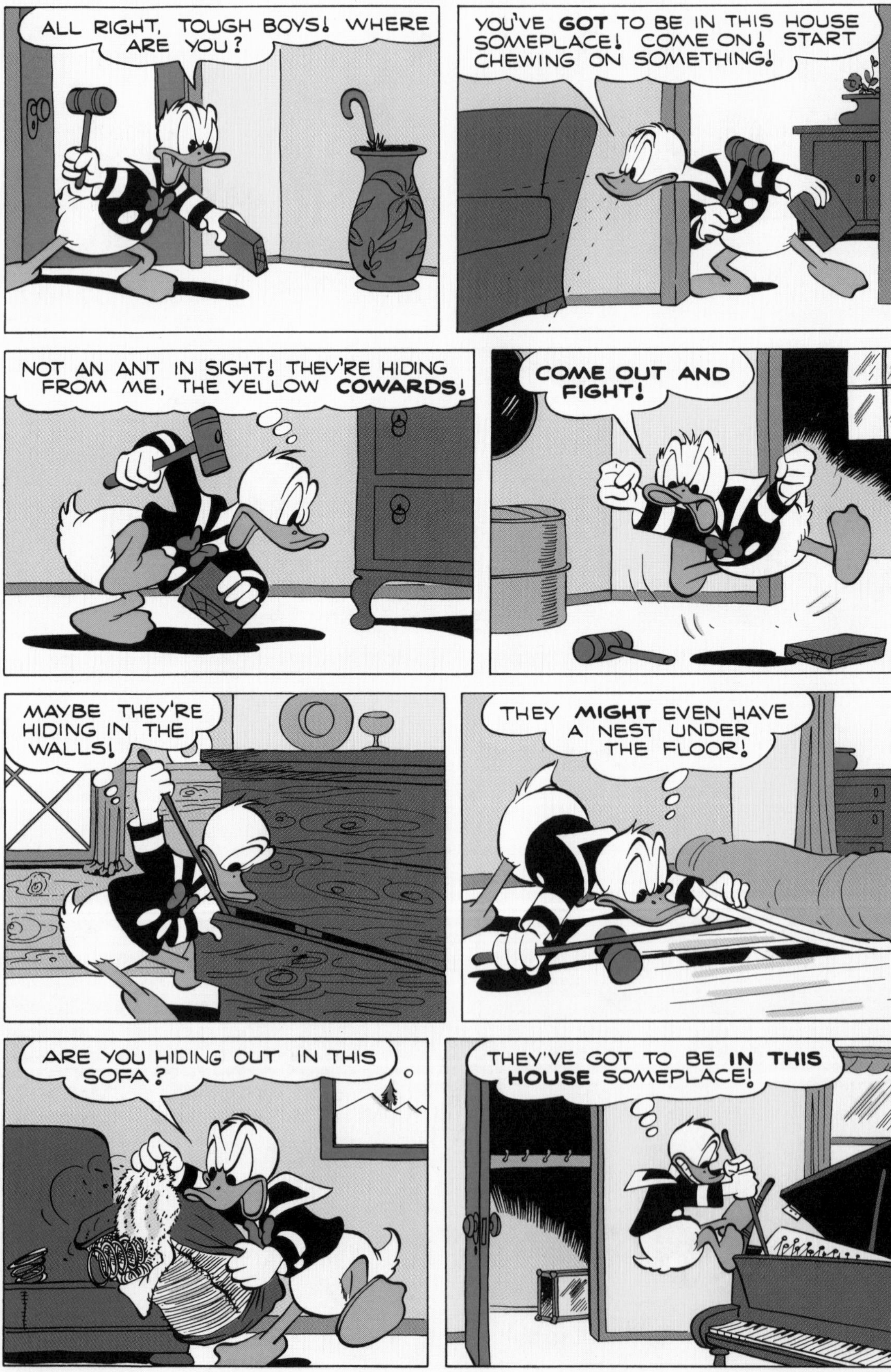
ALL RIGHT, TOUGH BOYS! WHERE ARE YOU?
YOU'VE GOT TO BE IN THIS HOUSE SOMEPLACE! COME ON! START CHEWING ON SOMETHING!
NOT AN ANT IN SIGHT! THEY'RE HIDING FROM ME, THE YELLOW COWARDS!
COME OUT AND FIGHT!
MAYBE THEY'RE HIDING IN THE WALLS!
THEY MIGHT EVEN HAVE A NEST UNDER THE FLOOR!
ARE YOU HIDING OUT IN THIS SOFA?
THEY'VE GOT TO BE IN THIS HOUSE SOMEPLACE!

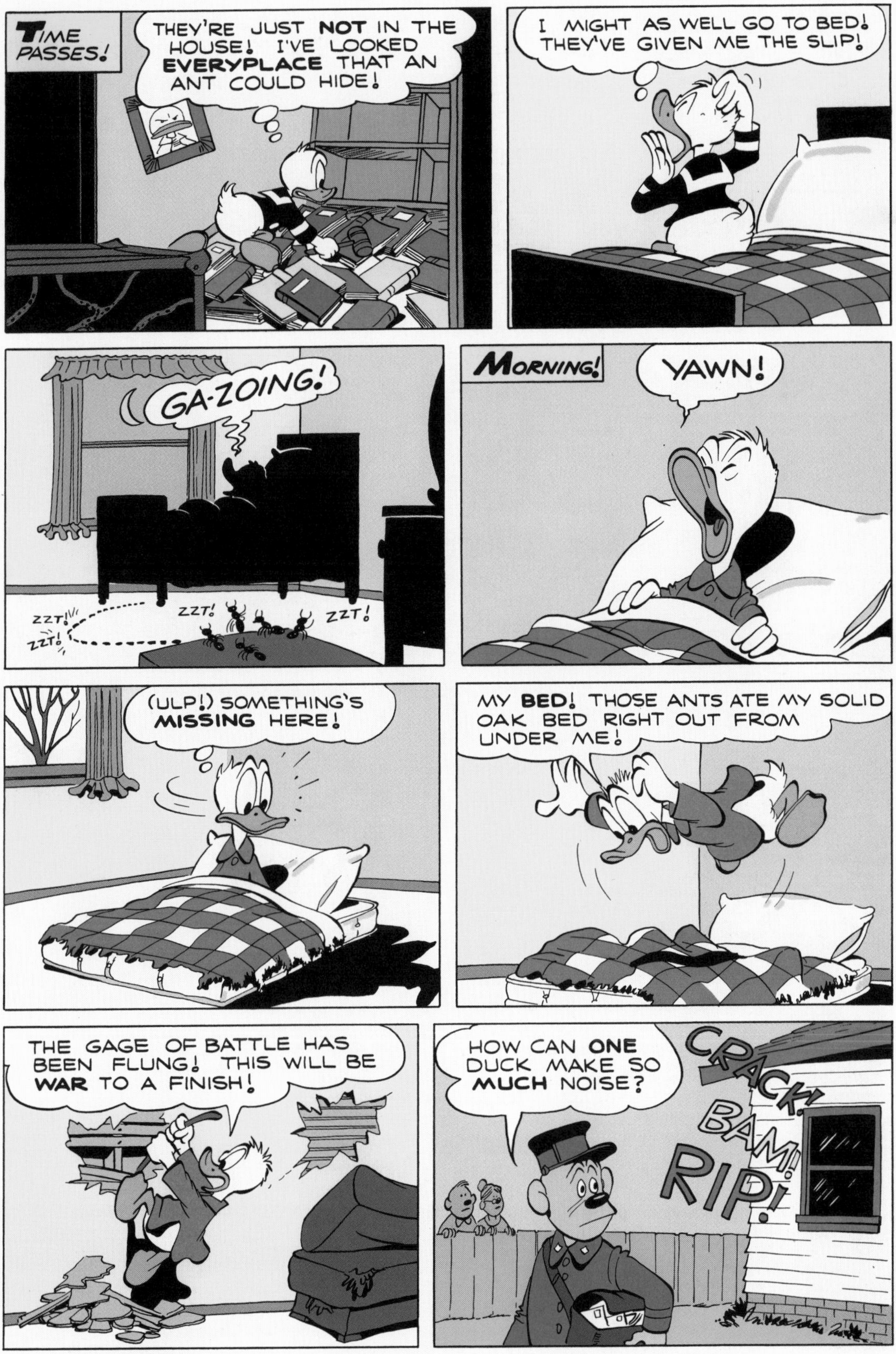
TIME PASSES!
THEY'RE JUST NOT IN THE HOUSE! I'VE LOOKED EVERYPLACE THAT AN ANT COULD HIDE!
I MIGHT AS WELL GO TO BED! THEY'VE GIVEN ME THE SLIP!
GA-ZOING!
ZZT!
ZZT!
ZZT!
ZZT!
MORNING!
YAWN!
(ULP!) SOMETHING'S MISSING HERE!
MY BED! THOSE ANTS ATE MY SOLID OAK BED RIGHT OUT FROM UNDER ME!
THE GAGE OF BATTLE HAS BEEN FLUNG! THIS WILL BE WAR TO A FINISH!
HOW CAN ONE DUCK MAKE SO MUCH NOISE?
CRACK!
BAM!
RIP!

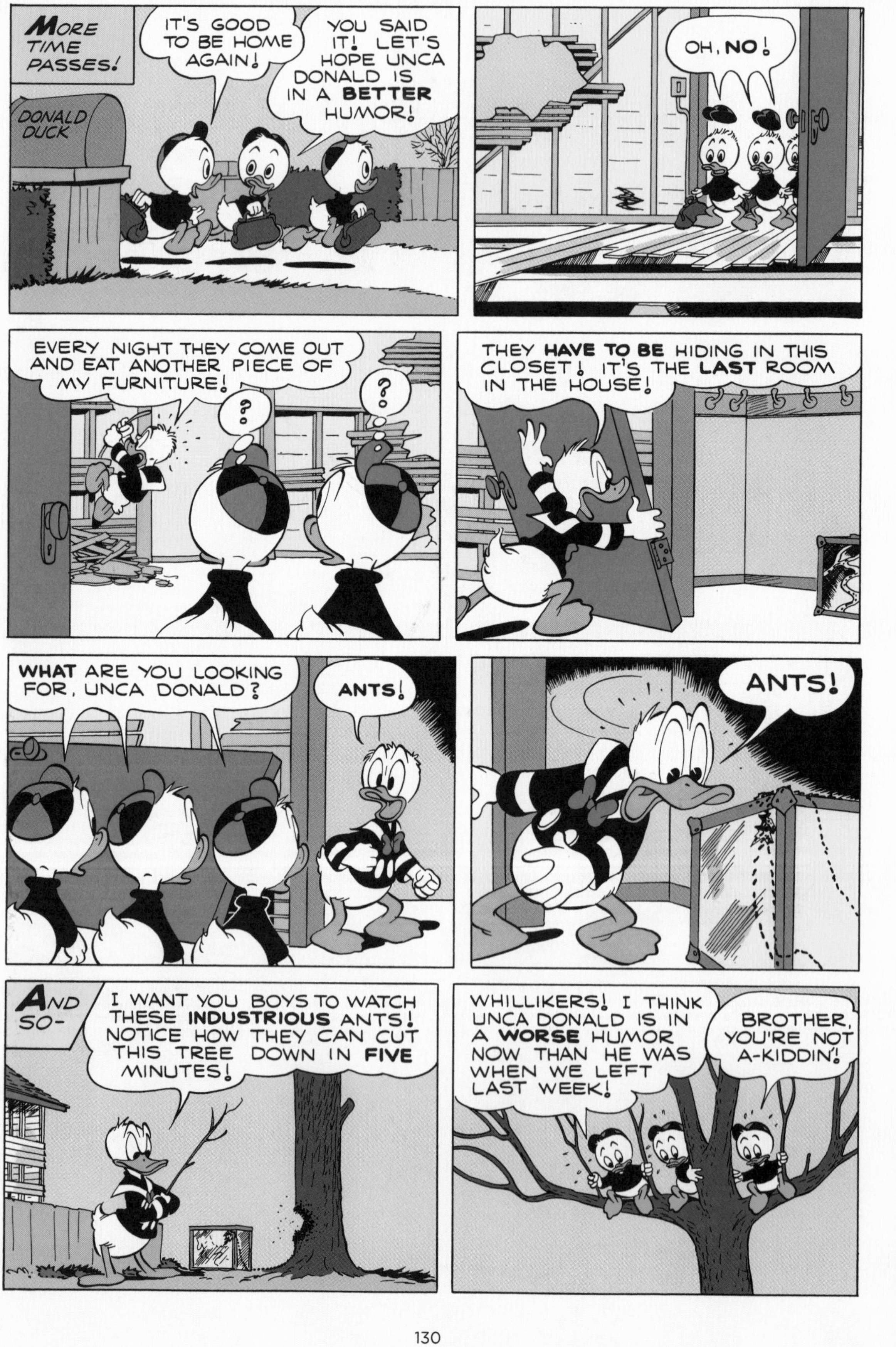
MORE TIME PASSES!
DONALD DUCK
IT'S GOOD TO BE HOME AGAIN!
YOU SAID IT! LET'S HOPE UNCA DONALD IS IN A BETTER HUMOR!
OH, NO!
EVERY NIGHT THEY COME OUT AND EAT ANOTHER PIECE OF MY FURNITURE!
?
?
THEY HAVE TO BE HIDING IN THIS CLOSET! IT'S THE LAST ROOM IN THE HOUSE!
WHAT ARE YOU LOOKING FOR, UNCA DONALD?
ANTS!
ANTS!
AND SO-
I WANT YOU BOYS TO WATCH THESE INDUSTRIOUS ANTS! NOTICE HOW THEY CAN CUT THIS TREE DOWN IN FIVE MINUTES!
WHILLIKERS! I THINK UNCA DONALD IS IN A WORSE HUMOR NOW THAN HE WAS WHEN WE LEFT LAST WEEK!
BROTHER, YOU'RE NOT A-KIDDIN'!

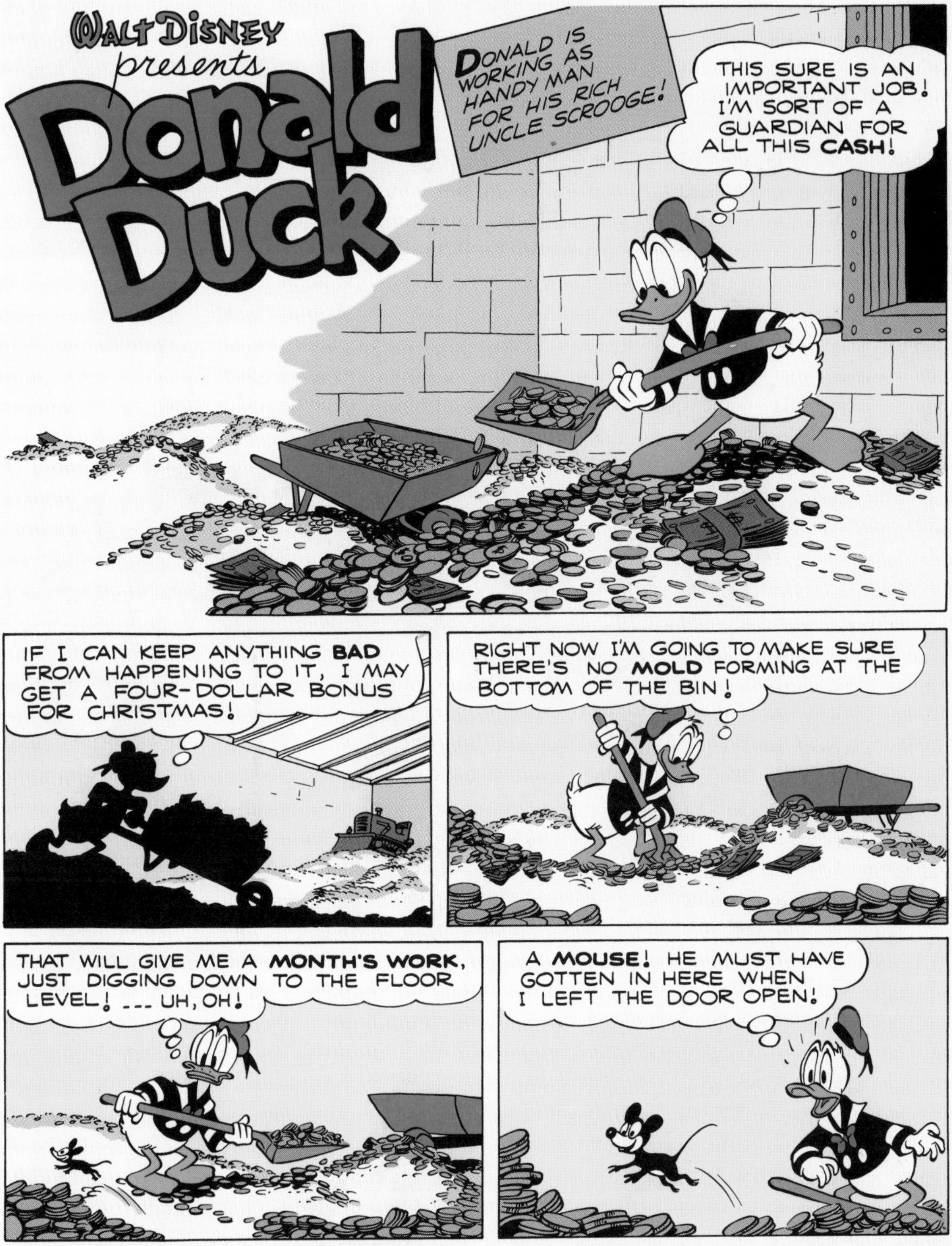
WALT DISNEY
presents
Donald Duck
DONALD IS WORKING AS HANDY MAN FOR HIS RICH UNCLE SCROOGE!
THIS SURE IS AN IMPORTANT JOB! I'M SORT OF A GUARDIAN FOR ALL THIS CASH!
IF I CAN KEEP ANYTHING BAD FROM HAPPENING TO IT, I MAY GET A FOUR-DOLLAR BONUS FOR CHRISTMAS!
RIGHT NOW I'M GOING TO MAKE SURE THERE'S NO MOLD FORMING AT THE BOTTOM OF THE BIN!
THAT WILL GIVE ME A MONTH'S WORK, JUST DIGGING DOWN TO THE FLOOR LEVEL! --- UH, OH!
A MOUSE! HE MUST HAVE GOTTEN IN HERE WHEN I LEFT THE DOOR OPEN!

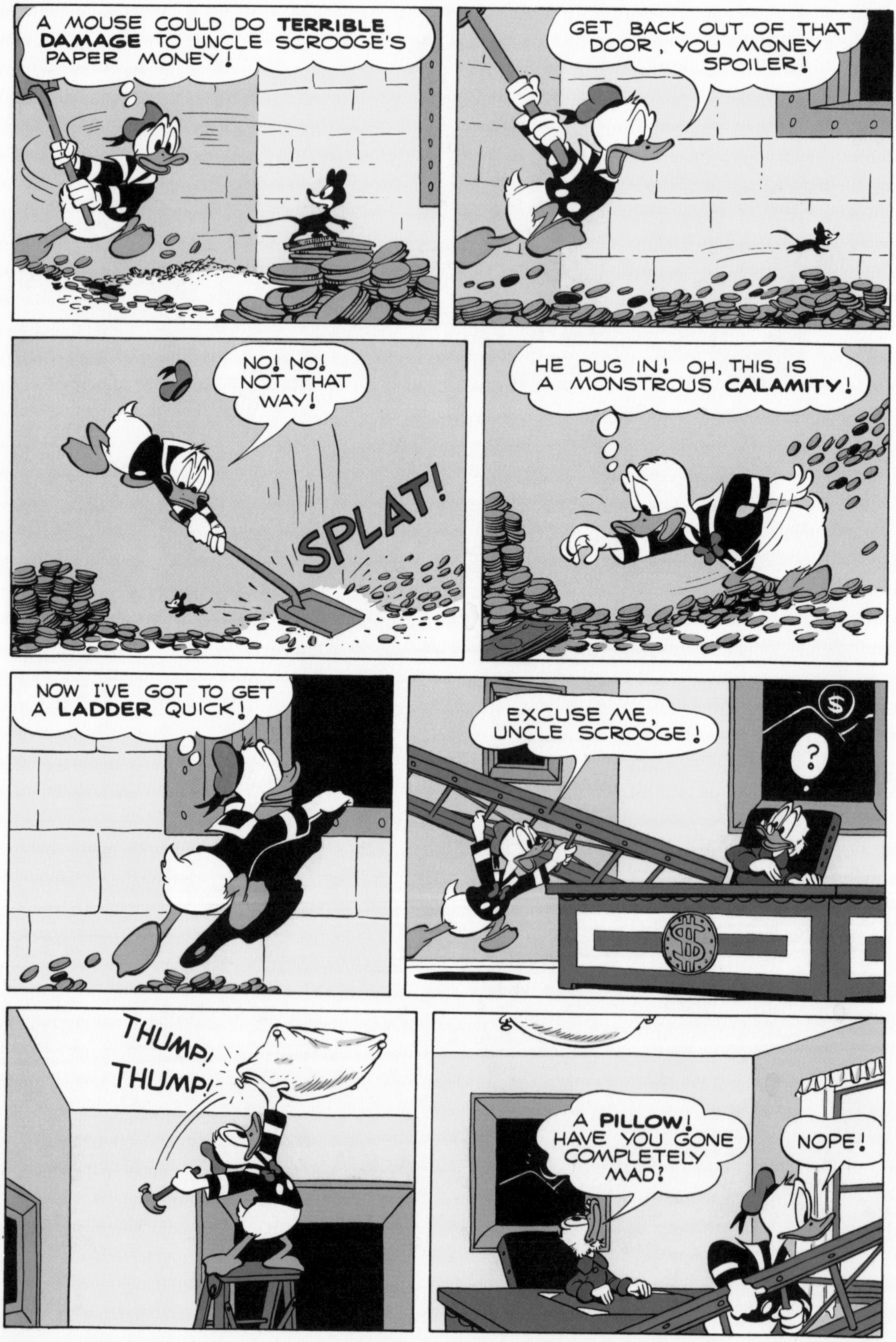
A MOUSE COULD DO TERRIBLE DAMAGE TO UNCLE SCROOGE'S PAPER MONEY!
GET BACK OUT OF THAT DOOR, YOU MONEY SPOILER!
NO! NO! NOT THAT WAY!
SPLAT!
HE DUG IN! OH, THIS IS A MONSTROUS CALAMITY!
NOW I'VE GOT TO GET A LADDER QUICK!
EXCUSE ME, UNCLE SCROOGE!
?
THUMP! THUMP!
A PILLOW! HAVE YOU GONE COMPLETELY MAD?
NOPE!

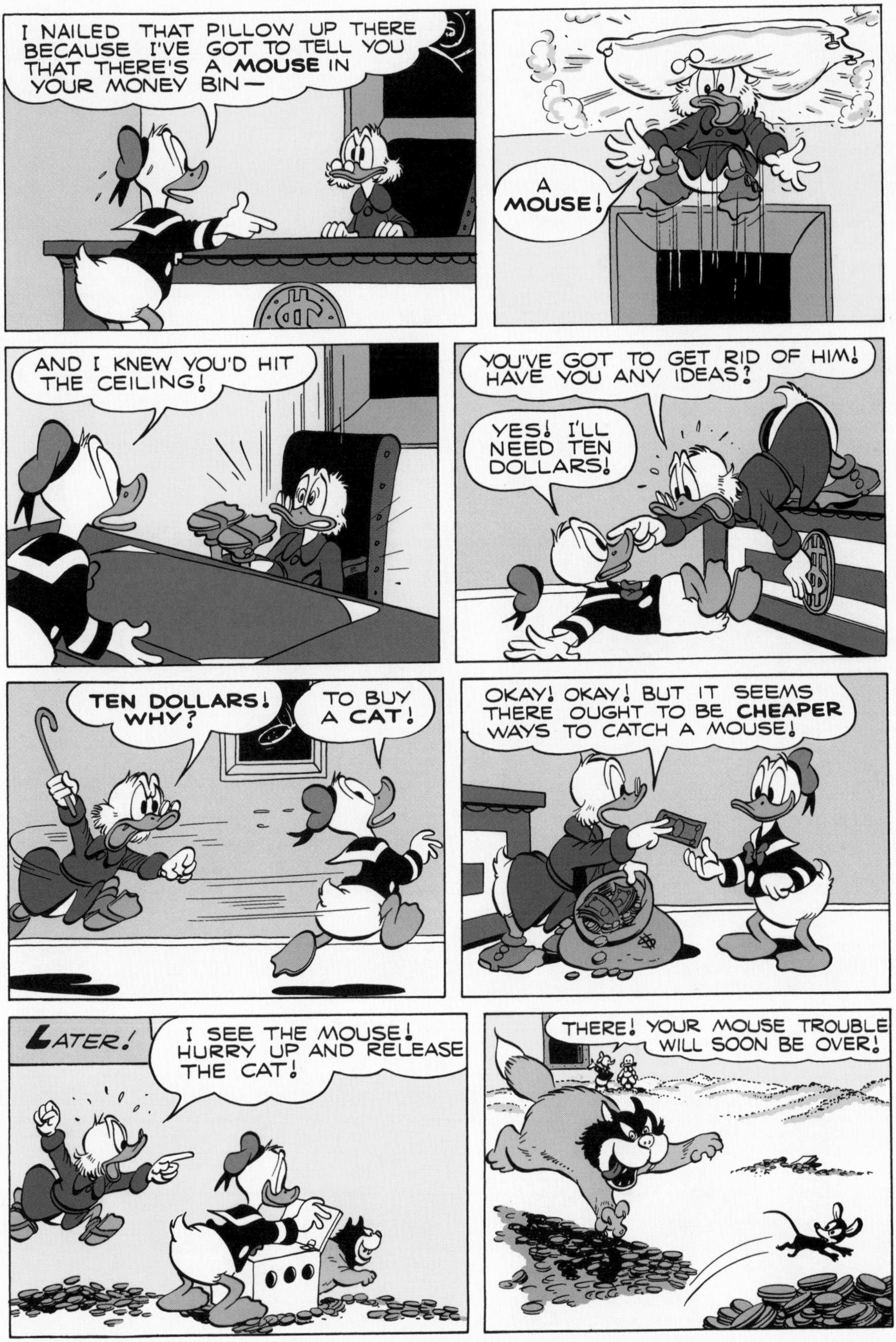
I NAILED THAT PILLOW UP THERE BECAUSE I'VE GOT TO TELL YOU THAT THERE'S A **MOUSE** IN YOUR MONEY BIN—
A **MOUSE**!
AND I KNEW YOU'D HIT THE CEILING!
YOU'VE GOT TO GET RID OF HIM! HAVE YOU ANY IDEAS?
YES! I'LL NEED TEN DOLLARS!
TEN DOLLARS! WHY?
TO BUY A **CAT**!
OKAY! OKAY! BUT IT SEEMS THERE OUGHT TO BE **CHEAPER** WAYS TO CATCH A MOUSE!
LATER!
I SEE THE MOUSE! HURRY UP AND RELEASE THE CAT!
THERE! YOUR MOUSE TROUBLE WILL SOON BE OVER!

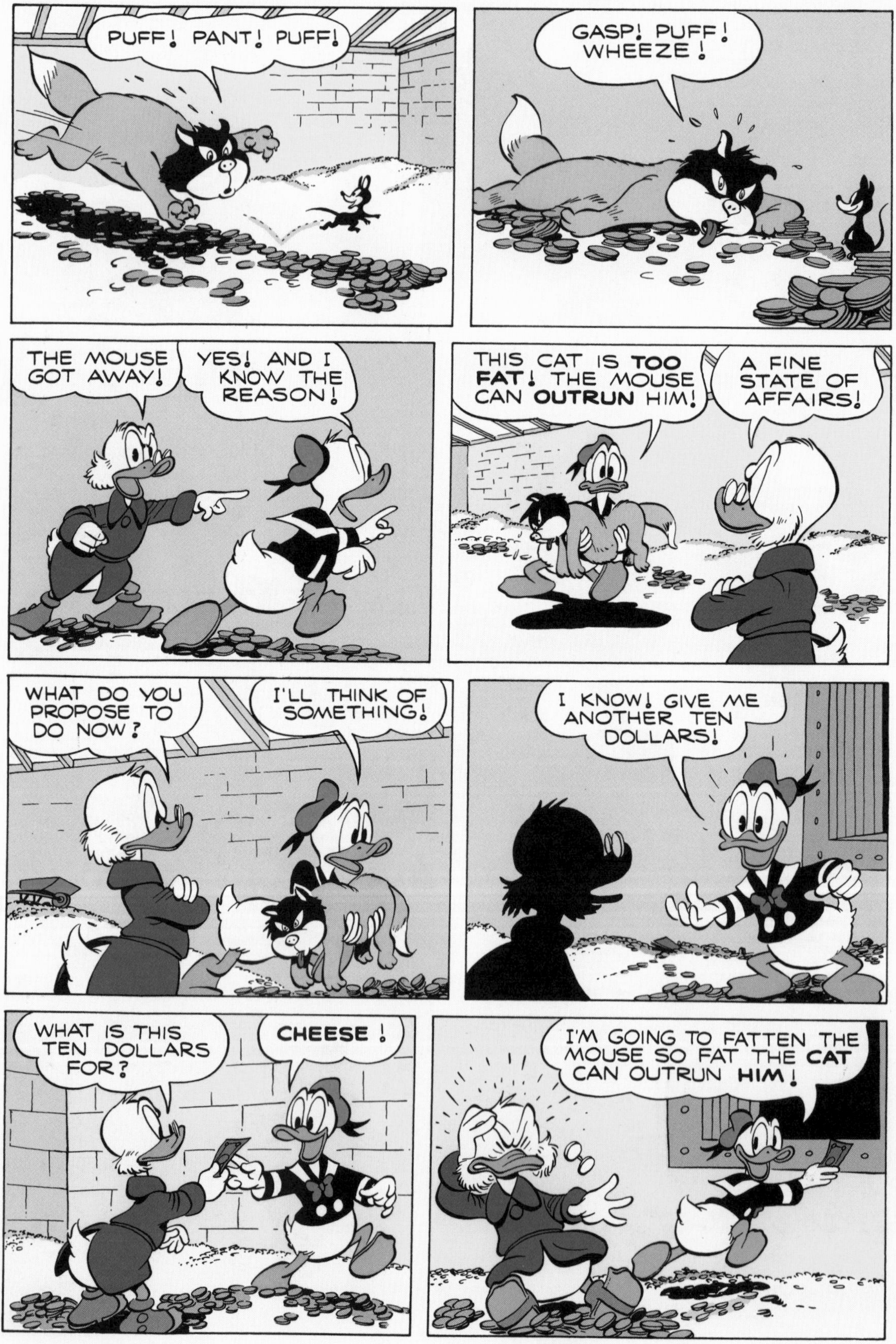
PUFF! PANT! PUFF!
GASP! PUFF! WHEEZE!
THE MOUSE GOT AWAY!
YES! AND I KNOW THE REASON!
THIS CAT IS **TOO FAT**! THE MOUSE CAN **OUTRUN** HIM!
A FINE STATE OF AFFAIRS!
WHAT DO YOU PROPOSE TO DO NOW?
I'LL THINK OF SOMETHING!
I KNOW! GIVE ME ANOTHER TEN DOLLARS!
WHAT IS THIS TEN DOLLARS FOR?
CHEESE!
I'M GOING TO FATTEN THE MOUSE SO FAT THE **CAT** CAN OUTRUN **HIM**!

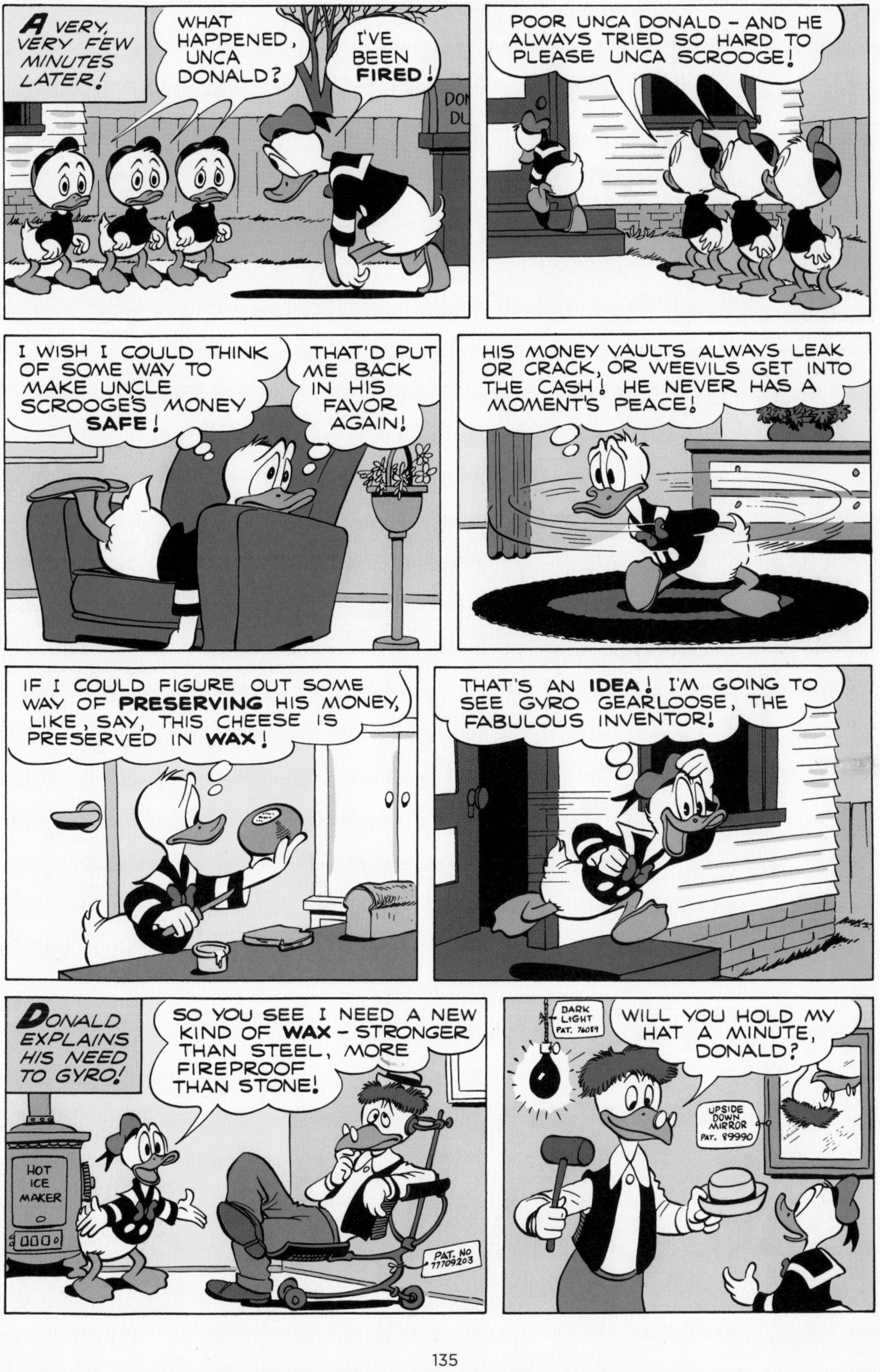
A VERY, VERY FEW MINUTES LATER!
WHAT HAPPENED, UNCA DONALD?
I'VE BEEN **FIRED**!
POOR UNCA DONALD – AND HE ALWAYS TRIED SO HARD TO PLEASE UNCA SCROOGE!
I WISH I COULD THINK OF SOME WAY TO MAKE UNCLE SCROOGE'S MONEY **SAFE**!
THAT'D PUT ME BACK IN HIS FAVOR AGAIN!
HIS MONEY VAULTS ALWAYS LEAK OR CRACK, OR WEEVILS GET INTO THE CASH! HE NEVER HAS A MOMENT'S PEACE!
IF I COULD FIGURE OUT SOME WAY OF **PRESERVING** HIS MONEY, LIKE, SAY, THIS CHEESE IS PRESERVED IN **WAX**!
THAT'S AN **IDEA**! I'M GOING TO SEE GYRO GEARLOOSE, THE FABULOUS INVENTOR!
DONALD EXPLAINS HIS NEED TO GYRO!
SO YOU SEE I NEED A NEW KIND OF **WAX** – STRONGER THAN STEEL, MORE FIREPROOF THAN STONE!
HOT ICE MAKER
PAT. NO 77709203
DARK LIGHT PAT. 76089
WILL YOU HOLD MY HAT A MINUTE, DONALD?
UPSIDE DOWN MIRROR PAT. 89990

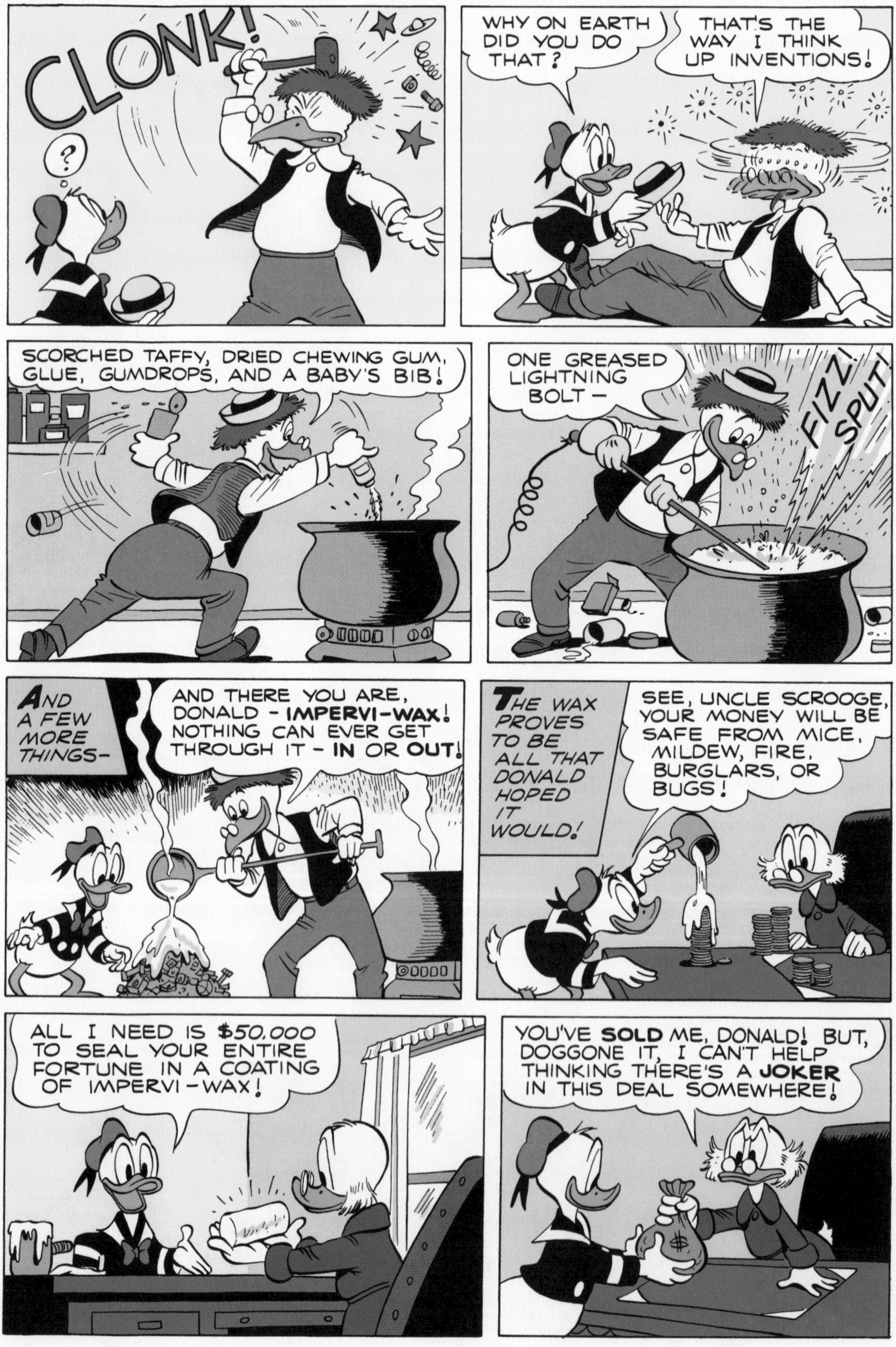
CLONK!
?
WHY ON EARTH DID YOU DO THAT?
THAT'S THE WAY I THINK UP INVENTIONS!
SCORCHED TAFFY, DRIED CHEWING GUM, GLUE, GUMDROPS, AND A BABY'S BIB!
ONE GREASED LIGHTNING BOLT –
FIZZ! SPUT!
AND A FEW MORE THINGS–
AND THERE YOU ARE, DONALD – IMPERVI-WAX! NOTHING CAN EVER GET THROUGH IT – IN OR OUT!
THE WAX PROVES TO BE ALL THAT DONALD HOPED IT WOULD!
SEE, UNCLE SCROOGE, YOUR MONEY WILL BE SAFE FROM MICE, MILDEW, FIRE, BURGLARS, OR BUGS!
ALL I NEED IS $50,000 TO SEAL YOUR ENTIRE FORTUNE IN A COATING OF IMPERVI-WAX!
YOU'VE SOLD ME, DONALD! BUT, DOGGONE IT, I CAN'T HELP THINKING THERE'S A JOKER IN THIS DEAL SOMEWHERE!

A WEEK PASSES! IT'S SWELL TO BE BACK ON THE PAYROLL AGAIN!

I'LL HAVE $14.40 EARNED BY THE TIME THIS IS FINISHED!

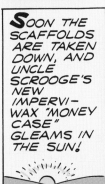

SOON THE SCAFFOLDS ARE TAKEN DOWN, AND UNCLE SCROOGE'S NEW IMPERVI-WAX "MONEY CASE" GLEAMS IN THE SUN!

IT'S ALL FINISHED, UNCLE SCROOGE!

MY MONEY! **SAFE** AT LAST!

NOW I'D KINDA LIKE TO COLLECT MY **WAGES!** I'M ABOUT BANKRUPT!

SURE! YES! (SIGH!)

I HAVE THE MONEY RIGHT HERE — OR HAVE I?

OH, ME! OH, MY! I FORGOT TO HOLD OUT ANY SPENDING MONEY!

YOU MEAN—

YES! **EVERY CENT** I HAVE IS SEALED IN THAT WAX CASE!

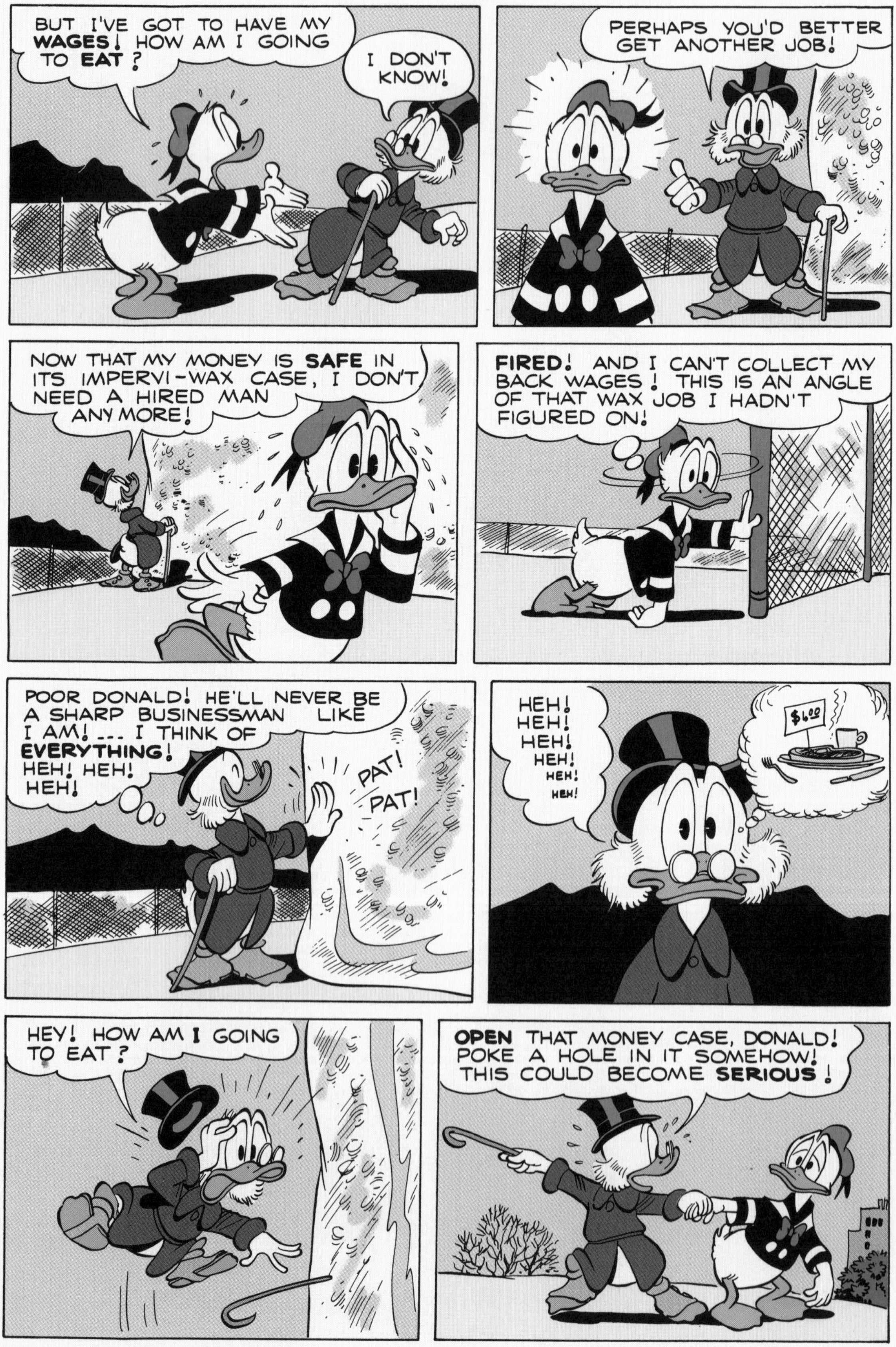
BUT I'VE GOT TO HAVE MY WAGES! HOW AM I GOING TO EAT?
I DON'T KNOW!
PERHAPS YOU'D BETTER GET ANOTHER JOB!
NOW THAT MY MONEY IS SAFE IN ITS IMPERVI-WAX CASE, I DON'T NEED A HIRED MAN ANYMORE!
FIRED! AND I CAN'T COLLECT MY BACK WAGES! THIS IS AN ANGLE OF THAT WAX JOB I HADN'T FIGURED ON!
POOR DONALD! HE'LL NEVER BE A SHARP BUSINESSMAN LIKE I AM! ... I THINK OF EVERYTHING! HEH! HEH! HEH!
PAT! PAT!
HEH! HEH! HEH! HEH! HEH! HEH!
$6.00
HEY! HOW AM I GOING TO EAT?
OPEN THAT MONEY CASE, DONALD! POKE A HOLE IN IT SOMEHOW! THIS COULD BECOME SERIOUS!

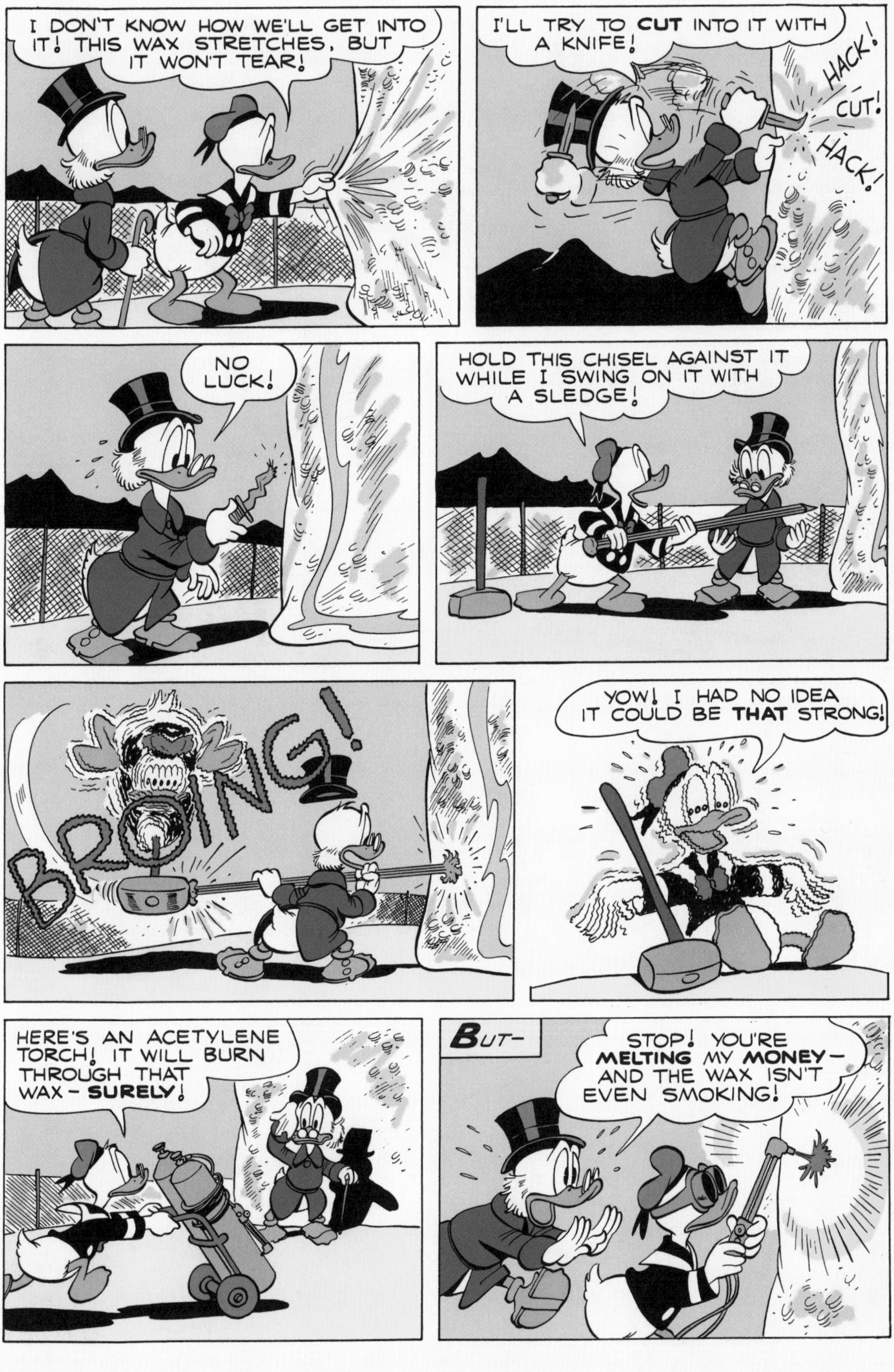
I DON'T KNOW HOW WE'LL GET INTO IT! THIS WAX STRETCHES, BUT IT WON'T TEAR!
I'LL TRY TO **CUT** INTO IT WITH A KNIFE!
HACK!
CUT!
HACK!
NO LUCK!
HOLD THIS CHISEL AGAINST IT WHILE I SWING ON IT WITH A SLEDGE!
BROING!
YOW! I HAD NO IDEA IT COULD BE **THAT** STRONG!
HERE'S AN ACETYLENE TORCH! IT WILL BURN THROUGH THAT WAX—**SURELY**!
BUT—
STOP! YOU'RE **MELTING** MY **MONEY**— AND THE WAX ISN'T EVEN SMOKING!

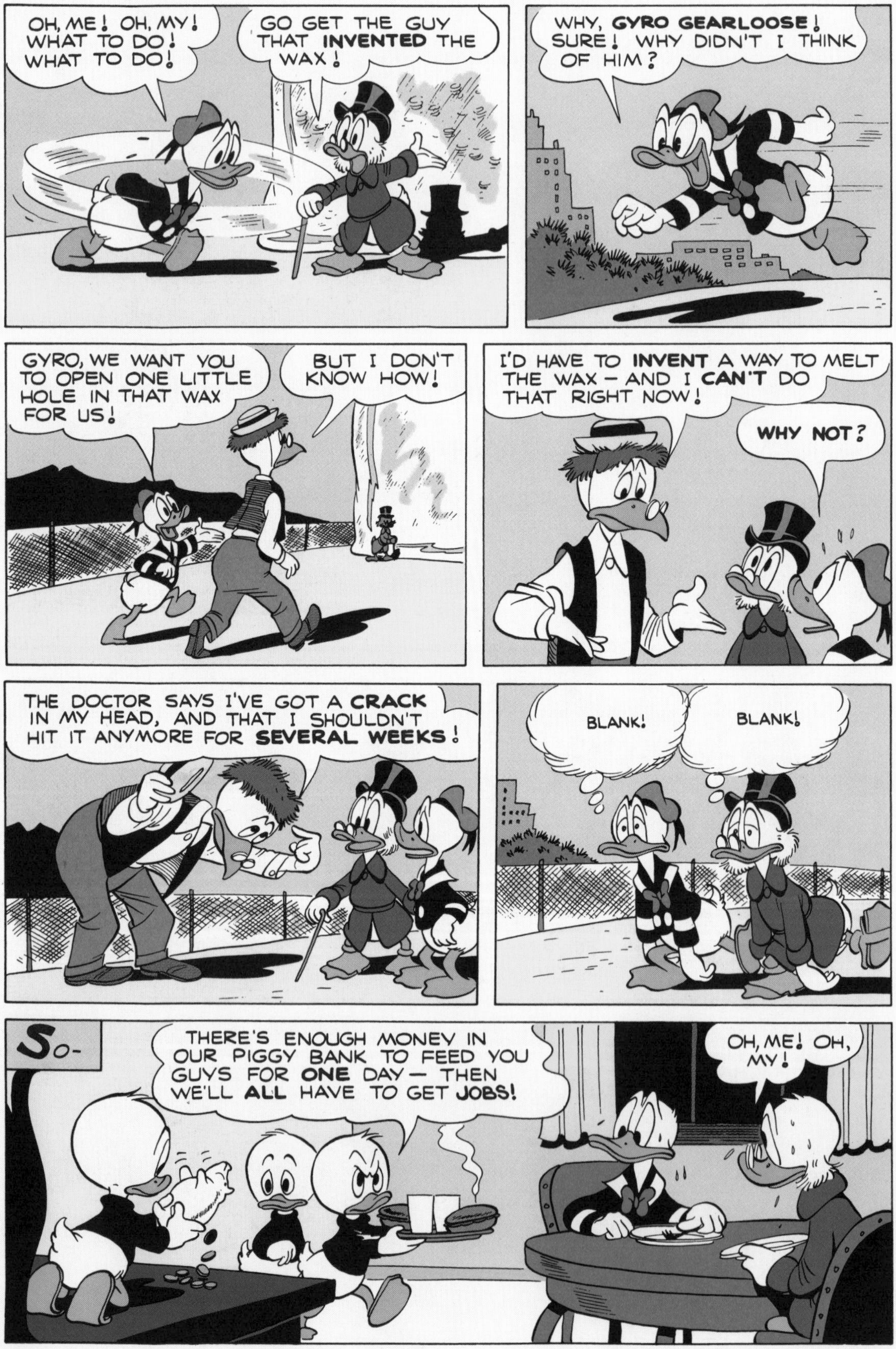
OH, ME! OH, MY! WHAT TO DO! WHAT TO DO!
GO GET THE GUY THAT **INVENTED** THE WAX!
WHY, **GYRO GEARLOOSE**! SURE! WHY DIDN'T I THINK OF HIM?
GYRO, WE WANT YOU TO OPEN ONE LITTLE HOLE IN THAT WAX FOR US!
BUT I DON'T KNOW HOW!
I'D HAVE TO **INVENT** A WAY TO MELT THE WAX — AND I **CAN'T** DO THAT RIGHT NOW!
WHY NOT?
THE DOCTOR SAYS I'VE GOT A **CRACK** IN MY HEAD, AND THAT I SHOULDN'T HIT IT ANYMORE FOR **SEVERAL WEEKS**!
BLANK!
BLANK!
SO-
THERE'S ENOUGH MONEY IN OUR PIGGY BANK TO FEED YOU GUYS FOR **ONE** DAY — THEN WE'LL **ALL** HAVE TO GET **JOBS**!
OH, ME! OH, MY!

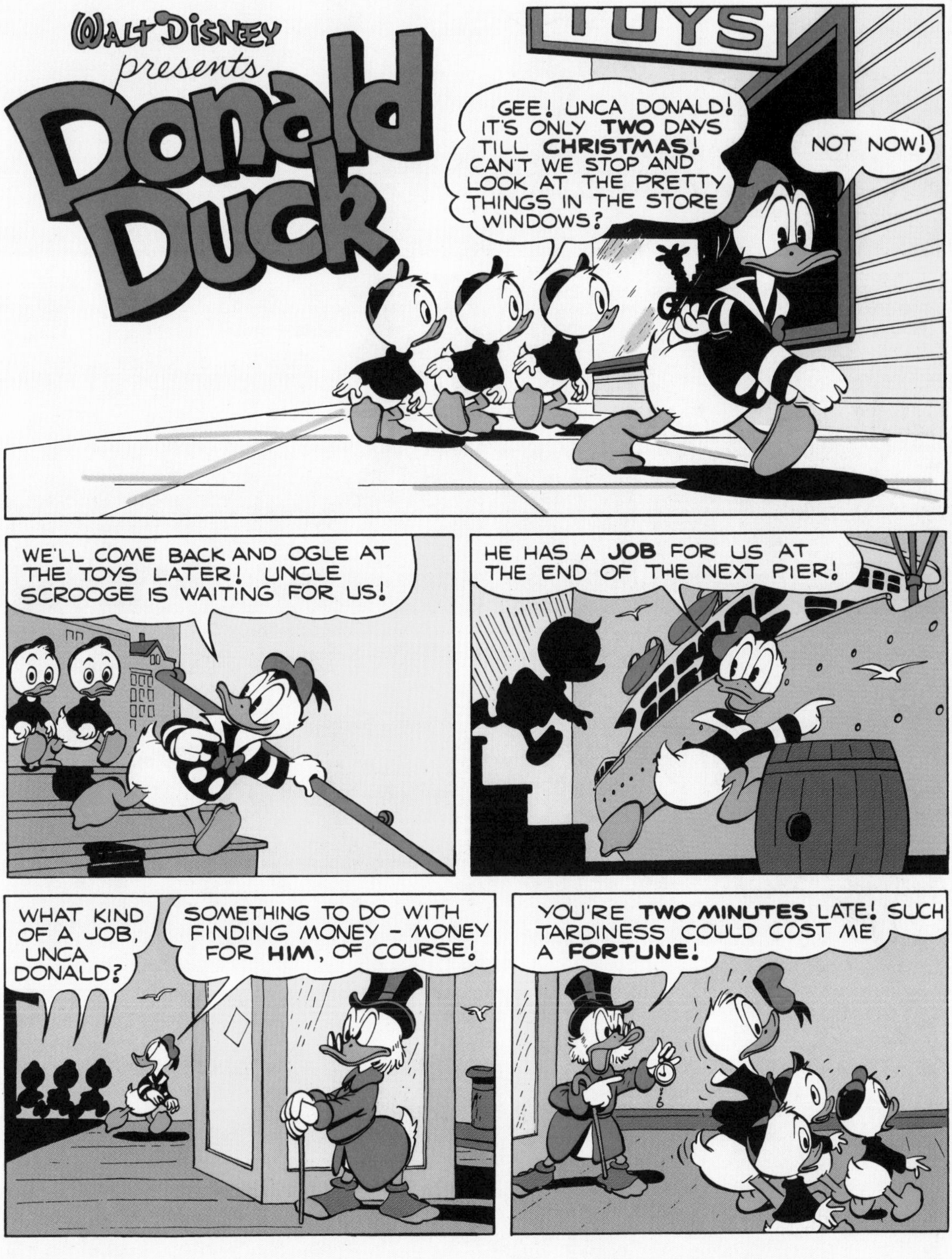
WALT DISNEY
presents
Donald Duck
TOYS
GEE! UNCA DONALD! IT'S ONLY TWO DAYS TILL CHRISTMAS! CAN'T WE STOP AND LOOK AT THE PRETTY THINGS IN THE STORE WINDOWS?
NOT NOW!
WE'LL COME BACK AND OGLE AT THE TOYS LATER! UNCLE SCROOGE IS WAITING FOR US!
HE HAS A JOB FOR US AT THE END OF THE NEXT PIER!
WHAT KIND OF A JOB, UNCA DONALD?
SOMETHING TO DO WITH FINDING MONEY - MONEY FOR HIM, OF COURSE!
YOU'RE TWO MINUTES LATE! SUCH TARDINESS COULD COST ME A FORTUNE!

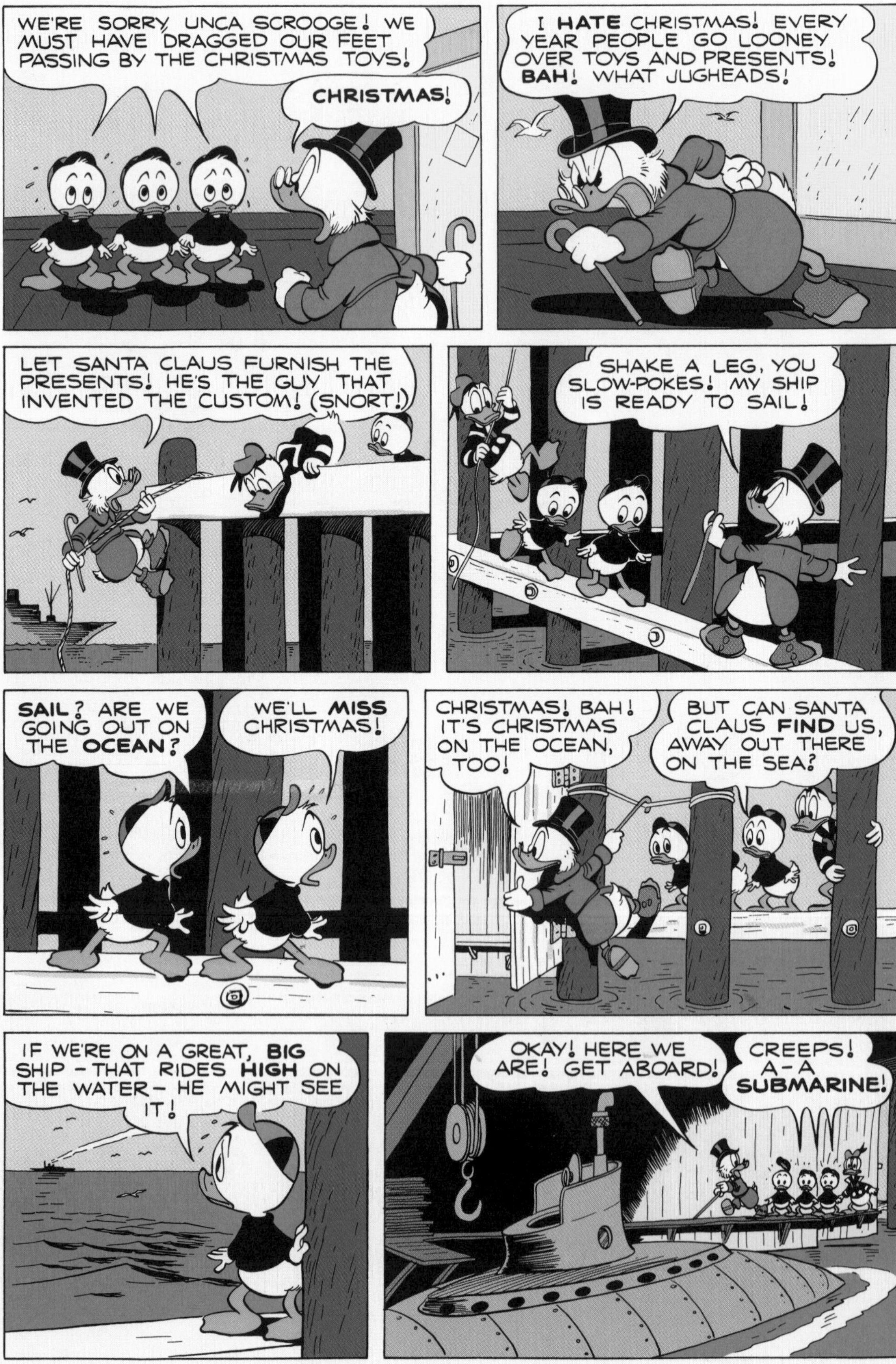
WE'RE SORRY, UNCA SCROOGE! WE MUST HAVE DRAGGED OUR FEET PASSING BY THE CHRISTMAS TOYS!
CHRISTMAS!
I HATE CHRISTMAS! EVERY YEAR PEOPLE GO LOONEY OVER TOYS AND PRESENTS! BAH! WHAT JUGHEADS!
LET SANTA CLAUS FURNISH THE PRESENTS! HE'S THE GUY THAT INVENTED THE CUSTOM! (SNORT!)
SHAKE A LEG, YOU SLOW-POKES! MY SHIP IS READY TO SAIL!
SAIL? ARE WE GOING OUT ON THE OCEAN?
WE'LL MISS CHRISTMAS!
CHRISTMAS! BAH! IT'S CHRISTMAS ON THE OCEAN, TOO!
BUT CAN SANTA CLAUS FIND US, AWAY OUT THERE ON THE SEA?
IF WE'RE ON A GREAT, BIG SHIP – THAT RIDES HIGH ON THE WATER – HE MIGHT SEE IT!
OKAY! HERE WE ARE! GET ABOARD!
CREEPS! A-A SUBMARINE!

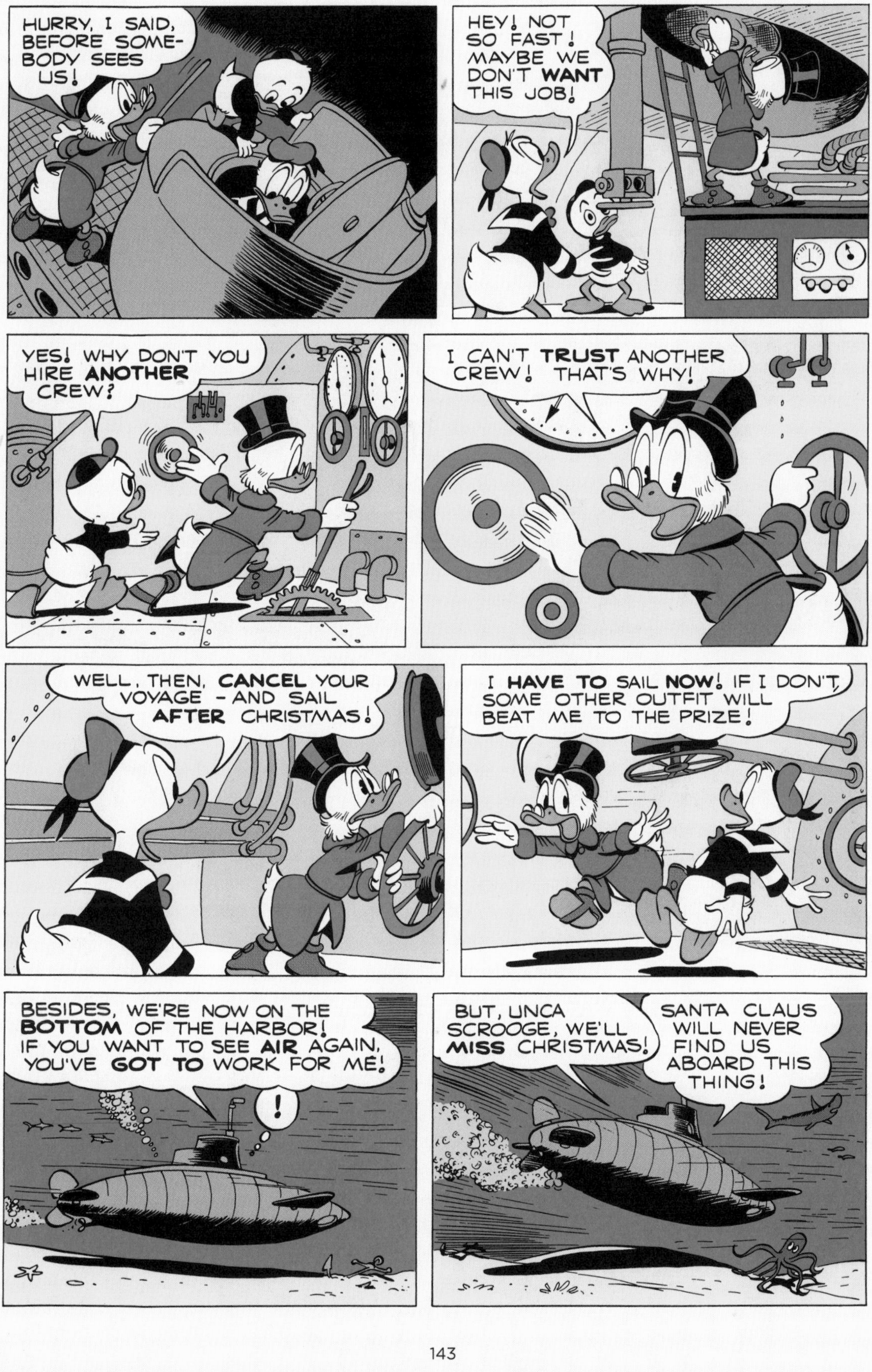
HURRY, I SAID, BEFORE SOMEBODY SEES US!
HEY! NOT SO FAST! MAYBE WE DON'T **WANT** THIS JOB!
YES! WHY DON'T YOU HIRE **ANOTHER** CREW?
I CAN'T **TRUST** ANOTHER CREW! THAT'S WHY!
WELL, THEN, **CANCEL** YOUR VOYAGE - AND SAIL **AFTER** CHRISTMAS!
I **HAVE TO** SAIL **NOW**! IF I DON'T, SOME OTHER OUTFIT WILL BEAT ME TO THE PRIZE!
BESIDES, WE'RE NOW ON THE **BOTTOM** OF THE HARBOR! IF YOU WANT TO SEE **AIR** AGAIN, YOU'VE **GOT TO** WORK FOR ME!
!
BUT, UNCA SCROOGE, WE'LL **MISS** CHRISTMAS!
SANTA CLAUS WILL NEVER FIND US ABOARD THIS THING!

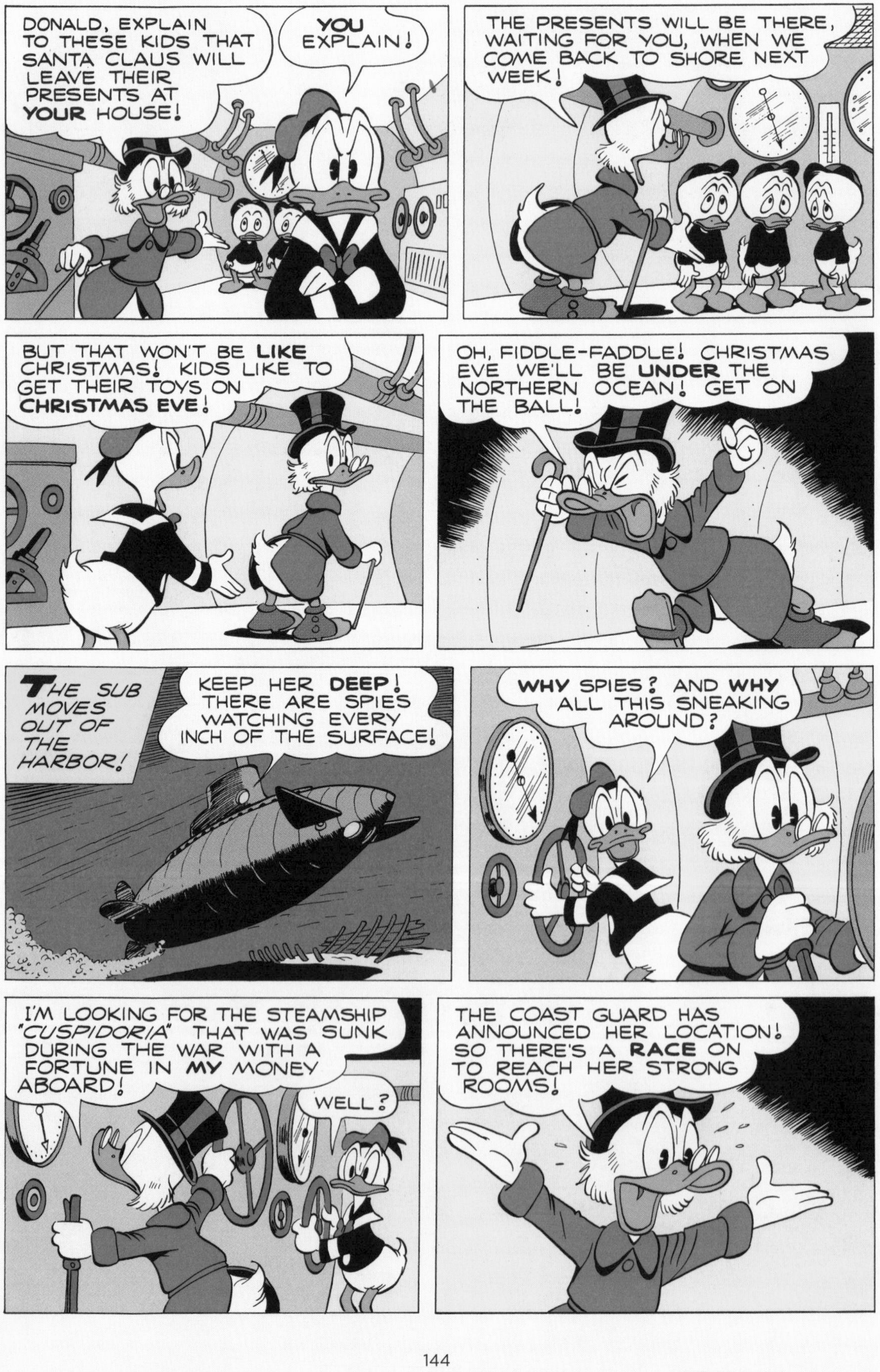
DONALD, EXPLAIN TO THESE KIDS THAT SANTA CLAUS WILL LEAVE THEIR PRESENTS AT **YOUR** HOUSE!
YOU EXPLAIN!
THE PRESENTS WILL BE THERE, WAITING FOR YOU, WHEN WE COME BACK TO SHORE NEXT WEEK!
BUT THAT WON'T BE **LIKE** CHRISTMAS! KIDS LIKE TO GET THEIR TOYS ON **CHRISTMAS EVE**!
OH, FIDDLE-FADDLE! CHRISTMAS EVE WE'LL BE **UNDER** THE NORTHERN OCEAN! GET ON THE BALL!
THE SUB MOVES OUT OF THE HARBOR!
KEEP HER **DEEP**! THERE ARE SPIES WATCHING EVERY INCH OF THE SURFACE!
WHY SPIES? AND **WHY** ALL THIS SNEAKING AROUND?
I'M LOOKING FOR THE STEAMSHIP *"CUSPIDORIA"* THAT WAS SUNK DURING THE WAR WITH A FORTUNE IN **MY** MONEY ABOARD!
WELL?
THE COAST GUARD HAS ANNOUNCED HER LOCATION! SO THERE'S A **RACE** ON TO REACH HER STRONG ROOMS!

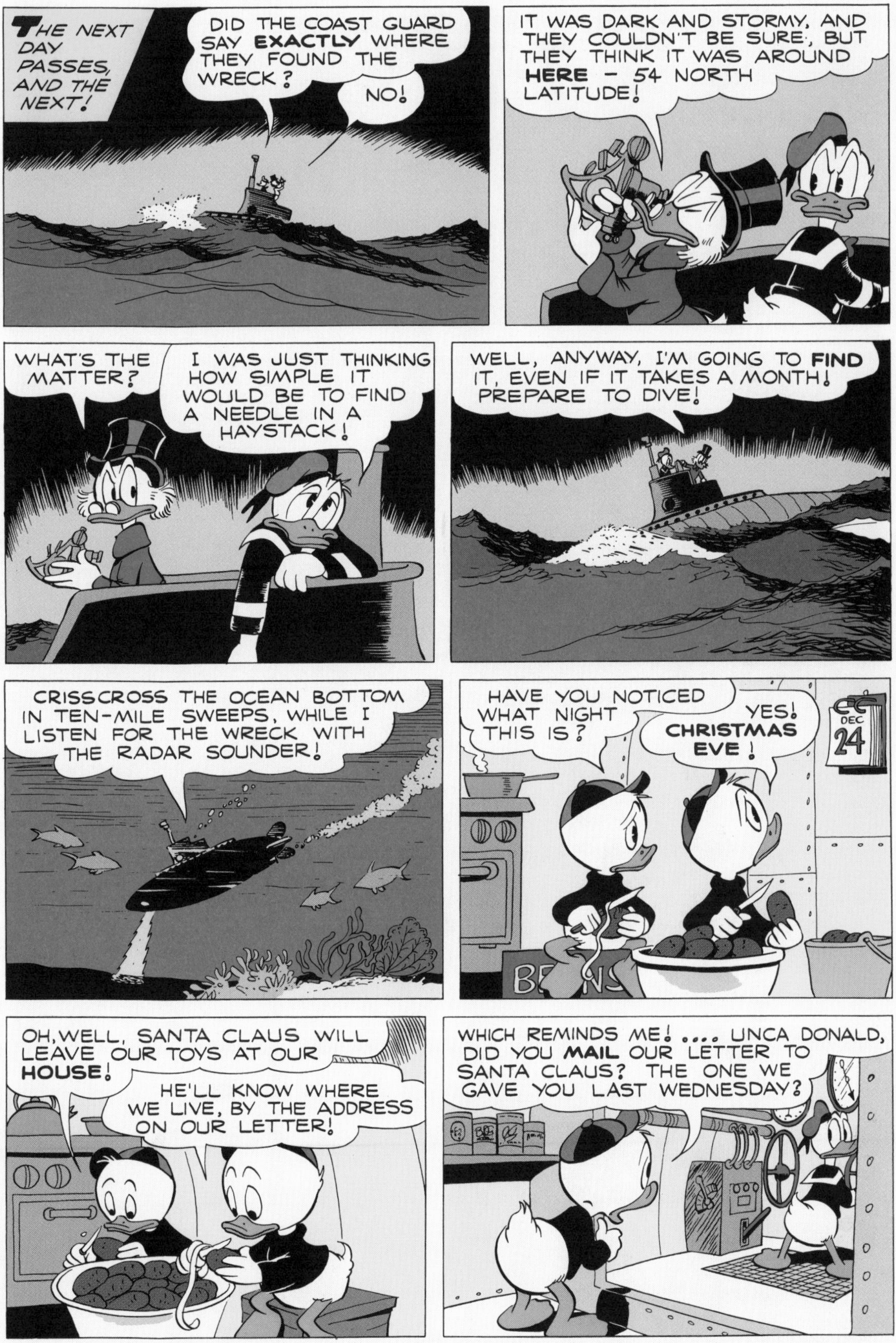
THE NEXT DAY PASSES, AND THE NEXT!
DID THE COAST GUARD SAY EXACTLY WHERE THEY FOUND THE WRECK?
NO!
IT WAS DARK AND STORMY, AND THEY COULDN'T BE SURE, BUT THEY THINK IT WAS AROUND HERE – 54 NORTH LATITUDE!
WHAT'S THE MATTER?
I WAS JUST THINKING HOW SIMPLE IT WOULD BE TO FIND A NEEDLE IN A HAYSTACK!
WELL, ANYWAY, I'M GOING TO FIND IT, EVEN IF IT TAKES A MONTH! PREPARE TO DIVE!
CRISSCROSS THE OCEAN BOTTOM IN TEN-MILE SWEEPS, WHILE I LISTEN FOR THE WRECK WITH THE RADAR SOUNDER!
HAVE YOU NOTICED WHAT NIGHT THIS IS?
YES! CHRISTMAS EVE!
DEC 24
OH, WELL, SANTA CLAUS WILL LEAVE OUR TOYS AT OUR HOUSE!
HE'LL KNOW WHERE WE LIVE, BY THE ADDRESS ON OUR LETTER!
WHICH REMINDS ME! .... UNCA DONALD, DID YOU MAIL OUR LETTER TO SANTA CLAUS? THE ONE WE GAVE YOU LAST WEDNESDAY?

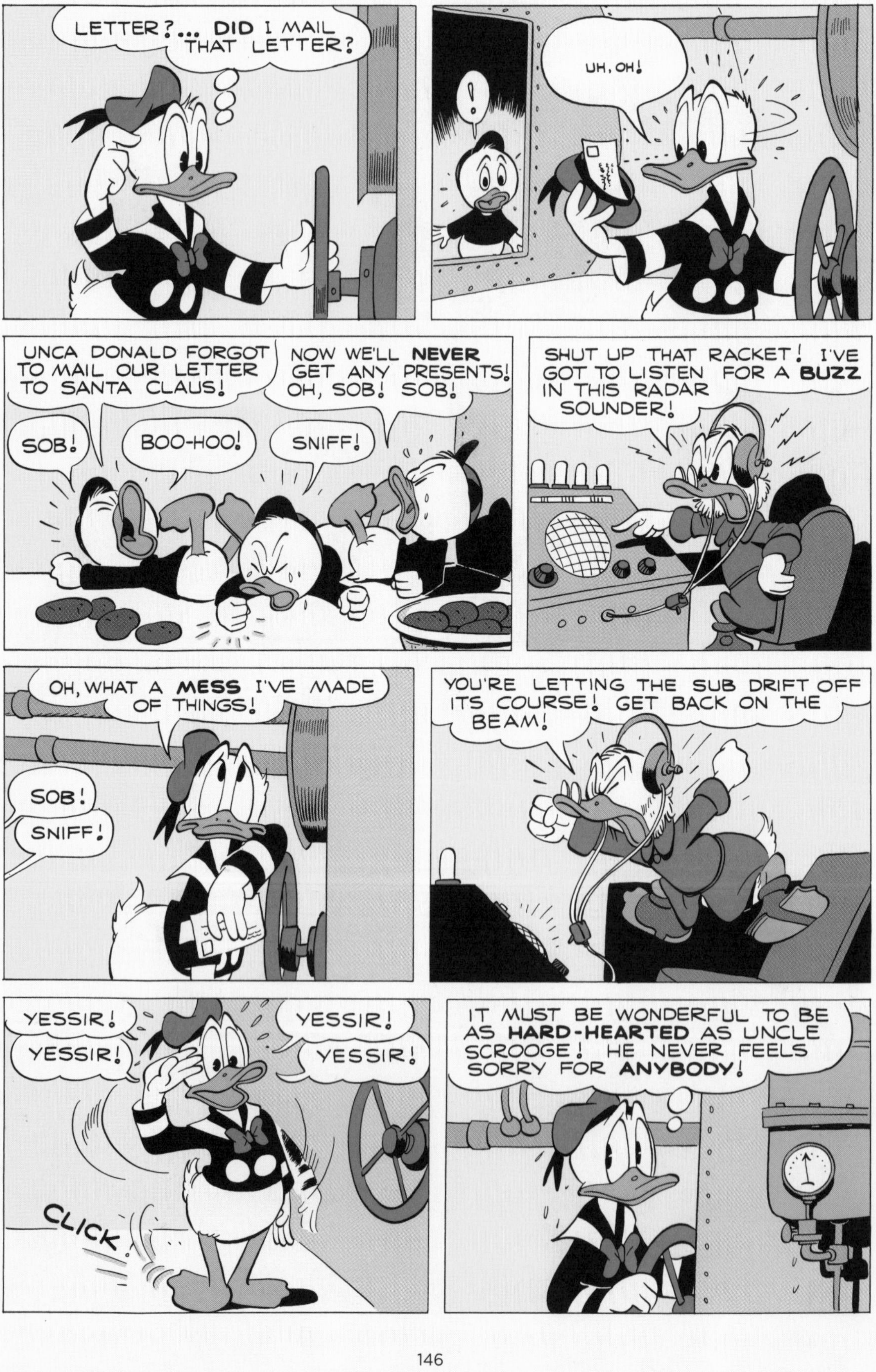
LETTER?... DID I MAIL THAT LETTER?
!
UH, OH!
UNCA DONALD FORGOT TO MAIL OUR LETTER TO SANTA CLAUS!
NOW WE'LL NEVER GET ANY PRESENTS! OH, SOB! SOB!
SOB!
BOO-HOO!
SNIFF!
SHUT UP THAT RACKET! I'VE GOT TO LISTEN FOR A BUZZ IN THIS RADAR SOUNDER!
OH, WHAT A MESS I'VE MADE OF THINGS!
SOB!
SNIFF!
YOU'RE LETTING THE SUB DRIFT OFF ITS COURSE! GET BACK ON THE BEAM!
YESSIR!
YESSIR!
YESSIR!
YESSIR!
CLICK
IT MUST BE WONDERFUL TO BE AS HARD-HEARTED AS UNCLE SCROOGE! HE NEVER FEELS SORRY FOR ANYBODY!

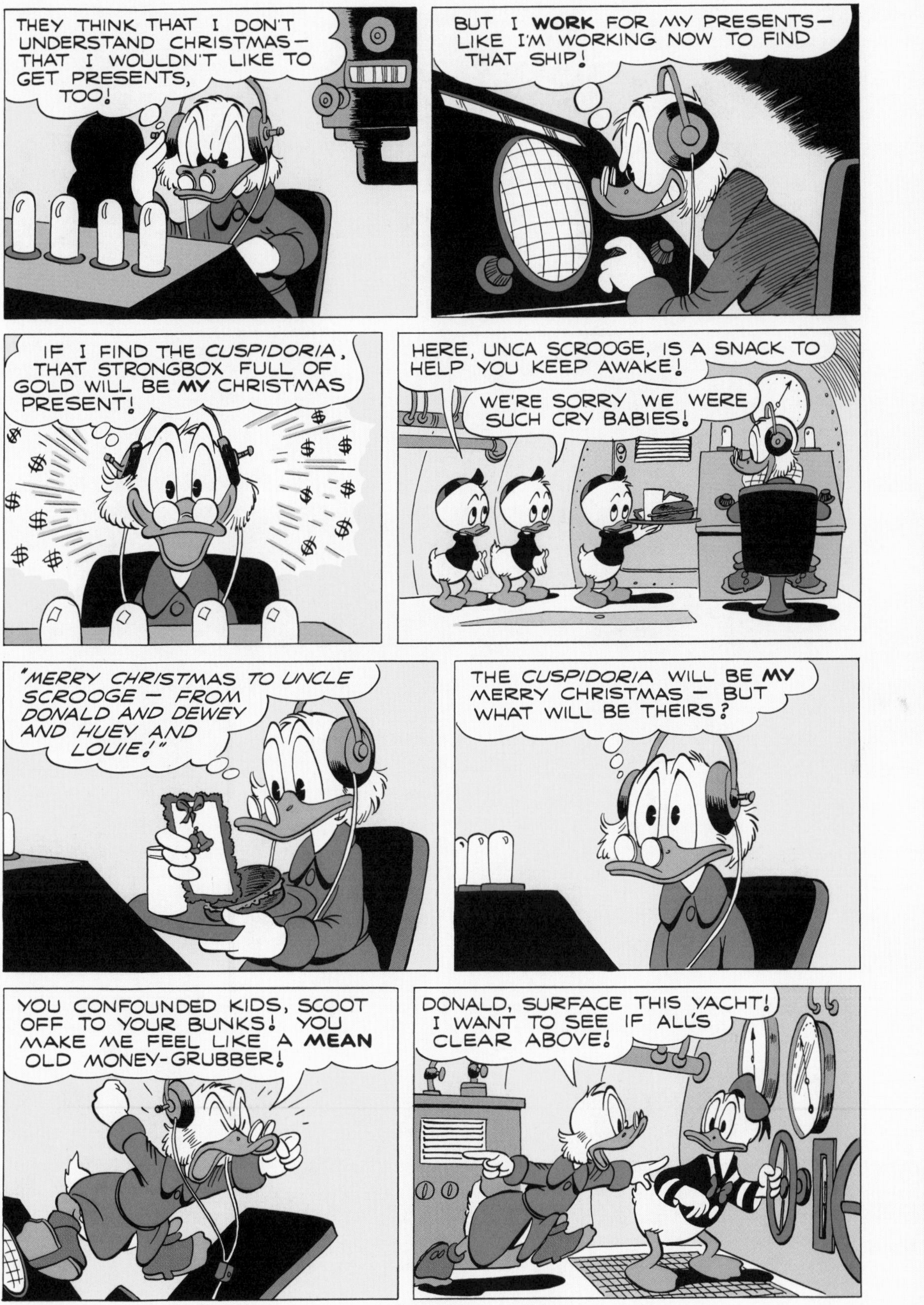
THEY THINK THAT I DON'T UNDERSTAND CHRISTMAS— THAT I WOULDN'T LIKE TO GET PRESENTS, TOO!
BUT I WORK FOR MY PRESENTS— LIKE I'M WORKING NOW TO FIND THAT SHIP!
IF I FIND THE CUSPIDORIA, THAT STRONGBOX FULL OF GOLD WILL BE MY CHRISTMAS PRESENT!
HERE, UNCA SCROOGE, IS A SNACK TO HELP YOU KEEP AWAKE!
WE'RE SORRY WE WERE SUCH CRY BABIES!
"MERRY CHRISTMAS TO UNCLE SCROOGE — FROM DONALD AND DEWEY AND HUEY AND LOUIE!"
THE CUSPIDORIA WILL BE MY MERRY CHRISTMAS — BUT WHAT WILL BE THEIRS?
YOU CONFOUNDED KIDS, SCOOT OFF TO YOUR BUNKS! YOU MAKE ME FEEL LIKE A MEAN OLD MONEY-GRUBBER!
DONALD, SURFACE THIS YACHT! I WANT TO SEE IF ALL'S CLEAR ABOVE!

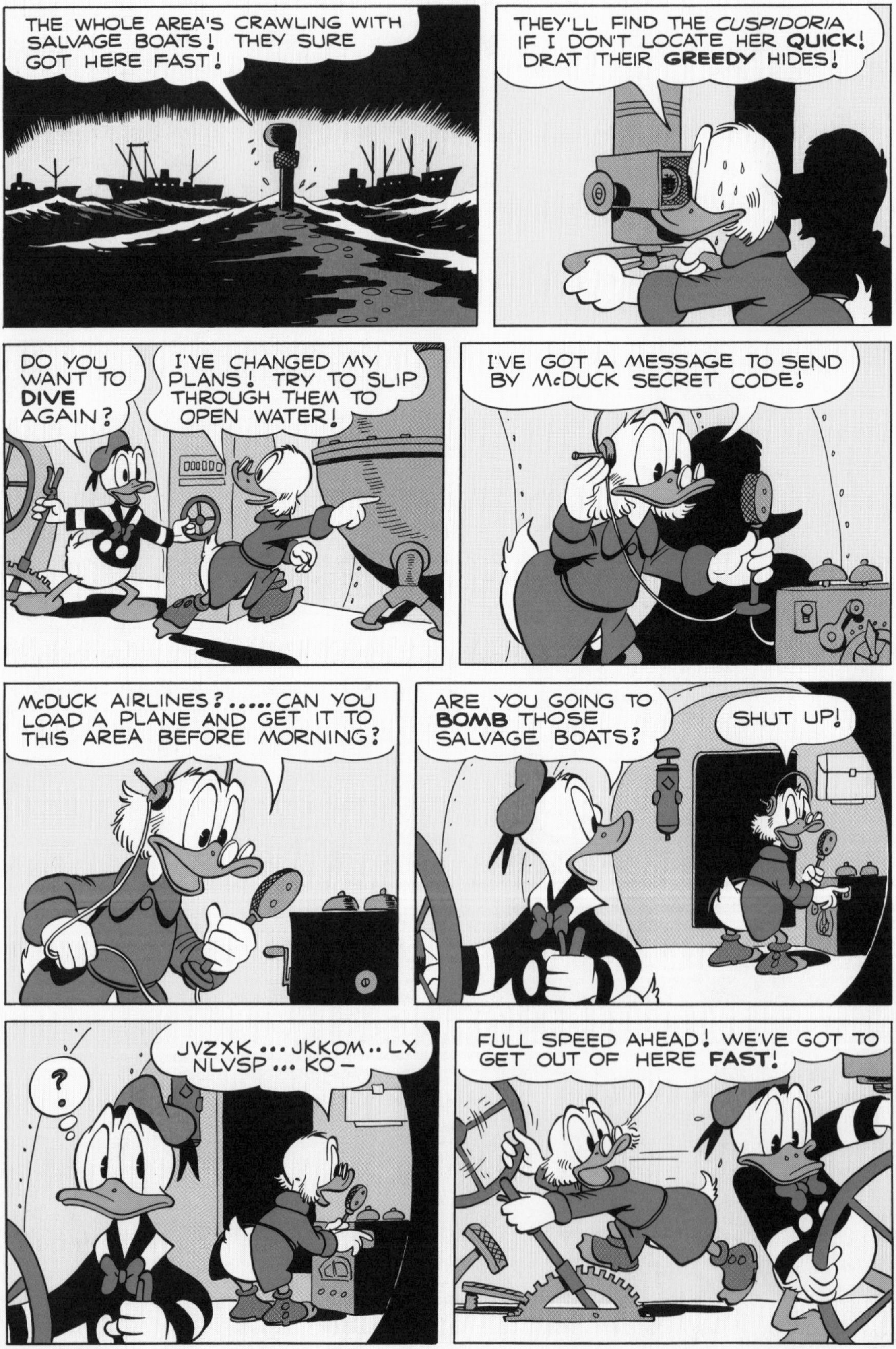
THE WHOLE AREA'S CRAWLING WITH SALVAGE BOATS! THEY SURE GOT HERE FAST!
THEY'LL FIND THE *CUSPIDORIA* IF I DON'T LOCATE HER **QUICK**! DRAT THEIR **GREEDY** HIDES!
DO YOU WANT TO **DIVE** AGAIN?
I'VE CHANGED MY PLANS! TRY TO SLIP THROUGH THEM TO OPEN WATER!
I'VE GOT A MESSAGE TO SEND BY McDUCK SECRET CODE!
McDUCK AIRLINES? ..... CAN YOU LOAD A PLANE AND GET IT TO THIS AREA BEFORE MORNING?
ARE YOU GOING TO **BOMB** THOSE SALVAGE BOATS?
SHUT UP!
?
JVZXK ... JKKOM .. LX NLVSP ... KO—
FULL SPEED AHEAD! WE'VE GOT TO GET OUT OF HERE **FAST**!

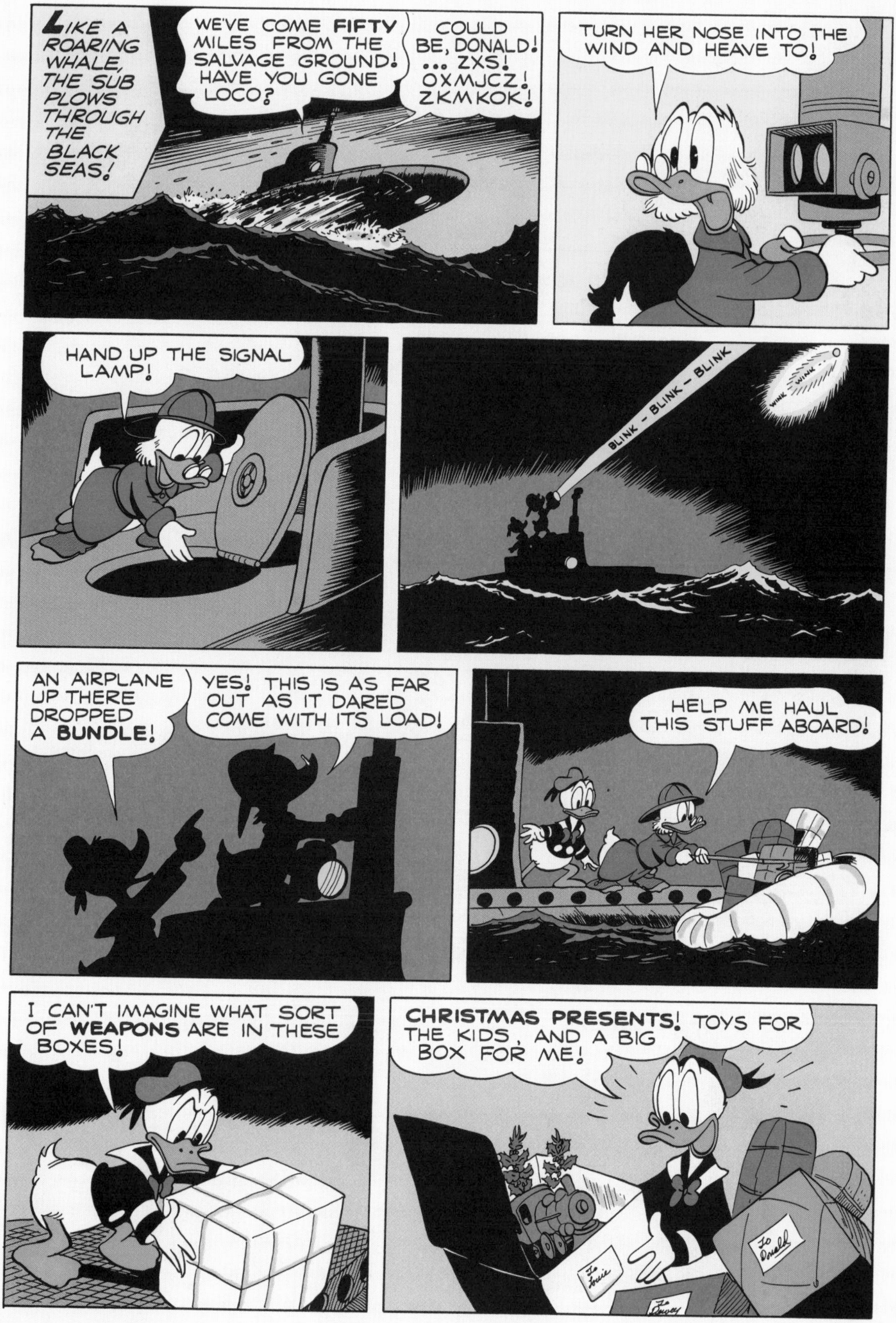
LIKE A ROARING WHALE, THE SUB PLOWS THROUGH THE BLACK SEAS!
WE'VE COME FIFTY MILES FROM THE SALVAGE GROUND! HAVE YOU GONE LOCO?
COULD BE, DONALD! ... ZXS! OXMJCZ! ZKMKOK!
TURN HER NOSE INTO THE WIND AND HEAVE TO!
HAND UP THE SIGNAL LAMP!
BLINK - BLINK - BLINK
WINK - WINK
AN AIRPLANE UP THERE DROPPED A BUNDLE!
YES! THIS IS AS FAR OUT AS IT DARED COME WITH ITS LOAD!
HELP ME HAUL THIS STUFF ABOARD!
I CAN'T IMAGINE WHAT SORT OF WEAPONS ARE IN THESE BOXES!
CHRISTMAS PRESENTS! TOYS FOR THE KIDS, AND A BIG BOX FOR ME!
To Donald

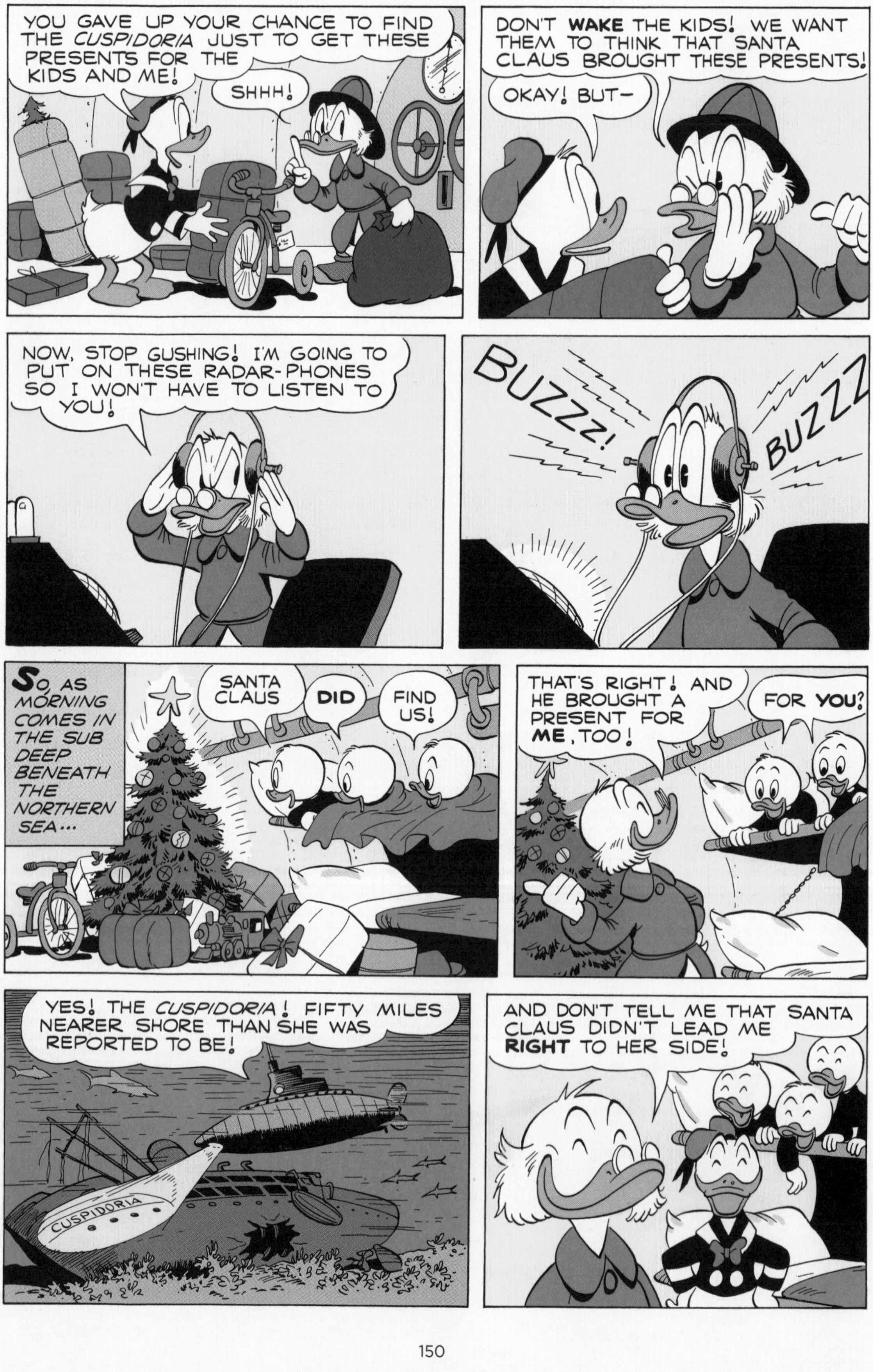
YOU GAVE UP YOUR CHANCE TO FIND THE CUSPIDORIA JUST TO GET THESE PRESENTS FOR THE KIDS AND ME!
SHHH!
DON'T WAKE THE KIDS! WE WANT THEM TO THINK THAT SANTA CLAUS BROUGHT THESE PRESENTS!
OKAY! BUT—
NOW, STOP GUSHING! I'M GOING TO PUT ON THESE RADAR-PHONES SO I WON'T HAVE TO LISTEN TO YOU!
BUZZZZ!
BUZZZ
SO, AS MORNING COMES IN THE SUB DEEP BENEATH THE NORTHERN SEA...
SANTA CLAUS
DID
FIND US!
THAT'S RIGHT! AND HE BROUGHT A PRESENT FOR ME, TOO!
FOR YOU?
YES! THE CUSPIDORIA! FIFTY MILES NEARER SHORE THAN SHE WAS REPORTED TO BE!
CUSPIDORIA
CUSPIDORIA
AND DON'T TELL ME THAT SANTA CLAUS DIDN'T LEAD ME RIGHT TO HER SIDE!

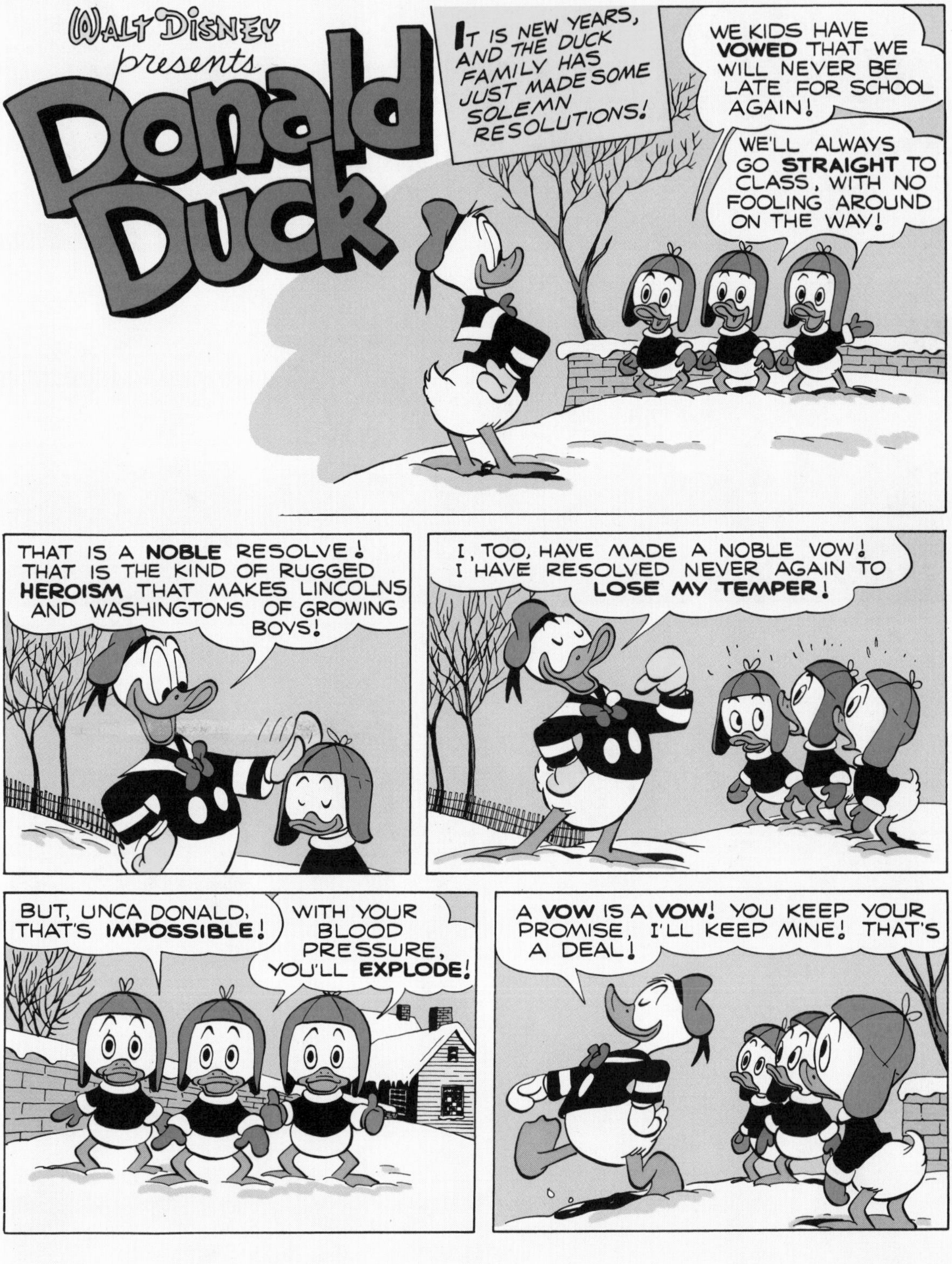
WALT DISNEY
presents
Donald Duck
IT IS NEW YEARS, AND THE DUCK FAMILY HAS JUST MADE SOME SOLEMN RESOLUTIONS!
WE KIDS HAVE VOWED THAT WE WILL NEVER BE LATE FOR SCHOOL AGAIN!
WE'LL ALWAYS GO STRAIGHT TO CLASS, WITH NO FOOLING AROUND ON THE WAY!
THAT IS A NOBLE RESOLVE! THAT IS THE KIND OF RUGGED HEROISM THAT MAKES LINCOLNS AND WASHINGTONS OF GROWING BOYS!
I, TOO, HAVE MADE A NOBLE VOW! I HAVE RESOLVED NEVER AGAIN TO LOSE MY TEMPER!
BUT, UNCA DONALD, THAT'S IMPOSSIBLE!
WITH YOUR BLOOD PRESSURE, YOU'LL EXPLODE!
A VOW IS A VOW! YOU KEEP YOUR PROMISE, I'LL KEEP MINE! THAT'S A DEAL!

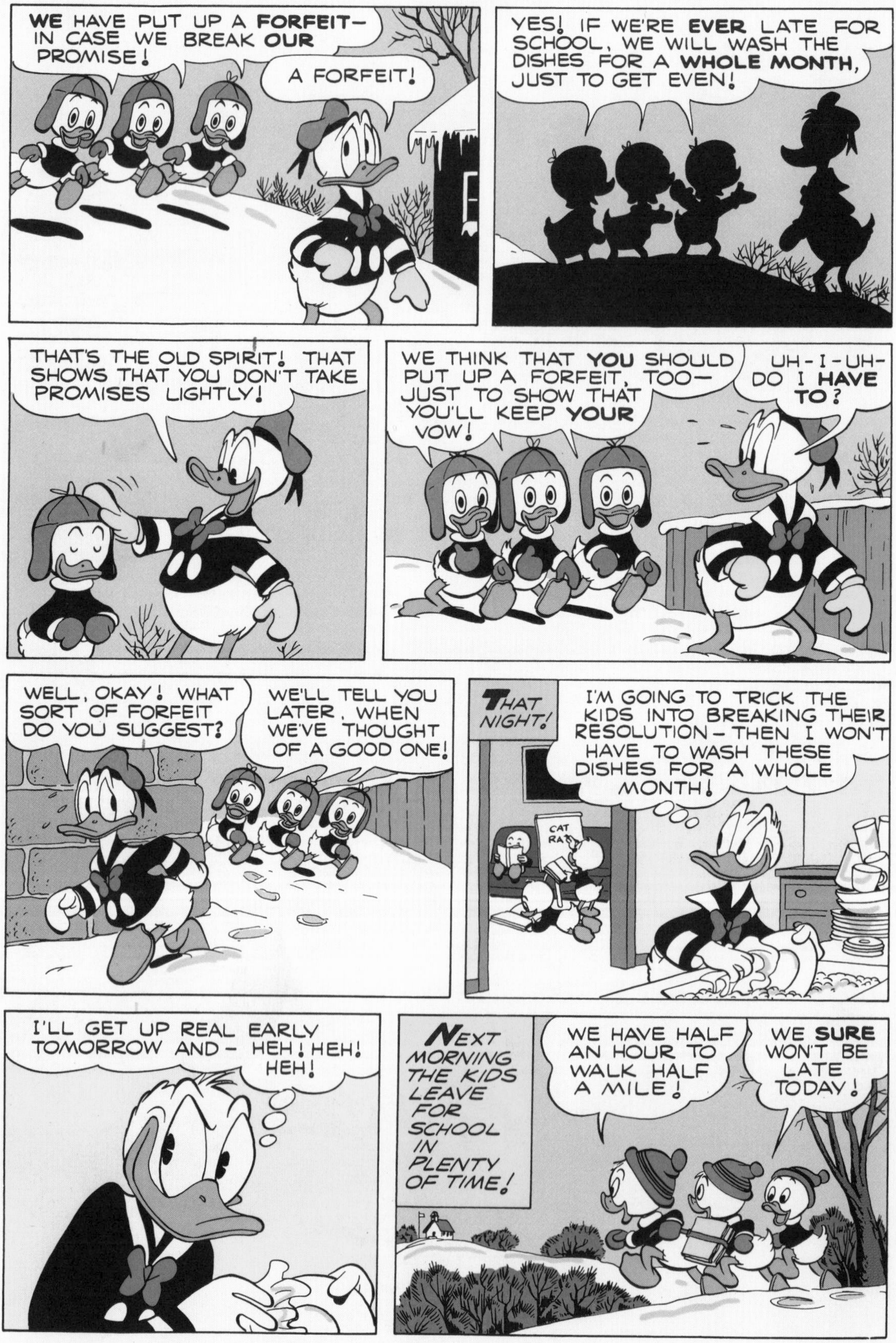
WE HAVE PUT UP A FORFEIT— IN CASE WE BREAK OUR PROMISE!
A FORFEIT!
YES! IF WE'RE EVER LATE FOR SCHOOL, WE WILL WASH THE DISHES FOR A WHOLE MONTH, JUST TO GET EVEN!
THAT'S THE OLD SPIRIT! THAT SHOWS THAT YOU DON'T TAKE PROMISES LIGHTLY!
WE THINK THAT YOU SHOULD PUT UP A FORFEIT, TOO— JUST TO SHOW THAT YOU'LL KEEP YOUR VOW!
UH-I-UH- DO I HAVE TO?
WELL, OKAY! WHAT SORT OF FORFEIT DO YOU SUGGEST?
WE'LL TELL YOU LATER, WHEN WE'VE THOUGHT OF A GOOD ONE!
THAT NIGHT!
I'M GOING TO TRICK THE KIDS INTO BREAKING THEIR RESOLUTION—THEN I WON'T HAVE TO WASH THESE DISHES FOR A WHOLE MONTH!
I'LL GET UP REAL EARLY TOMORROW AND— HEH! HEH! HEH!
NEXT MORNING THE KIDS LEAVE FOR SCHOOL IN PLENTY OF TIME!
WE HAVE HALF AN HOUR TO WALK HALF A MILE!
WE SURE WON'T BE LATE TODAY!

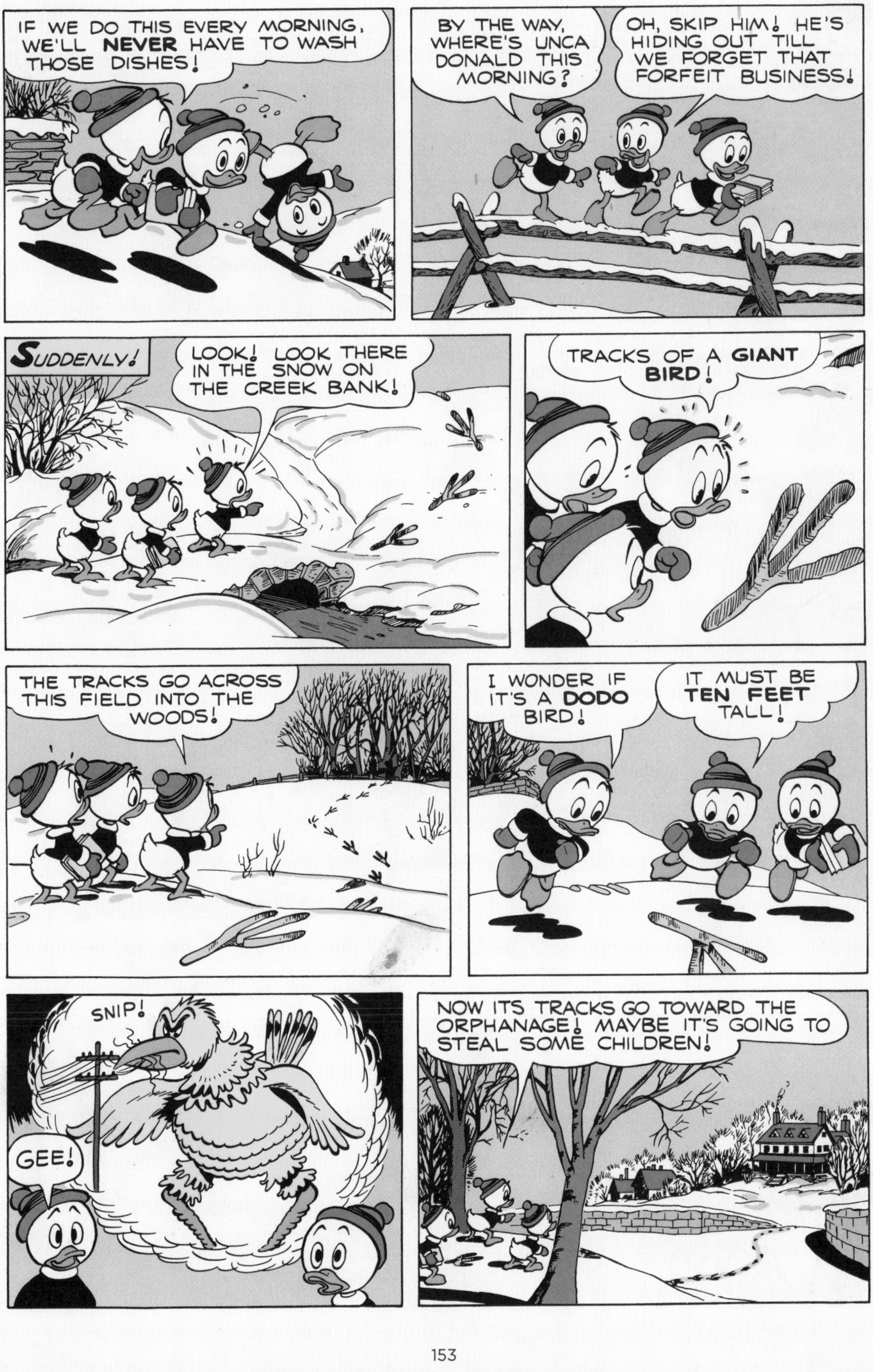
IF WE DO THIS EVERY MORNING, WE'LL **NEVER** HAVE TO WASH THOSE DISHES!
BY THE WAY, WHERE'S UNCA DONALD THIS MORNING?
OH, SKIP HIM! HE'S HIDING OUT TILL WE FORGET THAT FORFEIT BUSINESS!
SUDDENLY!
LOOK! LOOK THERE IN THE SNOW ON THE CREEK BANK!
TRACKS OF A **GIANT BIRD**!
THE TRACKS GO ACROSS THIS FIELD INTO THE WOODS!
I WONDER IF IT'S A **DODO** BIRD!
IT MUST BE **TEN FEET** TALL!
SNIP!
GEE!
NOW ITS TRACKS GO TOWARD THE ORPHANAGE! MAYBE IT'S GOING TO STEAL SOME CHILDREN!

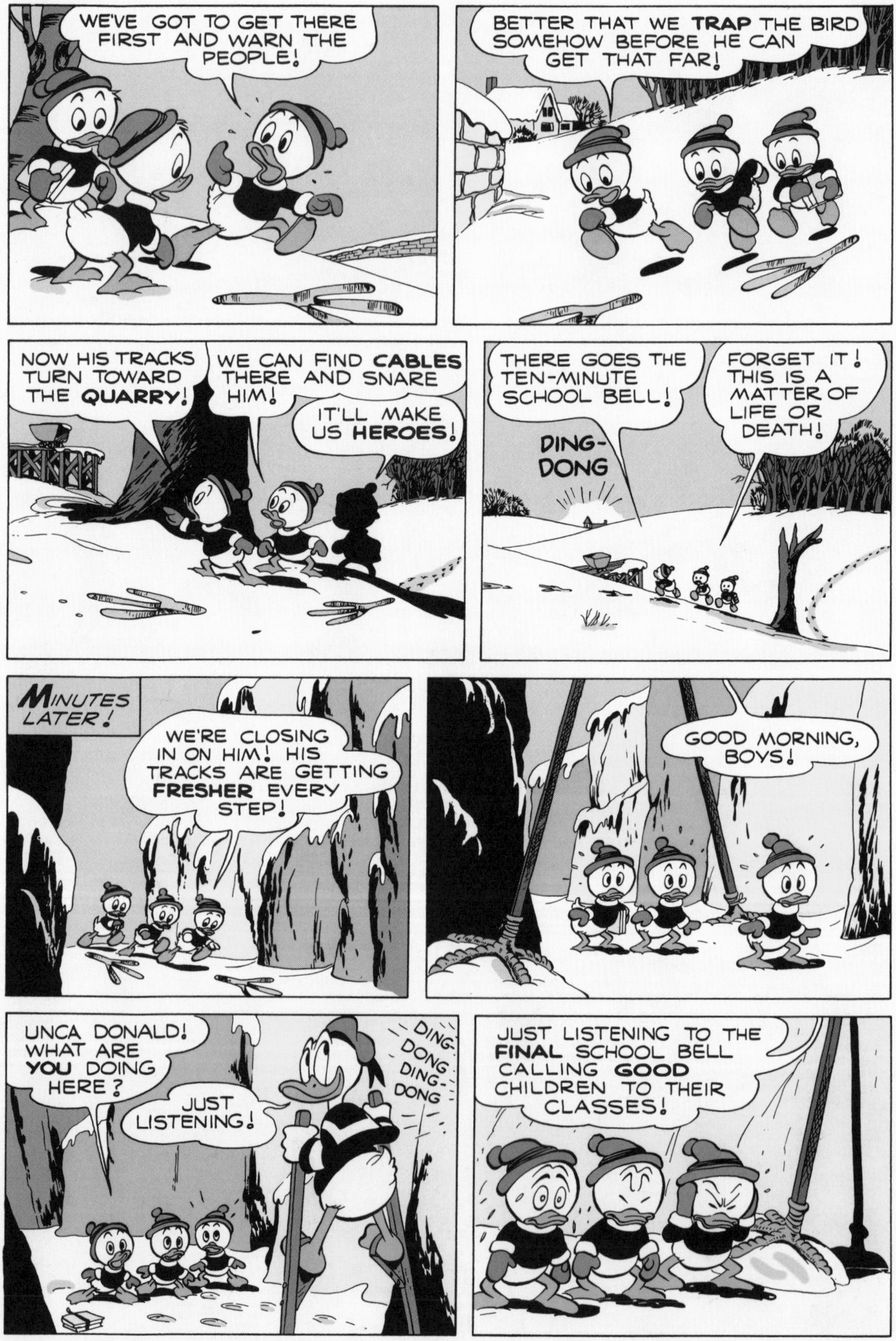
WE'VE GOT TO GET THERE FIRST AND WARN THE PEOPLE!
BETTER THAT WE **TRAP** THE BIRD SOMEHOW BEFORE HE CAN GET THAT FAR!
NOW HIS TRACKS TURN TOWARD THE **QUARRY**!
WE CAN FIND **CABLES** THERE AND SNARE HIM!
IT'LL MAKE US **HEROES**!
THERE GOES THE TEN-MINUTE SCHOOL BELL!
DING-DONG
FORGET IT! THIS IS A MATTER OF LIFE OR DEATH!
MINUTES LATER!
WE'RE CLOSING IN ON HIM! HIS TRACKS ARE GETTING **FRESHER** EVERY STEP!
GOOD MORNING, BOYS!
UNCA DONALD! WHAT ARE **YOU** DOING HERE?
JUST LISTENING!
DING-DONG DING-DONG
JUST LISTENING TO THE **FINAL** SCHOOL BELL CALLING **GOOD** CHILDREN TO THEIR CLASSES!

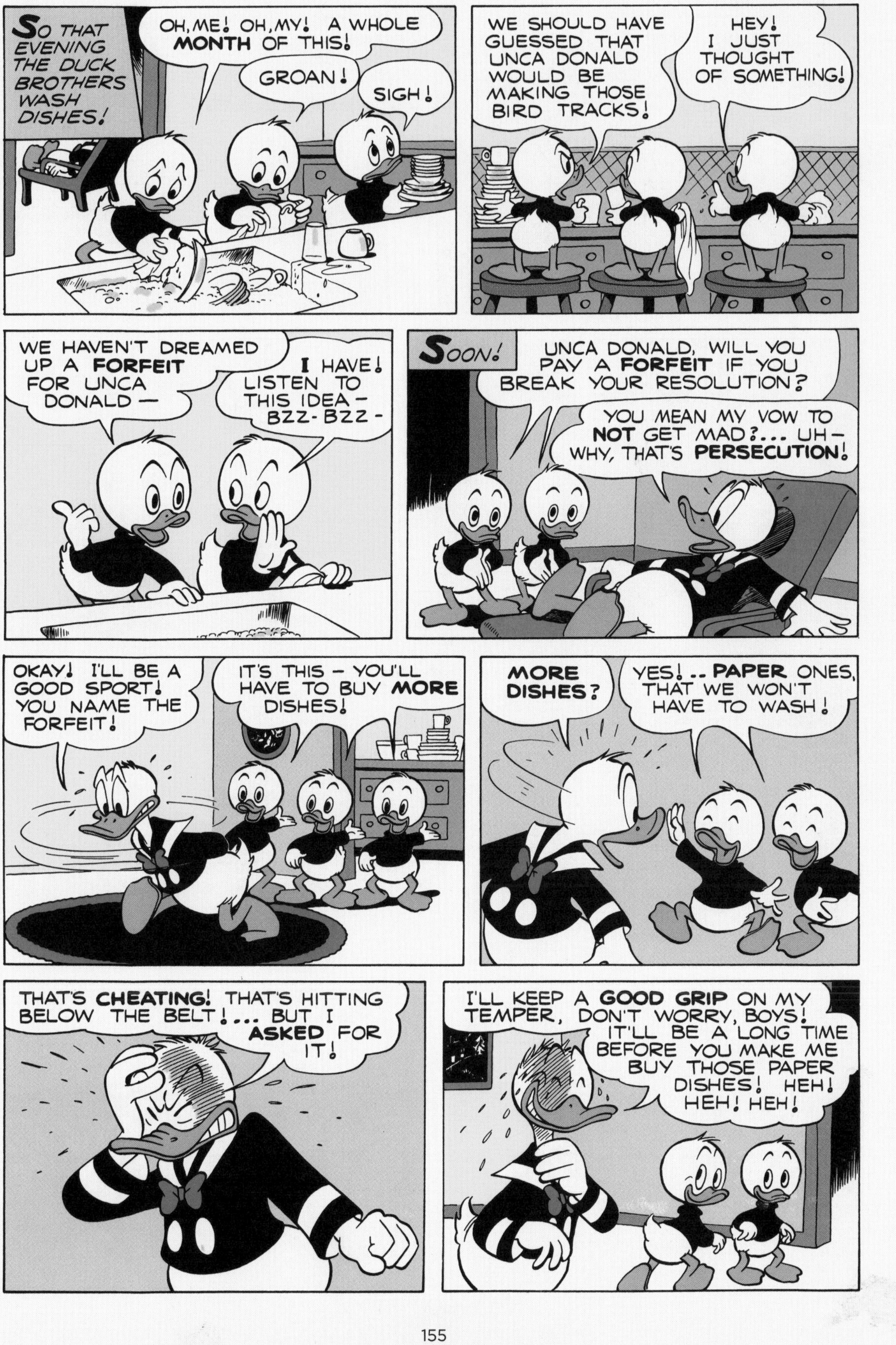
SO THAT EVENING THE DUCK BROTHERS WASH DISHES!
OH, ME! OH, MY! A WHOLE MONTH OF THIS!
GROAN!
SIGH!
WE SHOULD HAVE GUESSED THAT UNCA DONALD WOULD BE MAKING THOSE BIRD TRACKS!
HEY! I JUST THOUGHT OF SOMETHING!
WE HAVEN'T DREAMED UP A FORFEIT FOR UNCA DONALD —
I HAVE! LISTEN TO THIS IDEA — BZZ-BZZ —
SOON!
UNCA DONALD, WILL YOU PAY A FORFEIT IF YOU BREAK YOUR RESOLUTION?
YOU MEAN MY VOW TO NOT GET MAD?... UH— WHY, THAT'S PERSECUTION!
OKAY! I'LL BE A GOOD SPORT! YOU NAME THE FORFEIT!
IT'S THIS — YOU'LL HAVE TO BUY MORE DISHES!
MORE DISHES?
YES! .. PAPER ONES, THAT WE WON'T HAVE TO WASH!
THAT'S CHEATING! THAT'S HITTING BELOW THE BELT!... BUT I ASKED FOR IT!
I'LL KEEP A GOOD GRIP ON MY TEMPER, DON'T WORRY, BOYS!
IT'LL BE A LONG TIME BEFORE YOU MAKE ME BUY THOSE PAPER DISHES! HEH! HEH! HEH!

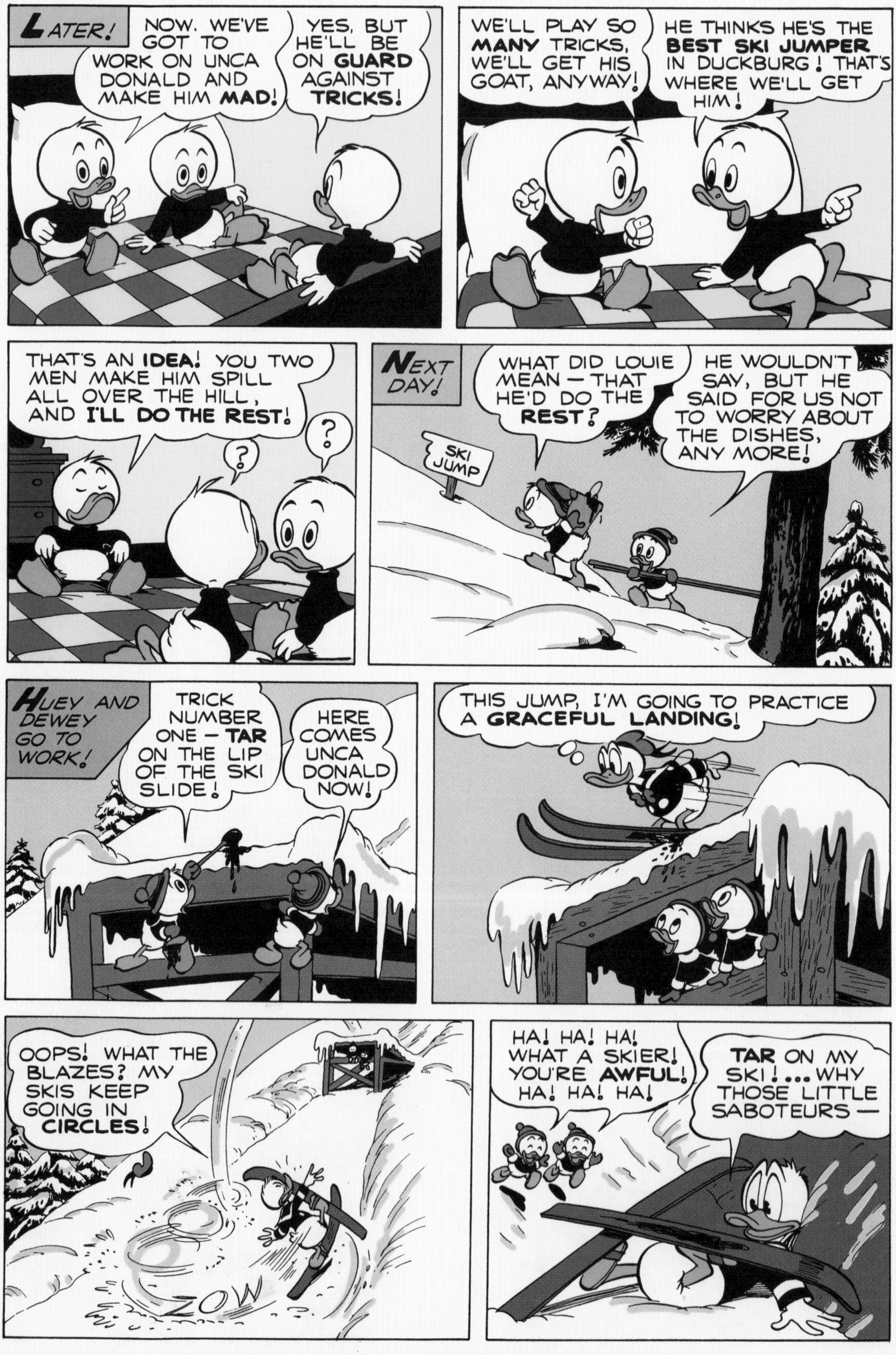
LATER!
NOW, WE'VE GOT TO WORK ON UNCA DONALD AND MAKE HIM MAD!
YES, BUT HE'LL BE ON GUARD AGAINST TRICKS!
WE'LL PLAY SO MANY TRICKS, WE'LL GET HIS GOAT, ANYWAY!
HE THINKS HE'S THE BEST SKI JUMPER IN DUCKBURG! THAT'S WHERE WE'LL GET HIM!
THAT'S AN IDEA! YOU TWO MEN MAKE HIM SPILL ALL OVER THE HILL, AND I'LL DO THE REST!
?
?
NEXT DAY!
SKI JUMP
WHAT DID LOUIE MEAN — THAT HE'D DO THE REST?
HE WOULDN'T SAY, BUT HE SAID FOR US NOT TO WORRY ABOUT THE DISHES, ANY MORE!
HUEY AND DEWEY GO TO WORK!
TRICK NUMBER ONE — TAR ON THE LIP OF THE SKI SLIDE!
HERE COMES UNCA DONALD NOW!
THIS JUMP, I'M GOING TO PRACTICE A GRACEFUL LANDING!
OOPS! WHAT THE BLAZES? MY SKIS KEEP GOING IN CIRCLES!
ZOW
HA! HA! HA! WHAT A SKIER! YOU'RE AWFUL! HA! HA! HA!
TAR ON MY SKI! ... WHY THOSE LITTLE SABOTEURS —

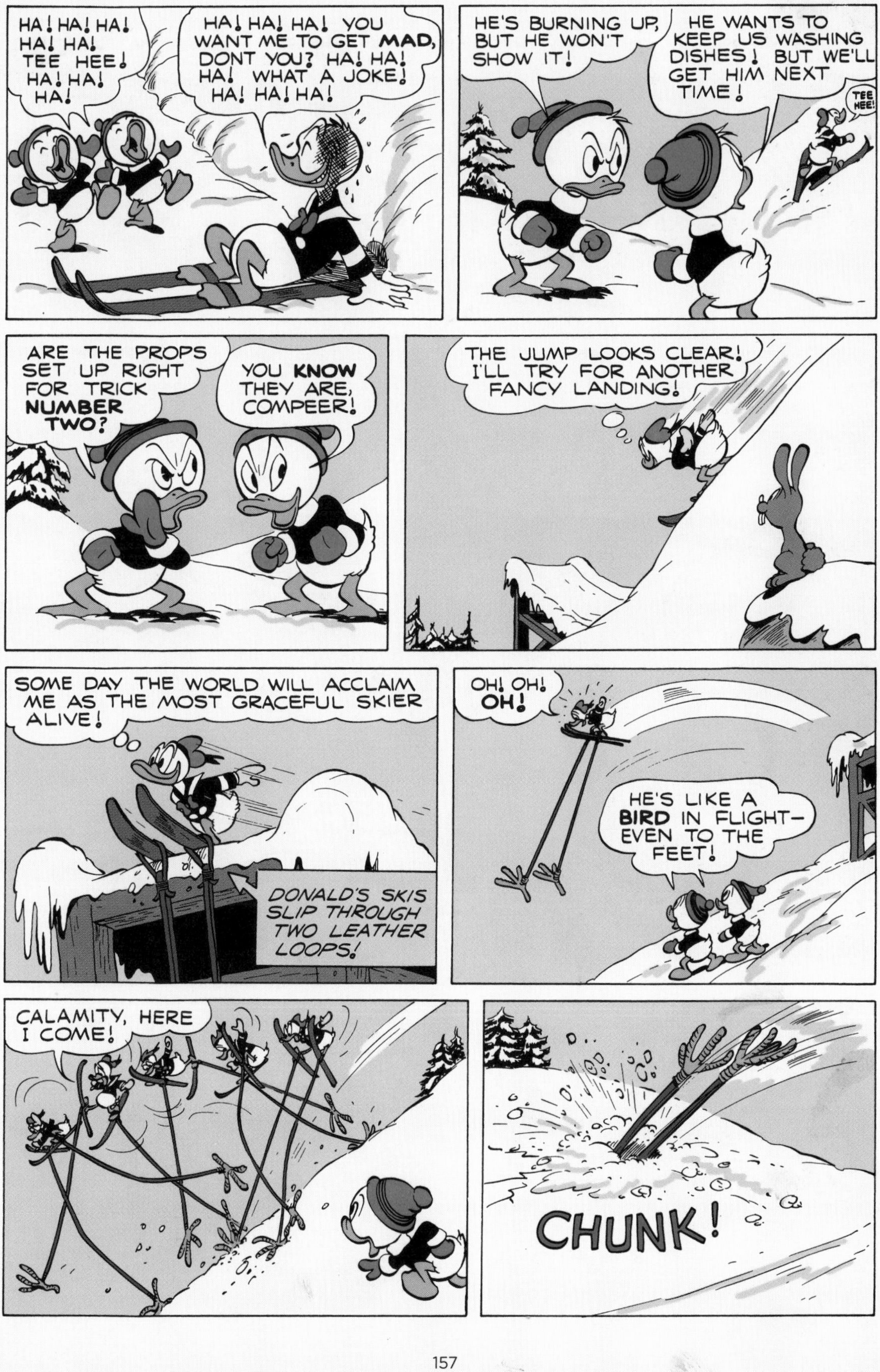

HA! HA! HA! HA! HA! TEE HEE! HA! HA! HA!
HA! HA! HA! YOU WANT ME TO GET MAD, DONT YOU? HA! HA! HA! WHAT A JOKE! HA! HA! HA!
HE'S BURNING UP, BUT HE WON'T SHOW IT!
HE WANTS TO KEEP US WASHING DISHES! BUT WE'LL GET HIM NEXT TIME!
TEE HEE!
ARE THE PROPS SET UP RIGHT FOR TRICK NUMBER TWO?
YOU KNOW THEY ARE, COMPEER!
THE JUMP LOOKS CLEAR! I'LL TRY FOR ANOTHER FANCY LANDING!
SOME DAY THE WORLD WILL ACCLAIM ME AS THE MOST GRACEFUL SKIER ALIVE!
DONALD'S SKIS SLIP THROUGH TWO LEATHER LOOPS!
OH! OH! OH!
HE'S LIKE A BIRD IN FLIGHT— EVEN TO THE FEET!
CALAMITY, HERE I COME!
CHUNK!

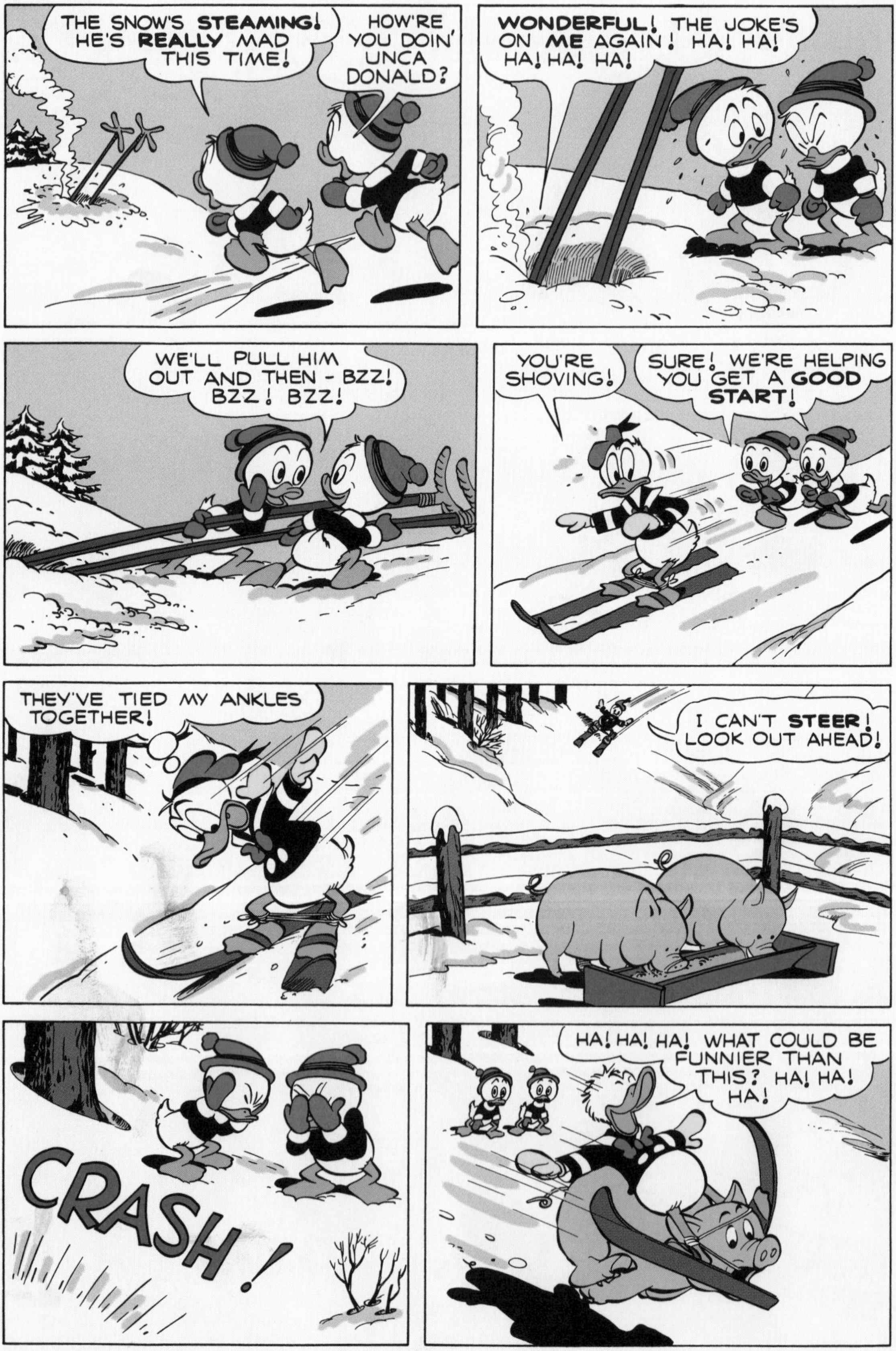
THE SNOW'S STEAMING! HE'S REALLY MAD THIS TIME!
HOW'RE YOU DOIN' UNCA DONALD?
WONDERFUL! THE JOKE'S ON ME AGAIN! HA! HA! HA! HA! HA!
WE'LL PULL HIM OUT AND THEN - BZZ! BZZ! BZZ!
YOU'RE SHOVING!
SURE! WE'RE HELPING YOU GET A GOOD START!
THEY'VE TIED MY ANKLES TOGETHER!
I CAN'T STEER! LOOK OUT AHEAD!
CRASH!
HA! HA! HA! WHAT COULD BE FUNNIER THAN THIS? HA! HA! HA!

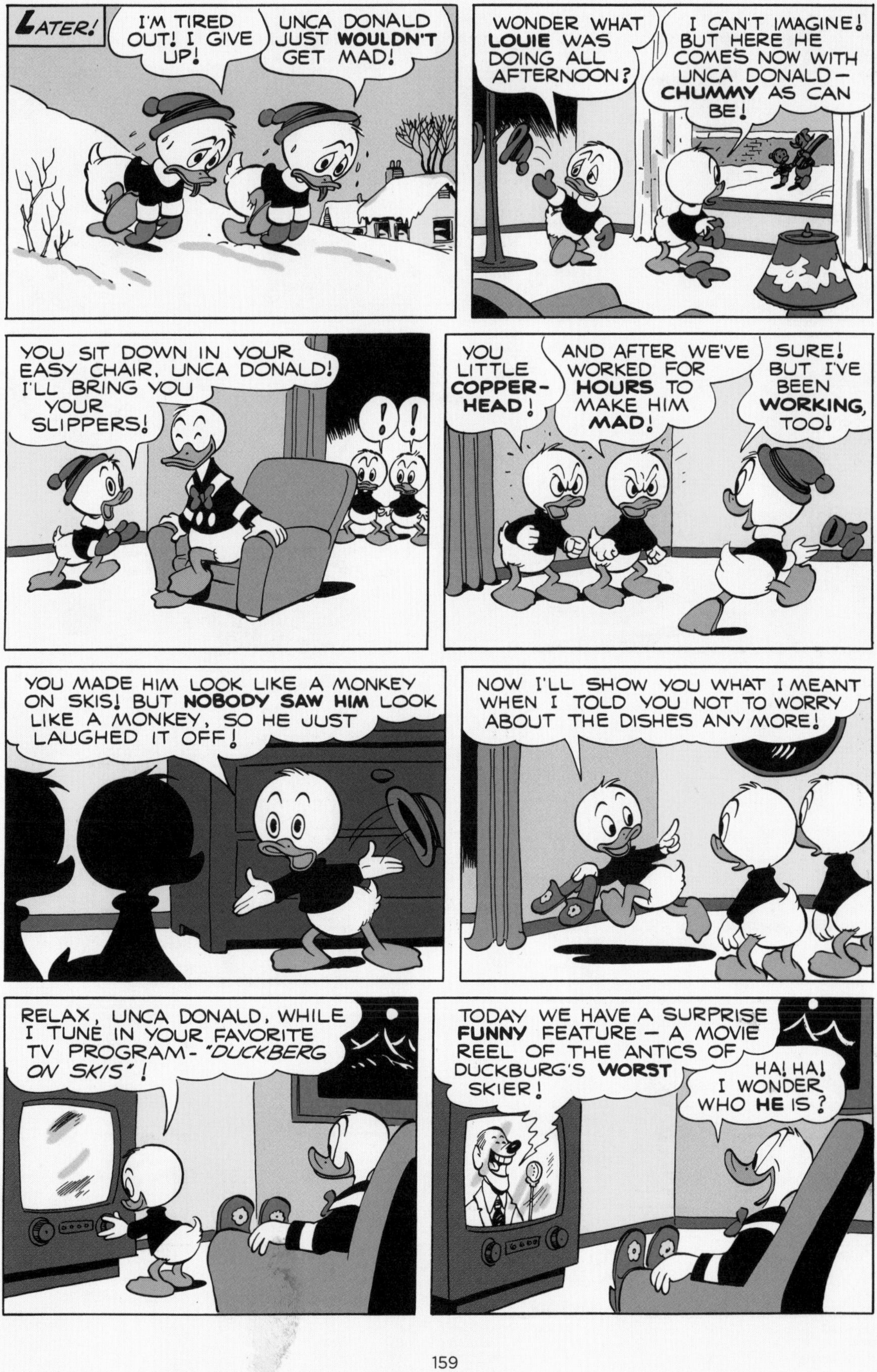
LATER!
I'M TIRED OUT! I GIVE UP!
UNCA DONALD JUST **WOULDN'T** GET MAD!
WONDER WHAT **LOUIE** WAS DOING ALL AFTERNOON?
I CAN'T IMAGINE! BUT HERE HE COMES NOW WITH UNCA DONALD—**CHUMMY** AS CAN BE!
YOU SIT DOWN IN YOUR EASY CHAIR, UNCA DONALD! I'LL BRING YOU YOUR SLIPPERS!
!
!
YOU LITTLE **COPPER-HEAD**!
AND AFTER WE'VE WORKED FOR **HOURS** TO MAKE HIM **MAD**!
SURE! BUT I'VE BEEN **WORKING**, TOO!
YOU MADE HIM LOOK LIKE A MONKEY ON SKIS! BUT **NOBODY SAW HIM** LOOK LIKE A MONKEY, SO HE JUST LAUGHED IT OFF!
NOW I'LL SHOW YOU WHAT I MEANT WHEN I TOLD YOU NOT TO WORRY ABOUT THE DISHES ANY MORE!
RELAX, UNCA DONALD, WHILE I TUNE IN YOUR FAVORITE TV PROGRAM—*"DUCKBERG ON SKIS"*!
TODAY WE HAVE A SURPRISE **FUNNY** FEATURE—A MOVIE REEL OF THE ANTICS OF DUCKBURG'S **WORST** SKIER!
HA! HA! I WONDER WHO **HE** IS?

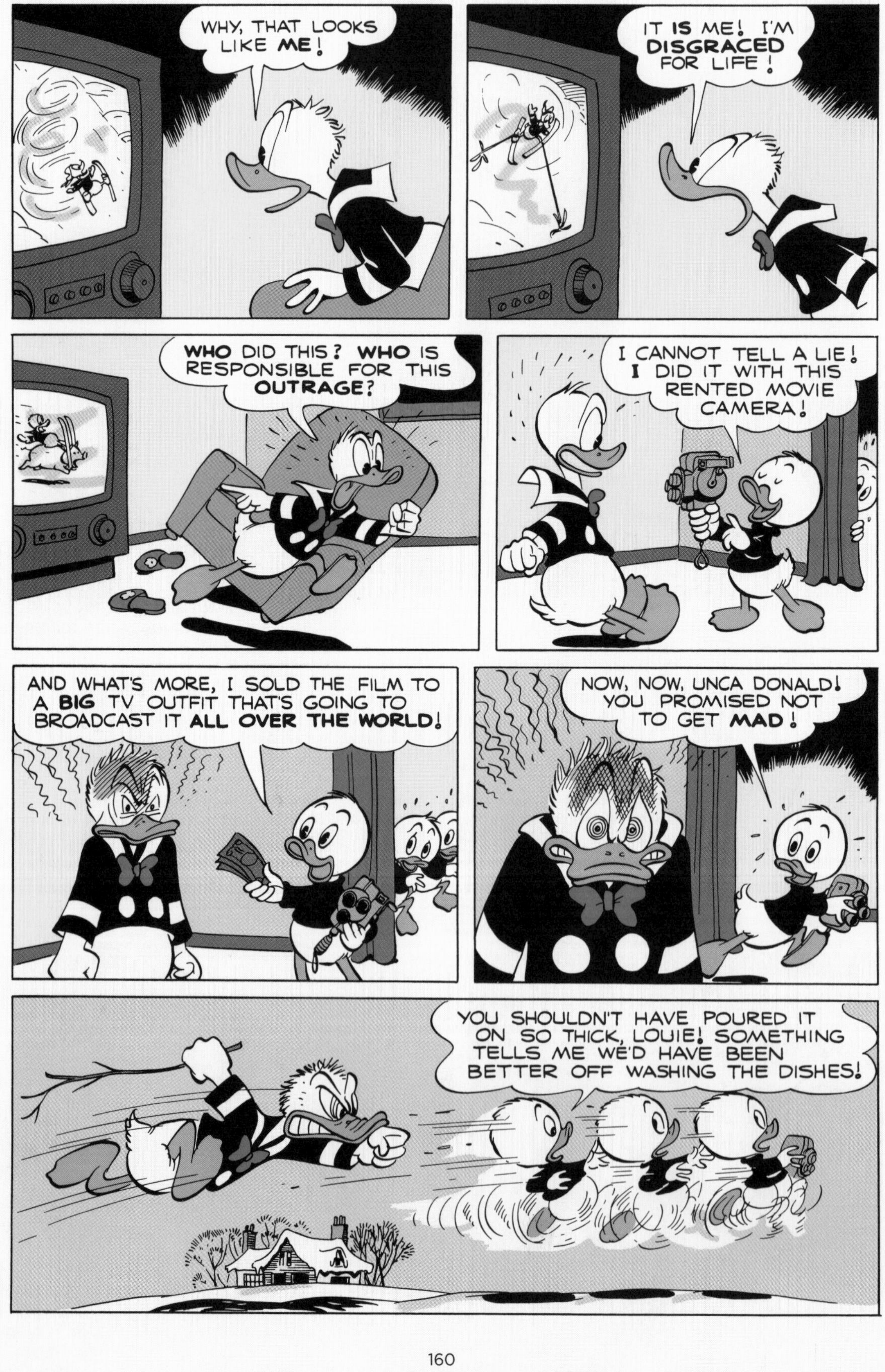
WHY, THAT LOOKS LIKE **ME**!
IT **IS** ME! I'M **DISGRACED** FOR LIFE!
WHO DID THIS? **WHO** IS RESPONSIBLE FOR THIS **OUTRAGE**?
I CANNOT TELL A LIE! **I** DID IT WITH THIS RENTED MOVIE CAMERA!
AND WHAT'S MORE, I SOLD THE FILM TO A **BIG** TV OUTFIT THAT'S GOING TO BROADCAST IT **ALL OVER THE WORLD**!
NOW, NOW, UNCA DONALD! YOU PROMISED NOT TO GET **MAD**!
YOU SHOULDN'T HAVE POURED IT ON SO THICK, LOUIE! SOMETHING TELLS ME WE'D HAVE BEEN BETTER OFF WASHING THE DISHES!

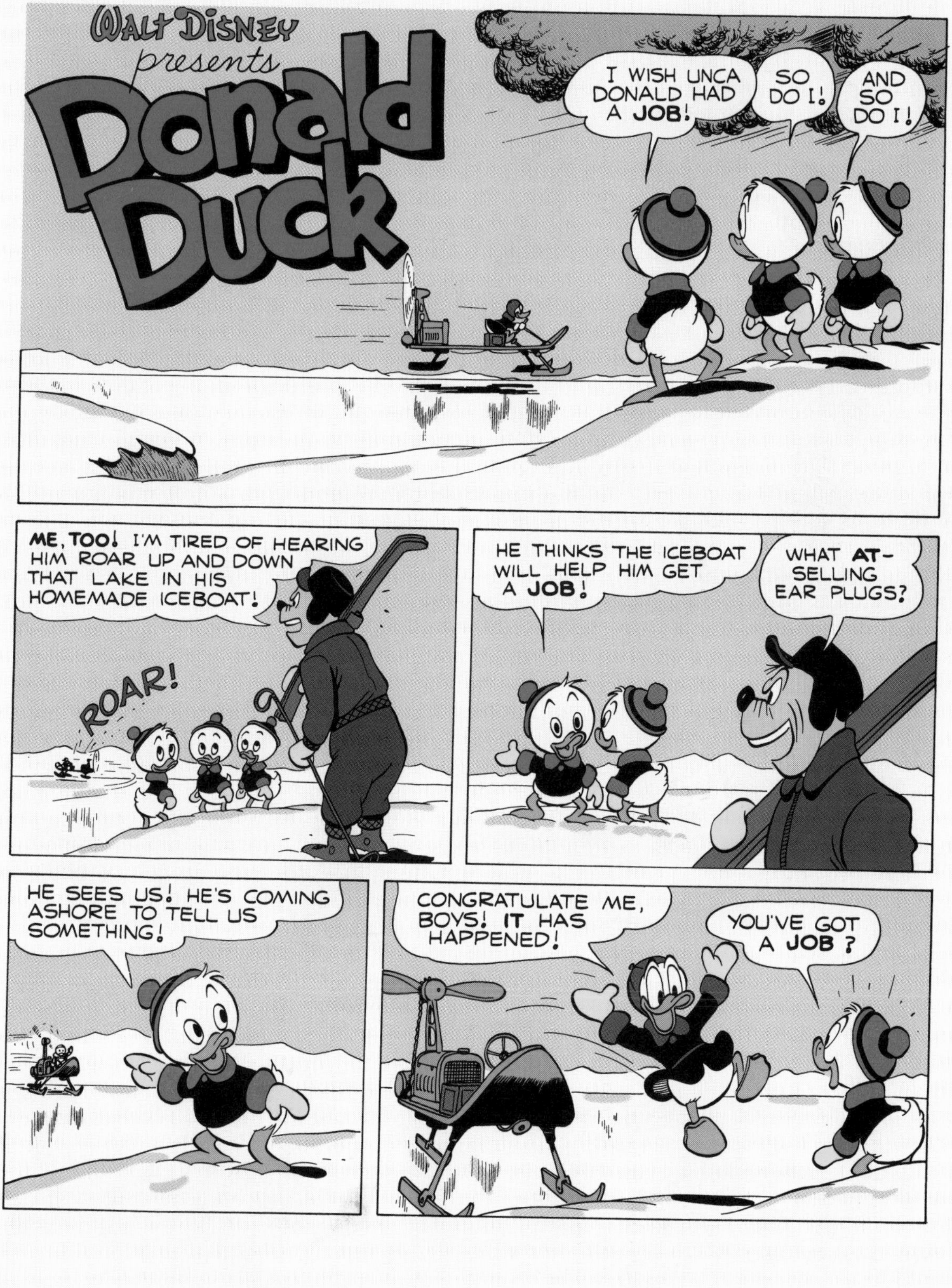
WALT DISNEY
presents
Donald Duck
I WISH UNCA DONALD HAD A JOB!
SO DO I!
AND SO DO I!
ME, TOO! I'M TIRED OF HEARING HIM ROAR UP AND DOWN THAT LAKE IN HIS HOMEMADE ICEBOAT!
ROAR!
HE THINKS THE ICEBOAT WILL HELP HIM GET A JOB!
WHAT AT— SELLING EAR PLUGS?
HE SEES US! HE'S COMING ASHORE TO TELL US SOMETHING!
CONGRATULATE ME, BOYS! IT HAS HAPPENED!
YOU'VE GOT A JOB?

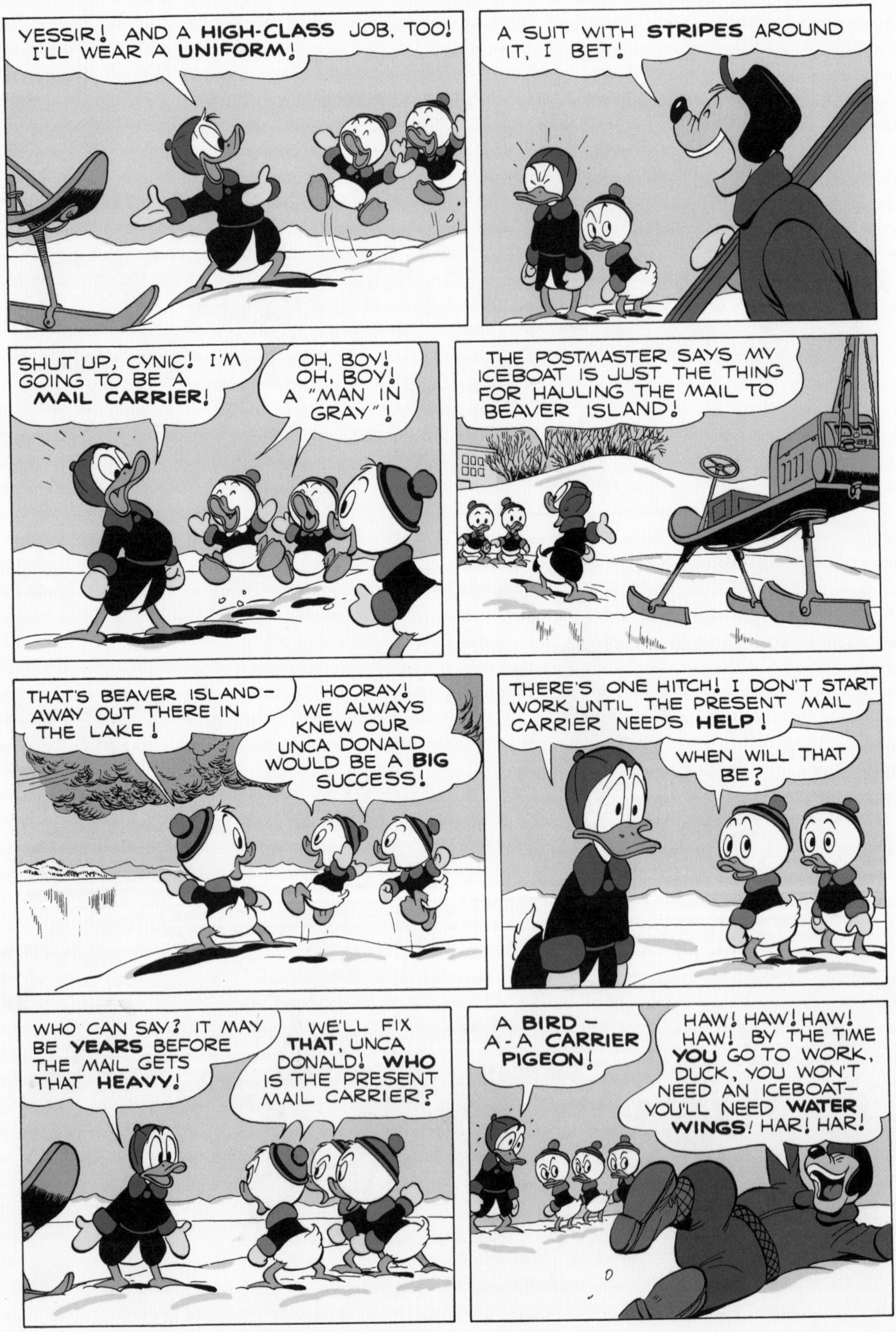
YESSIR! AND A HIGH-CLASS JOB, TOO! I'LL WEAR A UNIFORM!
A SUIT WITH STRIPES AROUND IT, I BET!
SHUT UP, CYNIC! I'M GOING TO BE A MAIL CARRIER!
OH, BOY! OH, BOY! A "MAN IN GRAY"!
THE POSTMASTER SAYS MY ICEBOAT IS JUST THE THING FOR HAULING THE MAIL TO BEAVER ISLAND!
THAT'S BEAVER ISLAND– AWAY OUT THERE IN THE LAKE!
HOORAY! WE ALWAYS KNEW OUR UNCA DONALD WOULD BE A BIG SUCCESS!
THERE'S ONE HITCH! I DON'T START WORK UNTIL THE PRESENT MAIL CARRIER NEEDS HELP!
WHEN WILL THAT BE?
WHO CAN SAY? IT MAY BE YEARS BEFORE THE MAIL GETS THAT HEAVY!
WE'LL FIX THAT, UNCA DONALD! WHO IS THE PRESENT MAIL CARRIER?
A BIRD – A-A CARRIER PIGEON!
HAW! HAW! HAW! HAW! BY THE TIME YOU GO TO WORK, DUCK, YOU WON'T NEED AN ICEBOAT– YOU'LL NEED WATER WINGS! HAR! HAR!

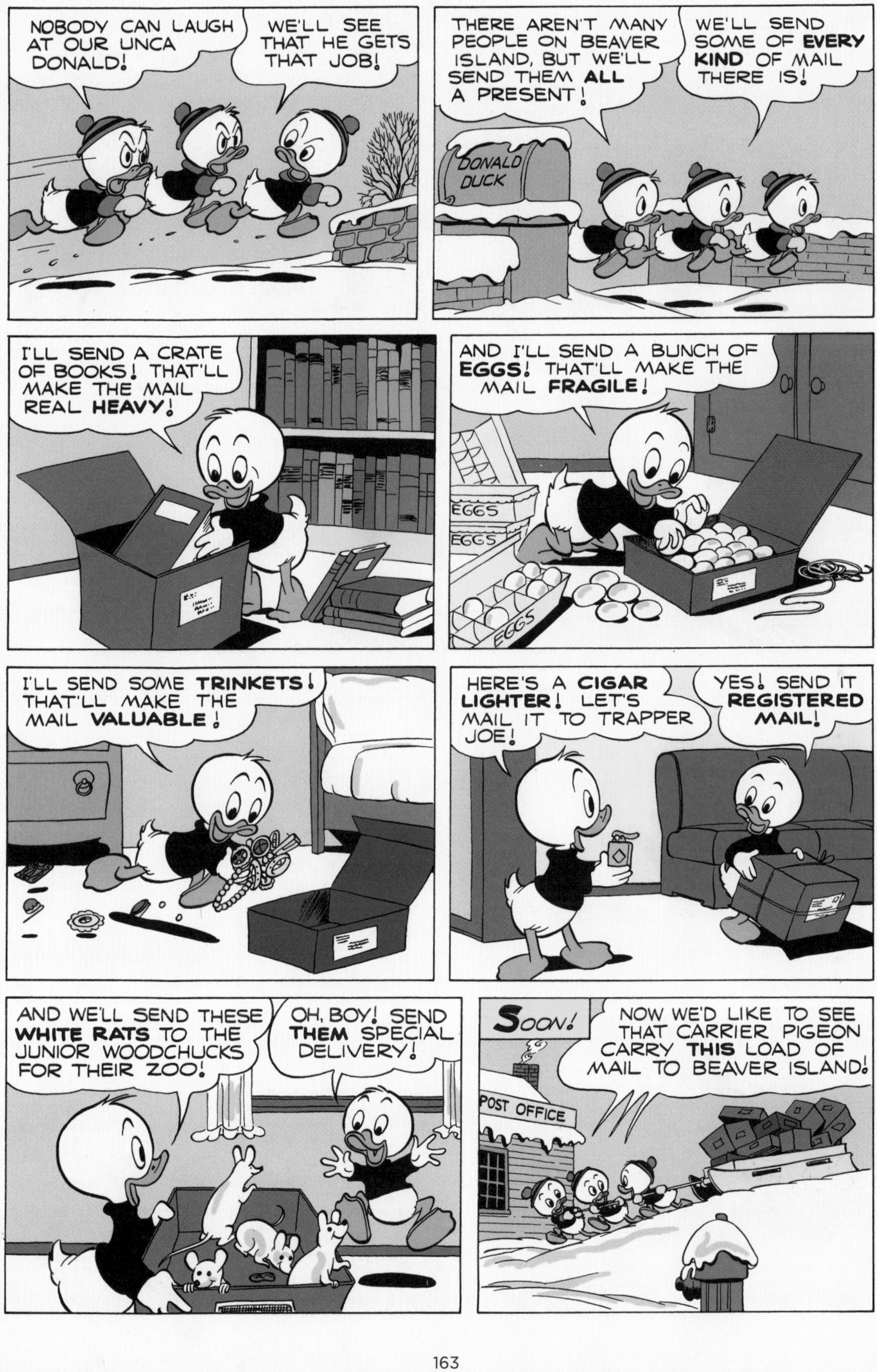
NOBODY CAN LAUGH AT OUR UNCA DONALD!
WE'LL SEE THAT HE GETS THAT JOB!
THERE AREN'T MANY PEOPLE ON BEAVER ISLAND, BUT WE'LL SEND THEM ALL A PRESENT!
WE'LL SEND SOME OF EVERY KIND OF MAIL THERE IS!
DONALD DUCK
I'LL SEND A CRATE OF BOOKS! THAT'LL MAKE THE MAIL REAL HEAVY!
AND I'LL SEND A BUNCH OF EGGS! THAT'LL MAKE THE MAIL FRAGILE!
EGGS
EGGS
EGGS
I'LL SEND SOME TRINKETS! THAT'LL MAKE THE MAIL VALUABLE!
HERE'S A CIGAR LIGHTER! LET'S MAIL IT TO TRAPPER JOE!
YES! SEND IT REGISTERED MAIL!
AND WE'LL SEND THESE WHITE RATS TO THE JUNIOR WOODCHUCKS FOR THEIR ZOO!
OH, BOY! SEND THEM SPECIAL DELIVERY!
SOON!
NOW WE'D LIKE TO SEE THAT CARRIER PIGEON CARRY THIS LOAD OF MAIL TO BEAVER ISLAND!
POST OFFICE

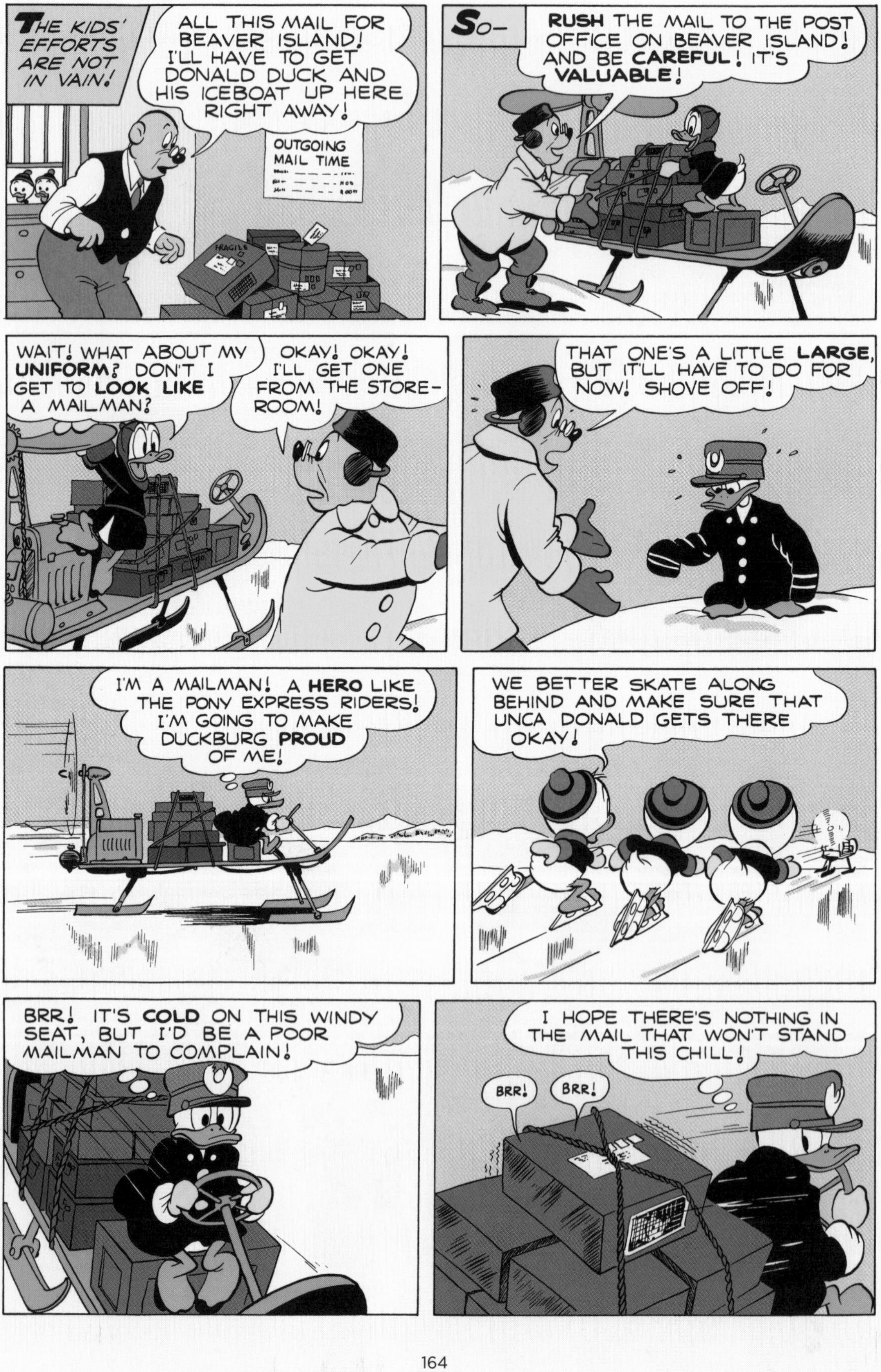
THE KIDS' EFFORTS ARE NOT IN VAIN!
ALL THIS MAIL FOR BEAVER ISLAND! I'LL HAVE TO GET DONALD DUCK AND HIS ICEBOAT UP HERE RIGHT AWAY!
OUTGOING MAIL TIME
FRAGILE
SO—
RUSH THE MAIL TO THE POST OFFICE ON BEAVER ISLAND! AND BE CAREFUL! IT'S VALUABLE!
WAIT! WHAT ABOUT MY UNIFORM? DON'T I GET TO LOOK LIKE A MAILMAN?
OKAY! OKAY! I'LL GET ONE FROM THE STORE-ROOM!
THAT ONE'S A LITTLE LARGE, BUT IT'LL HAVE TO DO FOR NOW! SHOVE OFF!
I'M A MAILMAN! A HERO LIKE THE PONY EXPRESS RIDERS! I'M GOING TO MAKE DUCKBURG PROUD OF ME!
WE BETTER SKATE ALONG BEHIND AND MAKE SURE THAT UNCA DONALD GETS THERE OKAY!
BRR! IT'S COLD ON THIS WINDY SEAT, BUT I'D BE A POOR MAILMAN TO COMPLAIN!
I HOPE THERE'S NOTHING IN THE MAIL THAT WON'T STAND THIS CHILL!
BRR!
BRR!

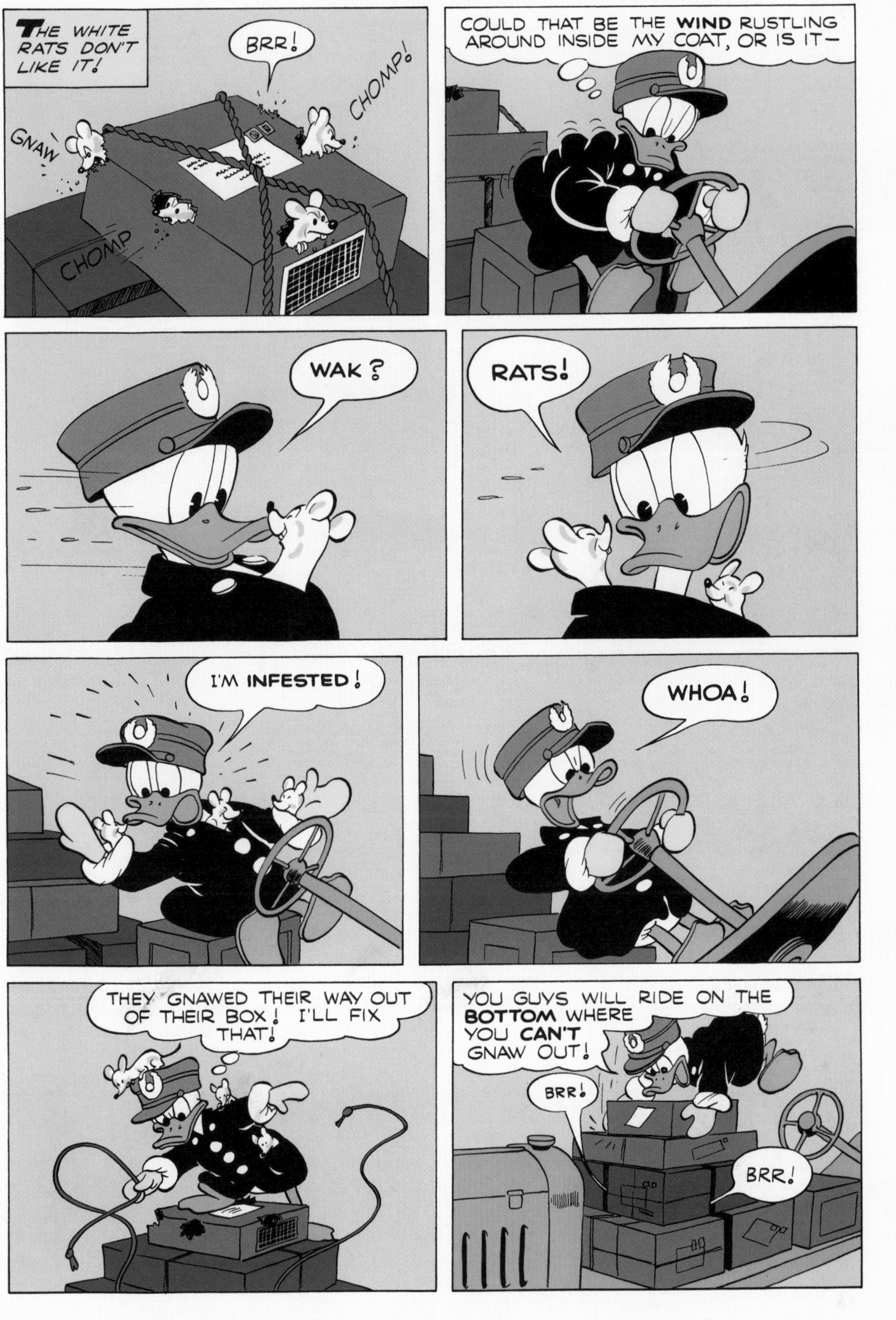
THE WHITE RATS DON'T LIKE IT!
BRR!
CHOMP!
GNAW
CHOMP
COULD THAT BE THE **WIND** RUSTLING AROUND INSIDE MY COAT, OR IS IT—
WAK?
RATS!
I'M **INFESTED**!
WHOA!
THEY GNAWED THEIR WAY OUT OF THEIR BOX! I'LL FIX THAT!
YOU GUYS WILL RIDE ON THE **BOTTOM** WHERE YOU **CAN'T** GNAW OUT!
BRR!
BRR!

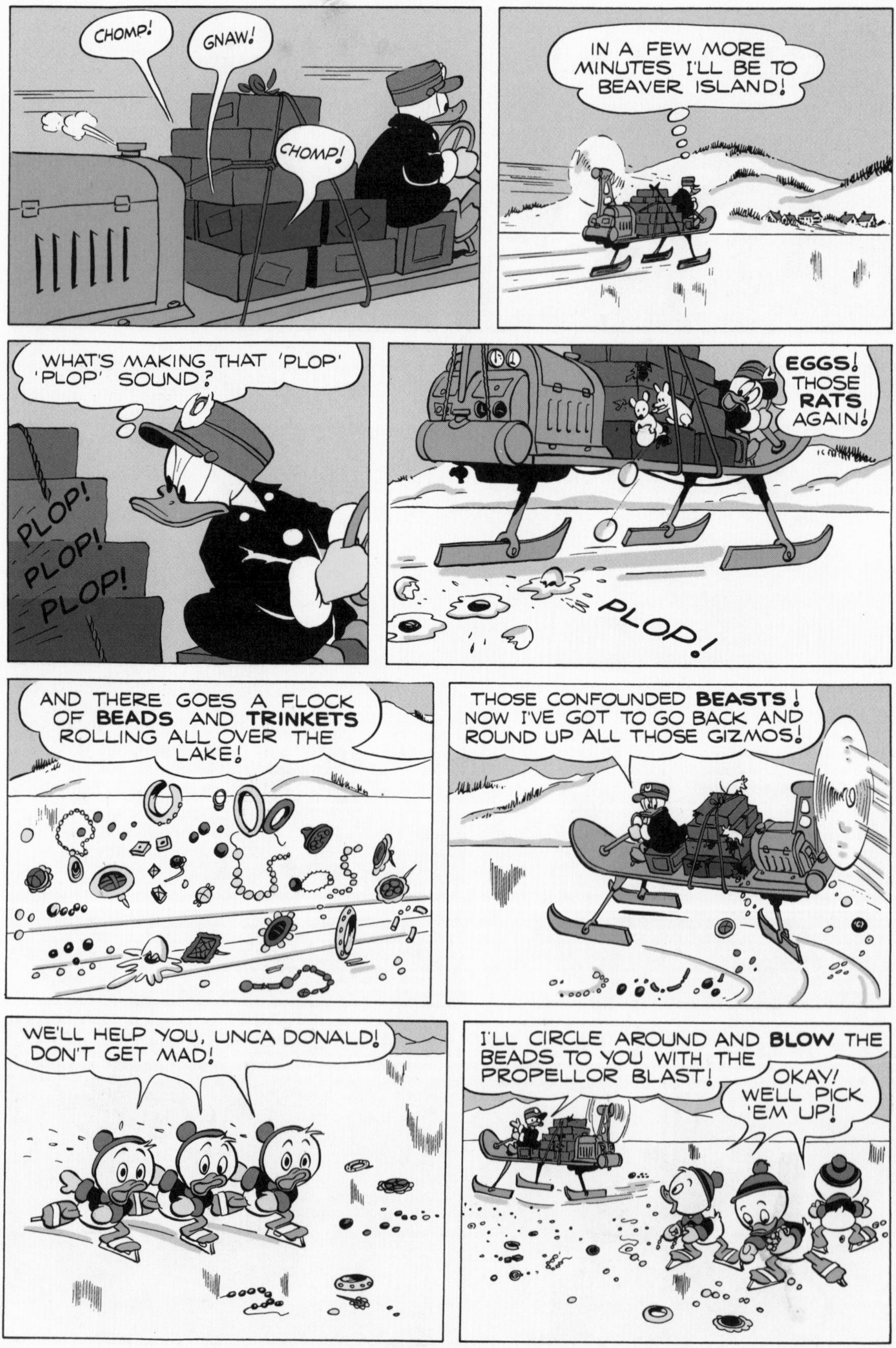
CHOMP!
GNAW!
CHOMP!
IN A FEW MORE MINUTES I'LL BE TO BEAVER ISLAND!
WHAT'S MAKING THAT 'PLOP' 'PLOP' SOUND?
PLOP! PLOP! PLOP!
EGGS! THOSE RATS AGAIN!
PLOP!
AND THERE GOES A FLOCK OF BEADS AND TRINKETS ROLLING ALL OVER THE LAKE!
THOSE CONFOUNDED BEASTS! NOW I'VE GOT TO GO BACK AND ROUND UP ALL THOSE GIZMOS!
WE'LL HELP YOU, UNCA DONALD! DON'T GET MAD!
I'LL CIRCLE AROUND AND BLOW THE BEADS TO YOU WITH THE PROPELLOR BLAST!
OKAY! WE'LL PICK 'EM UP!

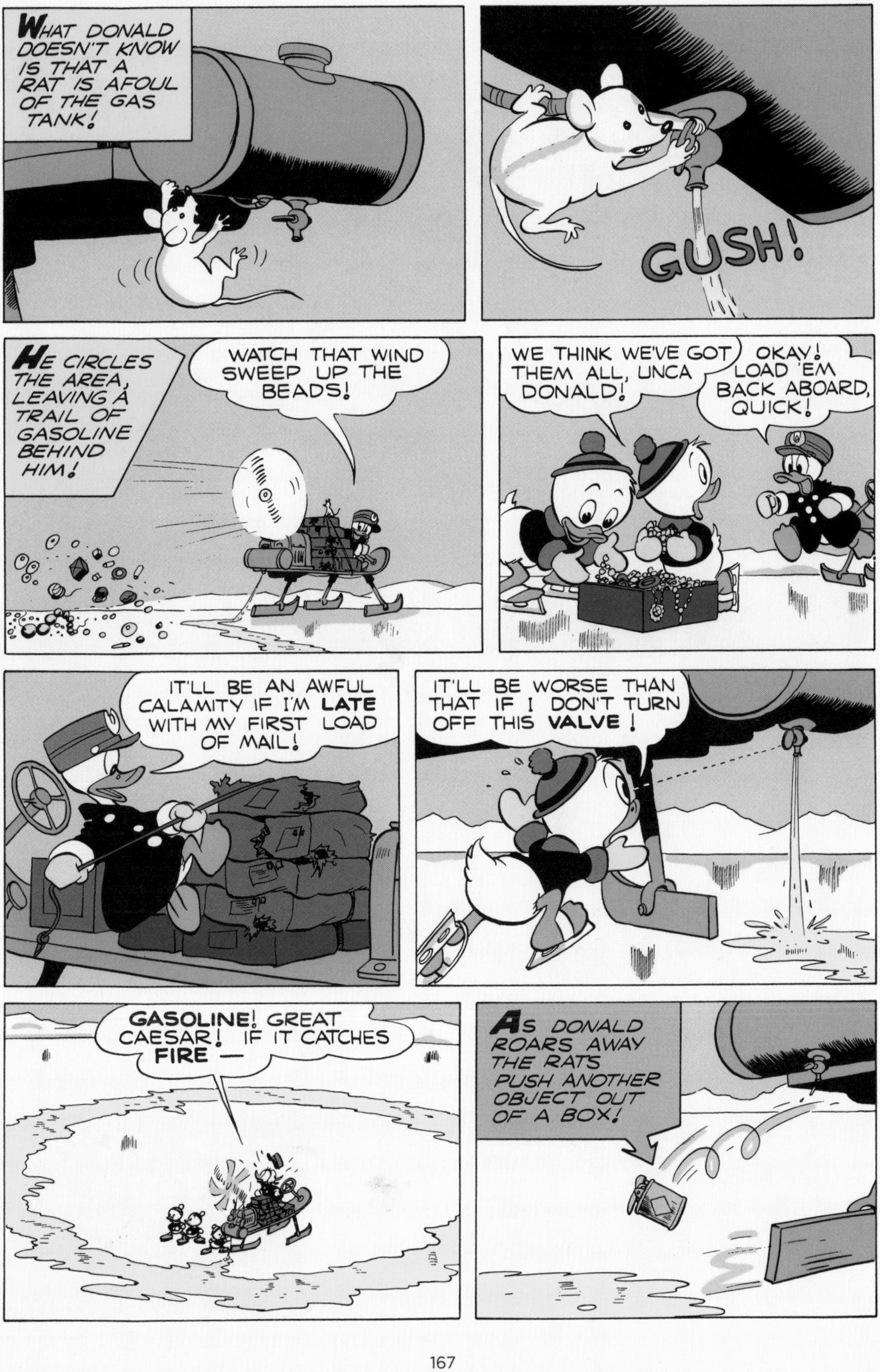
WHAT DONALD DOESN'T KNOW IS THAT A RAT IS AFOUL OF THE GAS TANK!
GUSH!
HE CIRCLES THE AREA, LEAVING A TRAIL OF GASOLINE BEHIND HIM!
WATCH THAT WIND SWEEP UP THE BEADS!
WE THINK WE'VE GOT THEM ALL, UNCA DONALD!
OKAY! LOAD 'EM BACK ABOARD, QUICK!
IT'LL BE AN AWFUL CALAMITY IF I'M LATE WITH MY FIRST LOAD OF MAIL!
IT'LL BE WORSE THAN THAT IF I DON'T TURN OFF THIS VALVE!
GASOLINE! GREAT CAESAR! IF IT CATCHES FIRE —
AS DONALD ROARS AWAY THE RATS PUSH ANOTHER OBJECT OUT OF A BOX!

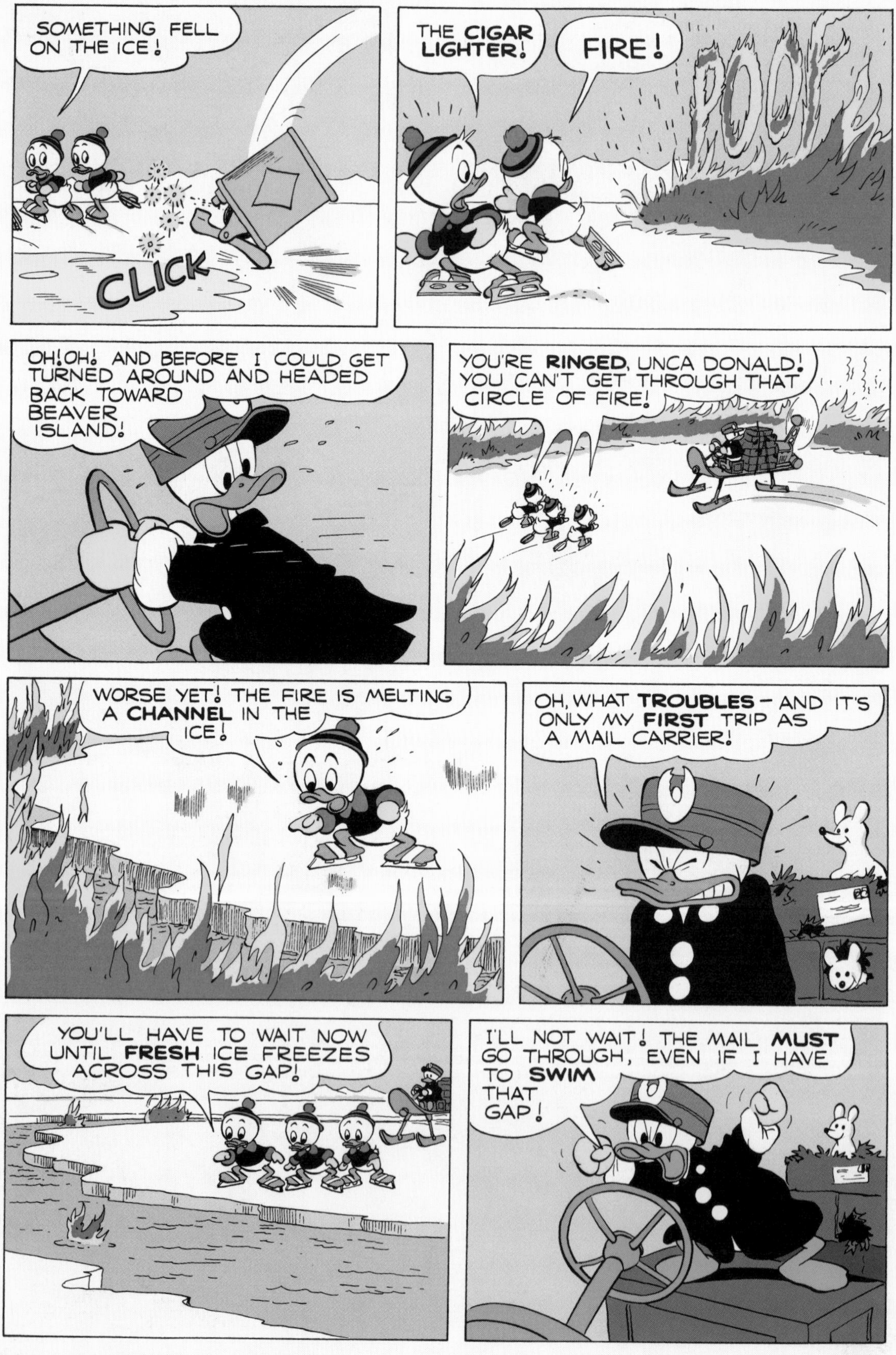
SOMETHING FELL ON THE ICE!
CLICK
THE CIGAR LIGHTER!
FIRE!
POOF
OH! OH! AND BEFORE I COULD GET TURNED AROUND AND HEADED BACK TOWARD BEAVER ISLAND!
YOU'RE RINGED, UNCA DONALD! YOU CAN'T GET THROUGH THAT CIRCLE OF FIRE!
WORSE YET! THE FIRE IS MELTING A CHANNEL IN THE ICE!
OH, WHAT TROUBLES – AND IT'S ONLY MY FIRST TRIP AS A MAIL CARRIER!
YOU'LL HAVE TO WAIT NOW UNTIL FRESH ICE FREEZES ACROSS THIS GAP!
I'LL NOT WAIT! THE MAIL MUST GO THROUGH, EVEN IF I HAVE TO SWIM THAT GAP!

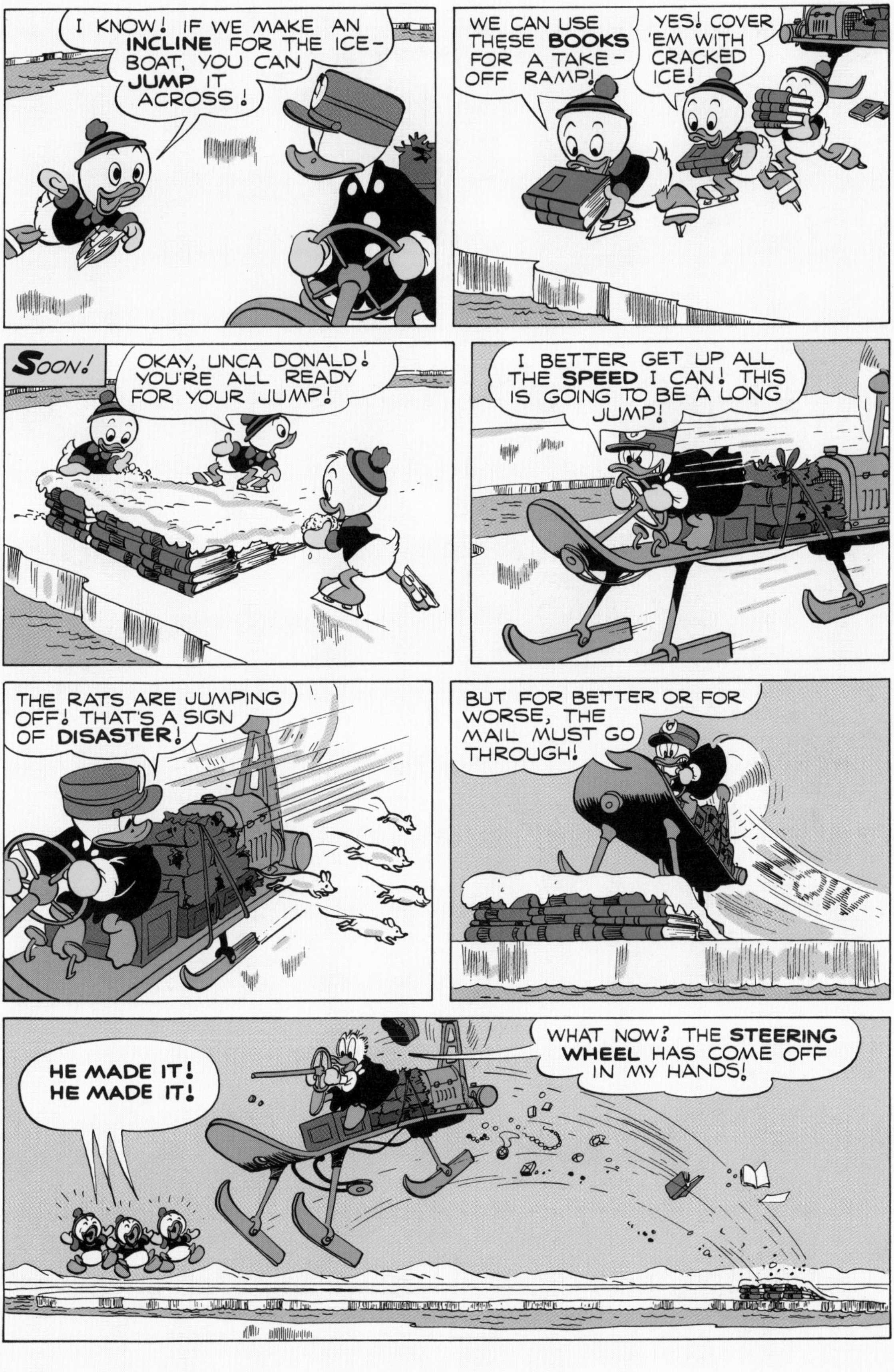
I KNOW! IF WE MAKE AN INCLINE FOR THE ICE-BOAT, YOU CAN JUMP IT ACROSS!
WE CAN USE THESE BOOKS FOR A TAKE-OFF RAMP!
YES! COVER 'EM WITH CRACKED ICE!
SOON!
OKAY, UNCA DONALD! YOU'RE ALL READY FOR YOUR JUMP!
I BETTER GET UP ALL THE SPEED I CAN! THIS IS GOING TO BE A LONG JUMP!
THE RATS ARE JUMPING OFF! THAT'S A SIGN OF DISASTER!
BUT FOR BETTER OR FOR WORSE, THE MAIL MUST GO THROUGH!
HE MADE IT! HE MADE IT!
WHAT NOW? THE STEERING WHEEL HAS COME OFF IN MY HANDS!

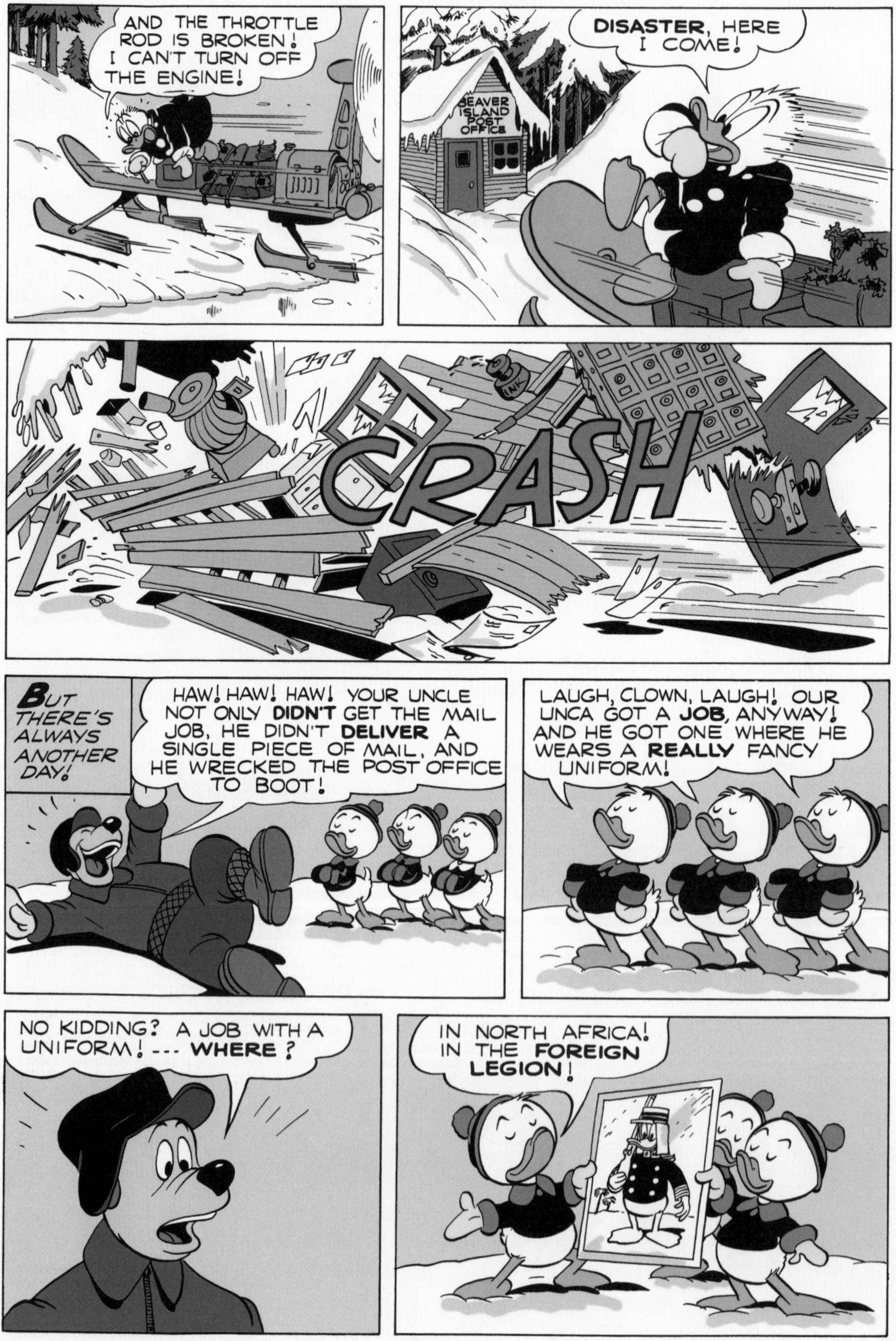
AND THE THROTTLE ROD IS BROKEN! I CAN'T TURN OFF THE ENGINE!
DISASTER, HERE I COME!
BEAVER ISLAND POST OFFICE
INK
CRASH
BUT THERE'S ALWAYS ANOTHER DAY!
HAW! HAW! HAW! YOUR UNCLE NOT ONLY DIDN'T GET THE MAIL JOB, HE DIDN'T DELIVER A SINGLE PIECE OF MAIL, AND HE WRECKED THE POST OFFICE TO BOOT!
LAUGH, CLOWN, LAUGH! OUR UNCA GOT A JOB, ANYWAY! AND HE GOT ONE WHERE HE WEARS A REALLY FANCY UNIFORM!
NO KIDDING? A JOB WITH A UNIFORM! --- WHERE?
IN NORTH AFRICA! IN THE FOREIGN LEGION!

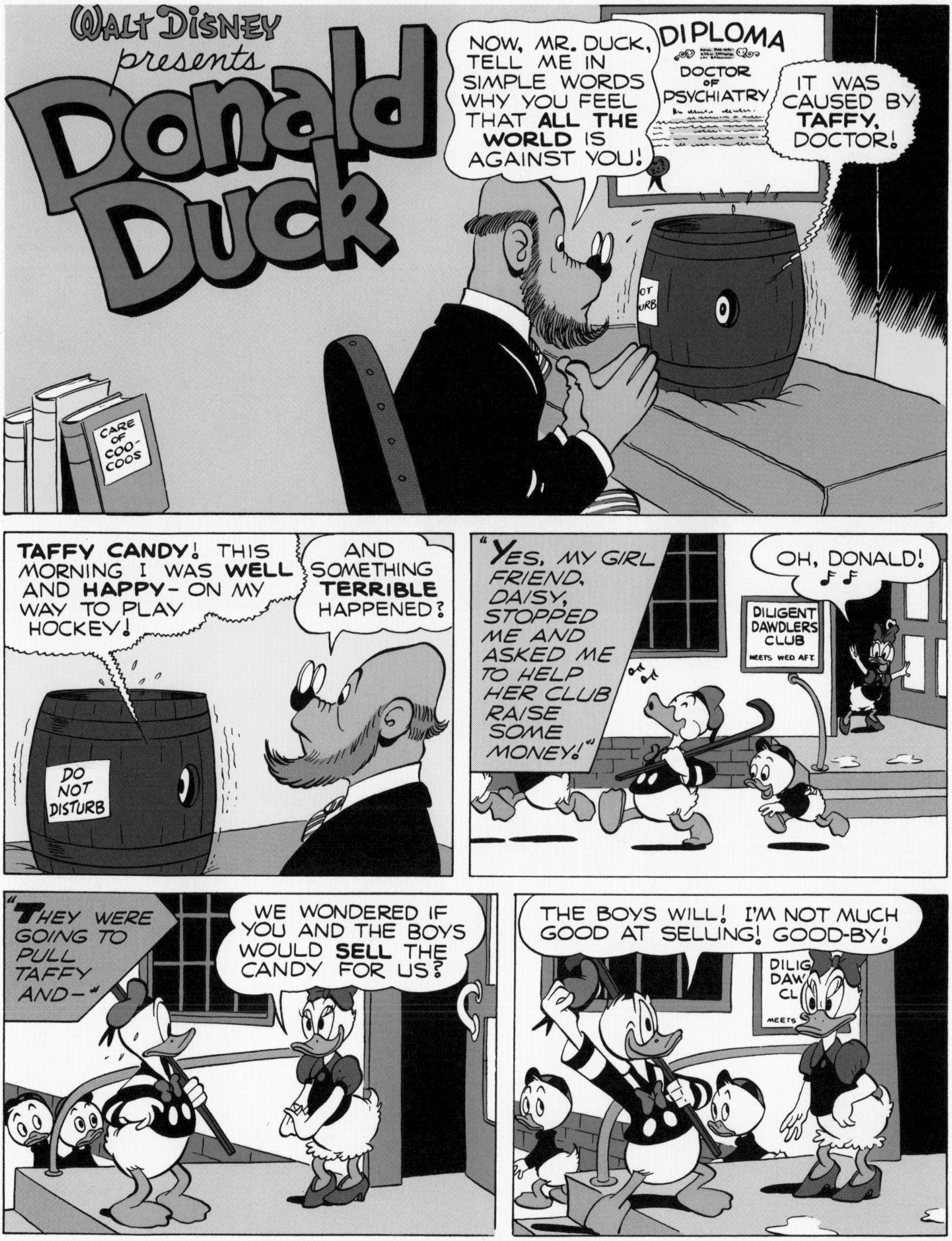

WALT DISNEY presents Donald Duck
NOW, MR. DUCK, TELL ME IN SIMPLE WORDS WHY YOU FEEL THAT ALL THE WORLD IS AGAINST YOU!
DIPLOMA
DOCTOR OF PSYCHIATRY
IT WAS CAUSED BY TAFFY, DOCTOR!
CARE OF COO-COOS
TAFFY CANDY! THIS MORNING I WAS WELL AND HAPPY- ON MY WAY TO PLAY HOCKEY!
AND SOMETHING TERRIBLE HAPPENED?
DO NOT DISTURB
"YES, MY GIRL FRIEND, DAISY, STOPPED ME AND ASKED ME TO HELP HER CLUB RAISE SOME MONEY!"
OH, DONALD!
DILIGENT DAWDLERS CLUB
MEETS WED AFT.
"THEY WERE GOING TO PULL TAFFY AND-"
WE WONDERED IF YOU AND THE BOYS WOULD SELL THE CANDY FOR US?
THE BOYS WILL! I'M NOT MUCH GOOD AT SELLING! GOOD-BY!

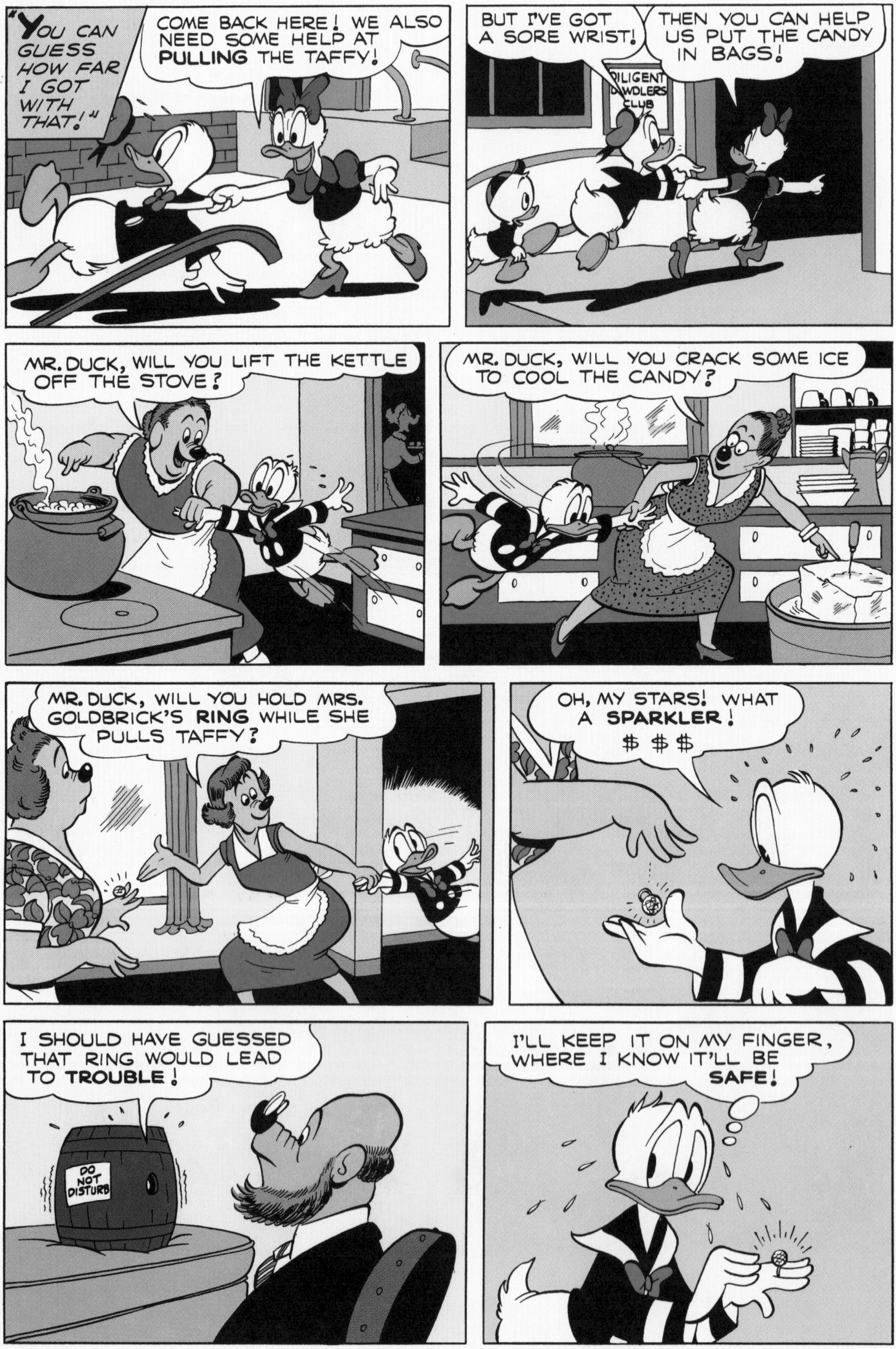
"YOU CAN GUESS HOW FAR I GOT WITH THAT!"
COME BACK HERE! WE ALSO NEED SOME HELP AT PULLING THE TAFFY!
BUT I'VE GOT A SORE WRIST!
THEN YOU CAN HELP US PUT THE CANDY IN BAGS!
DILIGENT DAWDLERS CLUB
MR. DUCK, WILL YOU LIFT THE KETTLE OFF THE STOVE?
MR. DUCK, WILL YOU CRACK SOME ICE TO COOL THE CANDY?
MR. DUCK, WILL YOU HOLD MRS. GOLDBRICK'S RING WHILE SHE PULLS TAFFY?
OH, MY STARS! WHAT A SPARKLER! $ $ $
I SHOULD HAVE GUESSED THAT RING WOULD LEAD TO TROUBLE!
DO NOT DISTURB
I'LL KEEP IT ON MY FINGER, WHERE I KNOW IT'LL BE SAFE!

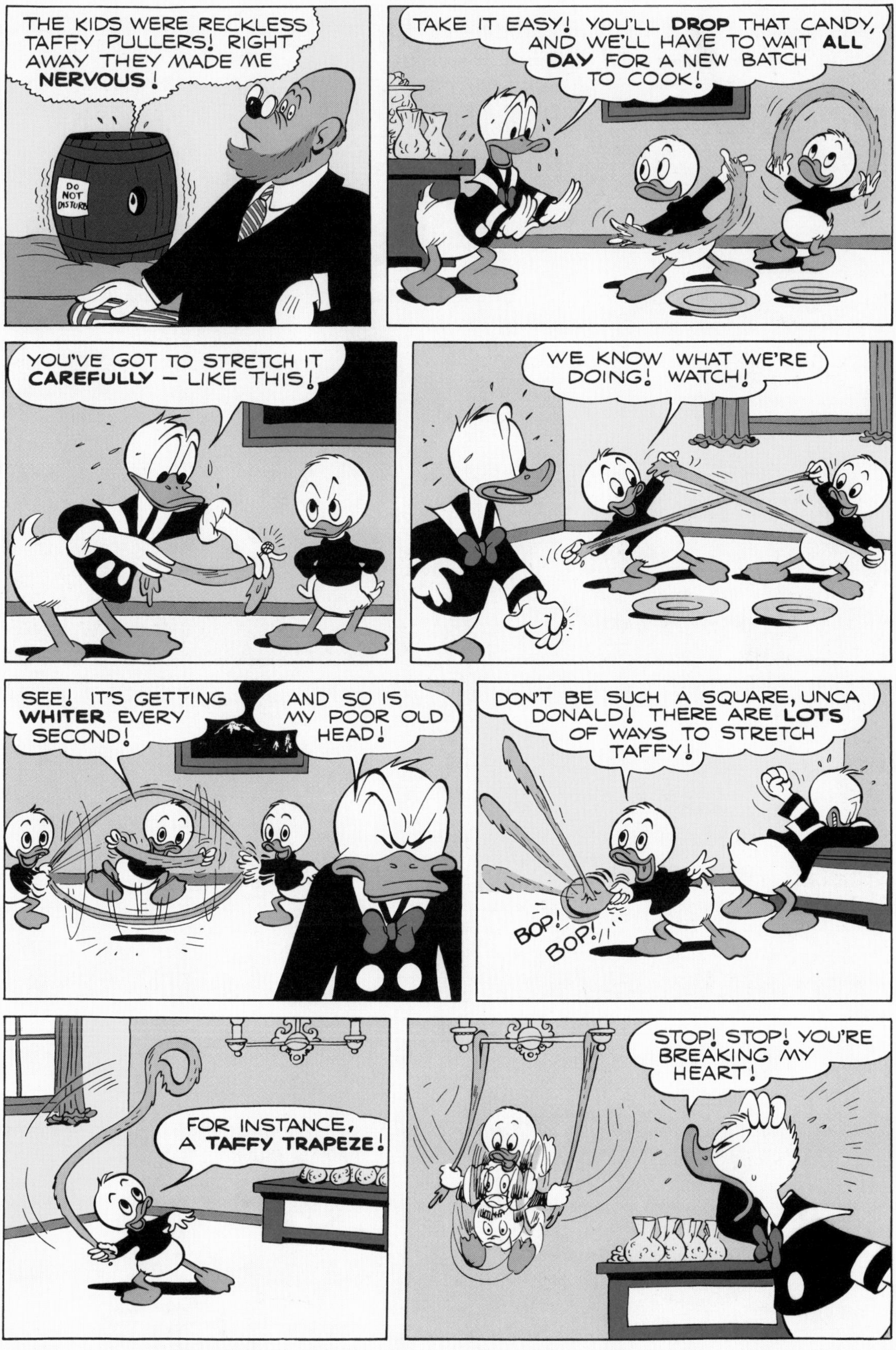

THE KIDS WERE RECKLESS TAFFY PULLERS! RIGHT AWAY THEY MADE ME **NERVOUS**!
DO NOT DISTURB
TAKE IT EASY! YOU'LL **DROP** THAT CANDY, AND WE'LL HAVE TO WAIT **ALL DAY** FOR A NEW BATCH TO COOK!
YOU'VE GOT TO STRETCH IT **CAREFULLY** – LIKE THIS!
WE KNOW WHAT WE'RE DOING! WATCH!
SEE! IT'S GETTING **WHITER** EVERY SECOND!
AND SO IS MY POOR OLD HEAD!
DON'T BE SUCH A SQUARE, UNCA DONALD! THERE ARE **LOTS** OF WAYS TO STRETCH TAFFY!
BOP!
BOP!
FOR INSTANCE, A **TAFFY TRAPEZE**!
STOP! STOP! YOU'RE BREAKING MY HEART!

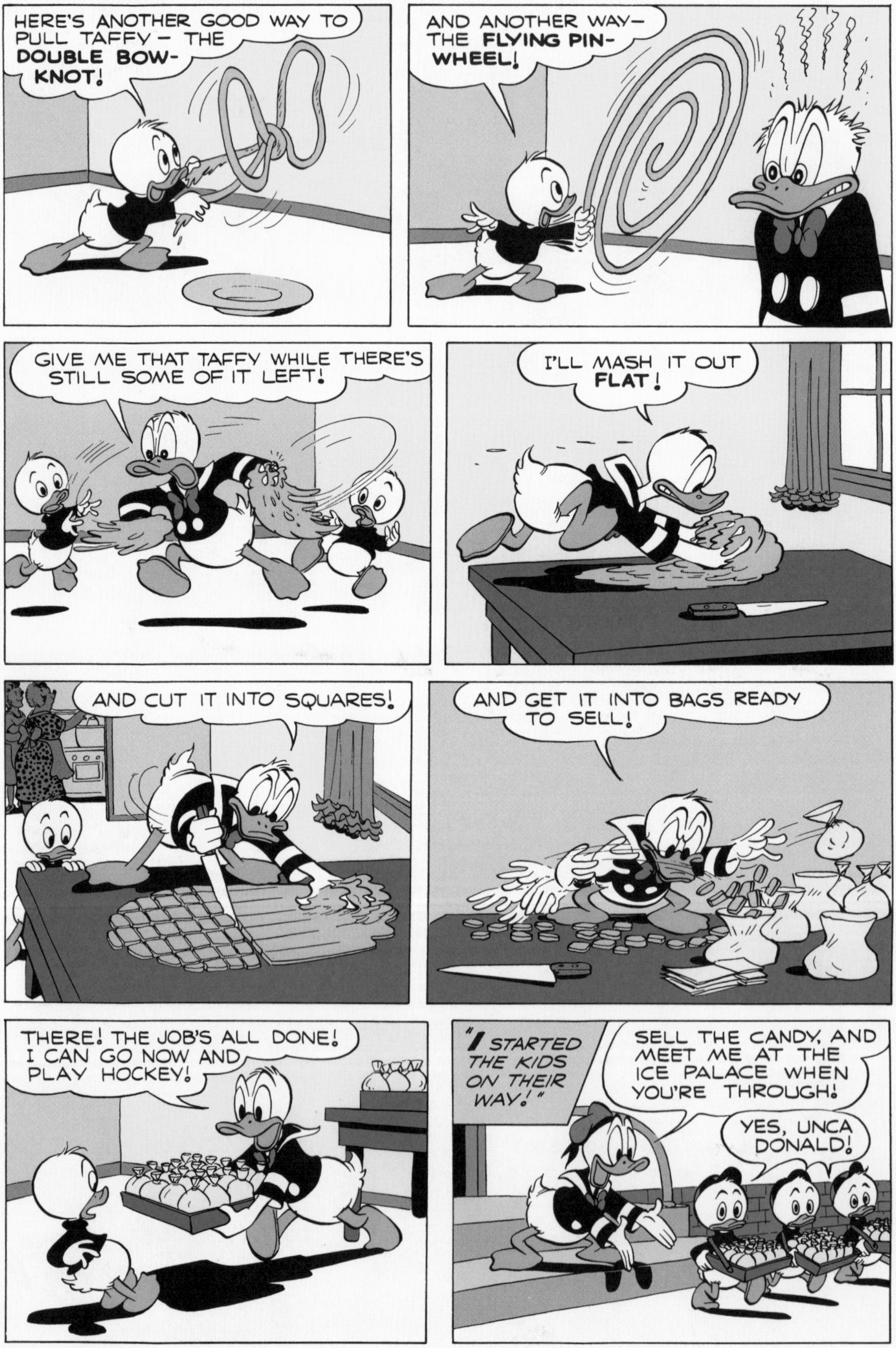
HERE'S ANOTHER GOOD WAY TO PULL TAFFY — THE DOUBLE BOW-KNOT!
AND ANOTHER WAY— THE FLYING PIN-WHEEL!
GIVE ME THAT TAFFY WHILE THERE'S STILL SOME OF IT LEFT!
I'LL MASH IT OUT FLAT!
AND CUT IT INTO SQUARES!
AND GET IT INTO BAGS READY TO SELL!
THERE! THE JOB'S ALL DONE! I CAN GO NOW AND PLAY HOCKEY!
"I STARTED THE KIDS ON THEIR WAY!"
SELL THE CANDY, AND MEET ME AT THE ICE PALACE WHEN YOU'RE THROUGH!
YES, UNCA DONALD!

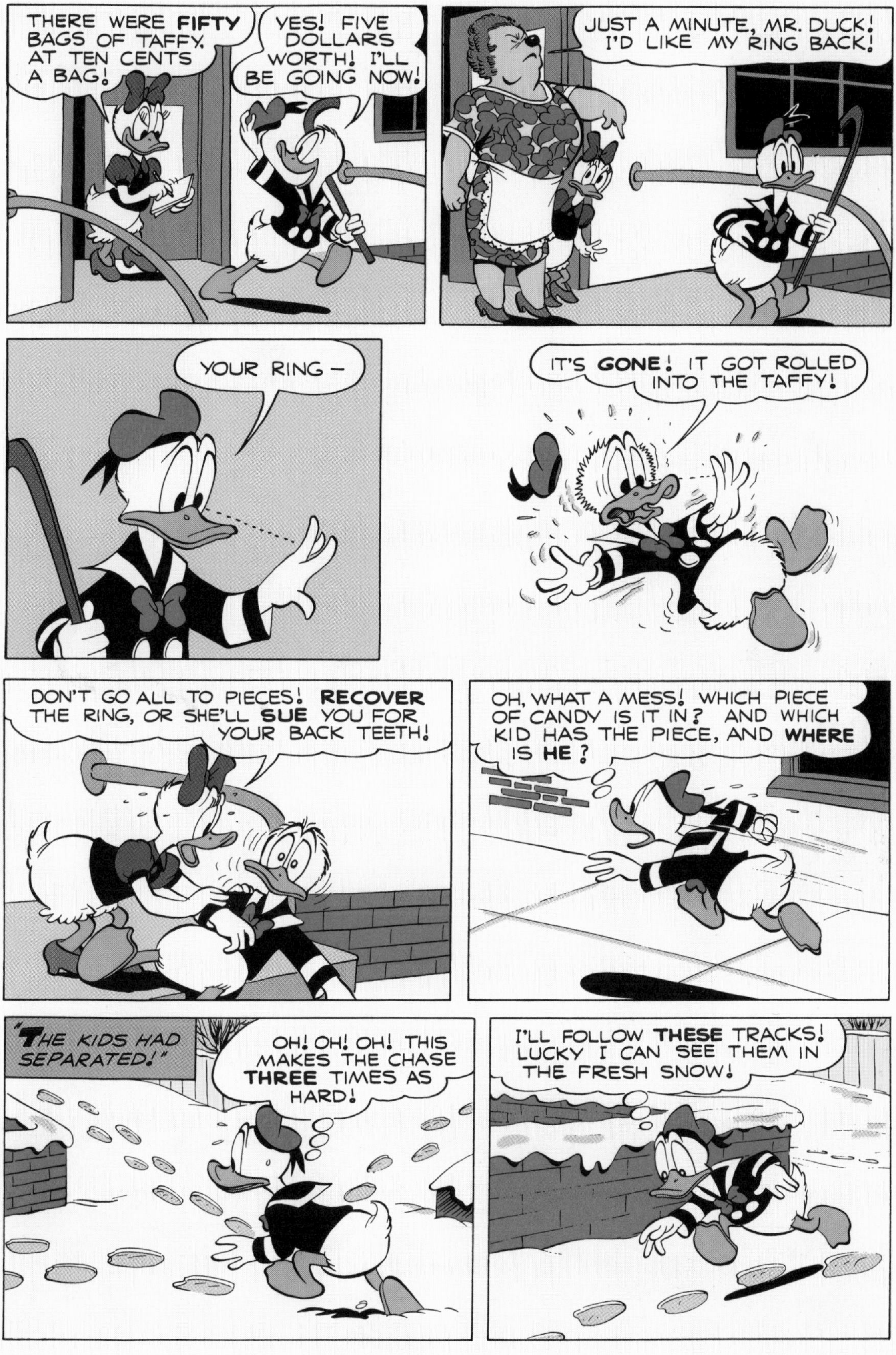
THERE WERE **FIFTY** BAGS OF TAFFY, AT TEN CENTS A BAG!
YES! FIVE DOLLARS WORTH! I'LL BE GOING NOW!
JUST A MINUTE, MR. DUCK! I'D LIKE MY RING BACK!
YOUR RING —
IT'S **GONE**! IT GOT ROLLED INTO THE TAFFY!
DON'T GO ALL TO PIECES! **RECOVER** THE RING, OR SHE'LL **SUE** YOU FOR YOUR BACK TEETH!
OH, WHAT A MESS! WHICH PIECE OF CANDY IS IT IN? AND WHICH KID HAS THE PIECE, AND **WHERE** IS **HE**?
"THE KIDS HAD SEPARATED!"
OH! OH! OH! THIS MAKES THE CHASE **THREE** TIMES AS HARD!
I'LL FOLLOW **THESE** TRACKS! LUCKY I CAN SEE THEM IN THE FRESH SNOW!

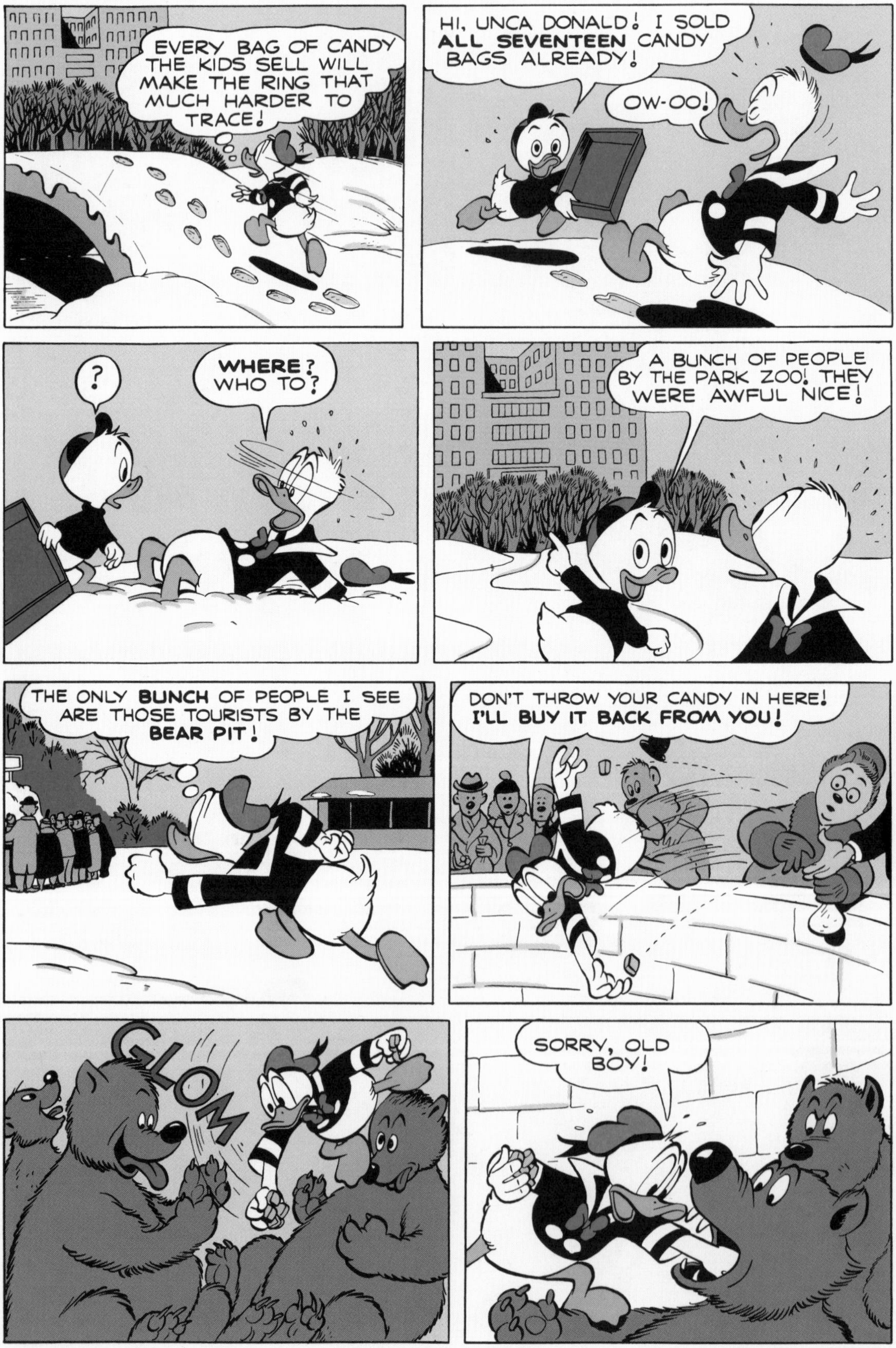
EVERY BAG OF CANDY THE KIDS SELL WILL MAKE THE RING THAT MUCH HARDER TO TRACE!
HI, UNCA DONALD! I SOLD ALL SEVENTEEN CANDY BAGS ALREADY!
OW-OO!
?
WHERE? WHO TO?
A BUNCH OF PEOPLE BY THE PARK ZOO! THEY WERE AWFUL NICE!
THE ONLY BUNCH OF PEOPLE I SEE ARE THOSE TOURISTS BY THE BEAR PIT!
DON'T THROW YOUR CANDY IN HERE! I'LL BUY IT BACK FROM YOU!
GLOM
SORRY, OLD BOY!

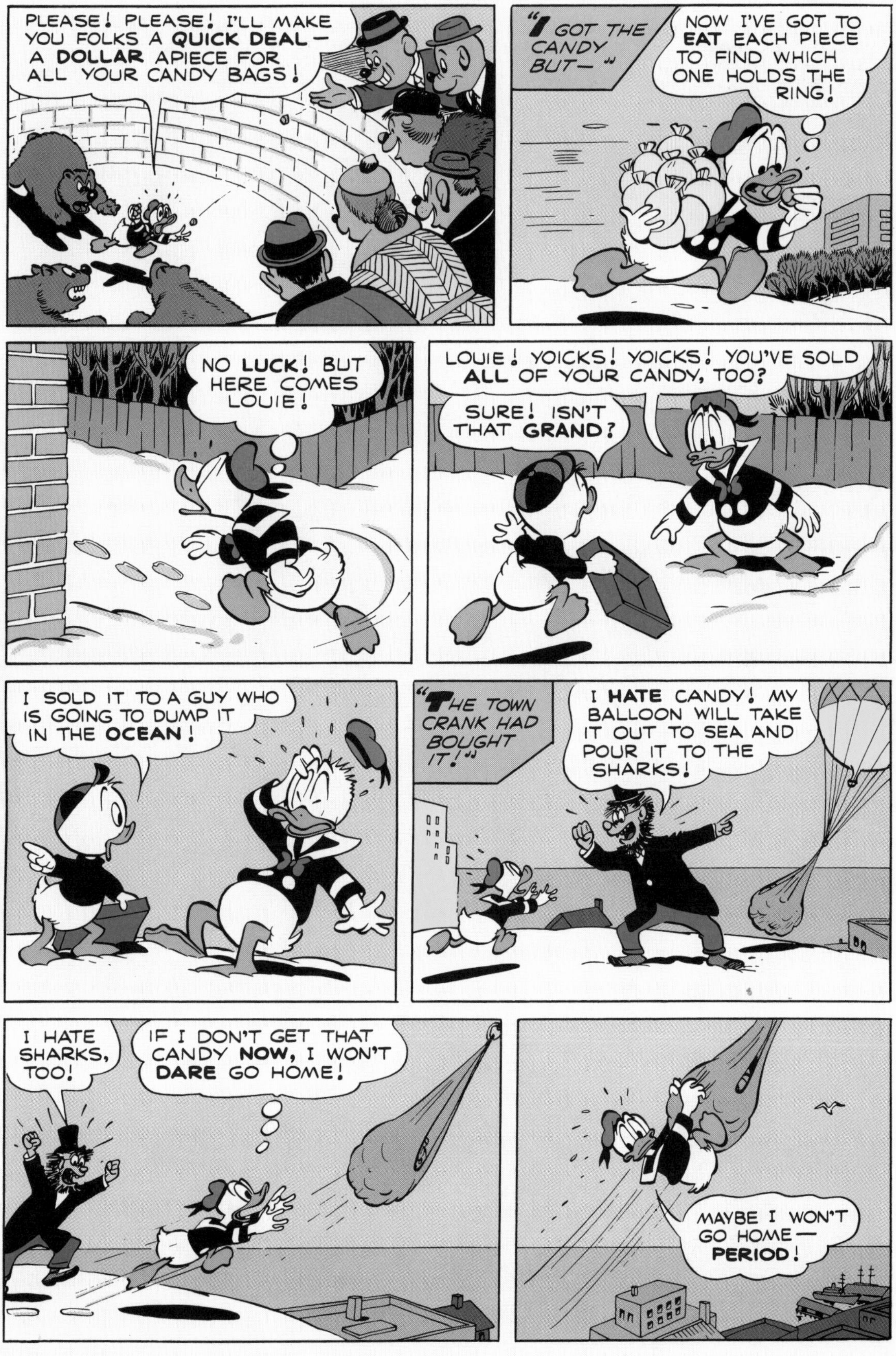
PLEASE! PLEASE! I'LL MAKE YOU FOLKS A QUICK DEAL— A DOLLAR APIECE FOR ALL YOUR CANDY BAGS!
"I GOT THE CANDY BUT—"
NOW I'VE GOT TO EAT EACH PIECE TO FIND WHICH ONE HOLDS THE RING!
NO LUCK! BUT HERE COMES LOUIE!
LOUIE! YOICKS! YOICKS! YOU'VE SOLD ALL OF YOUR CANDY, TOO?
SURE! ISN'T THAT GRAND?
I SOLD IT TO A GUY WHO IS GOING TO DUMP IT IN THE OCEAN!
"THE TOWN CRANK HAD BOUGHT IT!"
I HATE CANDY! MY BALLOON WILL TAKE IT OUT TO SEA AND POUR IT TO THE SHARKS!
I HATE SHARKS, TOO!
IF I DON'T GET THAT CANDY NOW, I WON'T DARE GO HOME!
MAYBE I WON'T GO HOME— PERIOD!

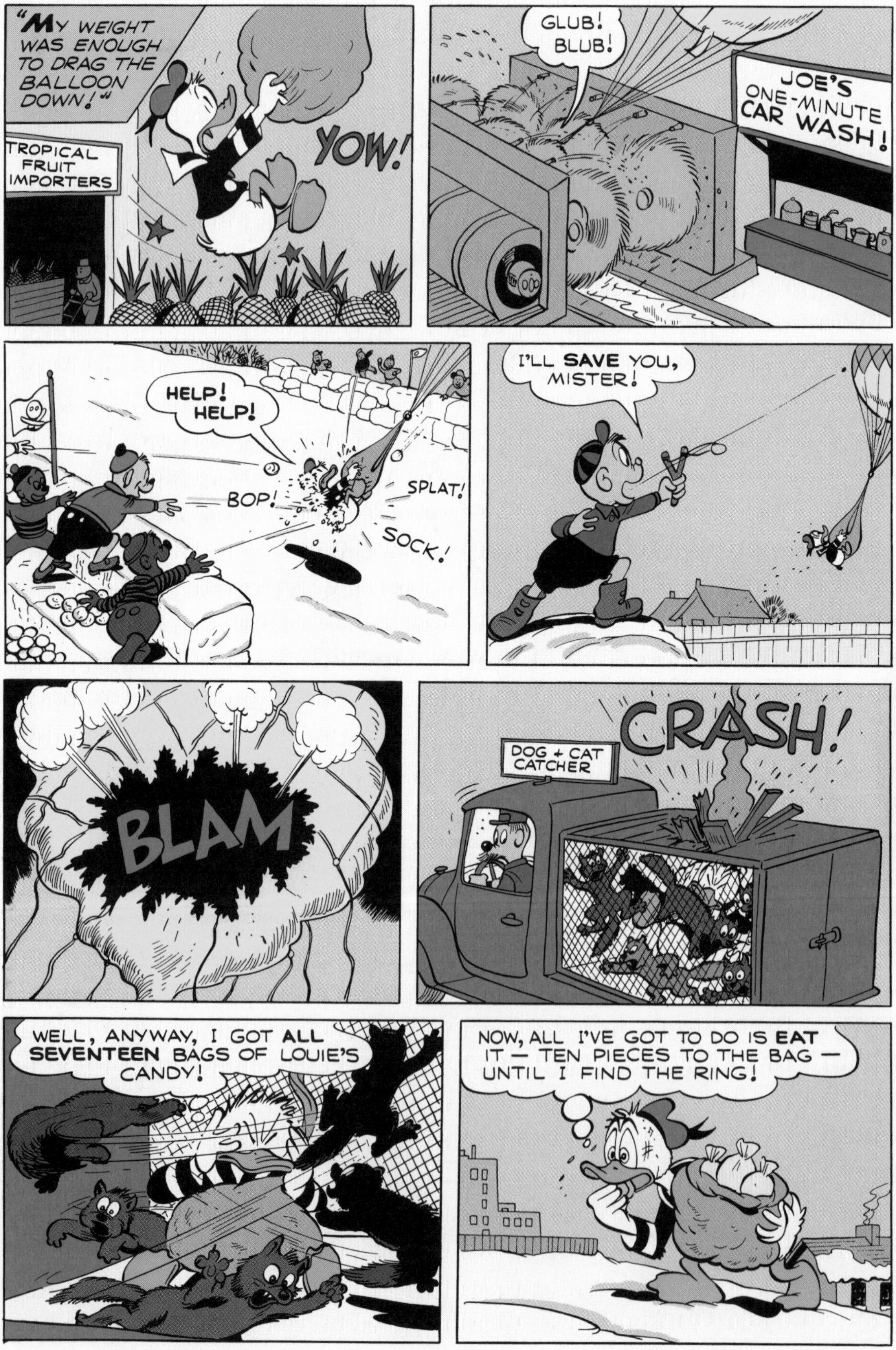
"MY WEIGHT WAS ENOUGH TO DRAG THE BALLOON DOWN!"
TROPICAL FRUIT IMPORTERS
YOW!
GLUB! BLUB!
JOE'S ONE-MINUTE CAR WASH!
HELP! HELP!
BOP!
SPLAT!
SOCK!
I'LL SAVE YOU, MISTER!
BLAM
DOG + CAT CATCHER
CRASH!
WELL, ANYWAY, I GOT ALL SEVENTEEN BAGS OF LOUIE'S CANDY!
NOW, ALL I'VE GOT TO DO IS EAT IT — TEN PIECES TO THE BAG — UNTIL I FIND THE RING!

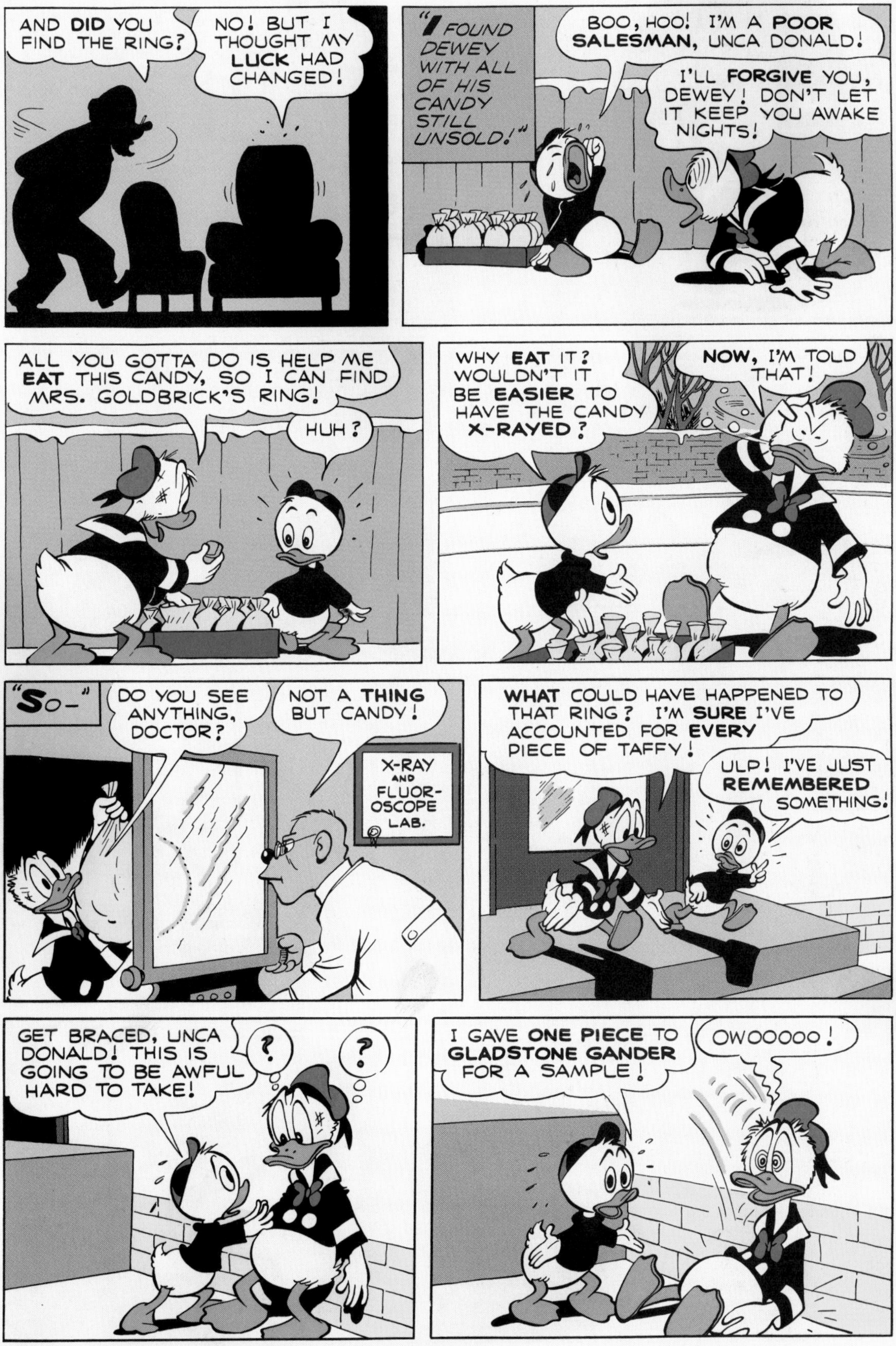
AND DID YOU FIND THE RING?
NO! BUT I THOUGHT MY LUCK HAD CHANGED!
"I FOUND DEWEY WITH ALL OF HIS CANDY STILL UNSOLD!"
BOO, HOO! I'M A POOR SALESMAN, UNCA DONALD!
I'LL FORGIVE YOU, DEWEY! DON'T LET IT KEEP YOU AWAKE NIGHTS!
ALL YOU GOTTA DO IS HELP ME EAT THIS CANDY, SO I CAN FIND MRS. GOLDBRICK'S RING!
HUH?
WHY EAT IT? WOULDN'T IT BE EASIER TO HAVE THE CANDY X-RAYED?
NOW, I'M TOLD THAT!
"SO-"
DO YOU SEE ANYTHING, DOCTOR?
NOT A THING BUT CANDY!
X-RAY AND FLUOROSCOPE LAB.
WHAT COULD HAVE HAPPENED TO THAT RING? I'M SURE I'VE ACCOUNTED FOR EVERY PIECE OF TAFFY!
ULP! I'VE JUST REMEMBERED SOMETHING!
GET BRACED, UNCA DONALD! THIS IS GOING TO BE AWFUL HARD TO TAKE!
?
?
I GAVE ONE PIECE TO GLADSTONE GANDER FOR A SAMPLE!
OWOOOOO!

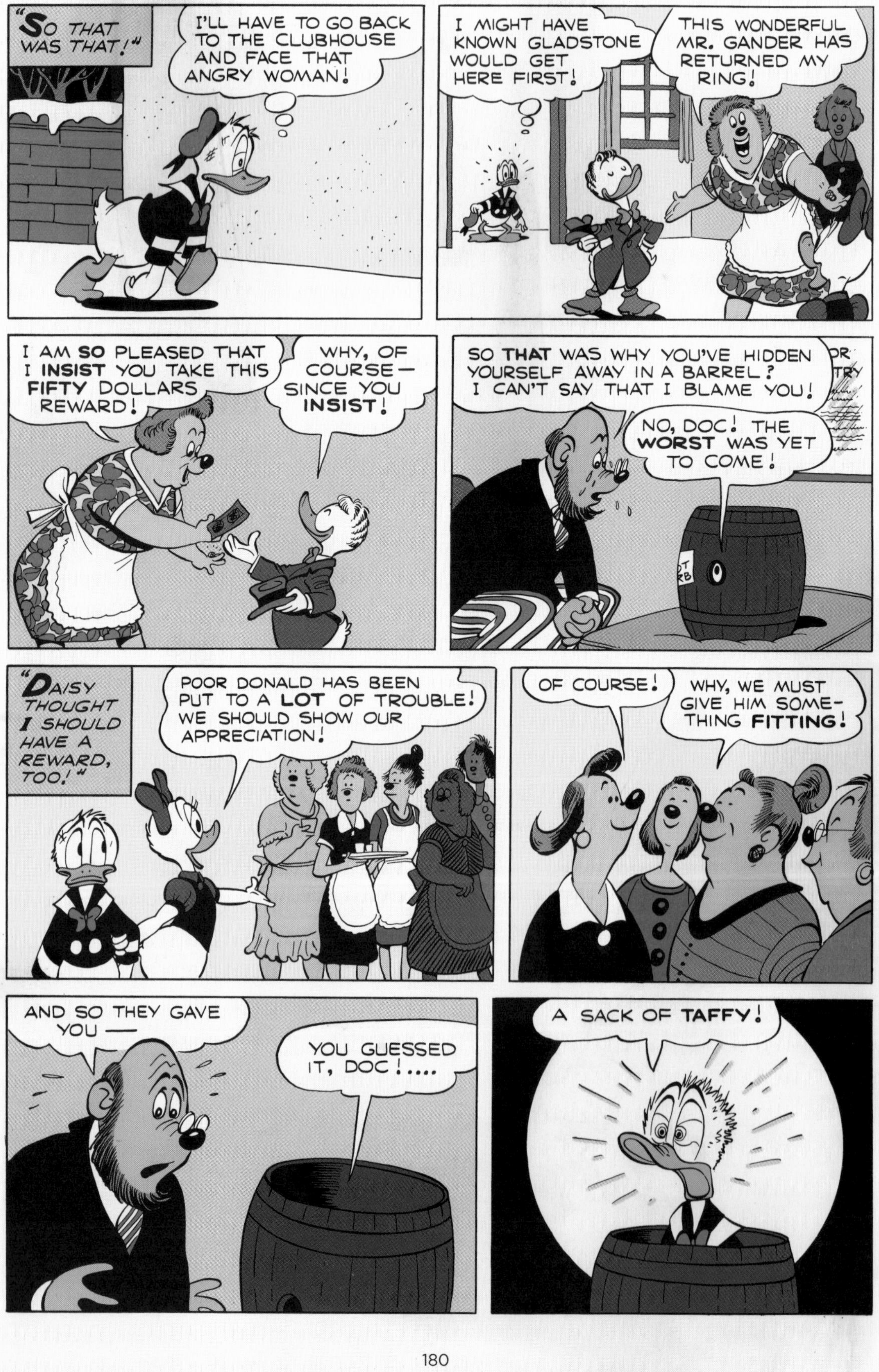
"SO THAT WAS THAT!"
I'LL HAVE TO GO BACK TO THE CLUBHOUSE AND FACE THAT ANGRY WOMAN!
I MIGHT HAVE KNOWN GLADSTONE WOULD GET HERE FIRST!
THIS WONDERFUL MR. GANDER HAS RETURNED MY RING!
I AM SO PLEASED THAT I INSIST YOU TAKE THIS FIFTY DOLLARS REWARD!
WHY, OF COURSE— SINCE YOU INSIST!
SO THAT WAS WHY YOU'VE HIDDEN YOURSELF AWAY IN A BARREL? I CAN'T SAY THAT I BLAME YOU!
NO, DOC! THE WORST WAS YET TO COME!
"DAISY THOUGHT I SHOULD HAVE A REWARD, TOO!"
POOR DONALD HAS BEEN PUT TO A LOT OF TROUBLE! WE SHOULD SHOW OUR APPRECIATION!
OF COURSE!
WHY, WE MUST GIVE HIM SOME-THING FITTING!
AND SO THEY GAVE YOU —
YOU GUESSED IT, DOC!....
A SACK OF TAFFY!

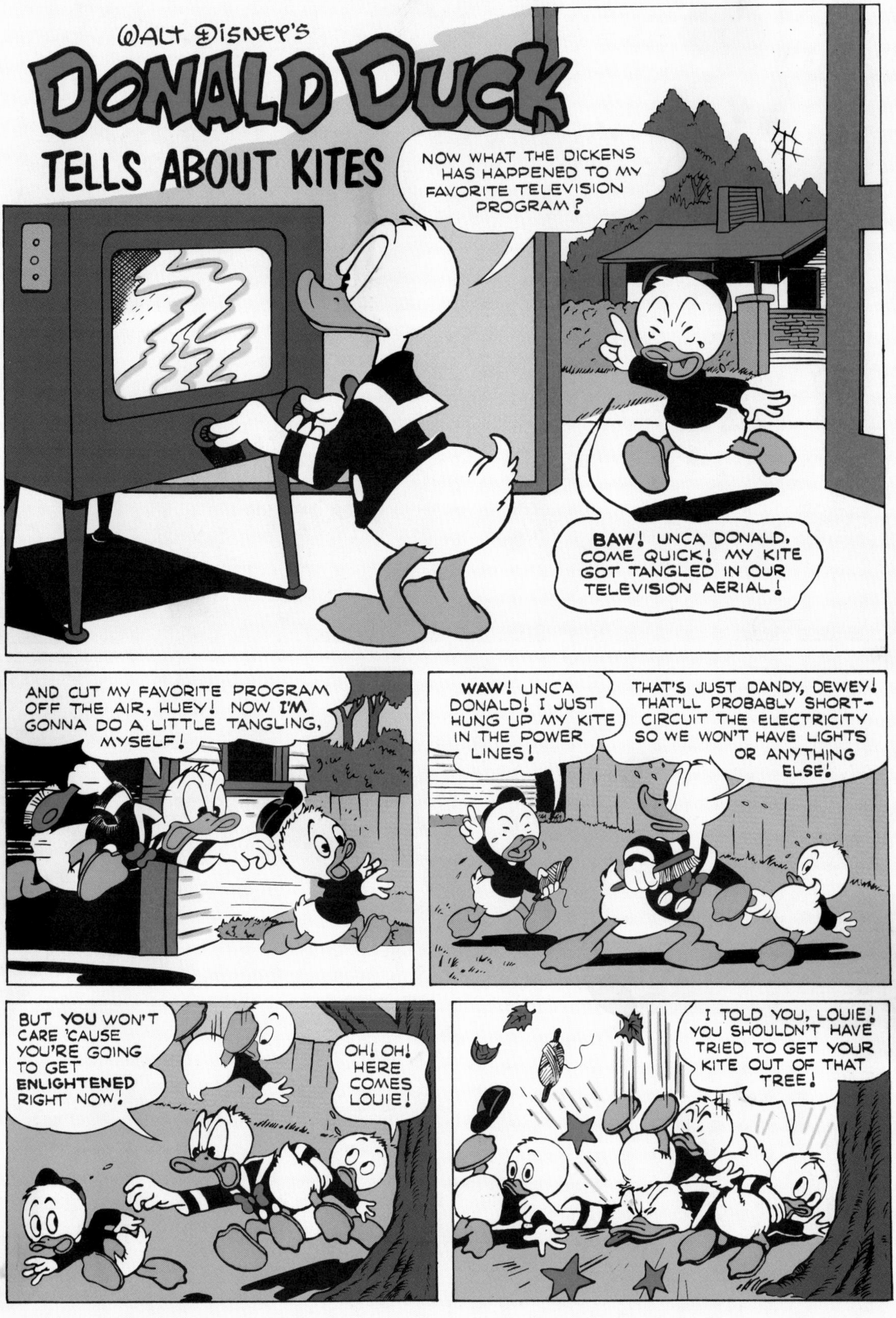
WALT DISNEY'S
DONALD DUCK
TELLS ABOUT KITES
NOW WHAT THE DICKENS HAS HAPPENED TO MY FAVORITE TELEVISION PROGRAM?
BAW! UNCA DONALD, COME QUICK! MY KITE GOT TANGLED IN OUR TELEVISION AERIAL!
AND CUT MY FAVORITE PROGRAM OFF THE AIR, HUEY! NOW I'M GONNA DO A LITTLE TANGLING, MYSELF!
WAW! UNCA DONALD! I JUST HUNG UP MY KITE IN THE POWER LINES!
THAT'S JUST DANDY, DEWEY! THAT'LL PROBABLY SHORT-CIRCUIT THE ELECTRICITY SO WE WON'T HAVE LIGHTS OR ANYTHING ELSE!
BUT YOU WON'T CARE 'CAUSE YOU'RE GOING TO GET ENLIGHTENED RIGHT NOW!
OH! OH! HERE COMES LOUIE!
I TOLD YOU, LOUIE! YOU SHOULDN'T HAVE TRIED TO GET YOUR KITE OUT OF THAT TREE!

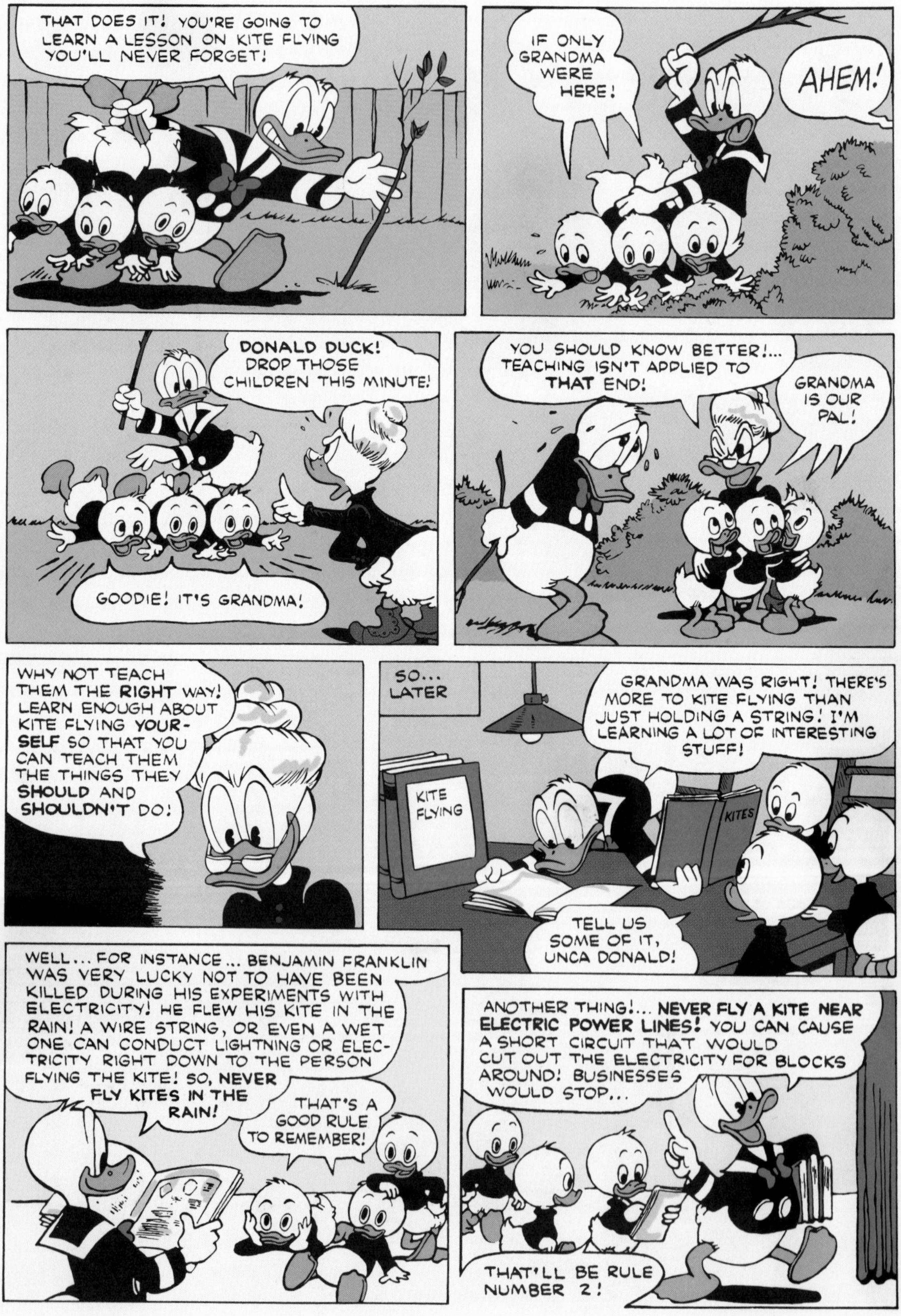
THAT DOES IT! YOU'RE GOING TO LEARN A LESSON ON KITE FLYING YOU'LL NEVER FORGET!
IF ONLY GRANDMA WERE HERE!
AHEM!
DONALD DUCK! DROP THOSE CHILDREN THIS MINUTE!
GOODIE! IT'S GRANDMA!
YOU SHOULD KNOW BETTER!... TEACHING ISN'T APPLIED TO THAT END!
GRANDMA IS OUR PAL!
WHY NOT TEACH THEM THE RIGHT WAY! LEARN ENOUGH ABOUT KITE FLYING YOURSELF SO THAT YOU CAN TEACH THEM THE THINGS THEY SHOULD AND SHOULDN'T DO!
SO... LATER
GRANDMA WAS RIGHT! THERE'S MORE TO KITE FLYING THAN JUST HOLDING A STRING! I'M LEARNING A LOT OF INTERESTING STUFF!
KITE FLYING
KITES
TELL US SOME OF IT, UNCA DONALD!
WELL... FOR INSTANCE... BENJAMIN FRANKLIN WAS VERY LUCKY NOT TO HAVE BEEN KILLED DURING HIS EXPERIMENTS WITH ELECTRICITY! HE FLEW HIS KITE IN THE RAIN! A WIRE STRING, OR EVEN A WET ONE CAN CONDUCT LIGHTNING OR ELECTRICITY RIGHT DOWN TO THE PERSON FLYING THE KITE! SO, NEVER FLY KITES IN THE RAIN!
THAT'S A GOOD RULE TO REMEMBER!
ANOTHER THING!... NEVER FLY A KITE NEAR ELECTRIC POWER LINES! YOU CAN CAUSE A SHORT CIRCUIT THAT WOULD CUT OUT THE ELECTRICITY FOR BLOCKS AROUND! BUSINESSES WOULD STOP...
THAT'LL BE RULE NUMBER 2!

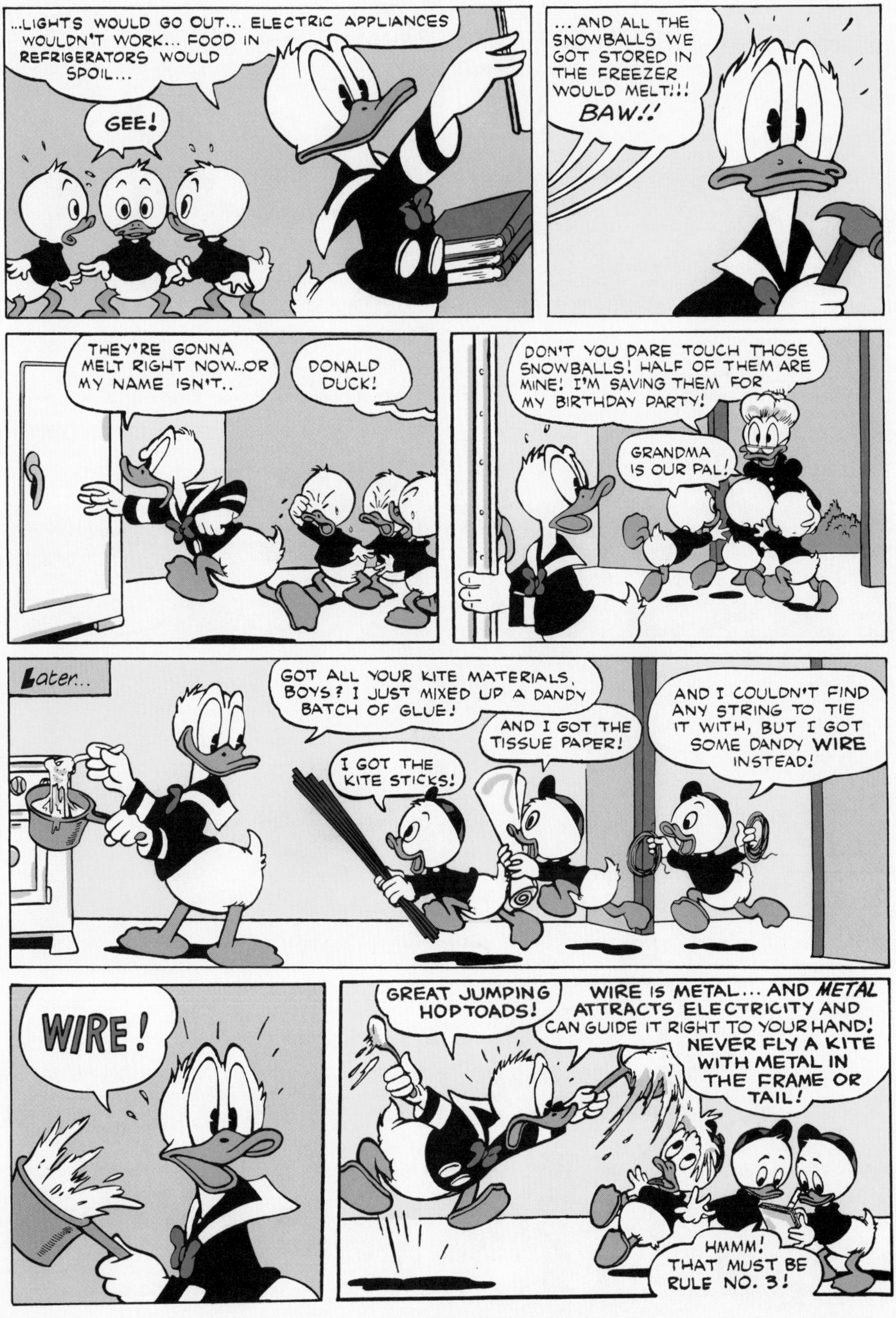
...LIGHTS WOULD GO OUT... ELECTRIC APPLIANCES WOULDN'T WORK... FOOD IN REFRIGERATORS WOULD SPOIL...
GEE!
... AND ALL THE SNOWBALLS WE GOT STORED IN THE FREEZER WOULD MELT!!! BAW!!
THEY'RE GONNA MELT RIGHT NOW...OR MY NAME ISN'T..
DONALD DUCK!
DON'T YOU DARE TOUCH THOSE SNOWBALLS! HALF OF THEM ARE MINE! I'M SAVING THEM FOR MY BIRTHDAY PARTY!
GRANDMA IS OUR PAL!
Later...
GOT ALL YOUR KITE MATERIALS, BOYS? I JUST MIXED UP A DANDY BATCH OF GLUE!
I GOT THE KITE STICKS!
AND I GOT THE TISSUE PAPER!
AND I COULDN'T FIND ANY STRING TO TIE IT WITH, BUT I GOT SOME DANDY WIRE INSTEAD!
WIRE!
GREAT JUMPING HOPTOADS!
WIRE IS METAL... AND METAL ATTRACTS ELECTRICITY AND CAN GUIDE IT RIGHT TO YOUR HAND! NEVER FLY A KITE WITH METAL IN THE FRAME OR TAIL!
HMMM! THAT MUST BE RULE NO. 3!

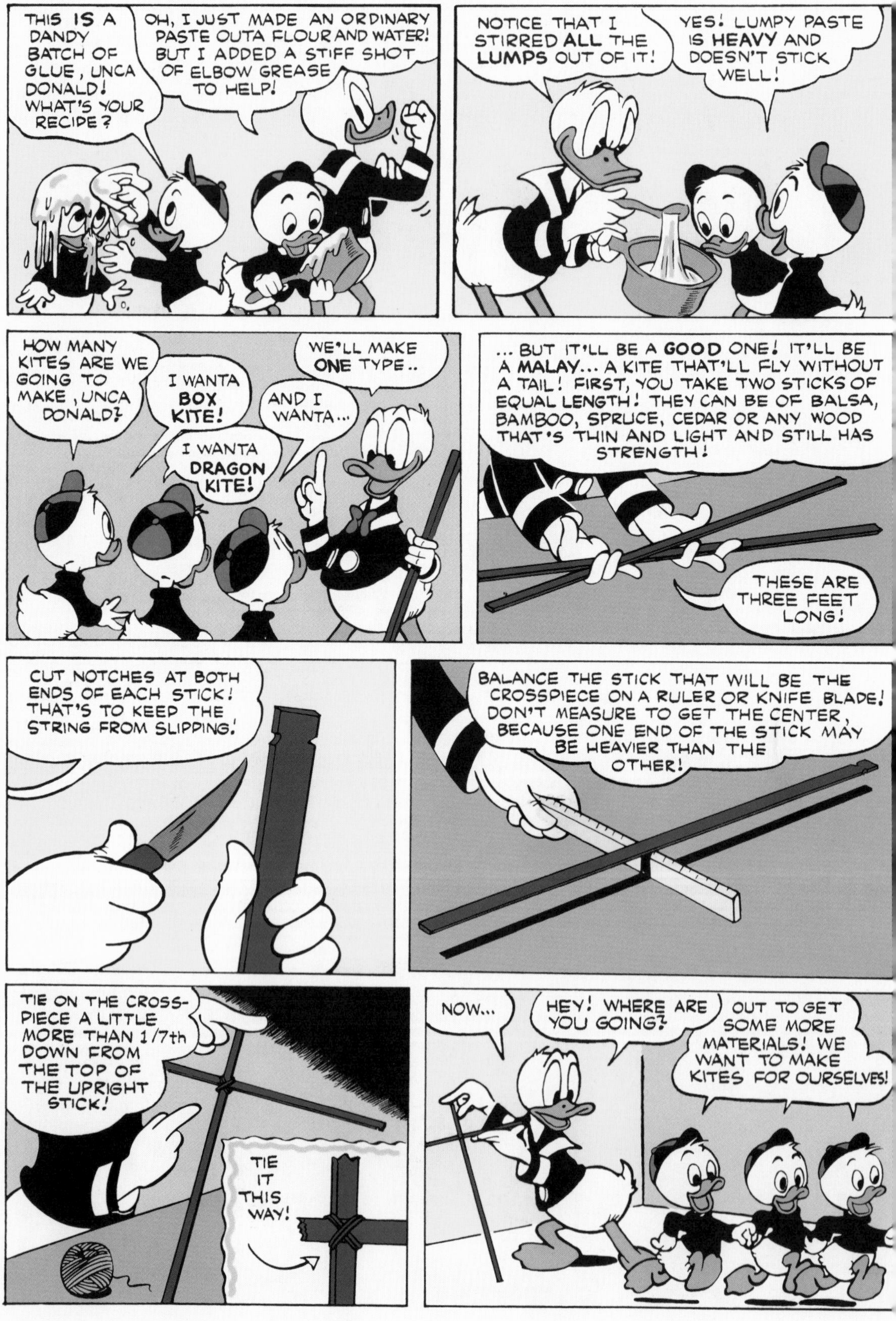
THIS IS A DANDY BATCH OF GLUE, UNCA DONALD! WHAT'S YOUR RECIPE?
OH, I JUST MADE AN ORDINARY PASTE OUTA FLOUR AND WATER! BUT I ADDED A STIFF SHOT OF ELBOW GREASE TO HELP!
NOTICE THAT I STIRRED ALL THE LUMPS OUT OF IT!
YES! LUMPY PASTE IS HEAVY AND DOESN'T STICK WELL!
HOW MANY KITES ARE WE GOING TO MAKE, UNCA DONALD?
I WANTA BOX KITE!
I WANTA DRAGON KITE!
AND I WANTA...
WE'LL MAKE ONE TYPE..
... BUT IT'LL BE A GOOD ONE! IT'LL BE A MALAY... A KITE THAT'LL FLY WITHOUT A TAIL! FIRST, YOU TAKE TWO STICKS OF EQUAL LENGTH! THEY CAN BE OF BALSA, BAMBOO, SPRUCE, CEDAR OR ANY WOOD THAT'S THIN AND LIGHT AND STILL HAS STRENGTH!
THESE ARE THREE FEET LONG!
CUT NOTCHES AT BOTH ENDS OF EACH STICK! THAT'S TO KEEP THE STRING FROM SLIPPING!
BALANCE THE STICK THAT WILL BE THE CROSSPIECE ON A RULER OR KNIFE BLADE! DON'T MEASURE TO GET THE CENTER, BECAUSE ONE END OF THE STICK MAY BE HEAVIER THAN THE OTHER!
TIE ON THE CROSS-PIECE A LITTLE MORE THAN 1/7th DOWN FROM THE TOP OF THE UPRIGHT STICK!
TIE IT THIS WAY!
NOW...
HEY! WHERE ARE YOU GOING?
OUT TO GET SOME MORE MATERIALS! WE WANT TO MAKE KITES FOR OURSELVES!

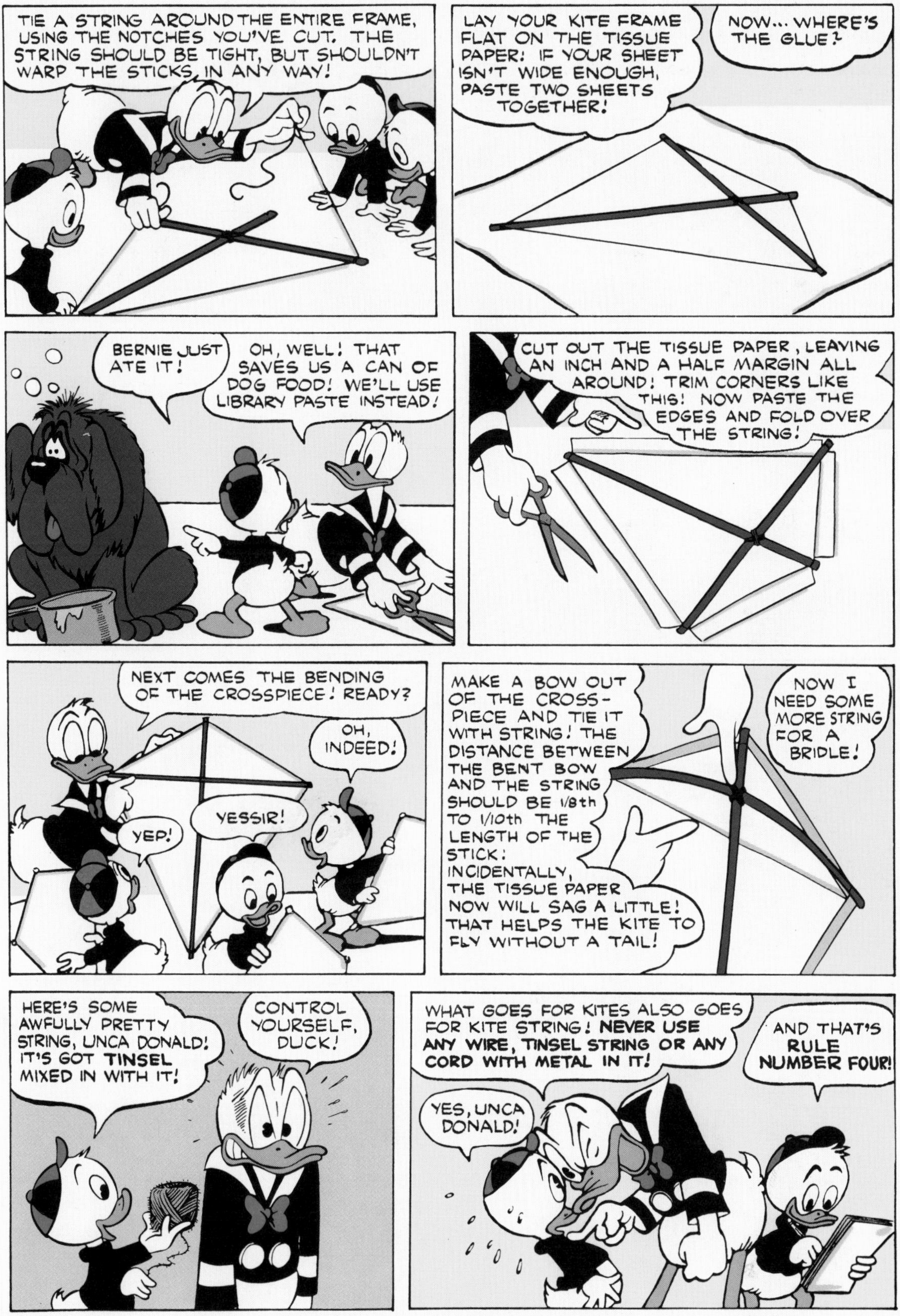

TIE A STRING AROUND THE ENTIRE FRAME, USING THE NOTCHES YOU'VE CUT. THE STRING SHOULD BE TIGHT, BUT SHOULDN'T WARP THE STICKS IN ANY WAY!
LAY YOUR KITE FRAME FLAT ON THE TISSUE PAPER: IF YOUR SHEET ISN'T WIDE ENOUGH, PASTE TWO SHEETS TOGETHER!
NOW... WHERE'S THE GLUE?
BERNIE JUST ATE IT!
OH, WELL! THAT SAVES US A CAN OF DOG FOOD! WE'LL USE LIBRARY PASTE INSTEAD!
CUT OUT THE TISSUE PAPER, LEAVING AN INCH AND A HALF MARGIN ALL AROUND! TRIM CORNERS LIKE THIS! NOW PASTE THE EDGES AND FOLD OVER THE STRING!
NEXT COMES THE BENDING OF THE CROSSPIECE! READY?
OH, INDEED!
YESSIR!
YEP!
MAKE A BOW OUT OF THE CROSS-PIECE AND TIE IT WITH STRING! THE DISTANCE BETWEEN THE BENT BOW AND THE STRING SHOULD BE 1/8th TO 1/10th THE LENGTH OF THE STICK: INCIDENTALLY, THE TISSUE PAPER NOW WILL SAG A LITTLE! THAT HELPS THE KITE TO FLY WITHOUT A TAIL!
NOW I NEED SOME MORE STRING FOR A BRIDLE!
HERE'S SOME AWFULLY PRETTY STRING, UNCA DONALD! IT'S GOT TINSEL MIXED IN WITH IT!
CONTROL YOURSELF, DUCK!
WHAT GOES FOR KITES ALSO GOES FOR KITE STRING! NEVER USE ANY WIRE, TINSEL STRING OR ANY CORD WITH METAL IN IT!
AND THAT'S RULE NUMBER FOUR!
YES, UNCA DONALD!

AH! HERE'S SOME STRING! YOU CAN USE EITHER PLAIN COTTON, OR NYLON CORD! HEAVY CARPET OR BUTTON THREAD IS GOOD FOR SMALL, LIGHT KITES! AND WRAPPING TWINE'S BEST FOR AVERAGE KITES!

THE BRIDLE CAN BE ATTACHED IN EITHER OF THESE TWO WAYS!

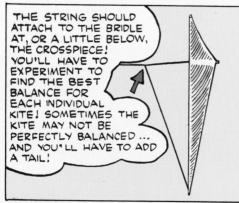

THE STRING SHOULD ATTACH TO THE BRIDLE AT, OR A LITTLE BELOW, THE CROSSPIECE! YOU'LL HAVE TO EXPERIMENT TO FIND THE BEST BALANCE FOR EACH INDIVIDUAL KITE! SOMETIMES THE KITE MAY NOT BE PERFECTLY BALANCED ... AND YOU'LL HAVE TO ADD A TAIL!

ALL OUR KITES ARE FINISHED, UNCA DONALD! WHAT NEXT?

STOP, HUEY! NEVER RUN INTO THE STREET!

LOOK, UNCA DONALD! MY KITE FLIES PERFECTLY!

YOU CAN BE HIT BY CARS... AND YOU MAY CAUSE A SERIOUS TRAFFIC ACCIDENT!

THAT'S RULE NUMBER FIVE!

SCREECH!

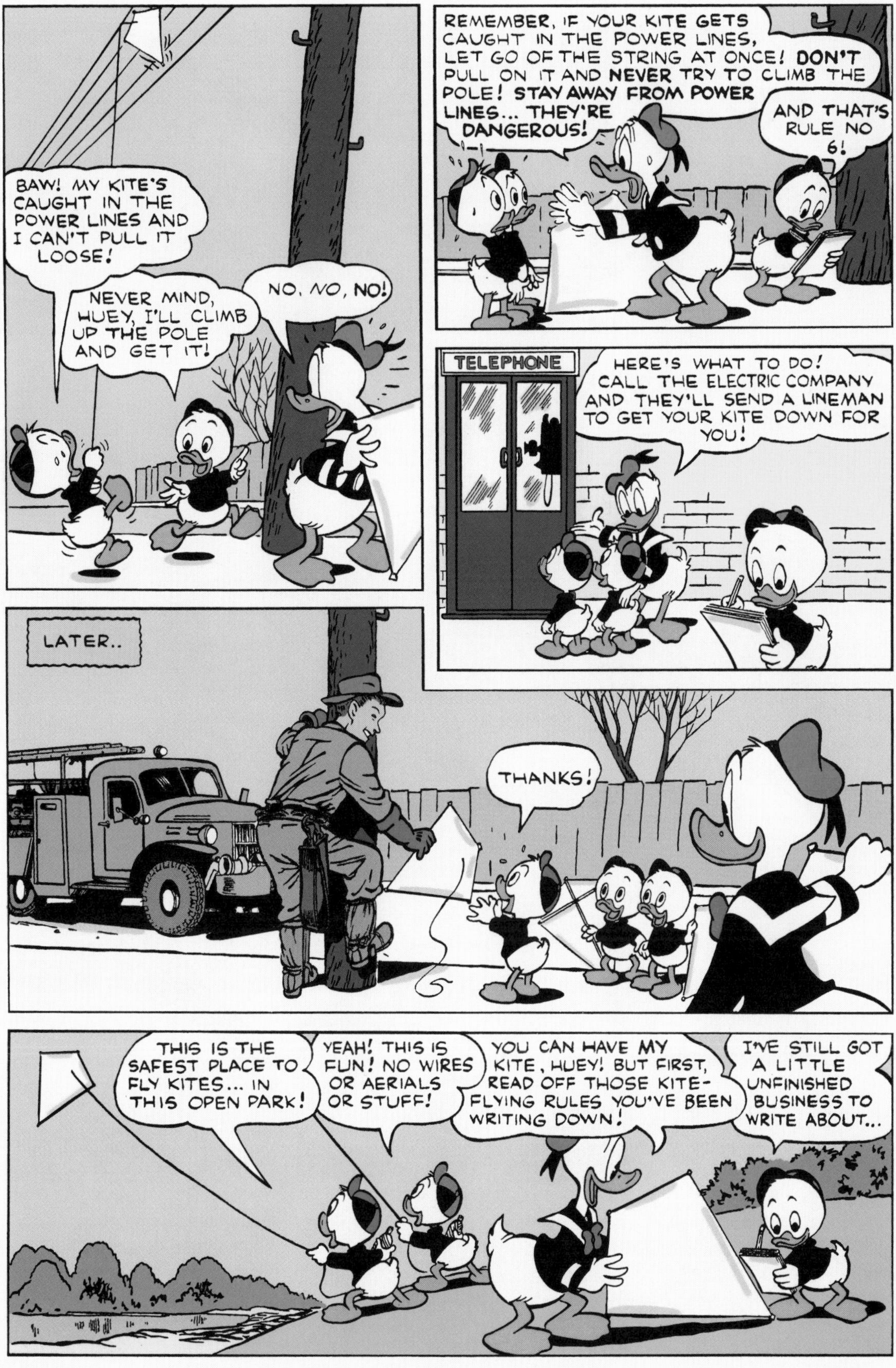
BAW! MY KITE'S CAUGHT IN THE POWER LINES AND I CAN'T PULL IT LOOSE!
NEVER MIND, HUEY, I'LL CLIMB UP THE POLE AND GET IT!
NO, NO, NO!
REMEMBER, IF YOUR KITE GETS CAUGHT IN THE POWER LINES, LET GO OF THE STRING AT ONCE! DON'T PULL ON IT AND NEVER TRY TO CLIMB THE POLE! STAY AWAY FROM POWER LINES... THEY'RE DANGEROUS!
AND THAT'S RULE NO 6!
TELEPHONE
HERE'S WHAT TO DO! CALL THE ELECTRIC COMPANY AND THEY'LL SEND A LINEMAN TO GET YOUR KITE DOWN FOR YOU!
LATER..
THANKS!
THIS IS THE SAFEST PLACE TO FLY KITES... IN THIS OPEN PARK!
YEAH! THIS IS FUN! NO WIRES OR AERIALS OR STUFF!
YOU CAN HAVE MY KITE, HUEY! BUT FIRST, READ OFF THOSE KITE-FLYING RULES YOU'VE BEEN WRITING DOWN!
I'VE STILL GOT A LITTLE UNFINISHED BUSINESS TO WRITE ABOUT...

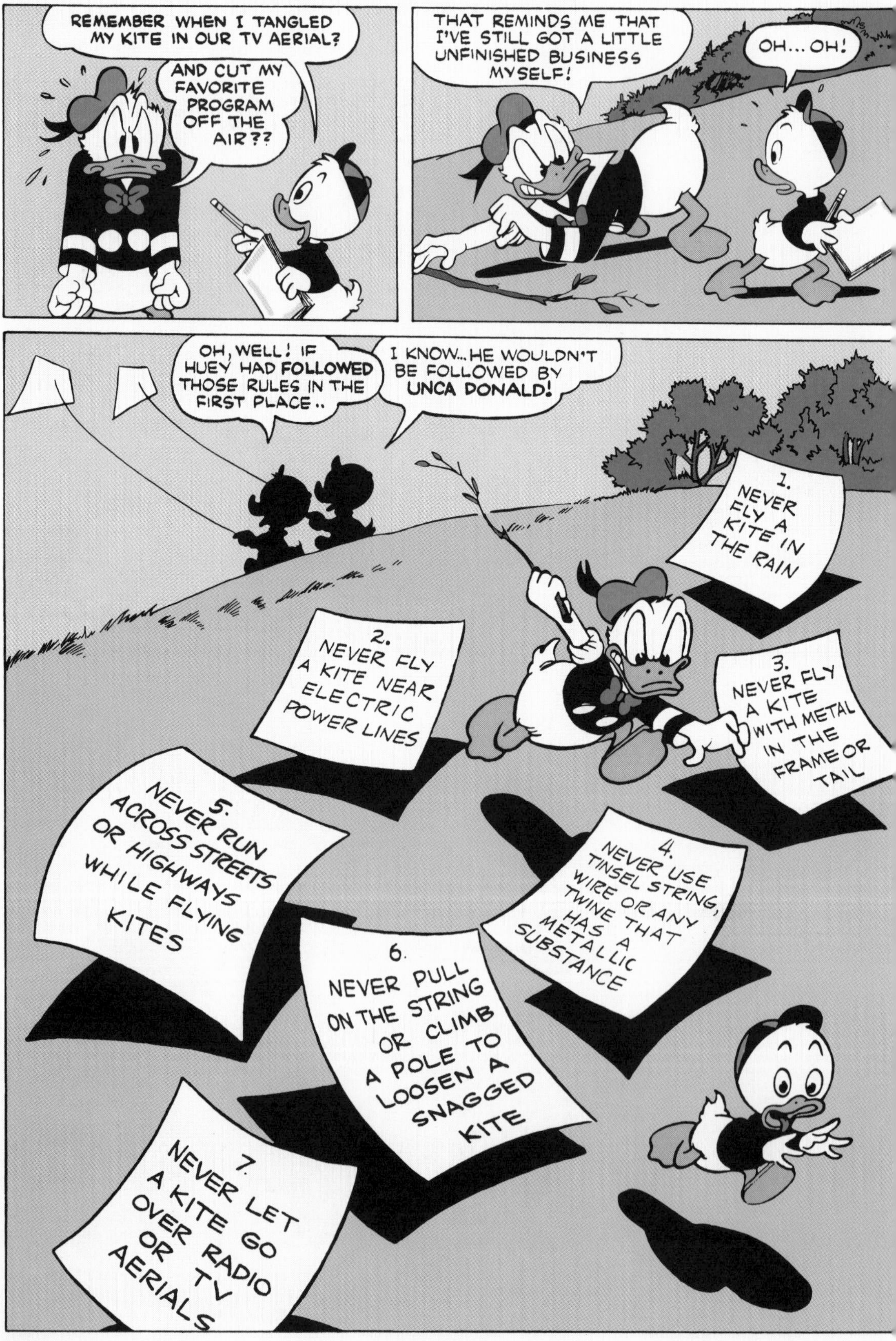
REMEMBER WHEN I TANGLED MY KITE IN OUR TV AERIAL?
AND CUT MY FAVORITE PROGRAM OFF THE AIR??
THAT REMINDS ME THAT I'VE STILL GOT A LITTLE UNFINISHED BUSINESS MYSELF!
OH... OH!
OH, WELL! IF HUEY HAD FOLLOWED THOSE RULES IN THE FIRST PLACE..
I KNOW... HE WOULDN'T BE FOLLOWED BY UNCA DONALD!
1. NEVER FLY A KITE IN THE RAIN
2. NEVER FLY A KITE NEAR ELECTRIC POWER LINES
3. NEVER FLY A KITE WITH METAL IN THE FRAME OR TAIL
4. NEVER USE TINSEL STRING, WIRE OR ANY TWINE THAT HAS A METALLIC SUBSTANCE
5. NEVER RUN ACROSS STREETS OR HIGHWAYS WHILE FLYING KITES
6. NEVER PULL ON THE STRING OR CLIMB A POLE TO LOOSEN A SNAGGED KITE
7. NEVER LET A KITE GO OVER RADIO OR TV AERIALS

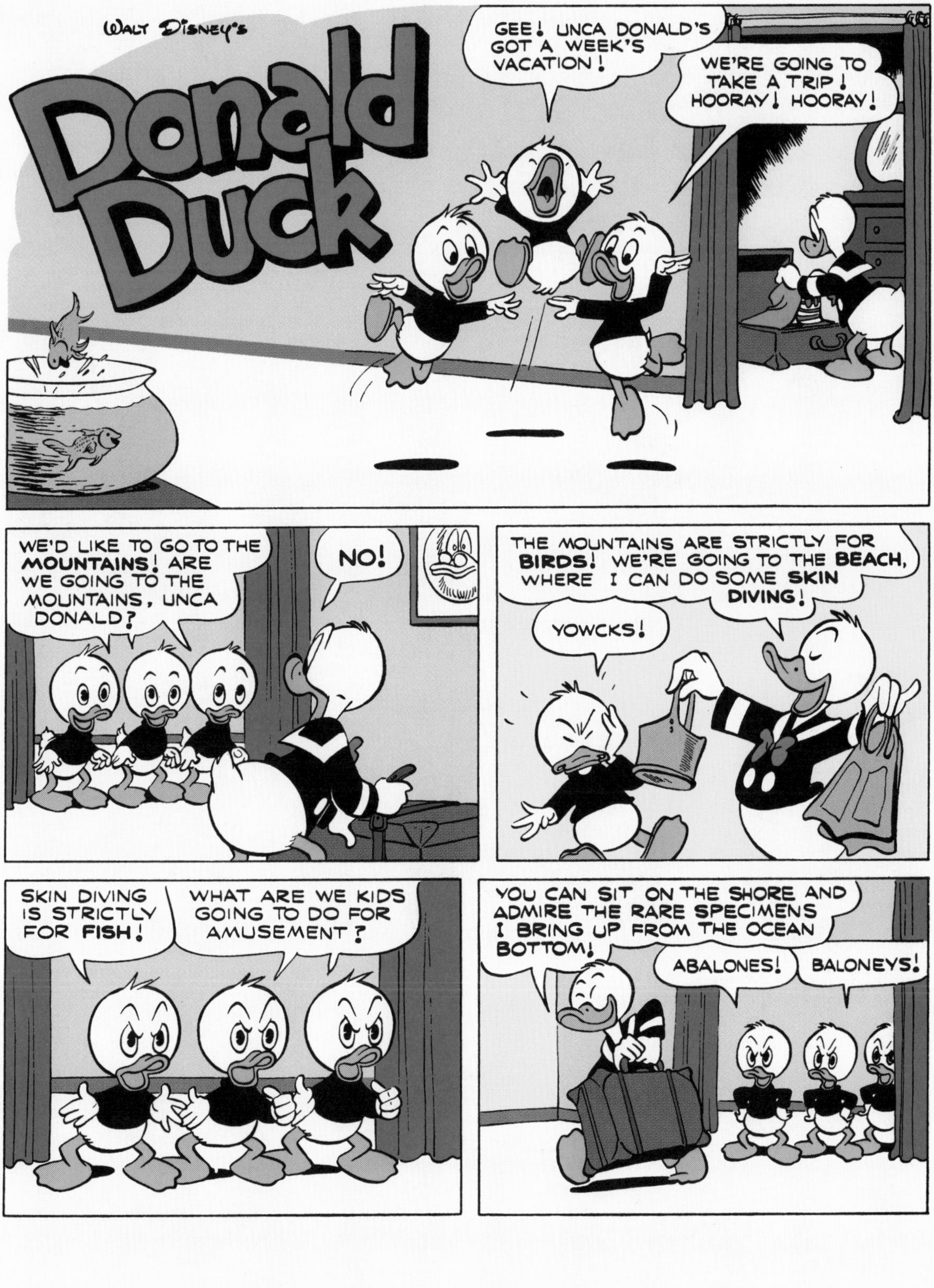
WALT DISNEY'S
Donald Duck
GEE! UNCA DONALD'S GOT A WEEK'S VACATION!
WE'RE GOING TO TAKE A TRIP! HOORAY! HOORAY!
WE'D LIKE TO GO TO THE MOUNTAINS! ARE WE GOING TO THE MOUNTAINS, UNCA DONALD?
NO!
THE MOUNTAINS ARE STRICTLY FOR BIRDS! WE'RE GOING TO THE BEACH, WHERE I CAN DO SOME SKIN DIVING!
YOWCKS!
SKIN DIVING IS STRICTLY FOR FISH!
WHAT ARE WE KIDS GOING TO DO FOR AMUSEMENT?
YOU CAN SIT ON THE SHORE AND ADMIRE THE RARE SPECIMENS I BRING UP FROM THE OCEAN BOTTOM!
ABALONES!
BALONEYS!

SOON, ON THE SHORE OF A ROCKY COVE!

AH! THE VAST SILENT WORLD BENEATH THE SEA! WHO KNOWS WHAT TERRORS OR TREASURES IT ENFOLDS?

ONLY THE BRAVEST OF THE BRAVE DARES PLUMB ITS MYSTERIOUS DEPTHS! ONLY THE STRONGEST OF THE STRONG DARES BATTLE ITS —

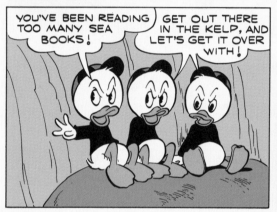

YOU'VE BEEN READING TOO MANY SEA BOOKS!

GET OUT THERE IN THE KELP, AND LET'S GET IT OVER WITH!

PHOOEY! YOU KIDS HAVE NO IRON IN YOUR BONES! YOU SHOULD YEARN TO EXPLORE THE MYSTIC FRONTIERS OF THE FATHOMLESS DEEP!

YOW! I STEPPED OFF A HIDDEN LEDGE!

YOW, AGAIN!

A SHARK HAS SCARED A WHOLE SCHOOL OF SWORDFISH TOWARD ME!

CHUNK

190

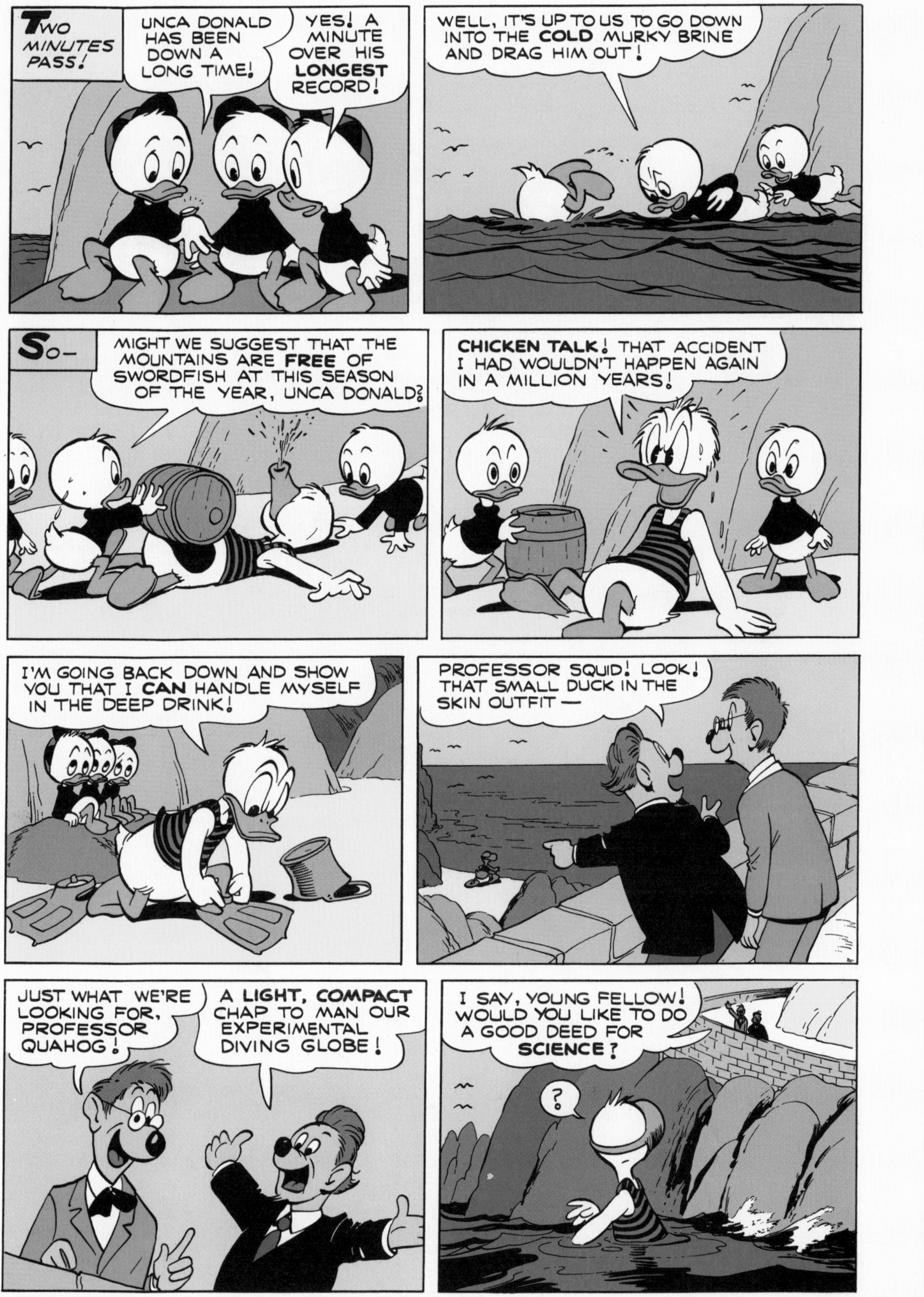
TWO MINUTES PASS!
UNCA DONALD HAS BEEN DOWN A LONG TIME!
YES! A MINUTE OVER HIS LONGEST RECORD!
WELL, IT'S UP TO US TO GO DOWN INTO THE COLD MURKY BRINE AND DRAG HIM OUT!
SO—
MIGHT WE SUGGEST THAT THE MOUNTAINS ARE FREE OF SWORDFISH AT THIS SEASON OF THE YEAR, UNCA DONALD?
CHICKEN TALK! THAT ACCIDENT I HAD WOULDN'T HAPPEN AGAIN IN A MILLION YEARS!
I'M GOING BACK DOWN AND SHOW YOU THAT I CAN HANDLE MYSELF IN THE DEEP DRINK!
PROFESSOR SQUID! LOOK! THAT SMALL DUCK IN THE SKIN OUTFIT—
JUST WHAT WE'RE LOOKING FOR, PROFESSOR QUAHOG!
A LIGHT, COMPACT CHAP TO MAN OUR EXPERIMENTAL DIVING GLOBE!
I SAY, YOUNG FELLOW! WOULD YOU LIKE TO DO A GOOD DEED FOR SCIENCE?
?

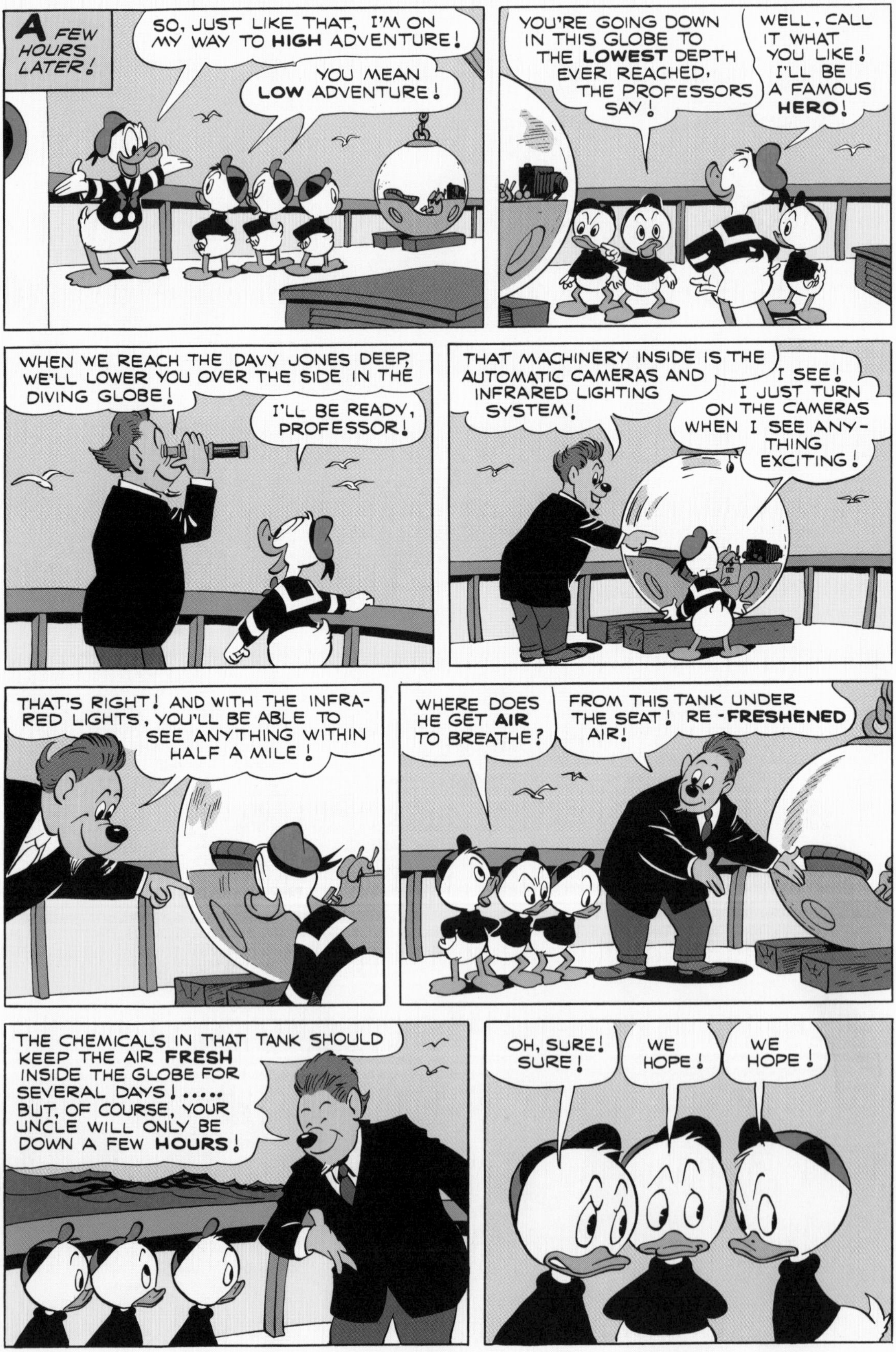
A FEW HOURS LATER!
SO, JUST LIKE THAT, I'M ON MY WAY TO **HIGH** ADVENTURE!
YOU MEAN **LOW** ADVENTURE!
YOU'RE GOING DOWN IN THIS GLOBE TO THE **LOWEST** DEPTH EVER REACHED, THE PROFESSORS SAY!
WELL, CALL IT WHAT YOU LIKE! I'LL BE A FAMOUS **HERO**!
WHEN WE REACH THE DAVY JONES DEEP, WE'LL LOWER YOU OVER THE SIDE IN THE DIVING GLOBE!
I'LL BE READY, PROFESSOR!
THAT MACHINERY INSIDE IS THE AUTOMATIC CAMERAS AND INFRARED LIGHTING SYSTEM!
I SEE! I JUST TURN ON THE CAMERAS WHEN I SEE ANYTHING EXCITING!
THAT'S RIGHT! AND WITH THE INFRA-RED LIGHTS, YOU'LL BE ABLE TO SEE ANYTHING WITHIN HALF A MILE!
WHERE DOES HE GET **AIR** TO BREATHE?
FROM THIS TANK UNDER THE SEAT! RE-**FRESHENED** AIR!
THE CHEMICALS IN THAT TANK SHOULD KEEP THE AIR **FRESH** INSIDE THE GLOBE FOR SEVERAL DAYS! ..... BUT, OF COURSE, YOUR UNCLE WILL ONLY BE DOWN A FEW **HOURS**!
OH, SURE! SURE!
WE HOPE!
WE HOPE!

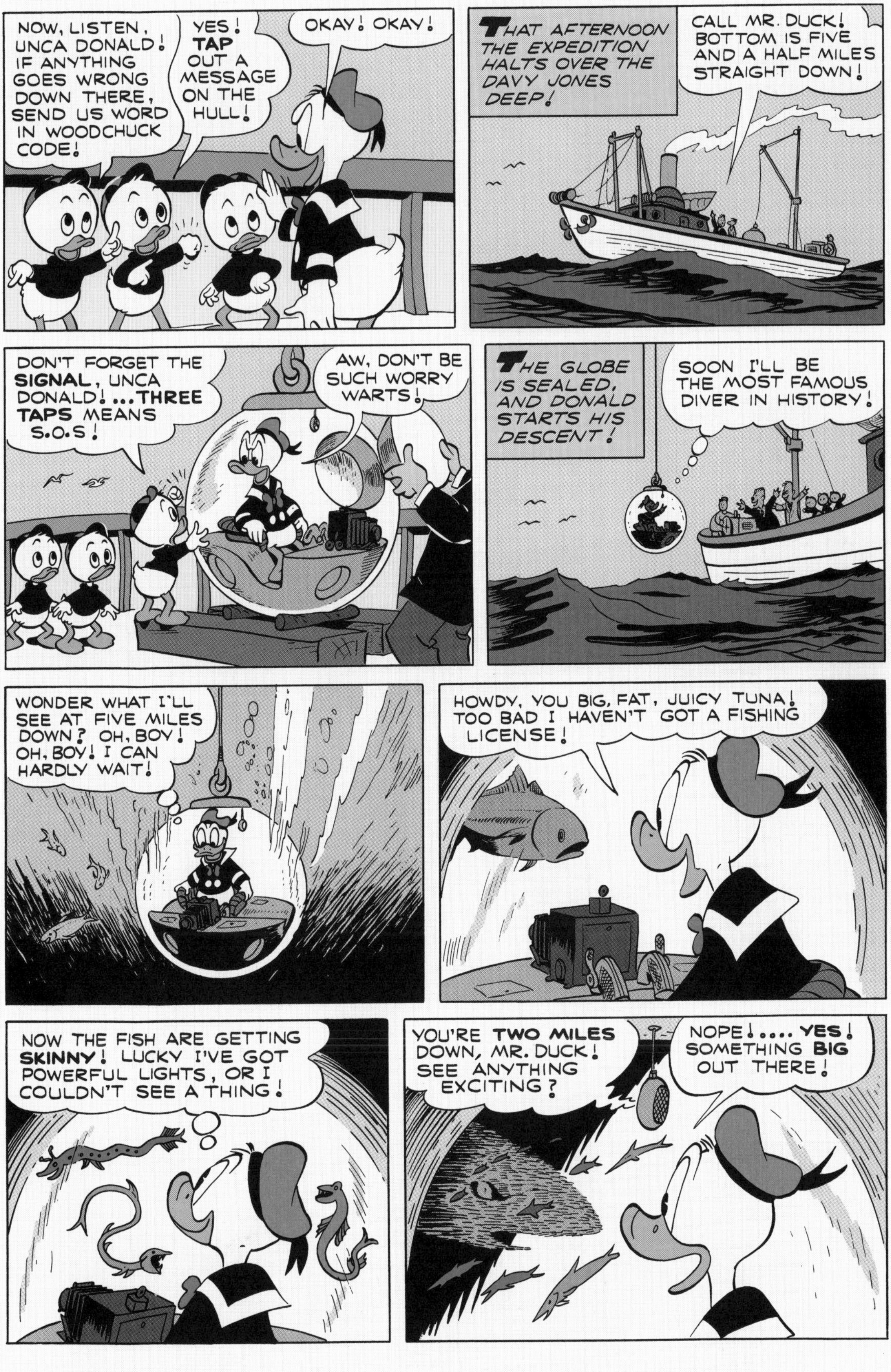
NOW, LISTEN, UNCA DONALD! IF ANYTHING GOES WRONG DOWN THERE, SEND US WORD IN WOODCHUCK CODE!
YES! TAP OUT A MESSAGE ON THE HULL!
OKAY! OKAY!
THAT AFTERNOON THE EXPEDITION HALTS OVER THE DAVY JONES DEEP!
CALL MR. DUCK! BOTTOM IS FIVE AND A HALF MILES STRAIGHT DOWN!
DON'T FORGET THE SIGNAL, UNCA DONALD! ...THREE TAPS MEANS S.O.S!
AW, DON'T BE SUCH WORRY WARTS!
THE GLOBE IS SEALED, AND DONALD STARTS HIS DESCENT!
SOON I'LL BE THE MOST FAMOUS DIVER IN HISTORY!
WONDER WHAT I'LL SEE AT FIVE MILES DOWN? OH, BOY! OH, BOY! I CAN HARDLY WAIT!
HOWDY, YOU BIG, FAT, JUICY TUNA! TOO BAD I HAVEN'T GOT A FISHING LICENSE!
NOW THE FISH ARE GETTING SKINNY! LUCKY I'VE GOT POWERFUL LIGHTS, OR I COULDN'T SEE A THING!
YOU'RE TWO MILES DOWN, MR. DUCK! SEE ANYTHING EXCITING?
NOPE! .... YES! SOMETHING BIG OUT THERE!

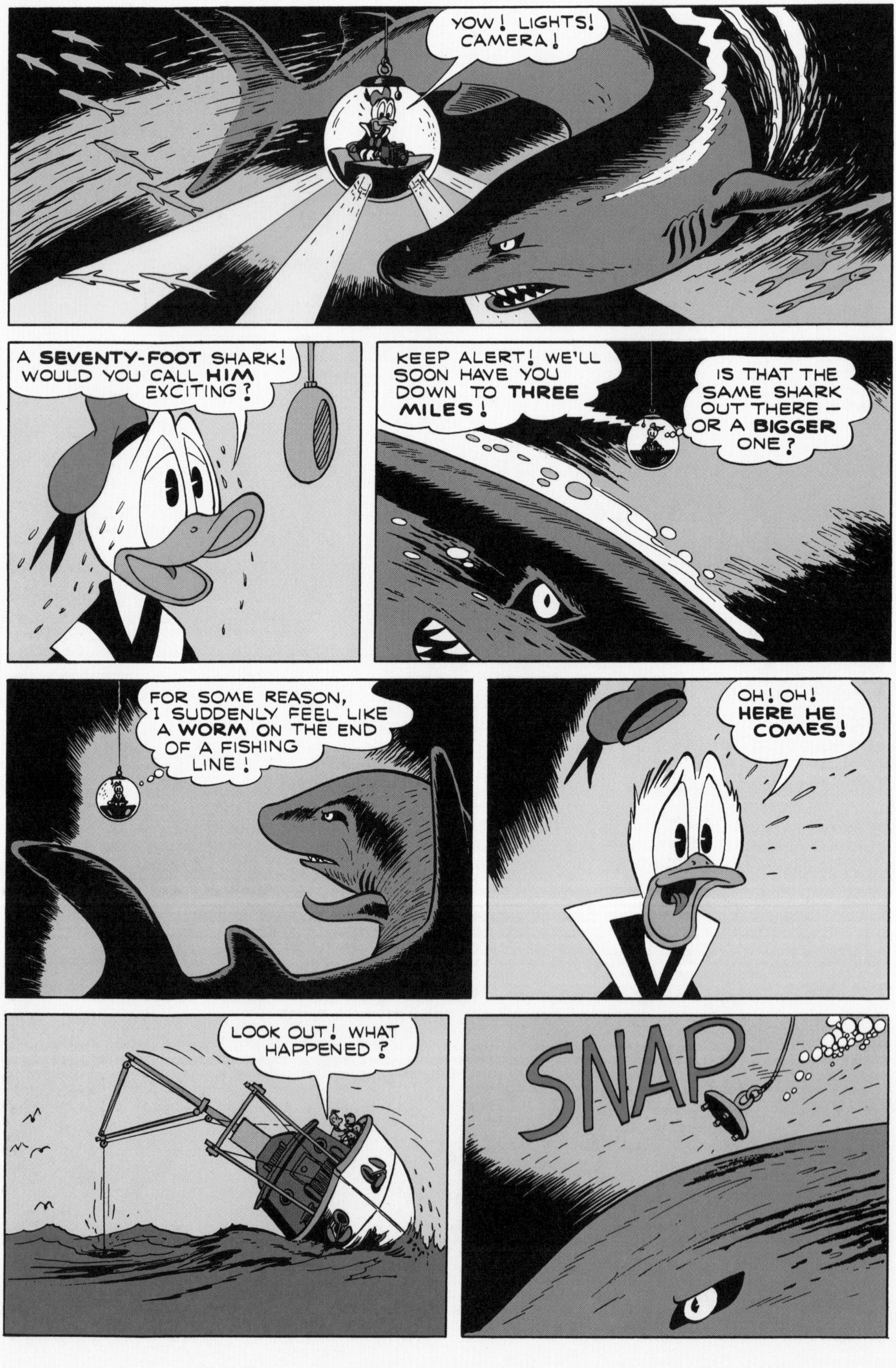
YOW! LIGHTS! CAMERA!
A SEVENTY-FOOT SHARK! WOULD YOU CALL HIM EXCITING?
KEEP ALERT! WE'LL SOON HAVE YOU DOWN TO THREE MILES!
IS THAT THE SAME SHARK OUT THERE — OR A BIGGER ONE?
FOR SOME REASON, I SUDDENLY FEEL LIKE A WORM ON THE END OF A FISHING LINE!
OH! OH! HERE HE COMES!
LOOK OUT! WHAT HAPPENED?
SNAP

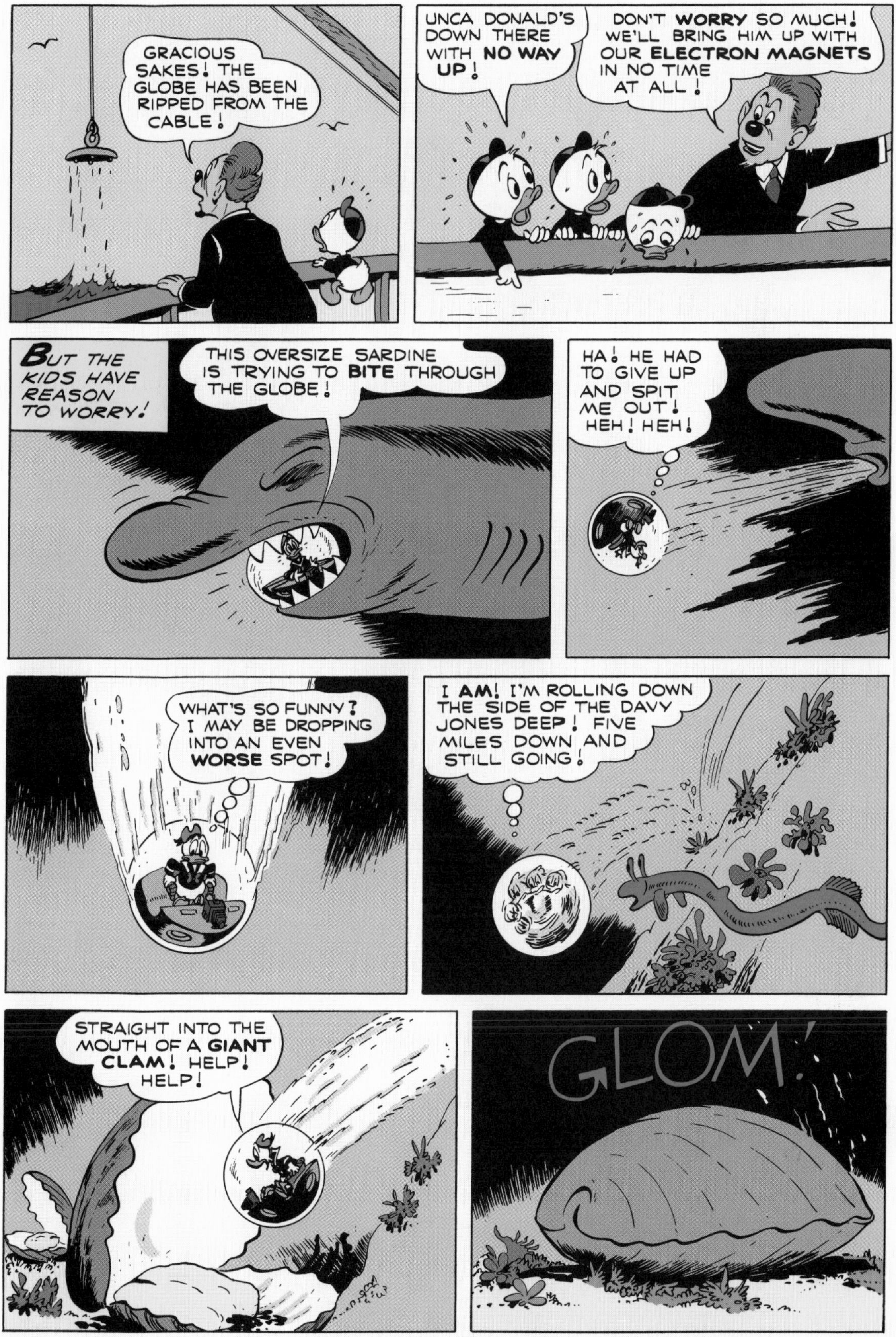
GRACIOUS SAKES! THE GLOBE HAS BEEN RIPPED FROM THE CABLE!
UNCA DONALD'S DOWN THERE WITH NO WAY UP!
DON'T WORRY SO MUCH! WE'LL BRING HIM UP WITH OUR ELECTRON MAGNETS IN NO TIME AT ALL!
BUT THE KIDS HAVE REASON TO WORRY!
THIS OVERSIZE SARDINE IS TRYING TO BITE THROUGH THE GLOBE!
HA! HE HAD TO GIVE UP AND SPIT ME OUT! HEH! HEH!
WHAT'S SO FUNNY? I MAY BE DROPPING INTO AN EVEN WORSE SPOT!
I AM! I'M ROLLING DOWN THE SIDE OF THE DAVY JONES DEEP! FIVE MILES DOWN AND STILL GOING!
STRAIGHT INTO THE MOUTH OF A GIANT CLAM! HELP! HELP!
GLOM!

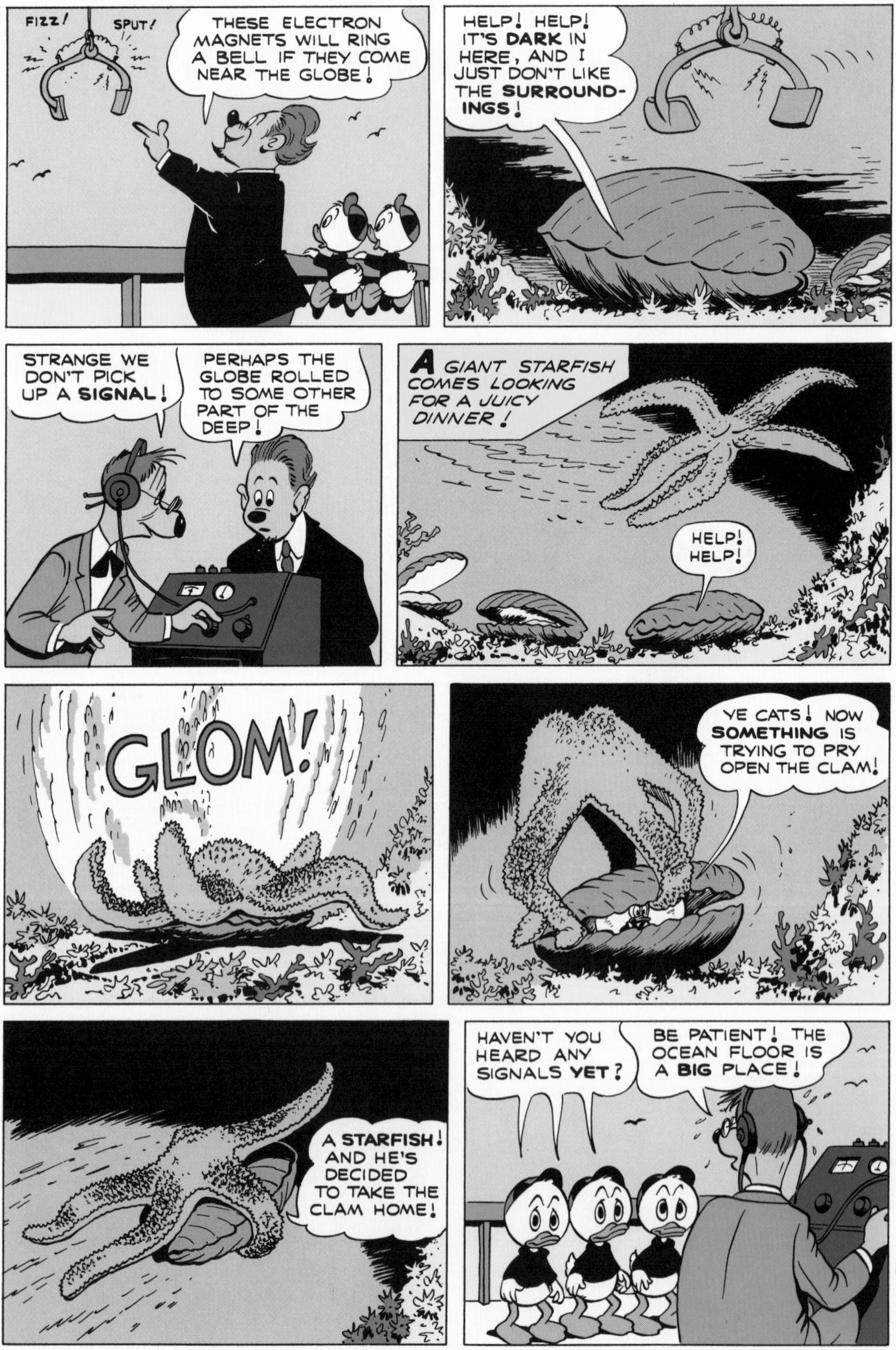
FIZZ!
SPUT!
THESE ELECTRON MAGNETS WILL RING A BELL IF THEY COME NEAR THE GLOBE!
HELP! HELP! IT'S DARK IN HERE, AND I JUST DON'T LIKE THE SURROUNDINGS!
STRANGE WE DON'T PICK UP A SIGNAL!
PERHAPS THE GLOBE ROLLED TO SOME OTHER PART OF THE DEEP!
A GIANT STARFISH COMES LOOKING FOR A JUICY DINNER!
HELP! HELP!
GLOM!
YE CATS! NOW SOMETHING IS TRYING TO PRY OPEN THE CLAM!
A STARFISH! AND HE'S DECIDED TO TAKE THE CLAM HOME!
HAVEN'T YOU HEARD ANY SIGNALS YET?
BE PATIENT! THE OCEAN FLOOR IS A BIG PLACE!

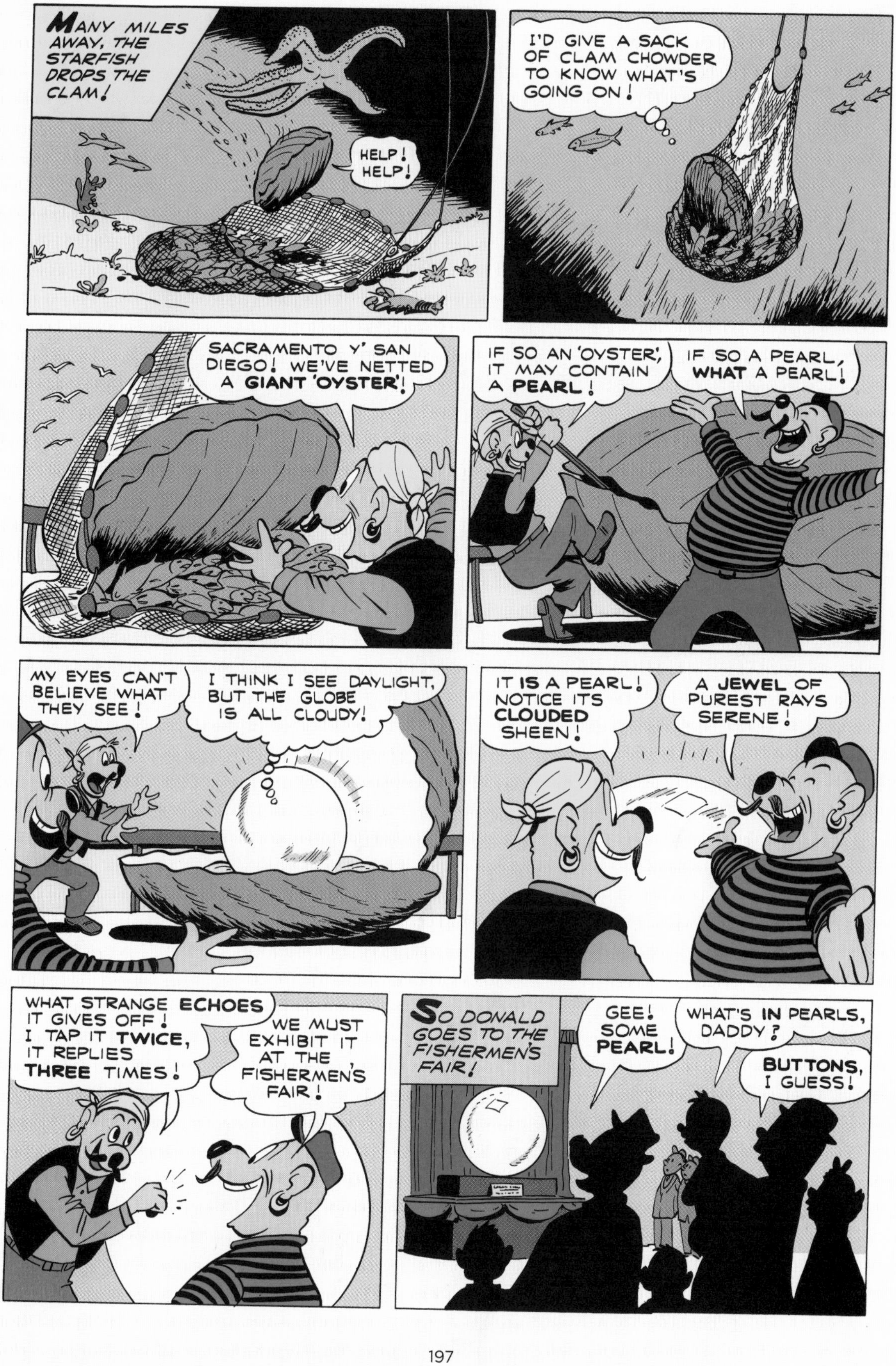
MANY MILES AWAY, THE STARFISH DROPS THE CLAM!
HELP! HELP!
I'D GIVE A SACK OF CLAM CHOWDER TO KNOW WHAT'S GOING ON!
SACRAMENTO Y' SAN DIEGO! WE'VE NETTED A GIANT 'OYSTER'!
IF SO AN 'OYSTER', IT MAY CONTAIN A PEARL!
IF SO A PEARL, WHAT A PEARL!
MY EYES CAN'T BELIEVE WHAT THEY SEE!
I THINK I SEE DAYLIGHT, BUT THE GLOBE IS ALL CLOUDY!
IT IS A PEARL! NOTICE ITS CLOUDED SHEEN!
A JEWEL OF PUREST RAYS SERENE!
WHAT STRANGE ECHOES IT GIVES OFF! I TAP IT TWICE, IT REPLIES THREE TIMES!
WE MUST EXHIBIT IT AT THE FISHERMEN'S FAIR!
SO DONALD GOES TO THE FISHERMEN'S FAIR!
GEE! SOME PEARL!
WHAT'S IN PEARLS, DADDY?
BUTTONS, I GUESS!

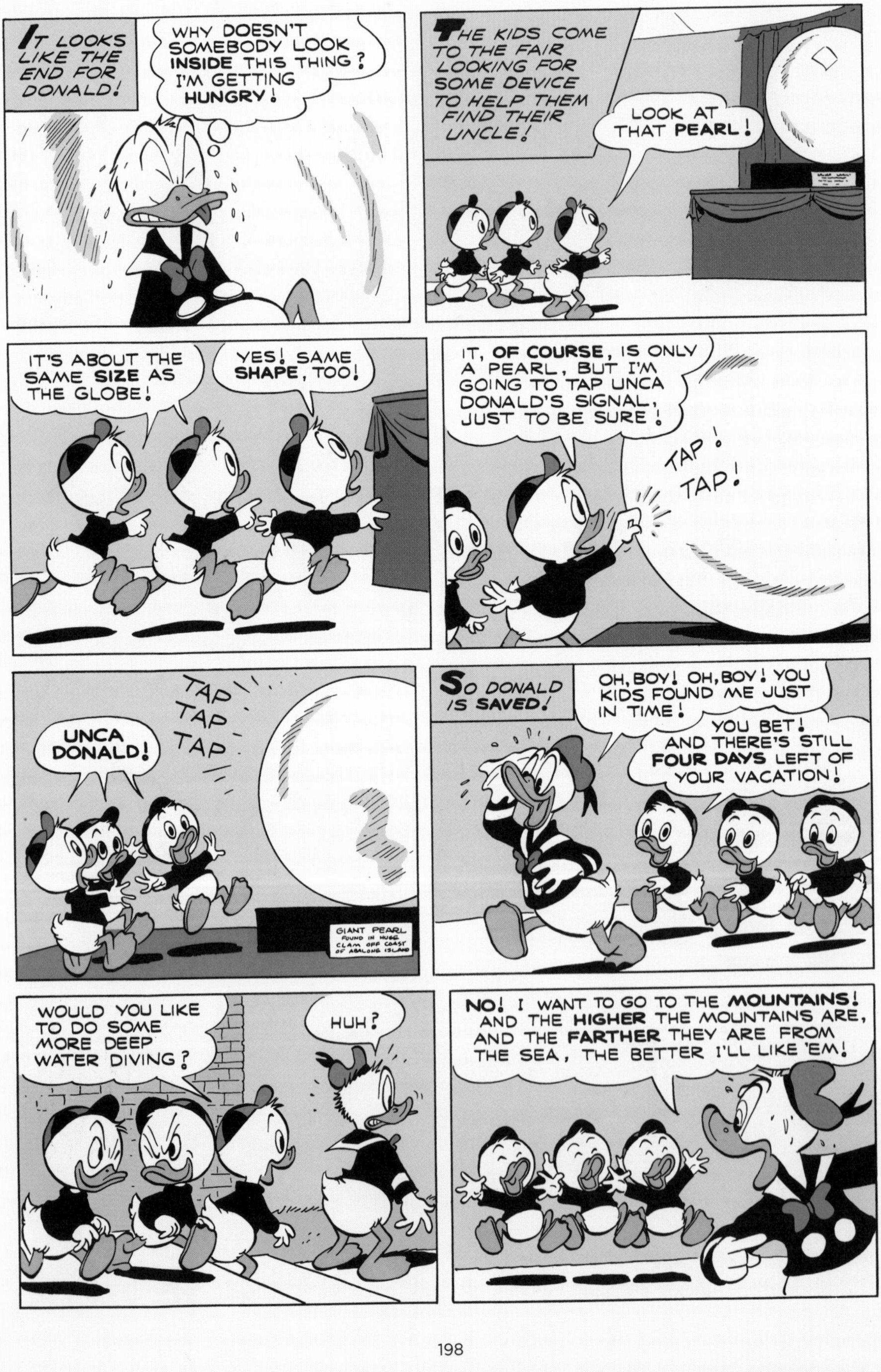
IT LOOKS LIKE THE END FOR DONALD!
WHY DOESN'T SOMEBODY LOOK INSIDE THIS THING? I'M GETTING HUNGRY!
THE KIDS COME TO THE FAIR LOOKING FOR SOME DEVICE TO HELP THEM FIND THEIR UNCLE!
LOOK AT THAT PEARL!
IT'S ABOUT THE SAME SIZE AS THE GLOBE!
YES! SAME SHAPE, TOO!
IT, OF COURSE, IS ONLY A PEARL, BUT I'M GOING TO TAP UNCA DONALD'S SIGNAL, JUST TO BE SURE!
TAP! TAP!
TAP TAP TAP
UNCA DONALD!
GIANT PEARL FOUND IN HUGE CLAM OFF COAST OF ABALONE ISLAND
SO DONALD IS SAVED!
OH, BOY! OH, BOY! YOU KIDS FOUND ME JUST IN TIME!
YOU BET! AND THERE'S STILL FOUR DAYS LEFT OF YOUR VACATION!
WOULD YOU LIKE TO DO SOME MORE DEEP WATER DIVING?
HUH?
NO! I WANT TO GO TO THE MOUNTAINS! AND THE HIGHER THE MOUNTAINS ARE, AND THE FARTHER THEY ARE FROM THE SEA, THE BETTER I'LL LIKE 'EM!

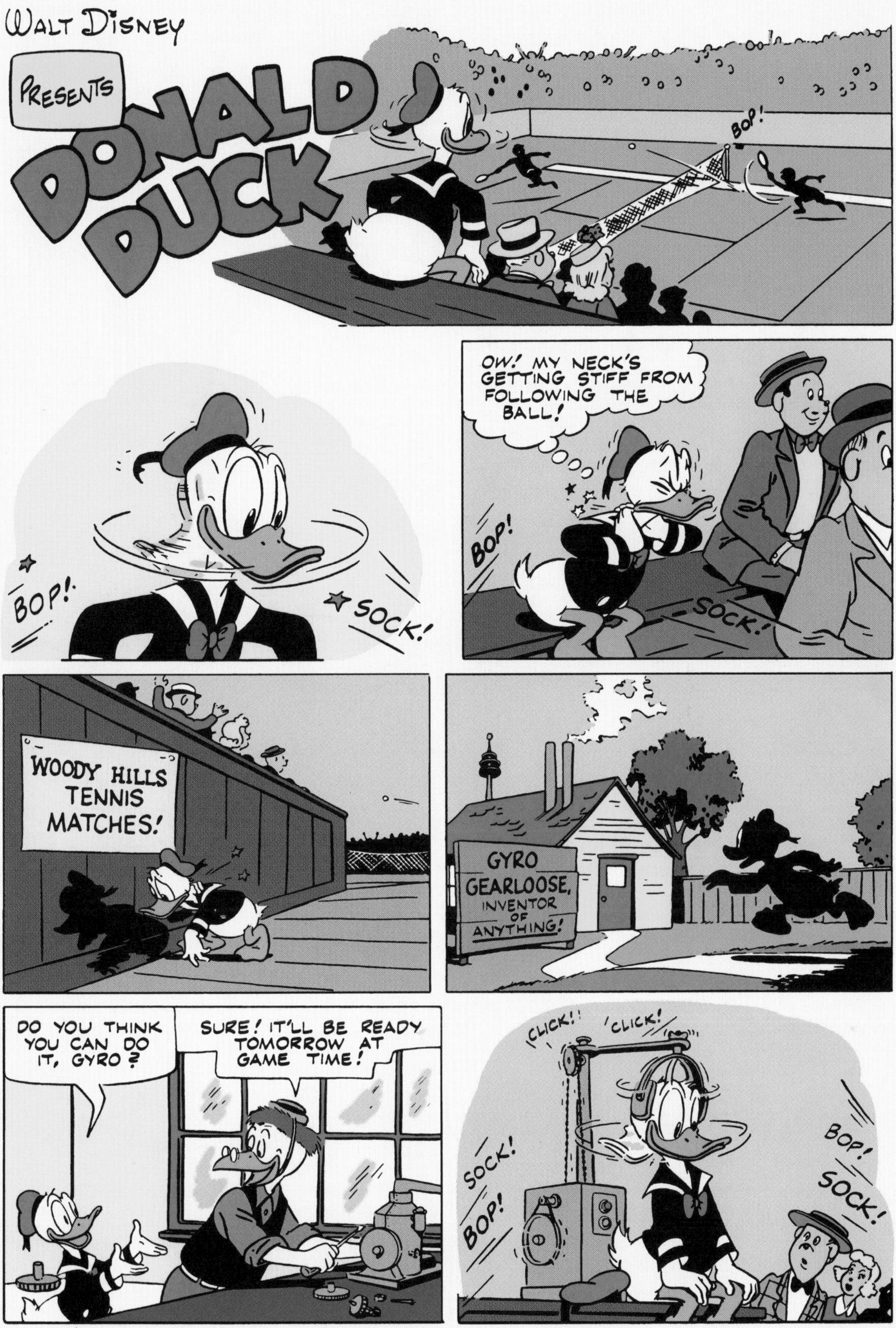

WALT DISNEY
PRESENTS
DONALD DUCK
BOP!
BOP!
SOCK!
OW! MY NECK'S GETTING STIFF FROM FOLLOWING THE BALL!
BOP!
SOCK!
WOODY HILLS TENNIS MATCHES!
GYRO GEARLOOSE, INVENTOR OF ANYTHING!
DO YOU THINK YOU CAN DO IT, GYRO?
SURE! IT'LL BE READY TOMORROW AT GAME TIME!
CLICK!
CLICK!
SOCK!
BOP!
BOP!
SOCK!

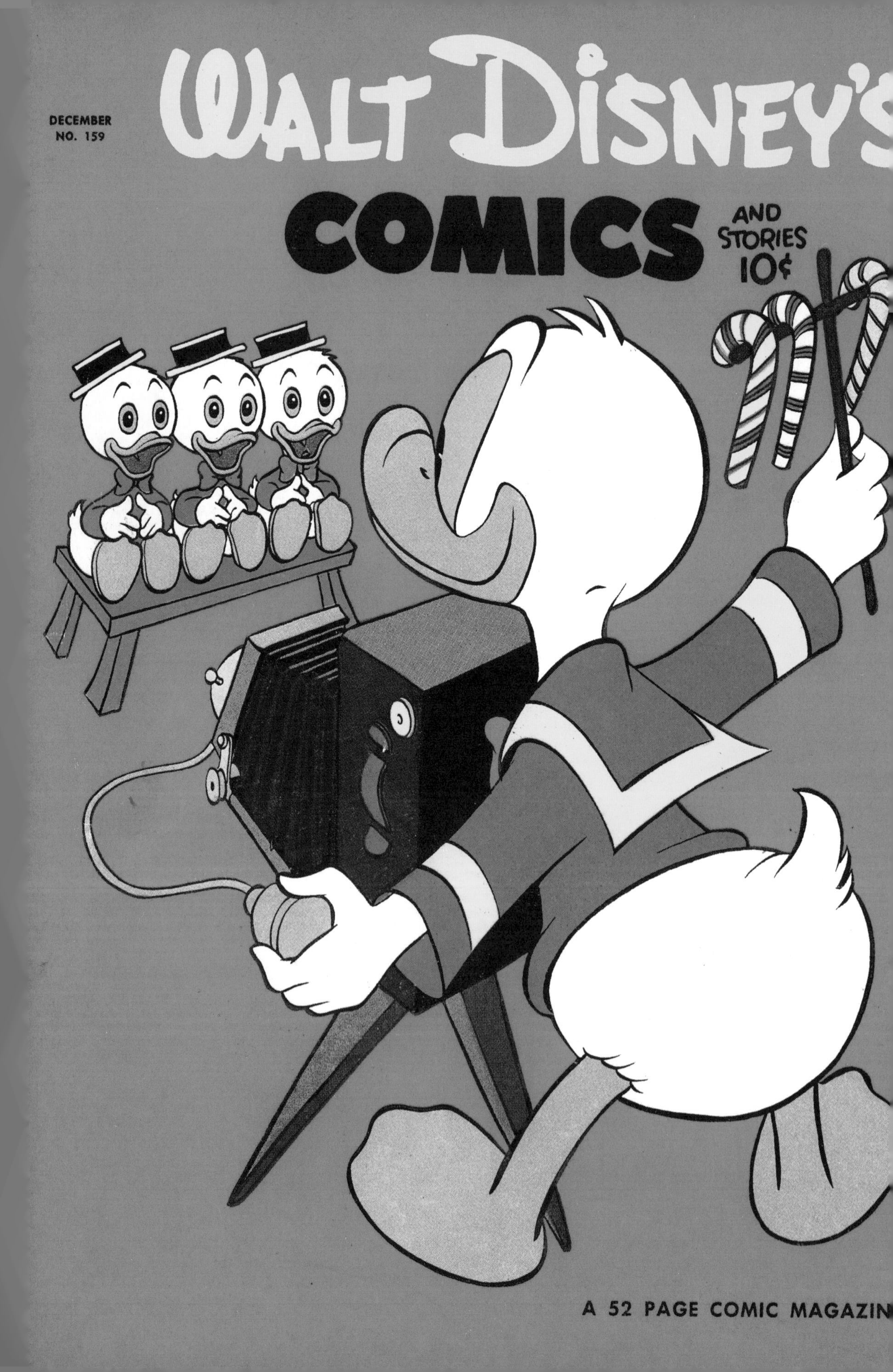
DECEMBER
NO. 159
WALT DISNEY'S
COMICS
AND STORIES
10¢
A 52 PAGE COMIC MAGAZIN

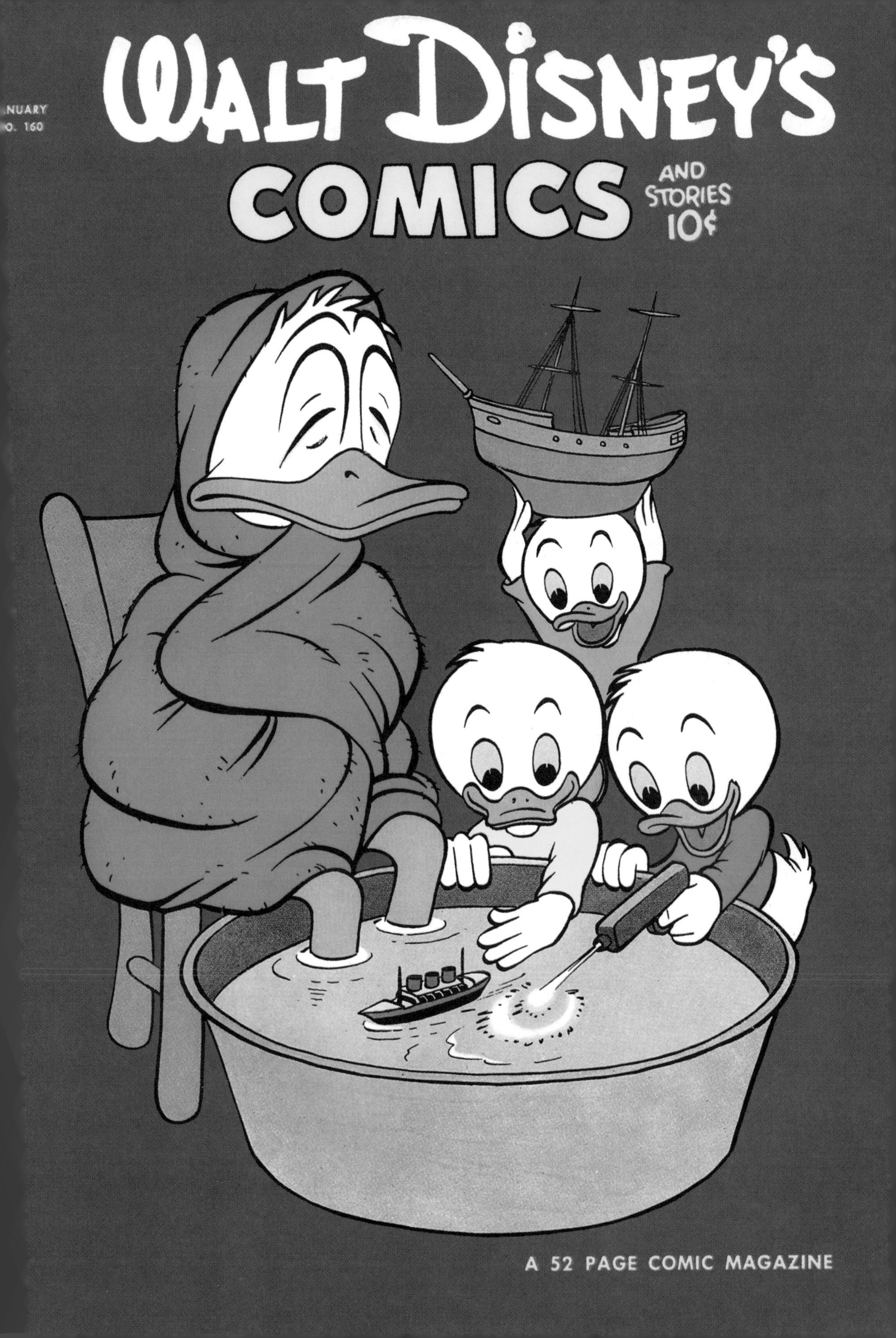

NUARY
O. 160
WALT DISNEY'S
COMICS
AND STORIES
10¢
A 52 PAGE COMIC MAGAZINE

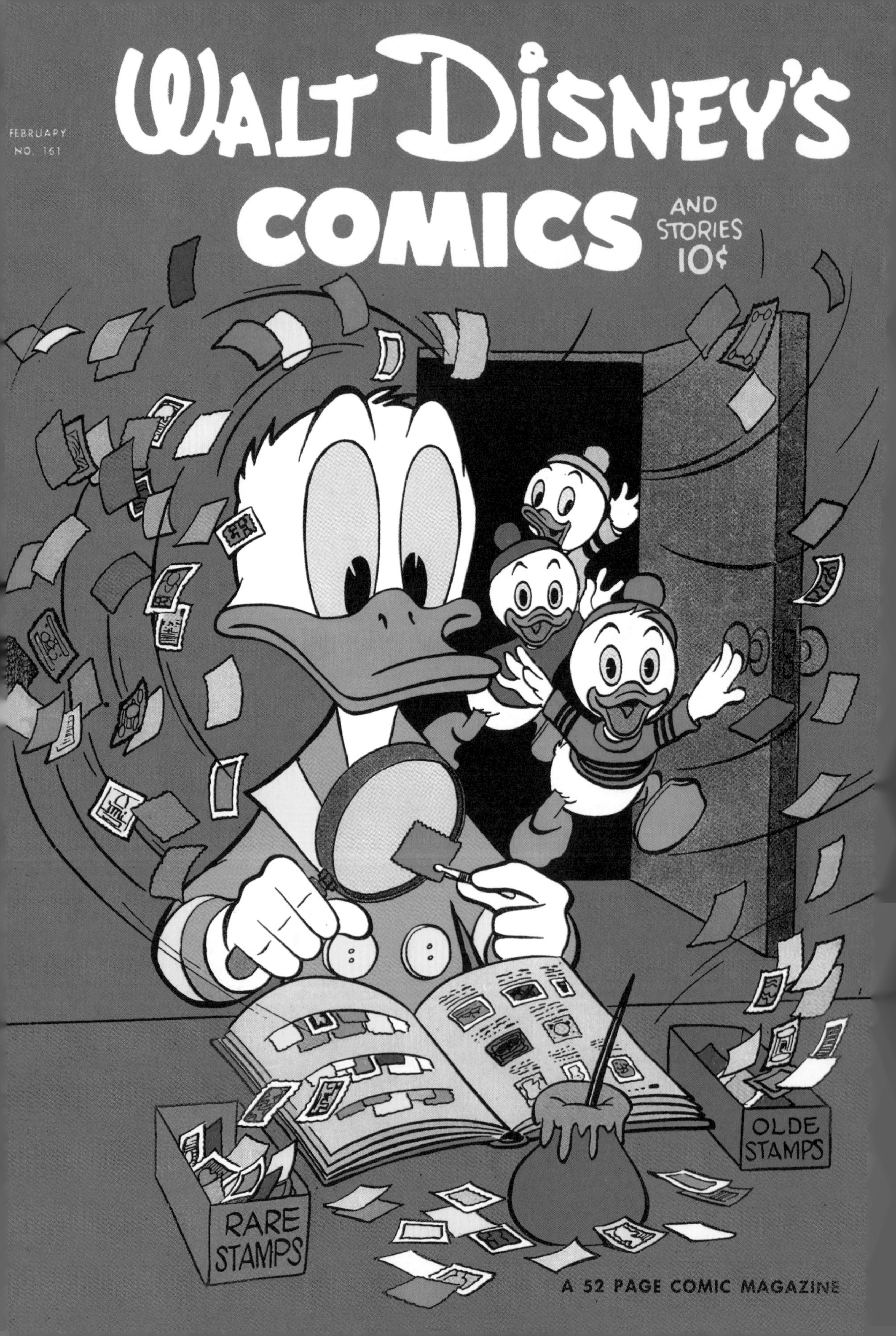

FEBRUARY
NO. 161
WALT DISNEY'S
COMICS
AND STORIES
10¢
OLDE STAMPS
RARE STAMPS
A 52 PAGE COMIC MAGAZINE

Story Notes

THE GHOST SHERIFF OF LAST GASP *p.1*

Over the years, the venerable Western has been mashed up with just about every genre you can think of — comedy, horror, martial arts, crime fiction, even science fiction, just to name a few. In "The Ghost Sheriff of Last Gasp," Carl Barks mixes the Western with the mystery and the ghost story.

Donald, irritated by cheesy Western TV shows ("they're an insult to the Old West") with their improbable sheriffs that his nephews like so much, takes Huey, Dewey and Louie to a genuine Western ghost town called Last Gasp. Once a boomtown, it was deserted in 1872 because of eerie sounds, supposedly from the ghost of sheriff Wild Bill Trueshot, the specter of the story's title.

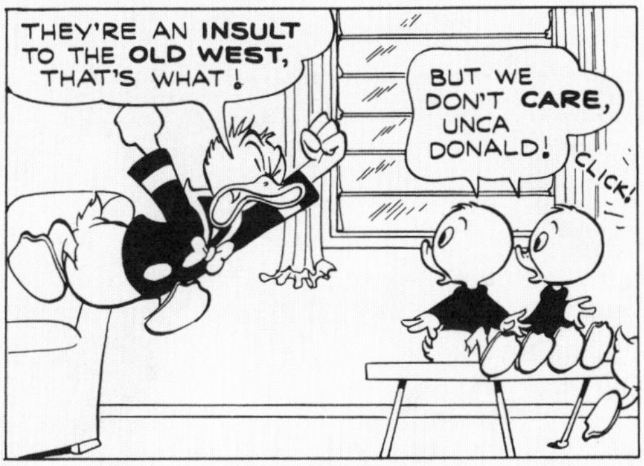
THEY'RE AN **INSULT** TO THE **OLD WEST**, THAT'S WHAT!
BUT WE DON'T **CARE**, UNCA DONALD!
CLICK!

Sure enough, when Donald and the boys arrive, they hear the eerie noises themselves. Barks ups the ante with some mysterious hostilities by seemingly inanimate objects, and Donald takes it as a challenge and gets ready to fight.

But Huey, Dewey, and Louie are on the case and soon track down the source of the spooky goings-on. They ultimately come face-to-face with the "ghost sheriff" himself — who is not what we might have been expecting after all these years. Recovering his courage, Donald challenges him to a duel, which results in the loss of the sheriff's "power" to continue his haunting ways.

Barks, as he did in his 1948 classic, "Sheriff of Bullet Valley" (*Walt Disney's Donald Duck: "The Old Castle's Secret,"* volume 6 in this series), satirizes Western fiction: the Old West sheriff isn't so tough even if his name pays homage to Western legend Wild Bill Hickok (he even says he doesn't want to be called Wild Bill Hiccup).

Westerns enjoyed an enduring popularity throughout the 1950s. In 1955, the year "The Ghost Sheriff of Last Gasp" was first published, the famous radio show *Gunsmoke* (1952–1961) debuted as a TV show (1955–1975) and went on to become the longest-running prime time live-action drama in the U.S.

— STEFANO PRIARONE

WISPY WILLIE *p. 11*

By the time "Wispy Willie" enters Barks's Duckiverse, Uncle Scrooge has already undergone his conversion from antagonistic tightwad to charismatic curmudgeon. Occasionally, Scrooge reprises his role as a profit-driven heavy for the sake of laughs. This inconsistency of character from story to story, and in some cases even from panel to panel, remains one of the greatest thrills of Barks's Ducks. Donald, Scrooge, and the nephews often surprise us with the spontaneity of their reactions to each other's folly and the effect makes every new predicament as engaging as it is capricious and unexpected. "Wispy Willie" provides several superb examples of that deliberately slippery continuity.

Scrooge and Donald face off so frequently that their combative stance seems iconic. Standing toe-to-toe and staring into each other's mugs, their postures provide a laughably familiar set of bickering bookends to "hold up" both ends of "Wispy Willie." The

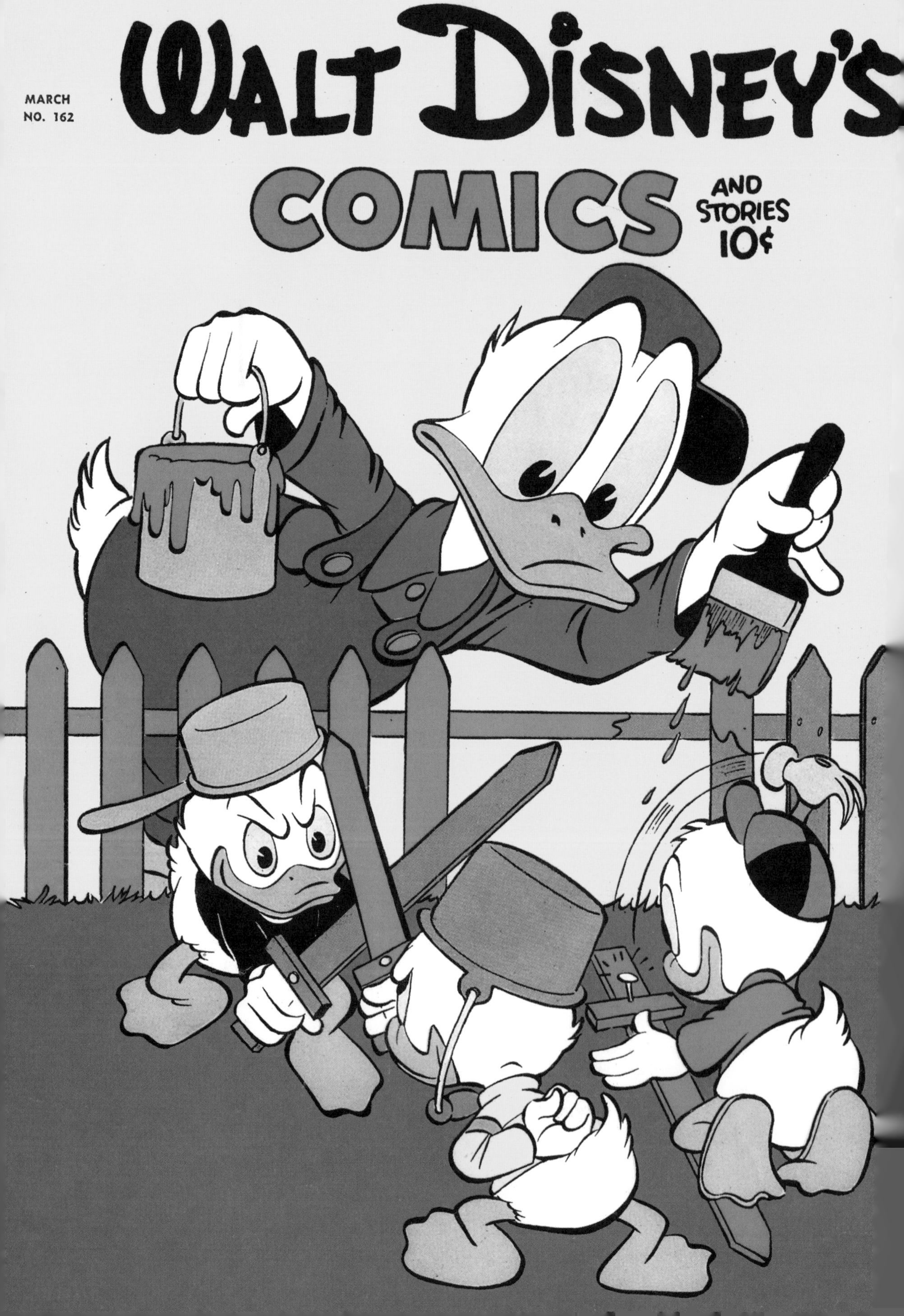
MARCH
NO. 162
WALT DISNEY'S
COMICS
AND STORIES
10¢

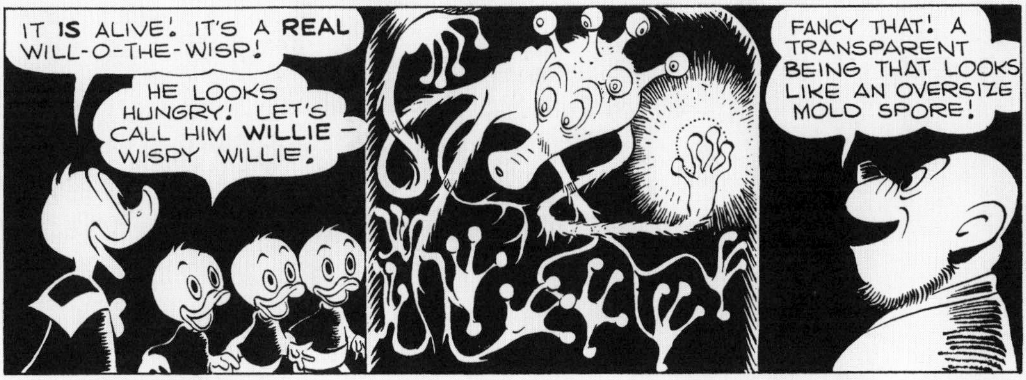
IT IS ALIVE! IT'S A REAL WILL-O-THE-WISP!
HE LOOKS HUNGRY! LET'S CALL HIM WILLIE — WISPY WILLIE!
FANCY THAT! A TRANSPARENT BEING THAT LOOKS LIKE AN OVERSIZE MOLD SPORE!

plot fodder is nothing new. Scrooge uses his enormous wherewithal in an attempt to avoid paying "more than a fair price," and Donald sticks to his guns, demanding satisfaction on his own terms. The shenanigans that follow provide Barks with a variety of "diabolical stratagems" and corny confrontations.

Meanwhile, the Scrooge/Donald battle escalates into one of Barks's many satires of the absurdity of progress, profit, property, and pride. Donald personifies the individualistic defender of his humble hovel, while Scrooge portrays the rapacious "big money" interest who stops at nothing to drive his ennobled nephew from his home. Such plots are rehashed across decades of screwball comedies and Westerns from *You Can't Take It With You* to *Shane*, but Barks tampers deliciously with the typical man vs. monopoly theme, ultimately leaving them both as ornery as ever.

This time, neither homesteader nor corporate titan play their hands very well. Scrooge's tricks are all too trite and desperate. Plagues of vermin, wicked witches rented from *Snow White* (complete with shoulder raven!), rampaging apes, and hissing dragons are too forced and fantastic to stir the bemused Donald, whose blasé attitude protects him from all forms of fear and intimidation. He merely smiles, shrugs off each assault, and ponders Scrooge's next move.

It's never completely certain if Donald sees through Scrooge's stale scheming, but Barks has a grand time lampooning his own penchant for wild adventures and exotic monsters. His TV dragon mirrors the sleeping beast of "The Golden Fleecing" (*Walt Disney's Uncle Scrooge: "The Seven Cities of Gold,"* volume 14). Barks's own terrifically fresh take on wicked witchery would arrive in 1961 when the mischievous Magica De Spell would begin her reign of terror.

This leaves, of course, the story's two best characters, the balmy Dr. Superthink and his moldy menace, Wispy Willie. Again, Barks's humorous reversals provide much of the fun. Superthink is so oddly charming that his "mad scientist" routine only unites the Ducks in mutual fondness for the supposedly "ghastly" root-munching will-o-the-wisp.

Willie himself is a triumph of Barksian comedic design. Though he appears in only six panels, his silent smiles, playful tentacles, and prodigious eyestalks exude warmth and delight from every angle. He is every bit the merry monster, in league with other marquee Barks creations like the silly sea serpent of "No Such Varmint" (*Walt Disney's Donald Duck: "Terror of the Beagle Boys,"* volume 10) or the Atlanteans of "The Secret of Atlantis" (*Walt Disney's Uncle Scrooge: "Only a Poor Old Man,"* volume 12). It's a shame that Willie gets so little time to shine his jack-o-lantern. He was a brief, brilliant contribution to Barks's Duck Family farce.

— DANIEL F. YEZBICK

THE HAMMY CAMEL *p. 21*

The rollicking "Hammy Camel" hangs on a commonplace premise pushed in ludicrous directions. The nephews' unusual holiday gift for Donald begins with a bargain that Scrooge himself might admire, yet Abdul refuses to accept his role as a "useful pet"

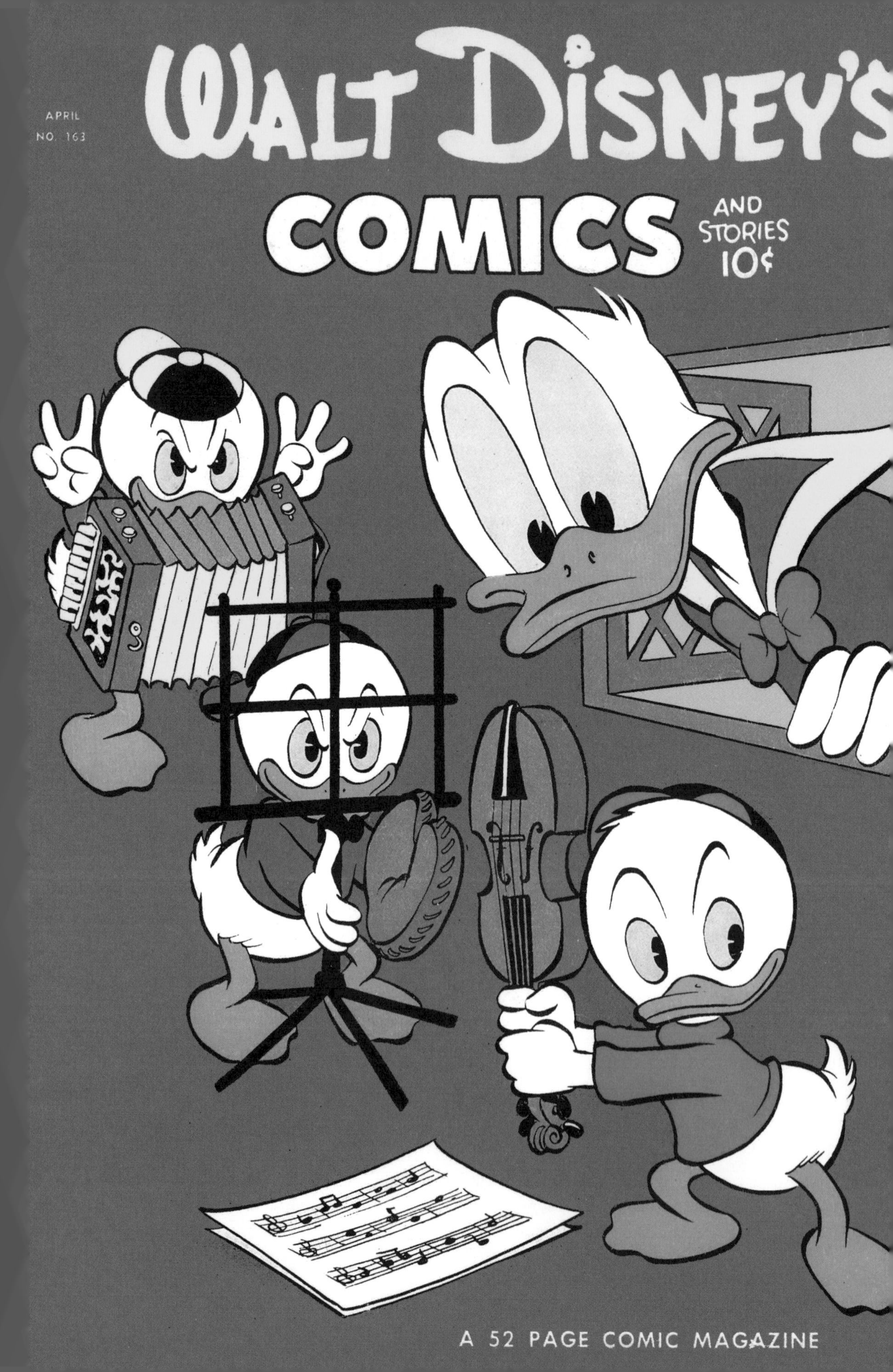
APRIL
NO. 163
WALT DISNEY'S
COMICS
AND STORIES
10¢
A 52 PAGE COMIC MAGAZINE

and prospecting pal. The resulting antics — involving soda-pop cowboys, uranium safaris, and super-whiz dishwashers — gleefully transcend commonplace miseries like daily chores, tight budgets, and domestic tedium. Laced with madcap fantasies of affluence, convenience, and efficiency, the story stands among Barks's broadest and goofiest explorations of how fun and adventure combat drudgery and poverty.

Nearly every scene introduces Barksian incongruities associated with mid-20th-century commerce, convenience, and convention. Subtle sight gags are evident early on. As the nephews enter the balmy "winter quarters" of the kaput circus, lush palms sway in the distance while a traditional evergreen wreath sits oddly in the opposite foreground. These kooky yuletide disparities continue through the opening panels as Donald's Christmas tree is contrasted with tropical palms seen through a window and peeking over a fence. The same pairings inform the later desert landscapes, where forlorn cacti, sages, and rocky outcroppings are coupled with more adamantly contemporary Cold War concerns like roadside soda stands and uranium deposits.

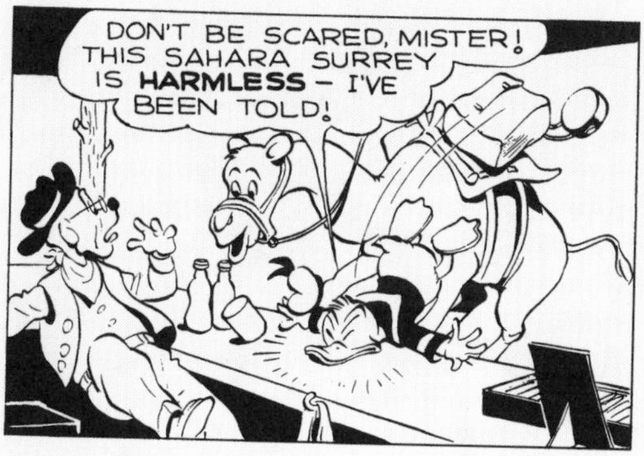
DON'T BE SCARED, MISTER! THIS SAHARA SURREY IS **HARMLESS** – I'VE BEEN TOLD!

Then there is Abdul himself, an affably obstinate foil for Donald's own blend of charm and chutzpah. As the tale unfolds, the oddball ungulate becomes a goofy signifier of shifting tradition. Here is an offbeat Christmas camel removed from any context involving stars, mangers, or myrrh. He exhibits no love for deserts, water, or work, preferring junk food, mooching, and playing to a crowd for applause. Abdul reaches his comedic zenith when he returns as a weird Marley-esque specter, reminding Donald and the kids of their obligations. Barks's glowing camel then becomes part of a screwball hodgepodge of Christmas imagery in a story that trumps everyone's expectations concerning leisure, labor, and landscape.

Signs of changing times and crass commercialism abound. The bankrupt Bungling Bros. Circus must sell their camel at a clearance price (50 cents), but the dusky dromedary will soon be "wowing the country" via television. Donald's urge to prospect references the government-sponsored "uranium rush" of the early 1950s where geologists and prospectors like Charles Steen, "the uranium king" of the Mi Vida mine, joined the mad dash to cash in on the demand for the raw material needed to build up America's atomic arsenal. Even the supposedly foreboding Parchneck Desert and Buzzard Bone Mountains brim with entrepreneurial soda jerks in cowboy costume, joyriding TV agents in ultra-flashy roadsters, and gargantuan "Glo-Go" highway ads painted over majestic buttes. All of these congeal into a wacky yuletide yarn of capitalist contrasts.

Mirroring his other Christmas tales, Barks concludes by emphasizing themes of charity and generosity. The lucky Ducks, now a-roll in dough and dishwashers, can't wait to share their windfall with a TV party for the rest of the clan. Here is Cold War holiday farce at its most absurdly techno-centric — uranium-colored TV camels and all!

— DANIEL F. YEZBICK

FIX-UP MIX-UP *p. 31*

Barks's Donald is fundamentally a positive character. Despite his short temper, he is intelligent, capable, enterprising, and dynamic — just witness his remarkable skills in "Master Rainmaker" (*Walt Disney's Donald Duck: "Trick or Treat,"* volume 13). In "Fix-up Mix-up," though, we mostly get to see his catastrophic side. Yes, he is enterprising and dynamic, but this time in a naive and immature way — he believes he can do it all after merely having read a manual the previous day, even though he really didn't understand it.

He is unrealistic about his capabilities and fails to recognize the importance of knowledge and experience, flaunting the

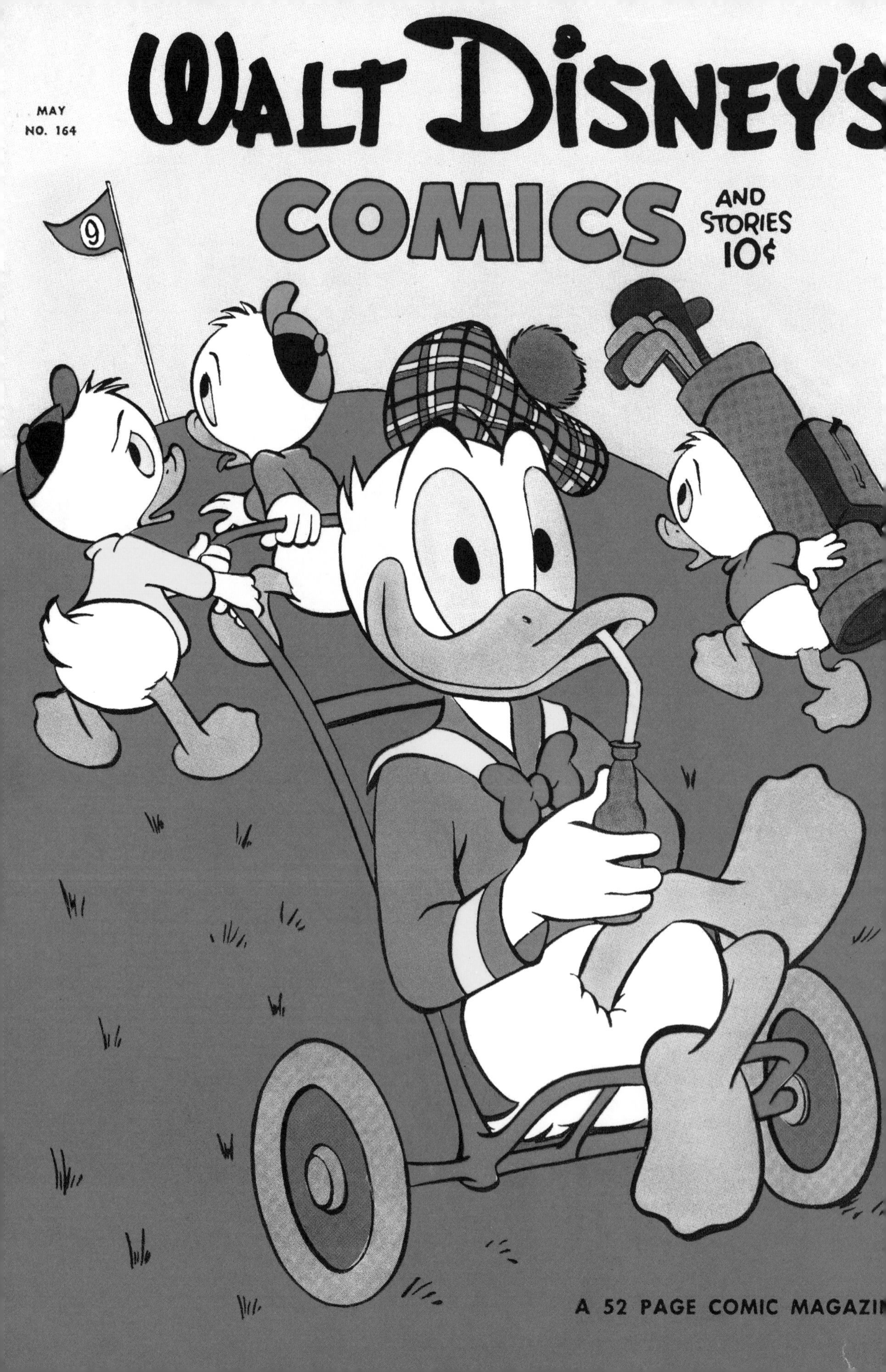
MAY
NO. 164
WALT DISNEY'S
COMICS
AND STORIES
10¢
9
A 52 PAGE COMIC MAGAZIN

same superficial attitude that attracts suckers to get-rich-quick schemes.

Barks despises that empty-headed mindset and punishes Donald mercilessly throughout the story. Donald dismisses the nephews' space toys as too technological and refuses to fix the blatantly impossible objects they bring in, such as the flattened trumpet and the concreted-in food mixer. But then he seems successful in repairing the meat grinder and the electric iron while the nephews mend the glass animals.

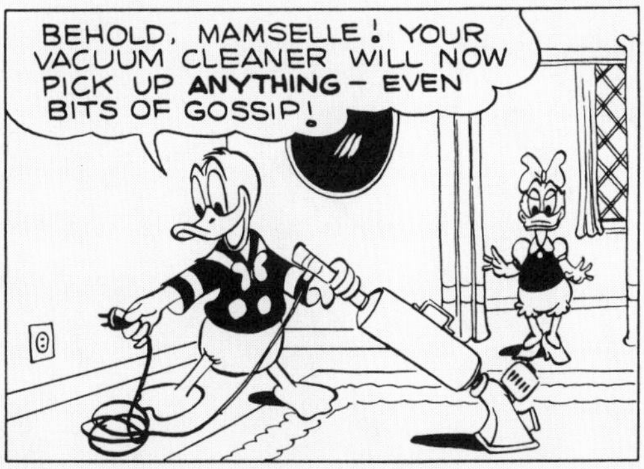
BEHOLD, MAMSELLE! YOUR VACUUM CLEANER WILL NOW PICK UP **ANYTHING** – EVEN BITS OF GOSSIP!

But that peak of achievement is short-lived. Disaster strikes, undoing all his previous accomplishments. Things get even worse as Barks piles on the disasters. Donald is able to bring the vacuum cleaner back to life, but he is incapable of keeping it under control, and he causes immensely more collateral damage than the meager earnings he would have made if everything had gone smoothly.

Our cocky anti-hero is painfully put back in his place — by the vacuum cleaner from hell.

— FRANCESCO STAJANO AND LEONARDO GORI

TURKEY TROT AT ONE WHISTLE *p. 41*

"Turkey Trot at One Whistle" is a brilliant example of why and how, even after decades have passed since their first publication, the stories and art of Carl Barks remain of immediate interest, bearing enjoyments yet to be discovered. Barks's concepts, staging, dialogues, dramatic action, and splendid images all come together like a well-paced motion picture, to inspire our imaginations and entertain our minds. No matter how involved, convoluted and far-fetched the Ducks' wild adventures may seem to be, by the time we reach the final panel we become true believers delighting in the outlandish plausibility, humor, pathos, and remarkable draftsmanship which are Barks's gifts to us.

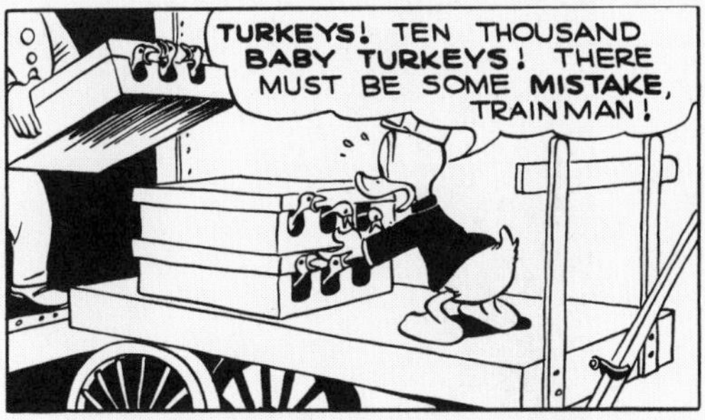
TURKEYS! TEN THOUSAND BABY TURKEYS! THERE MUST BE SOME **MISTAKE**, TRAINMAN!

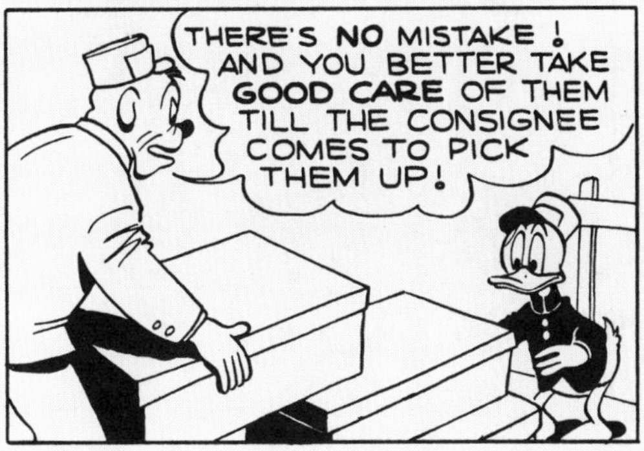
THERE'S **NO MISTAKE**! AND YOU BETTER TAKE **GOOD CARE** OF THEM TILL THE CONSIGNEE COMES TO PICK THEM UP!

I'll not walk readers through this storyline, as every one of the 79 drawings carries the plot along magnificently, and I don't want to spoil it. (And don't you dare peek ahead to the ending, even if you've read the tale a hundred times previously!)

The first page is like the opening of a major movie, with voiceover text and dialog, introducing us to where and why the action is about to unfold (One Whistle, Canada; population previously zero, now four). Panel one presents a close-up of the characters. Panel two pulls back to show the lonely desolation. Panel three provides an overhead glimpse of the action. And the bottom four panels introduce and solidify the dilemma. Even the boxcar and its wheels are drawn as blurs in the seventh panel, to show the action of the train racing from the station as Donald plaintively calls out, "What do I *feed* 'em?"

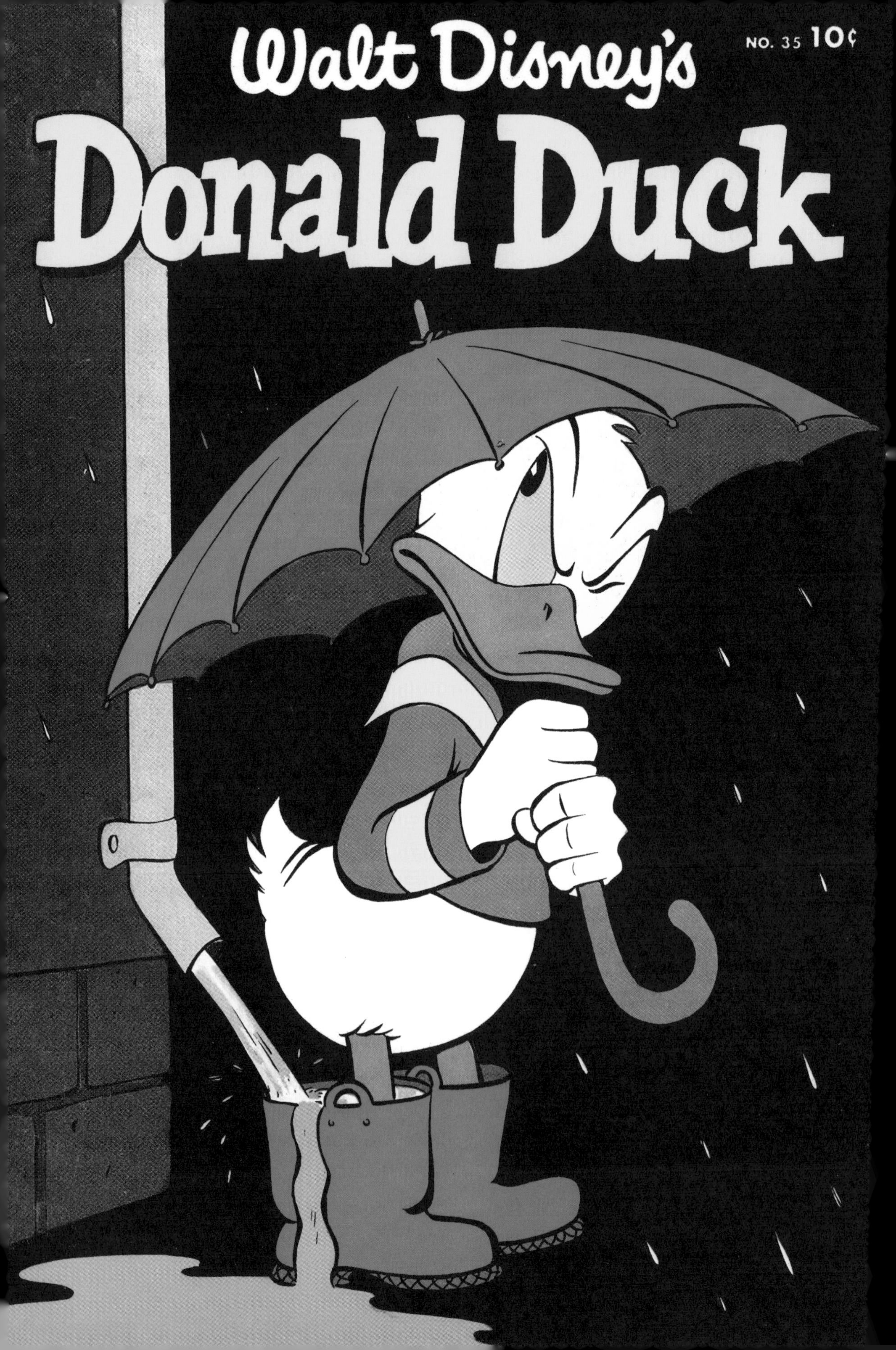
Walt Disney's
NO. 35 10¢
Donald Duck

What, indeed, does one feed starving baby turkeys that will eat anything and everything? And what perils will the Ducks face in the dark and frigid stormy night ahead? Especially when there's a train heading their way bearing a $4 million payload in gold, and the world's most notorious train robbers — Hairy Harry and his gang — are plotting to derail the train in the canyon!

— JOSEPH COWLES

RAFFLE REVERSAL *p. 51*

Let's face it, with a two-character cartoon series, how many times can you play out the same battle of wits? Admittedly, in any writer's hands, Donald and Gladstone's eternal feud can get a little *too* familiar. The stories usually go one of two ways: Donald's imminent victory is sabotaged by Gladstone's luck at the most inconvenient moment, or, completely by accident, Donald receives a greater reward than his no-good cousin.

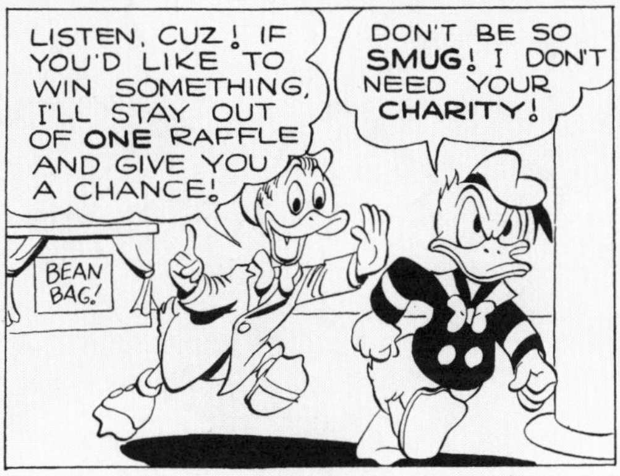
LISTEN, CUZ! IF YOU'D LIKE TO WIN SOMETHING, I'LL STAY OUT OF **ONE** RAFFLE AND GIVE YOU A CHANCE!
DON'T BE SO **SMUG**! I DON'T NEED YOUR **CHARITY**!
BEAN BAG!

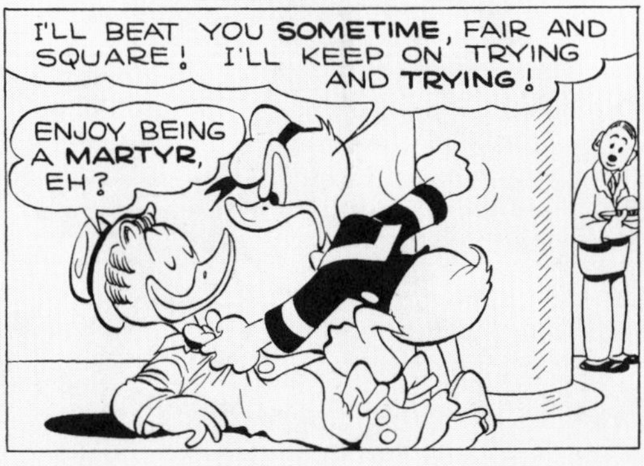
I'LL BEAT YOU **SOMETIME**, FAIR AND SQUARE! I'LL KEEP ON TRYING AND **TRYING**!
ENJOY BEING A **MARTYR**, EH?

"Raffle Reversal" does neither. It brings together elements from past Duck/Gander clashes and creates a refreshingly new take. Gladstone's luck seems to fail when Donald beats him in an auction raffle. Ah, but Donald doesn't see the treasure map Gladstone finds in the prize! But will Gladstone actually exert an effort to claim it? Or will the lazy bum scam Donald into doing the work for him — digging up what, by rights, belongs to Donald?

Gladstone pulled the oriental disguise routine in "Trail of the Unicorn" (*Walt Disney's Donald Duck: "Trail of the Unicorn,"* volume 8), and he was too lazy to dig up a prize he was literally sitting on in "Rival Beachcombers" (*Walt Disney's Donald Duck: "Lost in the Andes,"* volume 7). Barks revives these tropes for a new purpose: to show that neither cousin is worthy of our sympathy, as their only goal is to humiliate each other.

True, it's the underlying theme of all the Donald/Gladstone stories, but Barks brazenly displays it here, showing us quite a complex, unpredictable back-and-forth. We're never certain if Donald or Gladstone will come out on top. But when the stakes are so petty, could either Duck or Gander ever *truly* win?

Collectors take note: The reproduction of these pages is the sharpest ever seen. They are restored from newly discovered photostats of Barks's original art.

— THAD KOMOROWSKI

FLOUR FOLLIES *p. 61*

In his jack-of-all-trades tradition, Donald has been a peddler several times. More precisely, in this 10-pager he is — by his own admission — a "demonstrator" for the marvelous new flour produced by Uncle Scrooge's mills.

Considering what happens when Donald tries to bake a cake with it, we could coin a new saying here: "Where there's a flour, there's a flaw."

More generally, Carl Barks is making fun of the often-unintelligible instructions that accompany some products and medicines. In this case, being written in the ungrammatical Sowbuggian language, they are beyond unintelligible to an American Duck.

Barks once again uses a Dickensian approach to naming his supporting characters. The mustachioed Endless McChain is the rich

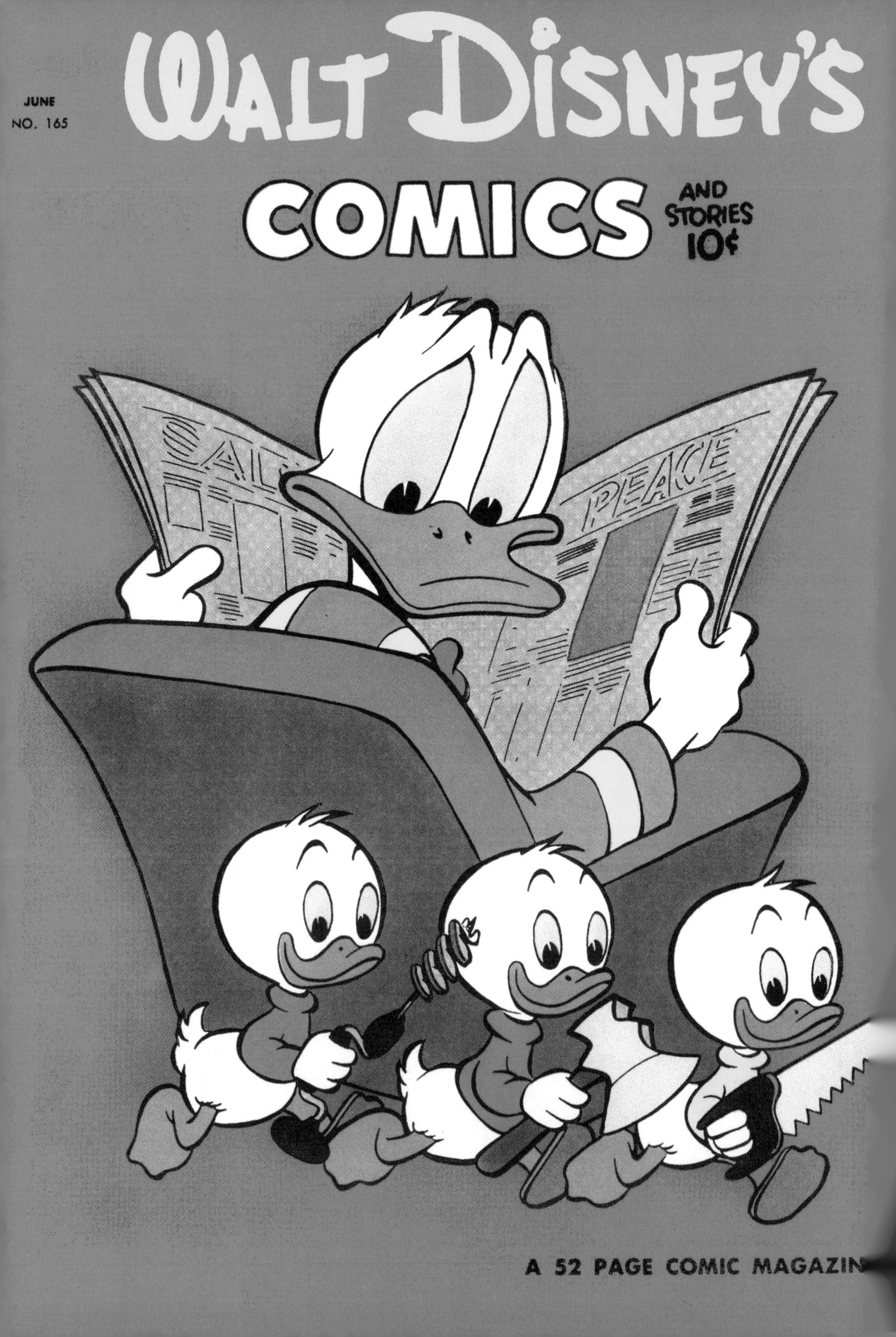
WALT DISNEY'S
JUNE
NO. 165
COMICS
AND STORIES
10¢
PEACE
A 52 PAGE COMIC MAGAZIN

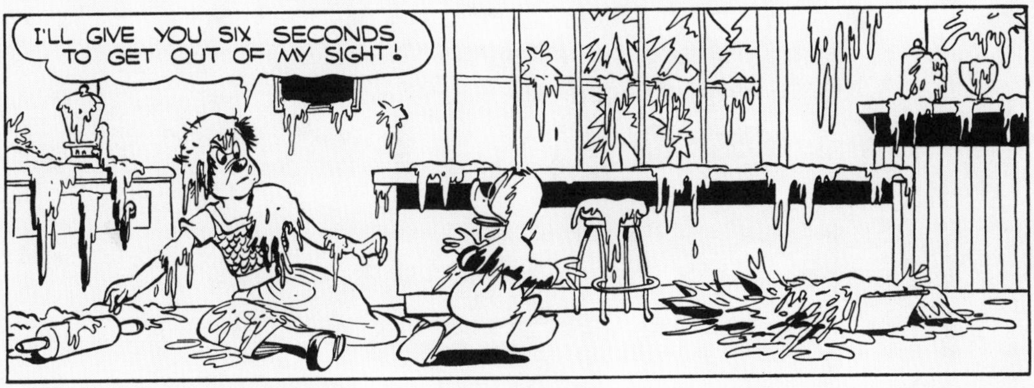
I'LL GIVE YOU SIX SECONDS TO GET OUT OF MY SIGHT!

owner of a food store franchise; Headline Heartless is the "meanest newspaper publisher in the world."

For the gingerbread-loving spinster Miss Penny Wise, Barks invokes the phrase "penny wise and pound foolish," which first appeared in Robert Burton's *The Anatomy of Melancholy* (1621). [By the way, on the cover of Scrooge's first solo comic book (*Walt Disney's Uncle Scrooge: "Only a Poor Old Man,"* volume 12), Barks named Scrooge's rowboat *Penny Wise*.]

Miss Penny Wise's appearance marks a turning point in the story, revealing a hitherto-unknown fact about Scrooge's past (she possesses an old note that could "ruin" Scrooge). Yet, differently from other events in Scrooge's life that Barks would later refer to, this one is only superficially dealt with here, and never mentioned in any other story.

Don Rosa, who would use most of these tidbits while building up his *Life and Times of Scrooge McDuck* [*Walt Disney Uncle Scrooge and Donald Duck: "The Last of the Clan McDuck,* Fantagraphics Books, 2015], chose not to use this one, considering it "no more than a quick, throwaway remark that was needed at one point of one story to make the ending make sense."[1]

— ALBERTO BECATTINI

[1] Don Rosa on INDUCKS — Disney Comics Mailing List, July 12, 1994.

THE PRICE OF FAME *p. 71*

There are times when Huey, Dewey, and Louie wish their Uncle Donald would be someone famous, rather than loafing at home or doing menial jobs like "delivery boy for a skunk oil factory," as Donald himself reveals at the beginning of this 10-pager. "The Price of Fame" is a great example of Carl Barks's ability to build up a plot until the initial situation is reversed at the end of the story.

"The Price of Fame" opens with Donald watching two famous musicians on TV — Perry Cougar and Lizardace, respectively parodying crooner Perry Como and pianist Valentino Liberace. Both were, in fact, starring in their own musical variety TV shows, *The Perry Como Chesterfield Show* and *The Liberace Show*, when Barks's story first appeared.

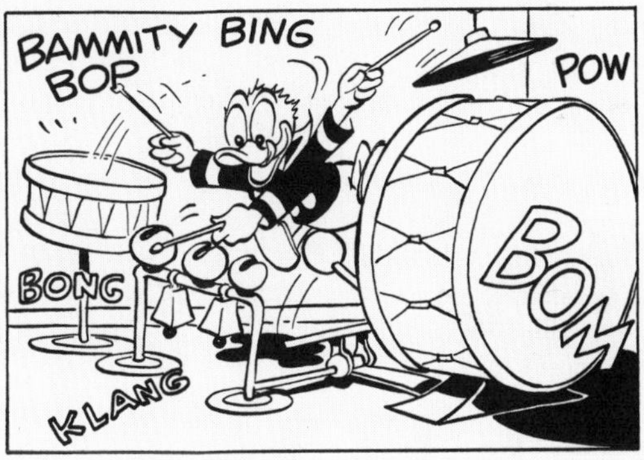
BAMMITY BING
BOP
POW
BONG
BOM
KLANG

Very often in Barks's Donald Duck 10-pagers, Donald shows talent for a particular job, but ultimately makes a mess of it. This time, instead, it is the nephews who make him aware of having a gift for music.

Thus, the bathtub singer swiftly develops into an ambitious vocalist whose repertoire includes such popular songs as "Who Threw the Overshoes in Missus Leary's Hash?," Barks's own version of George L. Giefer's

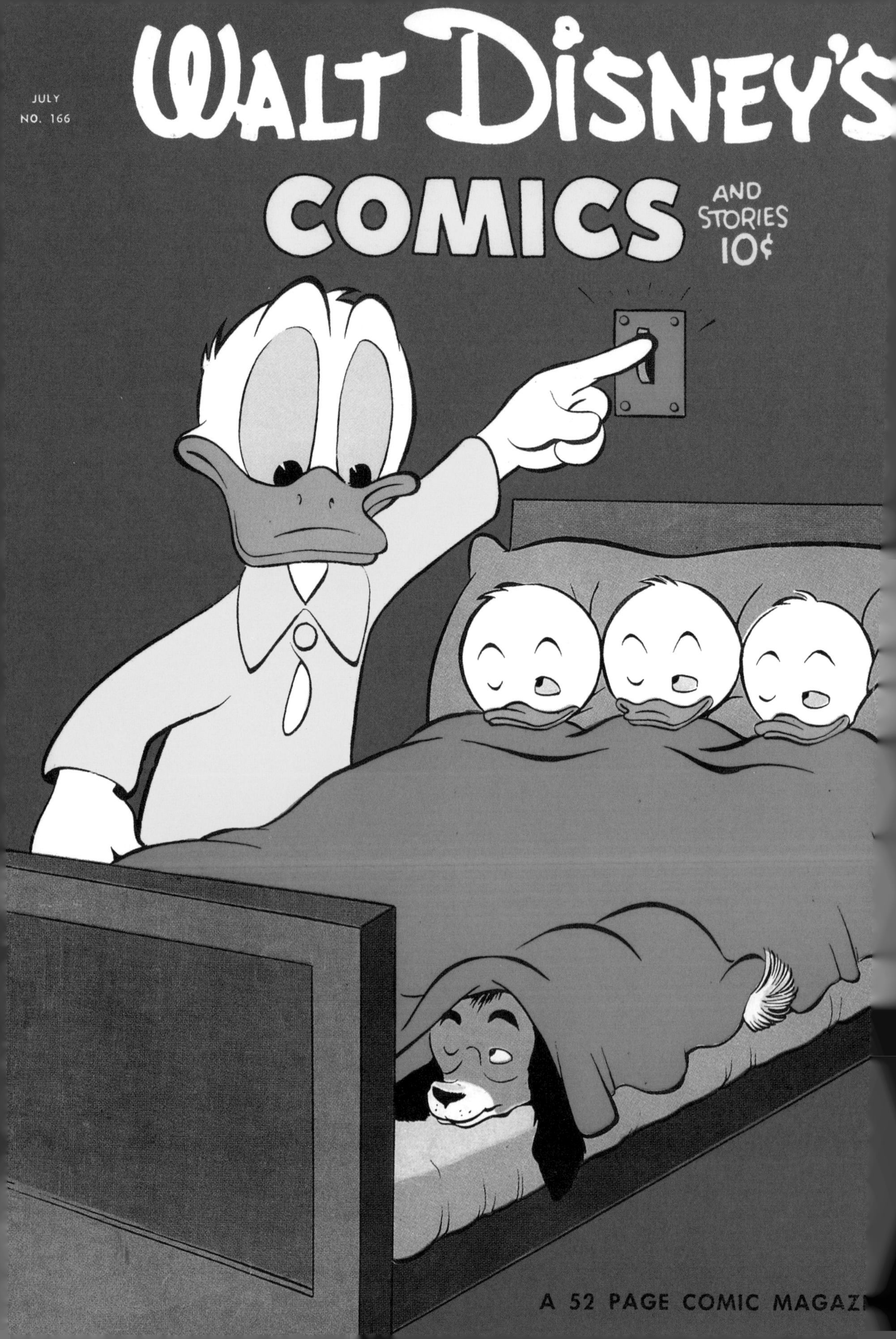
JULY
NO. 166
WALT DISNEY'S
COMICS
AND STORIES
10¢
A 52 PAGE COMIC MAGAZI

"Who Threw The Overalls in Mrs. Murphy's Chowder?" (1898).

From this point onward, the story is a veritable crescendo of gags — and jarring notes. Whereas the nephews grow more and more stressed, Donald turns from singing to playing a variety of instruments with an enthusiasm which borders on insanity, culminating in an open-air concert on a custom-made calliope.

Exaggeration is, thus, once again, the name of the game. Still, this time Barks chooses to stop his tale at the moment when Donald is being noticed by the media. Barks then diverts the reader's attention toward Donald's nephews, since *they* are the ones experiencing the real meaning of "What price fame?" firsthand.

— ALBERTO BECATTINI

MIDGETS MADNESS *p. 81*

Presenting Donald Duck as a pathetic sap in a world where everything that can go wrong does go wrong is tricky. "Overtly predetermined" best describes many a later Barks 10-pager in which Donald wreaks havoc using his Midas touch for failure. But Barks avoided that situation brilliantly in "Midgets Madness" by making what Donald is pathetic at as pathetic as the Duck himself. Forget regular NASCAR racing — Donald isn't even good enough for *midget* auto racing.

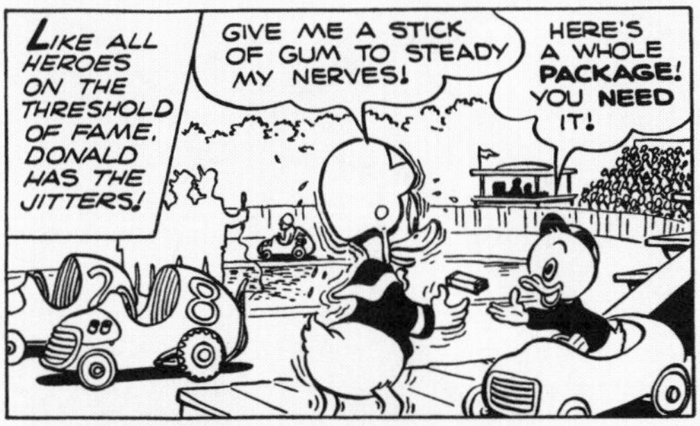
LIKE ALL HEROES ON THE THRESHOLD OF FAME, DONALD HAS THE JITTERS!
GIVE ME A STICK OF GUM TO STEADY MY NERVES!
HERE'S A WHOLE PACKAGE! YOU NEED IT!

Barks's biting opening page at the fairgrounds emphasizes just how infantile and plain stupid Donald's passion-of-the-month truly is. Grown men, hunched in their little cars, sneer in contempt at hopeful Donald as juvenile admirers look on. Donald only gets a break when a prissy "pro" gets a sore finger and needs him as a substitute driver. Donald starts off the first race by driving the wrong car, and it's all downhill from there.

Huey, Dewey, and Louie prove to be the more competent midget auto racers and, over the objections of Donald, the other drivers, and the irate spectators — who all feel the boys' presence on the racetrack in their "juvenile jalopies" makes the event undignified — set out, once again, to clean up their uncle's mess. In all this judgmental self-pity, Barks never lets us lose sight of one crucial fact: the kids' cars really aren't all that much smaller than the adults' cars.

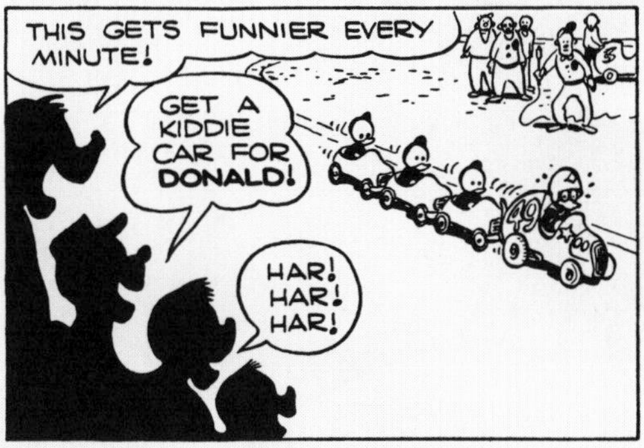
THIS GETS FUNNIER EVERY MINUTE!
GET A KIDDIE CAR FOR DONALD!
HAR! HAR! HAR!

"It is *my* fault that this glamorous attraction has come to *this!*" Donald grouses. Even though our hero is ultimately laughed out of town, when the farce is this outrageous it's hard to do anything *but* laugh at his failure.

— THAD KOMOROWSKI

SALMON DERBY *p. 91*

Carl Barks's luscious rendering of the great American landscape is like nothing else in world cartooning. The Pacific Northwest setting of "Salmon Derby" is a splendorous example of how his comic book wilderness evokes a distinctive, restorative charm reminiscent of John Muir's writings, the Hudson River painters, or Ansel Adams's photography.

Barks and his naturalist/artist wife and assistant, Garé, often invested their mutual love of the unspoiled outdoors into Duck

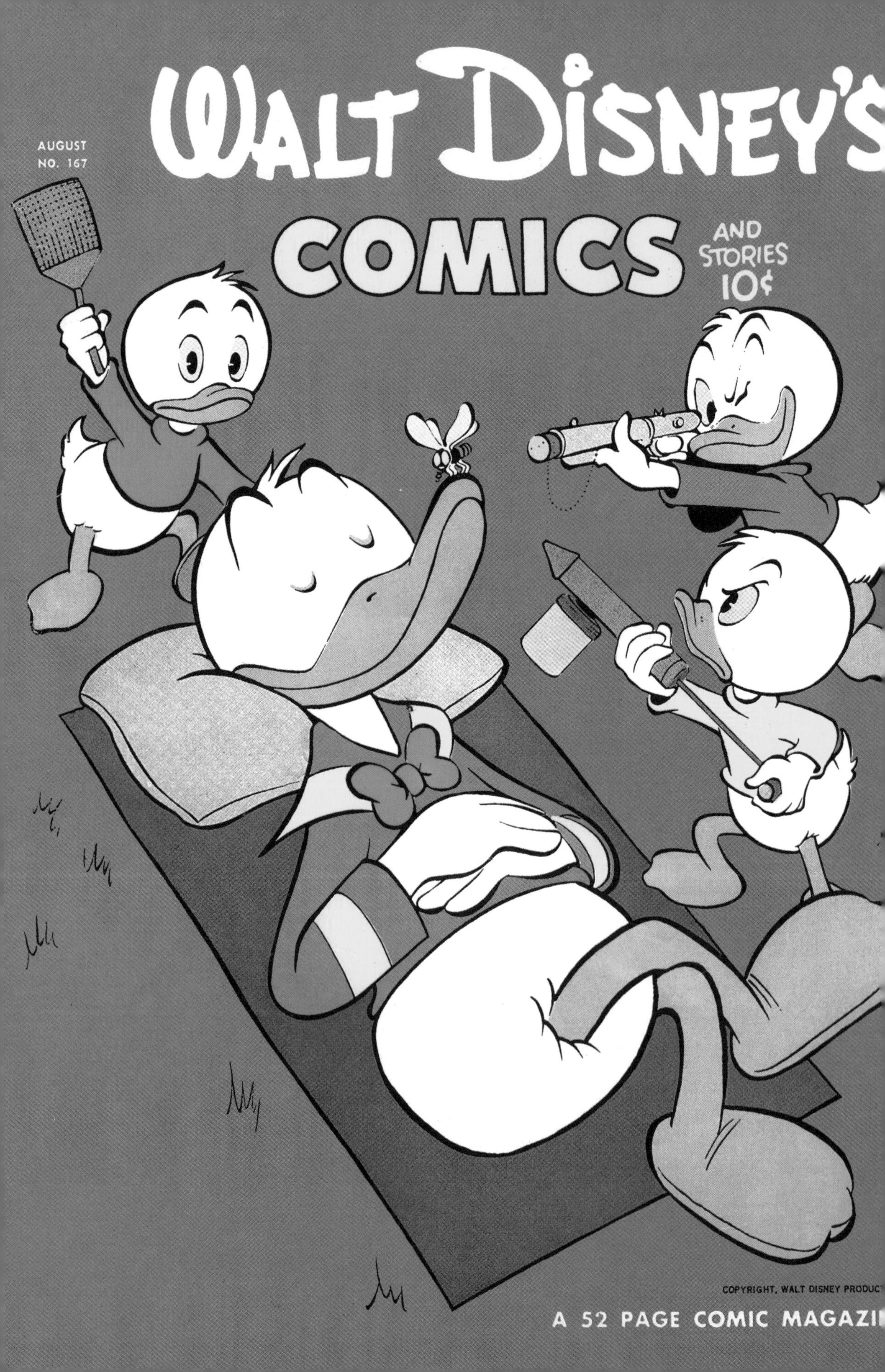
WALT DISNEY'S
AUGUST
NO. 167
COMICS
AND STORIES
10¢
COPYRIGHT, WALT DISNEY PRODUC
A 52 PAGE COMIC MAGAZI

tales of all sizes. Their elegantly rendered beaches, bays, forests, and fens are steeped in eco-environmental awareness, as well as subtle satirical comment on the supposedly "advanced" or "civilized" duck-tagonists who are generally kerflummoxed by the roughness and risk of surviving the wild.

Raw nature is everywhere, insistent and enduring, in this story's *mise-en-page*. Evergreen silhouettes, craggy cliffs, soaring gulls, and surly salmon deck every corner of each panel in a submersive effect common to Barks's exterior scenes.

The unspoiled forests from "The Land of the Pygmy Indians," (*Uncle Scrooge* #18, June–August 1957, not in this volume) and the dangerous deserts found in "Donald Duck in Old California" (*Walt Disney's Donald Duck: "Terror of the Beagle Boys,"* volume 10) both mirror this yarn's perpetual pine stands and mountainous vistas. Even the salmon themselves enjoy dynamic compositions rooted in the visual traditions of wildlife painting and *Field & Stream* photography.

Throughout this rustic farce, Barks and Garé also contrast Puget Sound's traditional wooden boat culture with monstrously mechanized custom convertible cars. Barks puts his special gift for skewering the egoism of American automotive culture to fine use, taking themes of high-torque speed, luxurious length, and uber-sporty prestige to comical extremes.

The final panel's brutally funny salvo of automobile envy sells the joke hard, as "the Ducks drive grandly homeward" complete

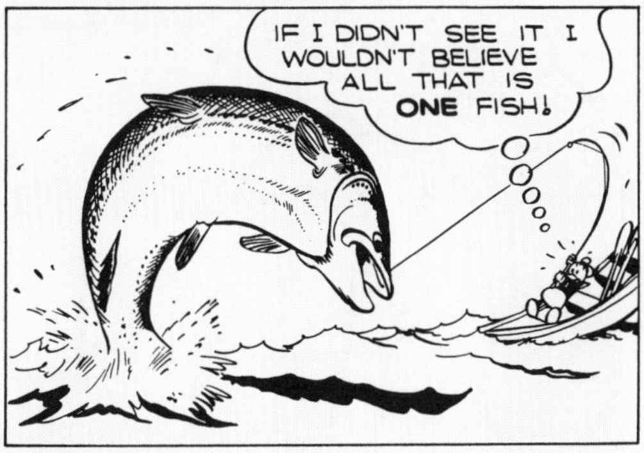
IF I DIDN'T SEE IT I WOULDN'T BELIEVE ALL THAT IS **ONE** FISH!

with smug chauffeur and smiley salmon hood ornament while Gladstone stews in his comparatively stubby "Snobmobile." Here on Duckaluk Bay, the comedic contrast between picturesque nature and streamlined snootiness makes for hilarious parody.

The actual derby is one of Barks's best satires on American leisure and competitive excess. In the verdant splash panel, the Ducks make meaningful connections with the vast

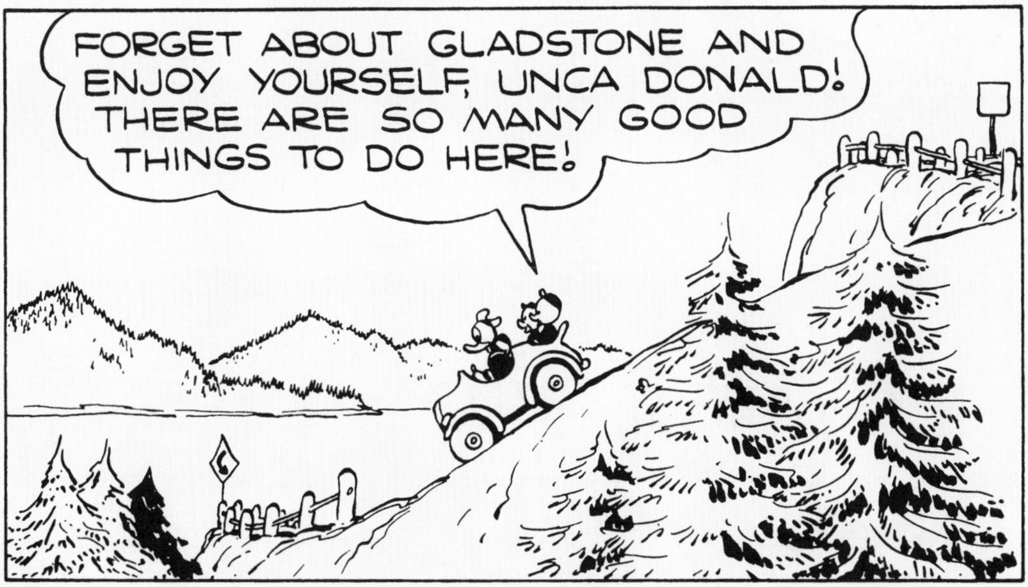
FORGET ABOUT GLADSTONE AND ENJOY YOURSELF, UNCA DONALD! THERE ARE SO MANY GOOD THINGS TO DO HERE!

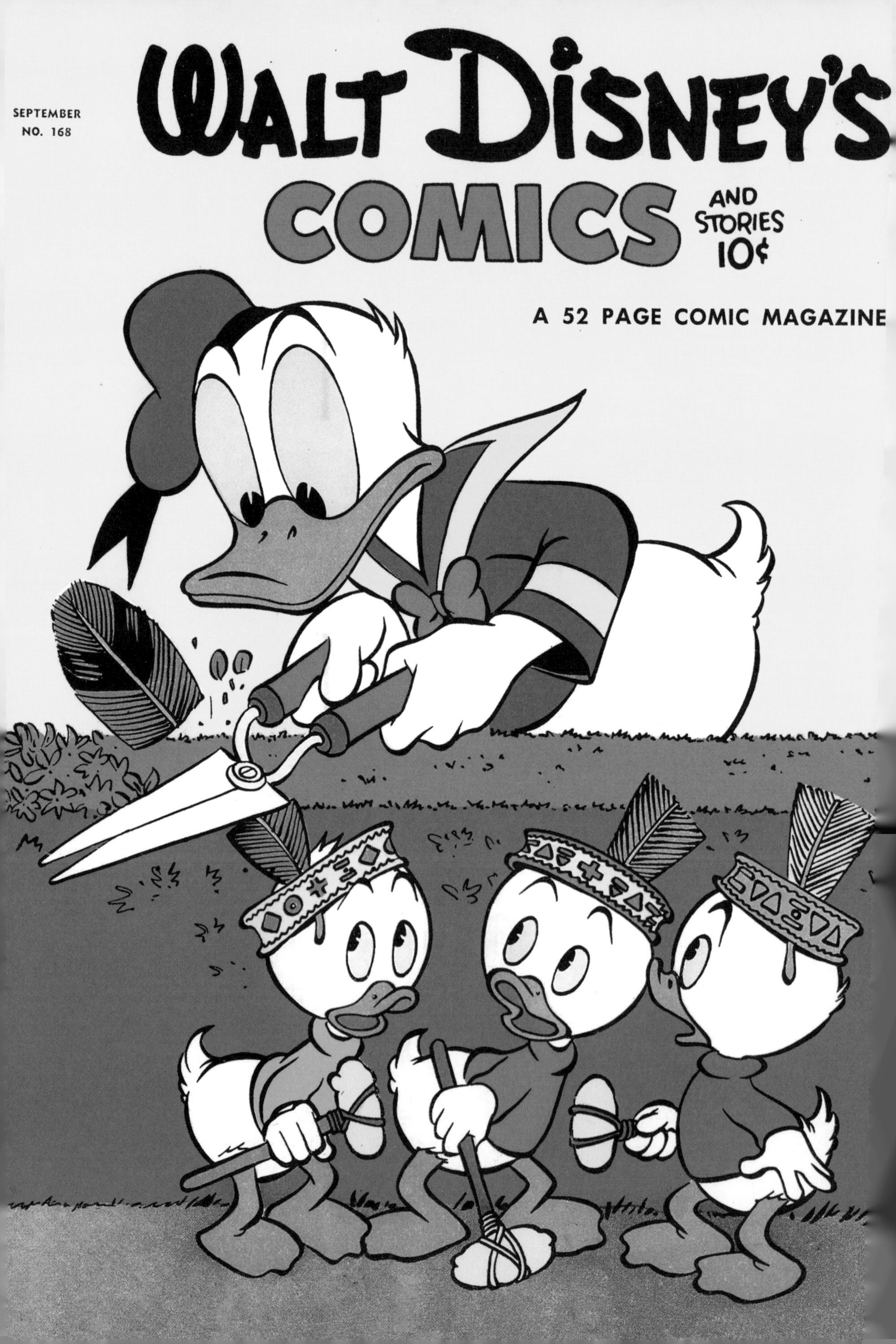
SEPTEMBER
NO. 168
WALT DISNEY'S
COMICS
AND STORIES
10¢
A 52 PAGE COMIC MAGAZINE

grandeur of "the beautiful country," but rather than relax and reflect, they are bamboozled by the promise of "luck" and "prizes." Before we turn the page, a potentially sublime vacation quickly devolves into the kind of forced debacle that today drives he-man reality spectacles like the Bassmaster Classic, *Deadliest Catch*, or *Wicked Tuna*.

The Ducks are not alone, either. Barks crams every frame with crowded boats and frantic fishermen hoping to weigh in and win big. Amid the eager throng, two scenes stand out.

First, the nephews encounter the wan frowns of a devastated father and son duo in one of Barks's most withering comments on the inevitable folly of confusing family pastimes with commercial gain. Their pathetic postures, reminiscent of the impoverished urchins from "A Christmas for Shacktown," (*Walt Disney's Donald Duck: "A Christmas for Shacktown,"* volume 11) are amplified by the distant string of boats filled with equally eager sportsmen about to meet similar disappointment and dismay.

In contrast to that 54-pound failure, the nephews meet up with a Native American who, despite some typically heinous Barksian stereotyping, comes off as more contented, charismatic, and charitable than anyone else in the story. Disdaining fancy autos and the promise of "100 prizes" — and the reality of heavy taxes — the wise old man's assistance garners a whopping 80-pounder, overcoming even Gladstone's unbearably good fortune.

The story's narrative core is, of course, yet another high-stakes duel between Donald, the striving "everyduck," and the privileged but undeserving Gladstone, whose daintily coiled headfeathers rate alongside the most irritating coiffure in comics. This particular rendition of their family feud seems especially satisfying because everybody from the nephews to the Native Americans to the very fish themselves seems to prefer Donald's jaunty, do-it-yourself mentality. They all contribute to Donald's eventual triumph over his pompous cousin.

Through a bizarre *speedboat ex machina*, Gladstone actually wins the salmon derby with "Donald's" fish. But Donald saves a child, becomes a full-fledged hero, and gets grandly rewarded, elevating his accomplishment well beyond the greedy gander's gains.

— DANIEL F. YEZBICK

CHELTENHAM'S CHOICE *p. 101*

"Cheltenham's Choice" is a sparkling example of what Carl Barks referred to as his "little morality tales."

In their tiny trailer, the Ducks and their pesky "mascot" are on a trip through the swampy South. Although cute, Cheltenham is destructive — chewing up curtains to build a nest in Donald's cuckoo clock and stealing keys to gnaw. His playful mischievousness backfires when he and the Ducks become locked out of the warm dry trailer during a rainstorm. To square things, Cheltenham

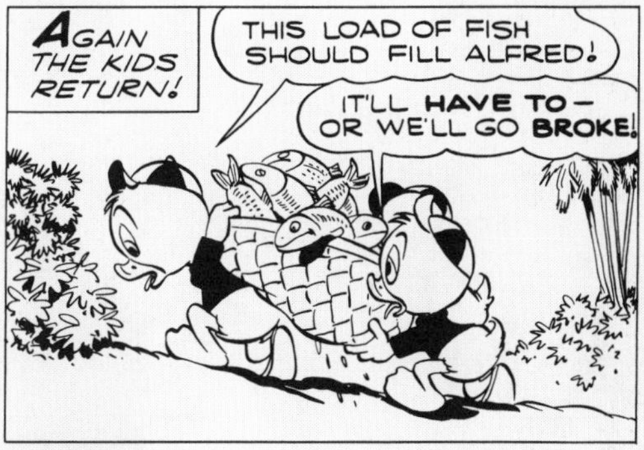
AGAIN THE KIDS RETURN!
THIS LOAD OF FISH SHOULD FILL ALFRED!
IT'LL HAVE TO — OR WE'LL GO BROKE!

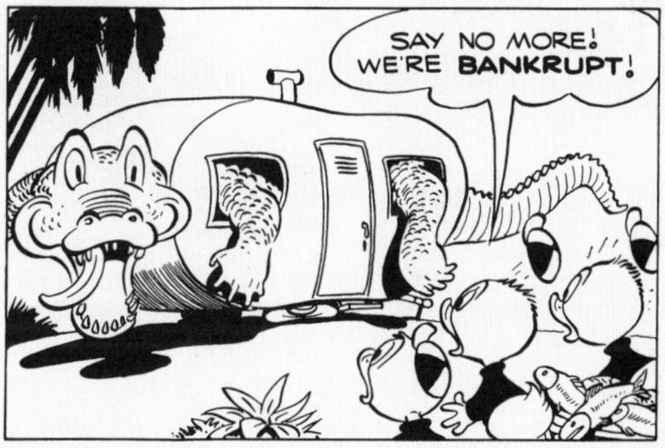
SAY NO MORE! WE'RE BANKRUPT!

returns the keys. But the next morning Donald vows there will be no more pets or mascots, and he abandons the chipmunk at the campsite.

They stop beside the sea, where Donald hopes to get in a few days of fishing — and where the kids find and adopt a baby alligator as a new mascot. Livid that his nephews have acquired yet another pet, Donald shamelessly plots to cure them of the habit. From a nearby farm, he rents a batch of alligators of various sizes to switch with one another and make his

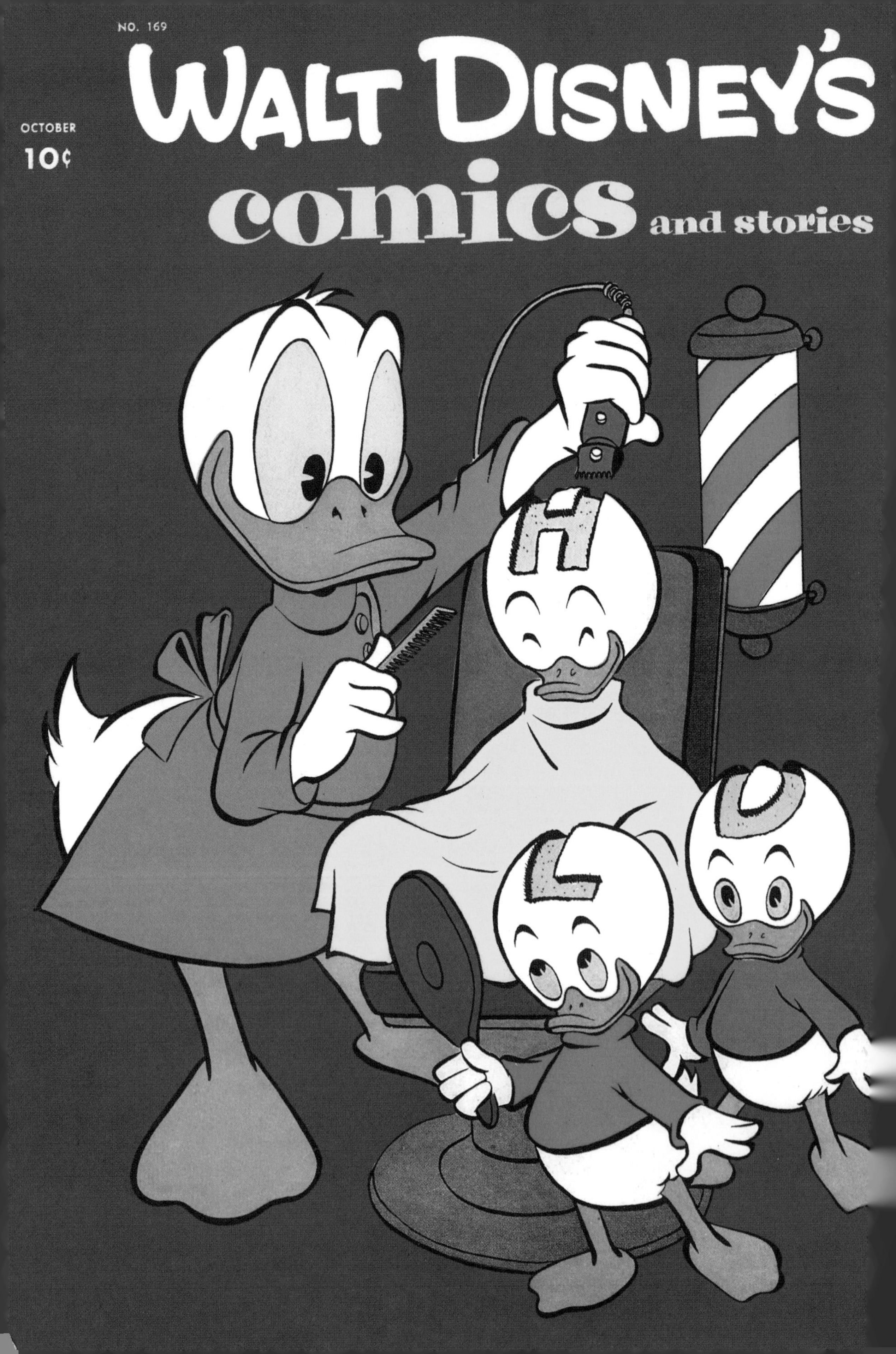
NO. 169
WALT DISNEY'S
OCTOBER
10¢
comics
and stories
H
L
D

nephews think Little Al is growing by leaps and bounds — and they'll have to empty their piggy bank to satisfy the gator's voracious appetite.

Donald gets his point across: there'll be no more pets for the Duck family.

But then Donald himself takes a fancy to a loud-beaked mynah bird, whose wisecracking jabber quickly lands the Ducks in the pokey.

It is only Cheltenham's unexpected return that enables Donald to introduce the mynah to the court as evidence of his own innocence and thus persuade the judge to dismiss the case.

In the final panel, Donald changes his mind about Cheltenham (even though he won't admit it), grants the plucky chipmunk a seat at the supper table, "and all is well with the Duck family again."

— JOSEPH COWLES

TRAVELING TRUANTS *p. 111*

Like many of Barks's 10-pagers, "Traveling Truants" is built on ferocious symmetry. If we divide the story into two parts — with the first six pages comprising part one, and the last four pages part two — we can see that Barks tells a story in part one that he repeats with variation in part two. Both parts begin with

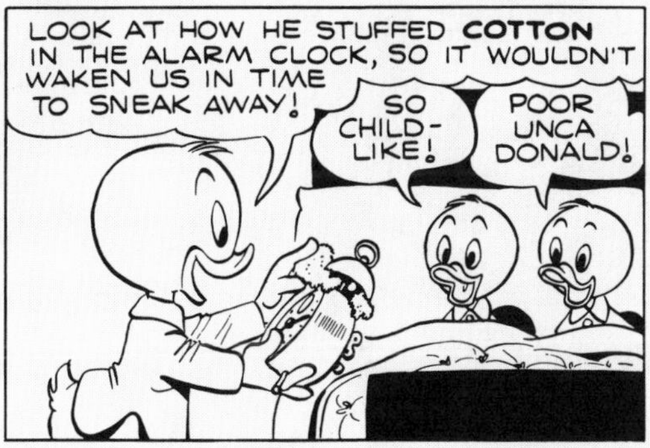
LOOK AT HOW HE STUFFED **COTTON** IN THE ALARM CLOCK, SO IT WOULDN'T WAKEN US IN TIME TO SNEAK AWAY!
SO CHILD-LIKE!
POOR UNCA DONALD!

a note about a journey. After two pages of setting up the conflict (and re-establishing the move/countermove aesthetic of the Donald vs. Ducklings relationship), Huey, Dewey, and Louie leave a note ("Good-by, Uncle Donald"), and the chase is on.

Later, on page 7, the nephews return home after their miserable hooky day, are fooled into believing that Donald has moved to Afghanistan, and leave another note, this one announcing their intent to follow him. Donald recognizes the narrative repetition-with-variation in a thought balloon in the last panel on page 7: *"Another chase* — and this one is for *real!"*

Animals complicate each chase. In part one, Donald sinks the nephews' boat and then scares them up a tree by convincing them that a dangerous lion is prowling through Beaver Island's shrubbery. In part two, however,

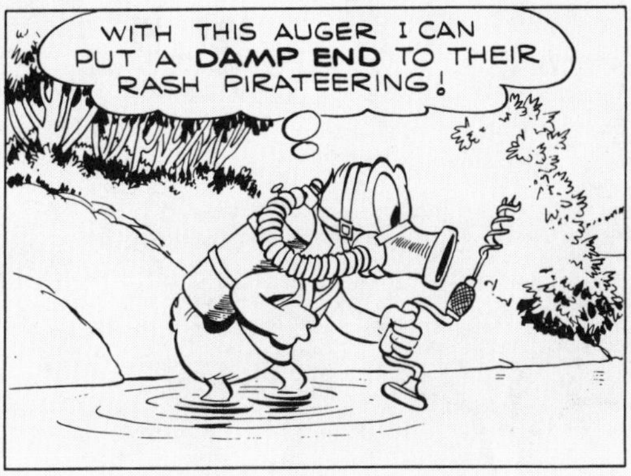
WITH THIS AUGER I CAN PUT A **DAMP END** TO THEIR RASH PIRATEERING!

Donald scrambles up a well frame to avoid a "bull." (Both the nephews and Donald see the dummy lion and the "bull" as silhouetted figures — difficult to see, indistinct, and thus more dangerous.)

Finally, the rain comes. After Donald seeds the clouds, Huey, Dewey, and Louie are drenched, and they return home ready for school — until Donald plays one trick too many with the Afghanistan lie. In Barks's karmic just-desserts universe, rain then falls on Donald as he is trapped atop the well.

By the end of the story, Donald learns the importance of education. At the beginning of "Traveling Truants," Donald anticipates that the nephews will try to skip school because — as the caption in the last panel on page 1 tells us, "He was young, once, himself!" In that panel, he reads a book called *Child Raising* by Hoocan Doit (love that name) and studies ways to "catch truant school children," even though he played hooky as a kid.

Although notes and signs pepper "Traveling Truants," Donald reads a book again

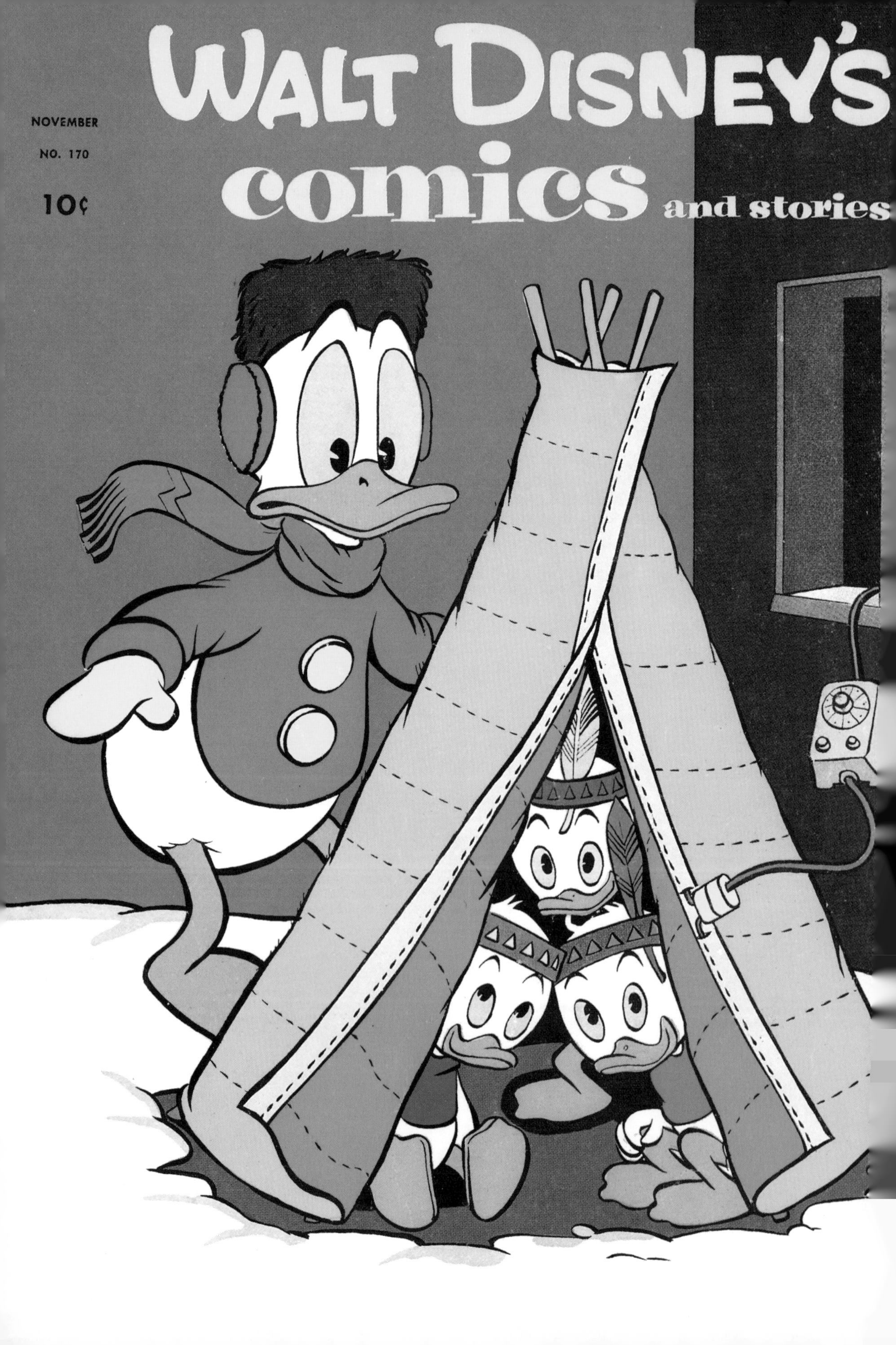

WALT DISNEY'S
NOVEMBER
NO. 170
10¢
comics
and stories

only at the end of the story, when he's back in the classroom himself, aware that he has more to learn, and that he should set a non-hypocritical example of a good student for his nephews.

Until, of course, the next 10-pager.

— CRAIG FISCHER

DONALD RANTS ABOUT ANTS *p. 121*

In "Donald Rants About Ants" — one of Carl Barks's great nightmare narratives, which centers on an unseen, alien threat — the artist employs his familiar device of having Donald's sanctimonious moralizing to the kids backfire.

The delightfully named Antofagasta Ax-Toothed Ants perfectly represent the home invasion paranoia evident in so much 1950s pop culture — the shot where they emerge from their cracked "city" in the dark of the night is straight out of the period's most feverish horror and sci-fi flicks. ZZZT! ZZT!

Barks is particularly good at combining the unnerving with the laugh-out-loud entertaining. Brilliant visual gags such as the receding ladder (helped by a clever kink to the panel border), or Donald waking up on just his mattress in the morning, are both funny and unsettling. His progressive derangement — tearing the stuffing out of his couch, taking a crowbar to his Steinway — doubly so.

The image of the Duck in his pajamas ranting about "a *war* to a finish," while tearing his own house apart is potent, potentially symbolic. And, characteristically for Barks, the worried looks of the neighbors and the mailman provide a leavening finish to the page, but without lessening its impact.

In the end, Barks cleverly ties Donald's rampage, which has turned his home inside out, into the universally recognizable — and at times downright maddening — frustration of seeking something and only finding it in the last place you look. ANTS!

— MATTHIAS WIVEL

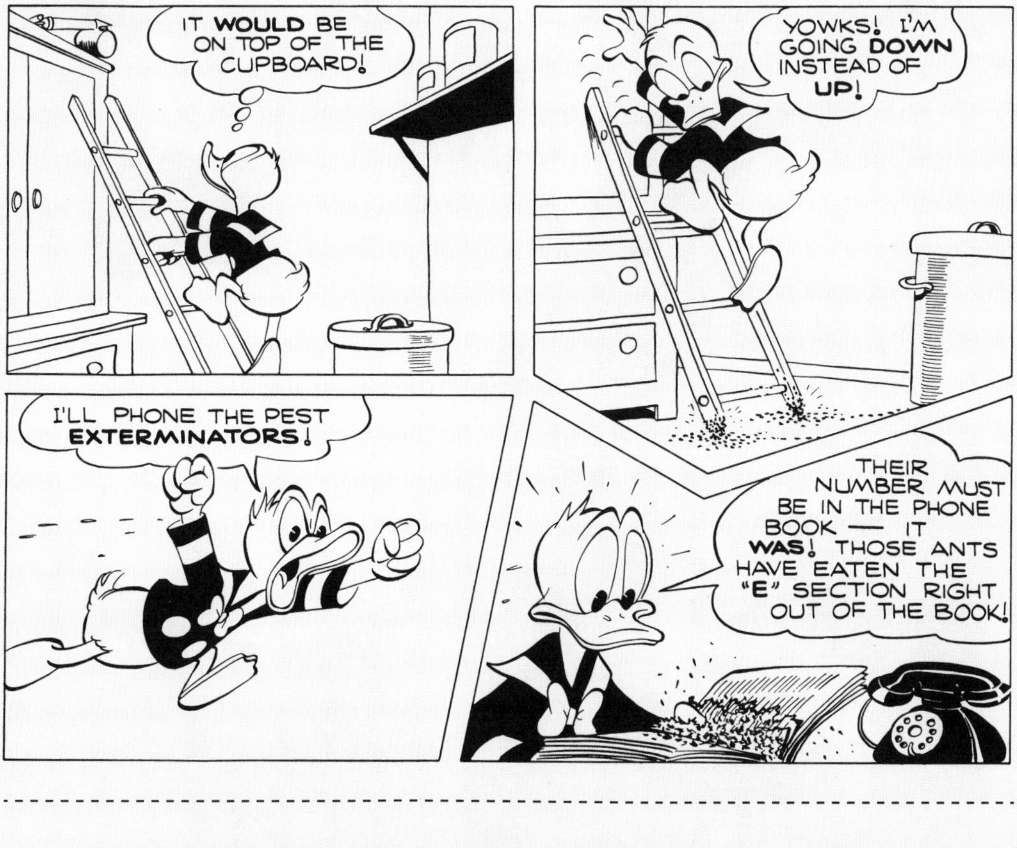
IT WOULD BE ON TOP OF THE CUPBOARD!
YOWKS! I'M GOING DOWN INSTEAD OF UP!
I'LL PHONE THE PEST EXTERMINATORS!
THEIR NUMBER MUST BE IN THE PHONE BOOK — IT WAS! THOSE ANTS HAVE EATEN THE "E" SECTION RIGHT OUT OF THE BOOK!

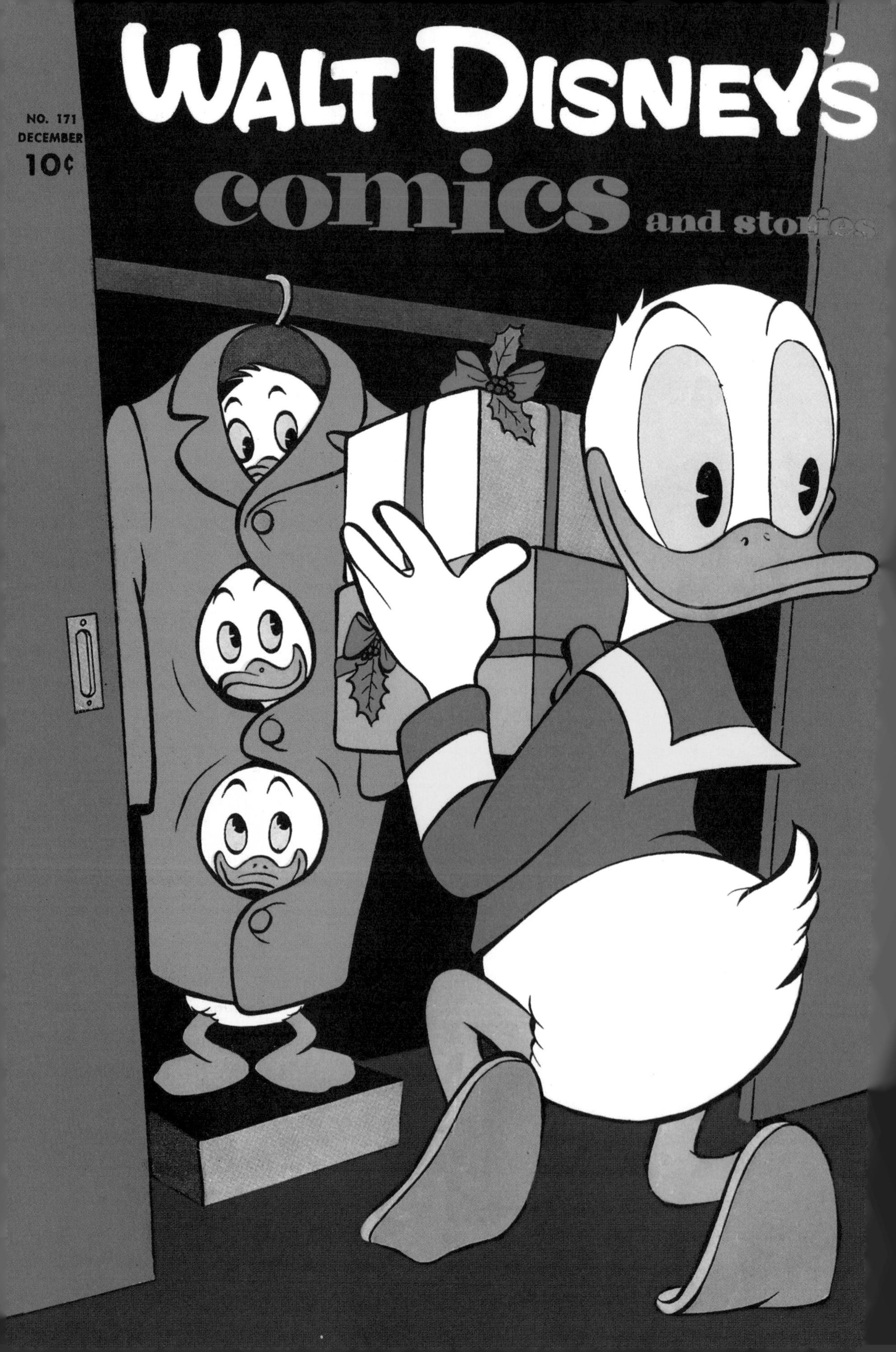
WALT DISNEY'S
NO. 171
DECEMBER
10¢
comics
and stories

TOO SAFE SAFE *p. 131*

A joke can still be good even if you already know the punch line before it's finished. It's all down to the execution. But a joke is profoundly weak if it takes too long to get to that spoiled punch line. And that, unfortunately, is an apt summation of "Too Safe Safe," a genuine dud in a seemingly unending string of classics in Barks's early 1950s Golden Age.

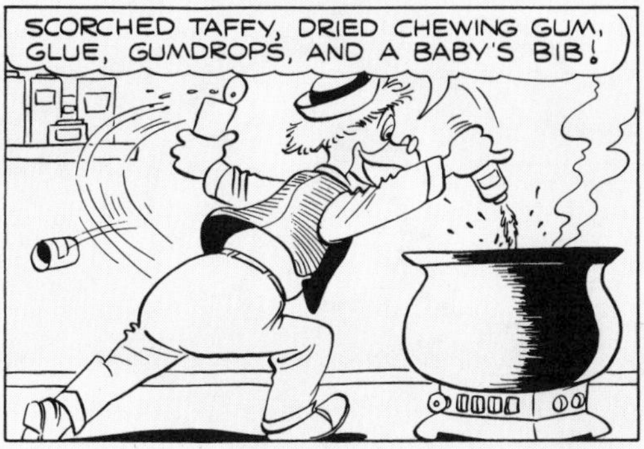
SCORCHED TAFFY, DRIED CHEWING GUM, GLUE, GUMDROPS, AND A BABY'S BIB!

Barks revisited ideas here that he'd already done better. Scrooge followed Donald's lame idea on how to handle his fortune in "Spending Money" (*Walt Disney's Donald Duck: "A Christmas for Shacktown,"* volume 11), and he unwisely converted all his coins to cash in "The Round Money Bin" (*Walt Disney's Uncle Scrooge: "Only a Poor Old Man,"* volume 12). Both those stories were 10-pagers, too, and the stakes built to higher and funnier outcomes than that of the bloated "Too Safe Safe."

Half the story meanders on a mouse invading Scrooge's money bin before Donald recruits Gyro Gearloose to invent a wax that will protect the money from harm. Gyro is not yet the charming eccentric he'd soon become but is, instead, a slightly deranged genius whose unorthodox method of coming up with ideas is Donald and Scrooge's downfall (and the subject of a cheerfully unpleasant line regarding Gyro's health at the story's conclusion).

What we knew all along — that an impenetrable wax also denies Scrooge access to his money — still has the potential to be truly funny stuff, if the methods to protect the money or break the wax were increasingly ridiculous. But Barks's heart clearly wasn't in it this time, and it's perfectly understandable. Like Gyro, when you're always operating at a high level, you need to take some time off — or risk cracking your head with your own genius.

— THAD KOMOROWSKI

SEARCH FOR THE CUSPIDORIA *p. 141*

The reoccurring theme of this volume is certainly Barks revisiting old ideas, and "Search for the Cuspidoria" may be the strangest amalgam herein. Barks's Christmas tropes abound in this story. Ducks isolated from the outside world during the holidays? Check. Donald forgets to mail the kids' letter to Santa? Got it. Scrooge rants about the cost of Christmas? Oh, you know it.

With its potpourri makings, "Search for the Cuspidoria" could never hope to reach the grandeur of Barks's earlier classics like "Letter to Santa" (*Walt Disney's Donald Duck: "Trail of the Unicorn,"* volume 8) or "Christmas for Shacktown" (*Walt Disney's Donald Duck: "A Christmas for Shacktown,"* volume 11), but Barks still manages to avoid the treacly crassness forced upon him in the 1940s Firestone giveaways and "The Golden Christmas Tree" (*Walt Disney's Donald Duck: "Lost in the Andes,"* volume 7).

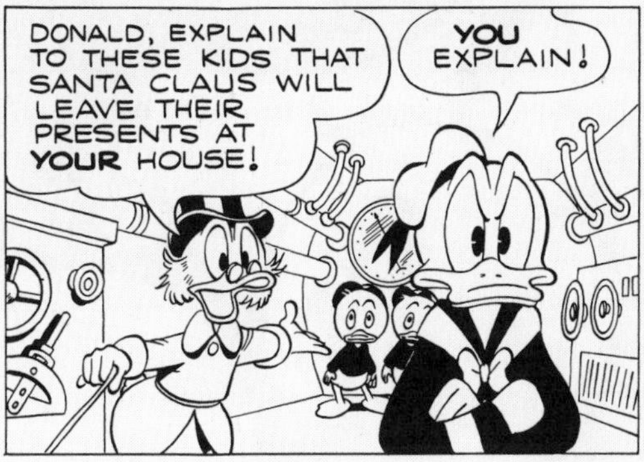
DONALD, EXPLAIN TO THESE KIDS THAT SANTA CLAUS WILL LEAVE THEIR PRESENTS AT YOUR HOUSE!
YOU EXPLAIN!

While those earlier stories had traditional wintertime-in-Duckburg settings, Barks provides refreshing atmosphere via Scrooge shanghaiing his nephews for the self-centered purpose of locating a sunken steamship with his money aboard. The possibility of the nephews missing out on Christmas morning

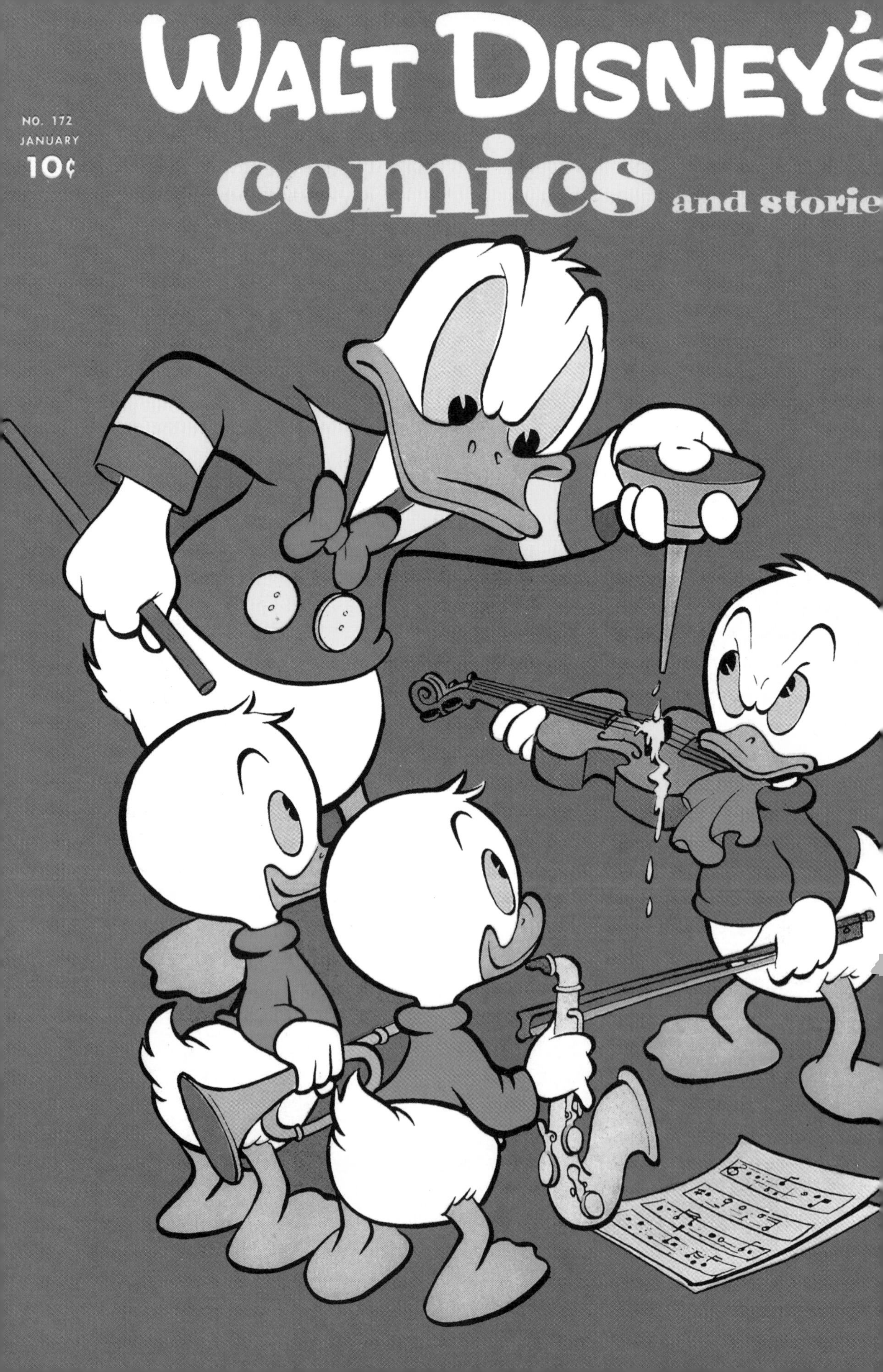
WALT DISNEY'S
NO. 172
JANUARY
10¢
comics
and storie

YOU CONFOUNDED KIDS, SCOOT OFF TO YOUR BUNKS! YOU MAKE ME FEEL LIKE A **MEAN** OLD MONEY-GRUBBER!

presents from Santa seems all too real as the lonely submarine dives deeper into desolate waters, and Scrooge deeper into his greed.

It wouldn't be a Christmas story without a change of heart, though, so Scrooge decides to miss his chance to reclaim the *Cuspidoria* in order to get a load of presents for the boys aboard. A little contrived, yes, but Scrooge hides his transformation so well — as if his obligations as an uncle are strictly business —

that we can't help but feel the miser deserves his happy ending. After all, it *is* Christmas.
— THAD KOMOROWSKI

NEW YEAR'S REVOLUTIONS *p. 151*

"New Year's Revolutions" is a reworking of "Donald Tames His Temper" (*Walt Disney's Comics and Stories* #64, January 1946, not in this volume). Ten years separate these stories, and Carl Barks has grown tremendously as an artist and storyteller in that time.

That older tale is fundamentally similar to the less-than-compelling animated cartoon version of Donald Duck: the kids try to get their uncle to blow his stack and thereby break his New Year's resolution. They succeed. End of analysis.

"New Year's Revolutions," on the other hand, enriches the concept by giving the nephews just cause in their skylarking. They've made their own resolution: they'll wash dishes for a whole month if they're late for school once. So, naturally, Donald tricks them into being late. In retaliation, the nephews come

CALAMITY, HERE I COME!

227

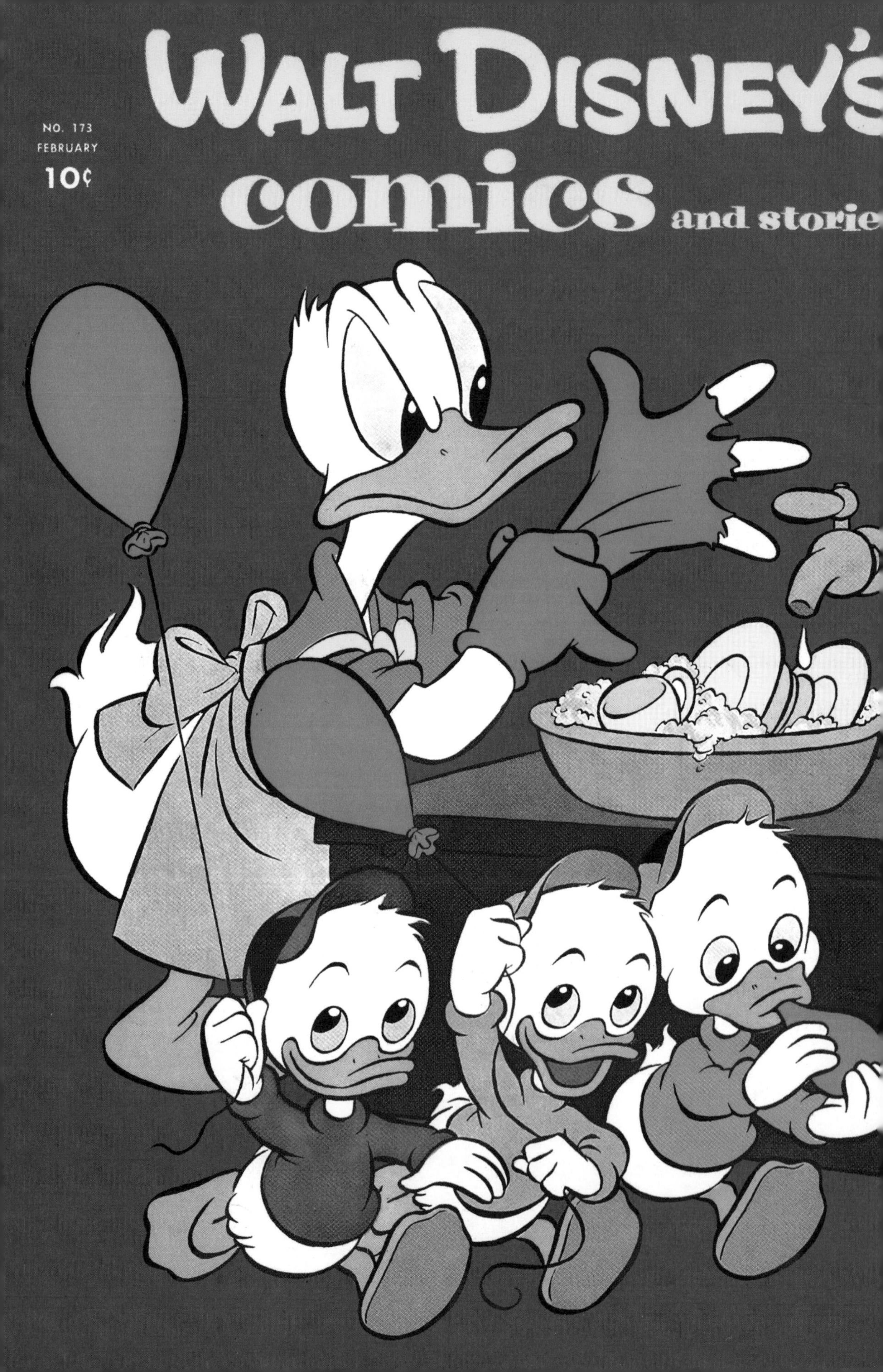

WALT DISNEY'S
NO. 173
FEBRUARY
10¢
comics
and storie

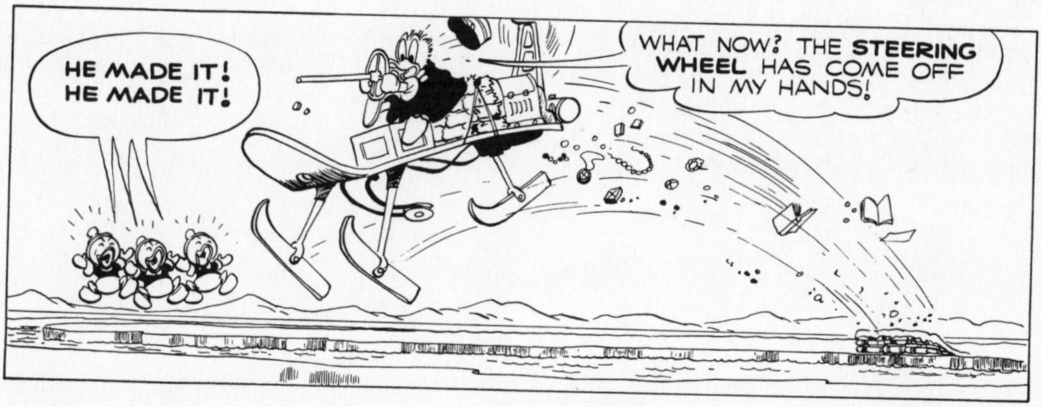
HE MADE IT! HE MADE IT!
WHAT NOW? THE STEERING WHEEL HAS COME OFF IN MY HANDS!

up with a forfeit for Donald if he loses his temper: he has to buy paper plates that they won't have to wash!

After suffering an embarrassing defeat, the nephews' sabotage of Donald's ski-jumping is far easier to take than the random acts of terror in that earlier story. What's more, Barks offers another twist: while Donald keeps his cool through the whole ordeal, the third nephew (Louie) is nowhere in sight.

Huey and Dewey are outraged by their brother's apparent absence, but there is more to be revealed in the grand scheme. As Louie says, "*Nobody saw him* look like a monkey, so he just laughed it off!"

Louie's role in the prank is too good to spoil for first-time readers, but suffice to say Donald does lose his temper, and the result is his blood boiling for an entire page. Even if the preceding pages were a loss (and they sure aren't!), those last panels alone are a masterwork of expressive cartooning and pacing, truly proving you couldn't mistake a Carl Barks comic book story for anyone else's.

— THAD KOMOROWSKI

ICEBOAT TO BEAVER ISLAND *p. 161*

Carl Barks's 10-pagers are like sonatas. Often, like a musical introduction, Donald has a new job. In "Iceboat to Beaver Island," he is (not for the first time and not for the last) a letter carrier — almost. He will only get the job of hauling mail to Beaver Island using his iceboat if the current mail carrier, an actual carrier pigeon, needs help.

The nephews want their uncle to get the job, so they send a collection of packages to Beaver Island that contain books, trinkets, a cigar lighter for Trapper Joe, and white rats to the local Junior Woodchucks (who seem to be everywhere) for their zoo.

Next comes a crescendo: Donald gets the job, but everything he is delivering (especially the rats) will bring destruction to the island. Needless to say, an open lighter on a gasoline-fueled machine means fire. Donald destroys the Beaver Island Post Office and doesn't deliver a single piece of mail.

Then the sonata comes to its conclusion: our "hero" does get a uniform — not the postal worker one he had longed for, but, rather, that of a Foreign Legion soldier. (He has to leave frozen Duckburg and escape to North Africa).

A cartoonist is in many ways akin to a musician, and Barks demonstrates a perfect feel for rhythm in the way he paces his stories — even the not-too-inspired ones like this.

The name "Beaver Island" was suggested to Barks by Western Publishing editors at the same time they were publishing the "Beaver Valley" comic book (*Four Color* #625, April 1955), an adaptation of the 1950 Disney-produced documentary *In Beaver Valley*.

— STEFANO PRIARONE

THE DAFFY TAFFY PULL *p. 171*

A volume like this, packed as it is with 10-page tales, admirably displays the wide-ranging subjects, conscientious craftsmanship, and inventive comedy of Carl Barks's shorter stories. Even at their most frantic, the narrative structure on display is economical and clear, and the action can readily be followed. Often these shorts begin with relatively mundane set-ups and ordinary emotional dispositions, only to rapidly progress through outlandish extensions of funny business and visual humor.

"The Daffy Taffy Pull" is a prime example — a frenzied farce of tight construction and smooth, if manic, evolution.

Making such laughable accelerations look easy is hard work. Throughout his career, Barks was his own harshest critic, and he labored diligently to meet the standards he set for himself. For instance, we know, thanks to the survival of a two-panel bottom tier and its following full page (below and opposite), that Barks replaced a fully rendered scene because he felt it did not measure up.

In Barks's final version, Donald's first taffy-retrieving ordeal erupts in the bear pit. That space in the story was originally occupied with a different, completely drawn-and-inked sequence in a hospital where Donald was forced to negotiate — to his financial disadvantage — with a group of nurses in order to regain the candy in their possession.

Evidence of this excised episode can still be seen in the form of the hospital building — named The Akin Bones Hospital in the outtake — in the backgrounds of the first and fourth panels on page 176.

What you see on this and the facing page is all that is known to have survived of Barks's self-rejected original sequence.

Why did Barks replace all that finished work? In correspondence, Barks allowed that the original was not funny enough. Worse, what humor the segment contained was largely verbal, so it would have been lost on his many pre-literate readers. Thus we get, in stark contrast, the dynamic, perilous — and highly accessible — ballet among the bears in the published version.

— RICH KREINER

DONALD DUCK TELLS ABOUT KITES *p. 181*

"Donald Duck Tells About Kites" is one of a series of electric power company giveaway comic books featuring instructions on how to make a kite and fly it safely, avoiding such threats as electrocution by power lines and death in traffic. Between the Pinocchio version in 1953 and the Br'er Rabbit version in 1955, Carl Barks got the assignment to draw the Donald Duck version in 1954.

A Western Publishing writer prepared the script, based on specific points the utility company wanted to drive home, so we should not expect a top-rank Barks tale, but the unknown writer is competent, and the story proceeds with aplomb.

The primary purpose, of course, is safety instruction. The lessons are presented in a humorous way with familiar characters to get kids to read it. Utility companies distributed these giveaway comics — which were printed on newsprint and lacked the slick covers of newsstand comics — in schools and elsewhere.

Western Publishing produced "Kite Fun Books" annually mainly for two California electric utilities — Southern California Edison and Pacific Gas and Electric — for more than 30 years starting in 1952. They also made them available to other utilities nationwide.

AKIN-BONES HOSPITAL
WAIT! STOP! DON'T ANYBODY EAT THAT CANDY!
DO YOU MEAN THIS TAFFY?
YES! IT'S GOT SOMETHING IN IT!
DIRT?

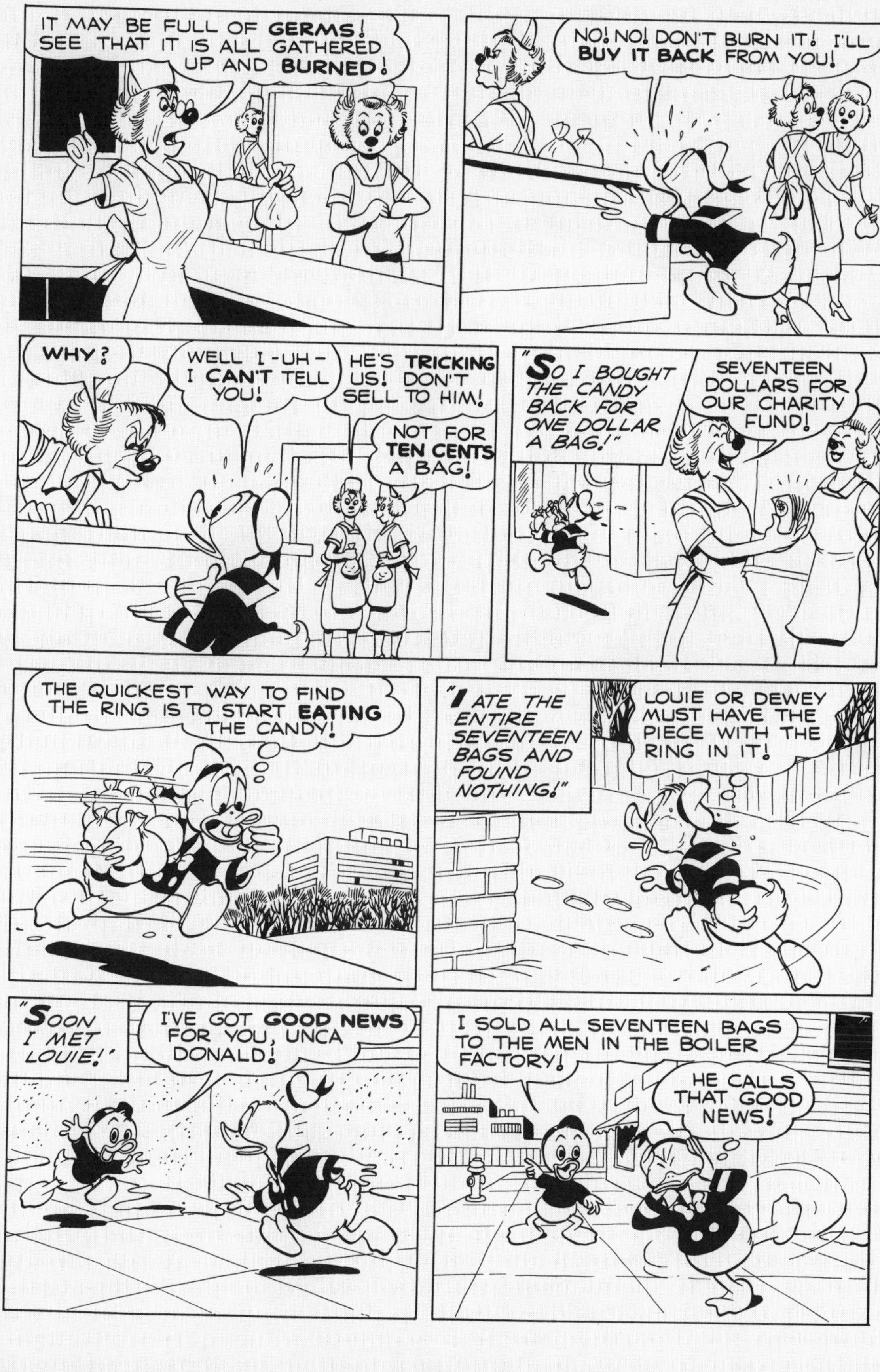
IT MAY BE FULL OF GERMS! SEE THAT IT IS ALL GATHERED UP AND BURNED!
NO! NO! DON'T BURN IT! I'LL BUY IT BACK FROM YOU!
WHY?
WELL I-UH- I CAN'T TELL YOU!
HE'S TRICKING US! DON'T SELL TO HIM!
NOT FOR TEN CENTS A BAG!
"SO I BOUGHT THE CANDY BACK FOR ONE DOLLAR A BAG!"
SEVENTEEN DOLLARS FOR OUR CHARITY FUND!
THE QUICKEST WAY TO FIND THE RING IS TO START EATING THE CANDY!
"I ATE THE ENTIRE SEVENTEEN BAGS AND FOUND NOTHING!"
LOUIE OR DEWEY MUST HAVE THE PIECE WITH THE RING IN IT!
"SOON I MET LOUIE!"
I'VE GOT GOOD NEWS FOR YOU, UNCA DONALD!
I SOLD ALL SEVENTEEN BAGS TO THE MEN IN THE BOILER FACTORY!
HE CALLS THAT GOOD NEWS!

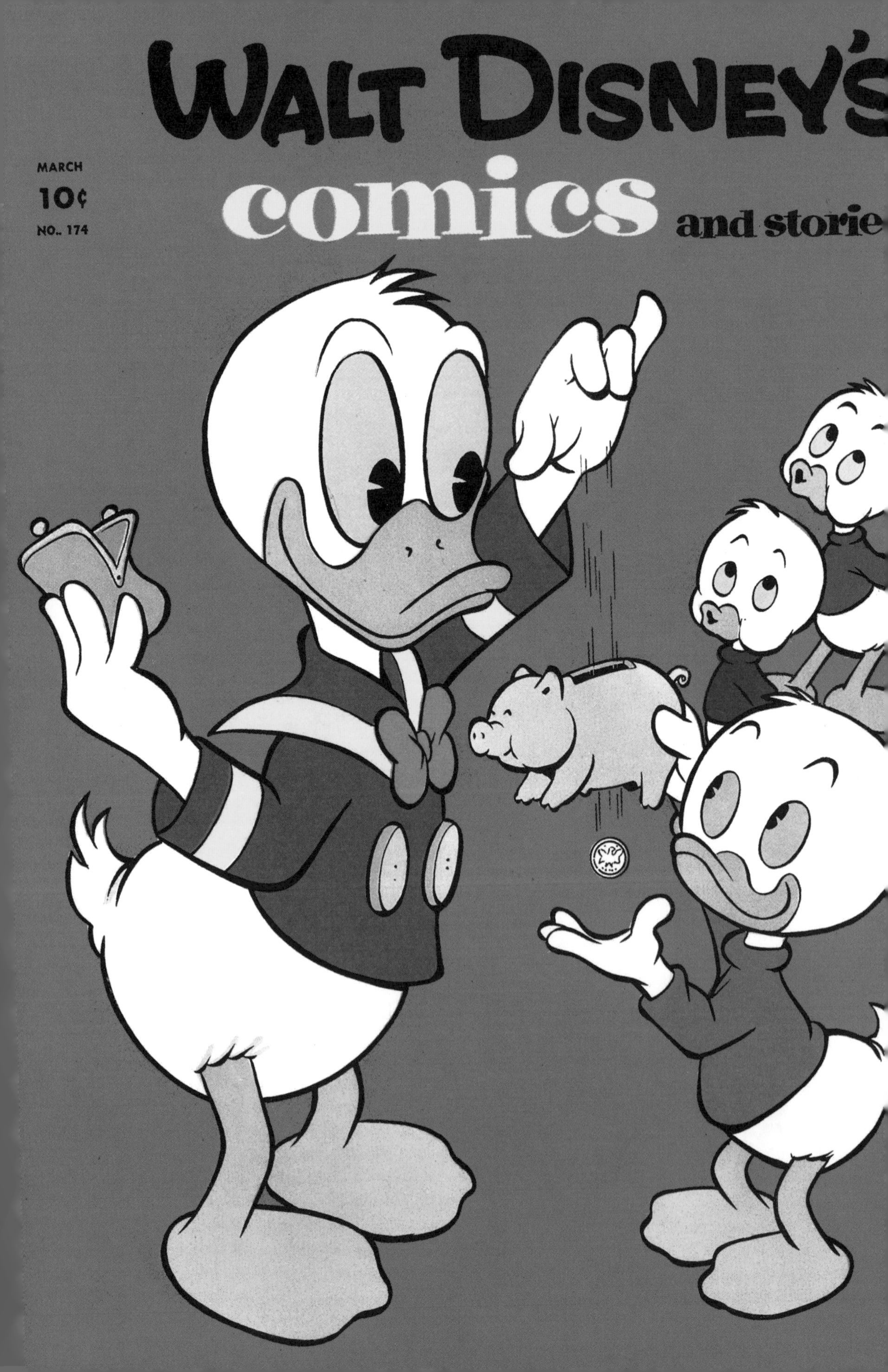
WALT DISNEY'S
MARCH
10¢
NO.. 174
comics
and storie

Apparently, Southern California Edison's edition was done first, and that is the version beginning on page 181. For the PG&E edition, the utility requested changes so it could have eight kite safety rules instead of SCE's seven.

To accommodate PG&E, Barks deleted two panels on page 7, added three new ones to fill the space, and added an eighth rule sheet on page 8. There are several dialogue changes, relettered by another hand. The key PG&E variant panels are shown on this page, but the panels shown in black-and-white have been clumsily re-inked by someone else.

Two other versions are known. Florida Power and Light's is the same as SCE's, except the Edison Company logo is removed from the truck door on page 7 and the word "Edison" is replaced by "Electric" in panel 2. There is also another known version, identical to the Florida Power version, except there is no company credit in the box on page 1, so it could have been distributed by other power companies, either remaining blank or with a local utility stamp or sticker in the box.

— KIM WESTON

A DESCENT INTERVAL *p. 189*

Among the hundreds of times Carl Barks sat down to bring forth the Donald Duck feature, there had to be occasions when he gazed at the drawing board without an idea in his head. This, I suspect, was one of them.

Hmm. How about skin diving? Gotta be something there. "What are we kids going to do?" lament Huey, Dewey, and Louie, echoing a grim foreboding in the cartoonist's mind, for

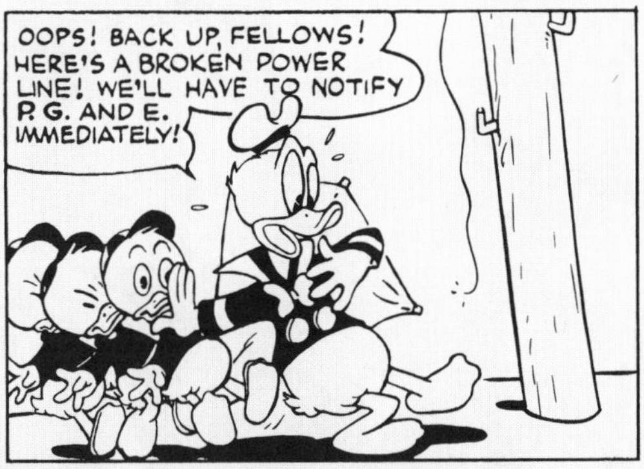
OOPS! BACK UP, FELLOWS! HERE'S A BROKEN POWER LINE! WE'LL HAVE TO NOTIFY P.G. AND E. IMMEDIATELY!

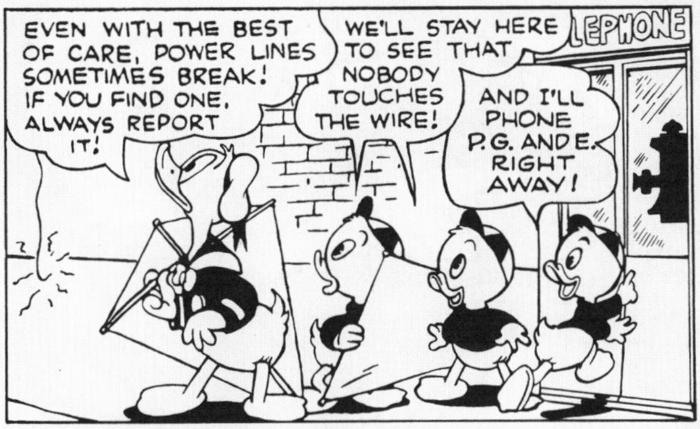
EVEN WITH THE BEST OF CARE, POWER LINES SOMETIMES BREAK! IF YOU FIND ONE, ALWAYS REPORT IT!
WE'LL STAY HERE TO SEE THAT NOBODY TOUCHES THE WIRE!
AND I'LL PHONE P.G. AND E. RIGHT AWAY!
LEPHONE

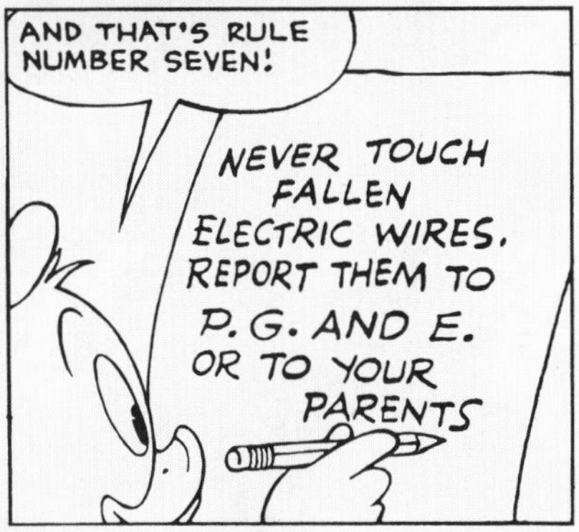
AND THAT'S RULE NUMBER SEVEN!
NEVER TOUCH FALLEN ELECTRIC WIRES. REPORT THEM TO P.G. AND E. OR TO YOUR PARENTS

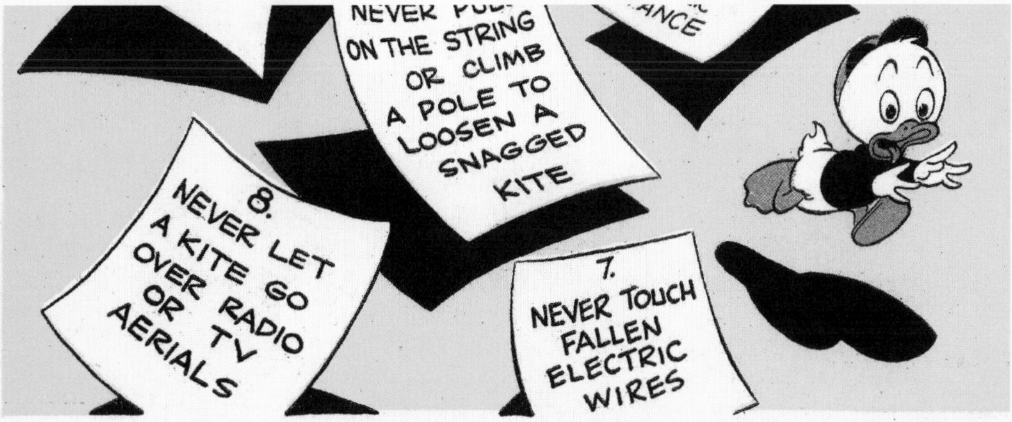
ON THE STRING OR CLIMB A POLE TO LOOSEN A SNAGGED KITE
8. NEVER LET A KITE GO OVER RADIO OR TV AERIALS
7. NEVER TOUCH FALLEN ELECTRIC WIRES

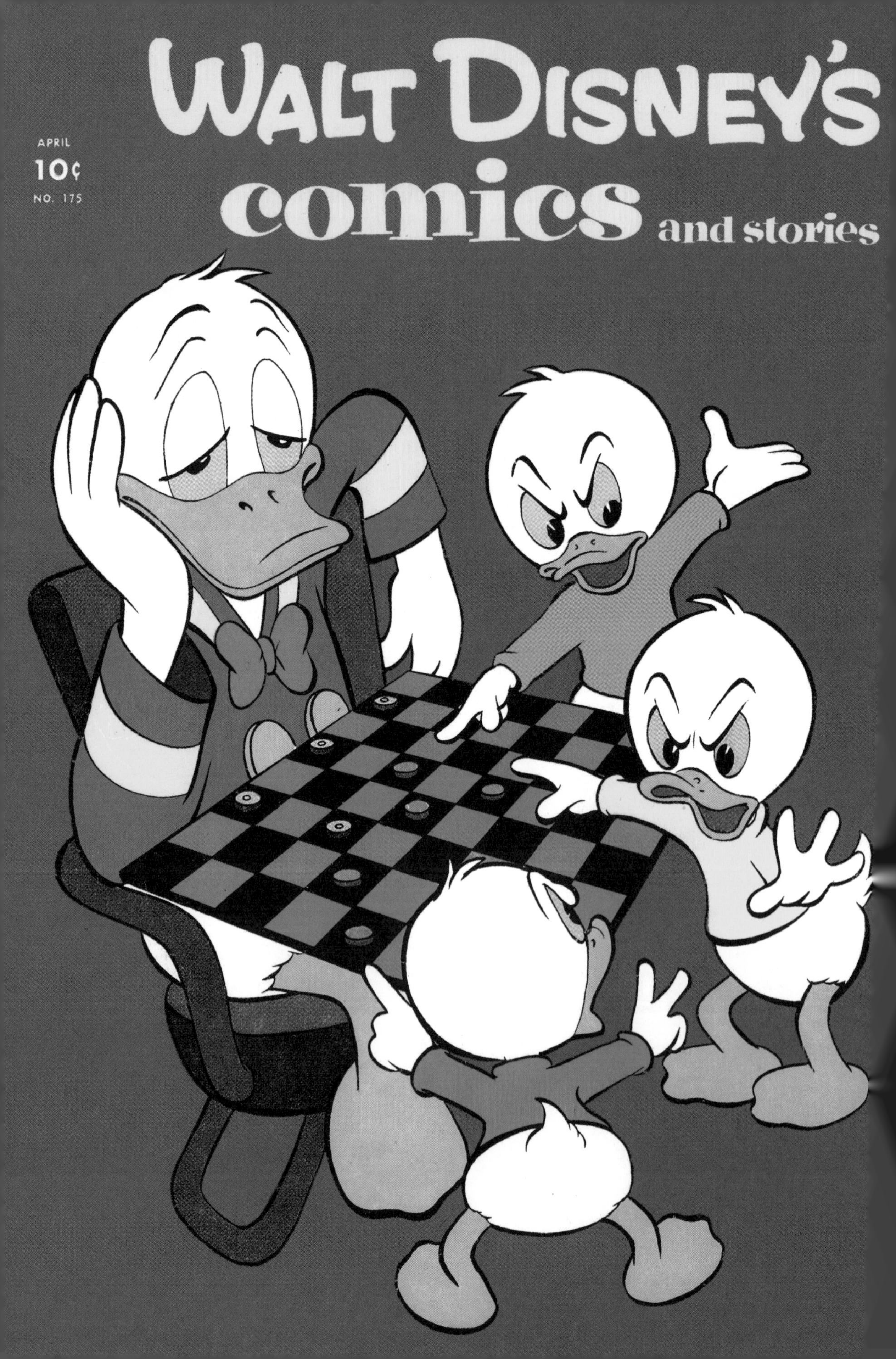
WALT DISNEY'S
APRIL
10¢
NO. 175
comics
and stories

indeed they have nearly nothing to do for the entire story.

So, into the drink. Whatever will Donald find there? Oh dear, oh dear, oh dear. How about swordfish? Swordfish are always good. But not today.

Maybe scientists can bail us out. Let's send Donald down in a diving bell — a small enclosed bubble at the end of a cable, the movements of which Donald does not control. So now we could have ... the big reveal of the giant shark. Not the first time, but it's that or a giant squid. Though of course the squid would be better for getting us off the end of this cable. But you know that shark bites with its teeth, babe, so you're out of that.

And rolling on the sea floor. Giant clam? Well, what can there be but a giant clam? Immobile creature of the sea floor. But supposing the fishermen dredge it up and mistake Donald's diving bell for a giant pearl and display it at a fair? That's *something*, that's a little chuckle.

You're entitled to a little indulgence after all the months of amusement you've provided.

The nephews find Donald's diving bell and rescue him, because of course the first thing you do when searching for someone lost at sea is to start combing the sidehows. So we're done for this month.

Next week, we start all over.

— R. FIORE

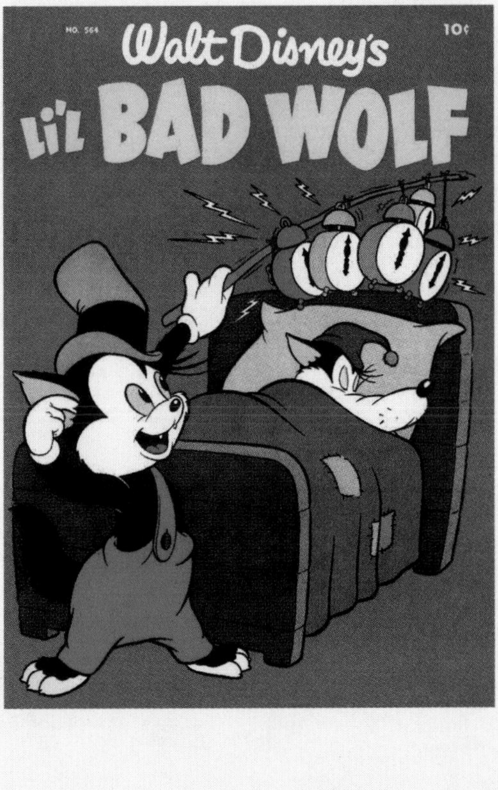
NO. 564
Walt Disney's
10¢
Li'l BAD WOLF

TENNIS MATCH *p. 199*
LI'L BAD WOLF'S ALARM CLOCKS

"Tennis Match" is a cute gag featuring another of Gyro Gearloose's impractical inventions concocted to solve an imagined problem. "Tennis Match" marks Gyro's first appearance in a one-page gag and only his sixth appearance since Barks had created him two years earlier.

Barks's work records for October 15, 1953, list "DD Tennis Match," but there is no published tennis gag drawn by Barks. "Tennis Match" was published about six months after Barks's submission, a typical lead time for comics, but it was drawn by Tony Strobl, and it is the only tennis match gag in any Duck comic book over the following five years or so.

In the 1970s, when I asked Barks about it, he told me that it looked familiar, but he could not confirm it was his.

But the use of Gyro, the sign in front of Gyro's workshop, the tennis subject matter, the timing of its publication, and Barks's recognition of it (despite its appearance in a *Donald Duck* issue with no other work by Barks and which he didn't even own a copy of), strongly suggests that this gag is that unidentified Barks tennis submission.

It's not hard to see "Li'l Bad Wolf's Alarm Clocks" (left) working just as well with the nephews and Donald. Barks submitted this gag as a cover idea sketch in December 1953, but it was Harvey Eisenberg who drew it as the cover to *Four Color* #564, May 1954.

Barks almost always scripted his own stories and gags. He rarely did scripts for other artists. "Tennis Match," and "Li'l Bad Wolf's Alarm Clocks" here, and "Talking Parrot" in *Walt Disney's Donald Duck: "Pixilated Parrot"* (volume 9) are the only known or suspected Barks Disney scripts drawn by others before Barks retired in 1966.

Barks continued to write scripts after 1966, but he didn't draw them, although he did draw a few covers in subsequent years.

— KIM WESTON

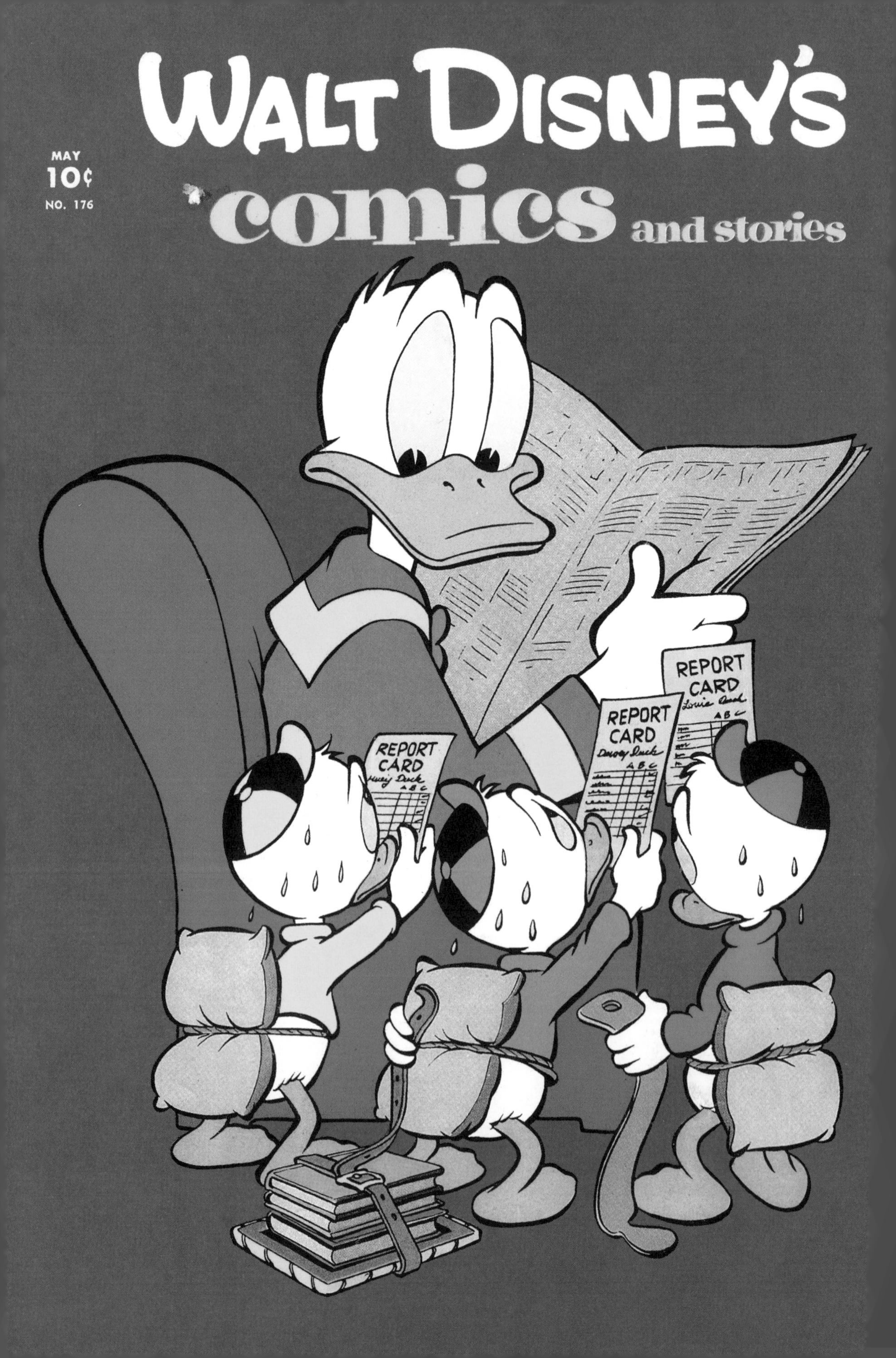
WALT DISNEY'S
MAY
10¢
NO. 176
comics
and stories
REPORT CARD
REPORT CARD
REPORT CARD

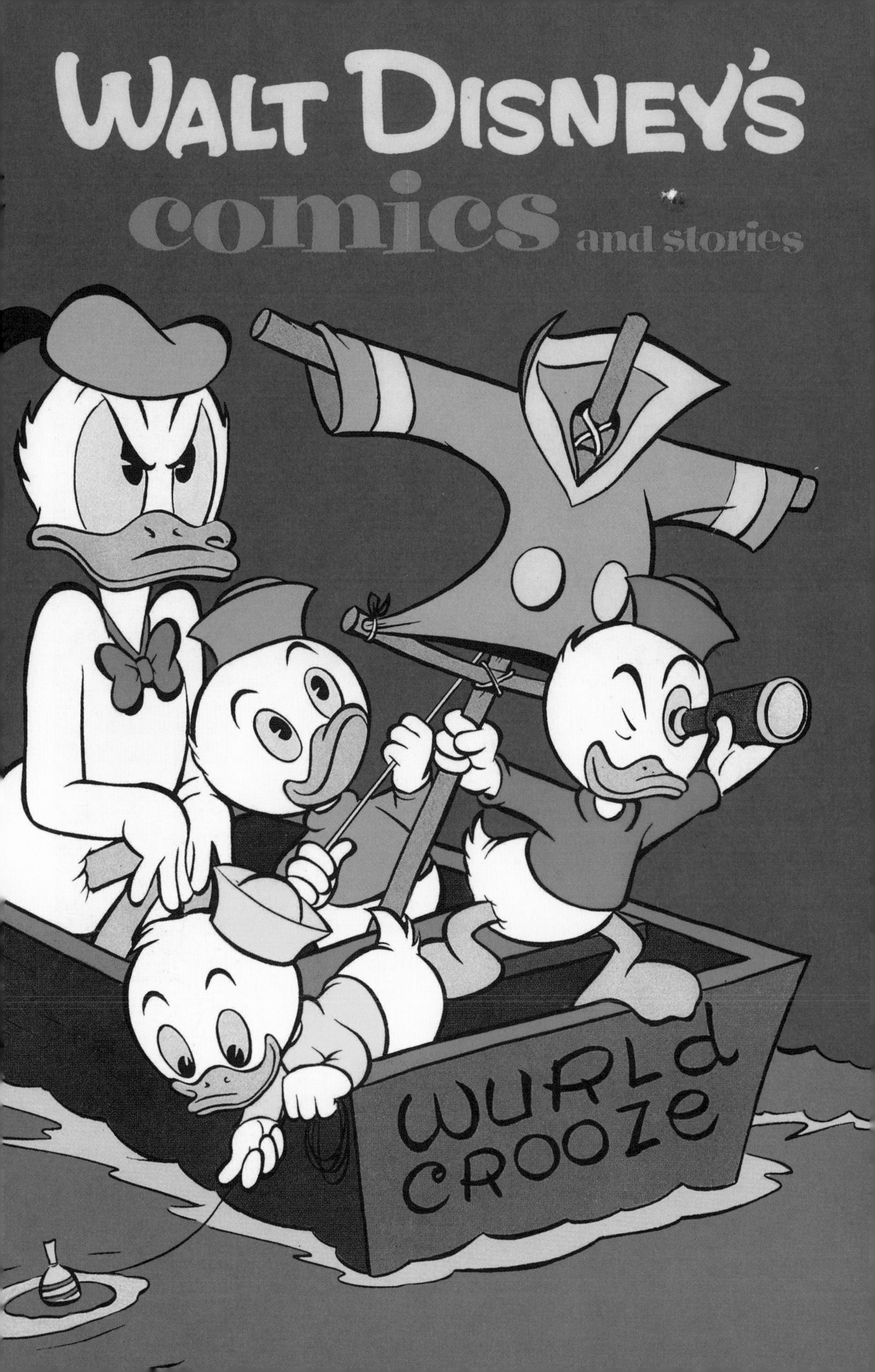
WALT DISNEY'S
comics and stories
WURLD CROOZE

Carl Barks

LIFE AMONG THE DUCKS

by DONALD AULT

ABOVE: *Carl Barks at the 1982 San Diego Comic-Con. Photo by Alan Light.*

"I was a real misfit," Carl Barks said, thinking back over an early life of hard labor — as a farmer, a logger, a mule-skinner, a rivet heater, and a printing press feeder — before he was hired as a full-time cartoonist for an obscure risqué magazine in 1931.

Barks was born in 1901 and (mostly) raised in Merrill, Oregon. He had always wanted to be a cartoonist, but everything that happened to him in his early years seemed to stand in his way. He suffered a significant hearing loss after a bout with the measles. His mother died. He had to leave school after the eighth grade. His

father suffered a mental breakdown. His older brother was whisked off to World War I.

His first marriage, in 1921, was to a woman who was unsympathetic to his dreams and who ultimately bore two children "by accident," as Barks phrased it. The two divorced in 1930.

In 1931, he pulled up stakes from Merrill and headed to Minnesota, leaving his mother-in-law, whom he trusted more than his wife, in charge of his children.

Arriving in Minneapolis, he went to work for the *Calgary Eye-Opener*, that risqué magazine. He thought he would finally be drawing cartoons full time, but the editor and most of the staff were alcoholics, so Barks ended up running the whole show.

In 1935 he took "a great gamble" and, on the strength of some cartoons he'd submitted in response to an advertisement from the Disney Studio, he moved to California and entered an animation trial period. He was soon promoted to "story man" in Disney's Donald Duck animation unit, where he made significant contributions to 36 Donald cartoon shorts between 1936 and 1942, including helping to create Huey, Dewey, and Louie for "Donald's Nephews" in 1938. Ultimately, though, he grew dissatisfied. The production of animated cartoons "by committee," as he described it, stifled his imagination.

For that and other reasons, in 1942 he left Disney to run a chicken farm. But when he was offered a chance by Western Publishing to write and illustrate a new series of Donald Duck comic book stories, he jumped at it. The comic book format suited him, and the quality of his work persuaded the editors to grant him a freedom and autonomy he'd never known and that few others were ever granted. He would go on to write and draw more than 6,000 pages in over 500 stories and uncounted hundreds of covers between 1942 and 1966 for Western's Dell and Gold Key imprints.

Barks had almost no formal art training. He had taught himself how to draw by imitating his early favorite artists — Winsor McCay (*Little Nemo*), Frederick Opper (*Happy Hooligan*), Elzie Segar (*Popeye*), and Floyd Gottfredson (*Mickey Mouse*).

He taught himself how to write well by going back to the grammar books he had shunned in school, making up jingles and rhymes, and inventing other linguistic exercises to get a natural feel for the rhythm and dialogue of sequential narrative.

Barks married again in 1938, but that union ended disastrously in divorce in 1951. In 1954, Barks married Margaret Wynnfred Williams, known as Garé, who soon began assisting him by lettering and inking backgrounds on his comic book work. They remained happily together until her death in 1993.

He did his work in the California desert and often mailed his stories into the office. He worked his stories over and over "backward and forward." Barks was not a vain man but he had confidence in his talent. He knew what hard work was, and he knew that he'd put his best efforts into every story he produced.

On those occasions when he did go into Western's offices he would "just dare anybody to see if they could improve on it." His confidence was justified. His work was largely responsible for some of the best-selling comic books in the world — *Walt Disney's Comics and Stories* and *Uncle Scrooge*.

Because Western's policy was to keep their writers and artists anonymous, readers never knew the name of the "good duck artist" — but they could spot the superiority of his work. When fans determined to solve the mystery of his anonymity finally tracked him down (not unlike an adventure Huey, Dewey, and Louie might embark upon), Barks was quite happy to correspond and otherwise communicate with his legion of aficionados.

Given all the obstacles of his early years and the dark days that haunted him off and on for the rest of his life, it's remarkable that he laughed so easily and loved to make others laugh.

In the process of expanding Donald Duck's character far beyond the hot-tempered Donald of animation, Barks created a moveable locale (Duckburg) and a cast of dynamic characters: Scrooge McDuck, the Beagle Boys, Gladstone Gander, Gyro Gearloose, the Junior Woodchucks. And there were hundreds of others who made only one memorable appearance in the engaging, imaginative, and unpredictable comedy-adventures that he wrote and drew from scratch for nearly a quarter of a century.

Among many other honors, Carl Barks was one of the three initial inductees into the Will Eisner Comic Book Hall of Fame for comic book creators in 1987. (The other two were Jack Kirby and Will Eisner.) In 1991, Barks became the only Disney comic book artist to be recognized as a "Disney Legend," a special award created by Disney "to acknowledge and honor the many individuals whose imagination, talents, and dreams have created the Disney magic."

As Roy Disney said on Barks's passing in 2000 at age 99, "He challenged our imaginations and took us on some of the greatest adventures we have ever known. His prolific comic book creations entertained many generations of devoted fans and influenced countless artists over the years.... His timeless tales will stand as a legacy to his originality and brilliant artistic vision."

Contributors

Donald Ault is Professor of English at the University of Florida, founder and editor of *ImageTexT: Interdisciplinary Comics Studies*, author of two books on William Blake (*Visionary Physics* and *Narrative Unbound*), editor of *Carl Barks: Conversations*, and executive producer of the video *The Duck Man: An Interview with Carl Barks*.

Alberto Becattini was born in Florence, Italy. He has taught high school English since 1983. Since 1978, he has written essays for Italian and U.S. publications about comics, specializing in Disney characters and American comics generally. Since 1992 he has been a freelance writer and consultant for The Walt Disney Company-Italy, contributing to such series as *Zio Paperone, Maestri Disney, Tesori Disney, Disney Anni d'Oro, La Grande Dinastia dei Paperi*, and *Gli Anni d'Oro di Topolino*.

Joseph Robert Cowles is a lifelong Donald Duck fan who became friends with Carl and Garé Barks when he was a teenager working at Disneyland in the 1950s. He publishes *The Carl Barks Fan Club Pictorial* and is the author of *The Barks Fan's Potpourri* and the pictorial dissertation *Recalling Carl*, in which he contends that Disney should be making feature films of Barks's stories. He also contributed materials and commentary to Egmont's *Carl Barks Collection*.

R. Fiore, he explains, makes his way in life working Square John jobs (when they let him) not far from Historic Duckburg. This marginal existence has even from time to time led onto the grounds of the Walt Disney Company, which is an interesting place. In his spare time he's been writing about comic strips and animation longer than you've been alive, my child.

Craig Fischer is Professor of English at Appalachian State University. His Monsters Eat Critics column, about comics' multifarious genres, runs at *The Comics Journal* website (tcj.com).

Leonardo Gori is a comics scholar and collector, especially of syndicated newspaper strips of the '30s and Italian Disney authors. He wrote, with Frank Stajano and others, many books on Italian "fumetti" and American comics in Italy. He has also written thrillers, which have been translated into Spanish, Portuguese, and Korean.

Thad Komorowski is an animation historian with a longstanding professional relationship with Disney comics. He translates stories for IDW's Disney comic books and is a regular contributor to the Carl Barks and Floyd Gottfredson archival collections from Fantagraphics Books. He is the author of *Sick Little Monkeys: The Unauthorized Ren & Stimpy Story* and co-author of a forthcoming history of New York studio animation.

Rich Kreiner is a longtime writer for *The Comics Journal* and a longtime reader of Carl Barks. He lives with wife and cat in Maine.

Stefano Priarone was born in Northwestern Italy about the time when a retired Carl Barks was storyboarding his last Junior Woodchucks stories. He writes about popular culture in many Italian newspapers and magazines, was a contributor to the Italian complete Carl Barks collection, and wrote his thesis in economics about Uncle Scrooge as an entrepreneur (for which he blames his aunt, who read him Barks's Scrooge stories when he was 3 years old).

Francesco ("Frank") Stajano began reading Disney comics in preschool and never grew out of it — the walls of his house are covered in bookshelves and many of them hold comics. He has written on Disney comics, particularly with Leonardo Gori, and had the privilege of visiting Carl Barks at his home in Oregon in 1998. In real life he is an associate professor at the University of Cambridge in England.

Kim Weston has a Bachelor of Arts and a Master of Science degree from Johns Hopkins University. He spent most of his career teaching physics and chemistry and still tutors at a local community college. He started collecting Carl Barks comics in 1956 and has been writing about Barks since the 1970s. He has contributed to many works of scholarship about Barks, including co-authoring a massive index of all of Barks's comics, including Donald Duck and Uncle Scrooge. He recently published *The Carl Barks Index*, an index to the first ten Fantagraphics Barks volumes.

Matthias Wivel is Curator of Sixteenth-Century Italian Painting at the National Gallery, London. He has written widely about comics for a decade and a half.

Daniel F. Yezbick grew up in Detroit, Michigan, reading Carl Barks's comics in Gold Key and Whitman reprints. Since then, he has wandered the nation in Barksian fashion, pursuing a variety of odd jobs including bartender, sheep wrangler, technical writer, and college professor. He now teaches comics, film studies, and writing courses at Forest Park College. His essays on Barks and Disney comics have appeared in a variety of anthologies including *Icons of the American Comic Book*, *Comics Through Time*, and *Critical Survey of Graphic Novels: History, Theme, and Technique*. He is the author of *Perfect Nonsense: The Chaotic Comics and Goofy Games of George Carlson* from Fantagraphics. He currently lives in South St. Louis with his wife, Rosalie, their two children, and one wise, old hound.

Where did these Duck stories first appear?

The Complete Carl Barks Disney Library collects Donald Duck and Uncle Scrooge stories by Carl Barks that were originally published in the traditional American four-color comic book format. Barks's first Duck story appeared in October 1942. The volumes in this project are numbered chronologically but are being released in a different order. This is Volume 15.

Stories within a volume may or may not follow the publication sequence of the original comic books. We may take the liberty of rearranging the sequence of the stories within a volume for editorial or presentation purposes.

The original comic books were published under the Dell logo and some appeared in the so-called *Four Color* series — a name that appeared nowhere inside the comic book itself, but is generally agreed upon by historians to refer to the series of "one-shot" comic books published by Dell that have sequential numbering. The *Four Color* issues are also sometimes referred to as "One Shots."

Most of the stories in this volume were originally published without a title. Some stories were retroactively assigned a title when they were reprinted in later years. Some stories were given titles by Barks in correspondence or interviews. (Sometimes Barks referred to the same story with different titles.) Some stories were never given an official title but have been informally assigned one by fans and indexers. For the untitled stories in this volume, we have used the title that seems most appropriate. The unofficial titles appear below with an asterisk enclosed in parentheses (*).

Some of the issues listed below had covers by Barks but contained no interior work by him. The following is the order in which the stories and covers in this volume were originally published.

***Walt Disney's Comics and Stories* #159 (December 1953)**
Cover
Wispy Willie (*)

***Walt Disney's Comics and Stories* #160 (January 1954)**
Cover
The Hammy Camel (*)

***Walt Disney's Comics and Stories* #161 (February 1954)**
Cover
Fix-Up Mix-Up (*)

***Walt Disney's Comics and Stories* #162 (March 1954)**
Cover
Turkey Trot at One Whistle (*)

***Walt Disney's Comics and Stories* #163 (April 1954)**
Cover
Raffle Reversal (*)

***Walt Disney's Comics and Stories* #164 (May 1954)**
Cover
Flour Follies (*)

Donald Duck #35 (May-June 1954)
Cover only

***Walt Disney's Comics and Stories* #165 (June 1954)**
Cover
The Price of Fame (*)

***Four Color* #564 (June 1954)**
Cover idea only;
Cover art by Harvey Eisenberg

***Walt Disney's Comics and Stories* #166 (July 1954)**
Cover
Midgets Madness (*)

***Donald Duck* #36 (July 1954)**
Tennis Match (*)
[a.k.a. "Tennis Watcher"]
script only; art by Tony Strobl

***Walt Disney's Comics and Stories* #167 (August 1954)**
Cover
Salmon Derby (*)

***Walt Disney's Comics and Stories* #168 (September 1954)**
Cover
Cheltenham's Choice (*)

***Walt Disney's Comics and Stories* #169 (October 1954)**
Cover
Traveling Truants (*)

***Walt Disney's Comics and Stories* #170 (November 1954)**
Cover
Donald Rants About Ants (*)

***Donald Duck Tells About Kites* (November 1954)**
Donald Duck Tells About Kites
art only; script by unknown

***Walt Disney's Comics and Stories* #171 (December 1954)**
Cover
Too Safe Safe (*)

***Walt Disney's Comics and Stories* #172 (January 1955)**
Cover
Search for the Cuspidoria (*)

***Walt Disney's Comics and Stories* #173 (February 1955)**
Cover
New Year's Revolutions (*)

***Walt Disney's Comics and Stories* #174 (March 1955)**
Cover
Iceboat to Beaver Island (*)
[a.k.a. "Worst Class Mail"]

***Walt Disney's Comics and Stories* #175 (April 1955)**
Cover
The Daffy Taffy Pull (*)

***Walt Disney's Comics and Stories* #176 (May 1955)**
Cover
The Ghost Sheriff of Last Gasp (*)

***Walt Disney's Comics and Stories* #177 (June 1955)**
Cover
A Descent Interval (*)